Where to find help in *The McGraw-Hill Guide*:

In the table of contents for Chapters 3 and 5–12, identify the chapter that corresponds to your writing assignment.

To set your writing goals, consider the guidelines that appear in the **Setting Your Goals** section of each chapter.

Where to find help in *The McGraw-Hill Guide*:

Chapters 3 and 5–12 are organized around four general writing goals:

1. To demonstrate **rhetorical knowledge**
2. To practice **critical thinking, reading, and writing**
3. To work through **writing processes**
4. To follow **conventions**

Successful writers adapt these goals to the particular needs of their situation. In Chapters 3 and 5–12, you will find clear guidance on how to think about the four goals and how to achieve them in relation to your specific assignment.

Where to find help in *The McGraw-Hill Guide*:

Chapters 3 and 5–12 all conclude with a guided **self-assessment** that will help you gauge how effectively your writing meets your goals.

All chapters include these helpful icons pointing out coverage of knowledge transfer and using digital technologies.

THE McGraw-Hill
GUIDE

Writing for College, Writing for Life

FOURTH EDITION

Duane Roen
Arizona State University

Gregory R. Glau
Northern Arizona University

Barry M. Maid
Arizona State University

Mc
Graw
Hill
Education

THE MCGRAW-HILL GUIDE: WRITING FOR COLLEGE, WRITING FOR LIFE, FOURTH EDITION

Published by McGraw-Hill Education, 2 Penn Plaza, New York, NY 10121. Copyright © 2018 by McGraw-Hill Education. All rights reserved. Printed in the United States of America. Previous editions © 2013, 2011, and 2009. No part of this publication may be reproduced or distributed in any form or by any means, or stored in a database or retrieval system, without the prior written consent of McGraw-Hill Education, including, but not limited to, in any network or other electronic storage or transmission, or broadcast for distance learning.

Some ancillaries, including electronic and print components, may not be available to customers outside the United States.

This book is printed on acid-free paper.

1 2 3 4 5 6 7 8 9 DOC 21 20 19 18 17

ISBN 978-0-07-811808-1
MHID 0-07-811808-5

Chief Product Officer, SVP Products & Markets: *G. Scott Virkler*
Vice President, General Manager, Products & Markets: *Michael Ryan*
Vice President, Content Design & Delivery: *Betsy Whalen*
Managing Director: *David Patterson*
Editorial Director: *Kelly Villella*
Executive Brand Manager: *Claire Brantley*
Director, Product Development: *Meghan Campbell*
Director, Product Development: *Lisa Pinto*
Executive Market Development Manager: *Nanette Giles*
Marketing Manager: *Marisa Cavanaugh*

Digital Product Analyst: *Janet Byrne Smith*
Director, Content Design & Delivery: *Terri Schiesl*
Program Manager: *Jennifer Shekleton*
Content Project Managers: *Lisa Bruflodt, Samantha Donisi-Hamm*
Buyer: *Susan K. Culbertson*
Design: *Debra Kubiak*
Content Licensing Specialists: *Shawntel Schmitt, DeAnna Dausener*
Cover Image: *Peter Kotoff/Shutterstock.com; Apirak Wongpunsing/Shutterstock.com*
Compositor: *Lumina Datamatics, Inc.*
Printer: *LSC Communications*

All credits appearing on page or at the end of the book are considered to be an extension of the copyright page.

Library of Congress Cataloging-in-Publication Data

Names: Roen, Duane H., author. | Glau, Gregory R., author. | Maid, Barry M., author.
Title: The McGraw-Hill guide: writing for college, writing for life /
    Duane Roen, Gregory R. Glau, Barry M. Maid.
Other titles: Writing for college, writing for life
Description: Fourth edition. | New York, NY: McGraw-Hill Education,
    2018. | Includes bibliographical references and index.
Identifiers: LCCN 2016025429 | ISBN 9780078118081 (alk. paper)
    0078118085 (alk. paper)
Subjects: LCSH: English language--Rhetoric.
Classification: LCC PE1408 .R643 2018 | DDC 808/.0420711—dc23 LC record available at
    https://lccn.loc.gov/2016025429

The Internet addresses listed in the text were accurate at the time of publication. The inclusion of a website does not indicate an endorsement by the authors or McGraw-Hill Education, and McGraw-Hill Education does not guarantee the accuracy of the information presented at these sites.

mheducation.com/highered

Brief Contents

Contents

"When I think about **setting my goals**, I think about my audience, my purpose, the rhetorical situation, my voice and tone, and the context, medium, and genre."

PART TWO   Using What You Have Learned to Share Information   74

5 Writing to Share Experiences   74

SETTING YOUR GOALS   75

Rhetorical Knowledge   76

Critical Thinking, Reading, and Writing   79

Knowledge of Conventions 146

Editing   146 • Genres, Documentation, and Format   147

 A Writer Achieves Her Goal: Elle Caminante's Final Draft   147

> **ELLE CAMINANTE,** STARVING ARTISTS: MYTH OR REALITY? (Exploratory Essay)   147

  Self-Assessment: Reflecting on Your Goals   152

7 Writing to Inform   154

SETTING YOUR GOALS FOR *INFORMATIVE WRITING*   156

 Rhetorical Knowledge   158

Writing to Inform in Your College Classes   158 • Writing to Inform for Life   158

Scenarios for Writing: Assignment Options   159

 Critical Thinking, Reading, and Writing   162

Learning the Qualities of Effective Informative Writing   163

Reading, Inquiry, and Research: Learning from Texts That Inform   164

> **CAROL EZZELL,** CLOCKING CULTURES (Article)   165
>
> **NIMH,** AUTISM SPECTRUM DISORDER (Article)   169
>
> **CRAIG BROADBENT,** (Annotated Bibliography)   174

 Writing Processes   176

Invention: Getting Started   176 • Exploring Your Ideas with Research   177 • Organizing Your Information and Research   181 • Constructing a Complete Draft   182 • Revising   187

 Knowledge of Conventions   189

Editing   189 • Genres, Documentation, and Format   189

 A Writer Achieves His Goal: Craig Broadbent's Final Draft   190

> **CRAIG BROADBENT,** WATCH FOR THE BLUE BARRELS (Informative Essay)   191

 Self-Assessment: Reflecting on Your Goals   196

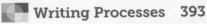
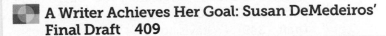
PART FOUR   Strategies for Effective Communication 419

13   Using Strategies That Guide Readers 419

14 Using Strategies for Argument   446

15 Using Strategies for Collaboration   471

16 Making Effective Oral Presentations   477

*"When I think about **achieving my goals,** I think about invention strategies to use, where I can find good ideas, whether I will need to conduct research, how I should organize my ideas, how my peers can help me improve my writing, and which writing conventions I need to check in my writing."*

PART FIVE   **Technologies for Effective Communication   485**

PART SIX   Using Research for Informed Communication   522

19   Finding and Evaluating Information   522

"When I think about assessing my goals, I think about whether I attained the outcomes I hoped for and how my audience responded to my writing."

21   Writing about Visual Texts

SETTING YOUR GOALS

 Rhetorical Knowledge
Writing about Visual Texts
Writing Assignment Options

 Critical Thinking, Reading, and Writing
Qualities of Effective Writing to Analyze Visuals
Reading to Learn about Analyzing Visual Texts

A Writer Achieves Her Goal: Frances Walker's Final Draft

FRANCES WALKER, "SOMETIMES SHE DREAMS" POETRY ANALYSIS (Student Essay)

Self-Assessment: Reflecting on Your Goals

To our students and colleagues, who offered us inspiration for this project. To Elizabeth Murphy, who guided our journey.

    D. R., G. G., and B. M.

To Maureen Roen, an accomplished writer, and to Harley Roen, a lifelong supporter.

    D. R.

For Courtney, with all my love. Thanks for sharing your life with me.

    G. G.

For Rachel and Seth, the most supportive son and daughter.

    B. M.

About the Authors

Duane Roen is Professor of English at Arizona State University, where he serves as Dean of the College of Integrative Sciences and Arts, Dean of University College, Vice Provost, and Coordinator for the Project for Writing and Recording Family History. At ASU he has also served as Head of Interdisciplinary Studies; Head of Humanities and Arts; Director of Composition; Co-Director of the graduate program in Rhetoric, Composition, and Linguistics; Director of the Center for Learning and Teaching Excellence; and President of the Academic Senate. At Syracuse University he served as Director of the Writing Program. At the University of Arizona, he was Founding Director of the graduate program in Rhetoric, Composition, and the Teaching of English, as well as Director of Graduate Studies in the Department of English. He has served as Secretary of the Conference on College Composition and Communication and President of the Council of Writing Program Administrators.

Duane has written extensively about writing across the curriculum; writing curricula, pedagogy, and assessment; writing program administration; writing family history; and collaboration, among other topics. In addition to more than 280 articles, chapters, and conference papers, Duane has published the following books: *Composing Our Lives in Rhetoric and Composition: Stories about the Growth of a Discipline* (with Theresa Enos and Stuart Brown); *The Writer's Toolbox* (with Stuart Brown and Bob Mittan); *A Sense of Audience in Written Discourse* (with Gesa Kirsch); *Becoming Expert: Writing and Learning across the Disciplines* (with Stuart Brown and Bob Mittan); *Richness in Writing: Empowering ESL Students* (with Donna Johnson); *Strategies for Teaching First-Year Composition* (with Lauren Yena, Susan K. Miller, Veronica Pantoja, and Eric Waggoner); *Views from the Center: The CCCC Chairs' Addresses, 1977–2005*; *The WPA Outcomes Statement: A Decade Later* (with Nicholas Behm, Greg Glau, Deborah Holdstein, and Edward White); and *The McGraw-Hill Guide: Writing for College, Writing for Life* (with Greg Glau and Barry Maid), now in its fourth edition. He is currently co-authoring a composition handbook (with Michael Day), co-editing a collection of essays on the Framework for Success in Postsecondary Writing (with Nicholas Behm and Sherry Rankins-Robertson), and co-editing a collection of essays on cognition in writing (with Patricia Portanova and Michael Rifenburg).

Gregory R. Glau was Director of the University Writing Program at Northern Arizona University from 2008 to 2015, and at Arizona State University from 2000 to 2008. Greg received his MA in Rhetoric and Composition from Northern Arizona University, and his PhD in Rhetoric, Composition, and the Teaching of English from the University of Arizona. With Linda Adler-Kassner of University of California–Santa Barbara, Greg is co-editor of the *Bedford Bibliography for Teachers of Basic Writing* (2001; 2nd ed., 2005); third edition 2010 (co-edited with Chitralekha Duttagupta of Utah Valley University). Greg also is co-author of *Scenarios for Writing* (Mayfield/McGraw-Hill, 2001). Greg has published in the *Journal of Basic Writing, WPA: Writing Program Administration, Rhetoric Review, English Journal, The Writing Instructor, IDEAS Plus,* and *Arizona English Bulletin.* Greg regularly presents at CCCC and has presented at WPA, MLA, RMMLA, the Western States Composition Conference, NCTE, and others. He (with Duane Roen and Barry Maid) is past Managing Editor of *WPA: Writing Program Administration.*

Barry M. Maid is Professor of Technical Communication at Arizona State University, where he led the development of the program in Technical Communication. He has spent most of his career in writing program administration. Before coming to ASU, he taught at the University of Arkansas at Little Rock, where, among other duties, he directed the Writing Center and the First Year Composition Program, chaired the Department of English, and helped create the Department of Rhetoric and Writing. He has written or co-authored chapters for more than twenty books, and some of his writing-across-the-curriculum work has recently been published (with several co-authors) in a nursing journal. Barry has co-authored articles on information literacy for library journals, and he is also the editor of *Information Literacy: Research and Collaboration across Disciplines* (with Barbara D'Angelo, Sandra Jamieson, and Janice Walker). His professional interests remain in writing in digital environments, writing program administration (especially program assessment), and partnerships between academic programs and industry. Barry enjoys long road trips and continues to visit the national parks of the West.

A Letter to Teachers from the Authors

It is an exciting time in higher education, especially in rhetoric and composition, where many innovations have defined the field in recent years. In light of current research, theory, and practice in the field, *The McGraw-Hill Guide* embodies these advances in ways that enrich the learning experiences of students. Elements that run throughout the *Guide* include:

- Teaching for transfer, to help students understand how their writing in composition classes will help them in their other college or university classes and in other parts of life

- Thorough coverage of genre, with examples and illustrations

- A focus on rhetorical purpose—using writing to get things done in the world

- Assignments that encourage students to use 21st-century digital technologies for crafting multimodal projects

- Flexible assignments that encourage students to focus on writing in any realm of life—academic, professional, civic, or personal

- Updated citation conventions used in the *MLA Handbook*, 8th edition

- Up-to-date sample student projects with examples from their invention work through peer review to finished academic essays

- Questions and guidance that help students to respond thoughtfully to peers' work—and to reflect critically on their own.

The national consensus among educators is that students succeed best when they are guided by outcomes and approach their assignments from a goals-based perspective. This is true for a wide range of faculty, whether full or part time, new or experienced: knowing and working with specific goals and objectives helps students to achieve those goals. We have structured *The McGraw-Hill Guide* to help students set goals for their writing, use effective composing strategies to achieve those goals, and assess their progress toward achieving them.

The student writing goals in *The McGraw-Hill Guide* are drawn from the learning outcomes established by the Council of Writing Program Administrators (CWPA) because we know how important they have been in shaping discussions about writing curricula. These learning outcomes demonstrate the value of the full range of knowledge sets and skills that writers need to develop, which include rhetorical knowledge; critical thinking, reading and composing; processes; and knowledge of conventions.

The current version of the CWPA Outcomes Statement for First-Year Composition—Version 3.0—emphasizes that digital tools are integral to a wide range of composing activities. As a result, they appear throughout the statement and throughout *The McGraw-Hill Guide*. When Duane was president of the Council of Writing Programs Administrators, he charged a task force to consider the role of digital technologies and visual tools in writing. The stellar work of that task force is reflected in the current version of the CWPA Outcomes Statement.

In addition to the newly revised CWPA outcomes that form our pedagogical framework, *The McGraw-Hill Guide* also includes the Modern Language Association's updated guidelines, whose new approach accommodates the evolving needs of research and documentation practices around a growing list of digital sources.

Just as Aristotle argued in *The Rhetoric* that writers should use "the available means of persuasion," we argue that 21st-century writers should use the full range of tools available to them, especially digital tools. Throughout the book we introduce students to the digital technologies that will help them in their research and writing, and we include digital technology icons alongside our instruction to emphasize these tools.

Learning is a lifelong journey that begins early—often in a classroom—and continues and changes throughout an individual's academic, professional, civic, and personal life. *The*

McGraw-Hill Guide prioritizes the transfer of knowledge and skills that students can use in settings other than first-year composition. We have added transfer icons throughout the chapters to draw students' attention to the ways that they can use writers' tools in other courses, as well as in their professional, civic, and personal endeavors.

We have enjoyed writing *The McGraw-Hill Guide* because it reflects our own experiences in the classroom, our research, and our many conversations with colleagues in the field. We hope that you enjoy using *The McGraw-Hill Guide* with your students as they strive to become the most effective writers possible. If there is anything that we can do to assist you, please let us know.

Sincerely,
Duane Roen
Gregory R. Glau
Barry M. Maid

How does **The McGraw-Hill Guide** help student writers succeed in their writing-intensive courses?

With *The McGraw-Hill Guide*, students apply a goals-oriented approach to their writing assignments using proven techniques related to student success. With *The Guide* students will understand the underlying principles on which their writing is assessed—by assessing it themselves—and will develop the strategies needed to support their writing development long after they have completed college.

First, the **Guide** helps students set goals for each writing assignment.

With *The McGraw-Hill Guide*, instructors can help students understand and set their writing goals using the assignment chapters in Parts Two and Three (Chapters 5–12). By following the unique instruction of *The Guide*, students will:

- Consider their writing goals
- Consider their writing contexts
- Transfer their writing skills

Consider their writing goals.

Students will learn to apply a goals-oriented approach to any writing situation, making effective choices by asking three questions:

- How do I set my goals?
- How do I achieve my goals?
- How do I assess my goals?

SET	**How do I set my goals?** **Setting Your Goals (p. 113)**
ACHIEVE	**How do I achieve my goals?** Rhetorical Knowledge: Understanding the rhetorical situation for your project (p. 115) **Critical Thinking, Reading, and Writing: Thinking critically about this type of writing (p. 120)** **Writing Processes: Establishing a process for composing your project (p. 133)** Knowledge of Conventions: Polishing your work (p. 146)
ASSESS	**How do I assess my goals?** **Self-Assessment: Reflecting on Your Goals (p. 152)**

Set, Achieve, Assess. Assignment chapters begin with outlines that show students how that chapter will help them to set, achieve, and assess their writing goals.

The *Setting Your Goals* feature, located near the beginning of Chapters 3 and 5–12, introduces the foundational concepts that will guide students' writing—rhetorical knowledge, critical thinking, writing processes, and knowledge of conventions. Based on the CWPA outcomes, these goals encourage students to establish a framework for their writing assignments grounded in sound rhetorical principles.

Each Setting Your Goals table relates to a type of writing. In this example, Setting Your Goals is framed specifically for persuasive writing.

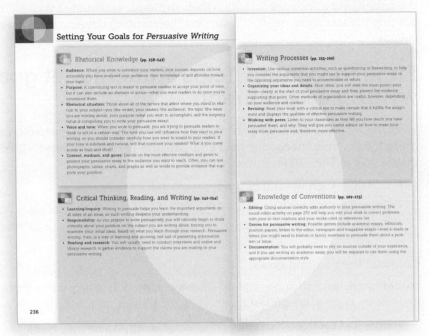

Consider their writing contexts.

Recognizing that writing is a lifelong journey, *The Guide* gives students and instructors the option—and the flexibility—of responding to writing scenarios based on academic, professional, civic, and personal contexts. Because *The Guide* focuses on all facets of a writer's life, it serves as a natural vehicle to help students as they learn to think of themselves as writers in academic, professional, civic, and personal situations.

Writing to Analyze for Life

In the professional, civic, and personal areas of your life, you also will construct analyses of various ideas, products, and situations.

The kind of analytical writing you do in your professional life will depend on your career, yet the odds are that at some point you will be asked to do an analysis and write a report on your findings. For example, an attorney analyzes legal rulings, the strengths and weaknesses of a client's case, and the arguments presented in court. A physician analyzes her patient's symptoms as she attempts to diagnose the illness and prescribe a cure.

Writing contexts. Each assignment chapter opens with specific writing contexts for the student to consider. In this example, students are presented with examples of analytical writing in professional, civic, and personal contexts.

Transfer their writing skills.

The McGraw-Hill Guide reinforces the premise that the knowledge learned and skills acquired in first-year composition classes equip students to compose not only in this and other courses but throughout their lives. *The McGraw-Hill Guide* incorporates research about transfer—the ability to carry over knowledge learned in one context and successfully apply that knowledge in another context—with its emphasis on reflective practice. Customizable assessment rubrics are available online in Connect Composition for each assignment, giving instructors the ability to show students how writing in different contexts can have an impact on their goals.

In each chapter a range of exercises asks students to reflect on their writing and on their perceptions of themselves as writers. Students will find many instances in which they are asked to consider how the writing they compose for the writing course might help them in other college classes. Instruction around transfer and activities that call upon students' metacognitive skills are tagged with this transfer icon.

Second, the *Guide* helps students achieve their goals.

After presenting the qualities of effective writing related to a particular purpose, each assignment chapter (3 and 5–12) then illustrates the steps of the writing process with clear examples of a student writer adapting to a specific writing situation. Designed to emphasize their goals as writers, each assignment chapter helps students to:

- Emphasize critical thinking and synthesize information
- Develop strategies for success
- Choose the appropriate genre
- Practice meeting writing goals

Emphasize critical thinking and synthesize information.

Chapter 3 introduces students to the importance of developing strong academic reading skills, which includes the ability to synthesize the ideas of others from diverse sources, and relates this as a critical pathway to achieving most writing goals. Every assignment chapter (chapters 5–12) then follows up on this concept in context with a section called "Synthesizing and Integrating Sources into Your Draft."

Develop strategies for success.

Based on the eight "habits of mind" that appear in the Framework for Success in Postsecondary Writing, developed by the CWPA, the National Council of Teachers of English (NCTE), and the National Writing Project and identified by the CWPA as "essential for success in college writing," Strategies for Success boxes offer students tips on how to develop their curiosity, openness, engagement, self-reflection, flexibility, creativity, persistence, and responsibility.

Strategies for Success.
Every writing assignment chapter features a Strategies for Success box. This example from Chapter 9, Writing to Convince, describes how the habit of mind "openness" strengthens a writer's argument.

Choose the appropriate genre.

Ways of Writing tables present examples of different genres relevant to the chapter topic and describe their advantages and limitations. *Genres Up Close* provides a closer look at one genre relevant to the chapter's writing purpose, including a literacy narrative, a profile, and a poster. An example of the genre follows each of these sections.

Ways of Writing to Analyze

Genres for Your College Classes	Sample Situation	Advantages of the Genre	Limitations of the Ge
Behavioral analysis	In your social psychology class, you are asked to construct a statistical analysis of the behavior in specific situations of male college students in groups, as compared to how they act individually in those same situations.	Your research and statistical analysis will provide your readers with useful information about behavior.	It is difficult to find enou reliable statistics for suc analysis; there sometime are time constraints that limit your research.
Rhetorical analysis	Your writing professor asks you to analyze the rhetorical appeals on a Web site.	This analysis will help you to understand how a Web site appeals to its readers.	This is only one way to examine a Web site.
Nutrition analysis	In your health and nutrition class, your professor asks you	You can provide useful information to readers.	Your analysis is not an evaluation of a diet, whi

Ways of Writing. This *Ways of Writing* table represents genres that relate to writing that analyzes.

Practice meeting writing goals.

The writing assignments in *The Guide* provide an array of writing possibilities, suggesting to students scenarios for constructing traditional and multimodal assignments. These Scenarios for Writing appear at the beginning of the chapter.

Writing for College

SCENARIO 1 **An Academic Paper Exploring a Career**

For this scenario, assume you are taking a career and life planning class—a class devoted to helping college students decide what discipline they might like to major in. This class gives you the opportunity to explore different career paths, to learn what the educational requirements are for various majors, and to find out what job opportunities will be available and what salaries and other forms of compensation different jobs might offer.

Writing for Life

SCENARIO 3 **Civic Writing: A Profile of a Local Agency**

What local nonprofit agencies exist in your area? What do you know about how they function? What do you know about the work that they do in your community? Do you interact with any local, county, state, or federal agencies or departments? What experiences (good or bad) have you had with such entities? Select one local nonprofit or government agency or organization in which you are interested and about which you would like to learn more. The agency or organization may be your city or county government, your local school system, or a nonprofit organization such as the United Way.

Third, *The Guide* helps students assess their goals.

The McGraw-Hill Guide gives students experience evaluating the work of their peers and responding to others' evaluations of their own work through *Writer's Workshop* activities and online peer-reviewing tools. Then, by reflecting on the writing process, students assess themselves. To help students assess whether they have achieved their goals, *The McGraw-Hill Guide* encourages students to:

- Learn effective strategies for assessing writing
- Collaborate with peers

Learn effective strategies for assessing writing.

Throughout *The McGraw-Hill Guide*, students are shown how to assess writing critically and rhetorically—whether written by a professional, another student, or themselves. Framed in the context of the core outcomes of the course, this skill has been shown to improve students' performance in their writing-intensive courses.

A compelling assortment of both professional selections and student samples—70 percent of which are new to this edition—features authors such as Laura Tohe, Jewell Parker Rhodes, John DeVore, Fernando Pérez, and Neal Gabler, with additional selections available online in the Connect Composition eReader.

Self-assessment questions at the end of each chapter ask students to consider what worked effectively for them (and what perhaps did not), what they would do differently on their next assignment, how what they learned might help them in their other classes, and so on.

Collaborate with peers.

Online, Connect Composition for *The Guide* provides several powerful tools that help students to improve their writing skills, better understand their readers, assess the impact of their writing, and revise to address the needs of their audience. With *The Guide*'s digital peer-review system, not only can students see and consider the comments of others, but they can also reflect on their work and develop a road map for revision based on the feedback they receive. Instructors can use Connect Composition to arrange peer groups and optimize the peer group experience.

Each writing assignment chapter in *The Guide* follows a student writer's progress as he or she constructs a sample paper—with examples that range from initial invention work to a first draft, to peer review and teacher feedback, to a final draft. Students thus can envision how they might follow such a path as they construct their own papers, understand what kind of feedback they may receive, and learn how to effectively work with those suggestions.

Fourth, Connect Composition for *The McGraw-Hill Guide* uses best-in-class educational technology to help students achieve first-year success.

Connect Composition helps instructors and students set, achieve, and assess their goals. Connect Composition is an assignment and assessment platform offering several powerful learning technologies that specifically support the critical outcomes of the composition course. *LearnSmart Achieve* and *SmartBook*, Connect's two adaptive learning environments, help students move through the knowledge and conceptual components of the course in a personalized, metacognitive way, giving them more confidence to engage in class discussions and communicate their ideas with peers and in their writing.

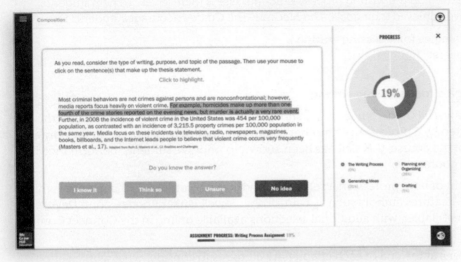

LearnSmart Achieve. Students can see their exact progress in each module, helping them pinpoint how much work they have left to complete, as well as the specific areas that require more study.

Power of Process promotes close, strategic reading and critical thinking, leading to richer, more insightful academic reading and writing in composition and beyond.

Power of Process guides students through an assigned text. With strategies selected by the instructor, which asking students to highlight, annotate, and respond to questions, Power of Process ensures that they slow down and truly engage with a reading or visual.

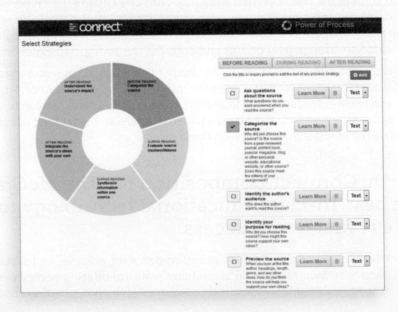

Connect Composition helps students understand, make progress on, and be reflective about their high-stakes composing assignments. The learning technologies and content in Connect Composition are meticulously developed with first-year college students in mind. This technology is designed outright to help students stay on course, transfer skills to other courses, and advance in their college careers.

Course administrators can deploy Connect Composition to establish consistency across sections, with a flow of assignments that reflect a department's curriculum and course outcomes and with reports that provide outcomes-based views of performance as well as measures of student engagement.

And Connect's deep assignment and grade book syncing with Blackboard and Canvas means it works *behind the scenes*—instructors and students access, complete, and document their work seamlessly through their local LMS interface.

Connect Composition Is an Economical, All-in-One Course Materials Solution

Handbook	☑
Rhetoric	☑
Reader	☑

Connect Composition for *The McGraw-Hill Guide* offers *all* of these common composition resources in **one place for one price**. And once students purchase Connect Composition, they can access it for four years.

The following tools and services are available with Connect Composition:

Feature	Description	Instructional Value
Simple LMS Integration	• Seamlessly integrates with every learning management system.	• Students have automatic single sign-on. • *Connect* assignment results sync to the LMS's gradebook.
LearnSmart Achieve	• Continuously adapts to a student's strengths and weaknesses to create a personalized learning environment. • Covers the writing process, critical reading, the research process, reasoning and argument, multilingual writers, grammar and common sentence problems, punctuation and mechanics, and style and word choice. • Provides instructors with reports that include data on student and class performance.	• Students independently study the fundamental topics across Composition in an adaptive environment. • Metacognitive component supports knowledge transfer. • Students track their own understanding and mastery and discover where their gaps are.

(continued)

Feature	Description	Instructional Value
SmartBook	• The first and only continuously adaptive reading experience *available for rhetorics*. Identifies and highlights content students have not mastered. • Provides instructors with reports that include data on student and class performance.	• The text adapts to the student based on what he or she knows and doesn't know and focuses study time on critical material. • Metacognitive component supports knowledge transfer. • Students track their own understanding and mastery and discover where their gaps are.
Power of Process	Guides students through the critical reading and writing process step by step.	• Students demonstrate understanding and develop critical thinking skills for reading, writing, and evaluating sources by responding to short-answer and annotation questions. Students are also prompted to reflect on their own processes. • Instructors or students can choose from a preloaded set of readings or upload their own. • Students can use the guidelines to consider a potential source critically.
Writing Assignments (with Peer Review)	• Allows instructors to assign and grade writing assignments online. • Gives instructors the option of easily and efficiently setting up and managing online peer-review assignments for the entire class.	• This online tool makes grading writing assignments more efficient, saving time for instructors. • Students import their Word document(s), and instructors can comment and annotate submissions. • Frequently used comments are automatically saved so instructors do not have to type the same feedback over and over.
Writing Assignments with Outcomes-Based Assessment	• Allows instructors or course administrators to assess student writing around specific learning outcomes. • Generates easy-to-read reports around program-specific learning outcomes. • Includes the most up-to-date Writing Program Administrators learning outcomes, but also gives instructors the option of creating their own.	• This tool provides assessment transparency to students. They can see why a "B" is a "B" and what it will take to improve to an "A." • Reports allow a program or instructor to demonstrate progress in attaining section, course, or program goals.
Connect eBook	• Provides comprehensive course content, exceeding what is offered in print. • Supports annotation and bookmarking.	The ebook allows instructors and students to access their course materials anytime and anywhere.

Feature	Description	Instructional Value
Connect eReader	Provides access to 31 additional readings that are assignable via *Connect*.	Sample essays provide models for students as well as interesting topics to consider for discussion and writing.
Insight for Instructors	• A powerful data analytics tool. Insight's visualizations are framed by questions and provide users with knowledge that they can act upon. • For instructors, Insight provides a quick view of student and class performance with a series of visual data displays that answer the following questions: • How are my students doing? • How is this student doing? • How is my section doing? • How is this assignment working? • How are my assignments working?	Instructors can quickly check on and analyze student and class performance.
Insight for Students	• A powerful data analytics tool that provides at-a-glance visualizations to help students understand their performance on *Connect* assignments. • Insight provides a view of the student's progress and performance in a series of visual displays that answer the following questions: • "How am I progressing?" which for classes larger than 10 students will show the student's individual assignment scores vs. the class average on that assignment. • "How am I doing?" which shows assignments across all courses the student is taking on Connect, allowing the student to spot assignments and even courses that may be particularly challenging.	Student Insight offers the student details on each *Connect* assignment. When possible, it offers suggestions for the student on how he or she can improve scores. These data can help guide the student to behaviors that will lead to better scores in the future.
Instructor Reports	• Allow instructors to review the performance of an individual student or an entire section. • Allow instructors or course administrators to review multiple sections to gauge progress in attaining course, department, or institutional goals.	• Instructors can identify struggling students early and intervene to ensure retention. • Instructors can identify challenging topics and adjust instruction accordingly. • Reports can be generated for an accreditation process or a program evaluation.

(continued)

Feature	Description	Instructional Value
Student Reports	Allow students to review their performance for specific assignments or the course.	Students can keep track of their performance and identify areas they are struggling with.
Pre- and Posttests	Offers precreated nonadaptive assessments for pre- and posttesting.	Pretest provides a static benchmark for student knowledge at the beginning of the program. Posttest offers a concluding assessment of student progress.
Tegrity	• Allows instructors to capture course material or lectures on video. • Allows students to watch videos recorded by their instructor and learn course material at their own pace.	• Instructors can keep track of which students have watched the videos they post. • Students can watch and review lectures from their instructor. • Students can search each lecture for specific bites of information.

Grade Book and Assignment Syncing

	Blackboard	Canvas	Angel, D2L, Moodle, Sakai, Pearson Learning Solutions (eCollege)
Single sign-on	X	X	X
Gradebook sync	X (auto-sync)	X (auto-sync)	X (manual sync)
Deep linking to assignments	X	X	

Support for Online Success

McGraw-Hill Education provides a variety of ways for instructors to get the help and support they need when incorporating new technology into a writing program. The learning technology in Connect was developed by experts to create a teaching and learning environment that engages learners with a wide variety of course assignments, suited for both online as well as hybrid or face-to-face courses. Users of Connect have several options for help in getting started, but also with developing courses and curricula that reflect best practices for incorporating learning technology.

- **Digital Faculty Consultants:** Instructors currently using Connect Composition are available to offer suggestions, advice, and training for new adopters. To request a Digital Faculty Consultant's assistance, simply e-mail your local McGraw-Hill representative.

- **Learning Technology:** Local McGraw-Hill representatives can provide local face-to-face training and support.

- **Digital Learning Consultants:** These specialists support instructors with initial setup and training as well as answer questions that may arise throughout the term.

- **Implementation Consultants:** When Connect Composition is adopted, the Implementation Consultant makes sure all facutly learn basic information about the platform, and course and assigment creation.

- **Implementation Managers:** An Implementation Manager maximizes usage in relation to course goals, course design, and tracking performance using reports and analytic insights.

In general, instructors are encouraged to contact us anytime they need help. Our Customer Support Team is available at 800-331-5094 or online at mpss.mhhe.com/contact.php.

Need a Connect Account?

Request access to Connect Composition from your local McGraw-Hill Education representative (www.mhhe.com/rep) or write to english@mheducation.com.

Reviewers

The McGraw-Hill Guide was developed with the guidance of the following instructors.

Abraham Baldwin Agricultural College Bonnie Asselin, Erin Campbell, Sandra Giles, Wendy Harrison, Jeff Newberry

Arizona Western College Jana Moore, Steve Moore, Anne-Marie Thweatt

Atlanta Metropolitan College Hristina Keranova, Kokila Ravi

Bakersfield College David Moton

Bellarmine University Olga-Maria Cruz

California State—Sacramento Angela Clark-Oates

Chesapeake College Eleanor Welsh

Cleveland Community College Tajsha Eaves

College of DuPage Jacqueline McGrath, Sheryl Mylan, Beverly Reed, Helen Szymanski

College of Saint Rose Megan Fulwiler, Jennifer Marlow

Community College of Aurora Susan Achziger

Cowley County Community College Marlys Cervantes, Julie Kratt

Dixie State University Tim Bywater, Cheri Crenshaw, Sean M. George, Randy Jasmine, Stephanie Millett

Drexel University Scott Warnock

El Paso Community College Gloria Estrada

Front Range Community College Donna Craine

Glendale Community College Alisa Cooper

Grand Rapids Community College Mursalata Muhammad

Guilford Technical Community College Jo Ann Buck, Carolyn Schneider

Harrisburg Area Community College Valerie Gray

Hawaii Pacific University—Honolulu Rob Wilson

Henderson Community College William Gary

Indiana University—Purdue University Indianapolis Steve Fox, Scott Weeden, Anne Williams

Iowa State University Sandy Hackemann, Susan Howard, Sheryl McGough, Dodie Marie Miller, John D. Miller, Carol Schuck

Ivy Tech Community College Carol Ann Chapman

James A. Rhodes State College Sally Angel, James Fallon

Johnson and Wales University James Anderson, Eileen Medeiros, Terry Novak

Kansas City Kansas Community College James Krajewski

Lake-Sumter Community College Patricia Campbell, Jacklyn Pierce, Menalie K. Wagner

Lee College David Hainline, Gordon Lee

Loyola Marymount University K. J. Peters

Madisonville Community College Gregory Dennis Hagan, Lawrence Roy, Jr.

Maryville University Jesse Kavadio

MCC-Longview Community College Dawnielle Walker

McLennan Community College Jim McKeown, Arvis Scott

Mississippi College Kerri Jordan, Jonathan Randle

Murray State College Jeana West

Northern Arizona University Jacquelyn Belknap, Valerie Robin, Nicholas Tambakeras

Northern Kentucky University, Kristi Brock

Oklahoma City Community College Angela Cotner, Michael Franco, Jon Inglett, Kim Jameson, Chris Verschage

Oklahoma State University Regina Ann McManigell Grijalva

Owens State Community College Tracy S. Darr, Brenna Dugan, Jen Hazel, Deborah Richey, Ellen Sorg

Pittsburg State University John Franklin

Prince Georges Community College Leela Kapai, Odeana Kramer, Wendy Perkins

Pueblo Community College Deborah Borchers

Purdue University—Calumet Karen Bishop Morris

Riverside City College Jason Spangler

Salt Lake Community College Lisa Bickmore

Samford University Kathy C. Flowers

Seminole State College of Florida Karen L. Feldman, Chrishawn Speller

Shawnee State University Neil Catpathios, Deborah S. Knutson

South Suburban College Laura Baltuska

Southeast Community College Kimberly Ann Fangman, Janet Kirchner

State Fair Community College Anneliese Homan

St. Louis Community College at Meramec Rich Peraud

St. Philip's College: Alamo Colleges John Michael Moran

Texas Christian University Charlotte Hogg

Triton College Alexandra Dragin, William Nedrow

University of Alabama at Birmingham Peggy Jolly, Cynthia Ryan, Rita Treutel

University of Alabama—Tuscaloosa Karen Gardiner, Steffen Guenzel, Jessica Fordham Kidd, Maryann Whitaker

University of Arizona Susan Miller-Cochran

University of Arkansas Sherry Rankins-Robertson

University of California—Irvine Lynda Haas

University of Central Florida Lindee Owens

University of Cincinnati Blue Ash College Sonja Andrus

University of Findlay Terri LaRocco, Ronald J. Tulley

University of Georgia Brandy James

University of Illinois—Chicago Nicole Khoury

University of Montana Amy Ratto Parks

University of South Alabama Larry Beason

University of Southern Indiana—Evansville Jill Kinkade, Paula M. von Lowenfeldt

University of Texas—El Paso Beth Brunk-Chavez, Christie Daniels, Judith Fourzan, Cira Montoya, Maggie Smith, Adam Webb, Judika Webb

University of Wisconsin—River Falls Jenny Brantley, Kathleen Hunzer, Lissa Schneider-Rebozo

Wilkes Community College Lisa Muir, Julie Mullis

Symposium Attendees

As part of its ongoing research in composition and in the design and administration of writing programs, McGraw-Hill conducts several symposia annually for instructors from across the country. These events offer a forum for instructors to exchange ideas and experiences with colleagues they might not have met otherwise. The feedback McGraw-Hill has received has been invaluable and has contributed directly to the development of *The McGraw-Hill Guide*.

Clark State Community College Laurie Buchanan

Cumberland County College James Piccone

East Carolina University Tracy Ann Morse

East Mississippi Community College Marilyn Ford

East Tennessee State University Martha Michieka

Full Sail University Rachelle Fox

Indiana University Purdue University Fort Wayne Debrah Huffman

Johnson County Community College Theodore Rollins

Northwest Vista College Jullie Moore-Felux

Robert Morris University Julianne Michalenko

Santa Fe College Melissa Flanagan

State College of Florida Angelique Medvesky

University of California—Irvine Lynda Haas

University of North Florida David MacKinnon

University of Southern Indiana Audrey Hillyer

Wayne County Community College Ella Davis

WPA Outcomes Statement for First-Year Composition

Introduction

This Statement identifies outcomes for first-year composition programs in U.S. postsecondary education. It describes the writing knowledge, practices, and attitudes that undergraduate students develop in first-year composition, which at most schools is a required general education course or sequence of courses. This Statement therefore attempts to both represent and regularize writing programs' priorities for first-year composition, which often takes the form of one or more required general education courses. To this end it is not merely a compilation or summary of what currently takes place. Rather, this Statement articulates what composition teachers nationwide have learned from practice, research, and theory.[1] It intentionally defines only "outcomes," or types of results, and not "standards," or precise levels of achievement. The setting of standards to measure students' achievement of these Outcomes has deliberately been left to local writing programs and their institutions.

In this Statement "composing" refers broadly to complex writing processes that are increasingly reliant on the use of digital technologies. Writers also attend to elements of design, incorporating images and graphical elements into texts intended for screens as well as printed pages. Writers' composing activities have always been shaped by the technologies available to them, and digital technologies are changing writers' relationships to their texts and audiences in evolving ways.

These outcomes are supported by a large body of research demonstrating that the process of learning to write in any medium is complex: it is both individual and social and demands continued practice and informed guidance. Programmatic decisions about helping students demonstrate these outcomes should be informed by an understanding of this research.

As students move beyond first-year composition, their writing abilities do not merely improve. Rather, their abilities will diversify along disciplinary, professional, and civic lines as these writers move into new settings where expected outcomes expand, multiply, and diverge. Therefore, this document advises faculty in all disciplines about how to help students build on what they learn in introductory writing courses.

 ## RHETORICAL KNOWLEDGE

Rhetorical knowledge is the ability to analyze contexts and audiences and then to act on that analysis in comprehending and creating texts. Rhetorical knowledge is the basis of composing. Writers develop rhetorical knowledge by negotiating purpose, audience, context, and conventions as they compose a variety of texts for different situations.

By the end of first-year composition, students should

- Learn and use key rhetorical concepts through analyzing and composing a variety of texts
- Gain experience reading and composing in several genres to understand how genre conventions shape and are shaped by readers' and writers' practices and purposes
- Develop facility in responding to a variety of situations and contexts calling for purposeful shifts in voice, tone, level of formality, design, medium, and/or structure
- Understand and use a variety of technologies to address a range of audiences
- Match the capacities of different environments (e.g., print and electronic) to varying rhetorical situations

Faculty in all programs and departments can build on this preparation by helping students learn

- The expectations of readers in their fields
- The main features of genres in their fields
- The main purposes of composing in their fields

---

[1]This Statement is aligned with the *Framework for Success in Postsecondary Writing*, an articulation of the skills and habits of mind essential for success in college, and is intended to help establish a continuum of valued practice from high school through to the college major.

CRITICAL THINKING, READING, AND COMPOSING

Critical thinking is the ability to analyze, synthesize, interpret, and evaluate ideas, information, situations, and texts. When writers think critically about the materials they use—whether print texts, photographs, data sets, videos, or other materials—they separate assertion from evidence, evaluate sources and evidence, recognize and evaluate underlying assumptions, read across texts for connections and patterns, identify and evaluate chains of reasoning, and compose appropriately qualified and developed claims and generalizations. These practices are foundational for advanced academic writing.

By the end of first-year composition, students should

- Use composing and reading for inquiry, learning, critical thinking, and communicating in various rhetorical contexts

- Read a diverse range of texts, attending especially to relationships between assertion and evidence, to patterns of organization, to the interplay between verbal and nonverbal elements, and to how these features function for different audiences and situations

- Locate and evaluate (for credibility, sufficiency, accuracy, timeliness, bias and so on) primary and secondary research materials, including journal articles and essays, books, scholarly and professionally established and maintained databases or archives, and informal electronic networks and internet sources

- Use strategies—such as interpretation, synthesis, response, critique, and design/redesign—to compose texts that integrate the writer's ideas with those from appropriate sources

Faculty in all programs and departments can build on this preparation by helping students learn

- The kinds of critical thinking important in their disciplines

- The kinds of questions, problems, and evidence that define their disciplines

- Strategies for reading a range of texts in their fields

 ## PROCESSES

Writers use multiple strategies, or *composing processes*, to conceptualize, develop, and finalize projects. Composing processes are seldom linear: a writer may research a topic before drafting, then conduct additional research while revising or after consulting a colleague. Composing processes are also flexible: successful writers can adapt their composing processes to different contexts and occasions.

By the end of first-year composition, students should

- Develop a writing project through multiple drafts

- Develop flexible strategies for reading, drafting, reviewing, collaborating, revising, rewriting, rereading, and editing

- Use composing processes and tools as a means to discover and reconsider ideas

- Experience the collaborative and social aspects of writing processes

- Learn to give and to act on productive feedback to works in progress

- Adapt composing processes for a variety of technologies and modalities

- Reflect on the development of composing practices and how those practices influence their work

Faculty in all programs and departments can build on this preparation by helping students learn

- To employ the methods and technologies commonly used for research and communication within their fields

- To develop projects using the characteristic processes of their fields

- To review work in progress for the purpose of developing ideas before surface-level editing

- To participate effectively in collaborative processes typical of their field

 ## KNOWLEDGE OF CONVENTIONS

Conventions are the formal rules and informal guidelines that define genres, and in so doing, shape readers' and writers' perceptions of correctness or appropriateness. Most obviously, conventions govern such things as mechanics, usage, spelling, and citation practices. But they also influence content, style, organization, graphics, and document design.

Conventions arise from a history of use and facilitate reading by invoking common expectations between writers and readers. These expectations are not universal; they vary by genre (conventions for lab notebooks and discussion-board exchanges differ), by discipline (conventional moves in literature reviews in Psychology differ from those in English), and by occasion (meeting minutes and executive summaries use different registers). A writer's grasp of conventions in one context does not mean a firm grasp in another. Successful writers understand, analyze, and negotiate conventions for purpose, audience, and genre, understanding that genres evolve in response to changes in material conditions and composing technologies and attending carefully to emergent conventions.

By the end of first-year composition, students should

- Develop knowledge of linguistic structures, including grammar, punctuation, and spelling, through practice in composing and revising
- Understand why genre conventions for structure, paragraphing, tone, and mechanics vary

- Gain experience negotiating variations in genre conventions
- Learn common formats and/or design features for different kinds of texts
- Explore the concepts of intellectual property (such as fair use and copyright) that motivate documentation conventions
- Practice applying citation conventions systematically in their own work

Faculty in all programs and departments can build on this preparation by helping students learn

- The reasons behind conventions of usage, specialized vocabulary, format, and citation systems in their fields or disciplines
- Strategies for controlling conventions in their fields or disciplines
- Factors that influence the ways work is designed, documented, and disseminated in their fields
- Ways to make informed decisions about intellectual property issues connected to common genres and modalities in their fields.

WPA Outcomes Statement for First-Year Composition (3.0), approved July 7, 2014. Copyright © 2014 by the Council of Writing Program Administrators. Used with permission.

Writing Goals and Objectives for College and for Life

Whenever you write, you strive to fulfill a goal. In school, you write papers and essay exam answers to demonstrate what you have learned and to communicate your ideas to others. Outside of school, you use writing to perform your duties in the workplace, to make your voice heard in your community, and to communicate with friends and family. Most discourse has a goal or **purpose:** to explain, to inform, to persuade, and so on.

Whatever the purpose, effective writers achieve their objectives. **Rhetoric** is the use of words—either spoken or written—as well as visuals to achieve some goal. Each chapter in this book has a *rhetorical* focus on what you as a writer want your writing to *accomplish*.

The first decision a writer makes is rhetorical: What would you like this writing to *do* for a particular group of readers—your **audience**—at a particular place and time? Once you have determined your goals, you are prepared to decide how much and what kinds of information your audience needs to know

© Nano Calvo/Alamy

and what will be convincing to this audience. You also decide how to collect this information and how to present it in an appropriate format. This rhetorical approach applies to writing that you do in various settings—not just in the classroom.

This chapter provides the context for the exploration of writing in subsequent chapters. Here we look at writing in the four areas of life, the course learning

goals, the concept of becoming a self-reflective writer, and strategies for success.

As you work through this chapter, think about the writing you will produce for this class, as well as for the other classes you are taking. How will the ideas in this chapter help you improve your writing?

Writing in the Four Areas of Your Life

Improving your ability to write effective college papers is an important goal of this course and this text. However, writing skills are vital not only in college but also in the professional, civic, and personal parts of your life.

Consider how you plan to spend the twenty-four hours in each day for the next week, the next month, the next year, the next four years, the next decade, and the next six decades. If you are like most students, during the next few years, you will devote much of your time to your academic studies. When you finish your academic studies, however, your time commitments will probably change. Although it is possible that you may still be a student half a decade from now, it is more likely that you will devote most of your time to the other three parts of your life—especially to your professional life.

Writing as a College Student

See Chapter 4 for writing-to-learn strategies.

You will be expected to do a great deal of writing in college because writing is a powerful tool both for learning and for demonstrating learning. Students who use writing to explore course material generally learn more—and get higher grades—than students who do not. The reason for this enhanced performance is fairly simple: writing is an effective way to become more involved with your course material in all of your college classes.

Writing as a Professional

Almost all jobs require some writing; some require a great deal of it. Furthermore, employers frequently list strong writing skills as one of the most important qualifications they seek in job candidates.

Surveys of employers consistently confirm the importance of writing in the work world: employers want to hire people who can write and speak clearly and effectively, think critically, solve problems efficiently, work well in teams, and use technology thoughtfully. The most competitive job seekers are those who begin honing these skills early.

Writing as a Citizen

As Thomas Jefferson frequently noted, democracies—and societies in general—work most effectively when citizens are well educated and involved. If you have strong feelings about certain issues and want to have a voice in how your society functions, you need to participate in your community. One important way to make your voice heard in a representative democracy is to write. You can write to elected officials at the local, state, and federal levels to let them know what you think about an issue and why you think the way that you do. In the civic part of your life, you often solve problems by working with others—neighbors or other citizens who are involved and interested in issues that affect them, their neighborhood, and their community.

Writing Activity

Balancing the Four Areas of Life

Working with two or three of your classmates, answer the following questions about the bar graph shown in Figure 1.1. Compare and discuss your responses. Your instructor may ask your group to share its findings with the rest of the class.

- Which group of bars (1, 2, 3, or 4) comes closest to representing the current balance in your life?

- Which group of bars comes closest to representing what you consider the ideal balance for someone enrolled full-time in college? For someone enrolled part-time? For a student with family responsibilities and/or a part-time or full-time job?

- Which group of bars best represents the balance that you would like to achieve a decade from now? Two decades from now? Five decades from now?

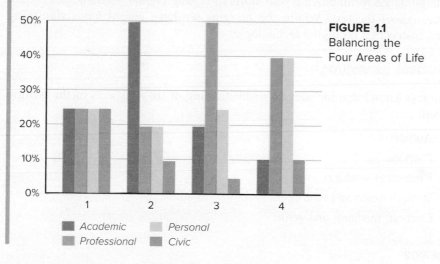

FIGURE 1.1
Balancing the
Four Areas of Life

Academic   Personal
Professional   Civic

Writing as a Family Member or Friend

Even though writing in the academic, professional, and civic areas of life is important, the writing that you do in your personal life at times can be the most important of all. We write—whether on paper or in cyberspace—to the people who are significant to us to accomplish life's daily tasks and to fulfill our needs.

Writing in the Four Areas in This Course

Because the academic, professional, civic, and personal parts of our lives are all important, this book offers numerous opportunities to write in all four areas. In each chapter in Parts 2 and 3, you have the option of writing in response to an academic or other type of situation. In addition, the writing assignments in these chapters are built around **scenarios**—simulated but realistic writing situations. Each scenario assignment provides a specific purpose for writing and a specific audience.

 ## Learning Goals in This Course

Whether you are writing for an academic, professional, civic, or personal audience and purpose, you will draw on the same set of writing skills. Your work in this course will help you to learn and to apply these skills to specific writing situations. To achieve this end, throughout the text we have incorporated the learning goals developed by the Council of Writing Program Administrators (CWPA), a national organization of instructors who direct composition courses. The goals are organized into four broad areas: rhetorical knowledge; critical thinking, reading, and writing; writing processes; and knowledge of conventions. Woven throughout are goals specific to using digital technologies in writing practice. Chapters include guidance for improving your skills in "Using Digital Technologies" boxes and throughout the text. Within the margins we have placed icons signifying focused instruction on digital technologies.

Rhetorical Knowledge

Rhetorical knowledge includes an understanding of these aspects of the writing situation:

- Audience
- Purpose
- Rhetorical situation
- Writer's voice and tone
- Context, medium, and genre

AUDIENCE

To write for others successfully, you need to tailor your writing to their expectations and needs. You need to focus on where there is a meeting of minds—yours and theirs—and where there is not. For example, if you were to write the following grocery list and take it to the store, you would probably know precisely what you had in mind.

Grocery List

cereal
milk
coffee
bread
paper

If you were sick, however, and had to rely on a close family member to do your grocery shopping for you, you might have to revise the list by adding a few more details.

Version of the Grocery List for a Family Member
Cereal
1% milk
Coffee beans
Multigrain bread
Sunday paper

If you handed the list to a neighbor, though, you would probably have to add much more specific information.

Version of the Grocery List for a Neighbor
Grape Nuts Flakes
1% milk (half gallon)
whole-bean Starbuck's Sumatra extra-bold decaf coffee
Grandma Sycamore's multigrain bread
the New York Times

In each case, you would adjust your list for the person who needs to act on the information. When you share a great deal of experience with your reader, you can leave gaps in information without causing serious problems. The fewer experiences you have in common with your audience, however, the more you need to fill in those gaps as you draft and revise, rather than after you have finished writing.

PURPOSE

In this book Chapters 3–12 focus on common rhetorical purposes for writing: to understand and synthesize texts, to learn, to share experiences, to explore, to inform, to analyze, to convince, to evaluate, to examine causes and effects, and to solve problems. In Chapter 3 you will learn to respond critically to a text and to synthesize texts. In Chapter 4 you will have opportunities to experiment with many forms of writing to learn, which will serve you in this course, as well as your other courses. In Chapters 5–12, you will have opportunities to engage with those purposes in some detail. In all the chapters, we will ask you to connect the concepts outlined to the other classes you are taking (and the writing you will do in those classes).

RHETORICAL SITUATION

When writers compose for a particular purpose, in response to the needs of a particular audience, they are responding to a **rhetorical situation.** A rhetorical situation consists of the following elements:

- Writer
- Purpose
- Audience
- Topic
- Context/occasion

Although each rhetorical situation is unique, there are general types of situations that require writers to use the appropriate conventions of format and structure.

For example, if you are writing a lab report for a biology course, your instructor will expect you to structure your report in a certain way and to use a neutral, informative tone. If you are proposing a solution to a problem in your community, your readers will expect you first to describe the problem and then to explain how your solution can be implemented, using a reasonable, even-handed tone and giving some attention to possible objections to your proposal.

WRITER'S VOICE AND TONE

A writer's **voice** is the personality or image that is revealed in the writer's text—the impression made on the reader. To establish a distinctive voice, a writer thoughtfully and consistently makes decisions about such elements as diction (word choice), syntax (sentence structure), and punctuation. For instance, think about a close friend whose use of a particular word or phrase clearly identifies that friend.

Tone is the writer's attitude toward the topic, the audience, and other people. Tone can reveal the extent to which a writer is respectful/disrespectful, patient/impatient, supportive/unsupportive, angry, happy, irritated, accommodating/unaccommodating, and the like. For example, Stephen Colbert, host of *The Late Show with Stephen Colbert*, will say something like, "I couldn't have said it better myself" when a political figure or celebrity has made a statement that many people find offensive or illogical. Everyone knows that his tone is ironic; he clearly means the opposite of what he is saying.

CONTEXT, MEDIUM, AND GENRE

The context for writing affects the writer's choice of medium and genre. For example, an executive who needs to announce a company's plan for furloughs

How would your writing change if you were writing to (a) a friend who is still in high school about your new roommate, and (b) a housing administrator to request a housing change?

© PhotoAlto/PunchStock RF

© Jamie Grill/JGC/Getty Images RF

(required time off without pay) to thousands of employees in several cities will probably choose to send a memo (the genre) via e-mail (the medium). This genre and this medium make sense in this context because companies often use memos for such announcements. Further, the medium of e-mail is cost-effective.

Context: Throughout this book you will have opportunities to write in a variety of **contexts,** or the circumstances that surround your writing, in all four arenas of life—the academic, the professional, the civic, and the personal. These opportunities appear in scenarios describing various rhetorical situations that give rise to writing. Consider what you would write if you were in the following rhetorical situations:

1. You want to convince the financial aid officer at your college that you need a scholarship to stay in school next semester.
2. After a disagreement with your spouse/fiancé/girlfriend/boyfriend, you want to write a letter to apologize for having said something that you regret.
3. After a disagreement with your supervisor at work, you want to write a letter to apologize for having said something that you regret.

As you contemplate these rhetorical situations, consider how the purpose, audience, topic, and context/occasion might alter what you will write. For instance, how does writing an apology to a love interest (no. 2 above) differ from writing an apology to your supervisor (no. 3 above)? In this case the purpose is the same, but the audiences differ.

Medium: A medium is a physical or electronic means of communication. **Media** include books, pamphlets, newspapers, magazines, CDs, DVDs, and the World Wide Web. As you develop projects for Chapters 5–12, you will be encouraged to use various media to communicate with your audience. Although you may want to use what feels most comfortable, you may also want to try forms of media that you have not used before.

Genre: *Genre* is a French word meaning "kind" or "type." Although people frequently use the word **genre** to refer to kinds of texts, such as a letter, a formal paper, a report, or a memo, people use this word in a wide variety of ways. You may have heard *genre* used to refer to the **content** of texts. For example, Shakespearean plays are labeled tragedies, comedies, or histories. If a friend tells you that she saw a film version of a Shakespearean tragedy last night, you could guess fairly accurately that she saw characters die as a result of foul deeds. Likewise, if another friend said that she had read résumés all morning, you would know that she was reading about people's educational and work backgrounds.

Genre also refers to different **forms** of texts. For example, think again about the friend who said that she had read résumés all morning. Résumés have not only standard content (educational and work background) but also a generally standard, easily recognized format.

From a rhetorical standpoint, you select the format or overall structure of the piece of writing you are constructing. A letter will have a salutation, a body, and a signature, although the structure of the body of that letter could vary widely—it could be organized in paragraphs or as a list, for instance. The point is that content can come in many kinds of packages. For example, in writing to convince people to wear seat belts, you could use any of the following: an academic paper, a flyer, a poster, or a Web site in which you present an argument in support of wearing seat belts; a poem, short story, play, or song about someone who died because he neglected to use a seat belt; an obituary; or a newspaper story.

You may choose from a wide variety of genres for writing projects in Chapters 5–12. In each of these chapters, you will find information about genres that are commonly used for that rhetorical purpose. For example, in Chapter 9, "Writing to Convince," you will find information about editorials, position papers, job references, and advertisements. In writing, *genre* means that you follow the conventions of a kind of writing and provide, generally, what readers expect from that genre. A paper for one of your college classes will usually be more formal and detailed than an e-mail you might write to your classmates asking them to vote in an upcoming election.

Rhetorical Analysis

For more information on rhetorical analysis, see Chapter 2.

A **rhetorical analysis** is an examination of the relative effectiveness of a particular text written for a particular audience for a particular purpose. It can include any of the previously mentioned features of rhetorical situations: audience, purpose, voice and tone, context, format, and genre. The average person does many rhetorical analyses each day. When someone says, "I don't think so," "yeah, right," or, "whatever," in response to a statement, that person is questioning the credibility of the speaker or the accuracy of the information. Although formal rhetorical analyses are more elaborate than this example suggests, the principle is the same.

Throughout this book, you will have opportunities to engage in rhetorical analysis. For example, at the end of each reading in Chapters 5–12, you will have an opportunity to write brief rhetorical analyses of those texts.

Critical Thinking, Reading, and Writing

To get the most out of your reading and to accomplish your goals as a writer, you need to develop and use critical thinking skills. In Chapter 2 we offer some informal reading and writing activities that promote critical thinking. Although these activities will help you read more thoughtfully, many of them are also tools for generating ideas and material for the more formal writing tasks you will do in all four parts of your life and, of course, in the other college classes you are taking.

In general, you engage in **critical thinking** when you examine an idea from many perspectives—seeing it in new ways. For example, when you write a formal argument, you will need to address others' objections to your ideas if you hope to persuade your audience to accept your point. As noted in Chapter 3, when you respond to texts or when you synthesize the ideas in several texts, you are thinking critically. You can also apply critical thinking to understand the relationships among language, knowledge, and power. That is, language often has a greater impact when it is used by people in positions of social, political, or economic power. When used effectively, language is often far more powerful than physical weapons. Many modern governments have written constitutions and written laws derived from those constitutions. The most politically and economically powerful people in societies tend to be those who use critical thinking and language most effectively to present their ideas.

Writing Processes

Although writing processes vary from writer to writer and from situation to situation, effective writers generally go through the following activities:

- Generating initial ideas
- Relating those ideas to the writing situation or assignment
- Conducting research to find support for their ideas
- Organizing ideas and support and writing an initial draft
- Revising and shaping the paper, frequently with the advice of other readers
- Editing and polishing the paper

The order of these processes can vary, and often you will need to return to a previous step. For example, while drafting you may discover that you need to find more support for one of your ideas; while revising you may find a better way to organize your ideas.

When writers revise, they add or delete words, phrases, sentences, or even whole paragraphs, and they often modify their ideas. After they have revised multiple times, they then edit, attending to word choice, punctuation, grammar, usage, and spelling—the "surface features" of written texts. Writers also revise and edit texts to meet the needs of particular readers.

Effective writers also ask others to help them generate and refine their ideas and polish their prose. Published writers in academic, civic, and professional fields rely heavily on others as they work, often showing one another drafts of their writing before submitting a manuscript to publishers.

Because effective writers get help from others, this book provides many opportunities for you and your classmates—your **peers**—to help one another. One key to working productively with others is to understand that they bring different backgrounds, experiences, knowledge, and perspectives to the writing task, so it is critical to treat what others think and say with respect, no matter how much you agree or disagree with them. You should also remember when working with others that the suggestions and comments they make are about your *text,* not about you.

Knowledge of Conventions

Conventions are the table manners of writing. Sometimes they matter; other times they do not. Writing notes to help yourself learn course material is like eating breakfast alone at home. In this situation, table manners are not very important. When you are having dinner with your employer or the president of your college, though, table manners do matter. The same principle applies when you write for readers. Effective writers know which writing conventions to use in particular settings.

To make their writing more appealing to readers, writers need to master many conventions: spelling, punctuation, sentence structure, and word choice. While some conventions are considered signs of the writer's respect for readers (correctly spelling someone's name, for instance), other conventions, such as punctuation, organization, tone, the use of headers and white space, and documentation style, help your readers understand what you are saying and where your information comes from.

Using Digital Technologies

Initially you might wonder, "Why is using digital technologies a learning goal for a writing course?" In fact, most writers use some kind of digital technology for parts of their composing process. Although many students choose to use pen and paper for note-taking or for the initial parts of their writing process, others write exclusively with a digital technology, taking notes on a laptop or tablet or even on a smartphone. At some point in the process, however, most students are likely to use a word-processing program.

Although you are likely aware that you will be using some kind of digital technology to produce your final drafts for your college assignments, digital writing will be a major part of the writing you do in all aspects of your life, whether you are sending an e-mail to a professor or supervisor, composing a text message to a friend, or updating your Facebook status. Part of what it means to compose using digital technologies is to understand the rhetorical strategies that are necessary in each different situation. You won't use the same strategies when you send a text message to a friend that you would when you e-mail an instructor. Likewise, the rhetorical strategies you use when updating your Facebook status are very different from the ones you employ when writing a paper for a course.

Further, using digital technologies strategically can help you throughout the process of composing. It is clearly easier to revise and edit using the functions of a word processor. However, a variety of technologies also make it extremely easy to share your work and review the work of others. You can share files simply by e-mailing them or sharing a flash drive, or you might choose to use a collaborative writing environment such as Google Docs or a wiki.

Finally, because research is often done electronically, it is essential to understand how to find credible online sources. To locate these sources, you need to understand how to use your college library's Web site as a portal to a wide range of scholarly databases and credible Web sites.

Writing Activity

Assessing Your Strengths and Weaknesses

In no more than two pages, assess your current strengths and weaknesses in each of the four goal areas: rhetorical knowledge; critical thinking, reading, and writing; writing processes; and knowledge of conventions. Also consider your proficiency in using digital technologies. Share your self-assessment with two or three classmates.

USING DIGITAL TECHNOLOGIES | **Sharing Digital Literacy**

You and your classmates can help each other get more out of the writing technologies that are available on your campus. Offer to show your friends or the members of your study group shortcuts and tools in programs you are familiar with. Don't be shy about asking friends and classmates for tips and tricks they've picked up while developing their projects. You can use your own computing knowledge as "social collateral" in classes because some students will be more comfortable than others with various programs. For example, you might show your classmates how to use some of the formatting tools in the word processor and ask others to show you how to use slide show presentation, spreadsheet, or sound file–mixing software.

Writing Activity

Assessing Your Uses of Digital Technologies

Think about the ways in which you have used digital technologies in the past year. In the grid below, list a few tasks that you have done with digital technologies. Compare your list with those of several classmates.

Digital Tool	Academic Situation	Professional, Civic, or Personal Situation
• E-mail	_____	_____
• Word-processing software	_____	_____
• Web browser (e.g., Mozilla Firefox, Safari)	_____	_____
• Web site composing tools (e.g., Dreamweaver)	_____	_____
• Presentation software (e.g., PowerPoint, Prezi)	_____	_____
• Other	_____	_____

Becoming a Self-Reflective Writer

By evaluating your strengths and weaknesses in each of the four learning outcomes, you have taken a step toward becoming a more reflective—and therefore a more successful—writer. Throughout this course, you will continue to build on this foundation. Toward the end of each chapter in Parts 2 and 3, you will be asked to reflect on the work you did for that chapter. Reflecting—in writing—on your own writing activities helps you learn what worked (and perhaps what did not work). That kind of activity will help you remember the most useful aspects of your process the next time you face a similar writing task. By reflecting on your learning and thinking of yourself as a writer, you increase the likelihood that your learning will transfer to other settings in the four arenas of life.

GENRES *Up Close*   Writing a Reflection

A meaningful form of thinking and writing, **reflection** is an opportunity to consider carefully the importance, value, or applicability of something. Reflection may improve your ability to learn a skill or acquire knowledge. A reflection includes two components:

- A description of what is being reflected on. For example, if you reflect on a lab experiment, you first need to describe the experiment. If you reflect on what you learned from reading a novel, you first need to summarize the novel. When you describe or summarize the subject of your reflection, you make it easier for your readers to understand it. In addition, the action of describing or summarizing helps you to focus your attention on the subject of your reflection.

- A thoughtful consideration of the subject of your reflection. For example, you could ask the following kinds of questions:
  - Why is the subject of my reflection important? How can I apply it?
  - What have I learned from this experience?
  - What do I know about _____? What do I still need to learn about _____?
  - What do my readers know about _____? What do they not know about _____? What do they need to know about _____?
  - Why am I engaged in this activity?
  - How can I apply this learning to other settings in my life—now and in the future?

In this book you will be asked to engage in many forms of reflection. The following example is an excerpt from a reflection by student writer Zack Peach, whose paper appears in Chapter 9. Notice how Peach addresses his knowledge and skills, as well as connections between the academic and personal arenas of his life:

> My passion for this topic encouraged me to devote lots of time and energy to writing a paper that would help other people understand how autism—Asperger's syndrome, in particular—affects the lives of people. Because I have lived with Asperger's syndrome for nearly two decades, I feel knowledgeable about the topic and compelled to use the term "Asperger's" even though it is no longer used as an official diagnosis for a particular form of autism.
>
> I enjoyed working on this writing project because it gave me an opportunity to consider the wide range of feelings that I have about the topic. I also enjoyed working with my peers, who asked me lots of questions about the topic and about my experiences. Their questions helped me to refine what I had said in earlier versions of the paper. They helped me see how I needed to elaborate on what I had said so that my thoughts would be easier to understand by people who have not experienced Asperger's or other forms of autism.
>
> I think that my writing skills are improving because of the invention work, drafting, revising, and editing that our teacher asks us to do. However, the more I write, the more I realize that learning to write is a lifelong journey. I'm eager to keep working at it.
>
> Most important, I feel that papers such as this one give me an opportunity to make a difference in the lives of other people.

Strategies for Success

Successful people use strategies that are effective in most areas of life. Recognizing this, several professional organizations—the Council of Writing Program Administrators, the National Council of Teachers of English, and the National Writing Project—have identified eight strategies—habits of mind—that can help writers achieve their goals:

- **Curiosity:** the desire to know more about the world
- **Openness:** the willingness to consider new ways of thinking and being
- **Engagement:** a sense of being involved in and committed to learning
- **Creativity:** the ability to use new and unusual approaches for generating, investigating, and representing ideas
- **Persistence:** the ability to remain interested in and involved with your projects, regardless of their length
- **Responsibility:** the ability to take ownership of your actions and understand the consequences of those actions for yourself and others
- **Flexibility:** the ability to adapt to situations, expectations, or demands
- **Metacognition:** the ability to reflect on your own thinking, as well as on the way that people in your culture tend to think

In Chapters 5–12 in this book, you will find suggestions for using these eight strategies to help you become a more effective writer. As you use these strategies, however, think about how they can help you to become more successful in anything that you attempt to do in life.

Text Credits

p. 13: Framework for Success in Postsecondary Writing (2011) by the Council of Writing Program Administrators (CWPA), the National Council of Teachers of English (NCTE), and the National Writing Project (NWP), January 2011; wpacouncil.org/files/framework-for-success-postsecondary-writing.pdf.

Reading Critically for College and for Life

In Chapter 1, we consider how writing skills will serve you in the academic, professional, civic, and personal areas of your life. This chapter focuses on an activity that reinforces and helps you improve your writing skills: **reading.** When we read, we make meaning out of words on a page or computer screen. We also "read" photographs and other visual images. Actually, then, reading is the active process of constructing meaning.

In this chapter, we ask you to consider how you currently read different kinds of material and give you some helpful reading strategies. Specifically, the chapter presents pre-reading strategies, strategies for reading actively, and post-reading strategies. All of these strategies will help you better understand what you read and use that information to make your own writing more effective.

In your college classes, you will be asked to read (and write) about all kinds of print and digital texts for all kinds of purposes. More often than not, you will use some of what you read in the papers that you write for your college classes. The

© Digital Division/Getty Images RF

connection between what you read and how you use that material in your writing requires you to read *critically.*

What does it mean to *read critically*? One thing reading critically does not mean is to be "nitpicky" or negative. Rather, when you read a text *critically*, you question what you read, make connections to other texts

you have read and to your own experiences, and think about how the information in the text might help you as you develop your own writing. To read critically means to read *thoughtfully*, to keep in mind what you already know, and to interact *actively* with the text. Critical readers underline, make notes, and ask questions as they read.

Why Read Critically? Integrating Sources into Your Own Writing

Why do you suppose that your instructor asks you to read critically and thoughtfully? In addition to reading to understand the information, a key reason to read critically and thoughtfully is so that you will be able to put the information and concepts you read about into your own writing, to support your own ideas.

Reading critically also has an added bonus: it helps you understand how the writing you read "works"—what makes that writing effective (or not) or how that writing connects to and affects (or doesn't affect) readers. As you read and learn to understand how the writing your instructors ask you to read *functions,* you will be able to construct more effective texts.

In your college classes, you will be asked to read *a lot*. Understanding what you read and relating what you read to what you already know is, to a large extent, what college is about. As you read for your college classes, consider how you might use that information in your own class papers or examinations. For example, if you know your philosophy instructor will ask you to construct a paper in which you outline and explain "philosophy of the mind," you should look for the terms *philosophy* and *mind* and anything that connects them as you read. Ask yourself:

- What is the main point, the thesis? How does it relate to what I already know? To what I'm reading for this class?

- How are important terms defined? How do the author's definitions compare to what I think the terms mean? What terms or concepts are not explained (and so I'll need to look them up)?

- How effective is the supporting evidence the author supplies?

- What did the author leave out? How does that omission affect his or her argument?

- What information in this text will help me construct my own paper?

You *use* what you learned from your reading by integrating those ideas into your own writing, by citing and paraphrasing the concepts you glean from your reading. You can read about using quotations in your own writing in Chapter 6. Chapter 20 discusses how to paraphrase and attribute those ideas correctly.

Writing Activity

How Do You Read?

Take a few minutes to answer the following questions:

- What kinds of books or magazines do you like to read? Newspapers? Web sites? Blogs?

- How does the way you read a text online differ from the way you read an article in a print magazine or newspaper?

- How do you read your college textbooks? How do the strategies you use to read a text for one course differ from those you use to read texts for another course?

- What strategies do you use to read long, complex nonfiction texts?

- What strategies do you use to help you understand and remember what you have read?

Share your answers with several classmates. How do your responses compare with theirs? What strategies do they use that might be helpful to you?

Using Pre-reading Strategies

When you write, you have a purpose in mind. As we note in Chapter 1, the reason for writing is your **rhetorical purpose**—what you hope to accomplish. Likewise, before you read, think about your rhetorical purpose: What are you trying to accomplish by reading? Are you reading to be entertained, to learn new information, to understand a complex subject in more detail, or for some other reason? If you consciously think about *why* you are reading, as well as *how* you plan to read a particular piece of writing, you will have a strategy you can follow as you begin reading.

Before you start to read any written work, take a few minutes to preview its content and design. Look for the following elements:

- The title of the work, or of the particular section you are about to read
- Headings that serve as an outline of the text
- Boxes that highlight certain kinds of information
- Charts, maps, photographs, or drawings
- Numbered or bulleted lists (such as this one) that set off certain information

Think about what you bring to your reading task: In what ways does the text seem similar to or different from others of this type or on this topic that you have already read? What can you bring to the new reading that you have learned from your past experiences? If you are actively involved in the reading process and if you think of reading rhetorically—that is, if you think about what you want to get from the reading—then you will start with a useful map for any text you read.

Next, skim the text by reading the first and last sections or paragraphs, as well as any elements that are highlighted in some way, such as boxes, section titles, headings, or terms or phrases in bold or italic type. Sometimes a box or highlighted section at the beginning of an article—often called an **abstract**—will give you a quick summary of what lies ahead.

As a final step before you start to read, consider again what you hope to accomplish by reading this particular text. Ask yourself:

- What information have I noticed that might help me with my writing task?
- How have I reacted so far to what I have seen in the text?
- What questions do I have?
- What in this text seems to relate to other texts that I have read?

Reading Actively

Now that previewing has given you a sense of what the text is about, you are ready to read actively. Here are some questions to ask yourself as you read:

- What is the writer's thesis or main point? What evidence does the writer provide to support that point? Does the writer offer statistics, facts, expert opinion, or anecdotes (stories)?

- How reliable is the information in this text? How conscientiously does the writer indicate the sources of his or her data, facts, or examples? How credible do these sources seem?

- What else do you know about this topic? How can you relate your previous knowledge to what this writer is saying? In what ways do you agree or disagree with the point the writer is making?

- Has the writer included examples that clarify the text? Are there photographs, drawings, or diagrams that help you understand the writer's main points? Graphs or charts that illustrate data or other statistical information? In what way(s) do the examples and visuals help you better understand the text? What information do they give you that the written text does not provide? What is the emotional impact of the photographs or other visuals?

- What information or evidence is not in this text? (Your past experience and reading will help you here.) Why do you think the author might have left it out?

- If you are reading an argument, how effectively does the writer acknowledge or outline other points of view on the issue at hand?

By asking questions like these and annotating as you read, you can read all kinds of texts critically, including visuals and Web pages.

For more on strategies for argument, including dealing with opposing views, see Chapter 14.

Annotating Effectively

When you **annotate,** you interact actively with the text as you read. To annotate a reading, make the following kinds of notes (Figure 2.1 on page 18):

- Underline the main point or thesis of the reading, or otherwise mark it as the key point.

- Underline key supporting points, and indicate in the margins next to the corresponding paragraphs why you think each point is important.

- List any questions you have.

- Respond to the text with your own remarks.

- Jot down key terms and their definitions.

- Mark sections that summarize material as "summary."

Reading Visuals

As a college student, you will most often be asked to read words on paper, but you can usually apply the same strategies you use to read sentences and

Writing Activity

Annotating "Power to the People: Why We Need Civilian Police Review Boards"

"Power to the People: Why We Need Civilian Police Review Boards" discusses an issue that is much in the news: citizens get shot (and often killed) by police officers, and it sometimes appears that the police are not accountable for their actions. One possible way to provide such accountability is to establish police review boards—independent groups that can investigate such incidents and hopefully determine what actually happened. Annotate the rest of this essay (Figure 2.1). As you work, keep in mind your own responses to the essay.

Your instructor may want you to share your annotations with several of your classmates, noting places where your responses are similar and where they may differ.

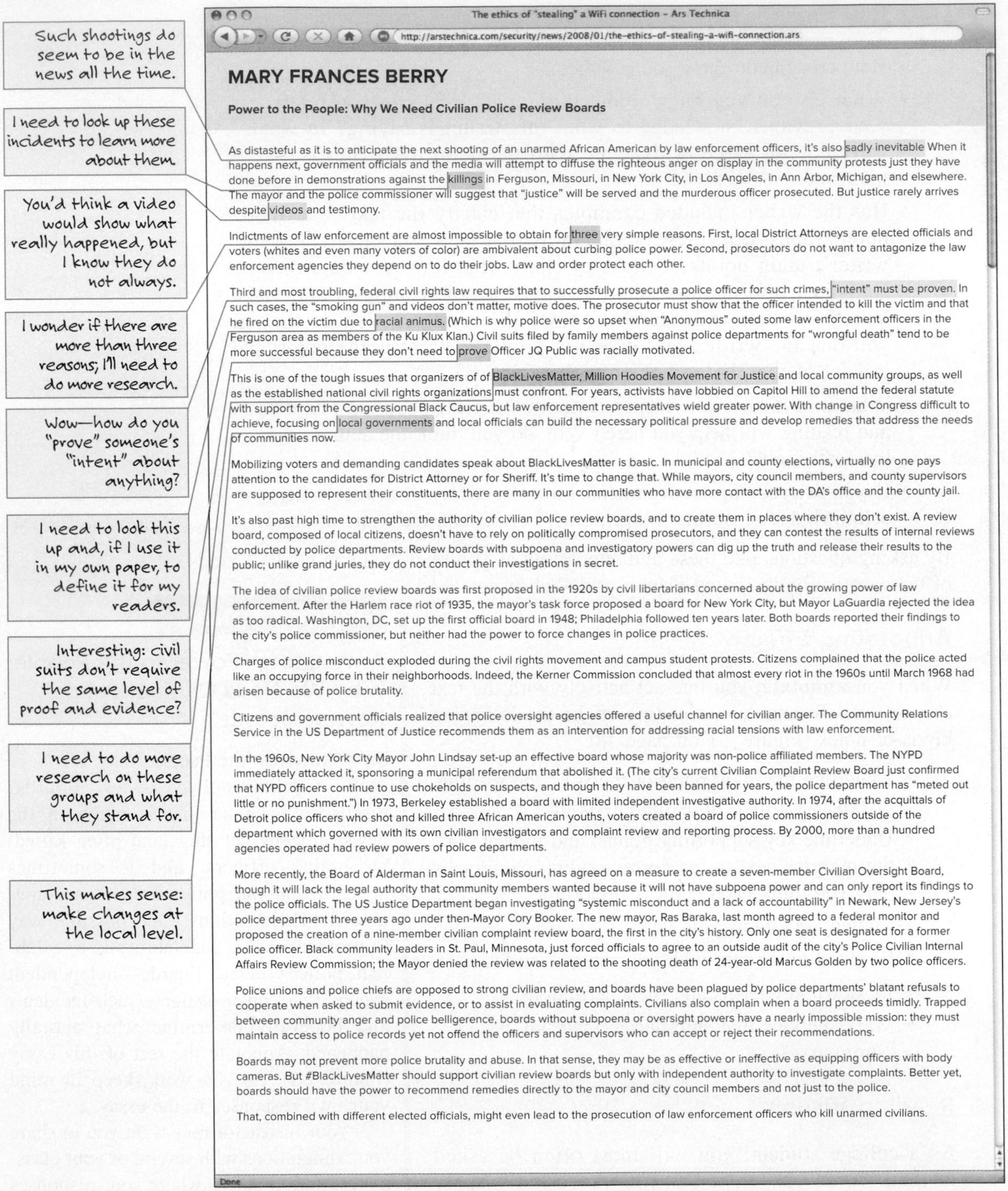

The ethics of "stealing" a WiFi connection – Ars Technica

http://arstechnica.com/security/news/2008/01/the-ethics-of-stealing-a-wifi-connection.ars

MARY FRANCES BERRY

Power to the People: Why We Need Civilian Police Review Boards

As distasteful as it is to anticipate the next shooting of an unarmed African American by law enforcement officers, it's also sadly inevitable When it happens next, government officials and the media will attempt to diffuse the righteous anger on display in the community protests just they have done before in demonstrations against the killings in Ferguson, Missouri, in New York City, in Los Angeles, in Ann Arbor, Michigan, and elsewhere. The mayor and the police commissioner will suggest that "justice" will be served and the murderous officer prosecuted. But justice rarely arrives despite videos and testimony.

Indictments of law enforcement are almost impossible to obtain for three very simple reasons. First, local District Attorneys are elected officials and voters (whites and even many voters of color) are ambivalent about curbing police power. Second, prosecutors do not want to antagonize the law enforcement agencies they depend on to do their jobs. Law and order protect each other.

Third and most troubling, federal civil rights law requires that to successfully prosecute a police officer for such crimes, "intent" must be proven. In such cases, the "smoking gun" and videos don't matter, motive does. The prosecutor must show that the officer intended to kill the victim and that he fired on the victim due to racial animus. (Which is why police were so upset when "Anonymous" outed some law enforcement officers in the Ferguson area as members of the Ku Klux Klan.) Civil suits filed by family members against police departments for "wrongful death" tend to be more successful because they don't need to prove Officer JQ Public was racially motivated.

This is one of the tough issues that organizers of of BlackLivesMatter, Million Hoodies Movement for Justice and local community groups, as well as the established national civil rights organizations must confront. For years, activists have lobbied on Capitol Hill to amend the federal statute with support from the Congressional Black Caucus, but law enforcement representatives wield greater power. With change in Congress difficult to achieve, focusing on local governments and local officials can build the necessary political pressure and develop remedies that address the needs of communities now.

Mobilizing voters and demanding candidates speak about BlackLivesMatter is basic. In municipal and county elections, virtually no one pays attention to the candidates for District Attorney or for Sheriff. It's time to change that. While mayors, city council members, and county supervisors are supposed to represent their constituents, there are many in our communities who have more contact with the DA's office and the county jail.

It's also past high time to strengthen the authority of civilian police review boards, and to create them in places where they don't exist. A review board, composed of local citizens, doesn't have to rely on politically compromised prosecutors, and they can contest the results of internal reviews conducted by police departments. Review boards with subpoena and investigatory powers can dig up the truth and release their results to the public; unlike grand juries, they do not conduct their investigations in secret.

The idea of civilian police review boards was first proposed in the 1920s by civil libertarians concerned about the growing power of law enforcement. After the Harlem race riot of 1935, the mayor's task force proposed a board for New York City, but Mayor LaGuardia rejected the idea as too radical. Washington, DC, set up the first official board in 1948; Philadelphia followed ten years later. Both boards reported their findings to the city's police commissioner, but neither had the power to force changes in police practices.

Charges of police misconduct exploded during the civil rights movement and campus student protests. Citizens complained that the police acted like an occupying force in their neighborhoods. Indeed, the Kerner Commission concluded that almost every riot in the 1960s until March 1968 had arisen because of police brutality.

Citizens and government officials realized that police oversight agencies offered a useful channel for civilian anger. The Community Relations Service in the US Department of Justice recommends them as an intervention for addressing racial tensions with law enforcement.

In the 1960s, New York City Mayor John Lindsay set-up an effective board whose majority was non-police affiliated members. The NYPD immediately attacked it, sponsoring a municipal referendum that abolished it. (The city's current Civilian Complaint Review Board just confirmed that NYPD officers continue to use chokeholds on suspects, and though they have been banned for years, the police department has "meted out little or no punishment.") In 1973, Berkeley established a board with limited independent investigative authority. In 1974, after the acquittals of Detroit police officers who shot and killed three African American youths, voters created a board of police commissioners outside of the department which governed with its own civilian investigators and complaint review and reporting process. By 2000, more than a hundred agencies operated had review powers of police departments.

More recently, the Board of Alderman in Saint Louis, Missouri, has agreed on a measure to create a seven-member Civilian Oversight Board, though it will lack the legal authority that community members wanted because it will not have subpoena power and can only report its findings to the police officials. The US Justice Department began investigating "systemic misconduct and a lack of accountability" in Newark, New Jersey's police department three years ago under then-Mayor Cory Booker. The new mayor, Ras Baraka, last month agreed to a federal monitor and proposed the creation of a nine-member civilian complaint review board, the first in the city's history. Only one seat is designated for a former police officer. Black community leaders in St. Paul, Minnesota, just forced officials to agree to an outside audit of the city's Police Civilian Internal Affairs Review Commission; the Mayor denied the review was related to the shooting death of 24-year-old Marcus Golden by two police officers.

Police unions and police chiefs are opposed to strong civilian review, and boards have been plagued by police departments' blatant refusals to cooperate when asked to submit evidence, or to assist in evaluating complaints. Civilians also complain when a board proceeds timidly. Trapped between community anger and police belligerence, boards without subpoena or oversight powers have a nearly impossible mission: they must maintain access to police records yet not offend the officers and supervisors who can accept or reject their recommendations.

Boards may not prevent more police brutality and abuse. In that sense, they may be as effective or ineffective as equipping officers with body cameras. But #BlackLivesMatter should support civilian review boards but only with independent authority to investigate complaints. Better yet, boards should have the power to recommend remedies directly to the mayor and city council members and not just to the police.

That, combined with different elected officials, might even lead to the prosecution of law enforcement officers who kill unarmed civilians.

Done

Margin annotations (handwritten)

Such shootings do seem to be in the news all the time.

I need to look up these incidents to learn more about them.

You'd think a video would show what really happened, but I know they do not always.

I wonder if there are more than three reasons; I'll need to do more research.

Wow—how do you "prove" someone's "intent" about anything?

I need to look this up and, if I use it in my own paper, to define it for my readers.

Interesting: civil suits don't require the same level of proof and evidence?

I need to do more research on these groups and what they stand for.

This makes sense: make changes at the local level.

FIGURE 2.1 Example of Annotations on a Page

USING DIGITAL TECHNOLOGIES   **Using the Internet to Find Definitions**

Are you faced with a college reading assignment that contains unfamiliar language? When the glossary in the book just isn't enough, try searching for definitions online. A number of good dictionaries and thesauruses are available online. One research strategy is to use a Web search engine to find definitions of complex terms. For example, if you're looking for a working definition of *existentialism*, type "define: existentialism" (without quotation marks) into a search engine's search box. Often the results at the top of the list will include dictionary sites, academic Web sites, and technical sites that have developed working glossaries for students, experts, and professionals.

paragraphs critically to other types of texts as well. You might think that visuals are easier to read than written text, but this assumption is not accurate. In fact, you often have to pay more attention to visual images, not only because they are sometimes subtler than written text but also because you may not be accustomed to reading them critically.

Although the process of understanding photographs, bar and line graphs, diagrams, and other visuals may seem different from that of reading and understanding textual information, you are essentially doing the same kind of work. When you read a text, you translate letters, words, and sentences into concepts and ideas; when you read a visual image, you do the same kind of translation. Just as you read a local newspaper or other printed text for information, you also read the photographs in the newspaper or the images on your television or computer screen to be informed.

As you read visuals, here are some questions to consider:

- How can you use words to tell what the visual shows?
- If the visual is combined with written text, what does the visual add to the verbal text? What would be lost if the visual were not there?
- Why do you think that the writer chose this particular format—photo, line drawing, chart, graph—for the visual?
- If you were choosing or designing a visual to illustrate this point, what would it look like?
- How accurately does the visual illustrate the point?
- What emotions does the visual evoke?

Reading Web Sites

Today many of us read Web sites, which can include not only text, with type in different colors and various sizes, but also photographs or other visual elements, videos that we can click on to view, and music. To read Web sites actively and critically, you need to examine the information on your screen just as carefully as you would a page of printed text or a visual in a magazine or newspaper. Because there are more aspects of the text to examine and consider, however, and also because it is often more difficult to establish where a text on the Web comes from, active reading becomes even more important. Consider the following additional questions when you are reading a Web page:

- The uniform resource locator (URL) of a site, its address, can give you clues about its origin and purpose. For any page you visit, consider what the URL tells you about the page, especially the last three letters—*edu* (educational), *gov* (U.S. government), *org* (nonprofit organization), or *com* (commercial). What difference does it make who sponsors the site?

Writing Activity

Reading Text and Visuals in an Advertisement

Select a full-page advertisement from a newspaper or magazine, and read both the written text and the visual elements carefully, keeping in mind that nothing in an advertisement is left to chance. Each element, from the kind and size of the typeface, to the colors, to the illustrations or photographs, has been discussed and modified many times as the advertisement was developed and tested. On a separate sheet of paper, jot down answers to the following questions:

- What is this advertiser trying to sell?
- What kinds of evidence does the advertisement use to persuade you to buy the product or service?
- Does the advertiser appeal to your beliefs and sense of fairness (the rhetorical appeal of *ethos*—see page 27), and if so, how?
- Does the advertiser use factual data, statistics, or quotations from experts (the rhetorical appeal of *logos*—see page 27), and if so, in what way?
- In what ways does the advertisement appeal to your emotions (the rhetorical appeal of *pathos*—see page 27)?
- What strategies does the advertiser employ to convince you of the credibility of the ad's message?
- How effective is this advertisement? Why?
- How might the various elements of the advertisement—colors, photos or other visuals, background, text—be changed to make the ad more, or less, effective?
- How much does the advertisement help potential buyers make informed decisions about this product?

If your instructor asks you to do so, share your advertisements and notes with several of your classmates. What similarities did you find in the advertisements that you selected? In what ways did the advertisements make use of visuals? What were the most effective elements of the advertisements?

Writing Activity

Reading Web Pages: What You Can See

Using the questions on pages 20 and 22, read the following Web page. Respond in writing to as many of the questions as you can. Compare your responses with those of your classmates.

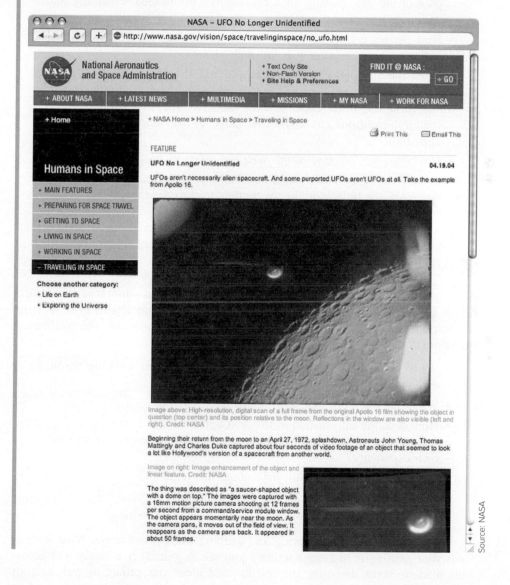

NASA – UFO No Longer Unidentified

http://www.nasa.gov/vision/space/travelinginspace/no_ufo.html

National Aeronautics and Space Administration

+ Text Only Site
+ Non-Flash Version
+ Site Help & Preferences

FIND IT @ NASA :   + GO

+ ABOUT NASA   + LATEST NEWS   + MULTIMEDIA   + MISSIONS   + MY NASA   + WORK FOR NASA

+ Home

+ NASA Home > Humans in Space > Traveling in Space

Print This   Email This

Humans in Space

+ MAIN FEATURES
+ PREPARING FOR SPACE TRAVEL
+ GETTING TO SPACE
+ LIVING IN SPACE
+ WORKING IN SPACE
– TRAVELING IN SPACE

Choose another category:
+ Life on Earth
+ Exploring the Universe

FEATURE

UFO No Longer Unidentified   04.19.04

UFOs aren't necessarily alien spacecraft. And some purported UFOs aren't UFOs at all. Take the example from Apollo 16.

Image above: High-resolution, digital scan of a full frame from the original Apollo 16 film showing the object in question (top center) and its position relative to the moon. Reflections in the window are also visible (left and right). Credit: NASA

Beginning their return from the moon to an April 27, 1972, splashdown, Astronauts John Young, Thomas Mattingly and Charles Duke captured about four seconds of video footage of an object that seemed to look a lot like Hollywood's version of a spacecraft from another world.

Image on right: Image enhancement of the object and linear feature. Credit: NASA

The thing was described as "a saucer-shaped object with a dome on top." The images were captured with a 16mm motion picture camera shooting at 12 frames per second from a command/service module window. The object appears momentarily near the moon. As the camera pans, it moves out of the field of view. It reappears as the camera pans back. It appeared in about 50 frames.

Source: NASA

- How reputable is the person or agency that is providing the information on this page? You can check the person's or agency's reputation by doing a Web search (using Google, Bing, or Yahoo!, for instance).
- What clues do you see as to the motives of the person or agency that is providing this information? Is there a link to an explanation of the purpose of the site? Usually, such explanations are labeled something like "About [name of organization or person]."
- How current is the information on this page? Can you find a date that indicates when the page was last updated?

For further details about evaluating information on the Web, see Chapter 19, "Finding and Evaluating Sources."

- Does the site make use of facts and statistics from credible sources (*logos*)? Is the site's author a recognized authority, and has he or she linked to other credible sites (*ethos*)? Does the site appeal to readers' emotions (*pathos*)? (See page 27 for more on these three appeals).
- How does the structure of the Web site affect its message?
- If there are links on the page, how helpful is the description of each link? Are the links working, or do they lead to dead ends?

Using Post-reading Strategies

After you have read an essay or other text actively and annotated it, spend a bit of time thinking about what you have learned from it and even writing in response to it. Review your annotations and answer the following questions:

- What is the main point or idea you learned from working through this text?
- What did you learn that surprises or interests you?
- How does the information in this text agree with or contradict information on this topic you have already read or learned from your own experience?
- What questions do you still have about this text?
- Where can you find answers to those questions?
- What in this reading might be useful in your own writing?

One useful method for storing and keeping track of what you have learned from your reading is to keep a writer's journal. A journal is a handy and accessible place to write down the information and ideas you gather, as well as your reactions to and insights about the texts you read. Other effective post-reading strategies include writing summaries, synthesizing information, and using your reading in your writing. Finally, you might be assigned to write a rhetorical analysis of a text you have read.

Starting Your Writer's/Research Journal

A writer's journal is a place where you keep track of the notes, annotations, and summaries that you make from your reading. Because any writing project longer than a page or two demands more information than you can usually store in your memory, it is vital to keep a written record of information that you discover. You can use the entries in your journal as the basis for group discussions as well as for writing tasks.

The information that you include in your journal can vary based on the needs of the project you are working on. The format and design will also vary to suit your purpose. In other words, your rhetorical situation will have an impact not only on the material you collect, the notes that you take, and the summaries and syntheses that you write (see pages 23–26 and Chapter 3), but also on the physical makeup of your journal. If you are working on a project that requires a large number of illustrations, for example, you will need to include space in your journal to store them.

It is usually a good idea to keep a journal of some sort for *each* writing project you are working on. Consider the following questions for each journal:

- What kinds of information (data, charts, anecdotes, photos, illustrations, and so on) should you collect for this project?
- What information will help you get your message across to your intended audience?
- What information might you jot down that may lead to more complex ideas? Why would more complexity be desirable?
- What questions do you have, and how might you go about finding answers to those questions?
- What kinds of illustrations might help you *show* what you mean?

As you write in your journal, you should note where ideas or quotations come from in the original texts so that you will be able to properly cite them in your own writing. Get in the habit of noting the information you will need to cite your source, including the page number an idea or quotation comes from.

For more on taking notes from and properly citing sources, see Chapter 20.

Writing Effective Summaries

After they have read and annotated a text, many readers find that summarizing it also helps them to understand it better. A **summary** is a concise restatement of the most important information in a text—its main point and major supporting points.

Writing Activity

Reading a Text Critically

Assume that for your criminal justice class, you have been asked to read the blog post "Power to the People: Why We Need Civilian Police Review Boards" by Mary Frances Berry, which appears on page 18. Berry wrote the piece for the *Beacon Broadside*, a blog sponsored by Beacon Press. Based on what you have learned in this chapter, consider how you should go about reading this text. Use the critical reading skills you have learned to do the following:

- Explain what you already knew about this topic just from the title.
- In a brief paragraph, explain what you did before you read this text. Did you skim it?
- Annotate the first paragraph.
- Jot down your answers to the following post-reading questions, using no more than two sentences for each response.
  - What were your initial reaction and response to this text?
  - What is the main idea you learned from working through this text?
  - Did you learn anything that surprises or interests you?
  - In what ways does the information in this text reinforce or contradict other texts you have read or what you know from your own experience?
  - What questions do you still have about this text?

Writing a Summary: To write an effective summary, start by listing the main points of the text, in effect outlining what you are reading. Remember, however, that a summary is more than just a list; a summary provides a brief narrative structure that connects these main ideas.

Writing Activity

Summarizing "Power to the People: Why We Need Civilian Police Review Boards"

In no more than one page, summarize "Power to the People: Why We Need Civilian Police Review Boards" (page 18). If your instructor asks you to, share your summary with several of your classmates.

STEPS FOR WRITING A SUMMARY

1. Read the text relatively quickly to get a general sense of what it is saying.
2. Read the text again. Mark or highlight a sentence that expresses the main point of each paragraph, and paraphrase that point—put it entirely into your own words—in the margin.

3. For a longer text, label the major sections. If the writer has provided subheadings, use them as they are or paraphrase them. If not, write sub-headings.

4. After considering what you have done in the first three steps, write a statement that captures the writer's main point or thesis.

5. Working backward from step 4, craft a paragraph—in your own words—that captures the gist of what the writer is saying.

Synthesizing Information in Readings

Synthesis calls for the thoughtful combination or integration of ideas and information with your point of view.

Suppose that you would like to see a particular movie this Saturday. You hope to persuade a group of your friends to accompany you. You have read several reviews of the film, you know other work by the director, and you have even read the novel on which this movie is based. At the same time, simply sending your friends all the information you have about the film might overwhelm them. Unless you effectively structure what you have to say, one piece of information may contradict some other point that you want to make.

For more help with writing a synthesis, see Chapter 3.

To organize your information, you could focus on what you see as the most compelling reasons your friends should see the film: the novel the film is based on, along with the director of the movie. You would then provide information to support your points:

- Specific examples to show how interesting the novel is

- Reviews or other information about the film to show how effectively the novel has been translated to film

- Other films by the same director that you know your friends like

When you synthesize effectively, you take the jumble of facts, data, information, and other knowledge you have on hand and put it into an understandable format that fulfills the purpose you want to accomplish. And, of course, when you cite reviewers' opinions (in the hope of convincing your friends of which movie to see), you will need to indicate where the comments came from—to properly attribute what the reviewers had to say and to lend their authority to your argument. Failure to properly attribute ideas to original sources constitutes plagiarism.

For more on avoiding plagiarism, see Chapter 20.

As we have noted, to fully understand information and then be able to synthesize it effectively, you must read critically, questioning, challenging, and engaging the text as you work through it. One strategy that will help you improve your critical thinking and reading is to work with others. When you work with your classmates, you hear their perspectives and ideas and have the opportunity to consider various points of view. Working with others also helps you learn to construct the most effective questions to ask to help you become an active reader.

Writing Activity

Synthesizing Information

Using what you have learned from this chapter on critical reading and synthesizing information, reread "Power to the People: Why We Need Civilian Police Review Boards" (page 18), and then select another article from a print or online source that takes an ethical stance on an issue related to public safety. Synthesize the issues outlined in both readings in no more than two pages. Remember that a synthesis is a thoughtful integration of your readings with your own point of view. Where do you stand on these ethical dilemmas? What else have you read in your college classes that relates to these ethical situations?

Using Your Reading in Your Writing

Information that you find in your reading can be used in many ways in your writing. If you have annotated the texts that your instructor asked you to read for a writing project in this course or another course, you can often use those annotations in your own writing. Likewise, if you have summarized sources for a research project, you can refer to and use those summaries to spot the important points of each text you have read, then use relevant information as evidence to support your main idea. If you have found statistical information in graphical form, or photographs, drawings, maps, or other illustrations, these too can become part of your text. Of course, it is always important to indicate where you found information, whose ideas you use in your text, and where statistical information came from in order to establish your credibility and avoid *plagiarizing*—representing the words or ideas of others as your own ideas or words.

In the chapters in Parts 2 and 3 of this book, you will read various selections. As you read these texts or conduct research in the library and on the Web to find support for your writing, you will find it helpful to use the reading strategies described in this chapter.

Constructing a Rhetorical Analysis

When you *analyze* something, you mentally "take it apart" to determine how the various parts or aspects function and relate to the whole. If you were to analyze, say, the winning team in last year's Super Bowl or World Series, you would examine the coaching, the players, the game plan, or perhaps all of these elements to determine how the parts of that team work together to make it the best. (For more on analysis, see Chapter 8.)

A rhetorical analysis is a way of looking at something, often a text, from a *rhetorical standpoint*. The purpose of examining a text from a rhetorical perspective and then constructing a rhetorical analysis of that text is to help you understand how it functions: how each aspect works to fulfill its purpose. If a text is trying to persuade you to believe something, you should examine how the various parts of that text work to *persuade*. If a text is intended to be informational (a newspaper article, for example), then you should look for evidence of how that text informs.

A rhetorical analysis includes a search for and identification of *rhetorical appeals:* the aspects of a piece of writing that influence the reader because of the credibility of the author *(ethos),* an appeal to logic *(logos),* an appeal to the emotions of the audience *(pathos),* or all three. The relationships among *ethos, logos,* and *pathos* can be represented as a triangle in which the author is related to an appeal to *ethos,* the audience or reader to the appeal of *pathos,* and the purpose of the text to the appeal of *logos:*

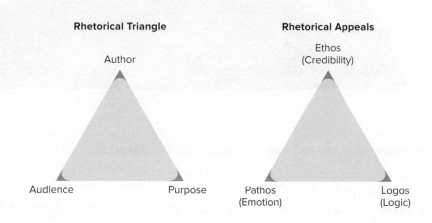

(For more on the rhetorical triangle, see Chapter 14.)

GENRES *Up Close* Writing a Rhetorical Analysis

The purpose of a rhetorical analysis is to examine an item—most often a text—to determine how the parts or aspects of the text function together to accomplish the author's purpose. Rhetorical analysis, then, is really a critical reading.

One way to understand how to use a rhetorical approach is to consider an advertisement. Consider the advertisement from Unicef—the United Nations Children's Fund—in Figure 2.2. How does a specific advertisement work to convince the audience? Most often, an advertisement is intended to persuade a reader to buy a product, but this advertisement clearly is different. In what ways is the ad in Figure 2.2 different from advertisements you normally see? What is the ad "selling"? What parts of the advertisement do you notice? What stands out? What about the pistol indicates that it is a plastic weapon? How do you react to the colors of the pistol? How does the expression on the child's face impact viewers of this advertisement? What kind of rhetorical appeal is the ad making? How does the text in the advertisement add to that appeal?

BAD WATER KILLS MORE CHILDREN THAN WAR.
SUPPORT THE 'ONE DROP OF WATER' PROJECT SMS "DROP" TO 99A TO DONATE 50 GEX. WWW.UNICEF.SE

unicef ✿

© Unicef.org

FIGURE 2.2
Advertisement for Unicef

In a rhetorical analysis, you will usually do the following:

- Identify the context of a piece of writing or a visual text (author, audience, and purpose).
- Identify the structure of the piece (chronological, cause/effect, problem/solution, topical, and so on).
- Identify the rhetorical appeals of the piece (*ethos, logos, pathos).*

Ethos appeals to a reader's beliefs, sense of ethics, and credibility, and to the trustworthiness of the speaker/author. When you read a text to identify the writer's *ethos,* look for the following characteristics:

- Language appropriate to the audience and subject
- A sincere, fair presentation of the argument
- Grammatical sentences
- A level of vocabulary appropriate for the purpose and level of formality

When you read a text to identify the rhetorical appeal of *logos,* look for the following characteristics:

- Literal (dictionary) meanings of terms or reasons, rather than metaphorical or connotative meanings
- Factual data and statistics
- Quotations from authorities and experts, properly cited

When you read a text to identify the rhetorical appeal of *pathos,* look for the following characteristics:

- Vivid, concrete language
- Emotionally loaded language (For example, calling your friend Ben "pig-headed" has a more negative connotation than calling him "stubborn." Likewise, describing your friend Jane as a "sheep" has a more emotional connotation than describing her as "meek.")
- Examples that evoke an emotional response
- Narratives of events that have an emotional impact
- Figurative language (when you describe one thing by comparing it with something else: "Courtney is as quiet as a sigh").

(For more on rhetorical appeals, see Chapter 14.)

Here are some questions that will help you pinpoint the rhetorical appeals in a text:

- Who is the intended audience? How do you identify the audience?
- What do you see as the writer's purpose? To explain? Inform? Anger? Persuade? Amuse? Motivate? Sadden? Ridicule? Is there more than one purpose? Does the purpose shift at some point within the text?
- Can you identify the rhetorical appeals in this piece of writing *(ethos, logos, pathos)*? What would you add to or omit from it to make the rhetorical appeals more effective?
- How does the writer develop his or her ideas? Narration? Description? Definition? Comparison? Cause and effect? Examples?
- What is the tone of the text? Do you react at an emotional level to the text? Does this reaction change at all throughout the text?
- How does the writer arrange his or her ideas? What are the patterns of arrangement?
- Does the writer use dialogue? Quotations? To what effect?
- How does the writer use diction? Is it formal? Informal? Technical? Does the writer use jargon? Slang? Is the language connotative? Denotative? Is the language emotionally evocative? Does the language change throughout the piece? How does the language contribute to the writer's aim?

For more on these strategies, see Chapter 13.

Writing Activity

Writing a Rhetorical Analysis

Apply the first three bullets on the previous page to the advertisement for Unicef on page 28. Share your responses with several of your classmates. How are those responses similar? How are they different?

Text Credits

p. 18: Berry, Mary Frances, "Power to the People: Why We Need Civilian Police Review Boards" *Beacon Broadside*, February 2015. Copyright © 2015 by Mary Frances Berry/ Used with permission of Beacon Press, Boston.

Writing to Understand and Synthesize Texts

© Inti St. Clair/Getty Images RF

Martin is a student in his first semester of college. As soon as he bought his books and examined the course syllabi for his classes, he knew that he would have a lot of reading to do. As part of his first-year composition class, Martin is learning about the process of critical reading. As noted in Chapter 2 (page 14), he found it especially useful to learn that "to read critically means to read *thoughtfully,* to keep in mind what you already know, and to *actively* interact with the text. Critical readers underline, make notes, and ask questions as they read."

Martin has taken this advice, becoming an active reader of the texts assigned in his classes. However, as he skims the assignments for the papers he will be asked to write this semester, Martin can see that he also will have a good deal of outside research to do for assigned course papers. An assignment for his political science class looks especially interesting but also worrisome. It asks students to read three articles and parts of a book and then to relate the information in these reading selections to one

another. Martin realizes that not only will he need to understand everything he reads in these selections, but he will also need to use that information in his own writing: he will need to *synthesize* it.

Reading this chapter carefully and thoroughly (and actively) will help you handle assignments such as the one Martin confronts: It will help you understand the information you read, form a critical response to it, and then synthesize the ideas from more than one source in your own college writing.

Setting Your Goals

- **Rhetorical Knowledge:** Because this chapter focuses on "understanding and synthesizing texts," your immediate goal is both to understand the information you will read in your classes and then to use that information effectively by synthesizing it in your own papers, using the instruction this chapter provides. As you read any text you will use as a source, you need to consider the purpose of the assignment you are responding to. (You can find this out by reading the assignments for your various classes.) How do those assignments ask you to explain and then synthesize the information in the essays and books you are required to read for your classes?

- **Critical Thinking, Reading, and Writing:** As you read critically and actively (see Chapter 2), think about how that reading relates to other texts you have read and other information you have learned. Think about what reading strategies you can use to discover the main areas of agreement. By making marginal notes and by annotating the texts as you read them, you will find it much easier to connect information and synthesize it in your own papers.

- **Writing Processes:** If your instructor assigns one of the writing assignment options on pages 32–33, think critically about your own writing process as you work on it: What kinds of invention activities do you find most useful? What organizational approaches help you best achieve your purpose? What kind of feedback helps you revise most effectively? Thinking critically about the answers to those kinds of questions will help you in the future, when you face a similar writing situation.

- **Knowledge of Conventions:** As you edit your work, think critically about how you used sources (your research), and be sure to cite them using the appropriate documentation style.

RHETORICAL KNOWLEDGE

In most of your college classes, much of what you will do involves reading, understanding, and working with texts. In these classes, you will read to glean information as well as to understand concepts. You will be asked to demonstrate that you know the information in your class texts, and often you will be asked to write about how the concepts you have learned relate to one another.

As noted in the opening to this chapter, there is useful advice on how to read critically and effectively all through this textbook, beginning with Chapter 2. As you may recall from that chapter, it can be useful to think about how you read various kinds of materials. Different reading strategies, such as annotating and keeping a writer's journal, can help you to read print texts as well as the texts and images in an advertisement or on a Web site. Finally, when you learn how to read a text critically, you will be able to summarize and synthesize the material you learn from it effectively. If you do so, you will be able to use that information effectively in your own writing projects.

"Ways of Writing to Understand and Synthesize Texts" on page 34 provides examples of genres you may use in your writing, both for college classes and for other areas of your life. The genres of writing you will be assigned will vary depending on the texts you are reading and the audience you are addressing.

Writing to Understand and Synthesize Texts

In this chapter, you will put into practice what you have learned about effective critical reading. We ask that you focus on the three terms in the title of this chapter:

- When someone asks you whether you **understand** a text, what does that question mean to you? How might you demonstrate that you have read and understood a piece of writing?

- When you are asked to **synthesize** texts, what does that term mean? How might you show that you can synthesize two or more texts?

Writing | Assignment Options

The most effective way to demonstrate your knowledge is to put that knowledge into practice. The two assignments that follow ask for brief pieces of writing that demonstrate your ability to respond critically to a text and to synthesize two texts.

OPTION 1

As you know, reading *critically* does not necessarily mean that you criticize a text or look at it in a negative way, but rather that you read actively, questioning as you read and making connections to other texts you have read. In other words, you work at reading to help you better understand—and then be able to use—the information.

Write a critical response to a brief reading selection, either one of the selections in this chapter (pages 36–47) or a selection chosen by you or your instructor. In your response, explain

- What new information you learned from the text
- How the information relates to what you knew about the subject before you read the text
- What questions you still have after reading this text
- How you and/or your readers will use that information

OPTION 2

In addition to writing responses to texts for your various college classes, you often will be asked to synthesize the ideas in two or more texts. When you synthesize, you show not only that you understand the texts you read, but that you can explain how the ideas and concepts in the two selections relate to one another. Find two reading selections on a similar topic and read and annotate them, or set up a table comparing the points the authors of the two readings make. Focus on several points each reading makes about the same concept or idea. The goal is to write an essay that provides a fair representation of both points of view on the issue, along with your own perspective. Some questions to consider and answer in your essay include the following:

- What information in the texts is similar, and in what ways?
- What information is different, and in what ways?
- What evidence in each text supports the assertions its author makes? What evidence in the other text supports other assertions or claims?

Rhetorical Considerations in Writing to Understand and Synthesize Texts

Before you begin writing in response to either of the options above, consider the various aspects of your writing situation:

Audience: Who is your primary audience? Who else might be interested in the subject that you are focusing on? Why?

Purpose: Your writing can have various purposes. For example, if you are writing in response to Option 2, your purpose is to inform readers of how the texts you read make similar or differing *claims* (arguable statements requiring support), how the evidence they use to back those claims is the same or different, and so on. That information will help your own readers become more informed about the issues or concepts those texts discuss.

Voice, tone, and point of view: Your instructor will advise you on whether you should use the pronoun *I* in your text, or whether you should write in the third person (avoiding *I*) as you write your critical response (Option 1) or synthesize the information in two texts (Option 2). In either case, your tone should be neutral.

Context, medium, and genre: You will need to understand the situation that establishes the occasion to write. How will your writing be used? If you are writing for an audience beyond the classroom, consider what will be the most effective way to present your information to this audience.

For more on choosing a medium and genre, see Chapter 17 and Appendix C.

Ways of Writing to Understand and Synthesize Texts

Genres for Your College Classes	Sample Situation	Advantages of the Genre	Limitations of the Genre
Review of the Literature	Your psychology professor asks you to read several articles on a topic and then write a review in which you analyze each of them and finally present a synthesis.	This project should give you a better understanding of the subject of these articles.	This project is limited in scope. Since in fields like psychology the most current information is usually preferred, you'll need to make sure your review contains the most recent articles on this topic.
Essay Exam	In your political science class, you have to take an in-class essay exam in which you are asked to synthesize several political trends you have studied.	This kind of assignment allows you to show your instructor that you understand the course material.	A timed essay often limits your ability to show what you really know about a subject.
Academic Essay	Your sociology professor asks you to write an essay that synthesizes several of the theories of social behavior you have studied.	An academic essay will allow you to demonstrate your grasp of these theories.	Academic essays are often written in technical language, making it difficult for those outside of that particular field to understand them.
Critique	Your business instructor asks you to do a critical response to a business plan for a bike-repair shop near the campus.	Since you or people you know may be customers of the proposed business, your critical response may help the new business better understand its potential customer base.	You may not have enough information to completely understand the financial needs of the new business.
Critical Response	Your First-Year Experience instructor asks you to write a critical response to an article you've read about social media.	Looking at an article on social media critically may help you make better decisions about your own use of social media.	Since social media is now everywhere and rapidly evolving, and anyone can participate, you need to make sure of the accuracy and currency of the comments you're critiquing.
Genres for Life	Sample Situation	Advantages of the Genre	Limitations of the Genre
Recommendation Report	You are asked to analyze the phone needs of each department in your workplace. You must then synthesize your findings and recommend the best new phone system.	By looking at each department's needs, you are likely to come up with a global plan.	It's possible that one department has unique needs that you will miss in your search for a global solution.
Memo	After a reorganization at your company, you need to write a memo synthesizing the real effects of the change.	By providing your staff with a synthesis of recent changes, you provide them with truly useful information.	By presenting your staff merely with the basic facts, you may be ignoring some "human effects" of the recent changes.
Consumer Blog	You decide to create a blog for people in your neighborhood. In your blog you will synthesize reviews of local businesses offering consumer services.	By synthesizing the content of multiple reviews, you save your neighbors time.	Blogs need to be updated and maintained regularly.
Review of a competitor's product	Your boss asks you to use a product produced by a competitor and critique it.	By actually using a competitor's product, you will know how it really compares with yours.	You need to be careful that you don't have an internal bias toward your own product.
Response to a proposal to change the storm drainage in your neighborhood.	A group of your neighbors is concerned that a new plan from the city to alter the drainage in your area will damage the streets in your neighborhood and cause flooding.	You will let the city know that you are concerned that its proposal will have a negative impact on the quality of life in your neighborhood.	To be taken seriously, such responses to municipal projects need to be backed up by evidence—in this case, a report from a civil engineer would probably be required.

CRITICAL THINKING, READING, AND WRITING

Often, writing to understand texts takes place informally, in a classroom situation. You write a critical response to a text as a means of learning or to explain the ideas from a single text. In a synthesis you explain to readers how the information in a text is similar to or different from the information in the other text(s) you are synthesizing, or how the information in one text agrees or disagrees with (and thus supports or refutes) the claims made in other texts. The student examples that appear in the following sections will illustrate both forms of writing.

Qualities of Effective Writing to Understand and Synthesize Texts

Effective writing that responds to a text or synthesizes two or more texts engages your readers because the information you present is offered in a compelling way and, in a synthesis, is combined with your own carefully considered point of view.

Readers expect the following qualities in writing that demonstrates understanding of texts or that synthesizes two or more reading selections:

- **Clear, complete explanations of the main points of the text or texts.** So that your reader will be able to understand your response or synthesis, you need to make sure that the main ideas in the text or texts you are considering are clearly and completely explained. Look for terms that readers might not know, and define them. Explain concepts that are difficult to understand

- **An informative thesis and evidence to support it.** Your critical response to the text or texts should be clearly articulated in a *thesis statement*—a statement of your main point—and backed by evidence such as examples or quotations.

- **Similarities and differences clearly explained in a synthesis.** You can, of course, emphasize the areas you consider most important. For example, perhaps the texts present a similar point of view or argument, but differ in these areas:

  - *The kinds of evidence they present.* One text, for example, might use data (numbers, statistics) while the other might use anecdotes or expert testimony.

  - *The emphasis placed on certain ideas or concepts.* Determining which ideas each author is emphasizing gives you a sense of what each author thinks are the most important aspects of the subject being discussed.

For more on comparison and contrast, see Chapter 13.

- **Relationships clearly outlined and explained.** The relationships between ideas and concepts and information in the texts you synthesize need to be clearly explained so your readers can see those relationships and connections in the same way that you see them. Explain in detail in what ways the texts agree and disagree with each other.

Reading to Learn about Understanding and Synthesizing Texts

As a student in a first-year writing class, you've made the decision to begin a college education. The following three readings present information with regard to the national debate concerning the value of that education. Historically, the assumption in the United States was that a college degree led to better employment opportunities. More recently, with the rising cost of college, that assumption has been called into question by some politicians. Both of these readings address that discussion by presenting data, including visual data, to support their perspectives.

PAUL FAIN

EDITORIAL

The New Bachelor's Payoff

Paul Fain is a news editor for *Inside Higher Ed*, an online trade publication for higher education. Previously, he worked for *The Chronicle of Higher Education*, a traditional higher education trade publication. He has also written for *The New York Times*, *Washington City Paper*, and *Mother Jones*. He has won several journalism awards.

Doubts about the labor-market returns of bachelor's degrees, while never serious, can be put to rest.   1

Last month's federal jobs report showed a rock-bottom unemployment rate of 2.8 percent for workers who hold at least a four-year degree. The overall unemployment rate is 5.7 percent.   2

But even that welcome economic news comes with wrinkles. A prominent financial analyst last week signaled an alarm that employers soon may face a shortage of job-seeking college graduates. And the employment report was a reminder of continuing worries about "upcredentialing" by employers, who are imposing new degree requirements on jobs.   3

"Presumably, these educated workers are the most productive in our information economy," wrote Guy LeBas, a financial analyst with Janney Montgomery Scott, in a report *Bloomberg Business* and other media outlets cited. "At some point in the coming year, we're going to risk running out of new, productive people to employ."   4

Anthony P. Carnevale concurred with LeBas. As director of the George-town University Center on Education and the Workforce and a top expert on the labor-market returns of degrees, Carnevale has long railed against dubious arguments about the payoff from college being overrated.   5

"We're headed for full employment" of bachelor's-degree-holding workers, he said.   6

It's a challenge decades in the making. Carnevale cites research that has found colleges lagging badly in producing talent. Since 1983, the job market has outpaced higher education with a cumulative total of 11 million positions for workers with "usable knowledge," which he defines as "degrees with labor-market value."   7

These days, demand for positions in the knowledge economy grows by 3 percent each year, Carnevale said, while higher education meets only 1 percent of that growth.   8

That's where employers step in. Carnevale's center last week released a report that broke down the $1.1 trillion colleges, government agencies and employers spend each year on higher education and job training in the United States. Employers chip in the most, the report found, spending $590 billion annually to train workers.   9

Of that amount, $413 billion paid for informal, on-the-job training. Colleges spent $407 billion on formal training, while employers spent $177 billion. However, the academy's rate of spending has outpaced that of employers, increasing by 82 percent since 1994 compared to 26 percent.   10

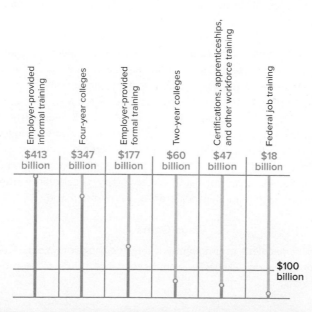

The report, dubbed "College Is Just the Beginning," also found that four-year-college graduates receive the most of the formal, employer-sponsored job training. Bachelor's degree holders account for 58 percent of employers' annual spending on formal training. 11

That fact, while somewhat counterintuitive, is because four-year-college graduates tend to get jobs that are specialized, complex and change over time, Carnevale said, particularly in STEM fields. 12

"Wherever the earnings are the strongest, that's where the training occurs," he said. "The more educated the workforce, the more training in the job." 13

Workers with an associate degree or some college credit but no degree received 25 percent of formal employer training. Those with a high school credential or less received 17 percent. 14

'Credential Creep'

The report's findings strongly suggest that a bachelor's degree often is required as a starting point for a job that requires more training—and one that pays well. So dropping out to go work for a tech company isn't a safe bet for most students. 15

"Formal employer-provided training typically complements, rather than substitutes for, a traditional college education," the report said. 16

The new federal jobs report in some ways bolsters the findings from a study released last fall by Burning Glass Technologies, a Boston-based employment firm that analyzes job advertisements. That research found that employers are more likely to replace workers who do not have bachelor's degrees with those who do. 17

One reason for this, according to Burning Glass, is that many "middle skills" jobs are becoming more technological and complex. Architectural drafters, for example, these days are expected to be "junior engineers," the report found. 18

But employers also appear to be screening applicants by requiring bachelor's degrees for positions that do not require nor are likely to require the kind of training one would get from a B.A. or B.S., according to the report, citing certain human resources and clerical jobs as examples. 19

This sort of credential creep is alarming to some economists, such as Richard Vedder, who directs the Center for College Affordability and Productivity and teaches economics at Ohio University. Vedder has written that an oversupply of bachelor's degrees creates its own demand. 20

Wage Gains

The virtually nonexistent unemployment rate for bachelor's holders poses a test to higher education, Carnevale said, beyond just trying to keep up with employer demand. 21

That's because the "wage premium" for workers with a four-year degree   22
relative to those who hold only a high-school credential, while large, has stagnated in recent years. As employers run out of graduates to hire, however, the
wage premium should climb again. That outcome would be further proof of
the value of a four-year degree.

Full-time workers with a bachelor's degree or more who are between the   23
ages of 25 and 32 have median annual earnings of $45,500, according to a
report the Pew Research Center released last year. Two-year-degree holders or
those with some college credits and no degree earn $30,000 while high school
graduates earn $28,000.

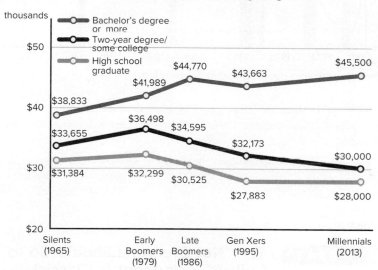

**Rising Earnings Disparity between Young Adults
with and without a College Degree**

Median annual earnings among full-time workers ages 25–32, in
2012 dollars

Another study, which the Federal Reserve Bank of San Francisco released last   24
year, tracked the fluctuating earnings premium for a four-year degree.

The premium was at its lowest in 1980, when bachelor's degree holders   25
earned 43 percent more, on average, than workers with just a high school
credential. In 2011, however, it was 61 percent, or $20,050 per year.

Carnevale predicted that gap would widen because of the high demand   26
for bachelor's degree holders. But it will take about two years for those effects
to show, he said.

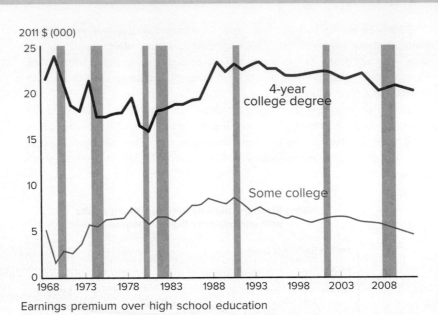

2011 $ (000)

Earnings premium over high school education

LeBas agreed that earnings gains of highly educated employees will outpace others. "Wage pressures among skilled workers will almost certainly rise further in the coming year," he wrote.   27

LIBBY NELSON

Libby Nelson is a writer for *Inside Higher Ed*, an online trade publication for higher education. She has worked in Scranton, Pennsylvania, for *The Times-Tribune* and has been an intern at *The New York Times*, the Minneapolis *Star-Tribune*, and the *St. Petersburg Times*.

EDITORIAL

The "Not Everyone Should Go to College" Argument Is Classist and Wrong

The economic return on investment for a college degree has never been higher. But the more that fact is discussed, the more some pundits seem to think the U.S. is at risk of an epidemic of unnecessary college-going that can be averted by singing the praises of highly skilled trades.   1

The latest, in *Businessweek*, is headlined "Let's Start Telling Young People the Whole Truth About College"—the whole truth being that a four-year degree isn't the only road to a stable, even lucrative, professional life.   2

Fair enough. (Though the economic evidence still comes down heavily   3
on the side of four-year college graduates being better off in the long run.) But
the argument that "everyone shouldn't go to college"—reiterated with dozens
of variations in the past few years—rests on some incorrect assumptions about
higher education in the U.S.

Many people imagine a bright line between college and vocational   4
education—PhDs on one side, plumbers on the other. That line doesn't exist,
and it hasn't for at least a generation. Particularly at two-year colleges, programs for future English majors and future auto mechanics often exist side-
by-side. One path might lead to an associate degree, the other to a certificate,
but they're both at a place called "college."

As higher education economist Sandy Baum wrote in a report for the Urban   5
Institute: "It is common to hear the suggestion that many students should forgo
college and instead seek vocational training. But most of that training takes
place in community colleges or for-profit postsecondary institutions."

The skilled trades are demanding workers with increasing levels of tech-   6
nical ability, and the market rewards those who have the credential to prove it:
About 30 percent of construction workers now have some kind of professional
license or credential, according to the Census Bureau. So do about 20 percent
of industrial workers. Workers without a traditional college degree, but with a
credential, earned more than workers with no credentials at all. They still earn
less than workers with a traditional degree.

Where do people earn these credentials? The vast majority—82 percent—of   7
workers with credentials other than a college degree, or in addition to a college
degree, earned them from an educational institution. In other words, to get
ahead in those skilled jobs so often promoted as the alternative to a college
education, they went to college.

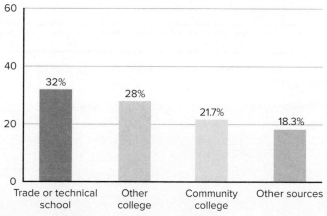

Where workers earned their credentials

Somehow, criticism of the cult of the college degree never pinpoints the   8
one group where a belief that "everyone should go to college" really is pervasive:
the upper middle class. Students from families in the top fifth of incomes have
gone to college in disproportionately high numbers since at least the 1970s.
About 80 percent of them now attend college right after high school. More than
half have a bachelor's degree by age 25.

It's more than plausible that some of those well-off students could be   9
happy and successful with a certificate in carpentry instead of a bachelor's
in business. Yet the calls to tell the truth about the value of a college degree
nearly always stop short of saying where—if too many people really do go to
college—that truth-telling is sorely needed.

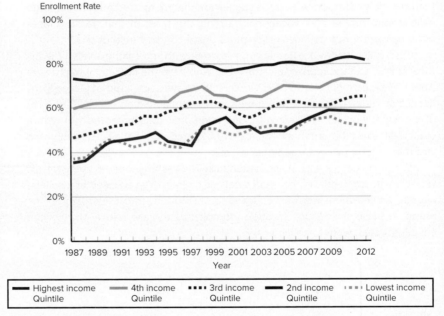

Postsecondary enrollment rates of recent high school graduates by family
income, 1987–2012

New School Year, Old Story: Education Pays

Wondering if your studies will pay off? Recent data from the U.S. Bureau   1
of Labor Statistics (BLS) suggest that they will. As past studies have
shown, as workers' level of education increases, their earnings rise and
unemployment rates fall.

The chart groups workers' earnings and unemployment by their high-   2
est level of educational attainment. Workers with a bachelor's degree, for
example, earned about $415 more a week than workers whose highest level
of education is a high school diploma. And the rate of unemployment for
workers with a bachelor's degree was about half that of those with no education beyond high school.

For students in graduate school, the payoff for a degree might be even greater.   3
Workers with a professional degree, such as lawyers and physicians, earned about
$612 more a week than did workers with a bachelor's degree—and over $1,000 more
per week than workers who have a high school diploma as their highest level of
education. Plus, at 2.4 percent, the unemployment rate for workers with a professional degree was also the lowest of any education level.

The numbers in the chart below are medians—meaning that half of all   4
workers earned more than that amount, and half earned less. As the chart
indicates, postponing work for school can pay off. But there are some financial
drawbacks. Students often forego a full-time paycheck while they are in school.

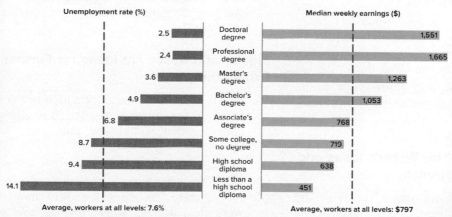

Unemployment rates and earnings for full-time wage and salary workers ages 25
and older, by educational attainment, 2011

Source: BLS, Current Population Survey.

And when estimating the financial benefit of additional education, students who take out loans to pay for school should consider the amount they will be obligated to repay. Data come from a special supplement to the BLS Current Population Survey. For more information, write to the BLS Division of Labor Force Statistics, 2 Massachusetts Avenue NE., Suite 4675, Washington, DC 20212; call (202) 691-6378; or visit www.bls.gov/CPS.

UNDERSTANDING A WRITER'S GOALS: QUESTIONS TO CONSIDER AND DISCUSS

Rhetorical Knowledge: The Writer's Situation and Rhetoric

1. **Audience:** How have the authors of these essays considered their audiences? In what ways do the graphs and charts help explain the data to an audience?

2. **Purpose:** Why did these authors write these essays? What did they hope to accomplish?

3. **Voice and Tone:** What are the writers' attitudes about the training that may be required after college?

4. **Responsibility:** How responsibly have these authors represented the interests of both students and businesses in this controversy? Why do you think that?

5. **Context, format, and genre:** How do the authors of each of these essays synthesize others' ideas?

Critical Thinking: The Writer's Ideas and Your Personal Response

6. To what extent do you agree with the arguments that these essays make? Why? How well does the chart in "New School Year, Old Story" resonate with you? Why?

7. How do these editorials challenge you to think about your own college education and what you hope to do after college?

Composing Processes and Knowledge of Conventions: The Writer's Strategies

8. How effective are charts in Nelson's essay? Why? How about the chart in the "New School Year, Old Story" essay? In what ways?

9. These essays cite many statistics. Which do you find the most compelling and convincing? Why?

Inquiry and Research: Ideas for Further Exploration

10. If you were to use the information in these essays to try to persuade a friend to attend college, what would you cite from the essays?

11. In "New School Year, Old Story" you read that "Workers with a bachelor's degree, for example, earned about $415 more a week than workers whose highest level of education is a high school diploma." How much did potential income influence your decision to attend college?

GENRES *Up Close*   **Writing a Critical Response**

Critical responses are common in all four areas of life. Thus, the practice you do now in critically responding will help you not only during but after your college years. In academic contexts, students are frequently expected to respond to assigned readings. In professional situations, workers respond critically to reports, memos, and proposals. In civic settings, voters respond critically to candidates' stump speeches and debate sound bites. In the personal area of life, people respond to a wide range of texts—product reviews, restaurant menus, labels on boxes and cans, and many others.

An effective critical response will encourage readers to think critically about the text under consideration. An effective response generally includes the following features:

- Enough details about the text so that readers can understand what it is about
- An accurate and fair representation of the text's main point
- A clear indication of the writer's perspective on the text

As you read the following critical response, consider how student writer Tracy Eckendorff has incorporated these features.

TRACY ECKENDORFF

Critical Response to "The New Bachelor's Payoff" by Paul Fain

CRITICAL RESPONSE

We hear it all the time—the connection between having a bachelor's degree and getting a high-paying job is beyond dispute. With the title "The New Bachelor's Payoff," Paul Fain states the article's bold promise of great rewards for college degree-holders. It continues by further declaring that not only is a bachelor's degree a requirement for landing high-paying employment, but that today's jobs also include supplemental training, provided by employers, to bolster their workers' skills.   1

In her first paragraph Eckendorff briefly summarizes the gist of Fain's article.

It took me a few readings to completely digest everything the author is saying before the full thrust of the article became clear to me. Fain starts with the upbeat numbers from a recent federal jobs report which cites an extremely low unemployment rate of 2.8 percent for college graduates. But clouds quickly arrive to darken this rosy economic outlook. Not only may employers soon find a lack of job-seeking graduates, but "upcredentialing" or "credential creep,"—requiring college degrees for jobs that did not traditionally need them—is causing serious concerns. Top education and workforce expert Anthony P. Carnevale points out that it has been years since higher education has turned out the talent needed for the technical jobs of today. To compensate for this trend, employers have been footing the bill   2

In this paragraph Eckendorff summarizes Fain's article in more detail.

for the additional training necessary to give its workers "usable knowledge." Out of the $1.1 *trillion* spent on training, almost one half of that comes from employers. As the article ends it points out how wages have been stagnant in recent years, but assures us that this is temporary. A "wage premium" for degree-holders is set to rise due to the inevitable increase in demand for college graduates. Despite a few hiccups in the current outlook, an increase in wages for degree-holders in the coming years, along with employer-provided training to supplement their skills, supports the long-term value of a college degree.

Eckendorff shows the nuances of Fain's points.

So although there is good news to report for those earning four-year college degrees, a combination of the dwindling supply of qualified graduates seeking employment, credential creep, and stagnant wages makes the picture more complicated. Despite these concerns, the necessity of a four-year degree appears to be solid. Due to the continued growth of technology, employers are now screening applicants by requiring degrees as a starting point in order to find employees who have an aptitude to learn the more complex skills required today. Employers then complement their employees' educations by providing additional training to acquire the talent that they need. This is fine for those who work in "middle skills" jobs, but the downside is that it means even jobs that traditionally did not require a degree now do. This credential creep, as economist Richard Vedder has written, generates its own demand. Anyone who has read a newspaper over the past few years knows that plenty of people with degrees are still not finding decent-paying jobs. This is one of the issues that is completely ignored by the author, who is writing for the publication *Inside Higher Ed*, giving a somewhat simplistic one-sided view of the inherent value of a college degree. The ever-rising costs associated with higher education cannot just be ignored. As wages have been stagnant, the cost of college has been skyrocketing. Not to mention the mountain of debt the average student incurs in getting their degree. How can this be "proof" that will "put to rest" any doubts I have about the labor-market returns of earning a degree?

3

Eckendorff comments on important omissions in the article.

Work Cited

Fain, Paul. "The New Bachelor's Payoff." *Inside Higher Ed*, 11 Feb. 2015, www.insidehighered.com/news/2015/02/11/bachelors-degrees-lead-employment-and-more-training.

UNDERSTANDING A WRITER'S GOALS: QUESTIONS TO CONSIDER AND DISCUSS

Rhetorical Knowledge: The Writer's Situation and Rhetoric

1. **Audience:** What does Eckendorff do to appeal to a wide audience?

2. **Purpose:** What has Eckendorff accomplished by writing this response?

3. **Voice and Tone:** What is Eckendorff's attitude toward Fain? Toward his position?

4. **Responsibility:** How accurately has Eckendorff presented the position that Fain takes in his article?

5. **Context, format, and genre:** At the beginning of the second paragraph, Eckendorff reflects on her own reading process. Why would a writer do that in a critical response?

Critical Thinking: The Writer's Ideas and Your Personal Response

6. How does Eckendorff's critical response help you to think critically about Fain's article?

7. How does Eckendorff's critical response affect your understanding of the value of a college education?

Composing Processes and Knowledge of Conventions: The Writer's Strategies

8. How effectively has Eckendorff paraphrased and summarized material from Fain's article? Why does Eckendorff begin her response by commenting on the title of the article?

Inquiry and Research: Ideas for Further Exploration

9. Write your own response to Fain's article, focusing on the ideas that interest you the most. How does your response differ from Eckendorff's?

10. As you prepare to write your response, think about what questions, in your role as "critical reader," you feel are most important to ask yourself about Fain's article. What makes those questions important?

WRITING PROCESSES

You may already recognize that you will engage in many writing processes as you invent and develop your ideas, draft, revise, and edit your writing to understand and synthesize texts. These processes are recursive. In other words, effective writers rarely work in a lockstep fashion but instead move back and forth among the different parts of the process. As you work on the assignment option that you have chosen (see pages 32–33), keep these processes in mind, as well as the qualities of effective writing to understand and synthesize texts (pages 35–36).

Invention: Getting Started

When you are writing to respond critically to a text or to synthesize information you have read in two or more texts, there are a few questions to keep in mind as you read the text or texts for the first few times and begin to develop your ideas. In addition, as you start your critical reading process, asking yourself questions like the following will help you as you read and analyze the text or texts and then produce your critical response or synthesis.

FOR A CRITICAL RESPONSE OR A SYNTHESIS:

- What is the purpose of the text or texts you are responding to critically?
- How solid is the author's argument?
- Do you have any issues with any of the author's assumptions?
- What is the author's main point?
- Does the author appeal more to facts or to emotions?
- To what extent do you believe the author?
- How do the writer's ideas relate to your academic, professional, civic, or personal interests?

FOR A SYNTHESIS:

- What is your purpose in synthesizing information from these texts? For example, are you simply trying to understand complex ideas, or are you trying to convince an audience of a particular point of view?
- Do the different texts you are synthesizing offer multiple perspectives on an issue or a topic or just different versions of the same perspective?
- What have you learned by reading, analyzing, and synthesizing these different texts?

The 'not everyone should go to college' argument is classist and wrong

Updated by Libby Nelson on July 16, 2014, 11:40 a.m. ET @libbyanelson libby@vox.com

TWEET (303) SHARE (1,334) +

DON'T MISS STORIES. FOLLOW VOX!

The economic return on investment for a college degree has never been higher. But the more that fact is discussed, the more some pundits seem to think the U.S. is at risk of an epidemic of unnecessary college-going that can be averted by singing the praises of highly skilled trades.

TV or newspaper editorial writers?

The latest, in *Businessweek*, is headlined "Let's Start Telling Young People the Whole Truth About College"—the whole truth being that a four-year degree isn't the only road to a stable, even lucrative, professional life.

Fair enough. (Though the economic evidence still comes down heavily on the side of four-year college graduates being better off in the long run.) But the argument that "everyone shouldn't go to college"—reiterated with dozens of variations in the past few years—rests on some incorrect assumptions about higher education in the U.S.

Here are Nelson's reasons.

Many people imagine a bright line between college and vocational education—PhDs on one side, plumbers on the other. That line doesn't exist, and it hasn't for at least a generation. Particularly at two-year colleges, programs for future English majors and future auto mechanics often exist side-by-side. One path might lead to an associate degree, the other to a certificate, but they're both at a place called "college."

This is interesting. People should get the training/education they need to do what they want to do.

As higher education economist Sandy Baum wrote in a report for the Urban Institute: "It is common to hear the suggestion that many students should forgo college and instead seek vocational training. But most of that training takes place in community colleges or for-profit postsecondary institutions."

The skilled trades are demanding workers with increasing levels of technical ability, and the market rewards those who have the credential to prove it: About 30 percent of construction workers now have some kind of professional license or credential, according to the Census Bureau. So do about 20 percent of industrial workers. Workers without a traditional college degree, but with a credential, earned more than workers with no credentials at all. They still earn less than workers with a traditional degree.

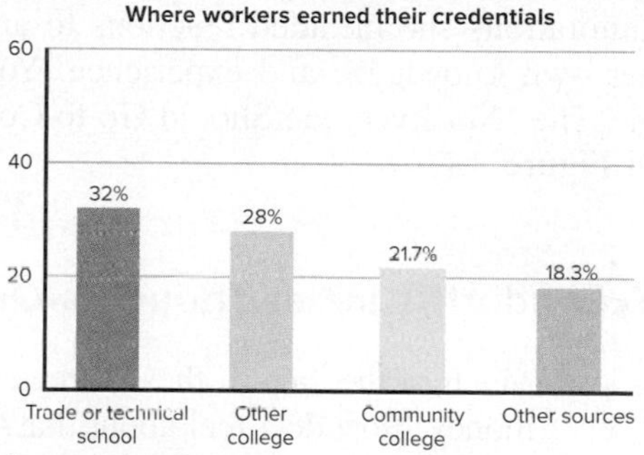

Where workers earned their credentials

Wow—I need to use these statistics in my paper.

Where do people earn these credentials? The vast majority—82 percent—of workers with credentials other than a college degree, or in addition to a college degree, earned them from an educational institution. In other words, to get ahead in those skilled jobs so often promoted as the alternative to a college education, they went to college.

Another important piece of information. Wonder if I can put it into a chart of some kind?

Somehow, criticism of the cult of the college degree never pinpoints the one group where a belief that "everyone should go to college" really is pervasive: the upper middle class. Students from families in the top fifth of incomes have gone to college in disproportionately high numbers since at least the 1970s. About 80 percent of them now attend college right after high school. More than half have a bachelor's degree by age 25.

Might be good information but confusing; maybe if I use it I should restate in some way?

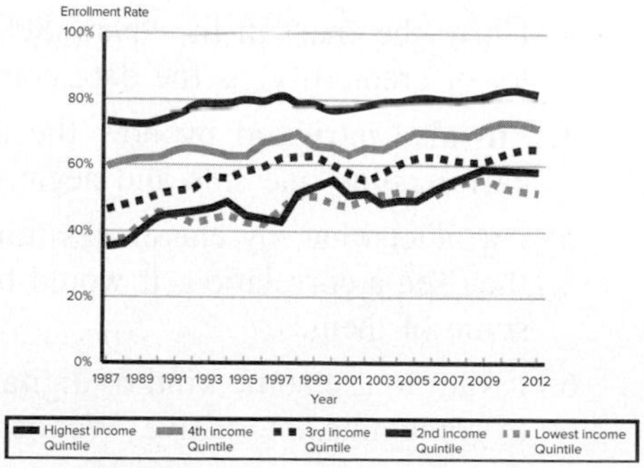

It's more than plausible that some of those well-off students could be happy and successful with a certificate in carpentry instead of a bachelor's in business. Yet the calls to tell the truth about the value of a college degree nearly always stop short of saying where—if too many people really do go to college—that truth-telling is sorely needed.

If I use this graph I'll have to simplify and explain terms like "quintile." Seeing these charts makes me wonder if I can use some of the statistics from Fain's essay, in a graph format.

FIGURE 3.1 Tracy Eckendorff's Annotations on "The 'Not Everyone Should Go to College' Argument Is Classist and Wrong"

- How similar or different are the thesis statements of the texts you are synthesizing?

- How similar or different are the examples each author uses to make his or her case?

- How do the various perspectives in the different texts you have read and analyzed help you to understand the subject?

- How could you add information in some format (data, for example) that you can present in a visual form (a chart or a graph)? What technology could you use for this?

- What is the purpose of your synthesis? For example, are you simply trying to understand complex ideas, or are you trying to convince an audience of a particular point of view?

For help with critical reading, see Chapter 2. For more on strategies for argument, see Chapter 14.

For her synthesis assignment, student writer Tracy Eckendorff chose three articles about the cost of going to college and the value of that education following graduation. You can read all three articles on pages 36–47. (Eckendorff's critical response to one of the articles is on page 47.) She began by reading the three articles critically, taking notes, and annotating them. In her notes and annotations she included reactions to and questions about the articles based on her own knowledge and experience. You can see her annotations on a portion of "The 'Not Everyone Should Go to College' Argument Is Classist and Wrong" in Figure 3.1.

Eckendorff's Initial Thoughts/Questions

1. Much of the data in these three essays show that the more college = more money. How do I feel about that? I wonder if all jobs happened to pay the same, what would I want to do?

2. Is some "mix" of formal education and on-the-job training a good idea?

3. I love the chart in the "New School Year, Old Story" essay, and it has a lot of credibility, as the data comes from the government.

4. I'm also intrigued by how the data "matches up," with positives (more earnings) on one side and negatives (less education) on the other.

5. I wonder what my classmates think about money and education—whether they see a correlation. It would be interesting to do a survey or interview some of them.

6. I want to use some kind of digital technology in my essay, or at least refer to something interactive. Wonder what I might find?

7. I wonder what correlations there are between "x" career and lifetime earnings? I'll bet I can find that kind of information.

8. Reading and writing about that kind of information will help me after I graduate, too.

9. I like the title of "The 'Not Everyone Should Go to College' Argument Is Classist and Wrong," but it asks a really good question: should everyone have at least some college? When and what?

10. I wonder how I can combine or at least highlight all of the facts and statistics and graphical information and use them in my own paper?

Writing Activity

Reading Critically and Taking Notes

Using the guidelines in Chapter 2 on reading critically, read the article or articles you have chosen, and take notes on your reactions and responses to the questions on page 48. You might annotate the article or articles, using the guidelines in Chapter 2.

Organizing Your Ideas and Details

Once you have generated ideas about the text you are responding to or the texts you are synthesizing, you might choose to organize your paper in a variety of ways. One possible way to organize your paper is to focus first on the title to see how that leads into the piece, as Tracy Eckendorff did in her critical response to Paul Fain's article (pages 36–40). Eckendorff then goes on to analyze and comment on the individual points Fain makes in the article. She comments both on the effectiveness of the points Fain makes as well as on some of his shortcomings.

In an academic essay where you have been asked to develop a synthesis of several texts, you will probably start with a description of what you are synthesizing. You might include a thesis statement in your introduction that articulates the main idea of your synthesis. You can then provide details from the texts you have read that support your thesis.

You might also organize a synthesis by briefly summarizing and analyzing each of the texts you have read in turn, leading up to your synthesis, which you would present at the end. This organization might be effective for a review of the literature on a particular topic.

For help with quoting and paraphrasing sources, see Chapter 20.

Constructing a Complete Draft

Once you have decided on the organizational pattern that you think will be most effective, go back over the notes you made during your invention process and see which points you want to include in your draft. Of course, you will need to make sure you can clearly articulate your critical response to the text you have chosen or your synthesis of two texts.

Writing Activity

Using your notes from your critical reading of the article or articles you have chosen and the organizational pattern you have decided on, write a complete first draft of your critical response or your synthesis. Remember that your ideas will likely change as you draft your paper.

As you write your first draft, you will need to consider whether it will be most effective to paraphrase parts of the text or texts you have read or whether using a direct quotation might be a better way to support a particular point.

Tracy Eckendorff's First Draft

After organizing her details, Tracy Eckendorff wrote a first draft of her synthesis essay. She contrasts the three articles by paraphrasing some of their points. As she wrote, Eckendorff concentrated on getting her ideas down; in later drafts she edited for style, grammar, and punctuation. (The numbers in circles refer to peer comments—see page 54.)

Just Go (to College)!
Tracy Eckendorff

By looking at the titles of the three pieces "The New Bachelor's Payoff," "New School Year, Old Story: Education Pays," and "The 'Not Everyone Should Go to College' Argument Is Classist and Wrong," you **1** get a hint at how all of the articles come to one overwhelmingly similar conclusion: attending college is the way to go, no question about it. You can see that coming just from seeing the word "pay" in two of the titles. For most people, this information is considered common knowledge and there is little debate about it. However, while these articles all make fundamental points that are in concert with each other, they write with separate, sometimes opposing voices, while reaching their similar outcomes. So with all of the common ground, what exactly are the points of departure? **2**

The most straightforward of the three, "New School Year, Old Story: Education Pays," comes from *Occupational Outlook Quarterly* (recently relaunched as *Career Outlook*), which is a voice out of the U.S. Bureau of Labor Studies (BLS). Because this is a government report it serves as a reliable source of statistics that should be free from personal bias or opinion. It states how those with a bachelor's degree, "earned about $415 more a week than workers whose highest level of education is a high school diploma." **3** Still, when I think about some of my older friends with multiple degrees who struggle to find stable work and are still far away from paying off their college debt, I'm not completely sure the connection is as strong as it looks.

One place where it is easy to see how these articles diverge a bit would be Libby Nelson's piece "The 'Not Everyone Should Go to College' Argument Is

Classist and Wrong," from the popular Web site *Vox*. A primary concern of hers lies with the erroneous "everyone shouldn't go to college" line of thinking that suggests that only certain kinds of skills require advanced training. The idea is that "future English majors and future auto mechanics" are involved in wholly separate pursuits. While this argument is not only classist, as she mentions in the title and throughout her piece, it is also simply incorrect. She points out that these people are all trained in the same place: college. According to the Census Bureau, construction workers make up 30% of those who "now have some kind of professional license or credential," as well as "about 20% of industrial workers." ❹ Nelson points out how one group is commonly considered exempt from the possibility of not needing to go to college (if there is an argument for that): the upper-middle class, a group that has 80% who graduate from a four-year college before they are 25. Suggesting that those holding PhDs and M.A.s are completely separate from the carpenters and plumbers of the world supports this awfully classist idea.

Paul Fain frames his article differently, ❺ which comes from a perspective more in line with an upper-middle-class point of view. Writing as an editor from the journal *Inside Higher Ed*, he is focusing on those who are earning a BA as the starting point of their education, and his article doesn't seem to venture beyond discussing the pursuit of a four-year degree, except to show that those don't who make less money. To be fair, he touches on issues of "credential creep" and "upcredentialing"—requiring degrees for jobs that previously had not needed them such as human resources or clerical work—and the concerns that some have with this problem. But the focus remains primarily with four-year degrees and the training of those who are in jobs which require BAs to begin with. Take a look at his choice of sources for his article. One is a financial analyst who points out how the working world is "running out of new, productive people to employ." The analyst's perspective refers only to the college-educated. Another source is an expert on the labor-market returns of degrees, who writes about how colleges are "lagging badly in producing talent" and not able to produce graduates with "'usable knowledge,' which he defines as 'degrees with labor-market value.'" But where does highly trained electrician or licensed industrial worker belong in this extremely narrow definition of labor market value?

All three of these articles support the strong connection between earning a degree and getting a better salary. ❻ College degrees matter, but it is important to include *all* kinds of colleges when we're talking about this issue. Still, one question that has stuck with me is how all three of these articles don't mention the dramatic ways in which the nature of knowledge and education are rapidly changing.

Works Cited

Fain, Paul. "The New Bachelor's Payoff." *Inside Higher Ed*, 11 Feb. 2015, www.insidehighered.com/news/2015/02/11/bachelors-degrees-lead-employment-and-more-training.

Nelson, Libby. "The 'Not Everyone Should Go to College' Argument Is Classist and Wrong." *Vox*, 16 July 2014, www.vox.com/2014/7/16/5904661/yes-everyone-should-go-to-college.

United States, Department of Labor, Bureau of Labor Statistics. "New School Year, Old Story: Education Pays." *Occupational Outlook Quarterly*, vol. 56, no. 3, Fall 2012, www.bls.gov/careeroutlook/2012/fall/oochart.pdf.

Student Comments on Eckendorff's First Draft

❶ Do you mean "me"? It can be awkward to use "you" in papers.

❷ Not also agreement?

❸ Are there more details and examples to show what you mean here?

❹ Are there more data on those who work at a trade?

❺ When will you show some divergences, as you promised them early in your paper?

❻ When will you show some divergences, as you promised them early in your paper?

 ## Revising

Revising means redoing your work after rethinking it. After you have finished your first full draft, you are likely to be too caught up in the ideas and language you have just written to be prepared to make real changes. It helps to put the draft of your critical response or synthesis aside for a day or so before coming back to it for revision. For example, you may think of another point to make about the text or texts you are responding to or synthesizing. However, because even experienced writers often find it hard to read their own work with fresh eyes, it also pays to have others look at your draft and provide you with comments. Classmates, friends, or family members can offer suggestions you might not have seen on your own. As you reread your critical response or synthesis draft, here are some questions to ask yourself:

- How effectively have I developed a response or synthesis of the ideas expressed in the text or texts I have read? Have I explained my response or synthesis by using specific examples from the original texts?

- How well do I know the audience I'm writing for? What have I done to make certain that my audience will understand my point of view?

- Are there any terms I use that my audience might not understand? Do I need to define or explain any of them?

- Would using some visuals help my readers understand my points better? Why?
- What kinds of visuals would help readers the most?

Technology can help you revise and edit your writing. For example, you can use the track-changes function of your word processor to try out your revisions and edits. After seeing what those changes might look like, you can choose to "accept" or "reject" those changes.

WRITER'S *Workshop* | **Responding to Full Drafts**

As you read and respond to your classmates' papers (and as they comment on yours), focus on the nature of critical response or synthesis in this assignment from a reader's perspective. Ask questions about their writing and respond to their ideas by exploring your reactions to their thoughts.

Working in pairs or groups of three, read each other's drafts, and then offer your classmates comments that will help them see both their papers' strengths as well as places where their ideas need further development. Use the following questions to guide your responses to each writer's draft:

- What is your first impression of this draft? Do you think the title is effective?
- What do you like about this draft? Provide positive and negative feedback to the writer.

- What is the writer's focus? How effectively does the writer maintain the focus throughout the paper?
- How effective is the critical response or synthesis? Where is the writer particularly effective? What suggestions could help the writer?
- How does the introduction help the reader understand the topic? What suggestions can you make to strengthen the introduction?
- How effectively has the writer analyzed the text or texts that are being used to develop the critical response or synthesis? Why?
- How effectively does the conclusion bring the critical response or synthesis to a close? How effectively does it sum everything up? What suggestions could strengthen the conclusion?
- What suggestions could strengthen the paper as a whole?

Responding to Readers' Comments

After receiving feedback on their writing from peers, instructors, friends, and others, writers need to decide how to respond. Although you should take seriously all comments from people who have read your work, you are not obligated to use all of them as you revise. Make sure you understand why your readers have made their comments and then, using your best judgment, incorporate their suggestions or answer their questions in your revisions as you see fit.

In the final version of Tracy Eckendorff's paper on pages 57–59, you can see how she responded to her peers' comments.

KNOWLEDGE OF CONVENTIONS

When effective writers edit their work, they attend to the conventions that will help their readers move through their writing effortlessly. These include genre conventions, documentation, format, usage, grammar, punctuation, and mechanics. By paying attention to these conventions in your writing, you make reading a more pleasant experience.

 ## Editing

In college classes, you may respond to or synthesize texts in response to essay examination questions asking you to—for example—find common threads in two or more readings. Editing a response to an in-class essay question can be challenging because time is limited, and you may not be allowed to consult any sources, including the course textbook. Because of these limitations, ask your instructor how carefully you will be expected to edit your essay during the examination. If your instructor expects you to edit a timed essay response, set aside a few minutes to do that task.

Of course, if your assignment is to write an out-of-class critical response to a text or a synthesis of texts, you will have time to edit your essay carefully. Put your writing aside for a day or two so that you can read it with fresh eyes. Also, ask classmates, friends, or tutors to read your paper and note areas that need further editing.

At this point in the process, you need to make sure everything in your project follows the conventions of grammar, usage, punctuation, and spelling. You can use the spell-check function of your word processing program to help, but be careful. If you've turned off the spell-check function while you've been writing, make sure you run it before your final edit. Remember, the spell-check function will not flag words that are spelled correctly but used incorrectly, such as *there* instead of *their*.

Genres, Documentation, and Format

For advice on writing in different genres, see Appendix C. For guidelines for formatting and documenting papers in MLA or APA style, see Chapter 20.

If you are writing an academic paper, follow the conventions for the discipline in which you are writing and the requirements of your instructor. If you have used material from outside sources, give credit to those sources, using the documentation style required by the discipline you are working in and by your instructor. If you are synthesizing two or more texts, you will need to document any quotations that you use from the texts.

A Writer Achieves Her Goal: Tracy Eckendorff's Synthesis

As you read the final version of Tracy Eckendorff's synthesis, consider what makes it effective. Following the reading, you will find some questions to help you consider Eckendorff's writing.

TRACY ECKENDORFF

Just Go (to College)!

SYNTHESIS

B y looking at the titles of the three pieces "The New Bachelor's Payoff," "New School Year, Old Story: Education Pays," and "The 'Not Everyone Should Go to College' Argument Is Classist and Wrong," readers get a hint at how all of the articles come to one overwhelmingly similar conclusion: attending college is the way to go, no question about it. Readers can see that coming just from seeing the word "pay" in two of the titles. For most people, this information is considered common knowledge and there is little debate about it. However, while these articles all make fundamental points that are in concert with each other, they write with separate, sometimes opposing voices, while reaching their similar outcomes. So with all of the common ground, what exactly are the points of departure as well as ideas that the essays agree on?

The most straightforward of the three, "New School Year, Old Story: Education Pays," comes from *Occupational Outlook Quarterly* (recently relaunched as *Career Outlook*), which is a voice out of the U.S. Bureau of Labor Studies (BLS). Because this is a government report it serves as a reliable source of statistics that should be free from personal bias or opinion. It states how those with a bachelor's degree, "earned about $415 more a week than workers whose highest level of education is a high school diploma." The report goes on to show that it not only pays to have a degree but that it keeps on paying as you climb the degree scale. "Workers with a professional degree, such as lawyers and physicians, earned about $612 more a week than did workers with a bachelor's degree—and over $1,000 more per week than workers who have a high school diploma as their highest level of education." Still, when I think about some of my older friends with multiple degrees who struggle to find stable work and are still far away from paying off their college debt, I'm not completely sure the connection is as strong as it looks.

One place where it is easy to see how these articles diverge a bit would be Libby Nelson's piece, "The 'Not Everyone Should Go to College' Argument

1

2

3

A peer reviewer thought that using "you" in a paper could be awkward, so Eckendorff changed it to "readers"

A peer reviewer asked about "agreement" between the essays, so Eckendorff clarified here.

A peer reviewer asked for more details and examples, so Eckendorff added the "Workers with . . ." quotation.

Is Classist and Wrong," from the popular Web site *Vox*. A primary concern of hers lies with the erroneous "everyone shouldn't go to college" line of thinking that suggests that only certain kinds of skills require advanced training. The idea is that "future English majors and future auto mechanics" are involved in wholly separate pursuits. While this argument is not only classist, as she mentions in the title and throughout her piece, it is also simply incorrect. She points out that these people are all trained in the same place: college. Just like with engineers, doctors, or lawyers, tradespeople are also included in the demand for workers with specialized technical skills. According to the Census Bureau, construction workers make up 30% of those who "now have some kind of professional license or credential," as well as "about 20% of industrial workers." Nelson points out how one group is commonly considered exempt from the possibility of not needing to go to college (if there is an argument for that): the upper-middle class, a group that has 80% who graduate from a four-year college before they are 25. Suggesting that those holding PhDs and MAs are completely separate from the carpenters and plumbers of the world supports this awfully classist idea.

This is in contrast to how Paul Fain frames his article, which comes from a perspective more in line with an upper-middle-class point of view. Writing as an editor from the journal *Inside Higher Ed*, he is focusing on those who are earning a BA as the starting point of their education, and his article doesn't seem to venture beyond discussing the pursuit of a four-year degree, except to show that those don't who make less money. To be fair, he touches on issues of "credential creep" and "upcredentialing"—requiring degrees for jobs that previously had not needed them such as human resources or clerical work—and the concerns that some have with this problem. But the focus remains primarily with four-year degrees and the training of those who are in jobs which require BAs to begin with. Take a look at his choice of sources for his article. One is a financial analyst who points out how the working world is "running out of new, productive people to employ." The analyst's perspective refers only to the college-educated. Another source is an expert on the labor-market returns of degrees, who writes about how colleges are "lagging badly in producing talent" and not able to produce graduates with "'usable knowledge,' which he defines as 'degrees with labor-market value.'" But where does highly trained electrician or licensed industrial worker belong in this extremely narrow definition of labor market value?

All three of these articles support the strong connection between earning a degree and getting a better salary. However, only Nelson takes a much broader view of the world of higher education to also include the training received by those involved in fields such as industrial work and specialized trades. In her article she quotes higher education economist Sandy Baum who says, "It is common to hear the suggestion that many students should forgo college and instead seek vocational training. But most of that training takes place in

4

5

A peer reviewer asked for more information on those who "work in a trade," so Eckendorff added this sentence.

A peer reviewer asked, "when will you show some divergences, as you promised them early in your paper?" Eckendorff changed her wording to clearly indicate that.

One of her reviewers asked Eckendorff to "flesh out and expand" her conclusion, which she does in this final draft.

community colleges or for-profit postsecondary institutions." College degrees matter, but it is important to include *all* kinds of colleges when we're talking about this issue. Still, one question that has stuck with me is how all three of these articles don't mention the dramatic ways in which the nature of knowledge and education are rapidly changing.

Works Cited

Fain, Paul. "The New Bachelor's Payoff." *Inside Higher Ed,* 11 Feb. 2015, www.insidehighered.com/news/2015/02/11/bachelors-degrees-lead-employment-and-more-training.

Nelson, Libby. "The 'Not Everyone Should Go to College' Argument Is Classist and Wrong." *Vox*, 16 July 2014, www.vox.com/2014/7/16/5904661/yes-everyone-should-go-to-college.

United States, Department of Labor, Bureau of Labor Statistics. "New School Year, Old Story: Education Pays." *Occupational Outlook Quarterly*, vol. 56, no.3, Fall 2012, www.bls.gov/careeroutlook/2012/fall/oochart.pdf.

UNDERSTANDING A WRITER'S GOALS: QUESTIONS TO CONSIDER AND DISCUSS

Rhetorical Knowledge: The Writer's Situation and Rhetoric

1. **Audience:** What knowledge does Eckendorff assume that her readers have or do not have? Why do you think that?

2. **Purpose:** What was Eckendorff's purpose in synthesizing the three readings as she did?

3. **Voice and Tone:** How does Eckendorff reveal her attitude toward Fain, toward Nelson, and toward all of the writers she considers?

4. **Responsibility:** How responsibly has Eckendorff presented the ideas from the three readings?

5. **Context, format, and genre:** Eckendorff wrote this synthesis for one of her classes. How has that context affected her synthesis?

Critical Thinking: The Writer's Ideas and Your Personal Response

6. How has Eckendorff helped you to understand the issues that Fain, Nelson, and the Bureau of Labor Statistics are addressing?

7. To what extent do your perspectives on the issues align with Eckendorff's perspectives? Why? Where do you disagree with her?

Composing Processes and Knowledge of Conventions: The Writer's Strategies

8. In places, Eckendorff directly compares the views of the three articles. Why do you think she does that?

9. In some places, Eckendorff quotes directly from the readings. In other places, though, she paraphrases or summarizes ideas in the readings. Why does she use a mix of strategies for presenting ideas from the readings?

Inquiry and Research: Ideas for Further Exploration

10. Conduct a library or Web search to find out more details about the importance of getting a college degree. If you were to advise Eckendorff on how to include some of those details in her synthesis, what would you suggest?

Self-Assessment: Reflecting on Your Goals

Now that you have considered how to respond critically to readings and synthesize them, think further about your learning goals by contemplating the following questions. If you are constructing a course portfolio, your responses to these questions can also serve as invention work for the portfolio.

 ## Rhetorical Knowledge

- *Audience:* How did the audience influence your approach to your critical response or to synthesizing texts?
- *Purpose:* How did your purpose influence your approach?
- *Rhetorical situation:* How did the rhetorical situation affect your approach?
- *Voice and tone:* How important was your voice in your critical response or in synthesizing the texts you chose? Why? What factors influenced your tone?
- *Context, medium, and genre:* How did the context affect the medium and genre you chose?

  ## Critical Thinking, Reading, and Writing

- *Learning/Inquiry:* What did you need to know about the topic of the article or articles you were responding to or synthesizing in order to write your critical response or synthesis effectively?
- *Responsibility:* What was your responsibility to readers when critically responding to a text or synthesizing two or more texts?
- *Reading and research:* What were some effective critical reading strategies that you used in developing ideas for your critical response or synthesis?
- *Skills:* How did critically responding or synthesizing help you to develop your skills in critical thinking, reading, and writing?
- What did you learn from the reading and writing for this assignment that might help you outside of this course? In your academic life? In your professional life? In your civic life? In your personal life?

Writing Processes

- *Invention:* What invention strategies were helpful as you approached this project? If you wrote a synthesis, what strategies helped you to compare texts?

- *Organizing your ideas and details:* What have you learned about organizing ideas when you respond to a text or synthesize several texts?

- *Revising:* What tools were useful in revising your critical response or synthesis to meet the needs of readers?

- *Working with peers:* How did peers help you to respond critically to a text or synthesize texts more effectively? What did you learn about working with others that will help you outside of this course?

- *Visuals:* How did you use visuals to strengthen your critical response or synthesis? If you did not use visuals, why did you choose not to use them? If you included visuals, what digital technologies did you use?

- *Writing habits:* What "writerly habits" did you find helpful when completing this project? Why?

 ## Knowledge of Conventions

- *Editing:* As you worked on this project, which editing skills served you well? What editing skills do you still need to develop further?

- *Genre:* What conventions of genre did you find most important in critically responding to or synthesizing the texts you chose?

- *Documentation:* What documentation style did you use to cite sources in your critical response or synthesis?

Refer to Chapter 1 (pages 12–13) to see a sample reflection.

Text Credits

4 Writing to Discover and to Learn

Most of the chapters in this book focus on learning to write for an audience—to accomplish a purpose involving other people. This chapter, though, provides some tried-and-true strategies for using writing to discover ideas and to learn—to accomplish a purpose for yourself. As you do more writing, you are probably noticing that it is a way of learning, of figuring out what you know and understand about a subject. The process of writing is also a way of coming to know and understand a subject better.

This chapter introduces strategies to help you to learn and to prepare for writing assignments. These tools can be used in academic, professional, civic, or personal settings. As discussed in Chapter 2, writing about what you read for your classes can help you learn that information better, not just by rewriting to summarize your notes, but by jotting down your questions and comments, reflecting on what you have read, and noting how any new ideas and information relate to other ideas and information. Relating ideas in a text to ideas in other texts, as you

© Fancy Photography/Veer RF

know from Chapter 3, is called *synthesizing*, and it is a strategy you will use in most of your college writing. In your professional life, consider how writing about what was useful in a recent business meeting, what problems came up, and what issues did not get solved might help you conduct more effective and efficient meetings in the future.

In almost any situation, writing (immediately afterward)

about what you *learned* from an experience will prepare you for similar situations you might face in the future. If you get into the habit of writing about the events and issues in your life, you likely will come to a more thoughtful and thorough understanding of those events and issues.

The strategies that follow are tools that writers have used to figure out what they have learned and what they still need to know.

Using Invention Strategies to Discover Ideas

As you begin to explore your subject, it is a good idea to use more than one invention activity to generate ideas. No matter what your purpose is for writing, you will need to generate information and knowledge about your topic through invention activities. Whichever of these strategies you use, a helpful accompanying activity is creating an audience profile. The "Genres Up Close" feature on page 65 walks you through the steps of this process.

Listing

Listing involves jotting down keywords that will remind you of ideas as you write more later. You might find it effective to establish categories within your lists to jog your memory. If you wanted to propose a solution to a problem, for example, you might organize keywords under "history of the problem," "how the problem affects my readers," "possible solutions," "failed solutions," and "objections to a solution."

Freewriting

When you freewrite, you simply write for a set time—perhaps five or ten minutes. You jot down, or type, everything that comes to mind, even if you cannot think of anything (in that case, you might write, "I can't think of anything to write," until your ideas start to flow).

Questioning

One way to generate information and ideas is to ask questions about your topic, audience, and purpose:

- What am I trying to accomplish in this paper?
- What do I already know about my topic?
- What might my readers already know?
- What would readers need to know to understand my point?
- What kind(s) of information (for example, graphs, tables, or lists) might be useful to *show* my readers (rather than just to tell them)?
- What kinds of details and explanations can I provide?
- Where might I learn more about this subject (in the library, on the Internet, by interviewing people)?

Answering the Questions *Who? What? Where? When? Why?* and *How?*

You can expand the questioning approach (above) by spending a few minutes jotting down answers to the reporter's questions: *who, what, where, when, why, and how.* You may find that your answers lead to still more questions:

- Whom does this subject affect? In what ways?

- Who is involved in making a decision about this subject?
- Who is my audience?
- What am I trying to get my audience to do?
- What can't I ask my readers to do?
- What is important here?
- What are the historical aspects of this topic?
- Where does all of this take place?
- When might something happen to affect this situation?
- When would I like something to happen?
- Why should my readers care about my paper?
- Why is this topic important?
- Why will _____ happen?
- How does the context—the "where"—affect the situation?
- How might _____ happen?
- How might _____ react to the topic I am writing about?

Brainstorming

When you brainstorm, you record on paper or on screen the information you already know about the topic you are exploring. Once you have written down several possible topics or ideas or possible ways to focus your paper, you may have an easier time finding the one that seems most promising.

Clustering

Clustering is especially useful for figuring out possible cause-and-effect relationships. For more on clustering and an example, see page 71.

Keeping Notebooks and Journals

Writers and learners frequently maintain notebooks and journals because these forms of informal writing are useful places for recording and exploring ideas. Leonardo da Vinci, for example, kept notebooks for years, compiling 1,566 pages of ideas in words and images.

Double-Entry Notebook

One useful type of notebook is what composition scholar Anne Berthoff calls a **dialectical notebook** or **journal.** In a dialectical notebook, you write notes on one page and then write your questions and comments about those notes on the facing page. The **double-entry notebook,** which is a type of dialectical notebook,

GENRES *Up Close* Writing an Audience Profile

An *audience profile* is a genre that helps writers understand their audience's needs. While understanding an audience's needs is only one part of the rhetorical situation, the more writers know about their audience, the better they are positioned to achieve their purpose and to present their information effectively. In fact, one of the first things experienced writers do when they start a writing project is to identify and analyze their audience. For example, determining whether the audience is knowledgeable about the topic can help writers choose the appropriate level of detail and decide how technical their language should be. The more writers know about their target audience, the more they can tailor the argument for the maximum impact on that audience. An informative pamphlet on the needs of children with autism in schools might provide different information, depending on its primary audience: parents and relatives of children with autism, parents of children attending classes with children who have autism, or school personnel.

When profiling their audience, writers need to ask themselves the following questions:

- Who is my audience?
- Does this writing task have only one audience, or are there multiple audiences?
- If there is more than one audience, how does each one differ from the others?
- What does my audience already know?
  - Are they experts in the field?
  - Are they knowledgeable laypeople?
  - Will I need to adjust my language and level of detail to meet my audience's needs?
- What does my audience need to know?
- Why is this information important to this audience?
- How do I expect my audience to use this information?

Here is a sample format you might use for an audience profile.

Main Audience
- What are their defining characteristics?

Secondary Audiences
- What are their defining characteristics?
- How do they differ from the main audience?

Audience's Knowledge of the Field
- What background (experience/education) do the audience members have?
- What are their assumptions about the information?
- Does their cultural context affect their view of the information? How?

What the Audience Needs to Know
- Why is this information important to my audience?
- How should I expect my audience to use this information?
- How might a graph, picture, table, chart (or some other visual that technology helps construct) help my audience understand my point?

Whether your instructor asks you to write an audience profile as a formal writing assignment or not, being able to profile an audience informally for every writing assignment you do is a valuable skill.

Writing Activity

Your Dialectical Notebook

Select one of your college classes and go over your notes for the most recent week of classes. Construct a dialectical notebook that outlines your notes and also your reactions to, comments on, and questions about those notes.

can be easily adapted to many contexts. The double-entry notebook has two columns. The left column is used to present whatever kind of information is appropriate to the context. Thus, in this column, you might record lecture, lab, field, or reading notes; list the steps in a math problem; construct a time line; or list events in chronological order. The right column is used to respond to, comment on, question, and apply the information in the left column.

For instance, Judy Bowden was enrolled in an art history course. To understand some of the artwork that she was studying in the course, Bowden frequently used the double-entry notebook. Because her journal was electronic, she could download public-domain artwork from the Web and paste it into the left column of her notebook. In the right column, she wrote about the work. Here is an example from Bowden's notebook.

Artwork	My Thoughts
 © SuperStock	This is the *Black Bull* cave painting from Lascaux, France. It's amazing that this and other paintings in the cave are 10,000 to 30,000 years old. It's also amazing that 2,000 paintings and drawings in the cave have survived for so long. The details seem very sophisticated for such an old piece of art. I wonder what the four teenagers thought when they discovered the cave on September 12, 1940. If I were in an anthropology course instead of an art history course, I wonder what other things we'd learn about this painting and the others.

Field Notebook

For more on field research, see Chapter 19.

Field notebooks are useful for students who are doing field research. A field notebook can take many forms, depending on the observations that you are making. For instance, Lindsay Hanson was enrolled in a summer session biology course for nonmajors. One of the requirements of the course was to pick a natural habitat and observe some life forms in that habitat. Lindsay chose to do some bird-watching in a marsh near her campus. She decided to set up her field notebook in columns with headings.

Date and Time	Location	Common Name	Scientific Name	Sex	Comments
6/6/16 6:20 p.m.	west shore of Widespread	red-winged blackbird	Agelaius phoeniceus	♂	The bird was sitting on the top of a weed, which was swaying in the breeze. Partly cloudy, 61°, windy
6/6/16 6:35 p.m.	south shore of Widespread	yellow-shafted flicker	Colaptes auratus	♀	The bird took off from some 8"–10" grass. Partly cloudy, 61°

Writing Activity

Writing Your Own Field Notebook

If you have a class that requires fieldwork, construct a field notebook that includes drawings or other images and your notes on your field research. If you do not have a class that requires field research, spend an hour at some location on your campus, observing and making notes on what you see in a field notebook. Use these reporter's questions to guide you:

- Who is there? What are they doing? How are they dressed? What are they carrying or working with?

- What does the place look like? Can you take photos or make drawings? What sounds and smells are in this place?

- Where is this place? How does it connect or relate to other places on campus?

- When did you visit? Why? What makes that time different from another time when you might observe this place?

- Why did you select this particular spot? What other locations did you consider? Why?

Rewriting Your Class Notes

Whether you use a double-entry notebook or some other method, make rewriting your class notes part of your own "homework" assignment each day:

- Put them into a readable and organized form.
- Think of questions about the information that had not occurred to you when you were taking the notes during class.
- Discover areas of interest that you want to find out more about.

Think of the "re" in the word *rewriting* and what it means: to resee, to reenvision, to reconsider, perhaps even to reorganize. When you rewrite your in-class notes, use the writing as a way to help you learn, not just by transcribing your notes, but by reconsidering them and asking questions, by reseeing what you wrote (and jotting down connections you make with other ideas and texts), and by reorganizing them so they make more sense than they might have made in class. Using even basic technology such as a word-processing program makes rewriting your notes easier.

 USING DIGITAL TECHNOLOGIES **Communicating with Study Groups and Partners**

When you take a college class, remember that your classmates can be a valuable resource. Create communication spaces online for you and your study partners. Exchange contact information with classmates, and use it. If your class has a course management system, like Blackboard, you can access your classmates through the e-mail link. Additionally, you will find collaboration space within the course shell. If you are taking a class at a location that does not have a learning management system, you may want to use a chat space like Google Chat, FaceTime, or Skype.

As you begin exchanging ideas and information within your group, make sure you cite sources if you or your group members are posting text or images from reference or online materials. With copyrighted work, you must obtain permission from the source before posting that person's intellectual property on a public site.

After each college class meeting, convert your in-class notes to e-notes in a computer document. Doing so encourages you to reread your notes and put them into a more readable form. Just reading them over again helps cement the ideas in your memory—and writing them down again helps you remember them, too. Also, your notes will be easier to read when exam time comes around. Finally, your notes will be searchable, and you can copy and paste them, as needed, into your college papers.

Minute Paper

A minute paper is a quick, useful way to reflect on a class lecture or discussion, a chance to jot down—in a minute or two—your answers to two questions:

For more on e-mail, instant messaging, and blogs, see Chapter 17.

- What is the most important thing that I learned in class today?
- What is the most important question that I have about today's class lecture/discussion?

For example, Conner Ames, who was enrolled in a general studies course in sociology, responded at the end of a particular class as follows:

1. Today we learned that group behavior often is different from individual behavior: people will act differently in groups than they might act alone. This is especially true for male adolescents when a group interacts with other male adolescent groups.

2. What are more of the real-life implications of group behavior (and I also want to know more about *why* young males like me act as they do when they're in a group)?

Muddiest Point

As its name suggests, the muddiest-point strategy involves jotting down a concept or idea that is unclear or confusing and, if possible, exploring it through writing. This does not mean looking up the definition of a concept, but instead writing about it to clarify your thinking.

Your muddiest point may come from a paragraph in a textbook that you are reading for a course, or it may come from a class lecture or discussion. In many instances, you may be able to work through your confusion by writing. At the very least, you will crystallize the issue and provide yourself with a reminder to raise a question during the next class meeting, in an office-hour visit, in an e-mail to the professor, or on the online discussion board for the course.

Preconception Check

A *preconception* is something you think you know about a subject before you learn more about it in class, through your reading, and from other sources of information. One strategy for overcoming preconceptions is to become aware of them. For instance, Tom Ambrose was enrolled in an astronomy course. As he read a chapter about the solar system, he encountered a subsection titled "Why Are There Seasons on Earth?" Before he read the subsection, he realized that he had some preconceptions about why the seasons occur. He wrote the following in his learning journal for that course:

> I think that Earth has the four seasons because of the elliptical path of the planet as it orbits the Sun. When that path takes us farthest from the Sun (December–March), we have winter. When the path takes us closest to the Sun (June–August), we have summer.

This short explanation may seem trivial, but it served to make Ambrose more attuned to the explanation in his astronomy textbook. When he read that the seasons are caused by Earth's tilt on its axis, he was better prepared to process that information. He noted:

> When I read the chapter, I realized the problem with my preconception. If the elliptical path of Earth's orbit were the cause of the seasons, then the whole planet would have summer at the same time. I forgot that when it's summer in the northern hemisphere it's winter in the southern hemisphere. In fact, Earth is farthest from the sun in July, when it is summer in the northern hemisphere.

Paraphrasing

One strategy you can use to make the material you are studying more understandable is to **paraphrase** it—to restate it in your own words. If you have ever tried to teach something to someone, you know that the act of teaching—explaining, demonstrating, answering questions—often aids your understanding of the subject or concept. This is the rationale behind paraphrasing—by explaining something in your own words, you come to understand it better.

Jack Johnson was taking an introductory physics course for nonmajors. Early in the course, the instructor mentioned "Occam's razor" but did not define it. Using a popular search engine to investigate the term, Johnson found that it is defined as the principle of economy or of parsimony. After reading several Web sites, Johnson felt he understood the term and wrote the following in his course journal:

> In a nutshell, Occam's razor means this: if two theories have equal explanatory power, choose the simpler one. That is, keep it simple, Stupid—K.I.S.S. In my geology class we discussed the Grand Canyon, and I kind of now see how the simplest answer to its formation—a river and other natural weather conditions, acting over a long period of time—actually makes the most sense. If I try to get too complicated about something, I need to remember Occam's razor: if two or more ideas seem to explain something, the simpler is probably the better answer.

For more on paraphrasing, see Chapter 20.

Organizing and Synthesizing Information

Finding and collecting information is part of learning, but effective learners need to organize and synthesize information to make it usable. As you conduct research and locate information that might be useful for your writing, do the following:

- Organize what you learn in a logical manner. Often an effective way to organize your notes is to put them into a digital document; you can then use its search function to locate particular words or phrases.

- Organize your notes by putting them into a spreadsheet like Excel. If you format the spreadsheet cells to "wrap text," you create a database of notes.

For more on summary and synthesis, see Chapters 2 and 3.

- As you take notes, synthesize the information: condense it into a brief form, where the important aspects are listed, along with the reference, so you can easily locate the complete information.

Invented Interview/Unsent Letter

In an invented interview, you are the interviewer. The interviewee could be a person or a character whom you are studying or a person associated with a concept that you are studying. If you *really* could interview someone for a college class, what would you ask that person? What issues or concepts would you focus on? It is often useful to put your questions into an unsent-letter format so that you have a specific audience you are writing to as you generate interview questions.

Here are some sample questions:

- In a geometry course, you might interview Pythagoras to ask him about the process that led to his development of the Pythagorean theorem.

- In an entrepreneurship course, you might interview Bill Gates to ask him what drove him to found Microsoft.

- In an anthropology course, you might interview a group of Cro-Magnons to ask about their interactions with Neanderthals.

- In a U.S. history course, you might ask President Harry Truman why he decided to drop atomic bombs on two Japanese cities in 1945.

Taking this concept of an invented interview further, you can conduct research to determine how your questions might have been answered if you had been able to conduct such an interview.

The key to writing such interviews is that you need to move beyond the limits of your initial response to an event or a person. Use the interview as an opportunity to explore a topic from an intellectual as well as an emotional perspective.

Using Charts and Visuals to Discover and to Learn

Just as charts, graphs, tables, photographs, and other visuals help readers understand what you write about, using visuals is often a way for writers to explore ideas and really see and understand what they are writing about.

Clustering and Concept Mapping

Concept maps, or *clustering*, can help us to visualize abstract ideas and also to understand relationships among ideas. Figure 4.1 shows how student writer Jessica Hemauer might have developed a cluster map to help her get started with her paper about living on a farm (you can read her complete essay in Chapter 5).

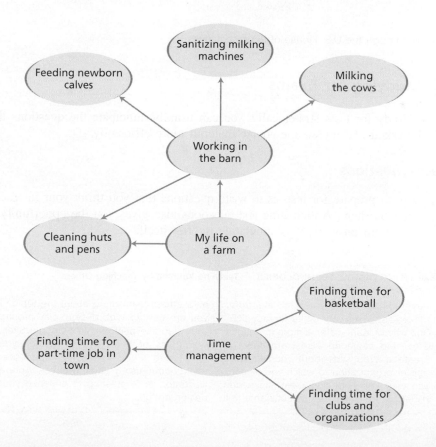

FIGURE 4.1

A Possible Cluster Map on the Topic of Living on a Farm

Process Flowchart

A process flowchart is another visually useful tool for converting information from verbal to visual form. A flowchart allows you to translate several paragraphs of information into a clear, succinct visual that can make difficult concepts easier to understand. Rather than focusing on relationships in a system (how ideas or concepts might connect to one another), a flowchart indicates how things *move* through a system.

In his political science course, Brian Flores studied the process by which a bill moves through the U.S. House of Representatives. After reading a few pages on the process, Brian converted the material into the flowchart shown in Figure 4.2.

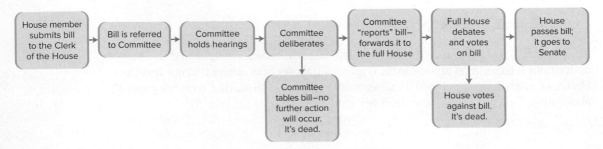

FIGURE 4.2   Following a Bill through the U.S. House of Representatives

Studying for Exams

If you study for tests strategically, you can usually anticipate the questions that will be asked and review the course material more efficiently.

Test Questions

One way to prepare for tests is to write questions that you think your instructor may pose on them. Anticipating test questions also gives you the opportunity to anticipate your answers, thus simulating the test itself.

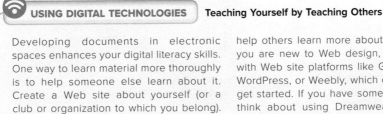

USING DIGITAL TECHNOLOGIES   **Teaching Yourself by Teaching Others**

Developing documents in electronic spaces enhances your digital literacy skills. One way to learn material more thoroughly is to help someone else learn about it. Create a Web site about yourself (or a club or organization to which you belong). Use your knowledge to create links, add visuals, and make connections that will help others learn more about the topic. If you are new to Web design, play around with Web site platforms like Google Sites, WordPress, or Weebly, which can help you get started. If you have some experience, think about using Dreamweaver, Adobe Illustrator, or Photoshop to enhance your design options.

If you are writing questions to prepare for a test, the first step is to ask the instructor about the kinds of questions that you should anticipate. Your instructor will probably indicate the formats that the questions will be in—for example, whether they will be multiple-choice, true/false, matching, short-answer, and/or essay questions—and might also indicate the levels of thinking they will require: comprehension, application, analysis, synthesis, and/or evaluation.

One of the most effective strategies for writing test questions is to go through your class notes and reading notes, marking sections that you think are likely to be covered on the test. Then, as soon as possible after class or after reading the textbook, write a few questions and think about the answers. If you write some questions each week, you will learn much more than if you wait until just before the test, and you will cover the material more thoroughly.

For advice on creating an effective Web site, see Appendix C.

Mnemonic Play

Although in many courses you will learn course material without having to memorize facts, there may be times when you need to develop memory aids for some material. Here is an example that may already be familiar to you. Erin Wilson was enrolled in a general science course for nonmajors. To help her remember the order of the planets in the solar system (before Pluto's status as a planet was changed), she used the sentence "<u>M</u>y <u>v</u>ery <u>e</u>ducated <u>m</u>other <u>j</u>ust <u>s</u>erved <u>u</u>s <u>n</u>ine <u>p</u>izzas." That is, the order, beginning with the planet closest to the Sun, is Mercury, Venus, Earth, Mars, Jupiter, Saturn, Uranus, Neptune, Pluto. Once Pluto was reclassified as a "dwarf planet," she used the sentence "My very educated mother just served us naan." Erin loves naan.

For advice on taking essay examinations, see Appendix B.

Text Credits

p. 66: Courtesy of Judy Bowen.

5 Writing to Share Experiences

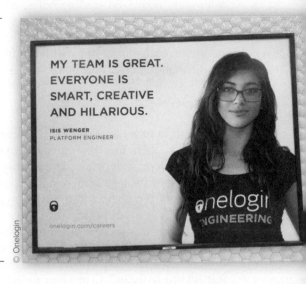

MY TEAM IS GREAT.
EVERYONE IS
SMART, CREATIVE
AND HILARIOUS.

ISIS WENGER
PLATFORM ENGINEER

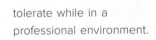

onelogin.com/careers

© Onelogin

In "You May Have Seen My Face on BART," a post that appears on the blog "The Coffeelicious" (https://medium.com/the-coffeeli-cious), Isis Anchalee, a platform engineer, shares an experience that taught her something about how women are viewed in her industry and in the culture at large. After appearing in an ad campaign aimed at recruiting talent for her company, OneLogin, Anchalee was dismayed by people's responses to her image. Comment threads on social media included remarks about her appearance—namely, that she did not resemble what commenters believed a tech engineer "should look like." In her blog post, Anchalee wrote:

> This industry's culture fosters an unconscious lack of sensitivity towards those who do not fit a certain mold. I'm sure that every other woman and non-male identifying person in this field has a long list of mild to extreme personal offenses that they've *just had to tolerate.* I'm not trying to get anyone in trouble, fired or ruin anyone's life. I just want to make it clear that **we are all humans,** and there are certain patterns of behavior that no one should have to tolerate while in a professional environment.

In telling her story on the Web, Anchalee was engaging in a common activity—sharing a meaningful experience with other people. On any given day, you share your experiences in a variety of ways. Writing about your experiences helps you as a writer because the act of writing requires reflection, which is a powerful tool for gaining insight into and understanding about life. Also, when you share your experiences with others, you are offering others insight into what has worked well—and not so well—in your life.

Setting Your Goals

- **Rhetorical Knowledge:** As you write, you'll need to consider the constellation of factors that make up your *rhetorical situation:* you (the writer), your readers (the audience), the topic (the experience that you're writing about), your purpose (what you wish to accomplish), and the exigency (what is compelling you to write). Readers—your *audience*—may or may not know you or the people you are writing about personally, but you will want to make your experience relevant to them. Your *purpose* may be to entertain your readers and possibly to inform and/or persuade them. You will have a *stance*—or attitude—toward the experience you are sharing and the people you are writing about. Your *voice* and *tone* may be amused, sarcastic, neutral, or regretful, among other possibilities. Finally, your writing *context,* the *medium* you are writing in (whether print or electronic), and the *genre* you have chosen all affect your writing decisions.

- **Critical Thinking, Reading, and Writing:** You will need to learn features of writing to share experiences so that you can do so effectively in any writing situation. As you write to share your experience, you will need to do so responsibly, representing them accurately and with sensitivity to the needs of others. You will draw on your own memories, memories of relatives and friends, photographs and documents, and ideas you develop from your reading and research.

- **Writing Processes:** It is best to choose invention strategies that will help you recall details about your experience or experiences. Generally, you will need to organize your ideas and details as a series of events. When you revise, you will read your work with a critical eye to make certain that it fulfills the assignment and displays the qualities of this kind of writing. At the revising stage, it often helps to work with peers, classmates, and others who can offer you comments on and questions about your work.

- **Knowledge of Conventions:** When writers share experiences, they tend to use dialogue to report what they said and what others said to them. When editing, you need to check to be sure you have followed the conventions for punctuating dialogue. If you have relied on sources outside of your experience, cite them using the appropriate documentation style. Finally, choose an appropriate genre; genres for sharing your experience include personal essay, memoir, autobiography, literacy narrative, magazine or newspaper essay, blog, letter, and accident report.

RHETORICAL KNOWLEDGE

When you write about your experiences in a private journal, you can write whatever and however you wish. When you write for other people, though, you need to make conscious choices about your audience; purpose; voice and tone; and context, medium, and genre.

Writing to Share Experiences

Throughout your college career, you will be called on to share your experiences in writing. Such writing can help you learn more effectively because it encourages you to reflect on your academic experiences. Further, much academic writing takes the form of **narratives**—stories about the physical or human world. For example, one of the best-known philosophers in history, Plato, used stories as powerful teaching tools. In the *Republic,* Plato tells "The Allegory of the Cave" to illustrate what it's like to think like a philosopher.

In your own academic life—your life in college—you may be asked to share experiences in the following ways:

- A math instructor may ask you to write about some experience in which you used a math principle or procedure to solve a problem in your everyday life.

- A music instructor may ask you to attend a concert and then write about the experience.

- An education instructor might assign you to observe a classroom and write about your observations.

As humans we tend to organize our lives as ongoing narratives. Although your life is one long narrative, within it are thousands of shorter narratives. Those are the kinds of events you will most likely focus on when you write to record and share experiences in the professional, civic, and personal parts of your life.

Star quarterback Peyton Manning was a professional athlete with a reputation for paying attention to detail. Sportswriter Peter King notes that when Manning was searching for a new team to join in 2011, he managed to remember, and acknowledge by name, every coach and assistant coach on every team he visited. This attention to detail helped him to make his final choice. While we don't know if Manning kept notes or has an extraordinary memory, for most of us, using writing to take notes and record details allows us to remember better. You can follow Manning's example of attention to details by using writing to record and analyze your **professional** experiences so that you can learn from them.

To participate effectively in **civic** life, writers also need to share their experiences. For democratic institutions to function effectively, citizens need to be involved with their government, especially at the local level.

In **personal** settings, you have many opportunities to record and share experiences every day. For example, at the wedding of two friends, you may be asked to tell the story of how you introduced them in high school.

"Ways of Writing to Share Experiences" on page 78 provides examples of genres you may use in your writing. The genres of writing you will be assigned will vary by the experiences you are sharing and your specific audience for those experiences.

Scenarios for Writing | Assignment Options

Your instructor may ask you to complete one or both of the following assignments, which call for you to write about your experiences. Each assignment is in the form of a *scenario*, a brief story that provides some context for your writing. The scenario gives you a sense of who your audience is and what you need to accomplish with your writing.

Starting on page 95, you will find guidelines for completing the assignment. Additional scenarios for college and life may be found online.

Writing for College

SCENARIO 1   A Memoir about the Impact of a Teacher

Throughout your formal education, you have studied with dozens of teachers. Some of them have been especially influential in helping you learn to succeed in academic settings—and, of course, their influence may have spilled over into the other three parts of your life. You may have chosen your future profession because of a specific teacher's influence.

Writing Assignment: The word *memoir* comes from the French word *mémoire,* which in turn comes from the Latin word *memoria,* meaning "memory" or "reminiscence." A memoir focuses on how a person remembers his or her life. Although the terms *memoir* and *autobiography* are sometimes used interchangeably, the genre of memoir is usually considered to be a subclass of autobiography. While an autobiography usually encompasses an entire life, a memoir is more likely to focus on memorable moments and episodes from a person's life.

Keeping in mind the qualities of a memoir, write about a teacher who was especially influential in a positive way in your academic life. Your memoir can be designed for a general academic audience, or it can be designed for a specific course in a specific discipline. As you remember and discuss in writing how this teacher influenced you as a student, include examples that show that influence.

Ways of Writing to Share Experiences

Genres for Your College Classes	Sample Situation	Advantages of the Genre	Limitations of the Genre
Academic essay	Your sociology professor asks you to construct an academic essay in which you share your family's holiday traditions.	This essay will help you understand how your traditions are unique and/or part of a larger culture.	It may be difficult to identify how your traditions are the same as or different from as those practiced by others in a short paper.
I-Search essay	In your technology and society class, you are asked to relate how you use the Internet to connect with friends and family.	An I-Search essay allows you to examine and explain your experiences with technology.	Because you are focusing on your experiences, it may be difficult to present that personal search in a formal assignment.
Academic reflection	After writing an extended argument for your economics class, you are asked to reflect on your writing process and explain what you might do differently next time.	This essay will help you understand your writing process and determine how to improve future performance.	You may have to provide evidence from your own writing and research, which may feel awkward.
Oral/visual presentation	Your humanities professor asks you to profile, in an oral and visual presentation, a period of art that is meaningful to you and explain why.	Perhaps each member of the class will present on a different topic. This gives you the chance to teach the class what you learned.	Because presentation time is limited, you will need to be selective and brief.
Project report	Your business professor asks you to write about your experience of working in a group on a marketing project.	This assignment will help you reflect on the group experience as well as your strengths and weaknesses as a collaborator.	You may feel you can't be honest about the group members who didn't work well with others.
Literacy narrative	Your writing teacher asks you to write about your earliest memories of learning to write.	A literacy narrative can provide insights into your current writing practices.	You may have only vague recollections of early writing experiences.

Genres for Life	Sample Situation	Advantages of the Genre	Limitations of the Genre
Letter to the editor	You want to construct a letter to the editor of your local paper, outlining your experiences with a local nonprofit agency.	A letter to the editor allows you to encourage others in your community to become involved with the agency.	Space is limited, and not everyone reads the local paper or all parts of it. It might not be selected for publication.
Memo	You want to let the president of your firm know of a recent experience you had with a training company that your business uses.	A memo allows you to convey information quickly and professionally.	A memo forces you to write concisely and specifically about your experiences; however, you might need more space.
Blog	You want to construct a blog about being a student at your university.	A blog is an easy and simple way for you to convey information to a wide audience.	Someone will need to monitor the blog for inappropriate comments.
Web page	You want to construct a Web page to describe your experience hiking a local nature trail.	Your Web page will give all readers the same information at the same time; you can update it when necessary.	You may not have the technical skills to construct an interactive Web site.
Poster	You want to construct a poster for a self-help fitness program, focusing on the notion that "I did it—so can you!"	A poster allows you to share your experience with the program clearly and concisely, yet with sufficient detail. The poster's visual impact should engage your audience.	If what your poster presents is too concise, readers will not believe that "they can do it too."

SCENARIO 2   A Literacy Narrative about an Influential Situation

This scenario asks you to construct a *literacy narrative*. Quite often, a literacy narrative is an account of a situation that helped you develop as a writer. One such situation would be how the actions of a parent or a teacher had a significant effect on how you approach writing today.

Writing Assignment: For your college newspaper or an alumni magazine, write a narrative account of a particular situation that you now understand had an influence on how you view writing, language use, or reading. Be sure to tell the story in detail, and then explain how you now understand how that particular occurrence changed you. Unlike a rhetorical analysis (see page 27), in which you explain how the various aspects of a text worked together, a literacy narrative is about your own writing process and how it has developed over time.

Rhetorical Considerations in Sharing Your Experiences

Before you begin the process of writing in response to one of the scenarios presented above, take a few minutes to consider the following aspects of your writing situation.

Audience: Who is your primary audience? Who else might be interested in this subject? Why?

Purpose: Your narrative could have several interrelated purposes. For example, if you are writing in response to Scenario 1, your narrative can serve both to entertain your audience by sharing your experience with them and to thank or honor others who contributed to your academic development.

Voice, tone, and point of view: Depending on the assignment, you may or may not be a major character in your narrative. If you are relating a story in which you are a participant, you have two roles: you are its writer, and you are also a major character in it. If you are not a participant, you will use the third-person point of view. Your attitude toward your characters will help determine the tone of your narrative. For example, your tone could be informal, such as in "Who Am I (What's My Name)?" by Fernando Perez (pages 89–93), or more straightforward and serious. What other attitudes could influence your tone?

Context, medium, and genre: You will need to understand the situation that creates the occasion to write. Keeping the context of the assignment in mind, decide on a medium and a genre for your writing. How will your writing be used? If you are writing for an audience beyond the classroom, consider what will be the most effective way to present your information to this audience.

CRITICAL THINKING, READING, AND WRITING

Before you begin writing to share your own experiences, read one or more examples to get a feel for writing about experiences. You might also consider how visuals could enhance your writing, as well as the kinds of sources you might consult.

Writing about experiences has several qualities—a clear sense of purpose, a significant point, a lively narrative, and an honest representation. The writer also has a responsibility to respect the privacy of anyone who appears in a narrative. The reading selections that appear in this section exemplify these qualities. Further, they may serve to stimulate your own inquiry and writing.

Qualities of Effective Writing about Experiences

Successful writing about experiences—often called *narrative writing*—engages your readers and keeps them interested. One of the best ways to engage readers when narrating your experiences is to incorporate real dialogue. Other strategies include providing telling details and description. The old advice to "show, don't tell" is especially important when writing about experiences.

Even when you are sharing experiences that seem self-evidently fascinating, you need to have a reason for writing about those experiences. In other words, you need to make a point.

Readers expect the following qualities in writing that shares experience:

- A clear sense of purpose. When you write about your experiences, provide readers with clues that will help them understand why you are sharing this narrative. Your tone is one important clue. The explanation and reflection that you include is another clue. If you are simply recording the event so that others can experience it vicariously, for example, you might include very little explanation or reflection. If, however, you want readers to learn something from your experience, or you are trying to convince them of something, you will probably use part of your paper to reflect on the significance of your experience.

- A significant point. Just as you need to have a clear purpose for what you are writing, you also need to use the experience to say something significant. Writers sometimes use their experiences to make a sweeping, clichéd point, such as "if I had known then what I know now," which usually leads to boring, obvious writing. Points have significance for readers when they are fresh and—often—unexpected.

  One way to show significance is to explain—with examples—how the event you are telling about affected you. You may or may not express your point in a thesis statement, however. Many writers who share their experiences use language, tone, and details to make their points implicitly.

- A lively narrative. Although your writing may include other elements, such as reflection, the foundation for writing about experience is a lively narrative. A narrative must answer the following questions: *Who? What? Where? When? Why?* and *How?* To answer these questions, you can use the following conventions of narrative writing:

For more on narration and description, see Chapter 13.

  - *Dialogue:* Natural-sounding dialogue helps make a piece of writing immediate and lively. Dialogue—what people have to say—brings a narrative to life. Dialogue also can reveal something about the character of the people in your narrative.

- *Vivid description:* Detailed descriptions of the people, or *characters,* mentioned in the narrative, the place where it occurs, and the actions that take place all help involve the reader in your story. Describing people, places, actions, and objects so that your readers can relate to them will help make your narrative memorable.

- *Point of view:* Although you will most often relate personal stories from your own point of view (first-person perspective, usually told using the pronouns *I* and *me*), it may be more interesting or effective to tell the story from a third-person perspective—perhaps from the point of view of another participant in the event (called the "third-person limited perspective") or from the point of view of an observer who knows what each participant is doing and thinking (called the "third-person omniscient perspective").

- *A climax or crisis:* Effective narrative *leads* to something: a point the writer wants to make or a concept the writer wants the reader to understand. By constructing your narrative to lead readers to your main idea or point, you keep them interested throughout your narrative. Sometimes, to build suspense, your narrative can lead up to a crisis, which may or may not have already been resolved.

- **An honest representation.** As you share your experiences, it's important to represent them to readers as accurately as possible. Although you can present your own perspective on any situation, it is usually important to present events without unnecessary embellishments, unless you are exaggerating for an obviously humorous purpose. Usually, you are not trying to convince readers to change their ways with this kind of writing, but to honestly relate your experiences so readers can understand their significance.

Reading to Learn about Writing That Shares Experiences

The selections that follow are examples of writing that shares experiences. As you go through each of the selections your instructor asks you to read, consider the following questions:

- How does the author make his or her experiences understandable and indicate their significance?

- What qualities of writing that shares experiences does each selection exemplify?

- How can you use the techniques of sharing experiences exemplified in the selection in your writing?

JOHN DEVORE

MEMOIR

Life in Chains: Finding Home at Taco Bell

Born in Texas, John DeVore is a blogger and editor-in-chief of *Internet Action Force*. His work has appeared in *The New York Times*, the *New Republic*, *Esquire*, and *Eater*, and he formerly cohosted the radio show *DeVore and Diana* on Maxim Radio. In 2015, his essay "Life in Chains: Finding Home at Taco Bell" won the James Beard Foundation's M.F.K. Fisher Distinguished Writing Award. In the essay featured here, DeVore writes about his experiences eating Mexican food at Taco Bell.

1   Taco Bell is the best Mexican food I ever ate. I will say this to your face over a plate of enchiladas suiza. You will shake your head at such transparent provocation. What a shocking thing to say at a restaurant that has the best tacos in New York City!

2   I won't even correct that assertion. There is no such thing as "the best tacos in New York City." There are only two kinds of tacos in New York City: adequate, and whatever is a little better than adequate. Unless we're talking Taco Bell. Which I will talk about, at length, even if you haven't asked a question that has anything to do with Taco Bell.

3   Yes, fast food is unhealthy. It preys on the poor by offering scientifically engineered food products that are devoid of nutritional value, but are richly emotionally satisfying. These products are intensely tasty, and most of all, cheap. Why spend five bucks on groceries? What can you get for five bucks at a grocery store anyway? A stalk of broccoli and a jar of mayo? Since we're at dinner, and I'm busy proselytizing, I'm not currently able to fact-check the following statement, but I'm pretty sure you can buy ten tacos for one dollar.

4   Taco Bell tacos are crunchy, crispy, meaty sailboats of spicy chemical flavor. The Taco Bell Cool Ranch Doritos taco shell is the most important invention of this century. But we've come this far, and you're halfway through your plate of organic, locally sourced, *New York Magazine*–celebrated Mexican tube casserole, so we have time to talk about Taco Bell. I'll order more chips and salsa. Now I'm going to hold up my fingers and wiggle them. This will signify we're flashing backwards in time.

5   The first meal I ate in New York City was a corned beef sandwich at a diner. When it was unceremoniously plopped down in front of me, I said to the waitress, "Thank you, ma'am."

6   I had just gotten off the plane from Texas. I was polite because good manners are the best way not to get shot in Texas. Politeness was nearly beaten into me. The waitress looked at me with dead eyes and said, "What do I look like, your ****ing mother?"

7   Then she stormed away, kicked open the kitchen door, and I'm pretty sure beat up the chef just because. *What a colorful New York character*, I thought.

She is terrifying and I am weak, my thoughts continued. So that's why I gave her a fifty percent tip. It was an expensive lunch.

Over the next few weeks I experienced New York cuisine. I would call my mother back in Texas from filthy payphones and tell her about all the delicious foods I was eating: dim sum, oysters, meatballs. Do you remember what it was like talking to someone on a pay phone? They always sounded so far away. As if one of you were standing at the bottom of a deep dark hole. There was a time when New York's only social network was a series of coin-fed boxes on the street connected by miles and miles of wires. 8

I'd end every conversation with my mother enthusiastically. I was going to gorge on kielbasa and pierogies! A job interview at a prestigious magazine company was coming up! It sure was a good idea to move to a city that didn't really want me there! 9

None of these things were true. Parents lie to their children about the cruelties of the world, and children grow up to return the favor to their parents. 10

This was the mid-nineties, a time when New York still went out of its way to make twenty-three-year-olds cry in public. I lived in an SRO and shared a bathroom with a ghost that left great gobs of green phlegm in the sink. I wasn't eating oysters; I was eating foods that didn't cost more than a dollar. Pizza slices, hot dogs, knishes. 11

My mother would finish each call saying, "Be safe, *mijo*." As a kid, I used to be so embarrassed when she'd call me "mijo" in front of my friends. It was bad enough that she looked different than me, but she also spoke in another language, a weird one. 12

As the weeks grew colder, I found myself blowing warmth into my hands like a forgettable Charles Dickens character. My work skills qualified me to answer phones or enter data into glowing green computer screens. 13

Then I moved to Queens. SROs are inexpensive places to die slowly, but moving to Queens is still cheaper. Queens is where America walks the talk. In school, we were taught that America is a country of immigrants. It's a nice idea, especially in comfortable suburbs where the lawns are mowed by workers who immigrate into the neighborhood at the crack of dawn and immigrate somewhere else by the time you get back from work. 14

Queens is an entire country of immigrants in 178 square miles. Hello, you're from Greece? Morocco? Bangladesh? Croatia? Senegal? I grew up in Virginia, but my family lives in Texas now. I guess I just emigrated from Texas to Queens! 15

In Queens, I found a small apartment with a toilet under a staircase buried deep in the borough. My neighbors were a large family of Mexicans. That large family probably would have liked an extra room to spread out. Which is probably why they always seemed to really, really hate me. 16

My mother spent years trying to get me to learn Spanish, but I never 17 wanted to take the time. Besides, who was I going to speak Spanish with in Virginia? To most Virginians in the 1980s, Mexicans were just the guys who Clint Eastwood shot in the movies. If I had learned Spanish I could have turned to this family and said "My good friends, stop hating me. I am lonely and hungry. Also, I am half-Mexican!" Then we'd fiesta?

Those were dark, cold days. Some people called those days "winter," but 18 not me. My phone calls home became more infrequent. I couldn't keep up the cheer. Every young person's mettle is tested when you move to New York. There were times I thought I should just pack up and die, which was just my way of saying move back to Texas.

Then, one weekend, instead of playing the game "Sleep All Day Because 19 Sleeping Is Free," I went walking through the streets looking for somewhere to spend three dollars. I was hoping to find a street-meat cart that served something more than charred gristle on a stick.

And that's when I saw the most marvelous sight. Glowing! In the distance! 20 Right there on Steinway Avenue! It was something I had never seen before. A fast food restaurant that combined two famous brands into one mighty, delicious Frankenstein's monster of empty calories. I beheld a restaurant that was, simultaneously, a Taco Bell and a Kentucky Fried Chicken. This didn't exist in Texas. But here, in New York City, these two franchises were turned into a two-headed snack shack.

Suddenly, I knew that everything was going to work out. I was home. 21

In elementary school, I had a stand-up routine I'd perform on the play- 22 ground for my white friends. I'd tell them that I was what you'd get if you crossed a redneck with a wetback: a wetneck! Pause for laughter. My mom is Mexican-American, you see. My dad is a white guy. Which means when I grow up, I'll drive a truck and steal my own hubcaps. You know why Mexicans don't barbecue? Because the beans fall through the grill.

This was how I survived, because racism is easy. That's why it's so evil. 23 Judging other people on the color of their skin is, literally, the least the human brain can do. Racism is the opposite of imagination.

I made fun of myself in order to keep my white friends laughing, because 24 sometimes all laughter does is reinforce tribal integrity. I wanted to be part of their tribe, because my tribe—half-breeds—was a small one at my school. We numbered uno. And we were secret.

After all, I was white. My brothers were darker, like my mother. But me? 25 I looked like a chubby little butterball. I was a spy under deep cover. No one suspected that I was different. Until they met my mom. My funny, feisty mom who loves books and paintings and movies and her family. She would passionately defend me when my teachers would question why I drew nothing but monsters. "He's an artist," she'd say.

During one of my birthday parties, to which I invited my friends from 26
elementary school, I was asked who that brown lady serving cake was. I said
she was my maid.

My mom and I were always followed by floorwalkers at department stores. 27
Once she spoke up when a man cut in a grocery store line, and a racial epi-
thet was muttered. When I got older, some people assumed I was the younger
boyfriend of a foreign woman, not her son.

Many years later, when I was an adult, I would admit my birthday party 28
betrayal to my mother. She laughed at my confession. She had always known
I was ashamed of her.

I remember asking my dad once if I was white, and he told me I was one 29
half him, and one half my mother. Simple. Then for dinner, mom made huevos
rancheros. That was one of her quick dinners. The next night we probably had
eggs again, only this time with biscuits and gravy. She was a good family cook.
Nothing fancy. Big portions.

My dad was a Depression-era kid from the South, so he ate chicken wings 30
like they were going to flap away from his mouth at any moment. He had terrible taste in food, but that's because when you grow up hungry, you'll happily
eat food that tastes terrible.

My mother dutifully learned the Dixie dishes of his childhood, including 31
exotic fare like spaghetti. Once upon a time, I think, spaghetti must have been
an alien cuisine in lush, banjo-loving places like Louisiana. But what does a
Latina from El Paso in the sixties know of such things? So with a little sleuth
work, she invented DeVore Spaghetti. DeVore Spaghetti features a spicy salsa
broth, boiled meatballs, and cheddar cheese. It is delicious because it tastes like
everyone is home for dinner and we're all silly and happy.

She would also make the food of her own childhood. Flautas, soup studded 32
with tiny *albondigas*, quesadillas. I loved a simple dessert that consisted of a
tortilla fried in oil, then dusted with cinnamon and a drizzle of maple syrup.
Her tamales were—they are—perfect. My favorite meal on Earth is my mom's
chiles rellenos. A chile pepper stuffed with cheese is what a poor family makes
when they can't afford meat because the chile flesh becomes tender, like a
slow-cooked cut of beef.

Mom wouldn't always eat my dad's beloved foods; she hated the fried giz- 33
zards he'd beg her to make. But she loved my old man dearly, and never complained when he'd ask her to make beef tongue. I'd stare at that slab of meat
and imagine a field of tongueless cows trying to moo.

She was also the kind of mother who never ate with her family. She was 34
a tornado of knives and skillets and wooden spoons. But once the food was
served, she just kicked back with a glass of milk. Sometimes she'd sit with us.
If we were at a restaurant, she'd order something modest. She didn't adore
food the way my dad did, and not because she didn't also come from humble

beginnings; she was raised on the Texas border by a father whose rifle was used to shoot at wild dogs.

But she did love Taco Bell. A summer break treat was a quick trip to Taco   35
Bell for tacos and burritos and a styrofoam cup of pinto beans, salsa, and cheese. When my mom was a kid, fast food was the dream. Imagine—literally anyone could afford to eat out! And not just boring and bland diner food, but high-tech food that was exploding with rainbows of taste-bud melting mystery powders! Food that you could eat not just at a table but in your car, the chariot of the future.

Taco Bell was easy, and inexpensive, and it was shamelessly Mexican.   36
Emphasis on "shameless": its garish facsimile of an entire nation's culture was seemingly dreamed up by the type of white person who gets drunk on tequila and wears a sombrero for comedic effect. It was still Mexican, though. In fact, it was both Mexican and American. All under one greasy roof.

But even though the restaurant's cartoonish decor bordered on   37
offensive, it was still a temple to a people and a cuisine that America couldn't ignore. Taco Bells were everywhere. In every strip mall. Off every highway exit. Even the racists, the immigrant-haters, the people who'd laugh at my elementary-school stand-up comedy routine would run for the border.

You can laugh or sneer at Taco Bell. Shake your head at its high fat and salt   38
content. Go ahead and lecture on what true Mexican food is. My mom would probably just roll her eyes at you, and take a broken yellow shard of crispy taco shell and use it to scoop up the pintos, cheese, and salsa.

I stood before that Taco Bell–KFC hybrid in Queens and felt like I had   39
come home. I went inside and ordered biscuits and a taco for three dollars, and filled my stomach. Finally, I thought to myself, a restaurant that represented my upbringing. My heritage. Maybe I wasn't the only person in Queens who silently ate at a Taco Bell–KFC and remembered parents who lived so far, far away.

We are now back in the present. So here we are, you and me, eating enchi-   40
ladas at this restaurant. I think it's a little easier to be biracial today. I hope it is. I still can't believe the President of the United States knows what it's like to have a mother who looks different.

Taco Bell is still the best Mexican food I've ever eaten. Because when   41
I eat it, I'm sitting with my mom, and her hair isn't gray, and my father's brutal death from cancer is so many years away, and she is so beautiful and I am so young and safe.

Just one bite of a seven layer burrito—not six, not five, but seven unbelievable   42
layers of goop—and we're laughing because I won't stop saying "Yo Quiero Taco Bell," and she wipes guacamole off my face and says, "Oh, *mijo.*"

UNDERSTANDING A WRITER'S GOALS: QUESTIONS TO CONSIDER AND DISCUSS

Rhetorical Knowledge: The Writer's Situation and Rhetoric

1. **Audience:** Much of DeVore's essay is personal, almost quirky. For whom do you think he wrote this essay?

2. **Purpose:** What do you see as DeVore's purpose in writing this essay?

3. **Voice and tone:** At first glance, this essay may appear to be about Taco Bell, and to some degree Taco Bell plays an important role. However, the essay is about much more. What specific uses of language can you cite to show what the essay is really about?

4. **Responsibility:** Within this essay, DeVore touches on the delicate topic of racism. At times he does so by alluding to racial stereotypes. Do you feel he has dealt with racism seriously enough?

5. **Context, format, and genre:** On some level DeVore's essay is a common genre, "small town boy comes to the big city." Yet, this is not really what the essay is about. How effective is he in using this common theme to make another point?

Critical Thinking: The Writer's Ideas and Your Personal Response

6. Food is culturally important to most of us. It's also an important component of all cultures. How does DeVore use fast food from a large chain to get his readers to think about his real message? How effectively does he achieve this goal? What is the basis of your judgment?

7. Although much of DeVore's essay is about his own biracial heritage, he also addresses how children relate to their parents. No matter what our current age, at one point, we all faced issues of how to relate to our parents. Does DeVore touch on issues you have felt? If so, does it help you to relate to his essay? If not, do you still understand his points?

Composing Processes and Knowledge of Conventions: The Writer's Strategies

8. DeVore has crafted his essay so that we begin reading it thinking it will be about food. He then uses food as a vehicle to explain how he first reacted to moving to New York City. Finally, he brings us back to a Taco Bell in his neighborhood in Queens. How effectively does this movement work for you? Why do you think that discovering the Taco Bell/KFC in Queens makes him feel more comfortable in his new environment? Do you like the way he led readers to that point? Why?

9. In the essay, DeVore uses the acronym "SRO." Did you know what it meant? Did you have to look it up? Would you have preferred he be more explicit in what he meant? Why?

Inquiry and Research: Ideas for Further Exploration

10. Like many people, DeVore moved away from his family and encountered new experiences. It is likely you have family members who also moved away to go to school, for a job, or to join the military. Interview them to see if their experiences mirrored any of those DeVore relates.

As illustrated by "Ways of Writing to Share Experiences" (page 78), experiences can be shared through many genres. The "Genres Up Close" feature explores doing so through a literacy narrative.

GENRES *Up Close*   Writing a Literacy Narrative

The literacy narrative has been a popular genre for decades, but it has become increasingly so in recent years. Readers are curious about how others, especially famous writers, have developed their writing and reading skills. When reporters and talk-show hosts interview well-known writers, they frequently ask about the writers' experiences with reading and writing, particularly early in life.

When writers craft literacy narratives, they often do the following:

- **Narrate their experiences with using language—reading and writing in particular situations.** As you craft a literacy narrative, think about those moments when you were most aware that you were using language as a reader, as a writer, or both.

- **Critically reflect on their experiences with using language.** As you craft a literacy narrative, think about the effects of particular experiences you have had with reading and writing. For example, if your first-grade teacher congratulated you for reading a book when you were six years old, how did that positive reinforcement affect your reading after that moment?

- **Think about how they developed ability and confidence as readers and writers.** That is, what have reading and writing allowed them to do in life? As you craft a literacy narrative, think about the ways that reading and writing have helped you to achieve certain goals. Think about how reading and writing have helped you to make a difference in the world.

- **Define "literacy" broadly.** As you consider your literacy experiences, be inclusive. In addition to reading and writing with words, how have you developed other similar or related skills? For example, what are your experiences with visual images? What are your experiences with information literacy (finding, evaluating, and using information)?

To explain how they became literate people, writers may use anecdotes to tell part of their literacy narratives. They also tend to tell stories about people who helped their development as writers and readers. A compelling story can help readers understand the impact of a particular event. Of course, strong positive role models can also motivate someone to keep reading or writing. In the selection by Fernando Pérez, "Who Am I (What's My Name)?" notice how Pérez uses both of these conventions to convey how he developed his lifelong commitment to reading and writing.

FERNANDO PÉREZ

Who Am I (What's My Name)?

LITERACY NARRATIVE

Fernando Pérez grew up in Los Angeles and earned a Master of Fine Arts degree in creative writing at Arizona State University. Currently living in Seattle, he teaches writing at Bellevue College. He was a finalist for the Andrés Móntoya Poetry Prize and the Crab Orchard Series in Poetry First Book Award. His work has appeared in literary magazines, including *Superstition Review*. In the following essay, Pérez writes about his own experiences with language and identity.

1   On the very first day of TA training, back in 2007, we were asked to think about how we were going to introduce ourselves to our students. They asked us to consider teacher identity in the classroom. Things like where we sat, what we wore and what we called ourselves were tossed around the discussion. Were we going to make them call us mister, miss, professor, or by our first names?

2   I had a bigger problem. Since the very first day I entered school as a young boy, my name took on another sound. *Fur nan-doe Pur-rez* fell from the lips of all of my teachers and classmates. My identity split. I was no longer just Fernando Pérez, as my parents pronounced it. It was at this point that my curiosity with the power of language grew. At home my name was always pronounced in Spanish. My folks and relatives said it correctly, but all of the new people in my life made me think that Spanish held only a place for intimates in the homes of cousins and grandparents. It's not that my relatives could only speak Spanish. In fact, we are quite assimilated. Most of us have actually held on to the language and culture of our Mexican roots while integrating successful American practices, careers, and attitudes.

3   I, however, internalized the split as the following: English belonged at school, among friends, and in the classroom; Spanish belonged at home. Whenever Spanish crossed into the English boundary that had been set, I would become nervous or embarrassed. I even began pronouncing my own name in English. The struggle with identity increased as I encountered far more Latino students in high school than I had ever had in my elementary and junior high where I was among only three.

4   Fast-forward to graduate school and TA training. My first semester at Arizona State University, I had a Poetry class with Professor and renowned poet, Alberto Ríos. I remember the first day he took roll. When he got to my name my face flushed with blood. He said my name in Spanish. The line had been crossed. This was the first time any teacher had ever said my name the way my mother does. What's more, I felt the guilt that I associated with the times my mother said my last name—usually reserved for moments of scolding. I remember asking my professor after class if he was embarrassed bringing Spanish into an "English" class. His answer has

stayed with me to this day. It was something along the lines of saying, "We are in the Southwest, and what's more, we are in a place of higher learning, where language and culture is not limited to those whose primary language is English." He continued to say that Spanish and any other language should be attempted by those who cannot speak it—at the very least a word or two here and there as a way of building bridges. From that moment on I felt empowered, yet I still accommodated my English language students by providing them the option of pronouncing my name in English, the way I had been used to hearing for half of my life. I felt content having at least provided the Spanish option as recognition for those students who knew my struggle.

Today, I don't provide the English option. Instead, I say my name in Spanish, provide *Ped-diss* as a way of sounding it, or tell my students that they can call me "Mr. P." Introductions are important. Identity is important. I share the history and struggle of reconnecting with my name on the very first day of every class. Seeing myself as belonging in this place of higher learning has been a struggle. I know that several students feel the same way. It is not surprising that students both at Arizona State University and now here at Bellevue College have come up to me after class and told me how much they can identify with the struggle of holding two different languages in their heads and how they have also struggled with the split in identity.

It is with identity and my name in mind that I had to speak up when my business cards here at Bellevue College were printed and my last name was misspelled. I was not insulted or even slightly stirred; I just knew that it would be important for me to ask that they be reprinted. I thought about how my cousin Carlos used to tease me when we were children, asking me, "I bet you don't even know where the accent mark goes in your last name." From that day forward, you better believe I learned it. It was important then for me to set an example for my Latino students that our names should be pronounced and spelled correctly, that they can be points of pride, and that the sounds they create are welcomed on this campus. It was an easy mistake for whoever printed the business cards to make. I don't consider it a micro-aggression in any way. How can anyone know how important a little accent mark is? In the end, what mattered was in the way my request to fix the problem was handled. No one raised an eyebrow, no one sucked their teeth, or rolled their eyes. The cards were changed and that was that. This was very reassuring to me as teacher of color at this school.

All aside, I find that my mere presence before these students of color is important. Teaching is a humbling vocation for me, but my face and my name are important for students to see, especially in an English class. I do find that my students of color, my Latino students especially, are eager to speak up and share their thoughts in class. They are eager to come up and establish a relationship with me after class as well. They want to tell me their stories and they want to know how I am adjusting to the weather and culture here. This is not to the exclusion of my white students. Because I care about education and learning, because I am excited about nerdy things, or articulate well, I find—understanding that I am making a sweeping generalization—my white students are eager to invest in me as well. They are curious about me at the very least, and I am certainly eager to invest and to be a bridge to all my students.

Whenever I take roll, I read my students' last names and ask them to tell me how they would like to be identified. This is an important way of empowering my students and honoring pluralism. How they identify themselves within the context of race, gender, or sexual orientation matters. I will be honest, it used to upset me inside that some of my students had "American" names they would ask to be called by—as a way, I thought, of accommodating English speakers. I used to want those students to accept their "foreign" names and allow me the room to learn how they were pronounced. When I think about it, I can only offer my anecdote about my name and the struggle I faced with identity as a model for my students. If they are not worried about it or if they are not ready to address that within their own lives, it is not up to me to push. Honoring their choice to be called what they ask to be called has been my pact. 8

One student last quarter shocked me then, when she asked me to call her "Skunk." Had she not been in my Creative Writing Poetry class, I might have found it difficult or odd, but I honored her request because she seemed sincere. As I got to know her through her writing and our conversations, I learned that she too was struggling with identity in her own way. Skunk identified culturally as Persian. If that weren't complex enough, she felt the burden of feeling out of place in a White-dominant society. She could have passed for being "white" but she didn't identify that way. She would say things like, her parents don't like her speaking Farsi in public or that they don't want her to date anyone whose culture comes from the Middle East. 9

Her own family and the dominant culture at large placed Skunk in the middle of complexity and confusion. Sometimes her confusion was self-imposed, but whatever the case, it was real and felt. 10

I worked with Skunk, nudging her to drop a line or two of Farsi into her poems. I told all my students that other languages or modes of speech were priceless nuggets in poetry. I think, if properly placed, other languages and modes of speech add a tremendous amount of flavor to any writing. Over 11 the course of the quarter I noticed subtle changes in Skunk's behavior. Her confidence improved. This quarter she is registered in my ENGL 101 class and when I took roll on the very first day, she wasn't embarrassed when I came across her last name—something she quickly discouraged me from saying in our Poetry Class. Skunk now goes by her given first name.

English Language Learners populate my classrooms as well. One such student in the fall quarter was Zaw. He was a quiet guy, rarely offering his thoughts during class discussion. I would carefully nudge him every now and then and one day after class he approached me. Zaw informed me some students feel uncomfortable speaking their minds because that is not how they are culturally used to doing things. He asked that I bear with him as he adjusted to my request to share his thoughts. I was happy that he felt comfortable sharing this with me. Zaw also told me that he felt stupid because he had an accent and because his English was limited. I quickly informed him that my pedagogy favors clarity of thought over mechanics and the use of "big" words. I told him that if it made him feel more comfortable he should consider writing out his ideas in his native language first and then work toward translating his ideas into English. I wanted him to know that his intelligence was not going to be measured by how well he spoke English. Zaw's attitude and confidence improved from that point on and he was further supported after we read and discussed "Mother Tongue" by Amy Tan in class.   12

I want my students to feel like they can come to me for anything. I don't pretend to know everything, but I inform them that we can work through their issues with writing or life outside of class, and that I will help them to find additional resources if necessary. Some students recognize and utilize my accessibility and support right away. For a variety of reasons, others do not.   13

Being so far away from my own forms of support/community has, at times, made the days seem very long. My family and friends are integral to my being. Transitioning into the new culture here at Bellevue College, the culture of the department, the quarter system, the Pacific Northwest (my apartment, the climate, the people), and all without my partner and while dealing with the recent loss of my grandmother, have shaken the ground I stand on. Remembering my identity, who I am and where I have come from in the midst of these challenges, has helped me to grow as an individual and as a teacher.   14

My identity is constantly being forged. I am working on the relationship I have with myself so that I may also improve the relationship that I have with others. I am learning to quiet the voices that say that I don't belong here and that I don't deserve this position or that I do not have anything to contribute to the department or the college.   15

I am becoming more deeply rooted in the belief that students have the   16
right to their own languages and that I am not a gatekeeper toward the "next
level" of the English language or writing. I want to encourage students to fall in
love with writing the way I did. I want them to enjoy their time in all of their
writing classes, whether they are required courses or not. I do not believe that
a student's writing will be transformed over the course of one short quarter,
but I do believe that their relationship to the subject and desire to continue on
this path can be fostered in my classroom.

Ultimately, I have come to accept that students respond to my style of   17
teaching, my accessibility, and who and how I am as a person. When students
invest in me, they begin quickly to invest in the class.

When I was an undergrad I made similar investments. I knew I wanted   18
to be a teacher when I sat as a student in Dr. Velvet Pearson's Intro to Poetry
Workshop at Long Beach City College. I liked how we sat in a circle and
each weighed-in on a poem. Everyone, from their own corner of the world,
with a fresh and different take, offering their perspectives on issues that
affect us as human beings made me realize how valuable this act can be.
It made realize that we learn from each other, not just the teacher, that our
voices matter, and that we need these human stories. Dr. Pearson was the
first English teacher that treated me like I was someone who was smart
and that made me feel like my contributions were valid. She got me excited
about writing, which made me invest in the journey that lay ahead of me
as a writer. That is, at least, what I took away from her class and what I hold
as an integral part of my pedagogy as an instructor today.

UNDERSTANDING A WRITER'S GOALS: QUESTIONS TO CONSIDER AND DISCUSS

Rhetorical Knowledge: The Writer's Situation and Rhetoric

1. **Audience:** Whom do you think Pérez is writing to? A general audience? An audience of people who may come to English as a second language or who may have used another language in their home when growing up? Or is he really writing to those of us who grew up speaking only English?

2. **Purpose:** Why do you think Pérez wrote this essay? On some level it seems as though he's simply declaring how he came to accept who he is. On other levels, it is as though he wrote this to better understand who he is. What do you think he learned about himself by writing this? Why?

3. **Voice and tone**: Pérez clearly has a message in his essay. Often when people try to make a point, their tone can be harsh and pedantic. How would you describe Pérez's tone? How effective do you think it is? Why?

4. **Responsibility:** Writers need to be responsible not only to their readers and themselves but also to their subjects. As a teacher, Pérez writes about some of his students. How responsibly does he do so? Can you give specific examples to support your judgment?

5. **Context, format, and genre:** Pérez's essay is an example of a "literacy narrative," a genre that tells a personal story of an event or events that had an impact on the development of the writer's language, reading, or writing skills. How did Pérez's essay help you understand how his experience with how personal names, including his own, are pronounced became important in his development as a person?

Critical Thinking: The Writer's Ideas and Your Personal Response

6. There is a subtext to this essay that if we aren't called by our real names then somehow we are limited as people. Pérez was fortunate enough to have as a teacher Alberto Ríos, who was able to help Pérez become who he really was in the classroom. Can you think of things besides names that might cause some people to be inhibited in some situations? What might they be?

7. First of all Pérez writes about his own educational experience. He then speaks about some of his students, Skunk and Zaw. What have you learned from his stories of Skunk and Zaw? Based on their stories, can you think of a situation where you may have meant well but acted in a way that didn't really help? What might that have been?

Composing Processes and Knowledge of Conventions: The Writer's Strategies

8. We commonly think of language as being rule driven and controlled by convention. Yet, Pérez explains how language is also related to our very identity. How might knowing only one set of conventions (like pronunciation) be limiting and cause problems? What are other situations where usage of conventions may be situational?

9. We often think that punctuation such as an accent mark is trivial. For Pérez it became far from trivial. What are some other situations, for whatever reasons, where punctuation is not trivial?

USING DIGITAL TECHNOLOGIES Organizing Your Files

Are your files stored in folders (directories) on your computer? If so, have you ever lost track of where you've stored a song, video, project, or paper? Before it happens again, take some time to organize your folders and files.

Start by looking at the names of all the folders you've already created. Did you use some principle for naming and organizing them? Are they named according to project or media type (such as music or video)? Or are the names more or less random? See if you can find relationships among the names of your documents, and look for ways to group documents into folders and files and store them together. Establish a separate folder for the different aspects of your life. For example, you might want a folder titled "School" and another titled "Music" or "Photos." Within those folders you might want to have a separate folder for each course or separate folders for different types of music or locations where photos were taken.

Taking a little time to organize your files and folders now can save you time and prevent confusion when you need to locate specific documents later. Once you have your files organized, you may want to consider backing up the folders to an external source such as a flash drive, an external hard drive, or a cloud account like Dropbox.

 # WRITING PROCESSES

In the pages that follow, you will engage in various writing processes to help you generate ideas and draft, revise, and edit your writing. As you work on the assignment scenario that you have chosen, keep these processes and the qualities of effective writing about experiences in mind (pages 80–81).

 ## Invention: Getting Started

As you begin to explore your subject, it is helpful to use more than one invention activity generate ideas. Especially when you are writing to share experiences, the more detail that you generate about the experience through invention, the better you will be able to convey the experience and its meaning to your readers. As you begin the process, consider the following questions:

- What do I already know about the experience that I am writing about?

- What feelings, attitudes, or notions do I already have about this experience?

- What questions can I ask about the experience? That is, what gaps do I have in my memory of it or knowledge about it that might help me understand what information a reader might need?

- Who would know about my experience (a relative or friend)? What questions might I ask that person in an interview?

- What do I know about my audience? What don't I know that I should know? Why might they be interested in reading my text?

- What might my audience already know about my subject? Why might they care about it?

For more on descriptive writing, see Chapter 13.

- To what extent will sensory details—color, shape, smell, taste—help my reader understand my topic? Why?
- What visuals might I use to help my readers understand my experience?

For help with strategies for discovery and learning, see Chapter 4.

Completing invention activities such as the ones suggested in the first writing activity should yield a wealth of information that you can draw on for your first draft. Consider sharing your invention work with several classmates or friends in order to understand your rhetorical situation more clearly and to generate more useful information.

Writing Activity

Listing, Questioning, and Freewriting

Get started with your paper by using listing, questioning, and freewriting. First, list keywords that will remind you of ideas and organize them in related categories, such as location, images, and sounds. Second, generate basic details of the event using the five questions commonly asked by reporters:

- *Who* are the participants in this event, and what information about those participants will help me share my experience?
- *What* are the participants doing and what are they saying?
- *Where* did the event occur?
- *When* did the event occur, and what is the significance of when it happened?
- *Why* did the participants do what they did? What motivated their actions?

Use freewriting (see page 63) to get your ideas down on paper. (For an example of freewriting, see page 134.)

Finally, if you already keep a journal, you might skim through it to find ideas for your writing. If you don't already keep a journal, you might do so while you are getting started on this writing project.

 USING DIGITAL TECHNOLOGIES   **Using Technology to Unjam Writer's Block**

You can use technology to "unjam" writer's block! Some writers find it hard to get started when faced with a new task. You can download images related to your topic, play a video from a popular Web site, or even use Twitter or texting to brainstorm with friends and classmates.

One helpful tip is to use the recorder on your phone or a digital voice recorder to talk out your ideas. State the information that you already know and your ideas about that information, and then as you listen back, take notes on what you said. This can help you get started.

JESSICA HEMAUER'S LISTING

For a memoir about her experience growing up on a farm, Jessica Hemauer, a student in a first-year composition course, generated the following list:

small town
farm chores—endless
Dad worked hard; we did too
coffee
siblings
Orange, multi-stained carpet
Oversized, cluttered table
Stuffed, pine shelves
Steep, creaky stairs
Bathroom
Basement
Loud, plastic runners covering the multi-stained orange carpet
Warm, rustic steel woodstove

Blinds
Navy blue, understuffed, corduroy sofa that has one cushion burnt b/c it was too close to the woodstove
White, clean carpet
Clean table set for 2
Neatly lined bookshelves
Round staircase with a wood banister

For help with listing, questioning, and freewriting, as well as other strategies for discovery and learning, see Chapter 4.

STUDENT WRITING EXAMPLES

Brainstorming (pp. 177, 343)

Freewriting (pp. 134, 256, 344, 393)

Criteria (p. 300)

Listing (p. 97)

Answers to Reporter's Questions (p. 256)

Organization (pp. 98, 182, 647)

Clustering (pp. 135, 298)

Interviewing (p. 216)

Research (pp. 136, 137, 178, 179, 217, 218, 258, 259, 302, 343, 346, 396, 396)

Reflection (p. 12)

Strategies FOR Success | Creativity

Successful writers are creative. However, being creative doesn't necessarily mean writing fiction or making up details about your experiences. It does mean that when you are writing a narrative, for example, you will need to discover a fresh new perspective on the story in order to be successful. When writing to share experiences, successful writers find ways to use specific details of the story to engage their readers, often taking a rather ordinary event such as a family dinner, or in John DeVore's case, a visit to Taco Bell, and presenting it in a new, creative way that makes a powerful statement.

For more on conducting interviews, see Chapter 19.

Organizing Your Ideas and Details

Once you have generated ideas and details about your subject using invention activities, consider how you might organize this material. The questions that you need to ask yourself when deciding on your organization are all rhetorical:

• Who is your audience?

• Why might they be interested in your narrative—and how can you make them interested?

• What is your purpose for writing—that is, what do you want your readers to understand about you or the event you are narrating?

The answers to these questions can help you decide what to emphasize, which in turn will help you choose an organizational strategy.

It is usually helpful to try *several* organizational strategies in early drafts because seeing your words on paper—in various ways—will help you decide what strategy will work best for you. Most often, writing about experiences is sequential: the writer starts at some specific point in the past and then moves to a later time or to the present.

An alternative would be to use the narrative technique known as **flashback.** In a flashback, commonly used in film, something that happened in the past is shown "just the way it happened," and then the narrator returns to the present to reflect on the event's significance.

Jessica Hemauer's Organization

Jessica Hemauer looked over her invention material and then put together a rough outline for her draft. She decided to begin her narrative at a crisis point:

Begin as a 10-year-old girl—waking up to feed calves
Describe daily family routine
Good feelings about being in charge when feeding calves
Describe parents
    Impact of their relationship on me
School WAS social life
    Being a farm girl made me different
    How I didn't fit in
Playing basketball in 8th grade
    Started to feel included—but worked harder than others
    Falling asleep in class
THE FAMILY MEETING
Freed from farmwork and being involved
Why I'm still different and that's ok

■ Constructing a Complete Draft

Once you have chosen the organizational approach that works most effectively for your audience and purpose, you are ready to construct the rest of your draft. Before you begin your draft, review all your invention material to see what needs to be included and what might be left out. To make these decisions, consider your purpose for sharing this experience with others: What is the significance of the experience? How can you help readers see the significance?

Synthesizing and Integrating Sources into Your Draft: Including Others' Perspectives in Narratives

When writers share experiences in first-person narratives, they primarily offer their own perspectives on events because they often are the leading characters in the narratives. However, most narratives also include other individuals who inter-act with the narrator. Writers can reconstruct interactions with other people by describing actions and by including dialogue. Although describing actions helps readers see what happened, those descriptions limit the perspective to that of the writer/narrator. Because multiple perspectives help readers see the story from several vantage points, effective writers often include dialogue—either by quoting it or by summarizing it.

In "Farm Girl," which appears on pages 104–108 of this chapter, Jessica Hemauer includes dialogue with some of the other people in her story. For example, in paragraph 18, Hemauer reconstructs the conversation with Ms. Cain, her teacher:

> One time my teacher, Ms. Cain, comes over to my wooden desk, where my head is resting on top of a math textbook. She taps her knuckles on the hollow wood and says, "Jessica, are you okay? Do you need to go to the health room?" Raising my head, embarrassed that she caught me sleeping, I say quickly, "No, Ms. Cain, I'm fine. I'm sorry for being rude and causing a disruption. I promise to be more attentive."

Although Hemauer could have described the dialogue by writing that her teacher asked if she was okay, she instead makes the teacher's concern more concrete by quoting the teacher's words.

Parts of a Complete Draft

Introduction: One of the qualities of a successful narrative is that it grabs and holds readers' attention. A number of strategies for beginning your narrative can help get your readers interested, including the following:

- **Start your narrative with a surprising event, comment, or piece of dialogue.** John DeVore starts his essay claiming that "Taco Bell is the best Mexican food" (page 82).
- **Start with interesting details** to draw the reader in through sensual, descriptive words and phrases.
- **Start with a comment that might cause your readers to reflect.** For example, Fernando Pérez begins his essay wondering how he should introduce himself to his students (page 89).

For more on introductions, see Chapter 13.

Body: The main part, or body, of your narrative is the place to tell your story. Use dialogue and descriptive details to develop the story and reveal the character of the people in your narrative. To hold your readers' interest, build your narrative to a crisis or climax, unless you are writing for an informative purpose and are required to maintain a neutral tone (or unless you are beginning at the crisis point of the narrative). Choose the verb tense that will best serve the purpose of your narrative. If you use past-tense verbs to narrate the experience, you remind readers that the event happened in the past and that you have had time to reflect on it. If you use present-tense verbs, you make the story seem as if it is happening now, and you will seem to reveal its significance to yourself and to your readers at the same time. Also, you might consider using photographs to complement your words.

INTEGRATING SOURCES

Including Others' Perspectives in Narratives (p. 99)
Quoting Sources (p. 139)
Paraphrasing Sources (p. 182)
Incorporating Numerical Data (p. 220)
Incorporating Partial Quotes (p. 262)
Creating Visuals to Show Your Data (p. 304)
Summarizing Information from Sources (p. 349)
Including Research Information (p. 398)

For more on conclusions, see Chapter 13.

Conclusion: Your conclusion should tie things together for your readers by explaining or suggesting the significance of the experience or experiences you have shared. Here are some strategies for concluding a paper in which you have shared experiences:

- Review the subject's most important aspects.
- Explain the subject's significance.
- Suggest avenues for a reader's further inquiry.
- Refer back to the introduction of your narrative.

Title: Rather than thinking of a title before you start writing, it is often more useful to construct a first draft and then consider possible titles. As with the introduction, an effective title for a narrative intrigues readers and makes them want to read the text.

Writing Activity

Constructing a Full Draft

Using the writing you did when selecting an organizational approach, write a complete draft of your paper that shares an experience.

Excerpts from Jessica Hemauer's First Draft

After deciding on her organizational approach, Jessica Hemauer wrote the first draft of her essay about growing up on a farm. The following excerpts are from her first draft. Like all first drafts, Hemauer's draft included problems with grammar, spelling, and punctuation. (The numbers in circles refer to peer comments—see pages 101–102.)

Farm Girl
Jessica Hemauer

BEEP! BEEP! BEEP! It's 5:00 a.m. My eyes are heavy with sleep and struggle to open. I think to myself, "A typical ten-year-old child does not have to wake up at five in the morning to do chores!" I hit the snooze button with disappointment, hoping desperately that the cows would for once, feed and milk themselves. Seconds away from falling back into a deep sleep, I hear the heavy footsteps of what could only be my father coming near my bedroom door. They stop and my door opens with a creak. "Jessica, are you awake yet?" my father asks. Without a word, knowing from the past that an argument doesn't get me anywhere, I stagger out of my warm twin bed, trudging dejectedly past the figure at the narrow doorway. I continue down the hall toward the small bathroom to find my sisters, Angie and Melissa, and my brother Nick already awake. ❶

We all proceed with our usual morning routine, which consists of washing our faces, brushing our teeth and taking turns on the white porcelain throne. In the lower level of the old farmhouse our outside clothes await. My mother made it a rule to keep them there so that they wouldn't stink up the rest of the house. As soon as you opened the door to the basement, you can smell the putrid aroma of cows that has seeped from our clothing into the damp cool air. ❷ We took our turns going down the steep, narrow steps, using the walls on either side for extra guidance. As we dressed not a single word was spoken because we all felt the same way, "I hate this!" Although most of the time our choice of vocabulary was much more creative. . . .

While Melissa and my father milked the 100 cows, Nick and Angie fed the cows, and I went to feed the newborn calves. ❸ Being the youngest in the family, this was my favorite chore because I rarely had the chance to look after someone or feel like I was taking care of them. I have always had older siblings who looked after me, watching every step I took, being sure that I didn't get into trouble. When feeding the calves, I was finally the one in charge. It was a nice feeling, being on the opposite end of the spectrum. They were my responsibility. I was in charge of them and caring for them during feeding time every morning and evening. Little did I know at that time, this was the beginning of a lifetime of responsibilities. . . .

. . . Typically, we would finish with the chores and return to the house around 7:30 in the morning.

When we made our way back to the farmhouse, we draped our clothes on a folding chair next to the washing machine in the basement and crawled up the stairs. The delicious smell of smoked bacon and cheese omelets grew more intense with each step. As our stomachs ached with hunger, we took turns in the shower, cleaning ourselves as fast as possible in order to get to the breakfast table. My brother would be the first to the table because as we all know, girls take longer to get ready than boys. My father would eat and be back outside on the farm by the time my sisters or I would run by the kitchen grabbing a glass of fresh squeezed orange juice and a piece of toast as we yelled frantically at the bus, "Wait!" It seemed our daily lives operated in shifts, not like a real family. ❹ . . .

When I finally arrived at school I had already been up for four hours doing chores on the farm in the bitter cold. The other kids in my private grade school just rolled out of their beds inside their subdivision homes an hour before the bell rang. The school day always went by fast. ❺ While my other classmates were thinking about what television show they were going to watch after school, I was thinking about the chores that await me once I get off the yellow school bus. . . .

Student Comments on Jessica Hemauer's Draft

❶ "I really liked the description of you getting up early and getting ready. I could almost feel the cold and smell the farm smells."

❷ "I like how the real details (like all of the smells) help me 'be there' with you."

❸ "I think you're writing this because you want to tell people that all those awful farm chores really helped you."

❹ "I think your point was that all the time you wanted to fit in, and then when you could do things normal kids do, you found out you were different anyway."

❺ "I'd like to hear more about school and the people there."

As with the comments you will receive from your instructor and classmates, Hemauer had to determine which comments and suggestions made sense—and then to revise her paper accordingly.

■ Revising

Finishing a complete draft may give you a justified sense of accomplishment. However, you still need to revise and then edit the draft. It is helpful to let your draft sit for a while after you have finished it. When you return to it, you are much more likely to find sections that need to be revised: places where

---

WRITER'S *Workshop* | **Responding to Full Drafts**

Working with one or two classmates, read each other's papers and offer comments and questions that will help each of you see your papers strengths and weaknesses. Consider the following questions as you do:

- What is your first impression of this draft? How effectively does the title draw you into the narrative? What do you like about the draft?

- How well does the introduction work? What is effective about it? What suggestions can you make on how to improve the introduction?

- What significant point is the writer making about the experience he or she is relating? How might the writer be able to make that point more clearly?

- Why is the writer relating this experience? What in this piece of writing helps you see why the experience was important to the writer?

- How lively is the narrative? Where has the writer gone beyond simply telling readers about the experience to showing it? How might the writer use more dialogue?

- How has the writer used description to make people, places, and scenes vivid for readers? Where is more description needed?

- How effectively does the story build in terms of reaching a climax and holding the readers' attention throughout? Are there any problems with logic in the way one action follows another? If so, where?

- Has the writer honestly explained the experience? If not, why do you question it?

- What could be added or changed to make the conclusion more effective? How well does it bring the narrative to a satisfying conclusion?

details need to be added, other places where details may need to be removed, and still others where some of your words or sentences need to be shifted from one place to another. Classmates may also offer feedback on your draft, and friends or family members might also be willing to read your draft and offer useful suggestions.

Responding to Readers' Comments

After receiving feedback from peers, teachers, writing tutors, and others, writers have to determine what to do with that feedback.

Consider carefully what your readers tell you. Some might not understand your point, or they may misunderstand something you wrote. It is up to you either to accept or to ignore their comments and suggestions. Others may offer perspectives that you may not have thought of. You may find that comments from more than one reader contradict each other. In that case, use your own judgment to decide which reader's comments are on the right track.

Jessica Hemauer's readers had the following reactions:

- Two readers liked some of the descriptive passages in the paper. Hemauer needed to consider whether more description could be added because this strategy had been effective.

- One reader outlined what seemed to be the point, or thesis, of Hemauer's paper. When you get such feedback on your papers, make sure that the reader does understand and reiterate your point. If the reader does not get your point, then perhaps you are not being clear and explicit enough.

In the final version of her paper, on pages 104–108, you can see how Jessica Hemauer responded to these comments, as well as to her own review of her first draft.

 # KNOWLEDGE OF CONVENTIONS

When effective writers edit their work, they attend to the conventions that will help readers understand their ideas. These include genre conventions, documentation, format, usage, grammar, punctuation, and mechanics. By attending to these conventions in your writing, you make reading a more pleasant experience for readers.

 ## Editing

After you revise, you need to go through one more important step: editing and polishing. When you edit and polish your writing, you make changes to your sentence structures and word choices to improve your style and to make your writing clearer and more concise. You also check your work to make sure it adheres to conventions of grammar, usage, punctuation, mechanics, and spelling.

Because it is sometimes difficult to identify small problems in a piece of writing you have been mulling over for some time, it often helps to distance yourself from the text before your last reading so you can approach the draft with fresh eyes. Some people like to put the text aside for a day or so; others try reading aloud; and some even read from the last sentence to the first so that the content, and their familiarity with it, does not cause them to overlook an error. Because checking conventions is easier said than done, though, we strongly recommend that you ask classmates, friends, and tutors to read your work to find sentence problems that you do not see.

Genres, Documentation, and Format

If you are writing an academic paper, follow the conventions for the discipline in which you are writing and the requirements of your instructor. If you have chosen to write a letter to a prospective employer, you should also follow the conventions of a business letter.

A Writer Achieves Her Goal: Jessica Hemauer's Final Draft

The final draft of Jessica Hemauer's essay "Farm Girl" follows. As you read Hemauer's essay, think about what makes it an effective example of writing about experiences. Following the essay, you'll find some specific questions to consider.

JESSICA HEMAUER

MEMOIR　Farm Girl

BEEP! BEEP! BEEP! It's 5:00 a.m. My eyes are heavy with sleep and struggle to open. I think to myself, "A typical ten-year-old child does not have to wake up at five in the morning to do chores!"　　1

I hit the snooze button, hoping desperately that the cows will, for once, feed and milk themselves. Seconds away from falling back into a deep sleep, I hear my father's heavy footsteps outside my bedroom door. They stop and my door opens with a creak. "Jessica, are you awake yet?" my father asks. Without a word, knowing from past experience that an argument won't get me anywhere, I stagger out of my warm twin bed, trudging dejectedly past the figure at the narrow doorway. I continue down the hall toward the small bathroom to find my sisters, Angie and Melissa, and my brother, Nick, already awake.

We all proceed with our usual morning routine, which consists of washing our faces, brushing our teeth, and taking turns on the white porcelain throne. In the lower level of the old farmhouse, our outside clothes await. My mother makes it a rule to keep them there so that they won't stink up the rest of the house. As soon as we open the door to the basement, we can smell the putrid aroma of cows that has seeped from our clothing into the damp cool air. We take our turns going down the steep, narrow steps, using the walls on either side for extra guidance. As we dress, not a single word is spoken because we all feel the same way, "I hate this!" However, most of the time our choice of vocabulary is much more creative.

Nick opens the basement door leading outside to the barn. There is a brisk and bitter wind accompanied by icy snowflakes that feel like needles digging into our faces. We don't turn back. We desperately want to, but we know my father is patiently waiting for us to help him milk and feed the cows before school starts at 8:30 a.m. We lift our scarves and pull down our hats so only our squinted eyes show. We lower our bodies to dodge the fierce winds and trudge a half mile to the red barn, which is somehow standing sturdily in the dreadful blizzard.

When we finally reach the barn, Nick, leading the pack, grabs the handle of the heavy wooden door and props it open for my sisters and me to pass through. Nick goes immediately to help my father herd the cows and get them into their proper stalls to be milked. Meanwhile, my sisters and I go to the milk house to sanitize the milking machines, prepare all the milking equipment, and set up a station with towels and charts of the cows that are being medicated.

While Melissa and my father milk the one hundred cows, Nick and Angie feed them, and I feed the newborn calves. Because I am the youngest in the family, this is my favorite chore because I rarely have the chance to look after someone or feel like I am taking care of him or her. I have always had older siblings who look after me, watching every step I take, making sure that I don't get into trouble. We all work together—that's critical. When I feed the calves, I am finally the one in charge. It is a nice feeling, being on the opposite end

2

3

4

5

6

One of Hemauer's peer readers wrote the following comment:

I like how the real details (like all of the smells) help me "be there" with you.

Notice the sensory details in this paragraph.

of the spectrum. They are my responsibility. Little do I realize it, but this is the beginning of a lifetime of responsibilities.

After the calves are fed, other chores have to be done. Cleaning out various huts and pens and laying down fresh straw are a part of our daily duties. This is the worst of the jobs I have to do. It is so dusty that I can hardly breathe at times, but we all know it has to be done so there is no sense complaining. My brother, sisters, and I work together to get the chores done as quickly as possible. Typically, we finish with the chores and return to the house around 7:30 in the morning. [7]

Again, note the sensory details in Hemauer's paper: the smells, being hungry, fresh OJ, and so on.

We make our way back to the farmhouse, drape our clothes on a folding chair next to the washing machine in the basement, and crawl up the stairs. The delicious smell of smoked bacon and cheese omelets grows more intense with each step. Our stomachs aching with hunger, we take turns in the shower, cleaning ourselves as fast as possible in order to get to the breakfast table. My father eats quickly and is back outside on the farm by the time my sisters or I run by the kitchen, grabbing a glass of fresh squeezed orange juice and a piece of toast as we yell frantically at the bus, "Wait!" It seems our daily lives operate in shifts, not like a real family. [8]

When I finally arrive at school, I have already been up for four hours doing chores on the farm in the bitter cold. The other kids in my private grade school have just rolled out of their beds inside their subdivision homes an hour before the bell rang. The school day always goes by fast. While my other classmates are thinking about what television show they are going to watch after school, I am thinking about the chores that await me once I get off the yellow school bus. [9]

School has always been my social life. I want to join teams or different clubs, but I always have to consider how my chores on the farm will get done, which makes it difficult for me to get involved. If I join a team that practices after school, I can't participate. If I join a club that meets before school, I can't attend the meetings. Being a farm girl means that I can't be like the other kids in my class. Not being able to participate in school activities like my friends makes me feel left out and depressed. The topic of conversation at the lunch table never involves me. [10]

Hemauer uses dialogue to engage her readers in the human interaction of her experience. Dialogue is an effective tool for making the experience more concrete.

"Hey, Carrie, how was basketball practice last night?" Susan asks as she pulls out a chair from the lunch table and sets her plastic tray down next to the tall, broad, blond-haired girl. [11]

"It was terrible! Coach was in such a bad mood!" Carrie shoves a handful of French fries into her mouth, spilling catsup down the front of her white tee shirt without noticing. "He made us run sprints for every shot we missed. And Kelly was missing all her shots last night. I'm so sore today." [12]

Carrie starts rubbing her legs when she notices the streak of catsup 13
on her shirt. She begins to wipe it off with one of her napkins, with little
success.

"Hey, Carrie, how was the student council meeting this morning? Did you 14
decide if we're going to have a formal dance this winter?"

"Yeah, we're having it on the Saturday before Christmas. Are you going 15
to come?"

I sit listening in silence. The twenty-minute lunch period always feels like 16
eternity. While everyone around me continues talking and laughing, I sit there
next to them silently eating my French fries, listening carefully, trying to laugh
at the right times.

In eighth grade I really want to play basketball, and after I beg and plead 17
with my parents, they finally say I can join the team as long as I continue to
help with chores in the morning before school and after practice. I quickly
agree. I become the basketball team's starting point guard. I am thrilled to be
on a team, and I finally feel like I am starting to have a life like the other kids.
Now I am included in the conversations at lunch, and I feel like a part of the
group. I never tell anyone that I have to go home after practice and work on
the farm, or that I wake up every morning at five to help with chores. None
of my friends, teachers, or coaches know. I don't think they would care and
I don't want them to know that I am different.

In high school I become more involved with the school. Coincidently, my 18
father's farm continues to grow. We are now up to two hundred cows, and
my dad still wants to expand the farm. During my freshman year I continue
to work on the farm before and after school, making sure that I can still play
on the basketball team. A few times a teacher catches me with my eyes closed
during class. One time my teacher, Ms. Cain, comes over to my wooden desk,
where my head is resting on top of a math textbook. She taps her knuckles
on the hollow wood and says, "Jessica, are you okay? Do you need to go to
the health room?" Raising my head, embarrassed that she caught me sleeping,
I say quickly, "No, Ms. Cain, I'm fine. I'm sorry for being rude and causing a
disruption. I promise to be more attentive."

Shortly after freshman year, my father arranges a meeting with my entire 19
family. He explains that he wants our farm to continue to grow, and this means
that he needs more help on the farm than his children can provide. In fact,
he says that he would rather not have us work on the farm anymore, unless
we want to. He would rather have us be more involved in school and go on to
college. After this meeting, I feel happy and relieved, and I can tell my father
is relieved too. He knows that my siblings and I have sacrificed our school
activities and social lives to help with the family business, and I know that this
is his way of saying thank you.

One peer reviewer
made this suggestion:

**I'd like to hear more
about school and
the people there.**

Note the details and
specific examples that
Hemauer provides to
really show what she
means (rather than
just telling).

From this moment on, I become more involved with my school. I join   20
the homecoming club, audition for musicals and plays, serve as the president of the student council as well as president of my class. I also become
more social with my friends. I even take on a waitressing job at a resort in
a neighboring town. During all these activities, I always notice that I stick
out from the group. In school people come up to me and ask how I manage
my time so well, without getting stressed out. When I'm with a group of my
friends, I always seem to be more mature than they are, leading the group
while others try to follow in my footsteps. When it comes to my job, I am
always on time, never calling in sick and never complaining about a task
I have been asked to do.

One night after work, I sit down in front of the full-length mirror in my   21
bedroom and start thinking about the past years. I had believed that joining
various clubs and social activities would make me fit in with my peers. But
in fact, it has not. I still stick out. And the more I think about it, the more
I realize why. My life growing up has been much different from the lives of
my peers. From an early age, I had to learn how to manage my time so that
I could do my chores and attend school. When I started to play basketball,
I had to manage my time even more carefully. I have always had a challenging amount of responsibility, and I have learned to complete tasks in a timely
fashion. The work that I had to do on the farm was far from glamorous.
I have done some of the worst jobs conceivable, so I have a higher tolerance for work than most people. Though I hated it growing up, working on
the farm has taught me many lessons about life, and it has shaped me into
the individual I am today.

Each day of my life there are times when I reflect back to working on   22
the farm. And every day people notice that I am different from the rest of
my peers. At school, teachers and organization leaders are impressed by my
time management skills and the amount of responsibility I take on. At work,
my boss continues to ask me where he can find some more hard working
people. I simply tell him, "Try hiring some farm girls. I hear they turn out
pretty good."

UNDERSTANDING A WRITER'S GOALS: QUESTIONS TO CONSIDER AND DISCUSS

Rhetorical Knowledge: The Writer's Situation and Rhetoric

1. **Purpose:** Why did Hemauer write this essay? How might different audiences see different purposes?

2. **Audience:** Whom do you see as Hemauer's audience? What can you point to in the text that supports your claim?

3. **Voice and tone:** How does Hemauer establish her *ethos*—her credibility—in this essay?

4. **Responsibility:** What is Hemauer's responsibility to her readers? To the members of her family? How does she fulfill those responsibilities?

5. **Context, format, and genre:** Hemauer has written a personal essay. When writing in this genre, writers try to relate their own personal experiences to much broader, more general human experiences. How has Hemauer used her personal remembrances of growing up on a dairy farm to help her readers, whose own lives may have been very different from that of a midwestern farm girl, relate to the essay?

Critical Thinking: The Writer's Ideas and Your Personal Response

6. Even though you may have had a much different childhood from Hemauer's, can you relate to some of her experiences? What does she do to develop interest in the subject of her essay?

7. What do you see as the significance of Hemauer's story?

Composing Processes and Knowledge of Conventions: The Writer's Strategies

8. How do descriptive and narrative details function in the essay? Point to several places where Hemauer "shows" instead of "tells."

9. How does Hemauer use dialogue in the essay? What other methods does she use to show readers what her life as a farm girl was like?

Inquiry and Research: Ideas for Further Exploration

10. Search the Web to find other narratives—even blog entries—in which college students reflect on their life and work experiences. How do they compare to Hemauer's narrative about her farm-life experience?

Self-Assessment: Reflecting on Your Goals

Now that you have constructed a piece of writing to share experiences, revisit your learning goals, which you and your classmates may have considered at the beginning of this chapter (see page 75). Here are some questions to help you focus on what you have learned from this assignment. Respond to the questions in writing, and discuss your responses with classmates. If you are constructing a course portfolio, your responses to these questions can also serve as invention work for the portfolio.

 ## Rhetorical Knowledge

- *Audience:* What did you learn about your audience as you wrote about your experience or experiences?
- *Purpose:* How successfully do you feel you fulfilled your purpose? Why?
- *Rhetorical situation:* What was your rhetorical situation? How have you responded to the rhetorical situation?
- *Voice and tone:* How did you reveal your personality? What tone did you use?
- *Context, medium, and genre:* What context were you writing in? What medium and genre did you choose, and how did those decisions affect your writing?

 ## Critical Thinking, Reading, and Writing

- *Learning/inquiry:* What did you discover about writing about experiences while you were working on this assignment? What did you discover about yourself? About your experiences?
- *Responsibility:* How did you fulfill your responsibility to your readers? To the people you wrote about?
- *Reading and research:* Did you rely on your memories, or did you conduct additional research for this assignment? If so, what sources did you consult? How did you use them?

Writing Processes

- *Invention:* What invention strategies were most useful to you? Why?
- *Organizing your ideas and details:* What organization did you use? How successful was it?
- *Revising:* What one revision did you make that you are most satisfied with? What are the strongest and the weakest parts of the paper you wrote for this chapter? Why?
- *Working with peers:* How did your instructor or peer readers help you by making comments and suggestions about your writing? List some examples of useful comments that you received. How could you have made better use of the comments and suggestions you received?
- *Visuals:* Did you use photographs or other visuals to help you describe your experience or experiences? If so, what did you learn about incorporating these elements?
- *Writing habits:* What "writerly habits" have you developed, modified, or improved on as you constructed the writing assignment for this chapter?

Knowledge of Conventions

- *Editing:* What sentence problem did you find most frequently in your writing? How will you avoid that problem in future assignments?
- *Genre:* What conventions of the genre you were using, if any, gave you problems?
- *Documentation:* Did you use sources for your paper? If so, what documentation style did you use? What problems, if any, did you have with it?

Refer to Chapter 1 (page 12) for a sample reflection by a student.

Text Credits

CHAPTER

6

Writing to Explore

Source: NASA

When you hear the word *exploration,* you may envision astronauts or explorers of earlier centuries, people who physically ventured to previously uncharted territory. When astronauts Neil Armstrong and Edwin E. "Buzz" Aldrin went to the moon in 1969, they were looking for answers to questions that humans have asked for thousands of years: What is the moon like? What is it composed of? What does Earth look like from the moon? More recently, the Hubble Space Telescope has enabled explorers to view remote parts of the universe, and today's space explorers are often not astronauts but robots—like the Mars Rover.

Although we commonly associate exploration with physical travel, there are many other kinds of explorations. Indeed, some of the most valuable explorations are those that take place in your own mind. Often, through the act of writing, you can discover new ideas or new perspectives.

Playwright Edward Albee once noted, "I write to find out what I'm talking about."

In addition to exploring what you already know, exploratory writing gives you the chance to ask questions and to consider what else you would like to find out.

In any exploration, whether in college or in the professional, civic, and personal areas of your life, you investigate a particular subject closely. You will often need to explore an idea or a concept—or a decision you need to make—in detail, from various perspectives, before you can really see and understand the overall situation.

Setting Your Goals for *Exploratory Writing*

 ## Rhetorical Knowledge (pp. 115-120)

- **Audience:** Because you are learning as you write, you will often be the main audience. Who else can you visualize reading your work? What will that person or those people expect to find in it? How can you appeal to those readers as well?

- **Purpose:** Your purpose might be simply to learn more about the topic, but often exploratory writing leads to the unexpected and unfamiliar, so you need to be prepared to be surprised.

- **Rhetorical situation:** Consider the many factors that affect what you write—you (the writer), your readers (the audience), the topic (the subject you are exploring), your purpose (what you wish to accomplish), and the exigency (what is compelling you to write). In an exploratory essay, you are writing to raise questions and to let them guide your inquiry; your readers are reading your text so that they can grapple with those same questions.

- **Voice and tone:** Generally, exploratory writing has an inquisitive tone. Of course, sometimes an exploratory essay can have a humorous tone.

- **Context, medium, and genre:** The genre you use to present your thinking is determined by your purpose: to explore. You will need to decide on the best medium and genre to use to present your exploration to the audience you want to reach. Think about how digital technologies can help you decide on the most effective medium and genre.

 ## Critical Thinking, Reading, and Writing (pp. 120-132)

- **Learning/inquiry:** By reading and writing as an explorer, you gain a deeper understanding of diverse and complex perspectives.

- **Responsibility:** You have a responsibility to represent diverse perspectives honestly and accurately.

- **Reading and research:** Your research must be accurate and as complete as possible to allow you to consider the widest possible array of perspectives.

Writing Processes (pp. 133-145)

- **Invention:** Choose invention strategies that will help you thoughtfully contemplate diverse perspectives.

- **Organizing your ideas and details:** Find the most effective way to present perspectives to your readers so they can easily understand them. Consider how using a spreadsheet may help you organize your information.

- **Revising:** Read your work with a critical eye to make certain that it fulfills the assignment and displays the qualities of effective exploratory writing.

- **Working with peers:** Your classmates will make suggestions that indicate parts of your text they find difficult to understand so you can clarify.

 ## Knowledge of Conventions (pp. 146-151)

- **Editing:** When you explore, you might tend to leave your thoughts—and sentences—incomplete. To help you avoid this pitfall, the round-robin activity in this chapter (on page 146) deals with sentence fragments. Consider using Google Docs or similar software for reviewing classmates' papers.

- **Genres for exploratory writing:** Possible genres include exploratory essays, profiles, and more informal types of exploratory writing such as blogs, journals, and diaries.

- **Documentation:** If you have relied on sources outside of your own experience, you will need to cite them using the appropriate documentation style. Think about how digital technologies can assist you in documenting sources accurately and consistently.

RHETORICAL KNOWLEDGE

When you write to explore, consider how your exploration will help you gain some greater understanding, how you can help your readers understand your topic in a new way, and why you want them to gain this understanding. Also, decide what medium and genre will help you communicate your exploration most effectively to your audience.

 ## Writing to Explore in Your College Classes

Your college classes give you wonderful opportunities to explore your current interests and discover new ones. Taking a college class in almost any field allows you to begin exploring that field, reading its literature, and listening to and interacting with people who are experts in the field. Each class you take also gives you the opportunity to explore the subject area via writing. During your college career, you may write the following kinds of papers:

- In a history class, your instructor may encourage you to explore several perspectives on the Cuban Missile Crisis in 1962. Such an exploration might then lead to a writing project in which you argue that certain events and factors were the actual causes of this crisis.

- In a nutrition class, your instructor may ask you to explore several perspectives on vegetarian diets. Here, too, your exploration could lead to a paper in which you demonstrate specific effects of vegetarianism or in which you argue for or against such a diet.

- For a communication course, your instructor may ask you to explore whether there is evidence that men and women have different communication styles.

For all of these writing situations, think about what you might need to do to communicate your ideas effectively: what information you might need to include, how you would describe your exploration, what visuals or examples you might use, and so on.

For information on writing a cause-and-effect analysis, see Chapter 11.
For information on writing to convince, see Chapter 9.

 ## Writing to Explore for Life

Just as you will undoubtedly write to explore in your academic life, you are likely to use different kinds of exploratory writing in other areas of your life. In much of the exploratory writing you will do in your *professional* life, you will find yourself exploring various options. A manager might ask to what extent hiring Ms. X instead of Mr. Y will make a difference to the business. A teacher might ask what effect one lesson plan would have on a group of students compared to a different lesson plan.

USING DIGITAL TECHNOLOGIES   Writing a Blog

The ultimate form of writing to explore might be a personal or professional online journal, or *blog*. A blog (a shortening of "Web *log*") can be a fun place to explore issues and events of the day while developing your voice, style, and expressive self. As you explore your topic and begin con- ducting research, use a blog to organize and to keep track of your research. Take a look at one writer's blog on her travels at *www.dr-randsdell.com/travel-muse-blog*. Ransdell's travels also help inform her books—as you will see when you read a bit of her blog.

People working for the good of a community often deal with *best options*—solutions to problems for which there may not be a single perfect result but rather many possible outcomes. Therefore, those involved in *civic* life can find explor-atory writing especially useful.

Your *personal* life offers many opportunities for exploratory writing. You may respond regularly to e-mails or notes from friends, family members, and class-mates in which you explore the possibilities for a group gift for someone import-ant to all of you, propose convenient times for getting together, or consider a new wireless carrier. You may keep a journal, where you can explore your thoughts, ideas, responses, and feelings privately.

For more on blogs, see Chapter 17.

The "Ways of Writing" feature (page 117) presents different genres that can be used when writing to explore.

Scenarios for Writing | Assignment Options

Your instructor may ask you to complete one of the following assignments that call for exploratory writing. Each assignment is in the form of a *scenario,* a brief story that provides some context for writing. The scenario gives you a sense of who your audience is and what you need to accomplish with your writing.

Starting on page 133, you will find guidelines for completing whatever assign-ment option you choose. Additional scenarios for college and life may be found online.

Writing for College

SCENARIO 1   An Academic Paper Exploring a Career

For this scenario, assume you are taking a career and life planning class—a class devoted to helping college students decide what discipline they might like to major in. This class gives you the opportunity to explore different career paths, to learn what the educational requirements are for various majors, and to find out what job opportunities will be available and what salaries and other forms of compensation different jobs might offer.

Ways of Writing to Explore

Genres for Your College Classes	Sample Situation	Advantages of the Genre	Limitations of the Genre
Academic essay	For your creative nonfiction class, you are asked to construct an essay exploring the writing styles of several authors you have read and studied.	Your exploration, using the conventions of an academic essay, will help you better understand the details of the writing styles of the authors you've studied.	An exploration often leads to more questions, which can be unsettling to a writer.
Internet exploration	Your writing professor has asked you to explore the Internet for reliable and relevant Web sites pertaining to your research topic and then post links to them with a summary of each on a discussion board for the class.	This activity will help you understand what electronic resources are available, as well as the range of quality.	Depending on your topic, there may be too much information to search through.
Exploratory paper	Your computer science instructor asks you to write an exploratory paper that proposes at least three viable solutions to a networking problem.	This activity will require that you envision multiple solutions rather than just one.	It can be difficult to write fairly about solutions you don't think will work.
Letter	You want to write a letter to your school newspaper that explores the ramifications of a proposed change in campus parking and encourages involvement in the decision.	The school newspaper will allow you to engage the appropriate audience about an issue that matters to them.	A letter to the editor allows only limited space, and you cannot use visuals to show what you mean. It might not be published.
Oral presentation	For your art class, you are asked to construct an oral and visual presentation exploring the local art scene by showing and discussing works from local artists.	The visuals in your presentation will allow your audience to see some of the art you are discussing.	Sometimes it is hard to get really good photographs of sculptures and other works of art. Aspiring artists may also not grant you permission to photograph their work.
Genres for Life	**Sample Situation**	**Advantages of the Genre**	**Limitations of the Genre**
Poster	You decide to construct a poster titled "Exploring _____" to help viewers understand what a specific nonprofit organization does.	Your poster is a visual way to help readers explore the purpose of your nonprofit organization.	A poster restricts the amount of space you can use; illustrations are needed to catch the eye of passing viewers.
Blog	You and two neighbors want to construct a blog to help everyone in your neighborhood explore possible ways to improve the area.	A blog lets your neighborhood interact and share community information.	A blog must be monitored for potentially offensive comments; not everyone will feel comfortable blogging.
Wiki	For your employer, you construct a wiki asking everyone in your organization to explore ways to serve the public more efficiently.	A wiki is an easy and uncomplicated way for everyone in your business to contribute their ideas while building on the ideas of others.	Someone will need to monitor the wiki for inappropriate entries and to collect suggestions.
Web page	You want to construct a Web page allowing members of your community to explore various options for raising tax revenue to benefit the community.	Your Web page can provide text, graphs, charts, and links to related areas.	Readers cannot interact with a static Web page.
E-mail profile	Your family is planning a large family reunion; you construct an e-mail profile of some possible locations.	Your e-mail lets you explore potential locations with a large number of people, with links to relevant Web pages.	An e-mail can get lengthy as family members respond; not everyone will feel comfortable using e-mail.

© Steve Debenport/E+/Getty Images RF

Writing Assignment: Select one college major or career that you may be interested in pursuing, and construct an exploratory paper (or PowerPoint or Prezi presentation) in which you consider the various aspects of that major or career from many angles, including the preparation you would need for it and the rewards and pitfalls you might encounter if you decide to pursue it. Asking and answering questions about the major or career you are considering will form the heart of your exploratory paper or presentation.

SCENARIO 2   A Profile Exploring a Personal Interest

In this writing option, you will explore a subject that interests you personally and write a profile of it. This assignment gives you the chance to explore something or someone you are interested in and would like to know more about.

Writing Assignment: Think of a subject that you would like to know more about— perhaps a type of music or musician, a sport, a college major, a popular singer or actor, a local hangout, a community center, or something completely different. This assignment offers you the opportunity to research and write about a topic you are interested in. Use this opportunity not only to learn about the subject but also to examine your perceptions of and reactions to it.

Writing for Life

SCENARIO 3   Civic Writing: A Profile of a Local Agency

What local nonprofit agencies exist in your area? What do you know about how they function? What do you know about the work that they do in your community? Do you interact with any local, county, state, or federal agencies or departments? What experiences (good or bad) have you had with such entities? Select one local nonprofit or government agency or organization in which you are interested and about which you would like to learn more. The agency or organization may be your city or county government, your local school system, or a nonprofit organization such as the United Way.

Writing Assignment: Investigate the nonprofit or government agency or organization you have chosen. Explore what it does, where and how it functions, where its funding comes from, who works for it, and how its functions relate to other aspects of your community. Then construct a paper in which you explain your exploration of the agency or organization. Include at least three illustrations that helped you understand the organization (charts or tables that show statistical data, photographs of its buildings or office areas, etc.). In your paper, explain what features of these illustrations helped you better understand the organization. Because this is not an informative paper, your focus should be on the exploratory process you used to learn about your subject.

Rhetorical Considerations for Exploratory Writing

Audience: Although your instructor is one audience for this paper, you are also part of your audience—this assignment is designed to help you think through some possible educational and career choices, to explore an interest, or to explore some of your personal beliefs. Your classmates are also your audience, because some of them may also be considering these issues and ideas. They will learn from your research and perhaps ask questions and think of ideas they had not yet considered. What might other students in your writing class, or in one of your other classes, learn from your research and exploration? Who else might be part of your audience?

Purpose: Your purpose is to explore the various aspects of your topic in enough detail and depth to lead you to a greater understanding of it and what you believe about it.

Voice, tone, and point of view: As you explore your topic, you will step back to consider whether any preconceptions you may have about it are accurate. Your stance should be objective, and you should be open to the different possibilities you will discover. The point of view you take should be one of questioning—what can you learn by exploring your topic?—but the tone you use can range from humorous to serious.

Context, medium, and genre: Because you will be exploring an area you are already interested in, you will have the incentive to learn more as you research and write. The knowledge you gain may benefit you later. For example, you may be able to use the information you have acquired from this assignment to write a causal analysis or a proposal paper. If you are writing for an audience beyond the classroom, what will be the most effective way to present your information to this audience? You might write a letter to a friend, prepare a formal report for colleagues at work, or construct a Web site.

For more on choosing a medium and genre, see Chapter 17 and Appendix C. For more on writing a causal analysis, see Chapter 11. For more on writing a proposal paper, see Chapter 12.

 # CRITICAL THINKING, READING, AND WRITING

Before you begin to write your exploratory paper, consider the qualities of successful exploratory writing. It also helps to read one or more examples of this type of writing. Finally, you might consider how visuals could enhance your exploratory writing, as well as the kinds of sources you will need to consult.

Unlike many other kinds of writing, where writers have a clear idea of their intent, exploratory writing frees writers to take intellectual chances and to see where different possibilities may lead. Although effective exploratory writing involves taking intellectual risks and finding alternatives that you may not have thought of before, your writing will not be successful if you simply write anything you please. Effective exploratory writing is based on reasonable options and uses information culled from solid research.

 ## Learning the Qualities of Effective Exploratory Writing

As you think about how you might construct an exploratory paper, consider that readers probably expect the unexpected from this kind of text. Effective exploratory writing will include the following qualities:

- **A focus on a concept or question.** Rather than focusing on a specific, narrowly provable thesis, exploratory writing is more open-ended. Writers are more than likely trying to answer a question, lay the groundwork for a solution to a problem, or re-define a concept. For instance, a writer might pose a question such as this: "Writers often use memoirs to explore their own past, and I wonder what memoir writing will look like in the future. How does technology change what we might record as we explore our past?" In her exploratory essay (page 122), Daphne Strassmann seems to answer the question, "Why do you use social media?" as doing so allows her to "deposit bits" of herself all over the Web.

- An inquisitive spirit. Any explorer begins with an interest in finding out more about the subject. Ask questions that you want to answer, and let the answers lead you to further questions. Although you need to ground your queries in reality, you should not feel constrained by conventional thinking. Albert Einstein used "thought experiments" to explore time and space in ways conventional experiments could not. As a result, he developed his revolutionary theory of relativity.

- A consideration of the range of perspectives in a subject. As you explore your subject, be willing to see it from different vantage points and to consider its positive and negative aspects. Effective exploratory writing looks at a topic from as many angles as possible. This can be difficult to do sometimes, because we often get locked into our own ways of thinking. In exploratory writing, however, it is vital to look at alternative views and to understand that others may have a different perspective from yours.

- Expansive coverage of a subject. Effective exploratory writing does not try to make a case or attempt to persuade you as writer or your reader of something. Rather, it examines many aspects of the topic, often developing a **profile** of its subject, as Daphne Strassmann does in "The Perils of a Perfect Memory" on page 122. Look at as much information about your subject as possible, while realizing that not all information is useful or relevant. Use your critical reading and thinking skills to help determine the reliability and relevance of the information you have gathered. Because exploratory writing is often inductive in nature, you might find it useful to organize your details in categories, using a cluster chart or listing.

For more on inductive thinking, see Chapter 14. For more on cluster charts and listing as strategies, see Chapter 4.

Reading, Inquiry, and Research: Learning from Texts That Explore

The following readings are examples of exploratory writing. Each offers perspectives on a subject. As you read each one, consider the following questions:

- What makes this reading an interesting and a useful exploration?

- After reading the selection, what else do you want to learn about the subject? Why?

- How can you use the writer's techniques of exploratory writing in your own writing?

DAPHNE STRASSMANN

The Perils of Perfect Memory: The New Past, According to Social Media

On her Twitter page, Daphne Strassmann self-identifies as a "Writer/Blogger/Latina Americana/ Somewhat Synesthetic/Omnigrant/ Mother/Wife." Her writing and research look into the "future of memoir in the digital age," the topic of the exploratory essay featured here.

Like most people these days, I willingly deposit bits of myself online every day, through shopping, commenting on friends' photos, posting pithy quips, and engaging in my newly found hobby of reviewing recent purchases. Isolated, these activities are disconnected material; woven together, they make me part of a new, vast community of casual storytellers. Despite their careless, seemingly ephemeral character, however, these stories have a new flavor of permanence, and material has never been so easily accessible to writers. Sites like Twitter, Facebook, or Instagram remind us and our followers where and how we have been, all the while creating parallel universes through our daily posts. The vast and specific nature of our online information has the capacity to behave as a spontaneous external hard drive to our own memories. We can have—increasingly, can't escape having—instant access to our past, seemingly bypassing the natural remembering process. Our hippocampus, it seems, can live on the Web.   1

Of course, future accessibility to the information we etch online, especially on social media, will vary depending upon who does the archiving. Yet as data storage becomes less expensive, the capacity capabilities grow and so does the amount of information held online. After all, in order to serve our needs, the Web must have infallible and non-perishable memory.   2

Certainly, this trove of online information will be a tantalizing and highly useful resource for future biographers and narrative nonfiction writers. And yet, for the memoirist, a source of indelible online information could be problematic.   3

Digital omnipresence shortens and stunts the distance to remembering— the crucial engine for memoir. Molded in the narrative nonfiction writer's hands, memory creates stories and feeds a compulsion to reflect on, understand, and validate personal experiences. The organic experience of remembering is still enveloped in mystery. Memoirists have a soft spot for that mystery, but we should concede that digital content will make the past, in some ways, less mysterious.   4

Some, like Viktor Mayer-Schönberger, author of *Delete: The Virtue of Forgetting in the Digital Age*, see the infallible memory of the Web as a big problem: "Because of digital technology, society's ability to forget has become suspended, replaced by perfect memory." Alas, memoir informed by perfect   5 memory would, I fear, lose its sensory appeal. Web memories might alter the memoirist's process, not only by providing infallible instant memory but also by usurping our own natural recollection processes.

Mayer-Schönberger also argues that that our online interactions make us feel watched and that, even if we are not in fact under surveillance, the sensation of being watched leads us to self-censor. In fact, writers online *are* often being watched—or, at least, seen—by readers. This, too, is a mixed blessing. On the one hand, social media, in particular, can help writers find a wider audience—that "platform" publishers are always talking about. Ideally, this audience will be invested in the work—but it could also be dissonant from it. For better and worse, the Web arms us with accidental connections.

Of course, if you're writing about your contemporaries, odds are good they're hanging around online, too, and maybe also watching you. Those characters—who in an earlier time might have been lost to us—travel across oceans and different decades to engage passively with our own recollections. They can disagree with our memories, question them, and, over time, even change them. They are unwelcome guests on e-mail, Facebook, or through the dream-like images of Instagram. We know what our college roommates, from thirty years ago, ate for breakfast this morning, and it can be difficult to gain distance from a character when she is still right there, hoping you'll "like" her handmade inspirational posters. These people, our characters, are persistently with us—and not just in our memories.

And, of course, they all have their versions of stories. That's always been true, but now the bar for commenting has been lowered significantly. That story you're telling about your halcyon days can become distorted or commandeered—tainted, even—as it passes through what we might call "the Facebook fact-check."

As it happens, I have some experience with this. I have an unpublished cultural memoir set in the Dominican Republic and Texas, concerning events that happened in the 1970s and '80s. In it, I piece together, much in the way my memory works, vignettes that touch on both the traumatic and the mundane. In great detail, I describe my aunt's palpable grief—she went from catatonic to howling in pain—on the afternoon we learned that my father had died piloting an air force plane. I mention how an uncharacteristically blonde, blue-eyed Dominican classmate derided some earrings my mother had brought back from a trip to Venezuela. If I had published this book in the early days of the Web, and especially before Facebook, and if, through a freak act of nature, a copy made it back to the Dominican Republic, someone might have quibbled about the narrative, recognized him- or herself in the story and related to or separated themselves from it. Maybe I would have received an e-mail or two with pointed questions: "Hey, did I really hurt your feelings when I said your earrings should be worn only by classless maids?" Or "Why would you write

6

7

8

9

about your aunt crying like that?" By contrast, that same interaction on Face-book or any other social media platform would be instantaneous and, for me, a huge distraction from my work. The mirror social media holds up to my work, so far, has intimidated me enough to keep me from publishing. Not because I have startling revelations that cast people in my life negatively, but because in my writer's mind, my past has its own past. I can't get lost in the reverie of recalling that past when so much of it is so present every time I update my Facebook status.

And yet, perhaps there's hope. I take heart in knowing that although social media supplies us with instant memory on steroids, the content itself can be ephemeral. The moment a corporate institution goes down, so does the content and so do your memories. Our data could be one hack or natural disaster or bankruptcy away from exposure or deletion. In many ways, the steady story-telling we're imprinting on the Web is no different than jotting an idea on the back of a napkin and misplacing it.   10

And perhaps that's for the best. We shouldn't rely too heavily on external digital memory. The noisy interactions on social media distract at every level, and the illusion of perfect recall is a siren's call. It's hard to resist since it's omnipresent in daily life, and so usable, but even the most assiduous curation of interactions on social media has a cost. If our postings on social media and the Web keep giving us perfect recall, then the story is authored for us; we become transcribers rather than storytellers. As writers, we delight in that moment when memory becomes story. We need to forget in order to engage in the essence of remembering.   11

UNDERSTANDING A WRITER'S GOALS: QUESTIONS TO CONSIDER AND DISCUSS

Knowledge: The Writer's Situation and Rhetoric

1. **Audience:** How does Strassmann's relationship with her social media network differ from her relationship with the readers of this essay?

2. **Purpose:** Why does Strassmann explain the Internet's capacity for "remembering" in such detail? Do you think that the Internet's "memory" allows people to be lazy in what they remember and subsequently write about?

3. **Voice and tone:** What is Strassmann's attitude toward social media?

4. **Responsibility:** According to Strassmann, what is a memoir writer's responsibility to her subjects? What about the responsibilities of a writer on social media? How does she compare and contrast them?

5. **Context, format, and genre:** Strassmann chose the genre of the memoir to explore and explain her feelings about the drawbacks of "perfect memory." Why do you think she chose that genre?

Critical Thinking: The Writer's Ideas and Your Personal Response

6. What does Strassmann mean when she writes that in using social media to recall the past "we become transcribers rather than storytellers"?

7. How does Strassmann's essay affect your own feelings about social media use? Why? Do you ever feel that others are "watching" you?

8. In paragraph 9, Strassman writes that, "The mirror social media holds up to my work, so far, has intimidated me enough to keep me from publishing." Would social media in some way inhibit your publishing your own exploratory memoir? Why?

Composing Processes and Knowledge of Conventions: The Writer's Strategies

9. How effective is Strassmann's analogy in which she compares writing on the Web to "jotting an idea on the back of a napkin" (paragraph 10)? Why?

10. If you had been "deposit[ing] bits" of yourself every day on the Internet, as Strassman says she does, do you think that would affect the accuracy of your memories?

11. Although Strassmann comments on the ideas of other people, including writers of memoir and users of social media, she does not quote anyone. Why do you think this is so? What might quotations have added to her essay?

Inquiry and Research: Ideas for Further Exploration

12. Read some of Daphne Strassmann's blog entries. How do they illustrate some of the points that she makes in her essay?

13. Ask a sibling or someone close to you to explore their own memories of a childhood event. How does that person's memory compare to your own?

GENRES *Up Close*   Writing a Profile

Because people are so curious about other people, they love to write and talk about them. To satisfy that craving, readers can find plenty of venues that offer profiles. Profiles of famous and not-so-famous people appear in magazines such as *People* and *Rolling Stone,* on radio news shows such as *All Things Considered* or *Weekend Edition* on National Public Radio, on television shows such as *E! News,* and especially on social networking sites such as Facebook. Social networking sites are especially popular because they allow ordinary people to read profiles of other ordinary people. A recent Web search using the term "Facebook," for example, yielded more than 16 billion sites. In fact, Facebook has more than 800 million users. That number is astounding, considering that Earth's population is approximately 7 billion.

Although profiles often focus on people, they also can describe places and events. Profiles have distinctive features. They usually do the following:

- **Provide some insight into the subject.** A profile takes readers behind the scenes to reveal details that are not widely known.

- **Include key details.** A profile describes its subject, offering details that appeal to the senses as well as dialogue and expert opinion.

- **Are logically organized.** Whether the organization is chronological or spatial, an effective profile holds readers' interest as it informs them about its subject.

As you consider the following profile of how social media had an impact on an environmental event, think about how it exemplifies the features of a profile.

MURIEL MACDONALD

PROFILE OF AN EVENT

1 Billion Impressions: The Digital Climate March

Muriel MacDonald is the content editor for social studies and for social media marketing for TINT. She composes some of TINT's tweets, edits TINT's blog, and "works with clients to tell their social hub success stories. She also works with clients to help them identify all the ways they can use social media hubs to achieve their goals." She is self-described as a "writer, techie, tree-hugger, musician, and hitchhiker."

In October 2010, Malcom Gladwell wrote a provocative piece for *The New Yorker,* "Small Change: Why the Revolution Will Not Be Tweeted." He argued that social media lacks the ability to form the kind of close, personal ties that push people to take the drastic action necessary to enact change.   1

Much has changed since 2010. Just two months after Gladwell's article was published the revolutions of the Arab spring showed the power of social media to do exactly what he feared it could not—to organize large groups of people to take big, drastic action, even in the face of danger. And while the debate about social media's role in movements for social change continues, the debate about whether or not it has a role at all is essentially over.   2

The Arab spring showed that the revolution will, in fact, be tweeted.   3

Gladwell's article was right in one respect: Twitter is not a tool for creat-   4
ing close social bonds—the kind of close social bonds that inspired the lunch
counter sit-ins of the 60s, for example. But it is a great tool for spreading ideas
to a wider audience than was ever possible without it. It is a tool for giving
the common people a voice, for creating your own attention, when traditional
news sources give you short shrift.

The People's Climate March Goes Viral

This past Sunday, 400,000 people took part in the People's Climate March in   5
New York City to demand action on climate change. The march made the front
page of *The New York Times*, but received the usual mix of coverage and inat-
tention that climate activists have come to expect from traditional news media.

The same day, there was a second climate march—one that made its own   6
coverage. It was a digital march that engaged participants across the globe on
the new battleground for change: social media.

In this march, the numbers were just as astounding. The organizers of the   7
People's Climate March estimate that on that day their digital campaign reached
600 million people in 70 countries. According to our Tint analytics, those
using the hashtag #peoplesclimate generated a jaw dropping 956.33 million
social impressions on Twitter alone.

We spoke with Thelma Young, Digital Organizer for the March, about how   8
social media is helping them to amplify the voices of their supporters.

TINT's website notes that it is "A self-service platform that allows organizations to create social hubs in minutes. [and so they can] engage audiences anywhere."

Digital March by the Numbers

On the day of the march, Thelma and the rest of the twelve person digital   9
team were ready. They had Tweetdeck tracking hashtag use on Twitter in real
time, and they had Tint pulling in related social posts from Twitter, Instagram,
Facebook, and YouTube, to be displayed in real-time on their website. Their
website's live social hub attracted nearly 400,000 visitors, presumably including
many that were not among the 400,000 busy marching in the streets that day.

The digital team took turns generating and moderating content—team   10
members took shifts on the ground, "embedded" at the march, where they took
pictures and posted to social platforms, while the rest of the team monitored
and moderated content from their control center where they watched the social
media attention roll in.

Twitter says that Tweetdeck is "The most powerful Twitter tool for real-time tracking, organizing, and engagement."

"Watching the feed come in from Twitter was crazy," Thelma told me. On   11
the day of the march, tweets rolled in at an average of 3 tweets per second. At
times, it was much faster than that.

At the end of the day, there had been 630,000 social posts about the march,   12
generating almost 1 billion social impressions.

The team used Tint to pull social posts through onto their website, approving posts with the iPhone app, which allowed them to swipe left or right to quickly accept or reject posts. At a certain point, they stopped moderating the overwhelming flow of content and let the tweets roll in, trolls and all.   13

People, Not Celebrities

In the days following the event, the celebrities present at the march have faded into the background, and the sheer numbers and diversity of the general crowd have become the story.   14

At first, the news focused on big names, like UN Secretary-General Ban Ki-Moon, Leonardo DiCaprio, Jane Goodall, and Sting. @PeoplesClimate themselves tweeted a screenshot of the Tint analytics showing the most influential contributors to their campaign, based on who had the most Twitter followers.   15

To a degree, celebrities are an important piece of the story. The list of the most influential tweeters is a wonderful and peculiar mix of politicians, media outlets, and entertainers, showing just how universal and diverse the climate movement has become: Obama tops the list, followed by *The New York Times*, Jason Mraz, *Rolling Stone* Magazine, the UN, and Chris Rock.   16

But amplifying the voices of celebrities is not the main benefit of social media for social justice campaigns. Rather, social media helped keep the march people-oriented. The press covered celebrities, but social [media] gave everyone a voice.   17

"Social media really helped spread the march far beyond New York itself," said Thelma, "It helped communicate that it was a *people's* march. Yes, we were on the cover of *The New York Times*, but everyone has their own personal photos and their own personal stories."   18

Social Media Meets Social Change

If the Arab Spring opened the debate about social media as a tool for social change, the People's Climate March closed it.   19

"People were talking about the march all across the Internet," said Thelma.   20

1 billion impressions crossing the borders of 70 countries has shown how effectively social media can be used to amplify the voices of a movement that has long suffered from a lack of traditional news coverage. In the coming months and years, the climate movement will doubtless continue to use social media to raise their voices. Other cause-oriented organizations can learn a lot by watching what they're doing.   21

If social media is the new place for mass organizing and serious conversations, then those who know how to encourage participation and utilize social to the fullest extent, will be best poised to make the big impactful changes that this world needs. As the marchers on Sunday shouted, "To change everything, you need everyone."   22

UNDERSTANDING A WRITER'S GOALS: QUESTIONS TO CONSIDER AND DISCUSS

Rhetorical Knowledge: The Writer's Situation and Rhetoric

1. **Audience:** Is this profile of how social media works suitable for a publication such as a blog?

2. **Purpose:** What do you think is MacDonald's purpose for narrating this event?

3. **Voice and tone:** What is MacDonald's attitude toward the People's Climate March and its coverage through social media? How does she convey that attitude?

4. **Responsibility:** What in the essay suggests that MacDonald feels a responsibility to raise awareness about the potential of social media to organize for social change?

5. Although you know some of the "famous people" MacDonald mentions, search for some of those you may be unfamiliar with. How do their names affect the credibility of MacDonald's text?

6. **Context, format, and genre:** What are the advantages of publishing this kind of profile in online format such as a blog?

Critical Thinking: The Writer's Ideas and Your Personal Response

7. What in her text might make you believe that MacDonald's focus on both the events of the Climate March and its coverage through social media was a good thing?

8. Given what MacDonald says about the potential for social media to help enact social and environmental change, especially in the future, what else would you like to know about the people and groups who are using it to this end? Why?

9. In paragraph 4, MacDonald writes that "Twitter is not a tool for creating close social bonds . . . [b]ut it is a great tool for spreading ideas to a wider audience than was ever possible without it." What other social media might do as effective a job as (or perhaps an even more effective job than) Twitter?

Composing Processes and Knowledge of Conventions: The Writer's Strategies

10. Why does MacDonald focus on specific data in her profile? What does she hope to illustrate by presenting her audience with data in the form of specific statistics? What does this information add to the profile?

Inquiry and Research: Ideas for Further Exploration

11. Conduct a Web search on groups that organize for change through social media. What do you find most interesting about what these groups have accomplished (or not accomplished)?

12. If there was a large event that used social media in the ways that MacDonald describes, do you think that you might get involved? Why?

PROFILE   Kiva Web Site www.kiva.org

Kiva is a nonprofit microfinance organization that provides loans to economically disadvantaged people around the world so that they can operate small businesses. Almost all of the loans are repaid to lenders, who often then provide loans to others. As you explore Kiva's Web site, consider what the writers have done to make it inviting to readers.

Source: Kiva

About Us
- Team
- Volunteers
- Board
- Finances
- History
- Statistics

How Kiva Works

About Microfinance

Social Performance

Support Us

Field Partners

How to become a
Field Partner

Kiva Fellows

App Gallery

Do More

Risk and Due
Diligence

Press Center

Help Center

About Us

The people behind Kiva include volunteers, Kiva Fellows, Field Partners, our board, and a team of employees (shown above) and contractors. The Kiva headquarters are located in San Francisco, California.

We are a non-profit organization with a mission to connect people through lending to alleviate poverty. Leveraging the internet and a worldwide network of microfinance institutions, Kiva lets individuals lend as little as $25 to help create opportunity around the world. Learn more about how it works.

Since Kiva was founded in 2005:

776,718 Kiva lenders

$321 million in loans

98.97% Repayment rate

We work with:

152 Field Partners

450 volunteers around the world

61 different countries

More metrics and stats >

Why we do what we do

Source: Kiva

UNDERSTANDING THE WRITERS' GOALS: QUESTIONS TO CONSIDER AND DISCUSS

Rhetorical Knowledge: The Writers' Situation and Rhetoric

1. **Audience:** How large is the audience for Kiva's Web site? Why do you think the audience is that size?

2. **Purpose:** What are the major purposes of Kiva's site?

3. **Voice and tone:** Although the authors of this Web site are anonymous, what attitude toward viewers does the site convey?

4. **Responsibility:** How does this Web site encourage responsible behavior?

5. **Context, format, and genre:** What features of the Web site's home page encourage readers to explore Kiva? How would you describe the links on the home page?

Critical Thinking: The Writers' Ideas and Your Personal Response

6. Visit the Web site for Kiva (www.kiva.org) and click on some of the links to pages that provide information about the organization. What information is most interesting?

7. What information is most useful to readers who want to learn more about Kiva?

Composing Processes and Knowledge of Conventions: The Writers' Strategies

8. Why do you think that the Kiva logo includes an image of a heart?

9. Why do you think that the Kiva home page includes so many photos of people, as well as information about each person featured on the page?

Inquiry and Research: Ideas for Further Exploration

10. Conduct a Web search with the terms "microfinance" and "microloan." Visit sites for several other organizations that offer such loans to see how they portray themselves. How do they differ from Kiva?

WRITING PROCESSES

As you work on the assignment you have chosen, remember the qualities of an effective exploratory paper, which are listed on pages 120–121. Also remember that writing is recursive—you might start with an invention activity or two and then conduct some research, which leads to more invention work and then a first draft. But then you might need to do more invention work to flesh out your draft and conduct more research to answer questions that come up as you explore your ideas further. And then you'll revise your draft and possibly find another gap or two. So while the activities listed below imply that writers proceed step-by-step, the actual process of writing is usually messier.

As you work on your project, save your computer files frequently because any work that you don't save could be lost. Savvy writers back up their computer files in two or more places—on an internal or external hard drive of the computer, on a USB flash drive, and to a cloud-based service, such as Dropbox.

Invention: Getting Started

The invention activities below are strategies that you can use to get some sense of what you already know about a subject. Whatever invention method(s) you use (or that your instructor asks you to employ), try to answer questions such as these:

- What do I already know about my subject?
- What preconceptions—positive, negative, neutral—do I have?
- Why am I interested in exploring this subject?
- What questions about the subject would I most like answers to? Who might I be able to talk to about this subject?
- What do I know about my audience? What can I say to interest them in my subject?
- What might my audience already know about my subject? What questions might they have?
- What is my purpose in exploring this subject? What would I like the end result of my research and writing to be? More knowledge? Information that I might use to pursue some goal?

If you do your invention work in electronic form, rather than on paper, you can incorporate this early writing more easily as you construct a draft.

As with any kind of writing, invention activities improve with peer feedback and suggestions. Consider sharing the invention work you have done so far with several classmates or friends in order to understand your rhetorical situation more clearly and to generate more useful information.

Elle Caminante's Freewriting and Clustering

Elle Caminante was taking a "career and life planning" class at her local community college, so she decided to respond to Scenario 1 on page 116. Elle was interested in a lot of areas—especially art—but she was not quite sure what she wanted to pursue as a career. Here is a portion of her freewriting, which reflects her questions and concerns about finding a career that she will enjoy:

> When I was a kid, I was sure I would grow up to be an artist. In fact, for a long time, my sister and I had a plan that she would write children's books and I would illustrate them. You start to realize as an adult, though, that dreams like that aren't always realistic. For one thing, I have no idea how to go about breaking into a career like that. And then the term "starving art-ist" comes to mind. I mean, they didn't come up with that phrase for noth-ing, and no college student wants to get into all this debt only to come out of school with no career options. So I've decided to explore what kinds of careers art majors can look forward to, along with some of the challenges and rewards of a career in the arts.
>
> I would like to talk to local artists, maybe even those who were art majors in college, and find out what they do now for a career. I also want to research the bios of famous artists, past and present, to get an idea of what their careers were like, especially *before* they became famous.
>
> Some questions I have are . . .

Elle Caminante also used listing to explore her ideas for a career. (See Chapter 5, page 97, for an example of this strategy.) Then she combined ideas from her freewriting and list into a cluster.

| **Writing** Activity |

Freewriting, Listing, and Clustering

Using the questions on page 133, freewrite for ten minutes, writing down every-thing you can think of about your subject. Even if you cannot think of anything to say, keep writing. Or list your ideas about the subject. Develop categories for your list to help you brainstorm.

Once you have gathered your ideas using one of the above methods, cluster them to determine how they relate to one another.

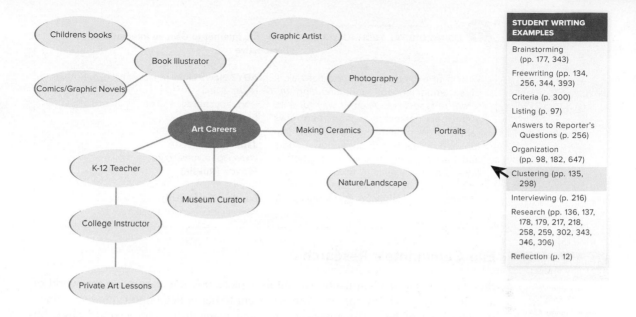

STUDENT WRITING EXAMPLES

Brainstorming (pp. 177, 343)

Freewriting (pp. 134, 256, 344, 393)

Criteria (p. 300)

Listing (p. 97)

Answers to Reporter's Questions (p. 256)

Organization (pp. 98, 182, 647)

Clustering (pp. 135, 298)

Interviewing (p. 216)

Research (pp. 136, 137, 178, 179, 217, 218, 258, 259, 302, 343, 346, 306)

Reflection (p. 12)

Exploring Your Ideas with Research

Although your opinions and ideas—and especially your questions—are central to any exploratory writing that you do, answer the questions you raise as you explore your subject. Getting those answers usually requires research, which can include reading books and periodical articles at the library, reading articles in your local newspaper, interviewing people who know more than you do about your subject, and conducting searches online, among other means. The information that you discover through your research can help you respond to the questions that prompted your exploration.

Before you start your research, review your invention work to remind yourself of all that you know about your subject and the questions you have about it. Use the reporter's questions—*who, what, where, when, why,* and *how*—to get started. After you have decided what information you need, determine what kind of research will help you to gather that information. Then conduct research in the library and on the Internet.

You could conduct several kinds of research in response to the scenarios on pages 116–119. For Scenario 1, for example, in which you explore potential majors, you might visit the Web sites of various departments at your school to gather information about degree programs, courses offered, and careers of alumni. You might also visit the Web sites of companies that hire graduates in the fields that you are exploring. You could even search newspapers and the Internet to find job advertisements in those fields. You might interview graduating seniors to ask them about their experiences in the majors that you are exploring or people who hold the kinds of jobs that require those majors. Finally, you could search for and read blogs maintained by people who write about their professional fields and careers.

For help with locating sources of information, see Chapter 19; for help with taking notes and documenting your sources, see Chapter 20.

USING DIGITAL TECHNOLOGIES   Using the Internet to Gain an International Perspective

Writing to explore involves the hard work of experiencing and understanding *different perspectives.* A good way to learn about new perspectives is to read news reports from around the world, including those published in foreign newspapers and newsmagazines. Most major publications are now available in English translation. The following are some examples of Web sites maintained by foreign news organizations:

ABYZ News Links (A List of Links to Foreign News Sites)
www.abyznewslinks.com
French News
www.france24.com/en/
Japan Times
www.japantimes.co.jp/
Pravda (Russia)
http://english.pravda.ru/
London Times (UK)
www.timesonline.co.uk/tol/news/

Elle Caminante's Research

Student writer Elle Caminante wanted to explore possible careers in the world of art. In addition to browsing the Web, she went to her college library and examined recent issues of her school newspaper, some magazines, and several books. To find helpful articles, she used the search term "art—careers." She used the same search term to search her school's online library indexes. She also made a note to speak with local artists, for their personal perspectives. Based on what she read, she made some notes to herself in order to try to find some direction. Here are some of Caminante's notes toward a research plan:

- Check local business downtown to see if they sell works by local artists. They might provide useful contact information.

- Look at the college Web site for an idea of careers within the arts. Conduct more research on some of those careers.

- What about some of the artists and illustrators we think of as "famous" now? What were their early careers like? And did they face opposition from family and friends when they choose art as a major?

- Talk to local artists—there are a lot of them in this area who sell art at small businesses. I want to find out what other ways they get business and what kind of work they do either on the side or full-time with doing art on the side.

Writing Activity

Conducting Research

As you generate questions about your topic, consider where you might find the answers—books, journals, databases, the Internet, interviews, and so on. Begin to gather, read, or contact your sources. Manage your research by setting time (for example, two weeks) or quantity (say, ten sources) parameters to ensure that you meet your writing deadlines. Your instructor may specify the number and kinds of resources to focus on.

Reviewing Your Invention and Research

After you have conducted your research, review your invention work and notes. At this point, you may be tempted to decide on a **thesis statement**—a statement that summarizes the main point of your exploration. Even though you might already have a general idea of the conclusion your research is leading you to, it is often hard to know for certain what your thesis will be. Your thesis should come *from* your exploration. It is best to decide on your thesis after you have done a lot of invention work (listing, brainstorming, clustering, and so on) and research, or even after you construct your first draft.

For more on developing a thesis, see Chapter 13.

Strategies FOR Success | Curiosity

Successful writers are curious. Like good reporters, they ask questions, ask follow-up questions, and generally try to find out why things are the way they are and how things work. They like to explore ideas, problems, and various perspectives. Although curiosity is a powerful tool for approaching any kind of writing, it is especially helpful when you are writing to explore. To use your curiosity as you write to explore, pose the following kinds of questions and then consider many possible responses to them: How does the content of any of my courses relate to what I hope to accomplish in this writing project? Why do some people's views on my topic differ from those of others? What kinds of research will help me find answers to my questions? Who else has asked the kinds of questions I'm asking? Who has the answers to these questions?

As you seek answers to these and other questions, work with classmates to discuss possible approaches and answers. Curiosity can be contagious. When you and peers share your curiosity with one another, it can become more intense, driving everyone to ask more questions.

Organizing Your Ideas and Details

Because the purpose of writing an exploratory text is to examine an idea or concept from various perspectives, you will need to organize your thoughts in a useful manner. The questions that you need to ask yourself when deciding on your organization are all rhetorical:

- Who is your audience?
- Why might they be interested in your exploratory writing, or how can you make them interested in it? One way to emphasize the importance of your exploration to your audience is to show them why your subject is interesting to you.
- What is your purpose for writing—that is, why should your readers explore this topic with you?

Here is a brief outline of three possible organizational approaches to writing an exploratory paper:

Options FOR Organization
Options for Organizing an Exploratory Paper

Classify Ideas	Compare and Contrast Ideas	Relate Details Chronologically
Begin with your questions, perhaps from the least to the most important.	Note how many possible perspectives there may be on your subject and how they relate to one another.	Start from what happens first and move to later events.
Explain each question in detail and then provide possible answers.	Explore each perspective in detail.	Highlight events that were especially important to the subject and that will help readers get a better understanding of it.
Look at each question in detail. You may find that classifying both questions and answers is a useful method of organization.	Recognize that, because you began by noting multiple perspectives, comparison and contrast might be a useful method of organization.	Explore and explain various possible causes or effects, where they apply.
Offer follow-up questions that may lead to further exploration.	Explore your topic through various lenses to come to a better understanding of your subject, especially in relation to the different points of view on it.	End your paper at the present time, or with what seems like the final effect, if appropriate.
Perhaps conclude by suggesting that your exploration does not answer all the questions and that other, specified, questions now need to be asked.	Having presented multiple perspectives on your topic, indicate which conclusion your exploration has led you to.	

Constructing a Complete Draft

Once you know your subject, have recorded your ideas on paper or stored them in a computer file, and have conducted research, you are ready to construct your initial draft. It is possible that you will find a suitable organizational approach before you begin drafting, but you may also find it—or decide to change it—as you are drafting or even after you have constructed a draft. Also, as you write the first version of your exploratory paper, do not worry about editing your work.

Synthesizing and Integrating Sources into Your Draft: Quoting Information from Sources

Because effective writers use research, it is important to learn how to integrate sources in your own text. One way writers integrate sources is by incorporating direct quotations.

As mentioned in Chapter 20, there are a number of situations when using a direct quotation is most appropriate—for example, when you are quoting a primary source such as an expert you have interviewed. Generally, you should include a direct quotation—exactly what someone told you—when the comments are concise and support your own assertions. When someone you interview gives you an abundance of information, or if you interview a number of people, you may want to summarize their comments instead of using an exact quotation (for more on *summarizing*, see page 356; for more on *paraphrasing* someone's comments, see page 181).

Whether you are quoting a source directly or paraphrasing or summarizing the information, you should help readers by introducing the information so that they will understand why it is there and how it relates to the point you are making.

You will also need to document your source. For example, student writer Elle Caminante lets her readers know who Sky Martinez and Trace Glau are when she first mentions them. (See Caminante's final paper on pages 147–150.)

Note too that Caminante also asked both artists about their backgrounds, noting that Martinez "stumbled into painting" (paragraph 3), while Glau studied art for her undergraduate degree.

When you need to cite research, remember to do the following:

- Introduce the quotation (never just plop it into your text).
- Accurately report and document the source of the quotation.
- Explain how the quotation relates to your thesis.

One effective way to do these things is to surround any quotation with your own words: introduce the quotation and then connect that quote to your paper. Here is an example of how Caminante does so, in paragraph 5:

> Trace explains that many of the working artists she knows "join local artist groups, they attend art events to support their fellow artists," or even "join a co-op and work in the gallery that shows their artwork." For her, this is where a lot of the motivation to continue working and evolving as an artist comes from.

Parts of a Complete Draft

Introduction: One of the qualities of successful exploratory writing is that it grabs and holds readers' attention. There are a number of strategies for beginning your paper that will help you hook your readers:

- **Take your readers on the journey.** Let your readers know from the beginning that this is an exploration. Let them be your travel companions.

  The excerpt from "The Perils of Perfect Memory" by Daphne Strass-mann begins by noting that she "willingly deposit[s] bits of [her]self online every day . . ." and so her online "deposits" then become part of what she calls "a spontaneous external hard drive to our own memories." Readers will wonder if they do the same.

- **Ask one or more questions.** By asking questions, you present options and directions. Your exploratory writing will help you and your reader find solutions.

- **Set the stage by explaining the significance of your subject**, as Muriel MacDonald does in the first two paragraphs of "1 Billion Impressions: The Digital Climate March." MacDonald notes that while in 2010 Malcom Gladwell argued that "social media lacks the ability to form the kind of close, personal ties that push people to take the drastic action necessary to enact change," in fact social media has not only that kind of power, but much more.

Writing Activity

Constructing a Complete Draft

After selecting an organizational approach, write a complete draft of your paper that explores your topic. In exploratory writing, your thesis statement may not become apparent until after you have completed a first draft. Use as much detail as possible—the more you get down on paper initially, the easier it will be to flesh out and revise your paper later. Your first draft will likely lead to additional questions and answers you will want to include in your revision(s).

Body: The body of your paper will lead you and your readers through your exploration process. You may choose one or several different kinds of organization. You might try classification, for example, where by grouping ideas in like categories, you discover similarities. However, comparison and contrast, where you discover both similarities and differences, might be more helpful. Or you might discover that cause and effect is the most powerful kind of organization for your paper.

Conclusion: Following your exploration, your conclusion should leave your readers feeling satisfied.

- If in your exploration you discover that there will be consequences if certain events occur, you may choose to present these final consequences.

- If you discover that your exploration has led to even more questions, you may simply state the new questions that need to be researched.

- If your exploration does lead you to a reasonable conclusion, state that conclusion, explaining to readers how you reached it. Muriel MacDonald, for example, learns that social media has more power than previously imagined. She concludes by noting, "If social media is the new place for mass organizing and serious conversations," it can bring people together and so lead to real change—for "To change everything, you need everyone."

Title: You might think that you need to craft a title before you start writing, but often it is more useful to get a first draft down on paper or into a computer file and then consider possible titles. For an exploratory paper, your title should indicate your subject and give your reader a reason to want to explore it with you. The title "Why I Blog," for example, indicates that its author has a personal approach to his subject.

Elle Caminante's First Draft: Starving Artists

After doing research and deciding on an organizational approach, Elle Caminante was ready to begin her first draft. As she wrote, she did not concern herself with grammar, punctuation, or mechanics, but instead tried to get her questions and answers and ideas on paper. Note that Caminante started her paper by mentioning famous artists who initially struggled when they were starting out—one perspective about (and stereotype of) artists generally. She then went on, as suggested by one of the organizational methods described above, to explore her topic "through various lenses to come to a better understanding of [her] subject, especially in relation to the different points of views on it." (The numbers in circles refer to peer comments—see page 144.)

Starving Artists?
Elle Caminante

It is said that Van Gogh only sold one painting in his lifetime—and that was to a friend for a pittance; Charles Schulz had his early comic strips rejected over and over again and was even turned down for a job at Disney before his *Peanuts* comic strip took off; not until centuries after his death, did El Greco finally receive acclaim for his talent. ❶

In spite of the stereotype of the starving artist—someone who makes little to no money, but stubbornly slogs on in her or his creative endeavors, much to the dismay of family and friends—plenty of people have vibrant artistic careers. Several artists local to my community sell their art at small businesses like coffee shops and bookstores around town. Others have art on display at downtown galleries, while still others have their own websites from which they sell their work. I was able to get in contact with a couple of these local artists, Sky Martinez and Trace Glau, and ask them what their careers in the arts are like: how they promote and sell their art, and what kinds of careers support their creative work.

Sky is an artist who creates a lot of Native American and spiritual art. ❷ She does acrylic, watercolor, and oil painting, and also makes jewelry and ceremonial tools. Sky has no formal training in art, but she has always been able to draw and has felt compelled to express herself artistically. She stumbled into painting by accident, when a friend asked her if she could paint. When she said no, the friend asked, "Have you ever tried?" She decided she would give it a try, so she went out and bought some paint and poster board; she found that not only could she paint, but she loved it. Now some of her work is featured at a local gallery whose mission is to support emerging local artists.

Trace is a professional artist who works in a variety of media. She has done print-making, watercolor, and recycled art; she now does woodwork, primarily handmade wooden utensils. She says this is a good fit for her because, in her own words, "I wanted folks to be able to USE my artwork." Trace studied art as an undergraduate, focusing on studio arts because "Originally I wanted to teach K–12 and so I wanted a good firm foundation." She later decided she wanted to teach at the college level instead, so she went on to pursue a master's degree in education. She now teaches art part-time at the local community college in addition to producing her own art.

To both Sky and Trace, community plays a big role both in making art and in making any kind of a living off of it. Trace explains that many of the working artists she knows "join local artist groups, they attend art events to support their fellow artists," or even "join a co-op and work in the gallery that shows their artwork." For her, this is where a lot of the motivation to continue working and evolving as an artist comes from. Similarly, Sky is part of a local collaborative. ❸ One of the tremendous benefits of that for her is the opportunity to be mentored by more experienced artists, who give advice on both making and selling art. Additionally, she spends two to three hours a week volunteering at the gallery where her work is featured.

It is difficult to make a living only by producing art. Many artists decide on an art-related career to support themselves. ❹ One of these jobs that really appeals to me is that of becoming an art teacher; teaching allows artists to stay connected with the art community, to continue making their own art, and to help others grow artistically. Some of the possible avenues for art teachers are freelance art teachers, traditional K–12 teachers (elementary, middle, or high school), or college teachers. All of these options require a background in art and specific training.

To be a freelance art teacher, including a teacher in after-school programs and summer enrichment programs, artists usually need to have a bachelor's degree and a professional experience, or in some cases, just extensive experience—usually showcased in a portfolio. Requirements for this kind of work varies, so your best bet is just to do an internet search to see what's out there. There are a lot of great programs that work with youth or adults. The downside to positions like these is that they don't always pay well and they are often only temporary or contract positions.

To be a K–12 art teacher, ❺ artists generally have to earn a bachelor's degree in some area of art, usually art education, and then go through a teacher licensing or credentialing program. These programs are completed through a university and usually last about a year, including several months of student teaching. Student teachers work with a master teacher who has a lot of classroom experience; they learn how to put into practice all the things they've learned in their education programs and they get hands-on experience working with students. According the Bureau of Labor Statistics, K–12 art teachers make $50,000–$56,000 annually.

College art teachers or professors make an average of $76,000 a year, ❻ but again the process is more rigorous. Many colleges and universities require a Master of Fine Arts (MFA) degree with a particular specialization along with some teaching experience. This degree can take up to three years to complete after graduating with a bachelor's degree. Luckily, MFA students can often work as teaching assistants while they are completing their degree to gain some of the experience they will need. Then they can teach some art classes part time if they still need more experience before getting hired full time.

With so many of the current teaching opportunities ❼ available, artists do not have to starve to produce art. The key is to find a career that enhances the artistic side while still providing a paycheck. Teaching not only allows artists to make a living, but it also enables them to work with other artistic people and share what they've learned. As Sky stated in her interview with me, one of the best parts of being an artist is the ability to use art to "inspire and move in others what inspired and moved you in the first place."

Works Cited

Glau, Trace. Personal E-mail. 30 Nov. 2015.

Martinez, Sky. Personal Interview. 14 Dec. 2015.

Student Comments on Caminante's First Draft

❶ These are interesting as anecdotes, but I don't really see a thesis. What is this essay going to be about?

❷ What does this look like? It would be great to see some examples of both of these artists' work.

❸ What does this mean?

❹ You may want to join these sentences together so that this doesn't sound so choppy.

❺ Is there another way you can start this paragraph? This sounds just like the last one.

❻ I'm guessing you already know that you need to cite this.

❼ Do you know how many? That would be interesting and more specific.

 ## Revising

Revising means re-seeing and rethinking your exploratory text. The most effective way to revise your work is to read it as if you are reading it for the first time. Reading your work in this way is difficult to do, of course—which is why writers often put their work aside for a time. The more you can see your writing as if for the first time, the more you will respond to it as your real readers might, questioning and exploring it. As you reread the first draft of your exploratory writing, here are some questions to ask yourself:

• What are the most important questions, the ones I would really like to have answered? How well have I answered them?

VISUAL *Thinking* | Going beyond Words to Achieve Your Goals

For her assignment, student writer Elle Caminante decided to explore her interests in art and how she might find a career in that area. Art, of course, is a topic that lends itself to illustration, particularly with vivid, interesting, and often unusual photographs.

Because she was interested in counted cross-stitch, Elle sought out a local artist, Courtney Ann Glau, who for years has constructed beautiful pieces of art.

Figure 6.1 is an example of a regional design created by the Sani people, who reside in the Yunnan province of China. There are more than 35 thousand stitches in this piece, which measures 9" x 9" and has 22 stitches to the inch.

Artist Glau told student writer Caminante that counted cross-stitch blends many elements together (even-weave linen, silk floss, a range of colors, etc.) and they have to be perfectly "stitched" to create the piece of art.

Of course, Caminante would need to document the sources for any photos

© Greg Glau

FIGURE 6.1 An example of a regional design created by the Sani people of Yunnan province

she uses, and if she intends to make her project available online, she would need to determine whether the photos are protected by copyright and, if so, seek permission to publish them from the copyright holders.

- How well have I answered the questions that will help me understand every facet of my subject?
- How well do I understand the draft? What parts are confusing or need more information? What research might I need to conduct to clarify my ideas further?
- What information, if any, might I provide as a visual?

Technology can help you revise and, later, edit your writing more easily. Use your word processor's track-changes tool to try out revisions and editing changes. After you've had time to think about the possible changes, you can "accept" or "reject" them. Also, you can use your word processor's comment tool to write reminders to yourself when you get stuck with a revision or some editing task.

Because it is so difficult even for experienced writers to see their emerging writing with a fresh eye, it is almost always useful to ask classmates, friends, or family members to read and comment on drafts.

WRITER'S *Workshop* | Responding to Full Drafts

As you read and respond to your class-mates' papers (and as they comment on yours), focus on the exploratory nature of this assignment, but from a reader's perspective. Be sure to ask questions of their writing and respond to their ideas by exploring your reactions and responses to their thoughts.

Working in pairs or groups of three, read each others' papers, and then offer your classmates comments that will help them see both their papers' strengths and places where they need to develop their ideas further. Use the following questions to guide your responses to the writer's draft:

- What is your first impression? How interested are you in reading beyond the first paragraph? Why? Do you have any suggestions for improving the title?

- What do you like about the draft? Provide positive and encouraging feedback to the writer. How interest-ing, educational, or useful did you find this exploration? Why?

- What is the focus of the paper? How does the focus emerge as you read? How well do you understand how the writer comes to her or his conclusion?

- How easily can you follow the writ-er's thought process? Comment on how the writer's exploratory writing helps you better understand the questions or problems posed in the introduction.

- How thoroughly does the writer explore the subject? How might the writer explore it more fully?

- How viable are the differing perspec-tives? How appropriate are the writ-er's sources?

- Reread the conclusion: How logically does it follow from the rest of the paper? Were you surprised by the conclusion? What are other possible conclusions based on the informa-tion the writer has presented?

- What do you see as the main weak-nesses of this paper? How might the writer improve the text?

Responding to Readers' Comments

Once they have received feedback on their writing from peers, teachers, friends, and others, writers have to figure out what to do with that feedback. You may decide to reject some comments, of course. Other comments, though, deserve your attention, as they are the words of real readers speaking to you about how to improve your text. You may find that comments from more than one reader contradict each other. In that case, use your own judgment to decide which reader's comments are on the right track.

In the final version of Elle Caminante's paper, on pages 147–150, you can see how she responded to her peers' comments, as well as to her own review of her first draft.

KNOWLEDGE OF CONVENTIONS

When effective writers edit their work, they attend to the conventions that will help readers move through their writing effortlessly. By paying attention to these conventions in your writing, you make reading a more pleasant experience for readers.

 ## Editing

The last task in any writing project is editing—the final polishing of your document. When you edit and polish your writing, you make changes to your sentence structure and word choice to improve your style and to make your writing clearer and more concise. You also check your work to make sure it adheres to conventions of grammar, usage, punctuation, mechanics, and spelling, as well as genre conventions. Use the spell-check function of your word-processing program, but be sure to double-check your spelling personally. If you have used sources in your paper, make sure you are following the documentation style your instructor requires.

See Chapter 20 for more on documenting sources using MLA or APA style.

As with overall revision of your work, this final editing and polishing is most effective if you can put your text aside for a few days and come back to it

---

ROUND-ROBIN EDITING WITH A FOCUS ON

WRITER'S *Workshop* | **Round-Robin Editing with a Focus on Fragments**

Because exploratory writing often includes incomplete thoughts, writers sometimes inadvertently use sentence fragments to express their thinking. A sentence fragment is missing one or more of the following elements: a subject, a verb, or a complete thought.

Some fragments lack a subject, a verb, or both:

FRAGMENT   College sports are popular. *Generating lots of money for schools with successful teams.*

SENTENCE   College sports are popular. They generate lots of money for schools with successful teams.

Other fragments have subjects and verbs, but they begin with a subordinating word like *because* or *although* and so are not complete thoughts:

FRAGMENT   *Although I have played football in high school and college.* I'm not good enough to play on a professional team.

SENTENCE   Although I have played football in high school and college, I'm not good enough to play on a professional team.

Work with two peers to look for sentence fragments. For each fragment, decide whether to connect it to a nearby sentence or to recast it into a complete sentence.

with fresh eyes. Because checking conventions is easier said than done, though, we strongly recommend that you ask classmates, friends, and tutors to read your work to find sentence problems that you do not see.

To assist you with editing, we offer here a round-robin editing activity focused on sentence fragments, a common concern in all writing.

Genres, Documentation, and Format

If you are writing an academic paper, follow the conventions for the discipline in which you are writing and the requirements of your instructor. However, if you are exploring potential majors (Scenario 1), you might choose to write a letter or an e-mail message to family members. If you are doing a personal exploration (Scenario 2), you might want to write a journal entry. If you have chosen to do a personal exploration, you might avoid writing a blog entry, because blogs can have thousands of readers—including potential employers.

If you have used material from outside sources, including visuals, give credit to those sources, using the documentation style required by the discipline you are working in and by your instructor.

For advice on writing in different genres, see Appendix C. For guidelines for formatting and documenting papers in MLA or APA style, see Chapter 20.

A Writer Achieves Her Goal: Elle Caminante's Final Draft

As you read the final version of Elle Caminante's exploratory paper, consider what makes it effective. Following the reading you will find some questions to help you conduct an exploration of this paper.

ELLE CAMINANTE

Starving Artists: Myth or Reality?

EXPLORATORY ESSAY

It is said that Van Gogh sold only one painting in his lifetime—and that   1
was to a friend for a pittance. Charles Schulz had his early comic strips rejected over and over again and was even turned down for a job at Disney before his *Peanuts* comic strip took off. Not until centuries after his death, did El Greco finally receive acclaim for his talent. With stories like this, it's no wonder that the term "starving artist" has become so commonplace and has

One of Caminante's peer reviewers asked for a strong thesis statement, which Caminante added at the end of her first paragraph.

scared so many people away from pursuing an education or career in the arts. What people don't realize is that having an art-based career can allow them to make a living out of art.

In spite of the stereotype of the starving artist—someone who makes little 2 to no money, but stubbornly slogs on in her or his creative endeavors, much to the dismay of family and friends—plenty of people have vital artistic careers. Several artists local to my community sell their art at small businesses such as coffee shops and bookstores around town. Others have art on display at downtown galleries, while still others have their own Web sites from which they sell their work. I was able to get in contact with a couple of these local artists, Sky Martinez and Trace Glau, and ask them what their careers in the arts are like: how they promote and sell their art, and what kinds of careers support their creative work.

One of her peer reviewers suggested adding some examples of the artists' work, which Caminante did in Figures 1 and 2, below.

Sky is an artist who creates a lot of Native American and spiritual art 3 (see figure 1). She does acrylic, watercolor, and oil painting, and also makes jewelry and ceremonial tools. Sky has no formal training in art, but she has always been able to draw and has felt compelled to express herself artistically. She stumbled into painting by accident, when a friend asked her if she could paint. When she said no, the friend asked, "Have you ever tried?" She decided she would give it a try, so she bought some paint and poster board; she found that she could paint, and she loved it. Now some of her work is featured at a local gallery whose mission is to support emerging local artists.

Trace is a professional artist who works in a variety of media. She has 4 done printmaking, watercolor, and recycled art; she now does woodwork, primarily handmade wooden utensils (see figure 2). She says this is a good fit for her because, in her own words, "I wanted folks to be able to USE my artwork." Trace studied art as an undergraduate, focusing on studio arts because "originally I wanted to teach K–12 and so I wanted a good firm foundation." She later decided she wanted to teach at the college level instead, so she went on to pursue a master's degree in education. She now teaches art part-time at the local community college in addition to producing her own art.

A peer asked for an explanation of "collaborative," which Caminante provides here.

To both Sky and Trace, community plays a big role both in making art 5 and in making any kind of a living off of it. Trace explains that many of the working artists she knows "join local artist groups, they attend art events to support their fellow artists," or even "join a co-op and work in the gallery that shows their artwork." For her, this is where a lot of the motivation to continue working and evolving as an artist comes from. Similarly, Sky is part of a local collaborative, a group of artists who work together and encourage each other artistically. One of the tremendous benefits of that for her is the opportunity to be mentored by more experienced artists, who give advice on both making and selling art. Additionally, she spends two to three hours a week volunteering at the gallery where her work is featured.

© Grace Sky Martinez

FIGURE 1 A Native American ceremonial piece

© Trace Glau

FIGURE 2 Handmade wooden utensils

Because it is so difficult to make a living only by producing art, many 6
artists decide on an art-related career to support themselves. One of these jobs that really appeals to me is that of becoming an art teacher because teaching allows artists to stay connected with the art community, to continue making their own art, and to help others grow artistically. Some of the possible avenues for art teachers are freelance art teachers, traditional K–12 teachers (elementary, middle, or high school), or college teachers. All of these options require a background in art and specific training.

To be a freelance art teacher, including a teacher in after-school programs 7
and summer enrichment programs, artists usually need to have a bachelor's degree and a professional experience, or in some cases, just extensive experience—usually showcased in a portfolio. Requirements for this kind of work varies, so your best bet is to conduct an Internet search to see what's out there. There are a lot of great programs that work with youth, such as the Artists In Schools programs that many states sponsor, or with adults, like summer enrichment courses taught on college or university campuses. The downside to positions like these is that they don't always pay well and they are often only temporary or contract positions.

Becoming a K–12 art teacher is a longer process, but it's also more straight- 8
forward. Artists generally have to earn a bachelor's degree in some area of art,

A peer noted that two of Caminante's paragraphs began the same way, so here she changed the opening sentence of this paragraph.

usually art education, and then go through a teacher licensing or credentialing program. These programs are completed through a university and usually last about a year, including several months of student teaching. Student teachers work with a master teacher who has a lot of classroom experience; they learn how to put into practice all the things they've learned in their education programs, and they get hands-on experience working with students. According the Bureau of Labor Statistics, K–12 art teachers make $50,000–56,000 annually.

College art teachers or professors make an average of $76,000 a year, but again the process is more rigorous (United States, Dept. of Labor). Many colleges and universities require a Master of Fine Arts (MFA) degree with a particular specialization along with some teaching experience. This degree can take up to three years to complete after graduating with a bachelor's degree. Luckily, MFA students can often work as teaching assistants while they are completing their degree to gain some of the experience they will need. Then they can teach some art classes part time if they still need more experience before getting hired full time.

9

As of 2014, there were more than 70,000 art teachers employed in the U.S. at the postsecondary level alone (US Dept. of Labor). With all of the current teaching opportunities available, artists do not have to starve to produce art. The key is to find a career that enhances the artistic side while still providing a paycheck. Teaching not only allows them to make a living, but it also enables them to work with other artistic individuals and share what they've learned. As Sky Martinez stated in her interview with me, one of the best parts of being an artist is the ability to use art to "inspire and move in others what inspired and moved you in the first place."

10

Works Cited

Glau, Trace. Personal E-mail. 30 Nov. 2015.

Martinez, Sky. Personal Interview. 14 Dec. 2015.

United States, Department of Labor, Bureau of Labor Statistics. *Occupational Employment Statistics: Occupational Employment and Wages,* Mar. 2015, www.bls.gov/oes/2014/may/oes_nat.htm.

Caminante added a citation to show where her information came from.

A peer asked for more specific detail, which Caminante added here (with her source).

This paper follows MLA guidelines for in-text citations and works cited. Note that while URLs are optional, MLA strongly recommends including them when possible.

UNDERSTANDING A WRITER'S GOALS: QUESTIONS TO CONSIDER AND DISCUSS

Rhetorical Knowledge: The Writer's Situation and Rhetoric

1. **Audience:** Who is the intended audience for Caminante's essay? What in the essay makes you think so?

2. **Purpose:** What does Caminante hope will happen when people read her essay?

3. **Voice and tone:** How would you describe Caminante's tone in her essay?

4. **Responsibility:** How responsibly has Caminante reported information about being an artist to you, her audience? To herself? Explain your answers.

5. **Context, format, and genre:** Caminante wrote this paper for a college course. If you were an editor for your local newspaper, would you consider hiring Caminante to write about local artists? Why or why not?

6. In an exploratory essay, the writer starts with a premise and then follows one or more lines of inquiry to discover something new. Do you think Caminante has adequately explored the possibility of a career as an artist? Why or why not?

Critical Thinking: The Writer's Ideas and Your Personal Response

7. What is the main point of Caminante's essay? How well does she focus the essay?

How does she support her main idea? What questions do you still have about having a career as an artist?

8. How easily can you relate to what Caminante writes about? Why?

Composing Processes and Knowledge of Conventions: The Writer's Strategies

9. In what ways does Caminante establish her ethos, or her credibility, in this exploratory essay?

10. How effective are Caminante's introduction and conclusion? Why?

11. What do the two photographs add to Caminante's essay? What other visuals might she have used?

Inquiry and Research: Ideas for Further Exploration

12. In what other ways might Caminante have researched a career as an artist? What sources might she have investigated?

Self-Assessment: Reflecting on Your Goals

Now that you have constructed a piece of exploratory writing, go back and consider the goals at the beginning of this chapter (see pages 113–114). Reflecting on your writing process and the exploratory text you have constructed—and putting such reflections *in writing*—is another kind of exploration: you are exploring, thinking about, and commenting on your own work as a writer. Answering the following questions will help you reflect on what you have learned from this assignment:

 ## Rhetorical Knowledge

- *Audience:* What have you learned about addressing an audience in exploratory writing?
- *Purpose:* What have you learned about the purposes of exploratory writing?
- *Rhetorical situation:* How did the writing context affect your exploratory text?
- *Voice and tone:* How would you describe your voice in this project? Your tone? How do they contribute to the effectiveness of your exploratory essay?
- *Context, medium, and genre:* How did your context determine the medium and genre you chose, and how did those decisions affect your writing?

 ## Critical Thinking, Reading, and Writing

- *Learning/inquiry:* How did you decide what to focus on in your exploratory writing? How did you judge what was most and least important?
- *Responsibility:* How did you fulfill your responsibility to your readers?
- *Reading and research:* What did you learn about exploratory writing from the reading selections you read for this chapter? What research did you conduct? How sufficient was the research you did?
- *Skills:* As a result of writing this exploration, how have you become a more critical thinker, reader, and writer? What critical thinking, reading, and writing skills do you hope to develop further in your next writing project? How will you work on them?

Writing Processes

- *Invention:* What invention strategies were most useful to you? Why?
- *Organizing your ideas and details:* What organization did you use? How successful was it?
- *Revising:* What one revision did you make that you are most satisfied with? What are the strongest and the weakest parts of the paper or other piece of writing you wrote for this chapter? Why?
- *Working with peers:* How did your instructor or peer readers help you by making comments and suggestions about your writing? How could you have made better use of the comments and suggestions you received? How could your peer readers help you more on your next assignment? How might you help them more, in the future, with the comments and suggestions you make on their texts?
- *Visuals:* If you used photographs or other visuals to help present your exploration to readers, what did you learn about incorporating these elements?
- *Writing habits:* What "writerly habits" have you developed, modified, or improved on as you constructed the writing assignment for this chapter?

For help with freewriting and clustering, as well as other strategies for discovery and learning, see Chapter 4.

Knowledge of Conventions

- *Editing:* What sentence problem did you find most frequently in your writing? How will you avoid that problem in future assignments?
- *Genre:* What conventions of the genre you were using, if any, gave you problems?
- *Documentation:* If you used sources for your paper, what documentation style did you use? What problems, if any, did you have with it?

If you are preparing a course portfolio, file your written reflections so that you can return to them when you next work on your portfolio. Refer to Chapter 1 (page 12) for a sample reflection by a student.

Text Credits

Writing to Inform

© Bloomberg/Getty Imagees

We all deal with *information* every day of our lives. We learn about facts, ideas, and ways of doing things, and then communicate that information to others through spoken or written words and, at times, graphic or other visual means.

Many newspaper articles are examples of informative writing. The headlines from *The New York Times* online demonstrate that the primary goal of headline writers is simply to provide information. Readers don't expect headlines to contain elements of persuasion, argumentation, or evaluation.

We could argue, of course, that any type of writing has elements of persuasion, and by selecting certain words and emphasizing particular facts, a writer will influence a reader's response. However, the goal of most informative writing, especially the informative writing you will do in college, *is* to be as neutral as possible, so it is the writer's responsibility to present information impartially.

As a college student, you read informative writing in your textbooks and other assigned reading and are expected to write informative responses on tests and to provide information in the papers your instructors assign. While you may think that you encounter informative writing only in your textbooks and in newspapers or magazines, you can easily find examples of such reading and writing in each area of your life. In your professional life, for example, you may need to read (or construct) a training manual, while in your civic life, you may be called on to write a voter guide about two candidates, presenting their positions without revealing your personal views.

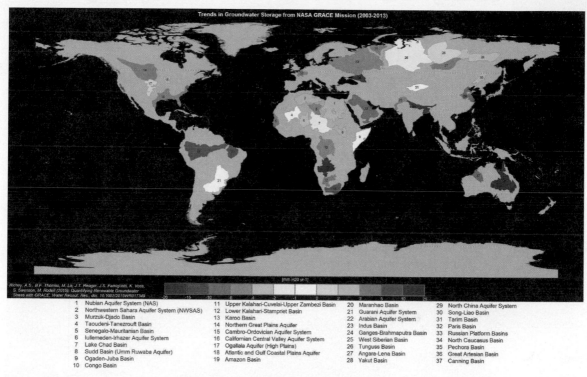

Trends in Groundwater Storage from NASA GRACE Mission (2003-2013)

[mm H20 yr-1]

Richey, A.S., B.F. Thomas, M. Lo, J.T. Reager, J.S. Famiglietti, K. Voss,
S. Swenson, M. Rodell (2015): Quantifying Renewable Groundwater
Stress with GRACE, Water Resour. Res., doi: 10.1002/2015WR017349

1 Nubian Aquifer System (NAS)	11 Upper Kalahari-Cuvelai-Upper Zambezi Basin	20 Maranhao Basin	29 North China Aquifer System
2 Northwestern Sahara Aquifer System (NWSAS)	12 Lower Kalahari-Stampriet Basin	21 Guarani Aquifer System	30 Song-Liao Basin
3 Murzuk-Djado Basin	13 Karoo Basin	22 Arabian Aquifer System	31 Tarim Basin
4 Taoudeni-Tanezrouft Basin	14 Northern Great Plains Aquifer	23 Indus Basin	32 Paris Basin
5 Senegalo-Mauritanian Basin	15 Cambro-Ordovician Aquifer System	24 Ganges-Brahmaputra Basin	33 Russian Platform Basins
6 Iullemeden-Irhazer Aquifer System	16 Californian Central Valley Aquifer System	25 West Siberian Basin	34 North Caucasus Basin
7 Lake Chad Basin	17 Ogallala Aquifer (High Plains)	26 Tunguss Basin	35 Pechora Basin
8 Sudd Basin (Umm Ruwaba Aquifer)	18 Atlantic and Gulf Coastal Plains Aquifer	27 Angara-Lena Basin	36 Great Artesian Basin
9 Ogaden-Juba Basin	19 Amazon Basin	28 Yakut Basin	37 Canning Basin
10 Congo Basin			

Source: UC Irvine/NASA/JPL-Caltech

This informative graphic and its accompanying text reflect data collected over a 13-year period by NASA to measure trends in groundwater storage. The goal of this graphic is to inform its audience. It does so effectively by emphasizing facts and using neutral language.

Setting Your Goals for *Informative Writing*

 Rhetorical Knowledge (pp. 158–162)

- **Audience:** Consider what your readers need to know—and how you can interest them in that information. What about your subject might your audience be *most* interested in? What information might readers consider unusual?
- **Purpose:** You want readers to understand the information you are sharing, so your writing must be clear. Considering what your audience might *do* with the information that you provide will help you decide how best to share it with them.
- **Rhetorical situation:** In an informational essay, you are writing to share information; your readers are reading your text to learn about (and—you hope—to understand) that information.
- **Voice and tone:** Generally, informational writing has a neutral tone. Sometimes, depending on the situation, an informational essay can have a humorous tone.
- **Context, medium, and genre:** The genre you use to present your information is determined by your purpose: to inform. Decide on the best medium and genre to use to present your information to the audience you want to reach.

 Critical Thinking, Reading, and Writing (pp. 162–175)

- **Learning/inquiry:** Because you are helping your readers learn about the subject of your text, decide on the most important aspects of your topic and explain them in a clear, focused way.
- **Responsibility:** You have a responsibility to represent your information honestly and accurately.
- **Reading and research:** Your research must be accurate and as complete as possible, to allow you to present thoughtful, reliable information about your subject.

Writing Processes (pp. 176–189)

- **Invention:** Choose invention strategies that will help you generate and locate information about your topic.
- **Organizing your ideas and details:** Find the most effective way to present your information to your readers so they can easily understand it.
- **Revising:** Read your work with a critical eye, to make certain that it fulfills the assignment and displays the qualities of good informative writing.
- **Working with peers:** Your classmates will make suggestions that indicate the parts of your text they found difficult to understand so you can work to clarify. Consider the ways that technology might improve the peer review process.

Knowledge of Conventions (pp. 189–195)

- **Editing:** Informative writing benefits from the correct use of modifiers, so the round-robin activity on page 190 focuses on avoiding misplaced or dangling modifiers.
- **Genres for informative writing:** Possible genres include newspaper or magazine articles, informative letters, informative essays, and Web documents.
- **Documentation:** If you have relied on sources outside of your experience, cite them using the appropriate documentation style. What are some ways that technology can make your documentation more accurate?

RHETORICAL KNOWLEDGE

When you provide information to readers, you need to consider what your readers might already know about your topic. You should also ask yourself, "What other information have I learned about through my research that would interest them and be helpful for them to know?" You will also need to decide what medium and genre will help you communicate that information to your audience most effectively.

Writing to Inform in Your College Classes

Much of the writing you will do for your college classes will be informative, as will much of the reading you will do. College textbooks are, almost by definition, informative. You would expect your American history textbook to provide accurate information about the Civil War, for example. The purpose of most of the reading you will do in college is to learn new information—and many writing assignments will require you to relate new facts and concepts to other facts and concepts you have already read and learned about, as in the following examples:

- Your psychology instructor may ask you to read several essays or books about recovered memory and to *synthesize* the information they contain—to explain to a reader the most important points made in each text and how the information in one text agrees or disagrees with the information in the others.

- Your art instructor may ask that you trace the development of a specific approach to art, providing examples and details that show its evolution over time.

- Your political science instructor may ask you to examine "presidential bloopers"—where presidential candidates did or said something awkward—and explain in writing how those instances affected the outcome of the election.

The "Ways of Writing" feature (page 160) presents different genres that can be used when writing to inform in your college classes.

Writing to Inform for Life

In addition to your academic work, you will also construct informative texts for the other areas of your life, including your professional career, your civic life, and your personal life.

Much of the writing done in professional settings is designed to inform and often to teach. If you have or have had a job, for example, consider how you would explain the details of your job to someone who is going to take it over: What information would that person need to know to do your job effectively? How could you best relay that information to your replacement? What you have just considered are the details that make up a training manual, a type of informative writing that most businesses have in one form or another.

Likewise, much civic writing is designed to provide information to the residents of a certain area to help them decide issues or take advantage of community resources and programs. Perhaps people who live in a neighborhood are being encouraged to participate in a community program such as a citizen's watch campaign, a civic event that would almost certainly require informative writing.

You will also do a great deal of informative writing in your personal life, ranging from notes to family members to Facebook conversations with relatives and friends. While you may feel more comfortable jotting down information for your friends and family than you do for other audiences, you probably feel especially obligated to provide accurate and useful information because you care about your personal relationships.

The "Ways of Writing" feature presents different genres that can be used when writing to inform for life.

Scenarios for Writing | Assignment Options

The following writing assignments call for you to construct informative texts. Each is in the form of a *scenario,* a brief story that provides some context for your writing. The scenario gives you a sense of who your audience is and what you need to accomplish. Starting on page 175, you will find guidelines for completing whatever assignment option you choose or that is assigned to you.

Writing for College

SCENARIO 1 Informative Essay on Littering

Your sociology class has been focusing on student behavior. Just last week a classmate mentioned the problem of trash on campus: "Our campus is a big mess because students just don't care," she said. "They ignore the trash cans and recycling boxes and just toss their garbage everywhere!"

Although this scenario focuses on littering, if you prefer you may write about some other issue on your campus. Your task is not to propose a solution for the issue; rather, your task is to inform other members of the campus community that a problem exists.

USING DIGITAL TECHNOLOGIES | **Using a Camera When Making Observations**

A digital camera or your cell phone camera can be an ideal tool for any assignment that asks you to make observations. Once you have transferred the photographs of your subject to your computer, it is easy to add them to your text. Be sure, though, to get written permission from anyone you photo- graph before using images of that person in your work. If your instructor allows you to submit your work electronically, you may wish to incorporate video and sound as well into your final project. You can do so by using a screen capture program such as Snagit, Jing, or QuickTime Player.

Ways of Writing to Inform

Genres for Your College Classes	Sample Situation	Advantages of the Genre	Limitations of the Genre
Academic essay	Your sociology professor asks you to make observations about the group behavior of a campus organization (the volleyball team, the debating club, and so on).	This project enables you to engage in primary research that you design; your readers can learn from your research findings.	It is difficult to be objective and present information in a neutral tone; you need to take lots of detailed notes to have sufficient research information.
Review of literature	Your economics teacher asks you to review the current literature on the causes of the Great Depression.	This project gives your reader a better understanding of the economic issues of the time period.	A limited number of texts can be examined, so your focus will be narrow. In many fields, the most current literature is seen as the most important.
Letter to your college newspaper	You want to write a letter to your school newspaper that informs students about an upcoming campus event sponsored by several student organizations.	Your letter will allow you to reach your intended audience and encourage them to attend.	In only a limited amount of space, you must provide all of the details so others will know what the event is, where it will be held, and when. It might not be published.
Profile	Your English professor asks you to make observations and construct a profile—a neutral description—about a place on your campus (the campus recreation center, for example).	You observe and take notes with lots of description, so your readers can "see" what the place looks like, who inhabits this place, what happens there, what the location is like, and so on.	The writer generally does not analyze why things happen in this place, so there is a limited understanding of why the place is as it is.
Narrated time-line	Your philosophy professor asks you to create a time-line of influential philosophers, showing when they lived and outlining their main ideas.	A time-line is a useful way to provide information, and is supplemented with text about the philosophers and their major ideas.	There is lots of ground to cover; it shouldn't be just a time-line showing when the philosophers lived. It will be difficult to describe complex thoughts and ideas and show relationships in limited space.
Genres for Life	**Sample Situation**	**Advantages of the Genre**	**Limitations of the Genre**
Brochure	You need to explain what a nonprofit organization does, what services it provides, and so on.	A brochure can provide readers with a brief overview of the agency's mission and services.	There is limited space for presenting information about the agency's specific services.
Information-sharing blog	You would like to share information about candidates in a local election.	A blog can be an easy way to update and share information with a wide audience.	Someone will need to monitor the comments for inappropriate posts. It should be updated often.
Fact sheet	You want to provide facts about a proposed tax increase for your neighbors, most of whom have children in the same school district as you.	A fact sheet allows you to present the details objectively so that your neighbors can make up their own minds.	It may be hard to remain neutral if you feel strongly one way or the other about the tax proposal.
Business comparison	The company you work for asks you to compare several locations for a possible expansion of the business.	By comparing and contrasting the details about each location, not advocating for one or the other, you let your readers make up their own minds.	With a vested interest in the decision, it is difficult to present information without making a recommendation.
Instructions	To help train new employees, you are asked to prepare a set of instructions for a specific task you do at work.	Step-by-step instructions will give enough detail for someone to understand and to complete the task.	It may be difficult to provide the right kind of detail—not too much and not too little.

Writing Assignment: Construct an informative paper, based on two sets of information: (1) your observations of the problem on campus, and (2) interviews you conduct with at least two of your classmates, asking them what their thoughts are on why some students don't use trash cans as they should, or on the alternate problem you have chosen to write about.

Writing for Life

SCENARIO 2 Civic Writing: Brochure for a Local Service Organization

Many colleges and universities have a service-learning class or classes that incorporate service-learning activities, such as volunteer work, into a class project. Service-learning opportunities include tutoring young children, helping with food banks, volunteering at rest homes, and other ways of serving the community in some manner.

Writing Assignment: Select a local nonprofit service agency and learn about services it provides to your community. Your research might include looking at the Web page for the agency, interviewing people who work there, examining any literature they provide, and volunteering with the agency (probably the best way to learn about it). Then construct a brochure for the agency that outlines the work it performs for the community. Think of this brochure as one the agency would actually provide and use. In other words, construct a brochure as if you actually worked for the agency and were asked to develop such a handout Include illustrations that help show what the agency does, the people it serves, and so on.

As with any writing assignment, consider who your audience might be and what they might already know about the agency. What else would you like them to know? What kind(s) of information would be useful to your audience? Are there photos or tables that might show what the agency does, how it spends any donations it receives, or something about the people who work there and the people the agency serves?

SCENARIO 3 Personal Writing: An E-mail Message about a Performance, Exhibit, or Sporting Event

Your friends and family members may sometimes ask you to provide information about—but not evaluations of—movies, concerts, TV shows, museum exhibits, or sporting events to help them make decisions about whether to spend money on them. For instance, if an art museum in your area were exhibiting works by the Dutch painter Vincent van Gogh, friends or family members who live some distance away might want to know which paintings were on display before deciding to spend their time and money on a visit to the exhibit.

Writing Assignment: In an e-mail to a friend or family member, describe a performance, exhibit, or sporting event that you recently saw or that is coming up. Try to avoid evaluating it. Instead, present what you know about the subject in a nonjudgmental, informative manner. While this e-mail basically contains your own information about the event, it always is useful to ask others—friends and relatives—for their own informative comments about the event or performance. Then you can add their insights to yours, which will provide even more useful information to the recipient of your e-mail.

Rhetorical Considerations in Informative Writing

Audience: Who is your primary audience? Who else might be interested in your subject? Why?

Purpose: As noted in Chapter 4, writing can be a powerful tool for learning, so use the information you collect and write about as a way to increase your knowledge of your subject, as well as the knowledge of your readers. Bear in mind as you write that your purpose is not to persuade readers to agree with an opinion you hold about your subject, but rather to inform them about it in neutral terms.

Voice, tone, and point of view: If you have a limited knowledge of your topic, your stance, or attitude, will be that of an interested investigator, and your tone will usually be neutral. If you are writing about a topic that you know well, take care to keep any biases out of your writing. If you are writing about a problem, present all opinions about the problem fairly, including those you disagree with. Your point of view will usually be third person.

For more on choosing a medium and genre, see Chapter 17 and Appendix C.

Context, medium, and genre: Keeping the context of the assignment in mind, decide on a medium and genre for your writing. How will your writing be used? If you are writing for an audience beyond the classroom, consider what will be the most effective way to present your information to this audience.

 # CRITICAL THINKING, READING, AND WRITING

Before you begin to write your informative paper, read examples of informative writing. You might also consider how visuals can inform readers, as well as the kinds of sources you will need to consult.

Writing to provide information has several qualities—a strong focus; relevant, useful information that is provided in an efficient manner; and clear, accurate explanations that enable readers to understand the information easily. The reading selections that appear in the next sections will stimulate your inquiry and writing. Finally, informative writing almost always requires that you go beyond your current knowledge of a topic and conduct careful research.

Learning the Qualities of Effective Informative Writing

As you think about how you might compose an informative paper, consider what readers expect and need from an informative text. As a reader, you probably look for the following qualities in informative writing:

- **A focused subject.** In *The Elements of Style,* his classic book of advice to writers, author and humorist E. B. White suggests, "When you say something, make sure you have said it. The chances of your having said it are only fair." White's comment is especially applicable to informative writing. The best way to "make sure you have said" what you want to say is to have a clear focus. What information about your subject is the most important? If you could boil down your information into one sentence, what would it be? Condensing the important aspects of your information into a single sentence forces you to craft a thesis statement, which in turn helps you connect all your details and examples back to that main point.

  For more on thesis statements, see Chapter 13.

- **Useful and relevant information.** People often read to gain information: They want to check on how their favorite sports team is doing, find the best way to travel from one place to another, or learn why high blood pressure is a health concern. How can you present your information so that readers understand what they might *do* with it and how it relates to their lives? Perhaps there is an unusual or a humorous angle on your subject that you can write about. And if you *synthesize* the information you have—explain the most important points made in each source you have consulted and how the information in one source agrees or disagrees with that in the other sources you have read—you will provide readers with a more thorough understanding of your subject.

  For more on synthesis, see Chapter 3.

- **Clear explanations and accurate information.** Information needs to be presented clearly and accurately so it is understandable to readers who do not have background knowledge about your subject. Consider your information as if you knew nothing about the subject. Examples are almost always a useful way to help explain ideas and define terms. Comparison and contrast can be useful when you need to explain an unfamiliar subject—tell the reader what a subject is like and what it is not like. One strategy that will help you write clear, accurate papers is to take careful notes when you conduct research.

  For more on using examples and comparison and contrast, see Chapter 13. For more on conducting research and taking notes, see Chapters 19 and 20.

For more on the use of visuals to enhance your explanations, see Chapter 18.

- Efficiency. Information should usually be presented concisely. To help readers grasp the information, you might want to provide them with a "road map," an outline of what you have in mind, at the beginning of the paper so they will know what to expect. Another way to present data efficiently is to "chunk" your writing—put it into sections, each dealing with a different aspect of the subject, making it easier for readers to understand. As you plan your paper, you should also consider whether it would be helpful to present your information in a table, graph, chart, or map. Consider how the title of your informative text not only will help readers understand your focus but also will help to draw them in, motivating them to read your paper.

Reading, Inquiry, and Research: Learning from Texts That Inform

The following reading selections are examples of informative writing. As you read, consider these questions:

- What makes this reading selection useful and interesting? What strategies does its author use to make the information understandable for readers?
- What parts of the reading could be improved by the use of charts, photographs, or tables? Why? How?
- How can you use the techniques of informative writing exemplified here in your writing?

CAROL EZZELL

Clocking Cultures

Show up an hour late in Brazil, and no one bats an eye- 1
lash. But keep someone in New York City waiting for
five or 10 minutes, and you have some explaining to do.
Time is elastic in many cultures but snaps taut in others.
Indeed, the way members of a culture perceive and use
time reflects their society's priorities and even their own
worldview.

Social scientists have recorded wide differences in 2
the pace of life in various countries and in how societies
view time—whether as an arrow piercing the future or as
a revolving wheel in which past, present and future cycle
endlessly. Some cultures conflate time and space: the Australian Aborigines' concept of the "Dreamtime" encompasses not only a creation myth but a method of finding
their way around the countryside. Interestingly, however,
some views of time—such as the idea that it is acceptable
for a more powerful person to keep someone of lower status waiting—cut across cultural differences and seem to be
found universally.

The study of time and society can be divided into the 3
pragmatic and the cosmological. On the practical side, in the
1950s anthropologist Edward T. Hall, Jr., wrote that the rules
of social time constitute a "silent language" for a given culture.
The rules might not always be made explicit, he stated, but they "exist in the air. . . .
They are either familiar and comfortable or unfamiliar and wrong."

In 1955 he described in *Scientific American* how differing perceptions of 4
time can lead to misunderstandings between people from separate cultures.
"An ambassador who has been kept waiting for more than half an hour by a
foreign visitor needs to understand that if his visitor 'just mutters an apology'
this is not necessarily an insult," Hall wrote. The time system in the foreign
country may be composed of different basic units, so that the visitor is not as
late as he may appear to us. You must know the time system of the country to
know at what point apologies are really due. . . . Different cultures simply place
different values on the time units.

Most cultures around the world now have watches and calendars, uniting 5
the majority of the globe in the same general rhythm of time. But that doesn't
mean we all march to the same beat. "One of the beauties of studying time is that
it's a wonderful window on culture," says Robert V. Levine, a social psychologist

Carol Ezzell has been a science
writer since the early 1990s and
currently works as a writer and
an editor at *Scientific American*,
specializing in biology and bio-
medicine. She has also worked for
Nature, Science News, Bio/World,
and the *Journal of NIH Research*.
An award-winning writer, Ezzell has
been recognized for her science
journalism by the National Association of Science Writers and the Pan
American Health Organization. In
2000, she won a Science in Society Journalism award for her article
"Care for a Dying Continent," about
how AIDS has affected women and
girls in Zimbabwe. This article was
originally published in the September 2002 issue of *Scientific American*. We find that our students
enjoy and learn from Ezzell's essay
and are sometimes surprised by
the information it contains.

at California State University at Fresno. "You get answers on what cultures value and believe in. You get a really good idea of what's important to people." Levine and his colleagues have conducted so-called pace-of-life studies in 31 countries. In *A Geography of Time,* published in 1997, Levine describes how he ranked the countries by using three measures: walking speed on urban sidewalks, how quickly postal clerks could fulfill a request for a common stamp, and the accuracy of public clocks. Based on these variables, he concluded that the five fastest paced countries are Switzerland, Ireland, Germany, Japan and Italy; the five slowest are Syria, El Salvador, Brazil, Indonesia and Mexico. The U.S., at 16th, ranks near the middle. Kevin K. Birth, an anthropologist at Queens College, has examined time perceptions in Trinidad. Birth's 1999 book, *Any Time Is Trinidad Time: Social Meanings and Temporal Consciousness,* refers to a commonly used phrase to excuse lateness. In that country, Birth observes, "if you have a meeting at 6:00 at night, people show up at 6:45 or 7:00 and say, 'Any time is Trinidad time.'" When it comes to business, however, that loose approach to timeliness works only for the people with power. A boss can show up late and toss off "any time is Trinidad time," but underlings are expected to be more punctual. For them, the saying goes, "time is time." Birth adds that the tie between power and waiting time is true for many other cultures as well.

6   The nebulous nature of time makes it hard for anthropologists and social psychologists to study. "You can't simply go into a society, walk up to some poor soul and say, 'Tell me about your notions of time,'?" Birth says. "People don't really have an answer to that. You have to come up with other ways to find out."

7   Birth attempted to get at how Trinidadians value time by exploring how closely their society links time and money. He surveyed rural residents and found that farmers—whose days are dictated by natural events, such as sunrise—did not recognize the phrases "time is money," "budget your time" or "time management," even though they had satellite TV and were familiar with Western popular culture. But tailors in the same areas were aware of such notions. Birth concluded that wage work altered the tailors' views of time. "The ideas of associating time with money are not found globally," he says, "but are attached to your job and the people you work with."

8   How people deal with time on a day-to-day basis often has nothing to do with how they conceive of time as an abstract entity. "There's often a disjunction between how a culture views the mythology of time and how they think about time in their daily lives," Birth asserts. "We don't think of Stephen Hawking's theories as we go about our daily lives."

9   Some cultures do not draw neat distinctions between the past, present and future. Australian Aborigines, for instance, believe that their ancestors crawled out of the earth during the Dreamtime. The ancestors "sang" the world into existence as they moved about naming each feature and living thing, which

brought them into being. Even today, an entity does not exist unless an Aborigine "sings" it.

Ziauddin Sardar, a British Muslim author and critic, has written about time   10
and Islamic cultures, particularly the fundamentalist sect Wahhabism. Muslims "always carry the past with them," claims Sardar, who is editor of the journal *Futures* and visiting professor of postcolonial studies at City University, London. "In Islam, time is a tapestry incorporating the past, present and future. The past is ever present." The followers of Wahhabism, which is practiced in Saudi Arabia and by Osama bin Laden, seek to re-create the idyllic days of the prophet Muhammad's life. "The worldly future dimension has been suppressed" by them, Sardar says. "They have romanticized a particular vision of the past. All they are doing is trying to replicate that past."

Sardar asserts that the West has "colonized" time by spreading the expec-   11
tation that life should become better as time passes: "If you colonize time, you also colonize the future. If you think of time as an arrow, of course you think of the future as progress, going in one direction. But different people may desire different futures."

UNDERSTANDING A WRITER'S GOALS: QUESTIONS TO CONSIDER AND DISCUSS

Rhetorical Knowledge: The Writer's Situation and Rhetoric

1. **Audience:** Who is the audience for Ezzell's essay? How can you tell?

2. **Purpose:** What realm (academic, professional, civic, or personal) does Ezzell's essay best fit into? Why?

3. **Voice and tone:** How would you describe Ezzell's tone in this essay? How does her tone contribute to her believability?

4. **Responsibility:** Ezzell discusses the notions of time across different cultures in her essay. How respectful of those cultures is she? Why do you think that?

5. **Context, format, and genre:** This essay was published during a time of worldwide fear of terrorism. How does that context affect your reading of this essay? The essay genre was developed to allow writers to discover other ways of seeing the world. How does Ezzell's essay display this feature of the genre?

Critical Thinking: The Writer's Ideas and Your Personal Response

6. What is the most interesting piece of information in Ezzell's article? Why? The least interesting? Why?

7. What is the main idea—or thesis—in Ezzell's essay? How well does Ezzell provide support for this idea? Why do you think that?

Composing Processes and Knowledge of Conventions: The Writer's Strategies

8. Ezzell uses information and quotations from experts throughout her essay. How does she present this information? What does the presence of these experts add to the essay?

9. Prepare a quick outline of this essay. What does this outline reveal about the way Ezzell has organized her information for readers?

Inquiry and Research: Ideas for Further Exploration

10. Prepare a list of questions that you still have about time and cultures. Interview several of your friends, asking them the questions that you have listed, and then explain, in no more than two pages, their answers to your questions.

NATIONAL INSTITUTE OF MENTAL HEALTH

Autism Spectrum Disorder

What Is Autism Spectrum Disorder?

Autism spectrum disorder (ASD) is characterized by:

- Persistent deficits in social communication and social interaction across multiple contexts;
- Restricted, repetitive patterns of behavior, interests, or activities;
- Symptoms must be present in the early developmental period (typically recognized in the first two years of life); and,
- Symptoms cause clinically significant impairment in social, occupational, or other important areas of current functioning.

The term *spectrum* refers to the wide range of symptoms, skills, and levels of impairment or disability that children with ASD can have. Some children are mildly impaired by their symptoms, while others are severely disabled. The latest edition of the *Diagnostic and Statistical Manual of Mental Disorders* (DSM-5) no longer includes Asperger's syndrome; the characteristics of Asperger's syndrome are included within the broader category of ASD. . . .

Early Signs & Symptoms

Symptoms of autism spectrum disorder (ASD) vary from one child to the next, but in general, they fall into two areas:

- Social impairment, including difficulties with social communication
- Repetitive and stereotyped behaviors.

Children with ASD do not follow typical patterns when developing social and communication skills. Parents are usually the first to notice unusual behaviors in their child. Often, certain behaviors become more noticeable when comparing children of the same age.

In some cases, babies with ASD may seem different very early in their development. Even before their first birthday, some babies become overly focused on certain objects, rarely make eye contact, and fail to engage in

A R T I C L E

The sections of text reproduced here are taken from a report produced by the National Institute of Mental Health (NIMH), a government agency, which outlines the symptoms of Autism Spectrum Disorder (ASD).

The report also touches on some possible causes, but notes that "Scientists don't know the exact causes of ASD, but research suggests that both genes and environment play important roles."

These excerpts focus on some of the symptoms exhibited by those with the disorder, along with some early "signs and symptoms" that might help parents in recognizing ASD.

Note that in the first section of this excerpt, the NIMH reports, "The latest edition of the Diagnostic and Statistical Manual of Mental Disorders (DSM-5) no longer includes Asperger's syndrome; the characteristics of Asperger's syndrome are included within the broader category of ASD. . . ."

For an argument in favor of *including* Asperger's syndrome as a separate disorder, see student writer Zack Peach's essay in Chapter 9.

typical back-and-forth play and babbling with their parents. Other children may develop normally until the second or even third year of life, but then start to lose interest in others and become silent, withdrawn, or indifferent to social signals. Loss or reversal of normal development is called regression and occurs in some children with ASD.

Social Impairment

Most children with ASD have trouble engaging in everyday social interactions. For example, some children with ASD may:

- Make little eye contact
- Tend to look and listen less to people in their environment or fail to respond to other people
- Rarely seek to share their enjoyment of toys or activities by pointing or showing things to others
- Respond unusually when others show anger, distress, or affection.

Recent research suggests that children with ASD do not respond to emotional cues in human social interactions because they may not pay attention to the social cues that others typically notice. For example, one study found that children with ASD focus on the mouth of the person speaking to them instead of on the eyes, which is where children with typical development tend to focus. A related study showed that children with ASD appear to be drawn to repetitive movements linked to a sound, such as hand-clapping during a game of pat-a-cake. More research is needed to confirm these findings, but such studies suggest that children with ASD may misread or not notice subtle social cues—a smile, a wink, or a grimace—that could help them understand social relationships and interactions. For these children, a question such as, "Can you wait a minute?" always means the same thing, whether the speaker is joking, asking a real question, or issuing a firm request. Without the ability to interpret another person's tone of voice as well as gestures, facial expressions, and other nonverbal communications, children with ASD may not properly respond.

Likewise, it can be hard for others to understand the body language of children with ASD. Their facial expressions, movements, and gestures are often vague or do not match what they are saying. Their tone of voice may not reflect their actual feelings either. Many older children with ASD speak with an unusual tone of voice and may sound sing-song or flat and robotlike.

Children with ASD also may have trouble understanding another person's point of view. For example, by school age, most children understand that other people have different information, feelings, and goals than they have. Children with ASD may lack this understanding, leaving them unable to predict or understand other people's actions.

Communication Issues

According to the American Academy of Pediatrics' developmental milestones, by the first birthday, typical toddlers can say one or two words, turn when they hear their name, and point when they want a toy. When offered something they do not want, toddlers make it clear with words, gestures, or facial expressions that the answer is "no."

For children with ASD, reaching such milestones may not be so straight-forward. For example, some children with autism may:

- Fail or be slow to respond to their name or other verbal attempts to gain their attention
- Fail or be slow to develop gestures, such as pointing and showing things to others
- Coo and babble in the first year of life, but then stop doing so
- Develop language at a delayed pace
- Learn to communicate using pictures or their own sign language
- Speak only in single words or repeat certain phrases over and over, seeming unable to combine words into meaningful sentences
- Repeat words or phrases that they hear, a condition called echolalia
- Use words that seem odd, out of place, or have a special meaning known only to those familiar with the child's way of communicating.

Even children with ASD who have relatively good language skills often have difficulties with the back and forth of conversations. For example, because they find it difficult to understand and react to social cues, some highly verbal children with ASD often talk at length about a favorite subject, but they won't allow anyone else a chance to respond or notice when others react indifferently.

Children with ASD who have not yet developed meaningful gestures or language may simply scream or grab or otherwise act out until they are taught better ways to express their needs. As these children grow up, they can become aware of their difficulty in understanding others and in being understood. This awareness may cause them to become anxious or depressed.

UNDERSTANDING A WRITER'S GOALS: QUESTIONS TO CONSIDER AND DISCUSS

Rhetorical Knowledge: The Writer's Situation and Rhetoric

1. **Audience:** How would you describe the audience that the National Institute of Mental Health (NIMH) had in mind when it produced this report?

2. **Purpose:** What purpose(s) would someone have for reading this report? In addition to its informative purpose, how is the report's writing also persuasive?

3. **Voice and tone:** To what extent do you believe what this report has to say? How does the report's tone contribute to its credibility? Why?

4. **Responsibility:** One important quality of any successful informative text is clarity, especially when the author is dealing with a complex subject. How does the report meet a government agency's obligation to its readers to be clear? Where might it have been clearer?

5. **Context, format, and genre:** Given this topic, it seems natural that this piece originally appeared in an online format (on the NIMH's Web site), with hyperlinks. When you read such an online article, do you ever click on its hyperlinks? Why?

Critical Thinking: The Writer's Ideas and Your Personal Response

6. What in the report do you want to learn more about? Why?

7. The report lists a lot of examples of what children with ASD do and do not do. Do these examples surprise you in any way?

8. If you saw some of the signs of ASD in a sibling or your own child, would you suggest having him or her tested?

Composing Processes and Knowledge of Conventions: The Writer's Strategies

9. Since this is a government report, you might have expected to find it boring and filled with dull facts and figures. Did you find the information in this excerpt interesting? Why?

10. The NIMH does not document the sources for this excerpt. Does this lack of documentation on where they got their information weaken this report? Why?

Inquiry and Research: Ideas for Further Exploration

11. Research a concept or issue on the Web. Make a list of the information you collect that seems contradictory. How might you reconcile those inconsistencies in order to determine what is accurate?

12. Read the entire report at *www.nimh.nih. gov/health/topics/autism-spectrum-disorders-asd/index.shtml*. Click on several of the hyperlinks. How did they help you understand this information?

GENRES *Up Close* **Writing an Annotated Bibliography**

As illustrated in "Ways of Writing to Inform" (page 160), information can be shared through many genres. Many instructors ask their students to construct annotated bibliographies as a means of helping them (1) understand what they are asked to read and (2) relate the information and ideas in an essay to information and ideas from other essays.

An **annotated bibliography** provides the citation for each work and a brief summary, or synopsis, describing what you learned from that specific text about your topic and, often, how that information relates to other information you read about. Annotated bibliographies are a research tool. You may be asked to develop an annotated bibliography as part of a research paper or even as the first step in writing a research paper.

Becoming proficient at writing annotated bibliographies will help you to use the information you learn from your college reading in your own writing.

When constructing an annotated bibliography, a writer should do the following:

- List the appropriate citation information for each work.

- Briefly summarize the cited work.

Below is a typical annotated bibliography entry, by student writer Craig Broadbent (his other invention work, draft, and final paper appear later in this chapter). Note that Broadbent also comments on how he might be able to use the information that he is annotating in his own writing.

"How Long Does Litter Last?" *United States, Department of the Interior, National Park Service,* 9 Sept. 2011, www.nps.gov/tuma/forkids/upload/HowLongDoesLitterLast.pdf.

This article by the National Park Service covers two things. The first is something of a game where students are asked to click on a link that will bring up drawings of a lot of different trash items. Other students are then asked to guess at how long that item will last before it decomposes. The second part of the article lists a number of products and how long they will survive before they decompose. I think I might be able to use these data in my own paper on recycling, but I will only be able to use the more interesting items, as there is a lot of information here.

ANNOTATED BIBLIOGRAPHY

Student writer Craig Broadbent crafted an annotated bibliography for his informative paper, and it formed the basis for the research he included in his writing (for some of Broadbent's invention work and research, see pages 177–178; an early draft of his paper appears on page 186 and the final draft of his informative paper is on pages 191–194). Note how Broadbent also includes some quotations. He is thinking ahead to what he will want to include in his paper, and jotting down actual quotations now will come in handy as he drafts.

"Reduce, Reuse, Recycle." *United States Environmental Protection Agency*, 15 Feb. 2015, www2.epa.gov/recycle.

Broadbent includes appropriate citation information for each entry.

This is an interesting page that includes all sorts of items that can be recycled and how/where to recycle them. Information from this government Web site includes several definitions I may be able to use in my paper. It offers advice on recycling electronics—something we all have questions about—and lots of useful information, including about what I think I'll focus on: the blue barrels. This page also lists the benefits of recycling as well as ways of reducing recycled things (like buying used items).

Roberts, Jim. Personal Interview. 15 Mar. 2016.

Broadbent briefly summarizes the information in each source that might be useful in his paper.

Jim Roberts is a student I know from my math class. I interviewed him and asked what he knew, if anything, about our college recycling program. "I've never heard of it," he said. "No one mentioned it during orientation. At least I don't recall anyone mentioning it." This information might be useful in my own paper, as it may indicate that the school is doing a poor job of promoting our recycling program.

RecycleMania Tournament. Recyclemania, www.recyclemaniacs.org. Accessed 16 Jan. 2016.

This Web site outlines what could be a useful suggestion for our college, something they call "RecycleMania." They claim that it is a "friendly competition among college and university recycling programs in North America and Canada. During 8 weeks each spring, schools compete to reduce waste, increase recycling and raise awareness of conservation issues across campus." This sounds like useful and interesting information I may be able to use in my paper.

The work that Broadbent did in constructing his annotated bibliography (only three of his entries are shown above) helped him as he crafted his informative paper, which focused on recycling on his own college campus. As an example, note how Broadbent used some of the material about "RecycleMania" in paragraph 11 in his own paper (see page 192):

> The EPA provides what might be a useful suggestion for our college, in that they help sponsor what they call "RecycleMania." "RecycleMania is a friendly competition and benchmarking tool for college and university recycling programs to promote waste reduction activities to their campus communities." ("Welcome"). Perhaps if we could get our own college involved we could make a huge difference in the environmental awareness of our own students.

UNDERSTANDING A WRITER'S GOALS: QUESTIONS TO CONSIDER AND DISCUSS

Rhetorical Knowledge: The Writer's Situation and Rhetoric

1. **Audience:** What might Broadbent have done to make his annotated bibliography helpful to a wider audience (for classmates, for example, who were writing on the same topic)?

2. **Purpose:** What is Broadbent trying to accomplish in this annotated bibliography?

3. **Voice and tone:** How has Broadbent established his credibility in this excerpt from his annotated bibliography?

4. **Responsibility:** What evidence do you have that Broadbent accurately reported on what he learned from his research?

5. **Context, format, and genre:** How does the format Broadbent uses match your understanding of the proper format for an annotated bibliography?

Critical Thinking: The Writer's Ideas and Your Personal Response

6. Broadbent quotes a classmate he interviewed, who claimed to know little or nothing about the campus recycling programs. What do you know about your own campus recycling efforts? How might you learn more?

7. In his annotation on "Reduce, Reuse, Recycle," Broadbent writes that, "Information from this government Web site includes several definitions I may be able to use in my paper." When is it useful, do you think, to include detailed definitions in your own papers?

Composing Processes and Knowledge of Conventions: The Writer's Strategies

8. Consult Chapter 20, "Synthesizing and Documenting Sources," to determine which style guide—MLA or APA—Broadbent is using. What evidence supports your conclusion?

9. In paragraph 9 of his final essay, Broadbent cites interviews he conducted with Jim Roberts and also Tracy Worsam, paraphrasing one and citing the other. Using the guidelines for quoting, paraphrasing, and summarizing (see pages 554–555 in Chapter 20, "Synthesizing and Documenting Sources"), explain why Broadbent may have chosen to paraphrase Roberts and quote Worsam.

Inquiry and Research: Ideas for Further Exploration

10. Do a Web search using the terms "recycling" and "EPA." In addition to what Broadbent cites in his annotated bibliography, what other government information about recycling can you find?

WRITING PROCESSES

As you work on the assignment scenario you have chosen, keep in mind the qualities of an effective informative paper (see pages 163–164). Also remember that writing is more a recursive than a linear process. You will keep coming back to your earlier work as you go through the activities listed below, adding to it and modifying the information to be more accurate as you conduct more research and become more familiar with your topic.

As you work on your project, make certain that you save your data frequently, backing up your computer files in two or more places.

Invention: Getting Started

Use invention activities to explore the information that you want to include in your first draft. It is useful to keep a journal as you work on any writing project, for your journal is a place where you can record not just what you learn but also the questions that arise during your writing and research activities.

For more on using journals, see Chapters 2 and 4.

Try to answer these questions while you do your invention work:

- What do I already know about the topic that I am writing about?
- What feelings or attitudes do I have about this topic? How can I keep them out of my text so that my writing is as free of bias as possible?
- What questions can I ask about the topic?
- Where might I learn more about this subject (in the library, on the Web)? What verifiable information on my topic is available?
- Who would know about my topic? What questions might I ask that person in an interview?
- What do I know about my audience? What don't I know that I should know? Why might they be interested in reading my text?
- What might my audience already know about my subject? Why might they care about it?
- To what extent will sensory details—color, shape, smell, taste, and so on—help my reader understand my topic? Why?

For more on descriptive writing, see Chapter 13.

- If I were to do a PowerPoint or Prezi presentation on recycling issues, what photos or charts or videos might I use?
- What visual aids might I use to better inform my readers?

Doing your invention work in electronic form, rather than on paper, lets you easily use this early writing as you construct a draft.

As with any kind of writing, invention activities improve with peer feedback and suggestions. Consider sharing the invention work you have done so far with several classmates or friends in order to understand your rhetorical situation more clearly and to generate more useful information.

Craig Broadbent's Brainstorming

Craig Broadbent, a first-year student, chose to respond to Scenario 1 on page 159. Broadbent decided that he would brainstorm to get onto paper what he already knew about the litter issue on his campus before he interviewed his friends about it:

—I see stuff every day—newspapers, those extra advertising things they put into the paper, cups, plates, and—especially—cigarette butts.
—It's always worst around where ashtrays are—that's really weird.
—The paper stuff is always worst around where the newspapers are.
—Oh—they do put a box or some container next to the paper stands for students to toss those inserts, if they don't want to read them. Not sure why so many end up on the ground.
—Bad in the men's rooms, too, at times—towels on the floor almost always.
—Classrooms: stuff tacked or taped to the walls, old soda cups and crumpled-up hamburger wrappers and old napkins and candy wrappers. . .

Broadbent also used freewriting and clustering to explore his topic. (See Chapter 6, page 135, for examples of these strategies.)

Writing Activity

Brainstorming

Working with the questions on page 176, spend a few minutes brainstorming—jotting down everything you can think of about your topic.

STUDENT WRITING EXAMPLES

Brainstorming (pp. 177, 343)

Freewriting (pp. 134, 256, 344, 393)

Criteria (p. 300)

Listing (p. 97)

Answers to Reporter's Questions (p. 256)

Organization (pp. 98, 182, 647)

Clustering (pp. 135, 298)

Interviewing (p. 216)

Research (pp. 136, 137, 178, 179, 217, 218, 258, 259, 302, 343, 346, 396)

Reflection (p. 12)

▮ Exploring Your Ideas with Research

Although you can sometimes draw exclusively on your experience in a piece of informative writing, especially in personal writing contexts, in academic, professional, and civic writing situations, you will usually need to include information gained from outside research.

Assume, for example, that you would like to inform a group of your friends about a local homeless shelter. You would probably want to list the services the shelter provides, indicate the various ways people can become involved with the shelter, and cite financial data on what percentage of each cash donation goes to support the shelter's clients. To provide this information to your readers, you would need to conduct some form of research.

Research provides you with the statistical data, examples, and expert testimony that will enable you to give your audience enough information, and the right kind of information, on your topic. As with any other aspect of your writing, the kind and amount of research you will need to do will depend on your rhetorical situation: who your audience is and what you are trying to accomplish. If you are writing a paper for a sociology course on aspects of male group behavior, you will need to locate articles in scholarly journals, as well as statistical data, which you could present in a chart. If you are writing about a problem in your community, you will need to read articles and government documents, and you might also interview government officials.

As you work on the scenario you have chosen (see pages 159–162), you could conduct several kinds of research. If you are researching a problem on campus

USING DIGITAL TECHNOLOGIES | **Using a Search Engine to Narrow a Potential Topic**

The results of a general search for sources can let you know if your informative topic is unwieldy. If a search using a search engine brings up thousands of Web sites with information about your topic, that topic is probably too broad. For example, when a search engine such as Google returns more than 36 million links for the topic "campus recycling," you need to narrow the topic so that your ideas and research will be more focused. Changing "campus" to "college" and searching on "college recycling" lowers the number of sites to about 12,000.

Adding search terms based on your specific interests and concerns can help narrow your exploratory Web search even more. (Tip: Separate your terms or phrases in the search window with quotation marks.) Adding the terms "benefits," "saving money," "sustainability" to the search brings the number of results down to about 80 sites—a lot to look through but a much narrower search with a tighter focus. And the top "hits" are all from educational institutions, many of which have recycling programs that are described in the research you have located—useful information for your own focus if you were writing a paper, as student writer Craig Broadbent is, on campus recycling.

or in your community, you might conduct interviews with students or residents affected by the problem. As an alternative, you might consider conducting a survey of a representative sample of students or community members. You will also need to observe the problem.

For help with locating sources of information, see Chapter 19; for help with documenting your sources, see Chapter 20.

Gather, read, and take notes on your topic from outside sources. You might use an electronic journal to record images, URLs, and other information that you find as you do your research. Such an e-journal makes it easy for you to add that information once you start drafting your paper.

Craig Broadbent's Research

For his informative paper on the litter problem on his campus, Craig Broadbent thought it would be useful to include data that show how long it takes certain waste products to decompose. By searching with the the phrase "How long does trash last?" in the Google search engine, he found this information at the Web site maintained by the National Park Service:

For more on using search engines, see Chapter 19.

Rate of Biodegradability	
Orange/banana Peels	2–5 weeks
Wool socks	1–5 years
Cigarette butts	1–5 years
Plastic-coated paper	5 years
Plastic bags	10–20 years
Plastic film containers	20–30 years
Nylon fabric	30–40 years

Rate of Biodegradability	
Leather	Up to 50 years
Tin cans	50 years
Aluminum cans & tabs	80–100 years
Glass bottles	1,000,000 years

Broadbent realized that this information, though interesting, was probably more than he needed, so he decided that he would narrow it down a bit when he added it to his informative paper.

Reviewing Your Invention and Research

After you have conducted your research, review your invention work and notes, and think about the information you have collected from outside sources. At this time, you may be tempted to decide on a thesis statement—a statement that summarizes your main point. Even though you might already have a general idea of what you want your informative paper to focus on, until you get some of your ideas and research on paper, it is often hard to know what your thesis will be. Your thesis should come *from* the writing you do about your topic. Once you have done a lot of invention work (listing, brainstorming, clustering, and so on) and research, you may be ready to decide on your working thesis. Or you can wait until after you construct your first draft.

For more on deciding on a thesis, see Chapter 13.

Writing Activity

Using Your Invention and Research to Help Focus Your Ideas

To help develop your thesis, review your invention and research notes:

- Look for connections between the pieces of information you have gathered. By doing so, you are synthesizing the information from your sources. Craig Broadbent noticed several instances where the recycling program on his campus seemed invisible. This discovery became the main idea of his paper.

- Decide on the most important piece of information you have collected. One approach is to start your paper with this information. To emphasize the invisibility of recycling on his campus, Craig Broadbent starts his paper with "We seem to have a case of invisible blue barrels on campus—when was the last time you saw one and what is unusual or unique about it?"

For more on synthesis, see Chapter 3.

Craig Broadbent's Review of His Research

Craig Broadbent wanted his paper to include some of the information about recycling that he learned from his research. He investigated the issue on his campus, he interviewed two of his classmates about it, and he did a brief search of back issues of the campus's newspaper, the *Campus Reporter,* for information about campus recycling. His review of his research helped him decide on an effective way to start his paper. Here are some of his notes:

1. Jim Roberts (roommate) told me that no one had mentioned the school's recycling program to him, at orientation or anywhere else.

2. Tracy Worsam (friend and classmate) told me that she'd even asked about the program at her orientation, and no one there seemed to know much about it, other than "we have some blue barrels around campus."

3. The last ten or twelve issues of the Campus Reporter had only one small advertisement and no articles about the program. Why so little? All of those things make me wonder if I should start with a question, perhaps like, "Why doesn't anyone on campus know about our recycling program?" And, maybe a title something like, "A big campus secret: Our blue barrels."

4. I also looked on the Web and found this information on the Environmental Protection Agency's (EPA) Web site (www.epa.gov/epawaste/nonhaz/municipal/pubs/msw_2010_factsheet.pdf).

Every ton of mixed paper recycled can save the energy equivalent of 165 gallons of gasoline.

Recycling just 1 ton of aluminum cans conserves more than 207 million Btu, the equivalent of 36 barrels of oil, or 1,665 gallons of gasoline.

Maybe I can use these in my paper to help readers understand the information more easily.

Strategies FOR Success | Responsibility

Writers of successful informational papers are responsible writers: they present their information honestly, accurately, and without bias. That careful approach allows readers to make up their own minds about the information.

Readers often use the information from their reading to help them make a decision, to support an idea in their writing, or to teach someone else. It is important, therefore, that you as a writer present accurate information and that you are aware of any biases, or preconceived ideas, you may bring to your writing about a topic—biases that might cause you to present that information in a way that is other than neutral.

Responsible writers also take care to present reliable data. For example, you cannot say "the majority of students who attend this college think that the school does a good job of recycling on campus" unless you have asked a sufficiently large and representative group of your schoolmates and are reasonably certain that you are presenting a true majority opinion.

Organizing Your Information and Research

Once you have some sense of what you would like your informative paper to include, consider how you might organize this material. The questions to ask yourself when deciding on your organization are all rhetorical:

- Who is your audience?
- Why might they be interested in your subject, or how can you make them interested in it? (One way to indicate why your subject is important to your audience is to explain how your audience will be affected by it.)
- What is your purpose for writing—that is, what do you want to *inform* your readers about?
- What are the most important ideas, concepts, or statistics that you want your readers to learn about from your text?

The answers to these questions can help you decide what you need to emphasize, which in turn will help you choose an organization.

Here are three possible organizational approaches for writing an informative paper:

Options FOR Organization
Options for Organizing Informative Writing

Capture Your Readers' Attention	Question Your Readers	Create a Context
Start with an unusual or surprising piece of information about your subject.	Begin with a question to help readers see why they might want to read about your topic.	Set the stage. What is the situation that your readers may be interested in?
Present the information, starting from the least unusual or surprising idea and moving to the most.	Outline the information, starting with the least significant piece of information and working toward the most important.	Broaden your initial explanation with specific details, quotations, and examples so your reader can "see" what you are writing about.
Use specific examples, quotations, statistics, and so on to illustrate your topic.	Use specific examples, quotations, statistics, and so on to illustrate your topic.	Compare and contrast your subject with another one, to help readers understand the information.
End your paper by restating a unique or surprising aspect of your topic.	Conclude by answering the question that you started with.	Conclude your paper by reinforcing your reader's connection to your topic.

Craig Broadbent's Organization

Craig Broadbent reviewed his invention material and then put together a rough outline for his first draft. He decided to start with a question and to use the second approach described above.

Set the stage, so to speak, by asking if readers know what the blue barrels are
    and how they work.
State my purpose: informational.
Explain recycling and how it works.
Include tables, photos, charts to show my ideas.
Explain the cost aspects of recycling.
Let people know how to find out more information.

Constructing a Complete Draft

Once you have chosen the organizational approach that works effectively given your audience and purpose, you are ready to finish constructing your draft. Look back over the information you have generated through your invention activities and collected through your research, as well as any comments made by your classmates. You should also reexamine your focus or your thesis (if you have one) and decide whether you need to modify it. If you do not have a thesis yet, consider whether you are ready to develop a working thesis.

Remember that you will learn more about your subject as you write, and your ideas will probably change as you compose the first draft of your informative essay. Consider, too, what visual aids your readers might find useful.

Integrating Sources into Your Draft: Paraphrasing Information from Sources

One effective way to present information is to paraphrase it: to put information from a source into your own words. This is especially true for information from interviews. You will discover once you start interviewing people that interviewees often ramble. Paraphrasing can help you present only the information that is pertinent to your subject.

Look at the notes Craig Broadbent had from his interviews of students:

Tracy Worsam:
I've been active in recycling efforts both at my high school and in my church. I just assumed this university would have a full-scale program. So I asked a whole bunch of people at orientation about what this school did. One person, I'm not even sure who, just pointed and said "we have some blue barrels around campus." I was really disappointed.

Jim Roberts:

I'm kind of interested in recycling and all kinds of green activities. I was expecting to hear how I could help during orientation. Unless I missed it completely, no one mentioned recycling at all—neither during orientation nor since I've been here. You're the first person I've met who seems interested in it.

Group interview with James Wilson, Stacy Marble, and Sam Addams:

Marble—Yeah, we and a few other guys all rent rooms in that house.

Wilson—Those of us who live here try to keep the place neat—but, you know, it's really the landlord's job to clean up the front yard.

Addams—No kidding. We wake up on Saturday morning and there are all those beer cans and other litter in the front yard. We hate it.

Marble—We can't stay up all night to see who's trashing our yard.

Addams—No, but you know, maybe a webcam would be cool.

Although the interviews provide relevant information, they also contain much extraneous detail. By paraphrasing, you can take only the relevant ideas you've gained from your interviews and state them in your own words. But remember: even though the words are yours, you still need to cite where you found the ideas.

Notice how Craig Broadbent integrated parts of his interviews into his final draft. In addition to comments from Roberts and Worsam, Broadbent included a sentence in paragraph 9 that paraphrased interviews with three other students— Wilson, Marble, and Addams: "They all told me that *they* never littered even though their yard was a mess (Wilson, Marble, and Addams)." Notice that this paraphrase gets to the heart of the matter while eliminating unrelated comments.

Parts of a Complete Draft

Introduction: Successful informative writing grabs and holds readers' attention. The following strategies can help you hook your readers:

- **Define any important terms that the reader might not know.** Defining terms does not mean listing their dictionary definitions, but rather explaining those terms in the context of your explanation of your subject. For an especially effective opening, you might get readers' attention by defining a familiar term in an unexpected way.

- **Start your text with unusual or surprising information.** What in the opening section of the National Institute of Mental Health's report on Autism Spectrum Disorder did you find new or surprising? What did you want to learn more about? Why?

- **Get down to business by bluntly stating your thesis.** A straightforward statement like "Denver's new sign code is causing businesses to lose money" often gets readers' attention. Journalists, who are trained to put the most important information up front, often use this approach.

- **Start with a provocative example or two.**

Body: Think of the body of your informative text as the place to provide all of the information that you want your readers to know and to understand. This is the section where you will present your data: quotations, graphs, tables, charts, and so on. The body of your paper is always the longest part, and although you are not trying to prove anything in an informative essay, you are providing information to your readers, and most of it will appear in this section. The body is also where you will synthesize the information you are providing.

For more on synthesis, see Chapter 3.

Conclusion: Your conclusion should tie your paper together for readers by explaining or suggesting the significance of the information you have given them: why it is useful or interesting to them. Here are some strategies for concluding an informative paper:

- **Summarize your main points.**
- **Explain the subject's most critical part.** Carol Ezzell uses a quotation from an expert to indicate what is most significant about her topic: "If you colonize time, you also colonize the future" (page 167).
- **Outline again the subject's most important aspects.**

Title: You might think that you need to craft a title before you start writing, but often it is more useful to get a first draft on paper or into a computer file and then consider possible titles. Your paper's title should indicate what your paper is about, but it should also capture your readers' interest and invite them to read further.

- **Use a title that readers will wonder about.** For example, "Clocking Cultures" makes readers wonder what this essay could be about.
- **Start with something current.** As more and more of us are diagnosed with some form of autism, the subject is much in current news reports.

Writing Activity

Constructing a Full Draft

Using the writing you did when selecting an organizational approach, write a complete draft of your informative paper.

VISUAL *Thinking* | Going beyond Words to Achieve Your Goals

To help his readers understand the information in his paper, Craig Broadbent decided to look for *visual aids* on the topic of recycling. As noted above, he had already found good information about how long trash lasts (page 178) and located some useful graphics (page 180), both of which he decided to use. Broadbent also wondered whether a photograph of some litter or a blue barrel might help, perhaps right at the start of his paper. He tried several images to get a sense of whether or not they would fit within his paper:

Watch for the Blue Barrels
Craig Broadbent

© Richard Newsteed/Flickr/ Getty Images RF

© Jeffrey Hamilton/Getty Images RF

© Robert Decelis Ltd/Digital Vision/Getty Images RF

None of these images seemed to be all that useful to Broadbent, so he kept searching on Google for images. Finally, he found a photograph that helped him show readers what he was discussing. He decided to put this image near the beginning of his paper.

Broadbent also deleted some of the information (such as "plastic film containers" and "plastic six-pack holders") from the data he found on how long trash lasts, so he would present only the most important information. He put that data into Table 1 in his final paper (page 192).

© Stockbyte/PunchStock RF

- Of the visuals Broadbent considered, which do you think best support his purpose?

- What kind of visual would you use to help readers understand the information about recycling?

Craig Broadbent's First Draft

After deciding on an organizational approach, Craig Broadbent was ready to begin his first, or working, draft. As he wrote, he did not worry about grammar, punctuation, mechanics, or proper documentation style; instead, he concentrated on getting his main ideas on paper. Here is the first draft of his recycling paper. (The numbers in circles refer to peer comments, which follow the draft below.)

Watch for the Blue Barrels
Craig Broadbent

Have you ever wondered what all of those blue barrels are, around campus . . . and if you know what they're for, do you wonder why students don't seem to use them? ❶

Joan Meyers, who coordinates our campus recycling program, says that it has been around for more than ten years now, but receives little publicity (Meyers). My purpose here is to outline what we're doing here on campus, what the costs and income are from the program, and finally, based on several interviews, to suggest reasons why students don't use the blue barrels.

Our campus program not only keeps the campus cleaner, since items are collected in the blue barrels instead of perhaps being thrown on the ground, but also makes some $5,000 a year for the school (Meyers). Ms. Meyers also told me that our college could make as much as $30,000 a year from recycling, if we all recycled all the newspapers, cans, etc., that we now throw away.❷ ❸

Students, though, don't use the program, sometimes because they're not aware of it. Student Jim Roberts told me that at orientation or anywhere else no one had mentioned the school's recycling program to him (Roberts). And Tracy Worsam even asked about the program at her orientation, and no one there seemed to know much about it, other than "we have some blue barrels around campus" (Worsam).❹

A search of several issues of the *Campus Reporter* perhaps explains why not many students are really aware of the blue barrel program. During the last few months, there has been only one small advertisement about the campus recycling program, and no articles about the program were published.

In order to know about and understand the recycling program, Meyers suggests that information be provided at all orientation meetings, and that weekly advertisements are run in the *Campus Reporter* (Meyers).❺

Student Comments on Craig Broadbent's Draft

❶ "I thought your introduction 'worked' and made me want to read more."

❷ "It seems to me that the strongest parts of your paper are the examples, especially all the statistics."

❸ "Perhaps a table or chart would help me see what you mean."

❹ "The weakest part is the interview information, which made me want to read more of what other people had to say."

❺ "Your conclusion was weak—maybe you could add what students ought to be doing now? Put another way, what do you want your readers to do with this (interesting) information?"

 ## Revising

Revising means reviewing and rethinking your informative text. The most effective way to revise your work is to read it as if you are reading it for the first time. Reading your own work in this way is difficult to do, of course—which is why writers often put their work aside for a time. The more you can see your writing as if for the first time, the more you will respond to it as your real readers might, questioning and probing and exploring it. As you reread the first draft of your informative writing, here are some questions to ask yourself:

- What else might my audience want or need to know about my subject?
- How else might I encourage my audience to learn more about my subject?
- What information did I find that I did not include in my paper? (Effective research always results in more information than you can include, so consider what you left out that you might include in your next draft.)
- Have I clearly explained any terms my readers might not know?
- Have I clearly synthesized the information I collected from all of my different sources?
- Could some of my information be more effectively presented as a graph, a chart, or in a photograph?

Technology can help you revise and edit your writing more easily. Use your word processor's track-changes tool to try out revisions and editing changes. After you've had time to think about the possible changes, you can "accept" or "reject" them. Also, you can use your word processor's comment tool to write reminders to yourself when you get stuck on a revision or some editing task. If you make a presentation about your topic in class, think about how you might be able to use a PowerPoint slide, or a chart or photograph, in your paper.

Because it is so difficult to see our own emerging writing with a fresh eye (even for experienced writers), it is almost always useful to ask classmates, friends, or family members to read and comment on drafts of your papers.

Responding to Readers' Comments

Once they have received feedback from peers, teachers, and others, writers have to decide what to do with that feedback. Because the text is *your* paper, you as the

WRITER'S *Workshop* | Responding to Full Drafts

As you read and respond to your classmates' papers (and as they comment on yours), focus on the informative nature of this assignment, but from a reader's perspective. Be sure to ask questions of their writing and respond to their ideas by exploring your reactions and responses to their thoughts.

Working in pairs or groups of three, read each others' drafts, and then offer your classmates comments that will help them see both their papers' strengths and places where they need to develop their ideas further. Use the following questions to guide your responses to the writer's draft:

- What is your first impression of this draft? How effectively does the title draw you into the paper? Why?

- What do you like about the draft? Provide positive and encouraging feedback to the writer.

- What is the writer's focus? If the paper loses focus, where does it do so?

- What part(s) of the text are especially informative? What information was interesting and/or new to you?

- Comment specifically on the introduction: What is effective about it? What suggestions can you make on how to improve it?

- What do you think is the author's thesis or main point? How could it be expressed or supported more effectively?

- In the main part of the paper, are there parts that are confusing? Where would you like more details or examples to help you see what the author means? What parts could use more explanation or definitions?

- How clear is the author's informative writing? If there are places that seem wordy or unclear, how might the author revise to address those problems?

- How accurate does the information seem? How does the author indicate the sources of statistics and other information that are not common knowledge?

- Reread the conclusion: How well does it tie everything together? To what extent does it make you want to learn more about this topic?

- What do you see as the main weaknesses of this paper? How might the writer improve the text?

- If you are working with a nontraditional text (a Web page, for example, or a brochure), what special attributes are present, and how effective are they?

- If there are visual aspects of the document, how effectively do they illustrate the point being made? How much do the visuals add to a reader's overall understanding of the information?

writer are responsible for dealing with reader responses to your work. You may decide to reject some comments, of course, and that decision is yours. Some of your readers might not understand your main point, or they may misunderstand something you wrote—so it is up to you either to accept or to ignore their comments and suggestions. Other comments, though, deserve your attention, as they are the words of real readers speaking to you about how to improve your text. You may find that comments from more than one reader contradict each other. In that case, use your own judgment to decide which reader's comments are on the right track.

 # KNOWLEDGE OF CONVENTIONS

When effective writers edit their work, they attend to the conventions that will help readers—the table manners of writing. These include genre conventions, documentation, format, usage, grammar, punctuation, and mechanics. By attending to these conventions in your writing, you make reading your work a more pleasant experience.

Editing

The last task in any writing project is editing. When you edit and polish your writing, you make changes to your sentence structure and word choice to improve your style and to make your writing clearer and more concise. You also check your work to make sure it adheres to conventions of grammar, usage, punctuation, mechanics, and spelling. Use the spell-check function of your word-processing program, but be sure to double-check your spelling personally. If you have used sources in your paper, make sure you are following the documentation style your instructor requires.

See Chapter 20 for more on documenting sources.

As with overall revision of your work, this final editing and polishing is most effective if you can put your text aside for a few days and come back to it with fresh eyes. We strongly recommend that you ask classmates, friends, and tutors to read your work as well.

To assist you with editing, we offer here a round-robin editing activity focused on finding and correcting problems with modifiers.

Genres, Documentation, and Format

If you are writing an academic paper, follow the conventions for the discipline in which you are writing and the requirements of your instructor. If you are constructing a brochure for a local service organization (Scenario 2), refer to the guidelines presented in Appendix C. If you have used material from outside sources, including

For advice on writing in different genres, see Appendix C. For guidelines for formatting and documenting papers in MLA or APA style, see Chapter 20.

WRITER'S *Workshop* | Round-Robin Editing with a Focus on Modifiers

Informative writing benefits from the careful use of modifiers—words or groups of words that describe or limit other words—such as adjectives, adverbs, infinitives, participles, prepositional phrases, and relative clauses. Working in small groups, read one another's papers, looking for two common problems: misplaced and dangling modifiers.

When a modifier is misplaced, it is too far away from the word or phrase it is modifying, so that it appears to be modifying something else. To correct the problem, the modifier needs to be moved.

MISPLACED Student Jim Roberts told me ~~at orientation or anywhere else~~ no one
                                              at orientation or anywhere else
had mentioned the school's recycling program to him∧.

A modifier is dangling when the word or phrase it modifies does not appear in the sentence to all. You can correct the problem by adding the word or phrase.

                                      students need to be provided with
DANGLING In order to know about the recyling program,∧ ~~Meyers suggests that~~
                                       ,*according to Meyers*
information ~~be provided~~ at all orientation meetings∧.

Compare notes to see if you have questions about modifiers, and consult a grammar handbook or ask your instructor for assistance.

visuals, give credit to those sources, using the documentation style required by the discipline you are working in and by your instructor.

 # A Writer Achieves His Goal: Craig Broadbent's Final Draft

The final draft of Craig Broadbent's essay "Watch for the Blue Barrels" follows. As you read Broadbent's essay, think about what makes it effective. Note, too, how he used the suggestions his classmates offered during peer review to make his informative paper more effective. Following the essay, you'll find some specific questions to consider.

CRAIG BROADBENT

Watch for the Blue Barrels

Have you ever wondered what all of those blue barrels that are scattered around campus are for . . . and if you know what they're for, do you wonder why students don't seem to use them? Those blue barrels are the heart of our campus-wide recycling program, and it is critical not only that students know what they are, but also that they *use* the barrels (see Fig. 1).

© Stockbyte/PunchStock RF

Fig. 1 A Blue Barrel for Recycling Waste. Source: Stockbyte/PunchStock RF

This is Broadbent's thesis sentence. Here he tells his readers that he will inform them about the campus recycling program and why they should take part.

Joan Meyers, who coordinates our campus recycling program, says that it has been in place for more than ten years now, but receives little publicity. My purpose here is to outline what we're doing about recycling on campus, to show what the costs and income are from the program, and finally, based on several interviews, to suggest the reasons that students don't use the blue barrels.

What is recycling and why should we care about it? Recycling is the reuse of some product. We all know that reusing plastic, aluminum cans, newspaper, glass, and other items by recycling them saves energy (and thus helps our air pollution problem) and can also save money. Recycling is environmentally sound—the more paper, plastic, and metal products that we can reuse, the less we have to make. That's the case even though things are usually not recycled into what they were to start with. That is, aluminum cans, Meyers told me, rarely are recycled to make more aluminum cans. But they *are* recycled and made into other products (frying pans, for instance). In addition to Meyers' examples, the United States Environmental Protection Agency mentions that there are more than 4500 products that are made from recycled material, including things such as car bumpers, ~~egg~~ cartons, and carpets. Therefore, recycling saves trees and other natural resources.

One peer suggestion Broadbent received was the following:

Perhaps a table or chart would help me see what you mean.

To address this reader's concern, Broadbent added this paragraph and also Table 1.

Not only that, but if certain items are *not* recycled, they can be around forever. That is, if we don't recycle some household items, they never seem to "waste away." For example, the National Park Service lists a number of items that can take close to forever to break down, or they *never* will go away, as shown in Table 1.

Table 1   Amount of Time It Takes Common Items to Break Down

Cigarette butts	1–5 years
Plastic-coated candy wrappers	5 years
Plastic bags	10–20 years
Tin cans	50 years
Aluminum cans and tabs	80–100 years
Glass bottles	100,000 years

Source: National Park Service, "How Long Does Litter Last?" 9 Sept. 2011, www.nps.gov/tuma/forkids/upload/HowLongDoesLitterLast.pdf.

Even seemingly minor items like cigarette butts can last as long as five years, and empty soda cans—unless they are recycled—can last for up to 100 years. And styrofoam and plastic can last forever.   5

Joan Meyers notes that our recycling program not only keeps the campus cleaner, since items are collected in the blue barrels instead of perhaps being thrown on the ground, but it also generates some $5,000 a year in revenue for the school. Ms. Meyers also told me that our college could make as much as $30,000 a year from recycling if we recycled all the newspapers, cans, and other waste that we now throw away. There is impressive savings involved in recycling: the University of Rochester was one of the EPA's Gold Achievement award winners for 2011, and they saved over $200,000 by recycling. The EPA provides details about UR's program: 6

The university effectively utilized online social networking tools, posters, fact sheets, articles, student group initiatives, and university staff and faculty to encourage participation in events and campaigns, including RecycleMania, the Go Green Pledge, Earth Day, Water Week, and E-Cycle Day. Through these efforts, more than 5,000 UR undergraduates learned about the importance of waste reduction on their college campus. To keep the students involved in UR's sustainability initiatives, they are offered the opportunity to write and edit for the "UR Green News" newsletter.   7

In all, UR's education and outreach efforts helped the university recycle nearly 3,400 tons of materials, resulting in a reduction of more than 8,000 metric tons of carbon dioxide equivalent. The university also saved more than $230,000 in 2010 through recycling revenues and avoiding disposal costs. ("2011 Wastewise Award Winners")   8

Recycling also saves in other ways, including energy (like gasoline and oil), as the EPA reports (see Fig. 2).   9

Students, though, don't use our recycling program, sometimes because they're not aware of it. Student Jim Roberts told me that no one had men-   10

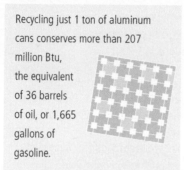

Recycling just 1 ton of aluminum cans conserves more than 207 million Btu, the equivalent of 36 barrels of oil, or 1,665 gallons of gasoline.

Fig. 2 Energy Savings from Recycling Aluminum. Illustration from "Municipal Solid Waste Generation, Recycling, and Disposal in the United States: Facts and Figures for 2010" (Environmental Protection Agency, Nov. 2011, www.epa.gov/epawaste/nonhaz/municipal/pubs/msw_2010_factsheet.pdf.

tioned the school's recycling program to him, at orientation or anywhere else. Another student, Tracy Worsam, even asked about the program at her orientation, but no one there seemed to know much about it, other than to say "we have some blue barrels around campus." Finally, I interviewed several students who live in that old house on the edge of campus. It's not really a fraternity but more of a boardinghouse. They all told me that they never littered, even though their yard was a mess (Wilson et al.). Maybe my interview with them—and the information I gave them about the blue barrel program—will help. Maybe if they understood recycling and had blue barrels in a convenient location, they would recycle plastic, paper, glass, and so on.

A search through several back issues of the *Campus Reporter* may explain why not many students are really aware of the blue barrel program. During the last few months, only one small advertisement about the campus recycling program has appeared in the *Reporter,* and no articles about the program were published.

The EPA provides what might be a useful suggestion for our college: a program they help sponsor called "RecycleMania." "RecycleMania is a friendly competition and benchmarking tool for college and university recycling programs to promote waste reduction activities to their campus communities." ("Welcome"). Perhaps if we could get our own college involved we could make a huge difference in the environmental awareness of our own students.

In order to know about and understand the recycling program, students need to be provided with information at all orientation meetings, and weekly advertisements need to be run in the *Campus Reporter,* according to Joan Meyers. In the meantime, students who would like to learn more about the recycling program on campus, and how they can help, can contact Meyers at JoanMeyers@Ourcollege.edu.

11

12

13

Another comment Broadbent received from his peer review session pointed out a problem:

The weakest part is the interview information, which made me want to read more of what other people had to say.

Note how he has now included a good deal of information from the students he interviewed.

Broadbent's peer made this comment on his earlier draft:

Your conclusion was weak—maybe you could add what students ought to be doing now? Put another way, what do you want your readers to do with this (interesting) information?

Note how he now addresses what students can do to become more involved with their campus recycling program.

This paper follows MLA guidelines for in-text citations and works cited. Note that while URLs are optional, MLA strongly recommends including them when possible. Access dates are also an optional element but should be included when no other date is available.

Works Cited

"How Long Does Litter Last?" *National Park Service*, 9 Sept. 2011, www.nps.gov/tuma/forkids/upload/HowLongDoesLitterLast.pdf.

Meyers, Joan. Personal Interview. 20 Jan. 2016.

"Municipal Solid Waste Generation, Recycling, and Disposal in the United States: Facts and Figures for 2010." *United States Environmental Protection Agency (EPA)*, Nov. 2011, www.epa.gov/epawaste/nonhaz/municipal/pubs/msw_2010_fact-sheet.pdf.

"RecycleMania Tournament." *Recyclemaniacs*, www.recyclemaniacs.org. Accessed 16 Jan. 2016.

"Reduce, Reuse, Recycle." *United States Environmental Protection Agency (EPA)*, 15 Feb. 2015, www2.epa.gov/recycle.

Roberts, Jim. Personal Interview. 20 Jan. 2016.

"2011 Wastewise Award Winners." *United States Environmental Protection Agency (EPA)*, 2 Nov. 2011, www.epa.gov/epawaste/partnerships/wastewise/events/2011awardees.htm.

Wilson, James, et al. Personal Interview. 20 Jan. 2016.

Worsom, Tracy. Personal Interview. 20 Jan. 2016.

UNDERSTANDING A WRITER'S GOALS: QUESTIONS TO CONSIDER AND DISCUSS

Rhetorical Knowledge: The Writer's Situation and Rhetoric

1. **Audience:** How effective is Broadbent at appealing to the audience that this information is intended for—students at a college or university? What can you point to in the essay to demonstrate what you mean?

2. **Purpose:** In addition to its informative purpose, what other purposes does this paper have?

3. **Voice and tone:** What is Broadbent's attitude toward his subject? How does he indicate this attitude in his tone?

4. **Responsibility:** What can you point to in Broadbent's informational essay that gives the text its *ethos*? To what extent do you believe the information that Broadbent presents here? Why?

5. **Context, format, and genre:** How has Broadbent's context—his college campus—affected his paper? How might he have written about the same subject differently in another context? The first sentence of Broadbent's essay directly engages the reader in a personal way that wouldn't be found in a formal report. Do you think Broadbent's informality here is appropriate for his audience? Will it succeed in getting his audience more fully engaged?

Critical Thinking: The Writer's Ideas and Your Personal Response

6. What ideas in Broadbent's essay seem the most important to you? Why?

7. How effectively does Broadbent inform the reader? What examples can you point to in the text that provide useful information?

Composing Processes and Knowledge of Conventions: The Writer's Strategies

8. How effective are the visuals that Broadbent includes? What is your opinion of the sources he uses? What other sources might he have consulted?

9. What is your opinion of Broadbent's conclusion?

Inquiry and Research: Ideas for Further Exploration

10. Go to your college's main Web page and search for "recycling." In no more than one page, outline what you learn.

Self-Assessment: Reflecting on Your Goals

Now that you have constructed a piece of informative writing, go back and consider your learning goals, which you and your classmates may have considered at the beginning of this chapter (see pages 156–157). Write notes on what you have learned from this assignment.

 ## Rhetorical Knowledge

- *Audience:* What did you learn about your audience as you wrote your informative paper?
- *Purpose:* How successfully do you feel you fulfilled your informative purpose?
- *Rhetorical situation:* How did the writing context affect your informational text? How did your choice of topic affect the research you conducted and how you presented your information to your readers? What do you see as the strongest part of your paper? Why? The weakest? Why?
- *Voice and tone:* How would you describe your voice in this essay? Your tone? How do they contribute to the effectiveness of your informational essay?

 ## Critical Thinking, Reading, and Writing

- *Learning/inquiry:* How did you decide what to focus on in your informative paper? Describe the process you went through to focus on a main idea, or thesis.
- *Responsibility:* How did you fulfill your responsibility to your readers?
- *Reading and research:* What did you learn about informative writing from the reading selections you read for this chapter? What research did you conduct? Why? What additional research might you have done?

Writing Processes

- *Invention:* What invention strategies were most useful to you? Why?

- *Organizing your ideas and details:* What organization did you use? How successful was it? Why?

- *Revising:* What one revision did you make that you are most satisfied with? Why? If you could make an additional revision, what would it be?

- *Working with peers:* How did your instructor or peer readers help you by making comments and suggestions about your writing? How could you have more effectively used the comments and suggestions you received?

- *Visuals:* Did you use photographs or other visuals to help you inform your readers? If so, what did you learn about incorporating these elements?

- *Writing habits:* What "writerly habits" have you developed, modified, or improved on as you constructed the writing assignment for this chapter?

Knowledge of Conventions

- *Editing:* What sentence problem did you find most frequently in your writing? How will you avoid that problem in future assignments?

- *Genre:* What conventions of the genre you were using, if any, gave you problems?

- *Documentation:* Did you use sources for your paper? If so, what documentation style did you use? What problems, if any, did you have with it?

Refer to Chapter 1 (page 12) for a sample reflection by a student.

Text Credits

p. 163: William Strunk, Elwyn Brooks White *The Elements of Style*, MacMillan, 1979. **p. 165:** Carol Ezzell, "Clocking Cultures." *Scientific American*, September 2002, pp. 74-75. Reproduced with permission. Copyright© 2002 Scientific American, Inc. All rights reserved. **p. 169:** "What Is Autism Spectrum Disorder" National Institute of Mental Health (NIMH), U.S. Dept. of Health and Human Services. http://www.nimh.nih.gov/health/topics/autism-spectrum-disorders-asd/index.shtml. **p. 191:** Environmental Protection Agency (EPA)."2011 Wastewise Award Winners." 15 Nov. 2011. http://www.epa.gov/epawaste/partnerships/wastewise/events/2011awardees.htm.

CHAPTER 8

Writing to Analyze

© Stockbyte/Punchstock RF

What are you afraid of?

To more clearly understand a subject such as the irrational fear of spiders or snakes, scientists analyze it, or break it down. An **analysis** examines an issue or topic by identifying the parts that make up the whole. You can gain a clearer understanding of your subject when you look closely at the individual pieces that constitute the whole. An analysis of a *phobia*, defined as an uncontrollable (and sometimes irrational) fear of some situation, object, or activity, would require you to examine the various aspects of that phobia.

Analyzing phobias is an area of study at colleges and universities. Here is an excerpt from an essay about anxiety disorders, which includes phobias, by a researcher at the University of Texas at Austin:

> Fear can be a good thing.
> Being afraid makes us heed severe weather warnings and keeps us from running across busy freeways. It is a survival mechanism for most, but for some people their fear has become consuming and out of control.

Since 1988 Dr. Michael Telch and the Laboratory for the Study of Anxiety Disorders (LSAD) in the Department of Psychology at The University of Texas at Austin have been researching treatments for anxiety-related disorders such as panic disorder, obsessive-compulsive disorder, social anxiety disorder, and specific phobias, including claustrophobia, arachnophobia and cynophobia (dog phobia).

"Anxiety is part of being a human being," Telch said. "The question is when does it become a disorder? Mother Nature gave us an alarm system of anxiety and panic to cope with threats. This signal system is critical to our survival. The bad news is that this mechanism is capable of sending a false alarm.

"It can become a disorder when the alarm is out of proportion to the threat," he added. "The hallmark is that the brain is receiving danger messages when the danger isn't there. While many people have these false alarms, it becomes a disorder when it interferes with daily functioning or when the response is above and beyond what is called for. Anxiety disorders are the largest—and one of the most treatable—classes of psychiatric disorders."

Rapid breathing, pounding heart and a desire to flee are typical—and reasonable—reactions to perceived danger, but for someone experiencing an anxiety disorder, these feelings become overwhelming. The fight or flight response kicks into overdrive when a person is experiencing the symptoms of an anxiety disorder. Research has shown that anxiety disorders in the U.S. cost more than $42 billion each year, about one third of the amount spent on mental health care in this country.

Although psychologists analyze subjects such as phobias to understand mental processes better, analysis can also be helpful in everyday life. You have probably analyzed the college you are currently attending: examining its catalogue to consider the variety of courses offered, perhaps reading through faculty lists to consider whom you might be able to study with, and considering other factors. Using analysis in your writing can help you come to a deeper understanding of your subject and share that understanding with your readers.

Setting Your Goals for *Analytical Writing*

Rhetorical Knowledge (pp. 202-207)

- **Audience:** Determine who will benefit from your analysis. What do the audience members probably already know? What will you need to tell them?
- **Purpose:** When you analyze a complex situation, process, or relationship, you can help others understand the subject more thoroughly.
- **Rhetorical situation:** In an analysis, you break down your subject into parts or categories to help your reader understand it more clearly. The situation that calls for the analysis helps you understand which details you need to look at most closely.
- **Voice and tone:** When you write an analysis, a detailed, thorough approach and a reasonable tone can increase your credibility to readers.
- **Context, medium, and genre:** Decide on the most effective medium and genre to use to present your analysis to the audience you want to reach. Think about how digital technologies might help to determine your choice.

Critical Thinking, Reading, and Writing (pp. 207-214)

- **Learning/inquiry:** By reading and writing analytically, you gain a deeper understanding of issues and the ability to make more informed decisions.
- **Responsibility:** Effective analysis leads to critical thinking. When you engage in analysis, you see the nuances of all the potential relationships involved in your subject.
- **Reading and research:** Analysis can involve close observation as well as interviews and online and library research.

Writing Processes (pp. 215–227)

- **Invention:** Use invention activities such as brainstorming, listing, and clustering to help you consider the parts of your subject and how they relate to one another.
- **Organizing your ideas and details:** If your subject is large, you might break it down into more understandable parts, or you might begin with individual parts and examine each one in detail. Consider using a spreadsheet or a database file to help you organize your information.
- **Revising:** Read your work with a critical eye to make certain that it fulfills the assignment and displays the qualities of good analytical writing.
- **Working with peers:** Listen to your classmates to make sure that they understand your analysis. Consider how digital technologies can help facilitate your work with peers.

Knowledge of Conventions (pp. 227–232)

- **Editing:** The round-robin activity on page 228 will help you check your analysis for wordy sentences. You could use an online tool such as Google Drive to share your drafts with peers.
- **Genres for analytical writing:** Usually, analyses are written as formal documents, so most of the time your analysis will be a formal report or an academic essay.
- **Documentation:** If you have relied on sources outside of your own experience, cite them using the appropriate documentation style. Consider how digital technologies can assist you in documenting sources accurately and consistently.

RHETORICAL KNOWLEDGE

An analysis is often an opportunity to help your readers understand a familiar topic in a new way. Whatever your topic, you will need to consider why you want them to gain this understanding. You will also need to decide what medium and genre will help you get your analysis across to your audience.

 ## Writing to Analyze in Your College Classes

Although academic disciplines vary widely, all of them require the use of analysis, because when you analyze something, you will come to understand it more completely. In your college career, you may be asked to construct written analyses in many of your classes:

- In a chemistry class, you might be asked to break down an unknown compound to find what elements are present and write a lab report on your findings.
- In a literature class, you might be asked to analyze how an author develops the hero of a novel to be a sympathetic character.
- In an American history class, you may analyze what political circumstances led to the ratification of an amendment to the U.S. Constitution.

Performing an analysis usually requires you to make close observations or conduct research so that you will have a command of your subject. Writing an analysis forces you to put your understanding of that subject into your own words.

The "Ways of Writing" feature presents different genres that can be used when writing to analyze in your college classes.

 ## Writing to Analyze for Life

In the professional, civic, and personal areas of your life, you also will construct analyses of various ideas, products, and situations.

The kind of analytical writing you do in your professional life will depend on your career, yet the odds are that at some point you will be asked to do an analysis and write a report on your findings. For example, an attorney analyzes legal rulings, the strengths and weaknesses of a client's case, and the arguments presented in court. A physician analyzes her patient's symptoms as she attempts to diagnose the illness and prescribe a cure.

Often the first impulse in civic life is emotional. You may become angry when the city council decides to demolish an old building, or you might enthusiastically support a local developer's plan to buy unused farmland. Your voice will be taken much more seriously by decision makers, however, if you engage in a balanced, in-depth analysis.

Interestingly, in our personal lives, we often tend to analyze events or conversations after they have happened. You may have had a conversation with a close friend that left both of you feeling unhappy. After the encounter, you replay

Ways of Writing to Analyze

Genres for Your College Classes	Sample Situation	Advantages of the Genre	Limitations of the Genre
Behavioral analysis	In your social psychology class, you are asked to construct a statistical analysis of the behavior in specific situations of male college students in groups, as compared to how they act individually in those same situations.	Your research and statistical analysis will provide your readers with useful information about behavior.	It is difficult to find enough reliable statistics for such an analysis; there sometimes are time constraints that limit your research.
Rhetorical analysis	Your writing professor asks you to analyze the rhetorical appeals on a Web site.	This analysis will help you to understand how a Web site appeals to its readers.	This is only one way to examine a Web site.
Nutrition analysis	In your health and nutrition class, your professor asks you to analyze several new diets.	You can provide useful information to readers.	Your analysis is not an evaluation of a diet, which often is what readers want.
Letter to your campus newspaper	Your ethics professor asks you to draft a letter to your college newspaper analyzing a campus problem.	Your college newspaper is a useful forum in which to publicize your analysis of the campus problem to the right audience.	A letter to the editor allows only limited space for your analysis. It might not be published.
Chemical analysis report	Your biology teacher asks you to construct a report on the toxicity of a specific group of chemicals when they are combined.	This report helps readers understand the interaction between chemicals. Such knowledge is critical whenever medicine is dispensed.	A chemical analysis report might not provide everything needed for your biology class.
Visual analysis	Your writing teacher asks you to analyze the visual features of advertisements for cellular phones.	A visual analysis will help you to understand that visuals can have as much impact on an audience as text.	A focus on visual elements can divert attention from verbal content.
Genres for Life	Sample Situation	Advantages of the Genre	Limitations of the Genre
Brochure	As part of a neighborhood group, you construct a brochure to analyze an issue for a school bond vote.	A brochure is a convenient format for distributing information.	A brochure offers limited space for your analysis of the school bond.
Web site	Your business offers a Web site that allows employees to input their salary, tax situation, and so on to help them determine the best way to invest their retirement funds.	This Web site is an interactive venue for employees to analyze their possible investment scenarios.	Sometimes Web sites can be difficult to use and take time to update with new information.
Wiki	You want to create a wiki that allows members of your community to share their analyses of a local issue.	A wiki is an uncomplicated way for interested parties to share their analyses.	Wikis can become long and convoluted; someone needs to monitor activity.
Brand analysis	Your company asks you to analyze several potential new lines of merchandise.	Your analysis will provide sufficient information to help the company make good business decisions.	It can be difficult to find adequate information for such an analysis.
Letter	In a letter that you will never send, you analyze a problem in a relationship with a friend to avoid similar problems in the future.	A "letter to yourself" helps you to honestly understand a problem.	Because you do not plan to send the letter, you might not put much effort into writing it.

the conversation in your mind, trying to take apart what was said by whom and figure out what went wrong. The "Ways of Writing" feature on page 203 presents different genres that can be used when writing to analyze in life.

Scenarios for Writing | Assignment Options

Your instructor may ask you to complete one or more of the following analytical writing assignments. Each assignment is a scenario, which provides some context for the analysis you will construct. The scenarios give you a sense of who your audience is and what you want to accomplish with your analytical writing, including your purpose; voice, tone, and point of view; context; and genre.

Starting on page 215, you will find guidelines for completing the assignment option that you choose or that is assigned to you.

Writing for College

SCENARIO 1   A Visual Analysis

Visuals are important and pervasive. Often, we see them in texts and use them in our own texts; sometimes, they stand alone. The visual elements of a text include not only photos, charts, and drawings but also the fonts used in that text. Here we will focus on an image.

To analyze an image, ask the same questions you would ask if you were to analyze a verbal text: What are the elements of the visual that make it work? How do those various aspects function together, complementing one another, to have the intended effect?

For practice, examine Figure 8.1, a billboard advertising a media player. Consider the elements that make up this ad and how they work together to tell a viewer about the product and to encourage that person to buy an iPod. See the "Genres Up Close" feature on page 214 for suggestions.

Writing Assignment: Assume you are part of an organizing committee for a campus event. It might be promoting an upcoming speaker on campus, a community service project, a social event, or any number of other possibilities. Your job is to design a poster to help promote the event. Design a draft of that poster. Then, based on your knowledge of analyzing visuals (Chapter 18), write an analysis of how your poster successfully evokes an effect and promotes the event to your intended audience.

Writing for Life

SCENARIO 2   Personal Writing: Constructing a Wiki to Share Family History

If you were asked to define the word *wiki*, where is the first place you might look? Perhaps on *Wikipedia*, where the entry both defines the term and demonstrates a working example. A wiki is a website that allows for collaborative editing of both content and structure. Visit the Wikipedia page for the term wiki and peruse its

FIGURE 8.1
Billboard Advertisement

contents and structure. Notice how many citations make up the reference list. Consider how an entry like this one—about an evolving digital technology—must have changed over time, as new contributions have been made. What, do you think, are the benefits and drawbacks to collaborating this way?

Writing Assignment: Assume that you would like to develop a system to analyze information about your family history. Because you have an extended family with aunts, uncles, cousins, nephews, and others all over the country, it makes sense to share the information they all have electronically. You could construct an e-mail list, but you want to develop something of an archive, so future generations of your family can access the information. You also want those who participate to be able to modify, analyze, and correct the information that others supply because sometimes the historical information we have about our family is not completely accurate.

A wiki is an effective way to accomplish this task because many family members can have access to and change inaccurate information that others post, as well as provide their own analyses. For this assignment, construct a wiki to share historical information about your family. There are many Web sources to help with this process: searching for "create wiki" will provide a large number of them.

SCENARIO 3   Professional Writing: A Business Report Analyzing Part of Your Future Career

Think forward to the day when you are ready to apply for jobs in your chosen field. Select an image or advertisement related to your future career—the position you plan to seek after you graduate from college. You might select the following, for example:

- A movie advertisement, if you are planning to work as an actor, director, or screenwriter, or in another role in the film industry
- An advertisement for a product produced by or a service provided by the company you hope to work for
- An image from a company's annual report
- A company's logo
- A Web page from a nonprofit or government agency for which you hope to work

Writing Assignment: For this writing project, analyze the image or advertisement that you selected. Your task is not to evaluate the image or advertisement, but rather to analyze its various aspects (color, point of view, text, size, and shading) to understand how the image or advertisement works.

Rhetorical Considerations in Analytical Writing

Audience: Although your teacher and classmates are the initial audience for your analysis, also consider a wider audience. What kinds of analysis will be most interesting to this group of readers?

Purpose: By researching and analyzing the problem, issue, concept, options, or object, you will provide your readers with an analysis that will allow them to make more informed decisions. What kinds of information will you include in your analysis to support your purpose?

Voice, tone, and point of view: You have probably chosen your topic because you have a personal interest in the subject. What preconceptions do you have? How can you avoid letting them affect your analysis? How can you use voice and tone to establish credibility, so your readers believe your analysis?

Context, medium, and genre: Keeping the context of the assignment in mind, decide on a medium and a genre for your writing. How will your analysis be used? Who might be interested in reading your analysis? If you are writing for an audience beyond the classroom, consider what will be the most effective way to present your analysis to this audience. Think about whether a digital format might be more effective for your analysis.

For more on choosing a medium and genre, see Chapter 17.

 # CRITICAL THINKING, READING, AND WRITING

Before you begin to write your analysis, consider the qualities of successful analytic writing. It also helps to read one or more examples of analysis to see these qualities in action.

 ## Learning the Qualities of Effective Analytical Writing

To help you and your readers better understand your subject, make sure your analysis includes the following qualities:

- A focus on a complex subject. Any subject worth analyzing—a political position, a book, a war strategy—will consist of many parts or features, and these parts will interact with one another in complicated ways.

- A thorough explanation of the parts and how they relate to one another. Your first step will be to identify the component parts or aspects of your subject and then consider how those parts function separately and together. For a subject such as a new school tax bond, you might consider aspects like the following:
- Benefits:
  - to the students
  - to the local tax base
  - to the teachers, administration, and support staff
- Problems and costs:
  - costs in the form of debt that will need to be paid off
  - interest charges
- What happens if the community does not fund the schools in this way?
  - Will school taxes need to be raised?
  - Will the quality of the school suffer?

After you have identified the parts or aspects of your subject, you need to gain a thorough understanding of each one so that you can explain it to your readers.

- **Research-based rather than personal-based writing.** A formal analysis usually requires research. Your understanding of the subject is seldom enough to inform a thorough analysis. If you were analyzing the bond proposal, for example, you would need to read the entire proposal, interview the officials or citizen groups behind it, and examine recent school budgets.

For more on conducting research, see Chapters 19 and 20.

- **A focused, straightforward presentation.** An effective analysis focuses on the subject's component parts, always working to show how they combine to make up the whole. All aspects of your text must focus on some central theme or idea that links all parts or aspects of the analysis.

  An analysis is usually neutral in tone—the writer's primary purpose is not to persuade, but rather to explain how the subject functions.

- **Insights.** Taking something apart to analyze it provides insights into how each part functions, how each aspect relates to every other aspect and to the whole.

For more on thesis statements, see Chapter 13.

- **A conclusion that ties parts together.** In an analysis, your conclusion does much more than just state your major claim (as a *thesis statement* usually does). In your conclusion, you have the opportunity to outline *how* the parts function together and also to explain whether you believe they function effectively or not.

Reading, Inquiry, and Research: Learning from Texts That Analyze

The reading selections that follow are examples of analytical writing. As you read the texts, ask yourself the following questions:

- What makes this analysis effective?
- What qualities of an effective analysis (see pages 207–208) do the selections exhibit?
- What parts of the analysis leave me with questions?
- How can I use these analytical techniques in my writing?

NATALIE KITROEFF

The Smartest People Are Opting Out of Law School

OPINION PIECE

Natalie Kitroeff reports on business education for *Bloomberg Business-week*. In this piece, Kitroeff analyzes the trend in lower Law School Admissions Test scores leading to admission of less-qualified candidates to law programs. Notice how she uses graphs to illustrate the details of her analysis.

American law schools have a brain drain problem. 1 Fewer people with high Law School Admission Test scores are applying to and enrolling in law school, and less-qualified students are filling their slots, new research shows.

As schools grapple with a persistent slump in young 2 Americans' interest in legal education, the programs seem to be compensating for their sudden unpopularity by taking in people who wouldn't have made the cut five years ago. As of March 2015, about half as many students with scores of 165 and above on the LSAT have applied to law school as did in 2010, according to a new analysis of the latest numbers from the Law School Admission Council, which administers the test. LSAT scores range from 120 to 180. Applications from students with lower scores are falling, too, but not nearly as sharply, as the second chart below shows.

The disenchantment with law school on the part of the people most likely 3 to get in shows up in the classroom head count, too: Around 5,400 people with the highest scores will enroll in law school this year, down from 9,400 in 2010, according to Jerome Organ, the University of St. Thomas School of Law professor who parsed the numbers.

Even as applications fall across the board, a growing number of people 4 with low scores are expected to show up to class. Some 8,700 low-scoring

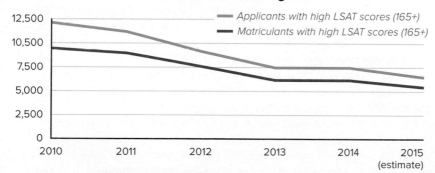

The Best and the Flightiest

— Applicants with high LSAT scores (165+)
— Matriculants with high LSAT scores (165+)

| | 2010 | 2011 | 2012 | 2013 | 2014 | 2015 (estimate) |

The Number of People with the Highest Test Scores Applying and Enrolling in Law School

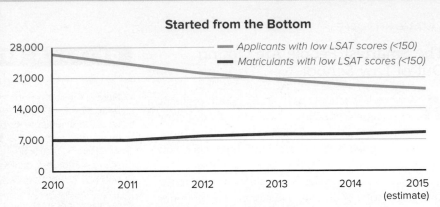

Started from the Bottom

Applicants with low LSAT scores (<150)
Matriculants with low LSAT scores (<150)

Law School Applicants and Matriculants with the Lowest LSAT Scores

students will likely start law school in 2015, up from 7,000 in 2010, according to Organ, who looked at LSAC data on the number of applicants as of March 6, 2015, and projected how much the pool would grow and how many would matriculate, based on averages from the previous three years.

"The top is eroding and the bottom is growing," says Organ, adding that   5
schools risk churning out graduates with less of a shot at becoming lawyers. "Four years from now, when those people graduate and take the bar, you'll have a much smaller percentage who are likely to pass the bar and a much larger percentage that are likely to fail." Research has shown that LSAT scores generally correlate with success during the first year of law school and with scores on the bar exam.

Indeed, several states have begun reporting results for the February 2015 bar   6
exam, and they are underwhelming: Scores on the multistate portion of the test dipped to their lowest point in five years, and pass rates are down across the country. The slump looks positively inspiring in comparison with the dark moment last fall, when states reported the single largest score drop for the July bar exam in four decades. After that bombshell, the National Conference of Bar Examiners, the organization that creates the exam, enraged some law schools after blaming the failing grades on a "less able" group of test takers. A group of 79 law deans jabbed back with a letter to the organization questioning "the integrity and fairness" of the test and openly questioning the need for a bar exam in the first place.

Still, as the bad marks pile up, some law professors are pointing the mirror   7
in law school's direction and asking deans to take a look.

"It's a reflection of the decline in the quality in graduates that law schools are   8
producing," says Derek Muller, a law professor at Pepperdine University, referring to the declining bar pass rates. "There's no question that schools have a moral imperative to consider the likelihood of success and the burden placed upon the students they admit, whether that's debt loads or probability of passing the Bar."

UNDERSTANDING A WRITER'S GOALS: QUESTIONS TO CONSIDER AND DISCUSS

Rhetorical Knowledge: The Writer's Situation and Rhetoric

1. **Audience:** Kitroeff wrote this piece for *Bloomberg Businessweek*. How effectively does she tailor this piece for people interested in business education? What does she do to address the interests of people who may not work in business?

2. **Purpose:** What does Kitroeff hope to accomplish in this piece? How does she want readers to respond?

3. **Voice and tone:** What can you point to in Kitroeff's tone that helps to establish her *ethos*?

4. **Responsibility:** What can you cite in this piece that shows how Kitroeff is fulfilling her responsibilities as a writer?

5. **Context, format, and genre:** Kitroeff wrote this piece as an essay. What other genre could she have used for treating this topic?

Critical Thinking: The Writer's Ideas and Your Personal Response

6. What is your initial reaction to Kitroeff's analysis? Why do you react that way?

7. If you are considering entering law school after completing a bachelor's degree, how might Kitroeff's analysis affect your plans?

Composing Processes and Knowledge of Conventions: The Writer's Strategies

8. Consider Kitroeff's overall organization by constructing a sentence or scratch outline of it (outline the text by writing, in one sentence next to every paragraph, what each paragraph says). How effective is this organization? Why? In what other ways might Kitroeff have organized the essay?

9. Kitroeff uses data to support her analysis. What other statistics could she have included? What effect would they have?

Inquiry and Research: Ideas for Further Exploration

10. Conduct a Web search to see how several law schools use data to describe the quality of their programs. Which data seem most compelling to you? What information can you find about how law schools help their alumni pass the bar exam?

KERRY MAGRO

ANALYSIS | ## Why Our Autism Community Loves Sheldon Cooper

Kerry Magro works as a social marketing director. Magro, who is on the spectrum, frequently speaks about autism across the United States.

When I was a kid I absolutely loved theater. My fascination with theater began when I was just starting grammar school. My parents had been using theater as part of my therapy to assist with my communication issues. Years later, when I became a self-advocate in college, I turned that fascination towards the world of films. I wanted to insure the entertainment industry was providing as realistic of a portrayal of individuals with autism as possible. This led to me helping out with the 2012 film *Joyful Noise* (starring Queen Latifah and Dolly Parton) that portrayed a character with Asperger syndrome.

As characters with autism appear in more plays, films and on television, I've received many questions regarding the trend. On my journey as an advocate I seem to always get a question or two about *The Big Bang Theory*'s main character Sheldon Cooper and whether or not he has Asperger syndrome.

Sheldon plays a scientific genius who works at a local university and shows several characteristics typical to those who have Asperger's, such as attention to detail, repetitive actions and a lack of social skills.

Although *The Big Bang Theory* states that Sheldon is not on the autism spectrum, Jim Parsons, who plays Sheldon on the show, has mentioned in several interviews how his character seems to exhibit some Asperger-like characteristics. Parsons isn't the only person who has suggested that certain scientific minds show characteristics of Asperger's. A few weeks ago, autism self-advocate Dr. Temple Grandin spoke at a conference I attended. She mentioned two other people she believed shared characteristics of Asperger's, Steve Jobs and Albert Einstein. Much like Sheldon, these two geniuses are seen as two brilliant minds that also have issues with social interaction.

Whether or not the Sheldon character has Asperger's, the show's popularity has brought this discussion to a large national audience, many of whom have high praise for Sheldon. I even heard this from a local boy with autism several weeks ago in a school that I visited. The boy wanted to grow up to be just like Sheldon! I have to admit that I have watched the show for years and I feel a connection to the character as well.

No matter why you watch the show, after talking to many individuals in our community, the biggest reason why people seem to be drawn to him is that he's absolutely genuine. He is who he is and doesn't pretend to be someone he isn't. He's just his own unique self.

I think that is something we can all relate to. We are all unique in our own   6
way. It goes with the old saying we have in the autism community how "If
you've met one person with autism, you've met one person with autism." For
our families, Sheldon shows that dreams we hope for our own kids like having
a job, being in a relationship and living independently can become reality.

Sheldon to me is one of the most unique characters we have on television   7
today. As an aspiring consultant in the field of autism awareness and education, it's a message I want to impart to others. Even though Sheldon may seem
different, a character like his should be treated with respect and tolerance. My
message of respect and tolerance is one I hope organizations focus on. The
wide spectrum of autism includes many truly unique individuals. Their stories
should be celebrated much like those of Sheldon, Albert and Steve.

UNDERSTANDING A WRITER'S GOALS: QUESTIONS TO CONSIDER AND DISCUSS

Rhetorical Knowledge: The Writer's Situation and Rhetoric

1. **Audience:** Kerry Magro wrote this piece for people who are interested in autism. How specifically does Magro focus on a subset of that broad audience?

2. **Purpose:** What is Magro trying to accomplish in this piece? How effective is he?

3. **Voice and tone:** What is Magro's attitude toward his readers? What makes you think that?

4. **Responsibility:** What does Magro do to show that he is a responsible writer?

5. **Context, format, and genre:** Kerry Magro wrote this piece as an essay for a blog. What other genre could he have used for treating this topic? What changes, if any, would Magro need to make if he were to rewrite this piece for a print magazine?

Critical Thinking: The Writer's Ideas and Your Personal Response

6. Because blog entries are often not vetted by editors, they can sometimes be biased. Do you detect any bias in Magro's piece? Explain.

7. If you have watched *The Big Bang Theory* and thought about Sheldon Cooper, how does Magro's analysis make you rethink your views of that character?

Composing Processes and Knowledge of Conventions: The Writer's Strategies

8. Consider Magro's mention of Steve Jobs and Albert Einstein. Why do you think that he chose to mention these two particular people? Are there others he could have mentioned here?

9. Magro uses personal experience to support his analysis. How effectively does he weave that experience into the analysis? How would it affect the analysis if he had not used personal experience?

Inquiry and Research: Ideas for Further Exploration

10. Conduct a Web search to see how others have addressed the topic of whether the character Sheldon Cooper is on the autism spectrum. What conclusions can you draw from those other analyses?

GENRES *Up Close*   Writing a Visual Analysis

On any given day, you are likely to encounter hundreds or even thousands of texts with visuals such as photos, diagrams, charts, maps, and graphs. For example, advertisements with visual elements appear in magazines, in newspapers, on billboards, as part of Web sites, and in various other media. The visuals that you see each day are as rhetorical as the words that you read. Because these kinds of visual elements are pervasive and often persuasive, readers and viewers need skills for analyzing them. Writing visual analyses helps to develop these reading and viewing skills. Consider, for example, Ben Evans' UNICEF visual analysis in Chapter 21.

A visual analysis will usually include the following features:

- **A copy of the image.** Seeing the image helps the reader understand the analysis, and reading the analysis helps the reader gain new insights into the visual.

- **A written description of the image.** The description can help guide readers' attention to specific features. Writing effective descriptions of images is an important skill in itself. If you're developing a Web site that uses images, provide a written description of each image when coding the site. Doing so makes the site accessible to screen readers that are used by visually impaired people.

- **An analysis of what the visual image is communicating—the rhetorical features of the visual.** As you craft your analysis, consider the material offered in Chapter 18, "Communicating with Design and Visuals." Also ask yourself the following kinds of questions:

  - What are the parts of the visual? How do the parts relate to the whole?
  - What story does the visual tell?
  - How do you react to the visual emotionally, intellectually, or in both ways?
  - What is the purpose of the visual?
  - How does the visual complement any verbal content in the text? (Most advertisements include both words and images.)
  - How is the visual placed in the text? Why do you think it is placed there?
  - How does this visual appeal to the intended audience? For example, a photo of Steve Lake (a catcher for the Chicago Cubs, Philadelphia Phillies, and St. Louis Cardinals in the 1980s and 1990s) playing in Game 7 of the 1987 World Series might appeal to a knowledgeable connoisseur of baseball, but it might not mean much to a casual fan of the game.
  - What would the text be like if the visual were missing?
  - What other visuals could work as well as, or even more effectively than, the current one? For example, in some situations a diagram might be more effective than a photo because it can reveal more details.
  - What design principles (see Chapter 18) has the writer used in the visual?

WRITING PROCESSES

As you work on the assignment you have chosen, remember the qualities of an effective analytical paper, which are listed on pages 207–208. Also remember that writing is rarely a neat series of well-defined steps. You might start with an invention activity or two and then conduct some research, which leads to more invention work and then a first draft; but then you might need to do more invention work to help flesh out your draft and conduct more research to fill in gaps in information; and then you will revise your draft and possibly find another gap or two. . . . Although the activities listed below imply that writers go through them step-by-step, the actual process of writing is usually messier.

Invention: Getting Started

Try to answer these questions while you do your invention work:

- What do I already know about the subject that I am considering for my analysis?
- What insights do I already have to offer?
- Where might I learn more about the topic I am considering? What verifiable information am I likely to find?
- What do I know about my audience?
- What might my audience already know about this topic? How can I make my insights convincing for them?
- What questions do I need to answer before I can begin (and complete) my analysis?

Writing Activity

Freewriting, Listing, and Interviewing

Using the questions above, jot down (freewrite) everything you can think of about your subject in ten minutes. Even if you cannot think of anything to say, keep writing.

Next, place your ideas in a sequence—whether from smallest to largest or least to most important. A list helps you categorize each aspect of your subject for an analysis. Once you have put your information in a list, you can move each item around as you see fit.

Finally, ask others what they know about your subject—what they see as its component parts, what they think are its important aspects, and how they think those parts or aspects work together. A useful way to conduct such interviews is to ask the *who, what, where, when, why,* and *how* questions that a newspaper reporter generally relies on.

Sarah Washington's Interviewing

Student writer Sarah Washington decided to write about a campus issue. When her instructor mentioned the issue of campus parking, Washington knew she had found her subject. In class, she used freewriting to get her initial ideas on paper and then decided to interview Michael Nguyen, who heads her college's Parking and Transit office. Here is a portion of that interview:

Question: Can you tell me a little about who you are and what your background is?

Answer: I have a degree—believe it or not—in Public Parking, and I'd worked with two businesses before I came here. When I started here, I had to start at the bottom and slowly worked my way up and I've had this position for nearly five years.

Q: What exactly does Parking & Transit do? What does it cost to park on campus?

A: P&T has 6,100 parking spaces available—most are in paved lots, but we also handle the Elm Street garage, which has six levels of covered parking, and the garage on Maple with five levels. We handle the cleaning, the paving and repair work, selling parking permits to students and faculty, and so on. We also patrol the campus, giving parking tickets to anyone illegally parked.

Lately, we've spent a lot of time talking to dorm residents, to see how we might provide better and more parking for their use. But it's a battle—we only have so much space on campus, and we're growing every semester in terms of students. That's a good problem to have.

Parking costs for the covered garage are $530 a semester, and for the surface lots it's $440 a semester. However, it costs the university about $500 to maintain a space in the garage, and about $400 a semester to maintain a surface space—so we more or less break even.

Q: When does most of your work take place?

A: Well, we're really busy right before classes start, selling permits. But we also get busy at mid-term as the lots and garages are pretty dirty by then—lots of litter—so there's an ongoing cleaning program. And we're busy all the time patrolling—we give out a lot of parking tickets.

Exploring Your Ideas with Research

Before you begin your research, consider what your focal point should be. For example, suppose you wanted to research how electronic telecommunications such as smartphones and the Internet are helping college students communicate electronically with their professors and classmates, enabling them to keep in touch and to share more information. You could choose to focus on how college students who take online courses communicate with classmates. Look over your invention work to remind yourself of all that you know about your subject, as well as the questions you came up with about it. Use the reporter's questions of *who, what, where, when, why,* and *how* to get started on your research. After you have decided what information you need, determine what kind of research you need to conduct in order to gather that information. Use an electronic journal to record images, URLs, interview notes, and other electronic pieces of information that you find as you conduct your research.

Writing Activity

Conducting Research

Consider your subject for analysis and, in no more than two pages, outline a research plan. In your plan, indicate the following:

- What you already know about your subject
- What questions you still have
- Who or what sources might be able to answer your questions
- Who (roommates, college staff, professors) might be able to provide other perspectives on your subject
- Where you might look for further information (library, Web, primary documents, other sources)
- When you plan to conduct your research

Sarah Washington's Research

Sarah Washington began her invention and research on college parking by writing down what she already knew and the questions she still had. During the early stages of her invention work, she realized that she was having an emotional response to the issue of parking—the lack of parking on campus made her frustrated and angry—and she really did not have good information about the reasons for the situation. She started her formal research by interviewing Michael Nguyen. She then interviewed others affected by college parking to find out what they thought about their situation, focusing on the reporter's *who, what, where, when, why,* and *how* questions; she also learned what other colleges do in terms of parking, examined how parking permits are issued, and determined whether the parking costs at her college are in line with what other, similar, colleges charge for parking.

After interviewing several people on campus, she made the following notes in her research journal.

There needs to be sufficient parking for all the students who live in campus housing who have or are allowed to have cars. Of course, this number could vary from semester to semester.

We have 6,100 parking places, in the garages and in surface lots (Nguyen interview).

There also needs to be sufficient parking for the staff who drive to work during regular business hours. Faculty needs are more difficult to determine. Their time on campus is inconsistent. While it is easy to know when they teach and hold office hours, other times (class preparation, grading, writing, researching in labs or the library, attending meetings, etc.) all vary from week to week. They need a parking spot, but they might not all be on campus at the same time. The trick is to figure out what percentage is likely to be on campus.

Mr. Nguyen told me that there were 13,845 total students enrolled this semester. Of that total, 6,735 live on campus. 2,700 of the resident students have cars. There are 512 full-time faculty and 193 part-time faculty. In addition, there are 398 staff people who work at the university.

Commuter students—there are about 6,500 of them, according to Mr. Nguyen—may be the group whose parking needs are most difficult to determine. They often lead complicated lives balancing school, work, and family obligations. They come to campus for class, but also likely come to campus at other times to use the library and other campus facilities, or to take part in other activities. It's difficult to determine when they will be on campus. I should ask some commuter students in my English class when they actually *are* at school—in class or at the library or whatever—to get some sense of how much that group of students is on campus.

Finally, all campuses need to provide parking spaces for visitors. Again, the needs of visitors vary. They can be prospective students, businesspeople, government employees, or industry leaders who need to meet with the faculty or administration. Sometimes they are members of the general public who want or need to use university facilities that may be open. Who can I talk to about how many visitors we have, on average?

Reviewing Your Invention and Research

For more on developing a thesis, see Chapter 13.

After you have conducted your research, review your invention work and notes, and think about the information you have collected from outside sources. You may be ready to decide on a working thesis statement—a statement that summarizes the main point of your analysis—at this point. Even though you might already have a general idea of the conclusion your analysis is leading you to, until you get

Strategies FOR Success | Persistence

Successful writers are persistent. They don't accept quick or easy answers. Instead, they take the time to delve deeply and thoughtfully into their subject. Since effective analytical writing is thorough, using persistence to examine and explain as many details as possible is necessary. If you are working in a field that has particular procedures in place, you have an obligation to use persistence in following the accepted procedures faithfully. For example, if you are working in a scientific field, you will need to document everything you do—from taking notes on your process, to constructing drawings that illustrate the process, to verifying measurements with specific instruments. You also must clearly and accurately present any statistical data, with all supporting evidence and detail, and you must explain relationships between variables in your experiment.

some of your ideas and research down on paper, it is often difficult to know what your thesis will be. It is helpful to decide on your thesis after you have done your invention work (listing, brainstorming, and clustering, for example) and research.

Organizing Your Information

When you have some sense of what your analysis will include, consider how you might organize this material. Here are some questions to ask yourself when deciding on your organization:

- Who is your audience?
- Why might they be interested in your analysis, or how can you make them interested in it?
- What is your purpose for writing—that is, why do your readers need this analysis?
- What is the most important aspect of your subject?

The answers to these questions can help you decide what you need to emphasize, which in turn will help you choose an organization.

Here are three organizational structures that you might consider.

For more on cause and effect, see Chapter 11; for more on classification, see Chapter 13.

Options FOR Organization
Options for Organizing an Analysis

Defining Parts	Classification	Relating Causes and Effects
Explain why the subject you are analyzing is important to your readers.	Start with a question about your subject that readers probably do not know the answer to.	Begin with information about your subject that may surprise your readers.
Provide examples of how readers might be affected by the subject.	Explain why knowing the answer to this question will benefit your readers.	Explain how an analysis of your subject will lead to more surprises and better understanding.
Provide background information so readers can see the whole subject of your analysis.	Use the writing strategy of *classification* to explain your subject, labeling and explaining each aspect or part.	Use the writing strategy of *cause and effect* to show how each aspect or part of your subject causes or is affected by the other aspects or parts.
Use a strategy of *description* to explain each aspect or part of your subject.	Provide specific examples to illustrate each category.	Provide specific examples to show what you mean.
Provide examples to show what you mean.	Conclude by showing how the aspects or parts function together to make up the whole of your subject.	Conclude by outlining how parts of your subject function together.
Conclude by showing how each aspect or part works with the others.		

▪ Constructing a Complete Draft

Once you have chosen the most effective organizational approach, you are ready to construct your draft. Consider how you might use the invention materials you generated and how you might integrate the research information you gathered.

As you write your first draft, remember the main point that you are trying to make. In an analysis, you will want to make sure that your discussion of the aspects of your subject helps to support what it is that you are trying to say about the whole.

There are many ways to write a first draft. It may seem to make the most sense to you to start at the first sentence and then move to the end; however, many writers, once they decide on their organization, write individual pieces of their draft and then put them all together.

Synthesizing and Integrating Sources into Your Draft: Incorporating Numerical Data

When writers incorporate numerical data from sources, they do not need to enclose numbers in quotation marks because it is not possible to paraphrase numbers. However, if a writer uses the exact words of a source to comment on those data, then quotation marks are required. For example, in the essay "Campus Parking: Love It or Leave It" (pages 228–231), Sarah Washington includes numerical data, which she gathered from Michael Nguyen and from the Web sites of other universities. Notice that she reports the data without any commentary from Nguyen or anyone else. Therefore, readers can assume that the following section of her analytical essay includes the exact numbers that Nguyen provided, but that the words are Washington's:

> When I interviewed Mr. Michael Nguyen, head of Parking and Transit, he gave me the following background information:
> —A total of 13,845 students are registered this semester.
> —Of those, 6,735 live on campus.
> —A total of 2,700 resident students (that is, students who live on campus) have cars.
> —There are 512 full-time faculty members; 193 part-time faculty.
> —There are 398 staff employees.

Even though Washington does not quote Nguyen, she credits him as a source when she introduces the data. Of course, in her list of works cited at the end of the essay, Washington also includes information about the source:

> Nguyen, Michael. Personal interview. 12 March 2016.

When integrating numerical data into your writing projects, keep in mind the following guidelines:

1. Double-check the source to make certain that you have reported the data accurately.
2. Do not place numbers in quotation marks unless you include commentary from the source.
3. Indicate the source in the body of your text and in your list of works cited or references.

Parts of a Complete Draft

Introduction: Regardless of your organizational approach, begin with a strong introduction that captures your readers' attention and introduces the subject you are analyzing. To do so, you might use one of the following strategies:

- **Explain (briefly) why an analysis of your subject might be of interest.** For example, in Kerry Magro's analysis, he notes how fascinated people are with the Sheldon Cooper character on *The Big Bang Theory*.

- **Provide a brief outline of what most people know about your subject.**

- **Explain (briefly) why your analysis is important.** You may want to look at how the topic affects one person and then generalize to show how it affects many people.

- **Provide a fact about the subject you are analyzing that will surprise or concern your readers.**

Body: You can use various writing strategies to effectively analyze your subject:

- **Classify and label each aspect of your subject.** In her analysis of the parking situation on her campus, student Sarah Washington classifies those who are likely to use parking spots as "students," "full-time faculty," and "staff."

- **Define the various parts of your subject—explaining what each is and how it relates to the other parts.** If you were to analyze a smartphone, for example, you would probably focus on the input options (keypad or touch screen), texting and phone capability, audio, video, and Web-browsing capability.

- **Compare and contrast each aspect of your subject, so readers can see the differences and similarities.** For instance, you might compare the functional features of two smartphones.

- **Focus on the cause-and-effect relationship of each aspect of your subject,** to show how one aspect causes, or is caused by, one or more other aspects. This approach would work well if you were analyzing a complex machine such as a car or an airplane.

For more on classification, definition, comparison and contrast, and causal analysis, see Chapters 11 and 13.

Conclusion: In your conclusion, review the major parts or aspects of your subject, explaining the following:

- How they relate to one another
- How they function together
- How all of the aspects of your subject lead to the conclusion you have reached

Title: As you compose your analysis, a title may emerge, but often it will not occur to you until late in the process. Because an analysis is by definition complex, you may not be able to summarize your main ideas in your title, but it should be something that catches your readers' attention.

VISUAL *Thinking* | Going Beyond Words to Achieve Your Goals

	Lots	Garages
MySchool	$440	$530
Texas	$127	$628
UAB	$130	$200
UTEP	$123.05	$231

You might discover that an effective way to show your analysis is by means of a chart or graph such as a flowchart, a pie chart, a bar graph, or a line graph. For example, Sarah Washington collected data when she was doing research for her analysis of campus parking. The data at the left is information Washington discovered about costs for parking at her school and three others. While collecting this data, she realized that comparing parking costs is difficult because some schools have a variety of parking options. This data reflects schools that offer both surface lots and parking garages.

If you wanted to show these data in a graph, you could present them in several ways. A line graph would look like this:

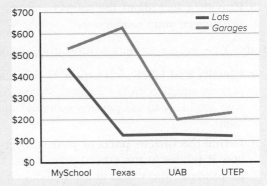

If you displayed the same data in a bar graph, the visual would look like this:

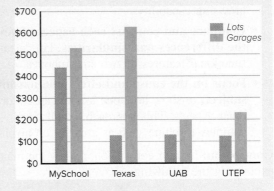

- What type of chart or graph most effectively shows and explains how the parking costs at Washington's school compare to costs at other schools? Why?

- How would it affect your audience's understanding if you used more than one kind of chart or graph in your analysis?

🔊 **USING DIGITAL TECHNOLOGIES** | Using Excel to Convert Data into Visuals

If you are using numbers and quantities as support for your analysis, working with a spreadsheet program like Microsoft Office Excel can be most effective. The Excel program can quickly convert your data into tables, graphs, and charts. If you are taking a class that uses advanced spreadsheet software such as SPSS (originally Statistical Package for the Social Sciences), you may want to use it for designing charts and graphs that illustrate data you are including in your project.

Sarah Washington's First Draft

Sarah Washington decided to start her first draft with a portion of her original freewriting as an opening paragraph. Note also that she uses headings for her report, which is excerpted below.

Because this is a first draft, Washington did not worry about errors in usage, grammar, punctuation, or spelling. She concentrated on getting her ideas down. (The numbers in circles refer to peer comments, which follow the draft on page 225.)

Writing Activity

Constructing a Complete Draft

Using the writing you did when selecting an organizational approach, write a complete draft of your analytical paper. Remember that your analysis will likely evolve as you write.

Campus Parking: Love It or Leave It
Sarah Washington

Like many others, I've been frustrated by the parking situation since I first started school here. . . . Every year it seems as though the parking fees go up, and every year it seems as though it's harder to find a good parking spot.❶

I finally decided to do something about it. I started by going to the Student Government Office to see if they had information on why the parking was so bad on this campus and what they were planning to do about it. I was told the best person to talk with was Michael Nguyen, the head of our parking department.

Campus Data

I interviewed Mr. Nguyen and received the following background information: There were 13,845 total students enrolled this semester. Of that total, 6,735 live on campus. 2,700 of the resident students have cars. There are 512 full-time faculty and 193 part-time faculty. In addition, there are 398 staff people who work at the university.❷

Analysis

Looking at those numbers, I was able to make the following quick determinations. If everyone drove themselves to campus and needed to be there at the same time, the campus would need 10,913 parking spots (the total of all the faculty and staff and students who are either nonresidential or have cars). That means the university would have to be looking at close to 11,000 parking spots, which is especially important because Nguyen told me that the campus presently has 6,100 parking spots.

My initial response was no wonder I always felt I could never find a parking spot.❸ However, I soon realized that even at 9:00 am on Monday not every one of those 11,000 people will be on campus and not everyone drives. I knew I had friends who lived in apartments close enough to campus that they walked to class. And, after talking to Nguyen, I realized that not only are all students not on campus at the same time, but all faculty aren't necessarily on campus at the same time either. In addition, some students, and to a lesser degree, faculty and staff, carpool. All of these variables act to reduce the number of parking spaces that is really needed.

We can get a better idea of how great the need really is by looking❹ at the following scenario. By looking at staff surveys done by the Parking Office, we learn that 15% of the staff either carpool or use some other means of transportation. That gives us around 340 spots that are necessary to support employees not counting the faculty.

If we then assume, at the busiest time of day, 60% of the full time faculty and 50% of the part time faculty need to be on campus, and they all drive their own vehicles and don't carpool, that will cause us to have an additional need of around 410 spots.

It may be more difficult to determine the real number of spots that students need. However, if we assume that at the time of highest traffic, 70% of students are there, we can see there will then be a need for approximately 5,000 student spaces—not counting the necessary 2,700 spaces by the resident halls.

Adding all of these numbers, we discover that the campus may need around 8,450 parking spots, or a little more than 76% of the initial estimate of more 11,000 spots. It also becomes evident that the campus really can use a lot more parking at peak periods—not my initial thought of 4,900 spots. . . .

Conclusion

I also became acutely aware that determining how many parking spots are needed is not an exact science. There are many variables and they may change from semester to semester. In addition to the raw numbers, I discovered that part of the problem exists as a result of the desirability of the lots. Everyone wants to be close to where they're going, but that "where" keeps changing. During the morning, students all want to park in the lots closer to the academic buildings where their classes were being held. Later in the day, more vehicles could be found in the lot that serves the student union and the library. One thing that might help is simply having students plan their days on campus a little better. For example, if they have classes in the morning and plan on staying on campus for most of the day, they might have a much easier time looking for a parking spot over by the library rather than the classroom buildings.❺

Student Comments on Sarah Washington's First Draft

❶ "Interesting introduction, but I'm not sure what the purpose of your paper is. Are you going to try to inform readers of parking problems or persuade us to do something?"

❷ "These numbers are confusing like this—maybe put them into a list?"

❸ "Also interesting, but you have a lot of your personal feelings in your paper. If I understood your paper's purpose, I'd know better whether it's appropriate for them to be in it."

❹ "Who is 'we' here? I'm not sure why you're using 'we'—sounds strange."

❺ "Now you're ending, and you're back to the number of parking spaces, without ever explaining what all that information about parking has to do with anything."

 ## Revising

Many writers find that it is useful to let their work "sit" for a time—to put it aside for a day or two and then revise it. When you approach your work this way, you will find it easier to notice parts that are not explained in enough detail, or examples that are confusing, or places where an illustration or graph might show what you mean more clearly than the text does.

As you revise your early drafts, wait before doing any editing. When you revise, you will probably change the content and structure of your paper, so time spent working to fix problems with sentence style or grammar, punctuation, or mechanics at this stage is often wasted.

When you reread the first draft of your analysis, here are some questions to ask yourself:

• What else might my audience want or need to know about my subject?

• How else might I interest my audience in my analysis of this subject?

• What did I find out about my subject that I did not include in my paper?

• Have I clearly explained any terms my readers might not know?

• Could some aspects of my analysis be better presented as a graph or chart?

Use your word processor's track-changes tool to try out revisions and editing changes. After you have had time to think about the possible changes, you can "accept" or "reject" them. Also, you can use your word processor's comment tool to write reminders to yourself.

WRITER'S *Workshop* | Responding to Full Drafts

Working in pairs or groups of three, read one another's papers, and then offer your classmates comments that will help them see both their papers' strengths and places where they need to develop their ideas further. Use the following questions to guide your responses to the writer's draft:

- What is your first impression of this draft? How effectively does the title draw you into the paper? Why?

- What do you like about the draft?

- What is effective about the introduction? What suggestions can you make on how to improve it?

- How well do you understand what the author is trying to do in this paper? Does the paper wander a bit? Where? What questions are left unanswered?

- How has the writer demonstrated an awareness of readers' knowledge, needs, and/or expectations for the analysis?

- How effective is this paper as an analysis? How has the writer covered—or failed to cover—all of the parts or aspects of the subject adequately? What other aspects of the subject should be included?

- What is your opinion of the author's insight into the subject? How meaningful is it?

- What do you think is the author's thesis or main claim for the analysis? How could it be expressed or supported more effectively?

- In the main part of the paper, are there parts that are confusing or concepts that are unclear? Where would you like more details or examples to help you see what the author means?

- Is the writer's tone straightforward and neutral?

- How accurate and appropriate is the supporting evidence? Are there any questionable statistics, inaccurate facts, or questionable authorities? How clearly does the author indicate the sources for statistics and other supporting information?

- How well does the conclusion tie everything together?

- If there are visual aspects of the document, how effectively do they illustrate the point being made?

- What do you see as the main weaknesses of this paper? How might the writer improve the text?

Because it is so difficult to see emerging writing with a fresh eye (even for experienced writers), it is almost always useful to ask classmates, friends, or family members to read drafts of your papers and comment on them.

Responding to Readers' Comments

Once they have received feedback from peers, teachers, and others, writers have to decide how to deal with those comments and suggestions. It is important to consider carefully what your readers are saying to you. You may decide to reject some comments, of course, because they are not consistent with your goals for your paper. For example, some readers may disagree with your point of view or conclusion. You may find that comments from more than one reader contradict each other. In that case, use your own judgment to decide which reader's comments are on the right track.

In the final draft of Sarah Washington's paper, on pages 228–231, you can see how Washington responded to readers' comments, as well as to her own review of her first draft.

 # KNOWLEDGE OF CONVENTIONS

When effective writers edit their work, they attend to the conventions that will help readers. These include genre conventions, documentation, format, usage, grammar, punctuation, and mechanics. By attending to these conventions in your writing, you make reading a more pleasant experience for your audience.

 ## Editing

The last task in any writing project is editing—the final polishing of your document. When you edit and polish your writing, you change your sentence structures and word choices to improve your style and to make your writing clearer and more concise. You also check your work to make sure it adheres to conventions of grammar, usage, punctuation, mechanics, and spelling. Use the spell-check function of your word-processing program, but be sure to double-check your spelling personally. If you have used sources in your paper, make sure you are following the documentation style your instructor requires.

See Chapter 20 for more on documenting sources.

As with overall revision of your work, this final editing and polishing is most effective if you can put your text aside for a time and come back to it with fresh eyes. It also helps to ask classmates, friends, and tutors to read your work as well.

To assist you with editing, we offer here a round-robin editing activity focused on finding and correcting problems with wordy sentences, a constant challenge for many writers (see page 228.) Consider using a digital technology such as Google Drive to collaborate with peers to edit one another's projects

Genres, Documentation, and Format

If you are writing an academic paper, follow the conventions for the discipline in which you are writing and the requirements of your instructor. If you are constructing a formal business report for Scenario 3, follow the model for a business analysis report.

For advice on writing in different genres, see the Appendix C. For guidelines for formatting and documenting papers in MLA or APA style, see Chapter 20.

If you have used material from outside sources, including visuals, credit those sources, using the documentation style required by the discipline you are working in and by your instructor.

WRITER'S *Workshop* | **Round-Robin Editing with a Focus on Wordiness**

Wordiness—using more words than necessary—is a common concern for writers and their readers. Wordy sentences take longer to read, and having a large number of them in your paper will increase your reader's workload and decrease your paper's effectiveness.

Work with two peers to edit one another's papers for wordiness. Use the track-changes and comment features in your word-processing program to make your edits and suggestions. Ask yourself questions like "Is the writer repeating herself?" and "Has the writer included phrases that don't add meaning to the sentence?" Circle sentences that can be made more concise, and make suggestions on how to tighten them. Compare notes to see if you have any questions about wordiness, and ask your instructor for assistance.

A Writer Achieves Her Goal: Sarah Washington's Final Draft

After meeting with peer reviewers, Sarah Washington continued to revise her paper and eventually constructed a finished draft. The final draft of "Campus Parking: Love It or Leave it" follows. As you read the essay, think about what makes it effective.

SARAH WASHINGTON

ANALYTICAL ESSAY   Campus Parking: Love It or Leave It

One classmate wrote this comment on Washington's paper:

Interesting introduction, but I'm not sure what the purpose of your paper is. Are you going to try to inform readers of parking problems or persuade us to do something?

In her revision, Washington clearly indicates what she is trying to accomplish: to analyze the parking situation.

Like many others, I've been frustrated by the parking situation since I first   1
started school here. While talking to other students, I've discovered that we're all not very happy about the parking. It's too expensive, and there are never enough spots. I've talked to other students who are juniors and seniors, and they say it's been like this since they started. Every year it seems as though the parking fees go up, and every year it seems as though it's harder to find a good parking spot. An analysis of the parking situation on campus will help anyone concerned with parking (and that includes most students) understand how parking "works" at our college. I am focusing my analysis on two aspects of campus parking: the number of spaces, including how many spaces are actually needed, and also the costs for parking on campus, especially compared to what other colleges charge.

Campus Data

When I interviewed Mr. Michael Nguyen, head of Parking and Transit, he gave   2
me the following background information:

A total of 13,845 students are registered this semester.

Of those, 6,735 live on campus.

A total of 2,700 resident students (that is, students who live on campus)
have cars.

There are 512 full-time faculty members, 193 part-time faculty.

There are 398 staff employees.

Analysis

Looking at the numbers Mr. Nguyen provided, I was able to make the following   3
quick determinations. If everyone drove to campus and needed to be there at
the same time, the campus would need 10,913 parking spots (the total of all
the faculty, staff, and students who are either nonresidential or have cars). That
means the university would have to provide close to 11,000 parking spots, or
around 4,900 additional spots. This is especially important because, according
to Nguyen, the campus presently has 6,100 parking spots.

However, even at 9:00 a.m. on Monday not every one of those 11,000 peo-   4
ple will be on campus, and not everyone who is on campus drives. I have
friends who live in apartments close enough to campus to allow them to walk
to class. And, after talking to Nguyen, I realized that not only are all students not
on campus at the same time, but all faculty aren't necessarily on campus at the
same time either. In addition, some students, and to a lesser degree, faculty and
staff, carpool. All of these variables act to reduce the number of parking spaces
really needed on campus. Clearly we need further analysis to understand the
severity of the parking problem.

Staff surveys done by the Parking office indicate that 15% of the staff either   5
carpool or use some other means of transportation. Therefore, around 340 spots
are necessary to support employees, not counting the faculty. If we then assume
that, at the busiest time of day, 60% of the full-time faculty and 50% of the part-
time faculty need to be on campus, and they all drive their own vehicles and
don't carpool, then the campus will need around 410 additional spots.

It may be more difficult to determine the real number of spots that students   6
need. However, assuming that at the time of highest traffic there are 70% of the
nonresident students present on campus, we can estimate that those students need
parking. At these times, then, the campus will need approximately 5,000 student
spaces—not counting the necessary 2,700 spaces by the resident halls.

Adding all of these numbers, we determine that the campus may need in
the neighborhood of 8,450 parking spots, or a little more than 76% of the initial
estimate of more 11,000 spots. It is evident that the campus really can use some

Washington
responded to one
of her peer review-
ers by placing this
information in a list
to make it more
readable.

In her earlier draft,
Washington got this
comment from one of
her peer reviewers
to this sentence from
her first draft: "My
initial response was
no wonder I always
felt I could never find
a parking spot."

**Also interesting but
you have a lot of
your personal feel-
ings in your paper.
If I understood your
paper's purpose, I'd
know better whether
it's appropriate for
them to be in it.**

Note that in her
final version she has
removed her personal
comment as she con-
tinues to outline the
details of her analysis.

A classmate asked
this question and
made this comment
on Washington's draft:

**Who is "we" here?
I'm not sure why
you're using "we"—
sounds strange.**

She revised her draft
to cut back on her
use of the word *we*,
which also helped to
make her sentences
more concise.

more parking at peak periods, perhaps as many as 2,300 spots—not my initial estimate of 4,900 spots.

Parking Costs

This analysis reveals that the college is close to the number of parking spots it needs, but cost is another part of the whole campus parking picture. Parking on our campus—which for students runs $440 per year—seems to be in the midrange. Some universities such as Iowa State University only charge students $148 per year to park. However, the University of Oregon charges students $360 for yearly parking (University of Oregon). Georgia Institute of Technology charges $776 ("Parking Permit Prices").

8

Other schools charge varying amounts:

9

The University of Nebraska: "perimeter parking " is $312 per year while "reserved parking" is $936 per year. There are two other levels, $504 and $612 per year, in between ("Permit Costs").

The University of Texas at Austin: students can park in surface lots for $127 a year, but if they want garage parking, it runs from $628 per year for commuters and $677 to $743 per year for residential students ("Student Permits").

Parking costs at our school, it appears, are not out of line with other colleges.

We can look at the graph in Fig. 1 to see how our school's costs compare to some others when looking at the difference in costs for parking in surface lots and parking garages.

Conclusion

Determining how many parking spots are needed on a campus is not an exact science. There are many variables involved and those variables may change from semester to semester. In addition to the raw numbers, I discovered that part of the problem with parking exists as a result of the desirability of the lots. Everyone wants to be close to where they're going, but that "where" keeps changing. During the morning, students all seem to want to park in the lots closer to the academic buildings where their classes are being held. Later in the day, more vehicles can be found in the lot that serves the student union and the library. Students can help the situation by simply planning their days on campus a little better. For example, if they have classes in the morning and plan on staying on campus for most of the day, they might have a much easier time finding a parking spot over by the library rather than in crowded lots near the classroom buildings. Where parking is concerned, a little strategy can go a long way.

10

In her first draft, Washington received this comment from a classmate:

Now you're ending, and you're back to the number of parking spaces, without ever explaining what all that information about parking has to do with anything.

Note how she now offers a more effective conclusion to her text.

Washington has provided a synthesis of the information she has analyzed.

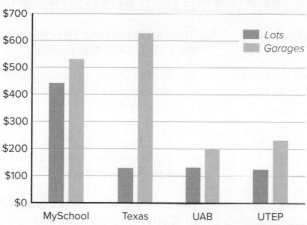

Fig. 1 The other schools, in addition to MySchool, are the University of Texas at Austin (Texas), the University of Alabama at Birmingham (UAB), and the University of Texas at El Paso (UTEP).

Works Cited

Northern Arizona U. "Parking and Shuttle Services." *Parking on Campus*, nau.edu/parking-shuttle-services/parking-on-campus/. Accessed 23 Feb. 2016.

Nguyen, Michael. Personal interview. 22 Feb. 2016.

"Parking Permit Prices." *Georgia Institute of Technology*, 2016, pts.gatech.edu/subsite1/Pages/Permit-Prices,-Payments,-Proration-and-Refunds.aspx.

"Permit Costs." *U of Nebraska—Lincoln Parking and Transit Services*, parking.unl.edu/permits/costs.shtml. Accessed 23 Feb. 2016.

"Student Parking Permits." *Student Parking Permits*, U of Texas at Austin, www.utexas.edu/parking/parking/student/. Accessed 23 Feb. 2016.

"Student Permits (Rules & Permits)." *Student Parking Permits*, U of Texas at El Paso, admin.utep.edu/Default.aspx?tabid=50699. Accessed 23 Feb. 2016.

"2016 - 2017 Parking Permit Price List." *Iowa State U*, www.parking.iastate.edu/permit/fees/. Accessed 23 Feb. 2016.

"UAB - Parking - Fees & Maps." *UAB - Parking - Fees & Maps*, U of Alabama at Birmingham, www.uab.edu/parking/parking/students/fees-location. Accessed 23 Feb. 2016.

This paper follows MLA guidelines for in-text citations and works cited.

UNDERSTANDING A WRITER'S GOALS: QUESTIONS TO CONSIDER AND DISCUSS

Rhetorical Knowledge: The Writer's Situation and Rhetoric

1. **Audience:** What audience does Washington have in mind for this essay? How can you tell?

2. **Purpose:** What can you point to in Washington's paper that indicates her purpose?

3. **Voice and tone:** How would you describe the tone Washington uses in her paper? Would a different tone (more strident, perhaps, or more subdued) have made her analysis more, or less, effective? Why?

4. **Responsibility:** How accurately does Washington represent statistical information? How credible is Washington's analysis? Why?

5. **Context, format, and genre:** Washington is writing as a college student concerned about parking on her campus. How does this context affect her use of language, and evidence in her analysis? Washington chose to write her analysis as an informal report. What impact does this genre have on you as a reader? Can you explain how by using this genre Washington's paper is more or less understandable than if she had chosen to just write an essay?

Critical Thinking: The Writer's Ideas and Your Personal Response

6. What is your initial response to Washington's analysis? What in her text causes your response?

7. To what extent does Washington's report give you insight into how parking might work at other public places serving large groups of drivers?

Composing Processes and Knowledge of Conventions: The Writer's Strategies

8. Construct a brief outline of Washington's analysis. How effective is her organization? Why?

9. How effectively does Washington use statistics or data to support her claims? How effectively does she visually represent statistics?

Inquiry and Research: Ideas for Further Exploration

10. At your library, find a journal or magazine that covers the area you think you want to major in, and locate an example of an analysis. In no more than two pages, explain why that text is or is not an effective analysis.

Self-Assessment: Reflecting on Your Goals

Now that you have constructed a piece of analytical writing, go back and consider your learning goals. Write notes on what you have learned from this assignment.

 ## Rhetorical Knowledge

- *Audience:* What have you learned about addressing an audience in analytical writing?

- *Purpose:* What have you learned about the purposes for constructing an analysis?

- *Rhetorical situation:* How did the writing context affect your analytical text? How did your choice of topic affect the research you conducted and the way you presented your analysis to your readers? What do you see as the strongest part of your analysis? Why? The weakest? Why?

- *Voice and tone:* How would you describe your voice in this essay? Your tone? How do they contribute to the effectiveness of your analysis?

 ## Critical Thinking, Reading, and Writing

- *Learning/inquiry:* What process did you go through to focus on a main idea, or thesis? How did you judge what was most and least important?

- *Responsibility:* How did you fulfill your responsibility to your readers?

- *Reading and research:* What did you learn about analytical writing from the reading selections you read for this chapter? What research did you conduct? How sufficient was the research you did?

- *Skills:* As a result of writing this analysis, how have you become a more critical thinker, reader, and writer?

- *Transferring skills and knowledge:* By writing an analysis, you have gathered information, examined that information closely, and reported on that information. What have you learned about yourself, as a writer, from this process? What skills can you transfer to writing and thinking tasks in other settings?

Writing Processes

- *Invention:* What invention strategies were most useful to you?
- *Organizing your ideas and details:* What organization did you use? How successful was it?
- *Revising:* What one revision did you make that you are most satisfied with? Why? If you could make an additional revision, what would it be?
- *Working with peers:* How did your instructor or peer readers help you by making comments and suggestions about your writing? How could you have made better use of the comments and suggestions you received?
- *Visuals:* Did you use photographs or other visuals to help explain your analysis to readers? If so, what did you learn about incorporating them?
- *Writing habits:* What "writerly habits" have you developed, modified, or improved on as you completed the writing assignment for this chapter?
- *Using digital technologies:* In completing your project for this chapter, what have you learned about using digital technologies for composing, for incorporating visuals, or for sharing your work with peers?

Knowledge of Conventions

- *Editing:* What sentence problem did you find most frequently in your writing? How will you avoid that problem in future assignments?
- *Genre:* What conventions of the genre you were using, if any, gave you problems?
- *Documentation:* Did you use sources for your paper? If so, what documentation style did you use? What problems, if any, did you have with it?

Refer to Chapter 1 (page 12) for a sample reflection by a student.

Text Credits

p. 198: Gerrow, Robin, "Fear Factor: Psychologists Help People Conquer Anxieties and Phobias." Copyright © 2002 The Univerity of Texas at Austin. Used with permission. **p. 209:** Kitroeff, Natalie, "The Smartest People Are Opting Out of Law School" *BloombergBusiness*, April 15, 2015. Copyright © 2015 by Bloomberg, L.P. Used with permission. **p. 209:** Source: LSAC via Jerome Organ. **p. 210:** Source: LSAC via Jerome Organ. **p. 212:** Magro, Kerry, "Why Our Autism Community Loves Sheldon Cooper" Autism Speaks Blog, August 13, 2014. Originally published at autismspeaks.org. Used with permission from the author, National Motivational Speaker Kerry Magro.

Writing to Convince

SET	**How do I set my goals?** Setting Your Goals (p. 236)
ACHIEVE	**How do I achieve my goals?** Rhetorical Knowledge: Understanding the rhetorical situation for your project (p. 238) Critical Thinking, Reading, and Writing: Thinking critically about this type of writing (p. 242) Writing Processes: Establishing a process for composing your project (p. 255) Knowledge of Conventions: Polishing your work (p. 269)
ASSESS	**How do I assess my goals?** Self-Assessment: Reflecting on Your Goals (p. 276)

"THE BIGGEST PYRAMID IN THE WORLD WITH A CHURCH ON TOP"

CHOLULA, PUEBLA

MEXICO

THE PLACE YOU THOUGHT YOU KN

DISCOVER MORE AT www.visitmexico

Courtesy of Mexican Tourism Board

Think of the last time you wrote something. Whether it was a formal academic paper, a letter, or an informal note such as a text message to a friend, your writing was most likely designed to convince someone about something—to persuade your reader that he or she should accept your particular point of view. In fact, most purposes for writing—to inform, to explain, to analyze—to some degree almost always involve persuasion.

You encounter **persuasive writing**—writing designed to convince readers to agree with the writer's position—many times a day. Notice, for example, the persuasive appeals in the advertisement here. The top line noting that Cholula, Puebla, has the "biggest pyramid in the world" and has "a church on top" is an ethical appeal because it shows that the ad writers are knowledgeable about the area's history and geography. At the same time, these historical details can be considered logical appeals because they are pieces of information. "The place you thought you knew" is, of course, an emotional appeal, as is the color photograph that showcases the breathtaking beauty of Cholula.

How effectively does this advertisement persuade you to visit this place?

Advertisements, of course, are clearly intended to persuade the reader to buy something—a product or service or trip to Mexico. For most of the persuasive writing you will do, you will have a more limited audience than the audience for an advertisement or a newspaper editorial, but the strategies that you will use to assert your point of view and persuade readers are the same.

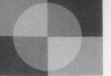

Setting Your Goals for *Persuasive Writing*

 ## Rhetorical Knowledge (pp. 238-242)

- **Audience:** When you write to convince your readers, your success depends on how accurately you have analyzed your audience: their knowledge of and attitudes toward your topic.
- **Purpose:** A convincing text is meant to persuade readers to accept your point of view, but it can also include an element of action—what you want readers to do once you've convinced them.
- **Rhetorical situation:** Think about all of the factors that affect where you stand in relation to your subject—you (the writer), your readers (the audience), the topic (the issue you are writing about), your purpose (what you wish to accomplish), and the exigency (what is compelling you to write your persuasive essay).
- **Voice and tone:** When you write to persuade, you are trying to persuade readers to think or act in a certain way. The tone you use will influence how they react to your writing, so you should consider carefully how you want to sound to your readers. If your tone is subdued and natural, will that convince your readers? What if you come across as loud and shrill?
- **Context, medium, and genre:** Decide on the most effective medium and genre to present your persuasive essay to the audience you want to reach. Often, you can use photographs, tables, charts, and graphs as well as words to provide evidence that supports your position.

 ## Critical Thinking, Reading, and Writing (pp. 242-254)

- **Learning/inquiry:** Writing to persuade helps you learn the important arguments on all sides of an issue, so such writing deepens your understanding.
- **Responsibility:** As you prepare to write persuasively, you will naturally begin to think critically about your position on the subject you are writing about, forcing you to examine your initial ideas, based on what you learn through your research. Persuasive writing, then, is a way of learning and growing, not just of presenting information.
- **Reading and research:** You will usually need to conduct interviews and online and library research to gather evidence to support the claims you are making in your persuasive writing.

Writing Processes (pp. 255-269)

- **Invention:** Use various invention activities, such as questioning or freewriting, to help you consider the arguments that you might use to support your persuasive essay or the opposing arguments you need to accommodate or refute.
- **Organizing your ideas and details:** Most often, you will state the main point—your thesis—clearly at the start of your persuasive essay and then present the evidence supporting that point. Other methods of organization are useful, however, depending on your audience and context.
- **Revising:** Read your work with a critical eye to make certain that it fulfills the assignment and displays the qualities of effective persuasive writing.
- **Working with peers:** Listen to your classmates as they tell you how much you have persuaded them, and why. They will give you useful advice on how to make your essay more persuasive and, therefore, more effective.

 ## Knowledge of Conventions (pp. 269-275)

- **Editing:** Citing sources correctly adds authority to your persuasive writing. The round-robin activity on page 270 will help you edit your work to correct problems with your in-text citations and your works-cited or references list.
- **Genres for persuasive writing:** Possible genres include academic essays, editorials, position papers, letters to the editor, newspaper and magazine essays—even e-mails or letters you might send to friends or family members to persuade them about a problem or issue.
- **Documentation:** You will probably need to rely on sources outside of your experience, and if you are writing an academic essay, you will be required to cite them using the appropriate documentation style.

RHETORICAL KNOWLEDGE

When you write to persuade, you need to have a specific purpose in mind, a strong sense of your audience, and an idea of what might be an effective way to persuade that audience. You need to make a point and provide evidence to support that point, with the goal of persuading your readers to agree with your position.

 ## Writing to Convince in Your College Classes

Many—if not most—of the papers you will be asked to write for your college classes will be persuasive. Although your college assignments will often specifically require that you inform or analyze, they will frequently include an element of persuasion. Here are some examples:

- In a literature course, your instructor might ask you to argue that the concept of the Oedipal complex is appropriate for analyzing Hamlet's behavior.
- Your sociology professor might ask you to develop and support a thesis about deviant behavior in prisons.
- Your mechanical engineering professor might ask you to argue for or against using a particular material in a specific situation.

 ## Writing to Convince for Life

Although persuasive writing is common in college and university courses, it plays an even larger role in professional, civic, and personal settings. Consider these examples of professional writing:

- A product development team needs to convince company executives to manufacture a product it has designed and tested.
- An attorney needs to ask fellow members of the local bar association to work *pro bono* (for free) for a specific group.
- A division manager needs to convince the human resources manager to hire a particular applicant.

Civic leaders and other participants in the political process—mayors, city council members, school board members, town supervisors, volunteers, and ordinary citizens—are also constantly involved in persuasion. In fact, it is difficult to imagine a political process without persuasion as its major component. For instance, concerned citizens might write to their city council to argue that a stoplight needs to be installed at an intersection where many accidents have occurred.

In personal settings, you constantly negotiate with those around you as you make life decisions, often working to convince others that your views ought to be accepted or that your ideas are more effective than theirs. For example, you might write to persuade a family member to send you money for tuition. Or you might write to a friend or family member to encourage him or her to have a medical test if that person is having trouble making a decision.

The "Ways of Writing" feature presents different genres that can be used when writing to convince in college and in other areas of life.

Ways of Writing to Convince

Genres for Your College Classes	Sample Situation	Advantages of the Genre	Limitations of the Genre
History essay	Your world history professor asks you to construct a paper in which you argue that specific events caused the Iraq war of 2003.	Your research will provide documented details of what led up to the war. It will help your readers understand the causal relationships.	Your essay may not offer a broad enough overview to give readers an idea of the total picture.
Letter to your campus newspaper	Your political science professor asks you to send a letter to your college newspaper encouraging your classmates to change the form of student government.	Anything published in a college newspaper will have a wide audience of people who have an interest in campus affairs.	You will have to make your argument in a limited amount of space. It might not be published.
Editorial for your local newspaper	For your writing class, you are asked to construct an editorial responding to public criticism about your campus: students driving fast through neighborhoods, loud parties at student-occupied apartment buildings, and so on.	Editorials are read by a local audience and are therefore useful for convincing local readers about an issue that is important to them.	You will have to make your argument in a limited amount of space and without visuals. It might not be published.
Oral presentation	Your environmental science professor asks you to prepare a ten-minute speech that convinces your classmates to attend a rally for a community clean-up.	Talking to your audience gives you the opportunity to engage them and gauge their level of interest.	Some listeners will "tune out," so you have to work to keep their attention.
Genres for Life	**Sample Situation**	**Advantages of the Genre**	**Limitations of the Genre**
Brochure	With several of your neighbors, you decide to construct a brochure that presents the benefits of raising taxes for your local schools.	A brochure can provide a quick overview of the arguments in favor of a tax increase.	Your argument must be presented in a limited amount of space.
Business letter	Your business is moving to a neighboring state, and you want as many employees as possible to make the move with your company.	A letter is a personalized way to explain the benefits of the new location.	Asking employees to make such a move is a difficult task; a letter might be too brief to be convincing.
Poster	To encourage people to attend an upcoming school event, you construct a poster that you will copy and place in various locations on campus.	A poster is a visual way to get readers interested. Posters can be placed in many places, ensuring broad exposure to your message.	A limited number of people will actually see and read the posters.
Web site	You want to create a Web site that will convince your community to vote for a mayoral candidate.	Your Web site can provide useful information for a particular demographic that is otherwise difficult to reach.	Some readers will only skim a Web site, and some do not have access.
Job application cover letter	You need to construct a cover letter in response to a job ad.	A cover letter lets you discuss and explain your background and experiences in a positive way, specific to the particular job.	Your background might not be a good match for the job, forcing you to "stretch" in your letter.

Scenarios for Writing | Assignment Options

Your instructor may ask you to complete one or more of the following assignments that call for persuasive writing. Each of these assignments is a *scenario,* which gives you a sense of who your audience is and what you need to accomplish with your persuasive writing.

Starting on page 255, you will find guidelines for completing whatever scenario you decide—or are asked—to complete.

Writing for College

SCENARIO 1 Academic Argument about a Controversial Issue

What controversial issues have you learned about in other college classes? Here are some possibilities:

- Political science: In what ways did the controversy over the Affordable Care Act, passed by Congress early in 2010, affect the results of the 2010 election?

- Business ethics: How effective is the threat of criminal punishment in preventing insider trading of stocks?

- Psychology: How should the courts use the concept of insanity to determine culpability in criminal cases?

Writing Assignment: Select a controversial issue or problem from one of your classes, and compose a paper convincing readers in that class that your position on the issue is valid.

SCENARIO 2 An Oral Presentation on an Issue That Matters to You

This scenario asks you to select an issue or a problem that matters to you and to construct and present a brief but convincing oral presentation to your class. Choose an issue that you are interested in, feel strongly about, and would like to explore in more detail. You can find some issues to choose from by filling in the blanks in these statements:

- I really wish someone would do something about _____.
- I'm always puzzled when I see _____.
- I hate it when someone tells me to _____.
- Downtown, _____ is a real problem.
- In the campus union, I wish they would _____.

As you construct your oral presentation, consider your audience. What might they already know about your subject? What are you trying to convince them of? Do you want them to take some action or simply to hear your argument? What kind of information (texts, statements, pictures, handouts) might be effective for this audience, your purpose, and your topic? What might be an effective way to present such information?

Writing Assignment: Construct a convincing oral presentation about an issue that is important to you. Your instructor will let you know if you can use PowerPoint, Prezi, or some other presentation software and will provide a time limit for your presentation.

Writing for Life

SCENARIO 3   Civic Writing: An Editorial about a Campus-Community Problem

Every college campus has problems, ranging from scarce parking, to over-crowded computer labs, to underage drinking, to too little community involvement. Some campus problems, such as too much traffic, extend into the surrounding neighborhoods.

Writing Assignment: Using the list of features of an editorial on page 252, write an editorial for your school newspaper in which you identify a campus problem that also affects the surrounding community and then persuade your readers that the problem exists and that it needs to be taken seriously. Although you need to do more than simply provide information about the problem (that is an informative paper, covered in Chapter 7), you do not need to suggest detailed solutions to the problem (that is a proposal, covered in Chapter 12). Your goal is to convince your readers that your campus has a problem and that this problem has a negative impact on the surrounding neighborhoods.

Underage drinking is an issue on many college campuses.

Rhetorical Considerations in Persuasive Writing

Audience: Although your instructor and classmates are your initial audience for this assignment, you might also consider other audiences for your persuasive writing. What would you like them to believe or do? How might they respond to your argument? How might you best convince them?

Purpose: Your main purpose is to make your audience aware of the issue and to convince them that it is significant and that your position is the most reasonable one. How can you achieve this goal? You might also want to convince them to *do something* about it. What are different ways to accomplish this goal?

Voice, tone, and point of view: Why are you interested in the issue? What are your attitudes toward the issue and the audience? How will you convey those attitudes to your audience?

Context, medium, and genre: Although you are writing this persuasive paper to fulfill a college assignment, most issues worth writing about are important beyond the classroom. How might your views make a difference to your community? Keeping the context of the assignment in mind, decide on the most appropriate medium and genre for your writing. If you are writing for an audience beyond the classroom, consider what will be the most effective way to present your argument to this audience. You might write an e-mail message to a friend, prepare a memo for colleagues at work, or write a brochure or op-ed piece for members of your community.

For more on choosing a medium and genre, see Chapter 17.

CRITICAL THINKING, READING, AND WRITING

As we have seen, effective persuasive writing focuses on an issue and provides sufficient and compelling evidence to convince readers that the writer's position on that issue is correct, or at least worthy of respect. Before you begin to write your own persuasive paper, read one or more persuasive essays to get a feel for this kind of writing.

 Learning the Qualities of Effective Persuasive Writing

Much of the writing that you do is intended to convince someone to agree with you about something, typically about an issue. An **issue** is a subject or problem area that people care about and about which they hold differing views. Issues of current concern in the United States include tax cuts, campaign finance reform, and school vouchers. Subjects about which people tend to agree—for example, the importance of education in general—are not usually worth writing arguments about.

Persuasive writing that achieves the goal of convincing readers has the following qualities:

- Presentation of the issue. Present your issue in a way that will grab your readers' attention and help them understand that the issue exists and that they should be concerned about it. For example, if you are attempting to convince buyers to purchase smartphones with antivirus protection, you first need to demonstrate the prevalence of smartphone viruses. Another way to present the issue is to share an anecdote about it or to offer some statistics that clearly demonstrate the existence and danger of viruses.

- A clearly stated, arguable claim. A **claim** is the assertion you are making about the issue. Your claim should be clear, of course; a confusing claim will not convince readers. Any claim worth writing about also needs to be arguable: a statement about which reasonable people may disagree. For example, "All smartphone users should purchase antivirus software" is an arguable claim; a reader could disagree by saying, "Smartphone viruses are not a major threat." However, no one would disagree with the statement "Computer viruses can be annoying and disruptive." Therefore, it is not arguable and so is not an effective claim for a piece of persuasive writing.

- An awareness of audience. Because your task as a writer is to convince other people, it is crucial to be aware of the needs, situations, and perspectives of your audience. In any audience, you can expect some members to be more open to your claim than others:

  - If someone already agrees with you, persuasion is unnecessary.
  - If someone mildly disagrees with you or is undecided, persuasion has a good chance of working.
  - If someone strongly disagrees with you, there is little chance that persuasion will work.

  Savvy writers devote their time and energy to addressing the second group of readers. It's usually not an effective use of time to address the first or third groups.

- Convincing reasons. Writers of convincing arguments offer support for what they are asking their reader to believe or to do. Think of the reasons you use to support your point as the other part of a *because* statement, with the claim being the first part. Here's an example: "Animal fur should not be used in clothing *because* synthetic fur is available and looks like real fur."

- Sufficient evidence for each reason. After considering the degree to which the audience agrees or disagrees with your claim, provide enough evidence, and the right kind(s) of evidence to convince your readers and, if applicable, persuade them to act accordingly. Evidence includes statistics, expert opinion, examples, and anecdotes (stories).

- Appeals based on the writer's logic, emotion, and character. Effective persuasive writers carefully decide when to use three kinds of appeals—*logos* (appeals based on logic), *pathos* (appeals to the audience's emotions), and *ethos* (appeals based on the writer's character or credibility). Appeals based on logic are generally the most effective. Emotional appeals can be effective with audience members who are predisposed to accept your claims. Appealing to an audience's emotions is risky, however, because critical thinkers will reject this type of appeal unless

 USING DIGITAL TECHNOLOGIES **Political-Discussion Posts**

One way to see argumentation and persuasion in action is to look at political-discussion posts on news Web sites. Choose a topic thread or news article, and as you skim or read the posts, ask yourself three questions about each post: (1) How much credibility does the writer seem to have on the topic he or she is discussing *(ethos)*? (2) How does the writer use factual information and logic to make his or her points *(logos)*? (3) What is your emotional reaction to the writer's remarks *(pathos)*? You can determine the weight a writer's comments probably carry with others by assessing that writer's credibility, reasoning, and emotional integrity. Be sure to assess the language writers use in response to each other as well.

it is accompanied by logical and ethical appeals. Appeals based on the writer's authority and credibility—ethical appeals—can be powerful, especially when coupled with logical appeals.

For more on strategies for argument, including dealing with opposing views, see Chapter 14.

- An honest discussion of other views. For any arguable claim or thesis, there will be at least one other point of view besides yours. To be effective, the writer of a persuasive text needs to acknowledge and deal with possible objections from the other side. You already make this kind of **counterargument** naturally. For example, when you are told that you "cannot register for this course because you have not completed the prerequisite," you probably already have an answer to that objection such as, "You're right, but I received approval from the dean because of my prior professional experience."

    If you think that another perspective has merit, you should certainly *acknowledge* it and even *concede* that it is valid. Another possibility is a Rogerian approach (see Chapter 14), in which both sides negotiate a compromise position. Perhaps you can offer a compromise by incorporating aspects of the other perspective into your thesis. Of course, if other perspectives on your issue are without merit, you will need to *refute* them by indicating how they are inappropriate, inadequate, or ineffective.

- A desired result. The goal of persuasive writing is to convince readers to change their minds about an issue or at least to give your view serious consideration. Often the goal is to get your reader to act in some way—vote for a candidate, write a letter to the school board, or buy some product.

Reading, Inquiry, and Research: Learning from Texts That Persuade

The readings that follow are examples of persuasive writing. As you read the persuasive selections your instructor assigns, consider the following questions:

- What makes this selection convincing?
- To what extent am I convinced by the writer's reasons and evidence? Why?
- What parts of the selection could be improved? In what ways?
- How can I use the techniques of persuasive writing exemplified here in my writing?

MARIAN WRIGHT EDELMAN

Still Hungry in America

OPINION PIECE

"There were some times where, you know, we wouldn't have that much food, and I would tell my mom, 'I'm not hungry, don't worry about it,' and I lost a lot of weight. I remember I used to be a size five, and I went from a size five to a size zero," a New York high school senior said in December.

In 1967, as a young civil rights lawyer in Mississippi, I was asked to testify before the Senate Subcommittee on Employment, Manpower, and Poverty in Washington about how the anti-poverty program in Mississippi was working. The Head Start program was under attack by the powerful Mississippi segregationist delegation because it was operated by church, civil rights, and Black community groups after the state turned it down. After defending the Head Start program, I told the committee I had become increasingly concerned about the growing hunger in the Mississippi Delta. The convergence of efforts to register Black citizens to vote, Black parents' challenges to segregated schools, the development of chemical weed killers and farm mechanization, and recent passage of a minimum wage law covering agriculture workers on large farms had resulted in many Black sharecroppers being pushed off their near feudal plantations, which no longer needed their cheap labor. Many displaced sharecroppers were illiterate and had no skills. Free federal food commodities like cheese, powdered milk, flour, and peanut butter were all that stood between them and starvation. I invited the Senators to come to Mississippi and hear directly from local people about the positive impact the anti-poverty program was making. They did.

I testified again with local community leaders in their subsequent hearing in Jackson—again sharing the desperate plight of hungry people—and urged the Senators to visit the Mississippi Delta with me to experience for themselves the hungry poor in our very rich nation, to visit the shacks and look into the deadened eyes of hungry children with bloated bellies, a level of hunger many people did not believe could exist in America. "They are starving and someone has to help them," I said.

Senator Robert Kennedy responded as did Senator Joseph Clark and Republican Senator George Murphy. So in April 1967 they visited homes in

Marian Wright Edelman, founding president of the Children's Defense Fund, has degrees from Spellman College and Yale Law School. She was the first African-American woman admitted to the Mississippi Bar. An activist for children's issues, she has convinced Congress to improve foster care, adoption policies, and child care. She has also advocated to protect children with disabilities, as well as children who are neglected, abused, and homeless.

In the following opinion piece, which appeared in *The Huffington Post* in February 2012, she writes to convince readers to take action to support federal programs that provide food to hungry children in America. As you read her opinion piece, consider whether she convinces you to support her cause.

1

2

3

4

Cleveland, Mississippi, asking respectfully of each dweller what he or she had had for breakfast, lunch, or dinner the night before. Robert Kennedy opened their empty ice boxes and cupboards after asking permission. I watched him hover, visibly moved, on a dirt floor in a dirty dark shack out of television-camera range over a listless baby with a bloated belly from whom he tried in vain to get a response. He lightly touched the cheeks, shoulders, and hands of the children clad in ragged clothes outside who responded to his question "What did you have for breakfast?" saying "We haven't had breakfast yet," although it was nearly noon. And he tried to offer words of encouragement to their hopeless mothers.

He kept his word to try to help Mississippi's hungry children and went immediately to see Secretary of Agriculture Orville Freeman the next day and urged him to get some food down there and to eliminate any charges for food stamps for people who had no income. Robert Kennedy's pushing, passion, and visibility helped set in motion a chain of events including a *60 Minutes* documentary on "Hunger in America" that led to reforms. But change was slow and incremental. Secretary Freeman did not believe there were people in Mississippi with no income who could not afford to pay $2 for food stamps and sent his own staff back with Peter Edelman, Robert Kennedy's legislative assistant, to retrace the Senators' trip. A series of reports in ensuing months funded by the Field Foundation and visits by doctors, including Robert Coles,[1] to examine poor children in Mississippi and other southern states documented that hunger was widespread not just in Mississippi but throughout the south and elsewhere in America.

But as more months passed without enough federal response, I complained in frustration during a visit with Senator Kennedy in Washington. When I told him I was stopping in Atlanta to see Dr. King, he urged me to tell Dr. King to bring the poor people to Washington to make hunger and poverty visible since the country's attention had turned to the Vietnam War and put poverty and hunger on the back burner. Dr. King responded positively and immediately, and began planning for the campaign. After Dr. King's assassination, the Poor People's Campaign was carried on by his staff, and I moved to Washington to help as Counsel and federal policy liaison. It was a watershed coming together of White, Black, Native American, and Latino poor seeking jobs and adequate income and an end to hunger.

Many have pronounced it a failure, but I differ and believe it made hunger a national issue and set into motion a number of positive steps that led to major expansions of the federal food safety net programs so many depend on today. After Robert Kennedy's assassination, the bipartisan McGovern committee continued hearings around the country, a range of hunger activists kept

5

6

7

---

[1]Child psychiatrist and author who chronicled the struggle to integrate schools in the South during the 1960s.

pushing the Nixon administration and Congress to improve the nutrition safety net, and President Nixon appointed a task force headed by Pat Moynihan, his Domestic Policy Advisor, which affirmed hunger was a major problem. President Nixon gave a speech saying hunger had no place in our rich land. A prod towards these steps was a second quiet Poor People's Campaign delegation, which came to Washington in 1969 and met with President Nixon and his Cabinet in the White House. In that meeting, Rev. Ralph Abernathy and other leaders urged action to end hunger, and President Nixon kept responding by saying he was seeking peace in Vietnam. A contentious press conference followed and a series of Congressional visits criticizing the President's weak response helped catalyze a series of steps, including a White House conference on nutrition and incremental expansions of child and family nutrition programs that made a huge difference for millions until they came under attack from Reagan administration budget assaults and attempts to eliminate a range of federal safety net programs.

Today, crucial programs like food stamps, the Women, Infants and Children (WIC) nutrition program, and school lunch, breakfast and summer feeding programs continue working to combat child and family hunger. Their implementation could be significantly improved, but in the current recession, they have proved to be indispensable lifelines for the millions of jobless families with no cash income in our rich nation—about six million or 1 in 50 Americans, *The New York Times* reported in 2010—for whom food stamps are the only defense against the wolves of hunger. Last year more Americans relied on food stamps to eat than at any time since the program began in 1939— *46 million.* Yet once again some voices are starting to wonder whether we *really* need robust anti-hunger programs in America, and whether there are *really* so many children out there who might otherwise go hungry. A recent skeptical *Wall Street Journal* article was titled "The Myth of Starving Americans." 8

The safety net has indeed made it harder to find starving children with bloated bellies like those Senator Kennedy met in Mississippi in 1967—thank God. But the quiet pangs of hunger and the documented signs of chronic malnutrition are still here, from rural Mississippi to inner cities to middle class suburbs where families have fallen on hard times. Hungry boys and girls are not imaginary figures like the fictional Dick and Jane but very real children like Jane Soliternik, a New York City high school senior and the recent recipient of a Children's Defense Fund's Beat the Odds® scholarship award. Jane has overcome many odds in her young life, including cardiac surgery, her father's death, and poverty—especially after her widowed mother was laid off from her job as a medical assistant during the Great Recession and couldn't find another job for more than two years. When unemployment benefits were exhausted, Jane and her mother lived on the Social Security payments Jane received following the death of her father. Jane was already facing multiple challenges, and 9 then hunger was added to the list: "There were some times where, you know, we wouldn't have that much food, and I would tell my mom, 'I'm not hungry, don't worry about it,' and I lost a lot of weight. I remember I used to be a size five, and I went from a size five to a size zero. So, you know, I try to not eat too much. I try to eat in school. They give me free lunch in school."

This makes Jane just 1 of 14 million children who participate in free or 10 reduced price school lunch programs during the year and are often "at nutritional risk" and go hungry when those meals aren't provided. Without this vital safety net, we might return to the scenes Senator Kennedy witnessed. Hunger in America is real and widespread and pretending hungry children do not exist or that families should be ashamed of their needs is shameful. Unemployed parents unable to find a job when jobs are scarce should not be blamed for their inability to put food on the table. Robert Kennedy always understood that in addressing the hunger emergency the real culprit was poverty and lack of jobs, wages, training, and education to provide hope for restless youths trapped into failure and jail rather than given opportunities. The same is true now. Until we solve that crisis, we will still have jobless parents, poor families, and hungry children in America. For now, when more than 16 million American children, one of every four children, are not sure where the next meal will come from, we have urgent work to do.

The Food Research and Action Council (FRAC) did release one small piece 11 of good news in January: a new poll showing American voters overwhelmingly oppose cutting food stamp assistance as a way to reduce government spending. "What this poll tells us is that, despite rhetoric and false claims about the program, Americans across the country see food stamps as a program that works and that is making a real difference for people," said FRAC President Jim Weill. "American voters won't tolerate hunger in our midst, and across party lines they support this valuable program." You and I need to make sure our leaders hear this message loudly and clearly.

UNDERSTANDING A WRITER'S GOALS: QUESTIONS TO CONSIDER AND DISCUSS

Rhetorical Knowledge: The Writer's Situation and Rhetoric

1. **Audience:** Who is the audience for this opinion piece? Whom is Edelman trying to convince?

2. **Purpose:** What is Edelman's primary purpose for writing this opinion piece? What does she want her audience to do?

3. **Voice and tone:** How does Edelman's voice come through in this reading? What evidence supports your view of her voice?

4. **Responsibility:** How has Edelman responsibly presented the issue of hunger to readers?

5. **Context, format, and genre:** Edelman wrote this column for *The Huffington Post,* a widely read online newsmagazine that publishes many opinion pieces. Why do you think *The Huffington Post* published this particular one?

Critical Thinking: The Writer's Ideas and Your Personal Response

6. What do you find most interesting in Edelman's column? Why?

7. How do you respond to the details about Edelman's own experience? How do those details support or undermine her case?

Composing Process and Knowledge of Conventions: The Writer's Strategies

8. How does Edelman use quotations in her column?

9. What persuasive appeals— *logos, ethos, pathos*—does Edelman use? How effectively does she use appeals? Why do you think so?

Inquiry and Research: Ideas for Further Exploration

10. Read other columns by Marian Wright Edelman. What do they have in common with this opinion piece?

ADVERTISEMENT

This advertisement appears on a Web site hosted by the WIC Works Resource System. WIC stands for "Women, Infants, and Children" and is a program of the Food and Nutrition Service of the United States Department of Agriculture. This particular ad was originally produced by the Oklahoma State Department of Health and is intended as a visual means to educate new parents on their new children from birth to one year of age. Did you know there was so much growth in an infant's feeding patterns in the first year? Did you find this ad to be an effective means for educating new parents? Why or why not?

I am ready for solids.
The American Academy of Pediatrics recommends exclusive breastfeeding until I am 6 months of age. Most babies are ready for solid food when they are 4 to 6 months old.

I will be ready for solid foods when I can...
- Sit supported with good head and neck control
- Open my mouth when I see a spoon
- Keep food in my mouth and swallow it

Even though I am starting solids, I still need my mom's milk or formula.
- If I am nursing, you will need to nurse me 6 to 8 times each day.
- If I am drinking formula, I will need about 30-45 ounces each day.

Now that I'm ready for some food...
- Please give me plain rice cereal at first. Rice is the least likely of the grains to cause an allergic reaction.
- At first, mix 1 tablespoon of cereal with 4-5 tablespoons of breastmilk or formula. The mixture should be very thin, like milk. In the beginning, just dip the tip of the spoon into the cereal and place in my mouth. I may not eat much the first few times but don't give up on me.
- Over the next couple of months, work up to 1-2 tablespoons per feeding and thicken the mixture by adding less breastmilk or formula.
- Next try barley and oatmeal cereals.
- Plase be patient with me! I will probably reuse new foods the first few times and make BIG messes!

Source: Oklahoma State Department of Health

UNDERSTANDING A WRITER'S GOALS: QUESTIONS TO CONSIDER AND DISCUSS

Rhetorical Knowledge: The Writer's Situation and Rhetoric

1. **Audience:** Who is the audience for this advertisement? What makes you think that?

2. **Purpose:** What language in the advertisement most clearly indicates the ad's purpose?

3. **Voice and tone:** The text in this advertisement seems to be written in the voice of the infant. What impact does this have on the audience?

4. **Responsibility:** How responsibly is the information presented?

5. **Context, format, and genre:** View the entire several-page advertisement here: wicworks.fns.usda.gov/wicworks/Sharing_Center/OK/FeedMeImYours.pdf. Each frame of this ad contains a picture of an infant and nutritional advice. What is the impact of the pictures in helping to make the points given in the text?

Critical Thinking: The Writer's Ideas and Your Personal Response

6. How persuasive do you find this advertisement? Why?

7. How do the persuasive features of this advertisement compared to those in Marian Wright Edelman's opinion piece on pages 245–248?

Composing Processes and Knowledge of Conventions: The Writer's Strategies

8. Why does the advertisement use multiple bulleted lists to get its information across?

9. Why does the advertisement choose to use the first person, as though the infant is speaking? Is it effective? Why or why not?

Inquiry and Research: Ideas for Further Exploration

10. Conduct a Web search to find other advertisements for child nutrition. How do their appeals (*ethos, logos, pathos*) compare to the appeals in this advertisement?

GENRES *Up Close*   *Writing an Editorial*

Writers use a range of genres to convince in professional, civic, and personal situations including editorials/opinion pieces, position papers, job reference letters, and business letters. Editorials are appropriate when you want to convince readers that you have a valid position on a controversial or debatable topic. An op-ed piece appears on the page opposite the editorial page in a newspaper or magazine; thus "op-ed" is short for "opposite editorial." However, it can also mean "opinions and editorials."

Features of effective op-eds or editorials include the following:

- They often respond to a previously published article in a newspaper.
- They are usually short (250–800 words).
- They include an opinion or stance.
- They make a point in the first few sentences.
- They indicate why the issue is important.
- They show respect for other points of view.
- They suggest or imply an action that readers can take.

As you read the following example of an editorial, consider in what ways McMillan's text matches the description above of an editorial or op-ed piece.

GLORIA MCMILLAN

EDITORIAL   ## Deep in the Heart of Pluto

Gloria McMillan is a research associate at the University of Arizona. She serves as the arts liaison to the Lunar and Planetary educational outreach committee. She writes about relationships between science and the arts.

This piece originally appeared in the *Arizona Daily Star*, on July 16, 2015. Although her essay attempts to persuade readers to become more interested in science, McMillan does so not by citing numbers and data but by appealing to human imagination.

Seen any faces in the clouds lately? We humans have an urge to put familiar patterns in all sorts of places, no matter how distant. 1

For some time we saw canals on Mars. We even saw a face on Mars until higher resolution photographs showed us otherwise. We (temporarily) are seeing mysterious "headlights" on the asteroid Ceres. 2

For just a day or two we saw a heart shape taking up part of the landscape of Pluto. We beheld Pluto's mysterious heart only until higher resolution photos broke the heart into what is probably an ice field from a recent impact and some rougher terrain nearby. 3

The transformation of these patterns illustrates imagination versus reality and rationality, one might say. But are imagination and rational curiosity opposed? We used to think that science and the arts were separate and opposed to each other. 4

Science fiction shows how much more interesting their relationship has become. It may not take even a year before some creative writer makes use of whatever data we get from Pluto to craft a story that promotes our sense of wonder, along with our desire to learn. 5

Kim Stanley Robinson has written Martian novels that take on many aspects of ecology and ethics in colonizing Mars. Before him, Ray Bradbury wrote *The Martian Chronicles* about how space exploration needed space ethics to prevent the wholesale destruction of others we might encounter in space. 6

Who did that inspire? Professor Peter Smith, the principal investigator of the Phoenix Mars Lander mission, which made the University of Arizona the first public university to have its own Mars mission. Smith read Bradbury's *The Illustrated Man* as a boy and got hooked on science for life. 7

But in the 1950s, when *The Martian Chronicles* first appeared, the horizon was clouded by fear of atomic warfare. In that decade, many people still regarded science fiction as a frivolous pastime for adolescents. 8

To defend the value of wondering about space and the future to those who believed science fiction held little to recommend it, Bradbury went around the country speaking to various groups. In the May 2, 1953, issue of *The Nation*, he also wrote about why science fiction helps us to learn about our world. Bradbury noted major advances in the communications technology of that time and wondered about a future in which people would use advanced forms of the newly invented transistor radios, noting: 9

> *I do not know whether tomorrow's street will be full of human beings with Seashell thimble-radios in their ears and the world's problems moved away from and neglected. Or whether by some miracle we may all carry supersonic stethoscopes to hear the heartbeat of every other human heart.* 10

Bradbury continues that humanity's techno-toys may take us to the stars or finish us off, but that neither outcome is a sure thing. Our dual abilities to be curious and to wonder make both science and the arts happen. 11

Working with art and science together, as science fiction does, may reawaken our young to the glories of the universe. Science may become more of a popular field again in this country. Attempting to strip wonder from science or science from wonder is a mistake. 12

And trying to be merely rational is like Dr. Jekyll trying to separate his nature into only the good side and to banish evil from his mind. We become half a person and the repressed comes back to haunt us as we become unable to make novel associations of ideas. 13

We need both imagination and logic because the worlds they co-create become tomorrow's realities. 14

Why go to Pluto? We are going because whatever data are transmitted from the digital cameras on the New Horizons mission, that heart we thought we saw on Pluto is important, too. 15

UNDERSTANDING A WRITER'S GOALS: QUESTIONS TO CONSIDER AND DISCUSS

Rhetorical Knowledge: The Writer's Situation and Rhetoric

1. **Audience:** McMillan wrote this essay for the readers of the *Arizona Daily Star*, the daily newspaper serving Tucson, Arizona, so we might assume she was writing for a "general audience." However, is there anything in her essay that makes you think she might have been targeting a more specific group? If so, who might that group be? What makes you think so?

2. **Purpose:** In what area of life (academic, professional, civic, personal) does "Deep in the Heart of Pluto" best fit? What makes you think so? In what ways might it overlap into more than one area?

3. **Voice and tone:** What is McMillan's attitude about those who might belittle science fiction? What does she do to try to convince them otherwise? Do you think she's effective? Why or why not?

4. **Responsibility:** McMillan writes about what seems to be a disconnect between science and the arts. Do you think such a chasm exists? What is her approach to this culturally assumed difference? Do you think she's right? Why or why not?

5. **Context, format, and genre:** McMillan's essay originally appeared in a daily newspaper. One of the hallmarks of newspaper writing is short paragraphs. McMillan employs that convention here. Do you think her short paragraphs help to make her essay more readable, or would you have preferred that she expand some of her points more fully? Give specific examples to back up your preference.

Critical Thinking: The Writer's Ideas and Your Personal Response

6. After reading McMillan's essay, are you reconsidering your own view about the relationship between science and the arts? Why or why not?

7. Consider other persuasive pieces that you have read. In what ways are they similar to or different from McMillan's essay?

Composing Processes and Knowledge of Conventions: The Writer's Strategies

8. McMillan begins her essay by mentioning images that humans have claimed to have seen on celestial bodies that have since been explained by science. Does her opening get you thinking about connections between science and human imagination in a positive way? If so, what does she do to accomplish this? If not, why do you think she failed?

9. Do you agree with the author that reading science fiction when young will help people develop an interest in science? Do you read science fiction? What effect do you think it has had on you? If you haven't read science fiction, why doesn't it hold any interest for you? Do you think you might better appreciate science if you did read science fiction? Why or why not?

Inquiry and Research: Ideas for Further Exploration

10. Think of a "connection," aside from space exploration, that might connect science and the arts. Research to see if that connection does exist.

WRITING PROCESSES

As you work on the assignment that you have chosen, remember the qualities of an effective and convincing persuasive paper, listed on pages 242–244. Also remember that while the activities listed below imply that writers proceed step-by-step, the actual process of writing is usually messier: you will keep coming back to your earlier work, adding to it and modifying the information to be more accurate as you conduct additional research and become more familiar with your issue.

If you are considering several issues for your persuasive text, put your notes into a separate computer document for each one. Once you determine the focus of your paper, it will be easy to access and use the notes on that issue.

Invention: Getting Started

The invention activities below are strategies that you can use to help you get some sense of what you already know about the issue you have chosen. Whatever invention method(s) you use (or that your instructor asks you to use), try to answer questions such as these:

- What do I already know about this issue?
- What is my point of view on this issue?
- Where might I learn more about this issue? What verifiable information is available?
- What might my audience already know? What might their point of view be?
- What do I know about my audience? What don't I know that I should know?
- What questions do I have about the issue?
- What are some other views on this issue?

Doing your invention work in electronic form, rather than on paper, lets you easily use your invention work as you construct a draft.

For more on strategies for discovery and learning, see Chapter 4.

Writing Activity

Questioning and Freewriting

Spend a few minutes jotting down answers to the reporter's questions about your issue: *who, what, where, when, why,* and *how.* You may find that your answers to these questions lead to more questions, which will help you focus on additional aspects of your subject to research.

Then, using the answers you noted above, freewrite about *one side* of your issue for ten minutes. Then freewrite about the *opposing side* of your issue, again for ten minutes. This activity will help you better understand and appreciate the arguments on both sides.

Student writer Zack Peach read an article in his college psychology class about how the new edition of the *Diagnostic and Statistical Manual of Mental Disorders* (*DSM*) had changed the definition of Asperger's Syndrome. People with Asperger's had been considered to have a "high functioning" version of autism, but the new version of the *DSM* (in Zack's words) "kind of lumped Asperger's into autism," which means that a patient's diagnosis might not be accurate, and as a result, treatment may not be correct. Zack was intrigued and decided to focus on that issue in an essay for his writing class.

Zack Peach's Answers to the Reporter's Questions

Student writer Zach Peach might ask—and try to answer through his research—the reporter's questions (*Who? What? When? Why? Where? How?*). (Note that the reporter's question of "Where?" does not really apply to this situation):

- Who is involved?

  Who does this change affect, and how are they affected? How might those with autism or those who had been diagnosed with Asperger's Syndrome be impacted? Would their diagnosis change now?

- What happened?

  The American Psychiatric Association changed its definition of Asperger's Syndrome to no longer having its own specific diagnosis. Does that marginalize some of those patients?

- When does the change take effect, and how will it be implemented?

  Zack wondered about those who previously had been diagnosed with Asperger's: would the new definition force doctors to change the treatment of those patients? Would it cause some new patients to be misdiagnosed? Would insurance coverage change?

- Why did the American Psychiatric Association change the definition of Asperger's Syndrome?

  Zach wondered why the Association changed the *DSM* definition of Asperger's Syndrome. Did some medical research (or some other reason) prompt such a change? Are there other such changes that happen when the *DSM* constructs a new edition?

- How might people who had Asperger's Syndrome react? Would they perhaps lose any assistance they might need to cope with situations they found themselves in, because of a change in diagnosis?

Zack Peach's Freewriting

Peach also used freewriting to explore his ideas. A portion of his freewriting appears here:

I'm wondering how this change—where Asperger's is no longer a specific diagno-sis—will hurt people (like me). On the one hand, Asperger's is part of autism (I can see that) but on the other, it's not anywhere as severe and so cannot be treated in the same way . . . but aren't they going to lump patients together now? Won't that screw up the treatments that some of them get? I mean (as a comparison) if one person breaks her wrist, and another breaks her arm, the both will have a splint and all, but won't their treatment be different in main ways?

Exploring Your Ideas with Research

Research is critical to any persuasive text, for if you cannot provide evidence to support your position, you probably will not convince your reading audience.

Although you may be able to use information from your own experience as evidence, you will usually need to offer verifiable information from sources, such as facts, statistics, expert testimony, and examples.

To find evidence outside of your own experience that you need to support your claim, look for answers to the following questions:

- What facts or other verifiable information can I find that will provide solid evidence to convince my readers to agree with my position?

- What expert testimony can I provide to support my claim? What authorities on my issue might I interview?

- What statistical data support my position?

- What are other people doing in response to this issue or problem?

For help with locating sources of information, see Chapter 19; for help with documenting your sources, see Chapter 20.

The subject you focus on and the kind of essay you are constructing help to determine the research you conduct. For example, for the scenarios earlier in this chapter, you could conduct several kinds of research:

- For Scenario 1 (page 240), which asks you to focus on a controversial issue, assume that you have decided to write about whether the threat of criminal punishment helps to prevent insider trading of stocks. What kinds of research might you conduct? At your library, a search of business publications such as *The Wall Street Journal, BusinessWeek,* and *Forbes* would be a good place to start. But you could also interview some local business executives to get their perspectives for your paper. And you could interview local law enforcement officials and attorneys to get their take on whether the threat of punishment helps stop insider trading.

- For Scenario 3 (page 241), where you focus on a problem in your campus community, that same kind of local research—interviewing your class-mates, for example—will provide useful information for your paper. Consider the comments you could get, for instance, if you were writing about an issue involving your classrooms, such as the condition of the building or the time classes are scheduled, or a campus issue, such as campus safety, student fees, or athletics. Speaking with campus officials and administrators will also give you useful information. In addition, a search of the campus newspaper archives in your college's library may provide good background information on your issue.

- One way to learn about other perspectives on your subject is to read online blogs or join e-mail lists that focus on your topic. These ongoing electronic conversations often can provide multiple perspectives and ideas on the issue you are writing about—which then can help you with your own thinking and research.

Writing Activity

Conducting Research

Using the list of qualities of effective persuasive writing, go through your invention activity notes to find the questions you still have and want to ask. Now is the time to determine the best way(s) to answer those questions. Would it be useful to:

- Conduct more library research in books?
- Interview people about your subject?
- Conduct more library research in journals?

Make a research plan. Where will you conduct your research, and when will you do so?

Student Example: An Excerpt from Zack Peach's Research

For my paper, I might be able to use some of what I read in my psychology class book. But then I also want to find some sources on autism and especially on Asperger's Syndrome, and how they really are not two distinct things but in ways they are different. That should help me explain how someone with Asperger's should not receive the same treatment as someone with autism.

I did check the *Random House Dictionary* through Dictionary.com and they had this definition for "autism":

> noun
> 1. *Psychiatry.* a pervasive developmental disorder of children, characterized by impaired communication, excessive rigidity, and emotional detachment: now considered one of the <u>autism spectrum disorders</u>.

And for Asperger's Syndrome, the same dictionary has this definition:

> noun, *Psychiatry.*
> 1. a developmental disorder characterized by severely impaired social skills, repetitive behaviors, and often, a narrow set of interests, but not involving delayed development of linguistic and cognitive abilities: now considered one of the <u>autism spectrum disorders</u>.

While both say they're "now considered one of the autism spectrum disorders," there are some important differences in those definitions, especially in how the Asperger's definition is much more specific. I hope I can discuss those differences in my paper.

Reviewing Your Invention and Research

After you have conducted your research, review your invention work and notes and the information you collected from outside sources. Once you have a general idea of the conclusion your research is leading you to, you can develop a "working" thesis statement: If you had to make a point now, based on what you have learned, what would it be? It is called a working thesis because your main point or thesis will inevitably change as you continue to conduct research and learn more. And, as you know, through the process of writing itself, you will learn about your topic, so give yourself permission to modify and develop this initial thesis statement as you draft and revise your text. Once you have written several drafts, received feedback on them, and revised them, you will be better able to determine what your final thesis statement should be.

For more on deciding on a thesis, see Chapter 13.

Writing Activity

Considering Your Research and Focusing Your Ideas

Using your research notes as a starting point, again use the reporter's questions of *who, what, where, when, why,* and *how* to get onto paper or into a computer file what you know about your issue. For example, if you were focusing on a campus-community problem, some of your research notes might look like these:

Who: Students and neighbors alike who are affected when lots of student cars are going through the neighborhood, often too fast, both when they come to campus and when they leave.

What: The biggest issues seem to be too many cars on neighborhood streets, too many of them speeding, and too many of them parking where they should not.

Strategies FOR Success: | Openness

Successful writers are open to new ideas and a wide range of perspectives. In writing to convince, openness is especially important because readers are more likely to accept your ideas if they think that you are open-minded. As you consider other perspectives, think about how they compare and contrast with your own ways of looking at the world. How does viewing an issue from another perspective enable you to see the world in new ways? If you find a new idea easy to accept, why is that the case? If you find a new idea difficult to accept, why is that so? If a perspective differs from yours, what distinguishes the two? What are the points of agreement? How can the two perspectives be combined to form yet another way of looking at the world?

Openness also applies to a writers' strategies for finding, gathering, using, and presenting information. For example, if you usually begin looking for information by doing a Google search, try a different approach, such as using some of the strategies described in Chapter 19, "Finding and Evaluating Information."

Open-minded writers listen to the ideas of others, and they consider the validity of those ideas without automatically ruling them out. An open-minded writer acknowledges opposing views and is willing to accept those that withstand critical scrutiny. Of course, it's important to know when to refute ideas that do not withstand critical analysis.

If you ignore or distort opposing views, readers will think you are either unaware or dishonest, which will quickly weaken or destroy your *ethos*—your credibility. Ignoring the other side of an issue, the objections that others might have to your point of view, actually weakens your position, as your readers may be aware of the objections and wonder why you did not deal with these other perspectives.

■ Organizing Your Information

Because the purpose of writing a persuasive text is to convince your readers to accept your point of view, you will need to organize your reasons and evidence strategically. The questions that you need to ask yourself when deciding on your organization are all rhetorical:

- Who is your audience? What is your readers' position on your issue likely to be? If they are undecided, you might try a classical or an inductive approach, both of which are discussed below. If they are likely to hold an opposing view, then a refutation approach, also discussed below, may be the better choice.
- Why might they be interested in your persuasive writing, or how can you make them interested in it?
- What is your purpose for writing—that is, why do you want to convince readers of this position?

See more on Aristotelian organization in Chapter 14.

When you construct a persuasive paper, determine the most effective organizational approach for your purpose and audience. One method of organizing an argument, called the *classical scheme,* was first outlined by Aristotle nearly 2,400 years ago. If you are using the classical scheme, this is the sequence you will follow:

introduction → main claim → evidence supporting claim → discussion of other perspectives (acknowledging, conceding, and/or refuting them) → conclusion

Aristotle's approach is also called the **deductive method** because you state your claim and then help the reader understand, or deduce, how the evidence supports your claim. The advantage of this method is that you state your position and make your case early, before your reader starts thinking about other perspectives.

Another organizational approach is commonly known as the **inductive method.** When using this approach, you first present and explain all of your reasons and evidence, then draw your conclusion—your main claim. The advantage is that your reader may come to the same conclusion before you explicitly state your position and will therefore be more inclined to agree with your point of view.

Because persuasive writing must usually acknowledge and incorporate or refute opposing viewpoints, a third organizational method starts by presenting the views of the other side. In this method, you first deal with objections to your claim and then state your position and provide reasons and evidence to support it. This is an especially effective strategy if the opposing view or views are widely held.

Here are three organizational structures that you might consider for your persuasive paper.

Options FOR Organization
Organizing a Persuasive Paper

The Classical (Deductive) Approach	The Inductive Approach	The Refutation Approach
Introduce the issue and state your thesis.	Introduce the issue.	Introduce the issue.
Explain the importance of the issue.	Offer reasons and evidence for your claim.	List opposing views.
Present your reasons and evidence—why readers should agree with you.	Draw your conclusion—your main claim.	Deal with each objection in turn.
Answer objections—either incorporating or refuting other points of view.	Deal with other viewpoints either before or after presenting your claim.	Introduce your position and explain why it makes sense, offering reasons and evidence.
Conclude—often with a call to action.	Conclude—often with a call to action.	Conclude—often with a call to action.

Constructing a Complete Draft

Once you have chosen the best organizational approach for your audience and purpose, you are ready to construct your draft. After you have reviewed your invention writing and research notes, developed a working thesis, and carefully considered all of the reasons and evidence you generated, construct a complete first draft.

As you work, keep the following in mind:

- You may discover that you need to do more invention work and/or more research as you write.

- As you try out tentative claims and reasons, ask your classmates and other readers about the kinds of supporting evidence they consider convincing.

- Consider whether photographs or other visuals might help support your thesis.

- If you become tired and the quality of your thinking or your productivity is affected, take a break.

For more on choosing visuals, see Chapter 18.

Synthesizing and Integrating Sources into Your Draft: Incorporating Partial Quotes in Your Sentences

Often, your research will provide you with lots of quotations, which means you have to determine how to incorporate the quotations you want to use into your text. One way to use quotations, whether they come from a source you interviewed or from source you read, is to incorporate them into your sentences, a using a phrase such as "she said" or "Johnson comments":

> Catherine Lord, a member of the American Psychiatric Association, states "The intent was that it would make diagnosis more straightforward. . . ."

Another method of incorporating a quotation is to integrate it into the structure of your sentence. For instance, in the following example, Zack Peach quotes from a book he read by providing information and context *before* the quotation:

> As mentioned by Tony Attwood in his book on Asperger's Syndrome, the *DSM-IV* did welcome Asperger's Syndrome as a diagnosis and movement of Pervasive Development Disorder and Autism onto Axis 1, the axis that meant signs can improve with early intervention. However, he notes, "there are problems with the diagnostic criteria in *DSM-IV*, and especially the differential criteria in the manual that distinguish between a diagnosis of Autism or Asperger's syndrome" (41–42).

When you incorporate quotations into your own writing, remember the following:

1. Always introduce the quotation (never just put it into your text without some words of introduction).
2. Accurately report and document where the quotation came from.

Parts of a Complete Draft

Introduction: Regardless of your organizational approach, you need to have a strong introduction to capture your readers' attention and introduce the issue. To accomplish these two goals in an introduction, you might do one or more of the following:

- **Share an anecdote that clearly exemplifies the issue.** Gloria McMillan mentions Peter Smith, the principal investigator of the Phoenix Mars Lander Mission, who became interested in science by reading science fiction as a boy.
- **Provide a brief history of the issue.** Marian Wright Edelman begins her argument (p. 245) with a history of efforts to protect and expand antipoverty programs.
- **Provide a fact or statistic about the issue that will surprise—and possibly concern—readers**. Zack Peach opens the final version of his paper with this:

> According to an estimate by the Centers for Disease Control and Prevention (CDC), in 2014 one in sixty-eight children was diagnosed with autism (CDC).

- **Explain (briefly) why your persuasive text is important.**
- **Ask an intriguing question about your subject.**

Body: You can use various writing strategies, including defining all terms your reader might not understand within the body of your text, to effectively persuade your reader. This is the area of your paper where you will need to provide supporting examples or other types of evidence for each reason you offer, use visual aids (photographs, charts, tables) to support your position, and use rhetorical appeals—*ethos, logos, pathos* (page 27)—to help convince your readers.

For more on rhetorical appeals and argument strategies, see Chapter 14.

Conclusion: In your conclusion, you need to restate or allude to your thesis and let your readers know what you would like them to do with the information they learned from your essay. Conclusions in persuasive writing often do the following:

- **Explain your main thesis or point—what you want to convince your reader about.**

- **Summarize how each supporting point adds evidence to support your main point.** In a long, involved argument, a summary can help readers recall the main points that you are making.

- **Reach out to the audience.** Marian Wright Edelman ends with an appeal to readers to make sure that "our leaders" hear the message about hunger.

- **Include a "call to action."** Gloria McMillan cites Ray Bradbury's 1953 article in *The Nation* where he explained how science fiction better helps us understand the world.

Title: As you compose your persuasive writing, a title should emerge at some point—perhaps late in the process. The title should reflect the point you are trying to make, and it should catch your readers' attention and make them want to read your essay. It may be risky to state your major claim in the title: If you state a controversial claim in your title, you run the risk that some readers will choose not to read your argument. However, there are times when stating a bold claim in the title is appropriate—especially if readers may not have even considered the topic.

VISUAL *Thinking* | **Going Beyond Words to Achieve Your Goals**

In his essay about the evolving definitions of autism and Asperger's Syndrome, Zack Peach gives a history of how mental health professionals have changed their thinking with regard to autism and Asperger's. To illustrate his point, Peach could include some examples of visuals that help explain his perspective, such as the poster in Figure 9.1. Using visuals to explain the distinctions he is writing about may help Peach's readers, as not all of them are familiar with the distinctions he is making.

What is....
ASPERGER SYNDROME?

A developmental disorder which falls within the Autism Spectrum. Asperger Syndrome, referred to by many as "High Functioning Autism," is a developmental disorder that is not widely understood. Main features of this disorder become obvious during early childhood and remain constant throughout life, although the common features and degree of actual impairment can vary. Rarely recognised before the age of three, it is more common in boys than girls. Core features of the syndrome are lack of social skills, limited ability to have a two way conversation and an intense interest in a particular subject. Most of these children attend normal primary schools.

COMMUNICATION

Poor conversation skills · Talks incessantly about one topic · Rarely makes eye contact · Concrete pedantic interpretation of language

Although these children are often highly articulate, content of speech may be abnormal, tending to be pedantic and often centering on one or two favourite topics. Sometimes a word or phrase is repeated over and over in stereotyped fashion. Usually, there is a comprehension deficit despite apparent superior verbal skills. Non verbal communication, both expressive and receptive is often impaired.

SOCIAL INTERACTION

Often teased and bullied by other children · The odd one out · Indifferent to physical contact

There tends to be impairment in two way social interaction due to an inability to understand the rules governing social behaviour. A lack of empathy with others and little or no eye contact may be evident. Can appear to be stuck at the egocentric stage of social and emotional development. They tend to perceive the world exclusively from their own point of view. Although interested in social relationships often social contact is made inappropriately.

SOCIAL BEHAVIOUR

Familiar routine very important · Eccentric, unusual behaviour · Inappropriate laughing or giggling · Solitary repetitive play

Social behaviour is often naive and peculiar. Can tend to become intensely attached to particular possessions often engaging in repetitive activities. Resistant to change, coping best when life is predictable. They prefer structure and may concentrate exclusively on matters in which they are interested. Are often known as loners who never quite fit in because of eccentric behaviour, peculiar ways of speaking and a lack of social skills.

COMMON FEATURES:
• Excellent rote memory, absorbs facts easily. • Generally performs well with maths, science and reading. • May be anxious and unable to cope with criticism or imperfection. • Often victims of teasing and bullying leading to withdrawal into isolated activities. • Can appear clumsy and have an unusual gait or stance. • Often seen as odd or eccentric. • Language often appears good but may have limited content and poor social understanding. • Self interested and lacks empathy.

ASPERGER SYNDROME SUPPORT NETWORK (VIC) INC. TELEPHONE: (03) 9845 2766
Assoc. No. A0043862N   A.B.N. 47 066 180 983

Source: Aspergers Victoria Inc.

FIGURE 9.1 A Poster Illustrating the Signs and Symptoms of Asperger's Syndrome

> **Writing** Activity
>
> ## Constructing a Complete Draft
>
> Using your invention work, your research, and the writing you did when select-ing an organizational approach for your persuasive paper, write a complete first draft. Remember that your argument will evolve as you write, so your ideas will most likely change as you draft.

Zack Peach's First Draft

In this brief draft, note how Zack Peach incorporates information and examples from his life, as well as from outside sources. As he wrote, Peach did not worry about grammar, punctuation, and mechanics; instead, he concentrated on getting his main ideas on paper.

Asperger's Syndrome, Autism, and You
Zack Peach

Autism refers to a range of complex disorders related to the brain and how it functions. Asperger's Syndrome is believed to be a milder form of autism. People with Asperger's tend to be higher functioning than people with more severe forms of autism and do not experience delays in language devel-opment. ❶

In recent years, the fifth edition of the *Diagnostic and Statistical Manual of Mental Disorders* (*DSM-V*), has excluded a definition for Asperger's Syndrome and includes its signs and symptoms under the umbrella term "autism spectrum disorder." My purpose here is to explain ❷ that Asperger's Syndrome is still a valid form of diagnosis. To properly explain the complexity of this issue, I will first explain what the *DSM* is and then describe both autism and Asperger's Syn-drome in more detail.

The *DSM* is the set of definitions for mental disorders used by mental health professionals to classify specific issues based on signs, symptoms, and periods of time and to give diagnoses and suggest specific kinds of treatment. ❸ By placing the diagnosis for Asperger's Syndrome along the autism spectrum, ❹ practitioners risk complicating diagnoses and compromising treatments for both disorders.

People with autism require methods, such as therapy, to help cope with the world and fit in. Donna Williams, author of *Autism: An Inside-Out Approach*, explains how when she was young all of the thoughts and feelings that went through her mind overwhelmed her. ❺ She describes autism not as a sense of "selfness," ❻ as implied in the translation of the word "autism," but of "otherness," where one feels a distinct lack of consistency of one's self. How severe these symptoms might be, how early signs are observed, and whether they are attributed to a delay in development or some other disorder, all determine where a person might be placed on the spectrum.

The change to the *DSM-V* has serious consequences, particularly for those who have come to accept their diagnosis as part of who they are and have built their lives around this understanding of themselves. Although people with Asperger's are able to function and adapt better than people elsewhere on the autism spectrum, the ease with which a person adapts to life depends on that person's access to a support system. The most effective way to improve the lives of people with Asperger's is to recognize the condition as a valid diagnosis and provide accurate treatment and support options for those who need it.

As ideas for further development, Zack made these notes at the end of his initial draft:

Define Asperger's and autism in greater detail

More specific examples showing differences between autism and Asperger's

Who are the experts on this topic—people with Asperger's?

Transitions.

Student Comments on Peach's First Draft

❶ These definitions aren't clear. Say more?

❷ Sounds like an informative paper—this assignment is to argue a point, I think.

❸ Do you have more information and background on the history?

❹ How, specifically, would having separate definitions help patients?

❺ Do you need a citation here?

❻ I like these quotations—they help me see what you mean.

▌ Revising

Once you have a full draft of your persuasive text, you still have much to do. First, however, you should set the draft aside so that you can gain some critical distance. You can then read it with fresh eyes. When you approach your work this way, you will find it easier to notice reasons that are irrelevant, evidence that is not fully developed, or places where a compelling visual might add to the impact of your argument.

As you work to revise your early drafts, do not be concerned about doing a great deal of heavy editing. When you revise, you will probably change the content and structure of your paper, so time spent fixing problems with sentence style or grammar, punctuation, or mechanics at this stage is often wasted.

When you reread the first draft of your persuasive writing, here are some questions to ask yourself:

- How clearly and persuasively am I making my point? Am I sure my readers can understand it? How easily will they be able to restate the thesis?

- How effectively does all of my evidence support that main point? (Have I included evidence that seems persuasive but that does not support the point I am arguing for?).

- Are there photographs, charts, or graphs that might help me make my point?

- Are there parts of my paper that might confuse a reader? If so, how might I clarify them?

- Do I restate or allude to my main point at the end of my paper and also explain to the reader what I would like him or her to *do* (to vote, to write a letter to the editor, to *do* what I have been arguing for)?

Technology can help you revise and edit your writing more easily. Use your word processor's track-changes tool to try out revisions and editing changes. After you have had time to think about the possible changes, you can "accept" or "reject" them. Also, you can use your word processor's comment tool to write reminders to yourself when you get stuck with a revision or some editing task.

Because it is so difficult even for experienced writers to see their emerging writing with a fresh eye, it is almost always useful to ask classmates, friends, or family members to read and comment on drafts of your persuasive writing.

WRITER'S *Workshop* | Responding to Full Drafts

Working with one or two classmates, read each paper, and offer comments and questions that will help each of you see your papers' strengths and weaknesses. Consider the following questions as you do:

- What is your first impression of this draft? How effective is the title at drawing you in? Why? What are your overall suggestions for improvement? What part(s) of the text are especially persuasive? What reasons could use more support? Indicate what you like about the draft, and provide positive and encouraging feedback to the writer.

- How tight is the writer's focus? Does the paper wander a bit? If so, where?

- How effective is the introduction? What suggestions can you make to improve it?

- What is the author's thesis or main claim? How could it be expressed or supported more effectively?

- Are there parts that are confusing? Where would you like more details or examples to help clarify the writer's meaning?

- How accurate and appropriate is the supporting evidence? How clearly does the author indicate the sources of statistics and other supporting evidence?

- Might visuals such as charts, tables, photographs, or cartoons make the text more convincing?

- How clearly and effectively does the writer present any opposing points of view? How effectively does the writer answer opposing viewpoints? How might the writer acknowledge, concede, and/or refute them more effectively?

- How well has the writer demonstrated an awareness of readers' knowledge, needs, and/or expectations? How might the writer demonstrate greater awareness?

- How carefully has the writer avoided logical fallacies?

- What could be added to or changed in the conclusion to make it more effective? How well does it tie everything together? If action is called for, to what extent does it make you want to take action?

Notes on Zack Peach's First Draft, from a Conference with His Instructor

After writing his first draft, Peach met with his instructor, who thought his topic was promising but indicated that he needed more examples about the differences between the wider term *autism* and the more specific issues involved with Asperger's Syndrome. That conversation included the following suggestions, which led to areas that were developed in more detail in Zack's final paper:

1. Provide more examples of why Asperger's differs from autism.
2. Add Zack's personal story to the final paper.
3. Explain how other problems can affect "Aspies."

4. Detail how *not* having the right diagnosis leads to patients getting weak or ineffective resources. In other words, they don't get the help they need.

5. Make it clear to your reader earlier in the paper that you're aware that the *DSM* considers Asperger's part of autism spectrum disorder.

Responding to Readers' Comments

Once they have received feedback on their writing from peers, instructors, friends, and others, all writers have to figure out what to do with that feedback.

The first thing to do with any feedback is to consider carefully what your readers have said about your text. In his case, Peach arranged a conference with his writing teacher, who helped him decide which specific terms needed to be better defined in order to make his argument clearer.

As with all feedback, it is important to listen to it carefully and consider what your reader has to say. Then it is up to you, as the author, to decide how to come to terms with these suggestions. It is especially important to deal with comments from readers indicating that they are unconvinced by your argument. You sometimes may find that comments from more than one reader contradict each other. In that case, you need to use your own judgment to decide which reader's comments are on the right track.

In the final version of his paper, you can see how Zack Peach responded to his instructor's comments, as well as to his own review of his first draft.

KNOWLEDGE OF CONVENTIONS

When effective writers edit, they attend to the conventions that will help readers process their work. These include genre conventions, documentation, format, usage, grammar, and mechanics. By attending to these conventions in your writing, you make reading a more pleasant experience for readers.

Editing

The final tasks in any writing project are editing and proofreading—the final polishing of your document. When you edit and polish your writing, you make changes to your sentence structures and word choices to improve your style and to make your writing clearer and more concise. You also check your work to make sure it adheres to conventions of grammar, usage, punctuation, mechanics, and spelling. Use the spell-check function of your word-processing program, but be sure to double-check your spelling personally. If you have used sources in your paper, make sure you are following the documentation style your instructor requires.

As with overall revision of your work, this final editing and polishing is most effective if you can put your text aside for a few days and come back to it

See Chapter 20 for more on documenting sources using MLA or APA style.

with fresh eyes. Because checking conventions is easier said than done, though, we strongly recommend that you ask classmates, friends, and tutors to read your work as well.

To assist you with editing, we offer here a round-robin editing activity focused on citing sources correctly.

WRITER'S *Workshop* | **Round-Robin Editing with a Focus on Citing Sources**

Working in small groups, look over both the in-text citations and the works-cited or references lists in your papers. For example, you might notice a problem with an in-text citation that is supposed to be in MLA style, such as this one:

> In the last line of the story, however, Rudebeck quotes Zach Krula, a freshman offensive lineman. Zach says,

"We've got a lot of great players, we might as well utilize them" (Rudebeck).

In MLA style, it is not necessary to include the source's name in parentheses if the name has been given within the text.

As you work with your peers, consult Chapter 20 of this text, which provides guidelines for using MLA or APA style when citing sources.

Genres, Documentation, and Format

If you are writing an academic paper in response to Scenario 1, you will need to follow the conventions for the discipline in which you are writing and the requirements of your instructor. If you are writing an editorial for your college newspaper (Scenario 3), you should check the newspaper's editorial page or its Web site to see what the requirements are for length and format and what information you need to include when you submit the editorial.

A Writer Achieves His Goal: Zack Peach's Final Draft

Zack Peach continued to revise and edit his paper, and constructed a finished draft, which follows. As you read the essay, think about what makes it effective. Following the essay, you'll find some specific questions to consider.

1"

↕ ¹/₂"
Peach   1

Asperger's Syndrome, Autism, and You

According to an estimate by the Centers for Disease Control and Prevention (CDC), in 2014 one in sixty-eight children was diagnosed with autism (CDC). Autism refers to a range of complex disorders related to the brain and how it functions. These disorders are based on a spectrum, which means that people diagnosed with autism experience it in varying degrees ("Autism Spectrum Disorder"). For example, Asperger's Syndrome is believed to be a milder form of autism. People with Asperger's may not have all the symptoms of autism, nor do they have the same number and degree of symptoms as a person on the severe end of the spectrum. They tend to be higher functioning than people with more severe forms of autism and do not experience delays in language development ("Asperger's Syndrome").

In recent years, there have been some controversies about the autism spectrum, most notably in response to the fifth edition of the *Diagnostic and Statistical Manual of Mental Disorders* (*DSM-5*), which excludes a definition for Asperger's Syndrome and includes its signs and symptoms under the umbrella term "autism spectrum disorder." My purpose here is to explain that Asperger's Syndrome is still a valid form of diagnosis and to argue that eliminating it from the *DSM-5* negatively impacts the ways in which people on the spectrum define themselves and go about their lives. To properly explain the complexity of this issue, I will first explain what the *DSM* is and then describe both autism and Asperger's Syndrome in more detail.

The *DSM* is the set of definitions for mental disorders used by mental health professionals to classify specific issues based on signs, symptoms, and periods of time and to give diagnoses and suggest specific kinds of treatment. The *DSM* has gone through several iterations, with experts refining, adding, and removing definitions of mental illnesses with each version. For example, in 1980, explicit diagnostic criteria were added in the third edition ("DSM"), allowing psychiatrists to identify patients' specific issues and determine the severity of their conditions. In May 2013, a group of mental health professionals who study and define the listed disorders advised placing autism, Asperger's, childhood disintegrative disorder, and pervasive developmental disorder under the single term of "autism spectrum disorder" in *DSM-5* ("Autism Spectrum Disorder Fact Sheet—*DSM-5*").

1"

1"   1"

1"

Title centered; major words capitalized.

Shortened version of title of source enclosed in parentheses.

Thesis statement.

According to an article from 2012, the *DSM* changed the diagnosis of Asperger's and autism for two reasons: to account for the variance in diagnosis from year to year by different practitioners and to standardize the term applied to a single set of symptoms ("*DSM-V* Changes"). "They're not necessarily different disorders," explains Catherine Lord of the American Psychiatric Association, "because, at least biologically, nobody can differentiate Asperger's from autism." Lord explains that the goal is "not to lose those people [with Asperger's] but to say they can be recognized within this broader concept of Autism Spectrum Disorders" (qtd. in Esposito). Although the *DSM-5* acknowledges that autism holds a spectrum, having specific definitions for at least a few sections, subgroups, and variations would help mental health professionals assist those whose diagnosis might be more accurately defined as Asperger's. By placing the diagnosis for Asperger's Syndrome along the autism spectrum, practitioners risk complicating diagnoses and compromising treatments for both disorders.

People on the autism spectrum do not suffer a particular long-term deficiency. Instead, their way of thinking and operating simply takes a different approach. Autism is defined by two key factors: persistent deficits in social communication and interaction across multiple contexts, and restricted, repetitive patterns of behavior, interests, and activities (CDC; *DSM-5*, 50). As noted in the *DSM-5*, most people with autism are very literal in their speech, and even when using common language skills "reciprocal social communication is impaired in autism spectrum disorder" (53). Some people with autism experience a form of sensory overload that feels as if something is assailing their senses. A light breeze might feel like a hand making contact with their body, a whisper like an indoor voice or unintelligible gibberish. Many people on the spectrum experience varying degrees of social sensitivity when dealing with new people or situations.

People with autism require methods, such as therapy, to help cope with the world and fit in. Donna Williams, author of *Autism: An Inside-Out Approach*, explains how when she was young all of the thoughts and feelings that went through her mind overwhelmed her (14). She describes autism not as a sense of "selfness," as implied in the translation of the word "autism," but of "otherness," where one feels

Peach 3

a distinct lack of consistency of one's self. This lack of consistency helps explain why people on the spectrum might be overly attached to routine, which gives them a sense of consistency and stability. How severe these symptoms might be, how early signs are observed, and whether they are attributed to a delay in development or some other disorder, all determine where a person might be placed on the spectrum. Because some people possess traits that indicate that they fall somewhere on the moderate range of the spectrum, it is important that Asperger's remain a valid diagnosis. At the same time, the *DSM* should provide a few guidelines on how to recognize Asperger's and differentiate it from other disorders or other points on the autism spectrum.

In fact, it is easy to misdiagnose those on the spectrum with something other than autism. People with Tourette syndrome and aphasia have been diagnosed as having characteristics of autism (Williams 22). Other similar disorders include Rett syndrome, selective mutism, ADHD, schizophrenia, language disorders and social/pragmatic communication disorders, and intellectual development disorders without the influence of autism (*DSM-5* 57-58). In short, diagnosing someone along the autism spectrum can be difficult. Eliminating the terminology used for specific diagnoses does not simplify the process nor lead to more accurate therapies and treatments. The fact of frequent misdiagnosis should prompt careful examination of the diagnostic criteria and support the argument for not narrowing the range of disorders falling under the heading of autism.

As one solution to the problem of misdiagnosis, Dan Coulter, author of *Life in the Asperger Lane*, encourages relevant organizations to publish updated information on the disorder and to advocate and fight for laws that would appropriately accommodate those who live with it ("Dealing"). Coulter's solution is a move in the right direction because it would mean engaging people with the knowledge that autism comes in more than just three levels of intensity. However, it does not address the primary issue of accurate diagnosis. Reinstating Asperger's Syndrome to the *DSM* would allow the caregivers to more effectively support people with Asperger's. If professional organizations and caregivers back the diagnosis, the "fight" for support and services will be shorter and more definitive.

Asperger's Syndrome is a specific condition within autism whose diagnosis impacts how people see themselves and how they lead their lives. The change to the *DSM-5* has serious consequences, particularly for those who have come to accept their diagnosis as part of who they are and have built their lives around this understanding of themselves. Although people with Asperger's are able to function and adapt better than people elsewhere on the autism spectrum ("Autism Spectrum Disorder"), the ease with which a person adapts to life depends on that person's access to a support system. When people with Asperger's are misdiagnosed, they are prevented from getting the help they need ("*DSM-V* Changes"). Therefore, the most effective way to improve the lives of people with Asperger's is to recognize the condition as a valid and distinct diagnosis and provide accurate treatment and support options for those who need it.

Works Cited

"Asperger's Syndrome." *Autism-Society*, 2015, www.autism-society.org/what-is/
      aspergers-syndrome/.

"Autism Spectrum Disorder." *National Institute of Mental Health*, Mar. 2016,
      www.nimh.nih.gov/health/topics/autism-spectrum-disorders-asd/index.shtml.

"Autism Spectrum Disorder Fact Sheet - *DSM-5*." *American Psychiatric Association*,
      2013, www.dsm5.org/Documents/Autism%20Spectrum%20Disorder%
      20Fact%20Sheet.pdf.

"CDC Estimates 1 in 68 Children Has Been Identified with Autism Spectrum Disorder."
      CDC. Centers for Disease Control and Prevention. 27 Mar. 2014, www.cdc.gov/me-
      dia/releases/2014/p0327-autism-spectrum-disorder.html.

Coulter, Dan. "Dealing with the Disappearing Asperger Diagnosis." *Oasis@MAAP*,
      2013, www.aspergersyndrome.org/Articles/DEALING-WITH-THE-
      DISAPPEARING-ASPERGER-DIAGNOSIS.aspx.

Diagnostic and Statistical Manual of Mental Disorders. 5th ed., American Psychiatric
      Association, 2013.

"DSM." *American Psychiatric Association*, 2016, www.psychiatry.org/psychiatrists/
      practice/dsm.

"*DSM-V* – What Do the Changes Mean?" *The Johnson Center for Child Health and
      Development* , 10 Apr. 2012, www.johnson-center.org/ blog/entry/105#.V21PvvkrK7o.

Peach   5

Esposito, Lisa. "Guideline Changes Set Asperger's Community on Edge." *WebMD*,

18 Apr. 2013, www.webmd.com/brain/autism/news/20130418/guideline-

changes-have-aspergers-community-on-edge.

Williams, Donna. *Autism: An Inside-Out Approach.* Jessica Kingston Publishers, 1996.

UNDERSTANDING A WRITER'S GOALS: QUESTIONS TO CONSIDER AND DISCUSS

Rhetorical Knowledge: The Writer's Situation and Rhetoric

1. **Audience:** What audience does Peach have in mind for this essay? How can you tell?
2. **Purpose:** What purpose(s) does Peach have for writing this essay? How well does he achieve his purpose(s)?
3. **Voice and tone:** How does Peach's voice and tone help to establish his *ethos*? Is his tone appropriate? Why or why not?
4. **Responsibility:** How effectively does Peach represent opposing views on the issue of not having Asperger's have its own specific definition, but rather having it defined as part of the autism spectrum?
5. **Context, format, and genre:** Does Peach convince you that a problem exists? Do you think his essay will spur anyone to action? Who might that be?

Critical Thinking: The Writer's Ideas and Your Personal Response

6. To what extent does Peach's text appeal to your emotions? In what way(s)?

7. What is Peach's main point, or claim? To what extent do you agree with it? Why?

Composing Processes and Knowledge of Conventions: The Writer's Strategies

8. How convincing is the evidence Peach supplies? What other evidence might he have used?
9. What organizational method does Peach use? How effective is it? What other method(s) might he have used?

Inquiry and Research: Ideas for Further Exploration

10. Conduct a search (at your school library or on the Web), focusing on Asperger's and autism. What new information did you find?

Self-Assessment: Reflecting on Your Goals

Now that you have constructed a piece of writing designed to convince your readers, review your learning goals, which you and your classmates may have considered at the beginning of this chapter (pages 236–237). Then reflect on all the thinking and writing that you have done in constructing your persuasive paper. To help reflect on the learning goals that you have achieved, respond in writing to the following questions:

 ## Rhetorical Knowledge

- *Audience:* What have you learned about addressing an audience in persuasive writing?
- *Purpose:* What have you learned about the purposes for constructing an effective persuasive text?
- *Rhetorical situation:* How did the writing context affect your persuasive text?
- *Voice and tone:* How would you describe your voice in this essay? Your tone? How do they contribute to the effectiveness of your persuasive essay?
- *Context, medium, and genre:* How did your context determine the medium and genre you chose, and how did those decisions affect your writing?

 ## Critical Thinking, Reading, and Writing

- *Learning/inquiry:* How did you decide what to focus on for your persuasive text? Describe the process you went through to focus on a main idea, or thesis.
- *Responsibility:* How did you fulfill your responsibilities to your readers?
- *Reading and research:* What did you learn about persuasive writing from the reading selections in this chapter? What research did you conduct? How sufficient was the research you did?
- *Skills:* As a result of writing this paper, how have you become a more critical thinker, reader, and writer? What skills do you hope to develop further?

Writing Processes

- *Invention:* What invention strategies were most useful to you?

- *Organizing your ideas and details:* What organizational approach did you use? How successful was it?

- *Revising:* What one revision did you make that you are most satisfied with? If you could go back and make an additional revision, what would it be?

- *Working with peers:* How did your instructor and peer readers help you by making comments and suggestions about your writing? List some examples of how you revised your text based on comments from your instructor and your peer readers. How could you have made better use of the comments and suggestions you received? How could your peer readers help you more on your next assignment? How might you help them more, in the future, with the comments and suggestions you make on their texts?

- *Visuals:* Did you use photographs, charts, graphs, or other visuals to help you convince your readers? If so, what did you learn about incorporating these elements?

- *Writing habits:* What "writerly habits" have you developed, modified, or improved on as you constructed the writing assignment for this chapter? How will you change your future writing activities based on what you have learned about yourself?

 Knowledge of Conventions

- *Editing:* What sentence problem did you find most frequently in your writing? How will you avoid that problem in future assignments?

- *Genre:* What conventions of the genre you were using, if any, gave you problems?

- *Documentation:* Did you use sources for your paper? If so, what documentation style did you use? What problems, if any, did you have with it?

If you are constructing a course portfolio, file your written reflections so that you can return to them when you next work on your portfolio. Refer to Chapter 1 (page 12) for a sample reflection by a student.

Text Credits

p. 245: Marian Wright Edelman, "Still Hungry in America," *The Huffington Post*, February 10, 2012 (http://www.huffingtonpost.com/marian-wrightedelman/hunger-in-america_b_1269450.html). Used with permission of Children's Defense Fund. **p. 252:** McMillan, Gloria, "Deep in the Heart of Pluto" *Arizona Daily Star,* July 16, 2015. Copyright © 2015 by Gloria McMillan. Used with permission. **p. 271:** Courtesy of Zack Peach.

CHAPTER 10

Writing to Evaluate

In 1997, the American Film Institute (AFI) announced a list of the hundred greatest American films. The list was chosen by a panel of "leaders from across the film community." In 2007, the AFI updated this list, which now includes one film released since 2000: *Lord of the Rings: The Fellowship of the Ring. Citizen Kane,* however, retained its spot at the top of the list. Following are the top twenty-five:

American Film Institute's Greatest Movies, 1–25

1. *Citizen Kane* (1941)
2. *The Godfather* (1972)
3. *Casablanca* (1942)
4. *Raging Bull* (1980)
5. *Singin' in the Rain* (1952)
6. *Gone with the Wind* (1939)
7. *Lawrence of Arabia* (1962)
8. *Schindler's List* (1993)
9. *Vertigo* (1958)
10. *The Wizard of Oz* (1939)
11. *City Lights* (1931)
12. *The Searchers* (1956)
13. *Star Wars* (1977)
14. *Psycho* (1960)
15. *2001: A Space Odyssey* (1968)
16. *Sunset Boulevard* (1950)
17. *The Graduate* (1967)
18. *The General* (1927)
19. *On the Waterfront* (1954)
20. *It's a Wonderful Life* (1946)
21. *Chinatown* (1974)
22. *Some Like It Hot* (1959)
23. *The Grapes of Wrath* (1940)
24. *E.T.—The Extra-Terrestrial* (1982)
25. *To Kill a Mockingbird* (1962)

Source: *AFI's 100 YEARS . . . 100 MOVIES (1998).*

Whether you agree with these rankings or not, for the AFI to compile the list, people had to evaluate movies based on specific criteria.

Evaluations are part of everyday life. When you decide which classes to take, what to eat for breakfast, or which candidate to support in an election, you decide

© New Line Cinema/Photofest

which choice is best for you and act accordingly. As you think about the choices you confront in your life, consider why you make the ones that you do.

You make such decisions by evaluating your available choices based on certain **criteria**, or standards. For example, if you are evaluating a product, you may consider factors such as price, brand name, location, and size.

Usually, you will base your evaluation on a combination of criteria—and you will inevitably weigh some criteria more heavily than others.

Whether you realize it or not, you have years of practice in judging the trustworthiness of others' evaluations and the relevance of the criteria they use. When a newspaper endorses a political candidate, your familiarity with the newspaper and its edito-

rial policy influences your view of that endorsement. If you are a movie fan, you have probably already come to some conclusions about the excerpt from the AFI's evaluation of the "Greatest Movies" based on your agreement or disagreement with its list of films. Your experience with everyday evaluations will help you determine the criteria for the evaluations you write.

Setting Your Goals for an *Evaluation*

 Rhetorical Knowledge (pp. 282-286)

- **Audience:** Determine who will benefit from your evaluation. Who needs to make decisions about the subject of your evaluation? What do the audience members probably already know about your subject? What will you need to tell them?
- **Purpose:** When you evaluate, you make a judgment based on specific criteria. Your purpose is not simply to say, "I think the Toyota truck is better than the Chevy," but to convince your reader to agree.
- **Rhetorical situation:** Consider the many factors that affect where you stand in relation to your subject. If you have some personal interest in your evaluation, you will have a different stance from that of a more neutral party.
- **Voice and tone:** When you construct an evaluation, you are trying to explain your reasoned judgment. You always want to support that judgment with specific examples and details so your readers can understand why your evaluation says what it does. Your tone should present your evaluation thoughtfully and reasonably—if you seem to "shout" at your readers, they will not agree with your evaluation.
- **Context, medium, and genre:** Decide on the most effective medium and genre to use to present your evaluation to the audience you want to reach.

 Critical Thinking, Reading, and Writing (pp. 286-296)

- **Learning/inquiry:** By observing, listening to, and/or reading about the subject of your evaluation, and then by writing about it, you gain a deeper understanding of its qualities and the ability to make more informed judgments about it.
- **Responsibility:** Effective evaluative writing leads naturally to critical thinking. When you evaluate something, you have to consider all aspects of your subject, not only to determine the criteria on which you will base your evaluation but also to construct a reasoned argument for your judgment.
- **Reading and research:** To evaluate a subject, you need not only to examine it in detail but also to examine similar items.

Writing Processes (pp. 297-312)

- **Invention:** Various invention activities can help you consider all aspects of the subject you are evaluating.
- **Organizing your ideas and details:** The act of evaluating necessarily means that you think about the various aspects of your subject. That process can help you organize your thinking, and later your writing, into categories, based on your criteria.
- **Revising:** Read your work with a critical eye to make certain that it fulfills the assignment and displays the qualities of effective evaluative writing.
- **Working with peers:** Listen to your classmates' thoughts and suggestions carefully to make sure that they understand your evaluation.

 ## Knowledge of Conventions (pp. 312-317)

- **Editing:** Effective evaluations usually require careful word choice. The round-robin activity on page 313 will help you check your evaluation for word choice.
- **Genres for evaluative writing:** In many situations, your evaluation will be a formal report or an academic paper. Evaluations written about movies, restaurants, or other products or services are not quite as formal as college assignments, however.
- **Documentation:** If you relied on sources outside of your experience, cite them using the appropriate documentation style. Consider how software can ensure that you cite accurately and correctly.

RHETORICAL KNOWLEDGE

When you write an evaluation, consider the criteria on which you will base your evaluation as well as how you will develop those criteria. What aspects of the work, product, service, or idea should you examine for your evaluation? How can you best make an evaluative judgment about it? You will also need to decide what medium and genre will help you get your evaluation across to your audience most effectively.

Writing to Evaluate in Your College Classes

As a college student, you will be expected to read and write evaluations in many of your classes:

- Your psychology instructor might ask you to read brief summaries of experiments and evaluate how well each experiment's design served to answer the research question.
- Your political science instructor might ask you to rate the effectiveness of a political campaign.
- Your business and marketing instructor might ask you to evaluate several potential store locations.

In much of your academic writing, you will also have to evaluate the sources and evidence you select to support your thesis statements.

The "Ways of Writing" feature on page 284 presents different genres that can be used when writing to evaluate in your college classes.

Writing to Evaluate for Life

In addition to the evaluations you will consider and write while in college, you will no doubt make evaluations every day in the professional, civic, and personal areas of your life.

In your professional life, your writing will often have an evaluative purpose. For example, if you are a manager with employees reporting to you, you will probably be asked to evaluate their performance. You may consider criteria that include both verifiable information (does your employee arrive at work on time?) and opinions (is he or she an effective leader?). You will need to provide evidence to support your judgments while sufficiently explaining your opinions.

In your civic life, you will often evaluate the political positions of local and national candidates for public office, along with ballot initiatives and referendums, and then make decisions or recommendations.

Without realizing it, we often make evaluations when writing in our personal lives. An e-mail to a relative may include comments about favorite restaurants, teachers, or newfound friends. On the one hand, we might feel more comfortable making evaluations for our friends and family. On the other, we may feel especially obligated to provide a useful evaluation because we care about the relationship.

The "Ways of Writing" feature on page 284 presents different genres that can be used when writing to evaluate in life.

Scenarios for Writing | Assignment Options

Your instructor may ask you to complete one or more of the following writing assignments that call for evaluation. Each of these assignments is in the form of a scenario, which gives you a sense of who your audience is and what you need to accomplish with your evaluative writing.

Starting on page 297, you will find guidelines for completing whatever scenario you decide—or are asked—to complete. Additional scenarios for college and life are online.

Writing for College

SCENARIO 1 Academic Evaluation: What Are the Rules?

You may currently live (or may previously have lived) in a communal setting such as a dormitory, a military barracks, a summer camp, or a house or apartment with roommates. In that setting, you are probably aware of rules and regulations, yet you may not have thought about whether they are fair or not, or even if there are punishments for not obeying the rules. Or you may be living with one or both of your parents, who probably insist on certain rules.

Consider questions such as these:

- What are the rules for living in the particular setting (communal or parental)? Are they fair and reasonable?

- Who is paying for the living quarters? Do they (should they) have total control of what happens in them?

- Should parents be allowed to place restrictions on college-age students who live at home? What rules would be reasonable?

- If an organization such as a college or the government controls the living quarters, can or should it monitor e-mail? Internet access?

Writing Assignment: Write an evaluation of the rules of the communal setting in which you currently live or once lived, or of your parent's or parents' rules. You will need to do some research on what the rules are and consider what you might use as criteria for evaluating them. Your audience will be your instructor and your classmates.

Ways of Writing to Evaluate

Genres for Your College Classes	Sample Situation	Advantages of the Genre	Limitations of the Genre
Career assessment	In your career and life planning class, you are asked to construct an evaluation focusing on possible careers you might pursue after you graduate: the kind of work, the pay, the possibilities for advancement, and so on.	The assignment requires you to think through your criteria and conclusions carefully and thoroughly.	You might not have time to gather really meaningful data if you lack the time to interview people pursuing the careers you are investigating.
History essay	In your world history class, you are asked to evaluate the perceived benefits of manned space flight.	This evaluation will require you to develop and apply valid criteria to reach a historical conclusion.	Historical events rarely occur in isolation, and no set of criteria will be all-inclusive.
Letter to your campus newspaper	Your mathematics professor asks you to write a letter using statistics drawn from interviews to evaluate a specific aspect of campus life (dining, grounds, and so on).	Anything published in a college newspaper will have a wide audience of people who have an interest in campus affairs.	A letter to the editor gives you limited space for your evaluation, and you may not have enough room to adequately make your case. It might not be published.
Business report	Your business instructor asks you to evaluate several marketing plans for a new product for college students.	An evaluative report allows you to identify criteria and then research what students might and might not purchase.	It does not allow for extraneous factors that may not be included in your research.
Genres for Life	**Sample Situation**	**Advantages of the Genre**	**Limitations of the Genre**
Brochure	As part of a community group, you want to publicize your evaluation of a sales tax increase that your community will be voting on.	Your evaluation, often with illustrations and in a compact form, will provide readers with evaluative criteria that will enable them to make a more informed decision.	A brochure provides limited space for your evaluation.
Letter	You are planning a family reunion, at which you expect nearly a hundred family members from around the country, and you want to evaluate possible locations.	A letter is an effective way to share information and to explain the criteria on which you are basing your evaluation.	Letters and responses to letters are slow; sending the letter by e-mail or posting it to a Web site is another option, but that may exclude some family members.
Blog	You start a blog that evaluates software programs used for education.	A blog is an easy and uncomplicated way for you to share your evaluations with a wide and interested audience.	Blogs often need monitoring for improper comments; sometimes a lot of information is generated that takes time to read through.
E-mail	You send an e-mail to coworkers that evaluates several digital storage options for your company.	An e-mail allows you to input links to the prospective companies' Web sites and ask for feedback.	Some people might feel they need more information than the e-mail includes.
Performance review	You are required to submit a performance review for several employees whom you supervise.	Often there is a form that provides specific criteria you can use to construct your evaluation.	Sometimes the criteria for an evaluation no longer fits the work the employee does; forms provide limited room for originality or extra comments and suggestions.

Writing for Life

SCENARIO 2 An Evaluation of a Subject You Are Curious About

For this scenario, select a work of art, a film, a television program, a product, a service, an event, or a place to evaluate—something you are interested in and would like to know more about. Your audience will be your instructor and your fellow classmates.

Writing Assignment: Choose a subject whose value you would like to consider. You may value it highly and want others to know about it, or you may think that it is highly overrated and want others to see why. Construct an evaluation in which you make your judgment known. Be sure to explain clearly the criteria on which you will make your evaluation, and then show how your subject meets—or does not meet—those criteria.

SCENARIO 3 Personal Writing: Evaluating a Cultural Event or Performance

In your personal life, you attend cultural events: museum exhibits, art shows (whether those of professional artists, photographers, or sculptors, or those of your friends), musical performances, plays, dance performances, and so on. Your college or university is a wonderful source of cultural events. How do you evaluate such cultural performances or events? On what criteria should they be evaluated? How much weight should you give one criterion in relation to others? How might your own criteria match up with those of other students who also attend the event or performance?

Writing Assignment: For this assignment, assume that your local newspaper or a local magazine has asked you to evaluate a recent cultural event or performance.

© Luke Stettner/Getty Images

In no more than 1,200 words, explain the criteria that you see as important, and then offer your evaluation of that event or performance. Consider how you might use visuals to help illustrate your evaluation.

Rhetorical Considerations in Evaluative Writing

Audience: Although your instructor and classmates are your initial audience for this assignment, who are other possible audiences? Consider whether the members of your audience will agree with you about the criteria for evaluating your subject, or whether you will need to convince them to accept your criteria.

Purpose: Your main purpose is to evaluate your subject in terms of the criteria you decide on. How will you persuade your audience to accept your judgment of it?

Voice, tone, and point of view: You have probably chosen your subject because you have a personal interest in it. What preconceptions about it do you have? How can you avoid letting them color your evaluation? How can you use voice and tone to establish credibility?

For more on choosing a medium and genre, see Chapter 17 and Appendix C.

Context, medium, and genre: Keeping the context of the assignment in mind, decide on a medium and genre for your evaluation. How will your evaluation be used? If you are writing for an audience beyond the classroom, consider what will be the most effective way to present your evaluation to this audience.

 # CRITICAL THINKING, READING, AND WRITING

Before you begin to write your evaluation, read one or more evaluations to get a feel for this kind of writing.

To write an effective, responsible evaluation, you need to understand your subject and the reasons for your evaluation of it. You will need to choose valid criteria, organize your writing logically, and present your evaluation in a way that fulfills your responsibility to your readers. To do this, you need to think critically about your own views, as well as those of any outside sources. Thinking critically does not necessarily mean that you will criticize, but rather that you will carefully consider which criteria are most and least important and how different aspects of your subject relate to each other.

 ## Learning the Qualities of Effective Evaluative Writing

As we have seen, most writing is purposeful. Focusing on the outcome should be the starting point for everything you write, and for an evaluation, you want to make a reasoned, thoughtful, and justifiable judgment. You need to outline the criteria on which you will base your evaluation and then explain how the subject of your evaluation fits the criteria.

Evaluative writing that achieves its goal has the following qualities:

- **Clearly defined and explained criteria.** Readers expect an evaluation to be based on specific criteria that are germane to the item being evaluated. You would evaluate an array of backpacks in a sporting-goods store using different criteria from those you would use to evaluate, say, a set of luggage. Readers deserve to have the criteria you use defined in detail so they can understand your reasoning.

  If you are evaluating a work of art, you should use—and explain— criteria appropriate for evaluating art—for example, aesthetic appeal, the impact the work has on the viewer, and how well it represents a specific genre.

- **Comparisons based on the criteria.** Especially when you are evaluating products or services, you will need to show how your subject can be measured against similar subjects and then explain this basis of comparison. You will compare like with like, showing how each aspect of the item you are evaluating rates in comparison with the same (or a similar) aspect of a similar item.

  You can make comparisons based on numerical information ("Tire brand C has a 50 percent longer tread life rating than Brand B, and twice as long as Brand A"). A table can help your readers see the basis of your claim.

Tire Brand	Tread Life Rating
Brand A	30,000 miles
Brand B	40,000 miles
Brand C	60,000 miles

Because numerical information is verifiable and is not a matter of opinion, it can be persuasive evidence for your overall evaluation.

Finally, you can make comparisons based on more subjective criteria, such as your definition of "quality": You might note that a backpack "should have this kind of fabric, this type of zipper, a lifetime warranty, and straps made out of this material." Then you could go on to outline how each backpack you are evaluating matches (or perhaps does not match) each of your criteria.

When you compare, it is important not to slant your evaluation by leaving out negative information or highlighting only those details that make the product, service, or work you favor seem to be the best. Instead, explain and compare honestly so your readers can reach their own conclusions about the effectiveness of your evaluation. You may find that the item you judge to be best is weak when measured on the basis of one or more of your criteria. It is vital to your overall credibility to account for such shortcomings. Just because something is comparatively weak in one or more areas does not mean that it cannot still come out on top in your evaluation.

- **Evidence that supports your claims.** To accept your evaluation, readers need to understand that you are not just making assertions about your subject, but that you have evidence to support your claims. Evidence can include the following:

  - *Testimony:* "I've owned Ford automobiles for twenty years, and they've never let me down."

  - *Statistical information:* "A recent study by the National Highway Traffic Safety Administration found that nearly 50 percent of the 11,500 cars, pickup trucks, vans, and sport-utility vehicles the agency checked had at least one tire with half-worn tread. Another 10 percent had at least one bald tire" (*Consumer Reports*).

  - *Detailed description:* The more details you can provide, the easier it will be for a reader to understand what you mean. For example, if you were evaluating netbook computers, you might explain your evaluation by discussing in detail the amount of memory in each netbook, the processor speed, screen size and quality, and price.

- **An analysis and explanation of how any visual elements affect your evaluation.** When they evaluate textbooks, teachers often consider how the visual elements in the books might help students learn more effectively. If you were a science teacher, for example, you might focus on the photographs or drawings in the various books under consideration and cite examples from the texts in your evaluative comments.

- **A clearly stated judgment.** Readers can either agree or disagree with your conclusions, but if you have written a successful evaluation, they will understand how you arrived at your judgment.

Reading, Inquiry, and Research: Learning from Texts That Evaluate

The following reading selections are examples of evaluative writing. As you read through the selections, consider the following questions:

- How clearly are the evaluative criteria explained?

- To what extent do I agree with the evaluation? Why?

- How well do I understand why the writer evaluated this subject as he did? That is, how clearly has the writer explained his judgment?

- How familiar am I with the subject that is being evaluated?

- What else would I like to know about the subject being evaluated?

- How can I use the techniques of evaluative writing, as demonstrated here, in my own writing?

DENNIS BARON

Don't Make English Official, Ban It Instead

OPINION PIECE

Dennis Baron is professor of English and linguistics at the University of Illinois. He is the author of *The Web of Language*, a blog in which he writes about language, the law, technology, and how they all interact.

It's International Mother Language Day, and once again the U.S. House of Representatives is considering legislation to make English the official language of the United States. Supporters of the measure say that English forms the glue that keeps America together. They deplore the dollars wasted translating English into other languages. And they fear a horde of illegal aliens adamantly refusing to acquire the most powerful language on earth. I would like to offer a modest alternative: don't make English official, ban it instead. 1

Opponents of official English remind us that without legislation, more than ninety-four percent of the residents of this country speak the national language. No country with an official language even comes close. Plus, today's non-English-speaking immigrants are picking up English faster than earlier generations of immigrants did. 2

Introducing an official English bill in Congress is an exercise in futility: one has been introduced every session for a couple of decades, but when crunch time comes, these bills don't pass. That's because members of Congress are afraid of alienating too many voters in their districts. Plus, requiring English could make people want to avoid it, like homework, or paying taxes. 3

Banning English may sound radical, but it's nothing new: proposals to ban English first surfaced after the American Revolution. Anti-British sentiment was so strong in the new United States that a few tea party patriots wanted to get rid of English altogether. They suggested replacing English with Hebrew, the language of the garden of Eden. French was another candidate to replace English, because it was thought at the time, and especially by the French, to be the language of pure reason. Then there was Greek, the language of the world's first democracy, so long as you weren't a woman, a slave, or a non-Athenian. It's not clear how serious any of these proposals were, though Roger Sherman of Connecticut supposedly remarked that it would be better to keep English for ourselves and make the British speak Greek. 4

Even though the British are now our allies, there is still a benefit to banning English. A common language can cause strife and misunderstanding. Look at Ireland and Northern Ireland, the two Koreas, or the Union and the Confederacy. Not to mention the average family, whose members share a common tongue but don't always get along so well. Banning English would prevent that kind of divisiveness in America today. 5

Also, if we banned English, we wouldn't have to worry about whose   6
English to make official: the English of England or America? of Washington or
Brooklyn? of Benedict Cumberbatch or Sarah Palin?

Another reason to ban English: it's hardly even English anymore. English   7
started its decline in 1066, when illegal French immigrants swam ashore at
Hastings demanding bilingual schools and wanting us to adopt the metric
system. Since then English has become a polyglot conglomeration of French,
Latin, Italian, Scandinavian, Arabic, Sanskrit, Celtic, Yiddish and Chinese, with
an occasional smiley face thrown in.

The French have banned English, so we should too. After all, they have   8
reason on their side.

We should ban English because it has become a world language. Remem-   9
ber what happened to all the other world languages: Latin, Greek, Proto-
Indo-European? One day they're on everybody's tongue; the next, they're dead.
Banning English would save us that inevitable disappointment.

Although we shouldn't ban English without designating a replacement for   10
it, there is no obvious candidate. The French blew their chance when they sold
Louisiana. It doesn't look like the Russians are going to take over this country
any time soon—they're having enough trouble holding on to Russia. German,
the largest minority language in the U.S. until recently, lost much of its appeal
after two world wars. Chinese is too hard to write, especially if you're not Chinese. There's always Esperanto, a language made up over a hundred years ago
to bring about world peace. We're still waiting for that. And if you took Spanish
in high school you can see that it's not easy to get large numbers of people to
speak another language fluently.

In the end, though, it doesn't matter what replacement language we pick,   11
just so long as we ban English instead of making it official. Prohibiting English
will do for the language what Prohibition did for liquor. Those who already use
it will continue to do so, and those who don't will want to try out what has been
forbidden. This negative psychology works with children. It works with speed
limits. It even worked in the Garden of Eden.

UNDERSTANDING A WRITER'S GOALS: QUESTIONS TO CONSIDER AND DISCUSS

Rhetorical Knowledge: The Writer's Situation and Rhetoric

1. **Audience:** Dennis Baron's *The Web of Language* can be found at https://illinois.edu/blog/view/25. Check the site's archive and then try to define who you think Baron's audience is. What makes you think so?

2. **Purpose:** How clear is Baron's purpose? If he really doesn't want a ban on English, what does he want? What does he write that supports your view?

3. **Voice and tone:** Perhaps the best way to describe the tone of this blog post is to call it "tongue-in-cheek." What features in the posting would lead you to come to that conclusion? Might you think otherwise? If so, what would have you think that way?

4. **Responsibility:** When authors write satire, they still must be responsible for what they write. How responsibly is Baron writing? Has he gone too far in any statement he has made? How comfortable are you with what he suggests? Why?

5. **Context, format, and genre:** Satire is a genre in which writers make statements that are so illogical, outrageous, or irreverent that educated readers know the statements aren't meant to be taken at face value. Give some examples of a statement or two that Baron uses. How do you respond when reading the statements you've chosen? Why?

Critical Thinking: The Writer's Ideas and Your Personal Response

6. What do you think Baron's real intent is in writing this blog post? What in his text makes you think so?

7. What was your response to Baron? How effective is he in achieving his goal? Did you think it was funny? Did you think it was childish? Did you think it was outlandish? Be specific in explaining how you determined your response.

Composing Processes and Knowledge of Conventions: The Writer's Strategies

8. In some ways, Baron's blog post is an evaluation of the effort by some members of the U.S. House of Representatives to make English the official language. He then presents a set of reasons, some more spurious than others, suggesting why they fail. Finally, he suggests, if their intent is to make everyone in the United States speak English, Congress should ban English. How effective is this evaluation? Why?

9. Some of what Baron says is, indeed, rooted in historical fact. For example, the Founding Fathers did discuss having a language other than English serve as the language of the new country. On the other hand, Baron sometimes stretches facts. English did undergo a marked change dating to 1066 when a conquering French army invaded England, but how well does that compare to what Baron calls "illegal immigrants"? Why? How easy is it to tell when Baron is stretching the truth? Point to specific examples that you might not be sure of.

10. Baron often uses language loosely here. He says, "The French blew their chance when they sold Louisiana." How do you respond to such language usage? Why?

Inquiry and Research: Ideas for Further Exploration

11. Baron refers to specific historic events. He also makes many assertions. How do you know which are reported accurately? Can you name any of those assertions that you would question? Where would you go to prove whether they are accurate or not, or perhaps simply an exaggeration of the truth?

GENRES *Up Close* Writing a Review

Critical reviews play an important role in daily life. Before people go to restaurants, movie theaters, concert halls, bookstores, or music stores, they often read reviews to help them make thoughtful decisions about how to spend their money. Before employers decide to hire job applicants, renew employees' contracts, or offer employees salary increases, they read reviews of those applicants and employees, in the form of letters of recommendation and annual performance evaluations. And before people spend large amounts of money on major repairs or renovations to their homes or apartments, they go online to read reviews of the contractors they are considering.

Although many critical reviews appear in print (newspapers, magazines, letters, reports), many also appear in audio form on radio shows such as *All Things Considered* and *Weekend Edition* on National Public Radio. They also appear in video form on television shows such as *Anderson Cooper 360* (CNN), *The O'Reilly Factor* (Fox), and *E! News* (E! TV). On the Internet, they can appear in written, audio, or video formats.

The critical review has some standard features:

- **A brief summary of what's being reviewed.** A summary helps readers make sense of the evaluation. For example, before passing judgment on a restaurant's décor, a reviewer needs to describe it so that readers can understand the points the writer is making about it—that the lighting is too dim or the bold color scheme is unattractive. Such a summary also helps readers decide if they are likely to agree with the reviewer's taste in restaurant décor. However, keep in mind that for some types of reviews, the reviewer needs to be careful not to provide too many details, or "spoilers." For example, giving away the ending of a mystery could ruin the film for some people who had planned to see it.

- **An evaluation or critique.** The evaluation focuses on the criteria that matter most to readers. Of course, the focus will vary depending on what is being reviewed. A movie review focuses on such criteria as acting, set design, sound track, special effects, character development, plot, directing, and editing. A restaurant review, however, focuses on décor, atmosphere, service, cost, menu, and flavor.

In the reviews that follow, notice how the reviewers attend to these genre criteria. In the two film reviews, for example, notice what standard film elements they summarize and critique. Consider how the writers' choices of what they evaluate affect your impressions.

STEVE MACFARLANE

Jurassic World

Of the dozen-plus name brands displayed in *Jurassic World*, none are as ubiquitous as the logo from Steven Spielberg's 1993 blockbuster *Jurassic Park*—having, in the world of Colin Trevorrow's sequel, proliferated and mutated across two decades' worth of signage, ball caps, ID badges, and other crude merchandising. Never-ending corporate expansion is very much the bailiwick of *Jurassic World*, whose screenplay is attributed to two separate teams of writers. It's a detail worth remembering each and every time Trevorrow's film betrays its own conglomerated-product anxiety.

1

Steve Macfarlane is a writer, film-maker, and online film critic. He has written for *Slant*, *Rotten Tomatoes*, *Metacritic*, and *BOMB Magazine*. He is also head programmer at the Spectacle Theater in Brooklyn, New York.

Paragraph 1: Provides an evaluation of the movie at the beginning of the review.

Two brothers, Zach and Bray (Nick Robinson and Ty Simpkins), are shuttled off to the revitalized Jurassic World theme park on Isla Nublar off the coast of Costa Rica, as a distraction from their parents' crumbling marriage; their aunt, Claire (Bryce Dallas Howard), is one of the park's administrators, so obsessed with her work that she barely remembers the boys are visiting. Meanwhile, a rugged ex-military velociraptor whisperer, Grady (Chris Pratt), is called in by the park's freewheeling, helicopter-piloting CEO, Simon (Irrfan Khan), to "evaluate the pattern of vulnerabilities" surrounding a new dinosaur: a crossbreed of tyrannosaurus and raptor known as the Indominus Rex, genetically engineered by the park's parent company, InGen. Seeing his scaly charges for the misunderstood animals they are, Grady opposes these experimentations, chiding Claire that "maybe progress should lose for once."

2

Paragraphs 2 and 3: Summarizes the movie briefly without giving away too many details, or "spoilers."

It's no surprise that *Jurassic World* falls victim to the same overelaborate plotting that's become de rigueur for its summer-blockbuster contemporaries. Everything goes calamitously wrong thanks to the usual shenanigans: the paddock door that can't close fast enough, the mysterious off-screen phone call, and a sneering security contractor, Hoskins (Vincent D'Onofrio), obsessed with deploying dinosaurs in otherwise human-led combat missions. (Observing a pack of Grady's raptors in concert, he muses breathlessly: "Just imagine if we had these puppies in Tora Bora!") But the film also chases a handful of theoretically admirable subtexts: There's a running gag about today's kids being too distracted to be wowed by mere in-the-flesh dinosaurs, and the park's boardroom doublespeak—with execs calling the reptiles "assets" instead of animals—verges on Verhoeven-level ridiculous. The case could be made that, stripped of its action scenes and near-death encounters (of which every major character survives at least three), *Jurassic World* is a goofy workplace comedy, centering on Claire's bizarre mix of klutziness and cold professionalism.

3

Focuses on the acting, a key criterion in film reviews.

None of this should count for much once the dinosaurs are front and   4 center, but that's where *Jurassic World* is truly depressing: The thrill of seeing these prehistoric beasts is subordinated to that of seeing them awkwardly airbrushed into the same frame as 21st-century humans. Grady and Claire's screwball romance plays out against painfully cheap-looking jungle backdrops closer to the tourist-corralling wait rooms of Universal Studios than a real live tropical island—and whenever Grady needs to run, jump, or roll out of the path of an incoming dinosaur, the disjunction between tangible footage and the pixelated filling enmeshing him is impossible to ignore. Action scenes are drawn in impossible swoops and pans, with artificial dolly shots and rack focuses often starting or ending long before perspective has managed to cut elsewhere; the meagerest sense of spatial plausibility evaporates whenever the camera needs to move. Even the most basic camera angles around the park see the actors green-screened against bogus panoramic vistas, cushioned by eerie under-rendered digital halos. Every third shot looks more like an early promotional still than a scene from an actual film.

Jurassic World can't tell whether it wants to be junk food or not, lovingly   5 poking fun at some Hollywood tropes while shamelessly indulging others. Claire's compassion and pluck come to the fore in a series of close shaves that see her saving her nephews' lives (if barely), while also losing more and more of her heretofore wardrobe. At a budget of 260 times that of Trevorrow's debut (*Safety Not Guaranteed*), *Jurassic World*'s aspirations to cautionary cynicism are bound from both sides by its franchise prerogatives; the end result can't satisfy either sensibility in full. For the umpteenth time, moviegoers will be left with that magical Spielbergian appreciation for a fear of death strong enough that it can keep a family together—but that won't stop them from also wishing the kids had gotten eaten.

MARY BETH GRIGGS

This is How *Jurassic World*'s Velociraptors Should Have Looked

R E V I E W

Mary Beth Griggs writes about science for popular publications such as *Scholastic*, *Popular Mechanics*, *USA Today*, and *Discover Magazine*. Although trained in geology and archaeology, she also writes about energy and the environment. This review of *Jurassic World* was published in *Popular Science*. Griggs' review is an interesting contrast to Steve Macfarlane's evaluation. As you read it, look for the differences in Griggs' focus and criteria.

Let's all take a moment to think about velociraptors.   1

In the quintessential dinosaur movies of the   2
Jurassic Park/World franchise, velociraptors were killing
machines that looked something like this:

© NBC Universal

Unfortunately, not all paleontologists were happy with the aesthetic choice.   3
See, for some time now, scientists have known that avian dinosaurs (those
related to birds) likely had feathers and probably looked a little more like this:

The very first sentence provides the main criterion for the evaluation.

© National News/ZUMA Press/Newscom

Many dinosaurs, including velociraptors, definitely had feathers. And now,   4
scientists have found a fossil that shows us what a fuzzy velociraptor would
have looked like.

In a paper published this week in *Scientific Reports*, researchers announced the   5
discovery of a dinosaur closely related to the velociraptor that definitely had feathers.

"This new dinosaur is one of the closest cousins of Velociraptor, but it looks   6
just like a bird. It's a dinosaur with huge wings made up of quill pen feathers,
just like an eagle or a vulture. The movies have it wrong—this is what Velociraptor would have looked like too," says Steve Brusette, co-author of the study.

Provides an evaluation of the film's representation of velociraptors by comparing the animation and special effects with recently published scientific reports.

The new dinosaur, named *Zhenyuanlong suni*, would have been about   7
5 feet long, and lived 125 million years ago. It is the largest dinosaur with feath-
ered, bird-like wings discovered so far. Given the size of the wings and the size
of the dinosaur, it likely didn't fly. The researchers speculate that the feathers
on the wings and tail could have been used for display instead.

UNDERSTANDING A WRITER'S GOALS: QUESTIONS TO CONSIDER AND DISCUSS

Rhetorical Knowledge: The Writer's Situation and Rhetoric

1. **Audience:** Although these are two very different essays, how different or similar are the audiences that Macfarlane and Griggs have in mind? Explain why.

2. **Purpose:** Although both Macfarlane and Griggs are writing about dinosaurs, their essays have different purposes. Explain the intent of both essays and explain your decisions.

3. **Voice and Tone:** Macfarlane and Griggs also have very different tones in their writing. Explain how you would define each of their tones and show what leads you to those choices.

4. **Responsibility:** Macfarlane is writing a movie review. What responsibilities do reviewers have to their readers? How well has Macfarlane fulfilled those responsibilities? What are Griggs' responsibilities? How effectively has she fulfilled them? Why? If you think her responsibilities are the same as Macfarlane's, why is this the case?

5. **Context, format, and genre:** Macfarlane's essay is a movie review, a standard kind of evaluation. How adequately has he evaluated the movie? Why? What else do you think he might have included in his review?

Critical Thinking: The Writer's Ideas and Your Personal Response

6. These two essays seem to have one thing in common: dinosaurs. What relationship, if any, exists between them beyond the dinosaur subject matter?

7. If you have seen the movie *Jurassic World*, which Macfarlane reviews, how accurate do you think his review is? Why? If you haven't seen the movie, how much does his review make you want to see it? Why?

Composing Processes and Knowledge of Conventions: The Writer's Strategies

8. To what extent does all the information that Macfarlane includes about other movies help or hinder your understanding of his review? Explain. To what extent is there an expectation that Macfarlane's readers have a certain level of movie knowledge to fully understand his perspective? Why?

9. Although Griggs opens by referring to the *Jurassic World* movie, her essay is not about a movie but about the dinosaurs themselves. To what extent does her using the reference to the popular movie help her to engage readers in a more scientific topic? Why?

Inquiry and Research: Ideas for Further Exploration

10. If after reading these two essays, you were asked to do further research on the topic, which topic would you choose: film or dinosaurs? Explain your choice.

11. After reading Macfarlane's review, do you think your understanding of the film would be enhanced if you knew more about Steven Spielberg, Colin Trevorrow, or the other *Jurassic Park* movies? To try to put all of it in context, look up reviews of the original *Jurassic Park* movies and compare them to what Macfarlane has written here.

12. One of Griggs' main points is that we now know that many dinosaurs had feathers much like present-day birds. Why do velociraptors in *Jurassic World* not have feathers? What might that reason be? If it's an artistic choice, what might have driven that choice?

WRITING PROCESSES

As you work on the assignment that you have chosen, remember the qualities of an effective and convincing evaluative paper, which are listed on pages 286–288. Also remember that while the activities listed below imply that writers proceed step-by-step, as you write, you will keep coming back to your earlier work, modifying your criteria and strengthening the support for your claim.

Strategies FOR Success | Engagement

Successful writers find ways to engage with their subject matter: they are interested in and involved with what they are writing about. To be engaged in your subject, it helps to select a topic to evaluate that interests you (if you have a choice of topic). If you have an interest in cars, for example, evaluating a particular car or some aspect of the automotive industry could be an engaging topic for you. If you are interested in a specific major or a particular career goal (to become an attorney, for example), then that subject will probably engage your interest. If you enjoy a particular genre of film, or a specific type of video game, that interest can inform your choice of topics.

Selecting a topic that engages you will help you ask pertinent questions about that subject, explore all of its most important features, and effectively compare or contrast it with other similar subjects. And selecting, focusing on, and working with an engaging subject will be more interesting and fun for you as you examine that subject in detail and then evaluate it. A successful evaluation also engages readers, so work with your classmates to determine what they think about your evaluation—and pay close attention to their comments and suggestions on how to improve your text.

Invention: Getting Started

Invention activities can help you clarify what you might want to evaluate before you begin your evaluation. Writers often find it useful to work through several invention activities for any particular writing task. Regardless of the invention activities you do, try to answer these questions while you work:

For more on discovery and learning, see Chapter 4.

- What do I already know about the subject that I am thinking about evaluating?
- What makes each potential subject suitable for evaluation?
- What criteria can I establish for my evaluation? On what basis should I make my judgment? How can I compare it with similar items?
- What kinds of explanation can I provide about each of my criteria?
- Where might I learn more about this subject?
- What verifiable information about my subject is available?

- Are any of my criteria potentially just a matter of opinion, and if so, how might I explain them?
- What might my audience already know about my subject? What do I know about my audience? What don't I know that I should know?

Writing Activity

Clustering

Clustering is an invention technique that can help you focus on a subject to evaluate and come up with criteria for your evaluation. Working with the questions here, spend a few minutes jotting down everything you can think of about the subject or subjects you want to evaluate or discussing them with classmates. Don't worry about putting this information into sentences or paragraphs; simply record it using any words that come to mind. Or try freewriting, which is writing continuously.

Once you have some ideas, you can then use clustering to see relationships between or among them. Put the subject you are focusing on into a circle in the center of a sheet of paper, and spend a few minutes creating a cluster of your ideas about the subject.

Annlee Lawrence's Clustering

Annlee Lawrence decided to write an evaluation of meals at some local fast-food restaurants. To get started, Lawrence brainstormed her initial thoughts, which turned out to be a series of questions. She continued her invention work by doing some freewriting and then clustering her ideas. Below is an example of a cluster Lawrence might have done for her evaluation of fast-food restaurants.

STUDENT WRITING EXAMPLES

Brainstorming (pp. 177, 343, 617)

Freewriting (pp. 134, 256, 344, 393)

Criteria (p. 300)

Listing (p. 97)

Answers to Reporter's Questions (p. 256)

Organization (pp. 98, 182, 647)

Clustering (pp. 135, 298)

Interviewing (p. 216)

Research (pp. 136, 137, 178, 179, 217, 218, 258, 259, 302, 343, 346, 396)

Reflection (p. 12)

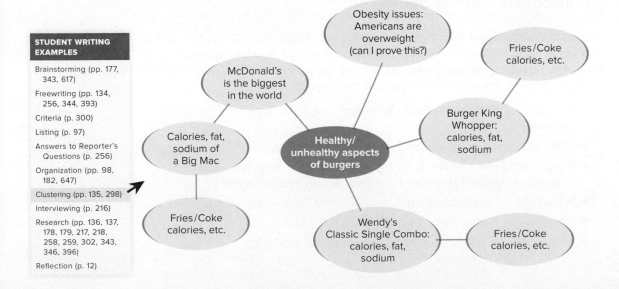

Constructing and Supporting Evaluative Criteria

To evaluate any subject, you need to begin by considering the basis on which you will make your evaluation, as well as how you might support your criteria. Consider the various aspects of the subject on which you might base your evaluation. Here are just a few possibilities:

- Physical aspects such as size, weight, shape, taste, smell, and sound (These criteria are often used in evaluating food products and restaurant meals, for example.)

- Quality (often measured by the warranty period, both in length of time and which parts of the product are covered under the manufacturer's warranty)

- Aesthetic aspects (for example, how the item feels to use, drive, listen to, sit in, wear), color, and proportion (you use these kinds of criteria when you purchase clothing)

- Entertainment-value aspects (If you are evaluating a TV action drama, for example, you might use criteria such as quality of the acting, number of action scenes in each episode, and level of interest in and appeal of the main characters.)

- Comparative aspects, such as the following:
  - Which career would give me the greatest satisfaction? Why?
  - What is the best place to study? Why?
  - Which political candidate should get my vote? Why?

In most evaluations, you will need to show how your subject can be measured against similar subjects and explain the basis of your comparison. If you are comparing two automobiles, for example, you could compare them in terms of price, gas mileage, and maintenance, among other criteria.

For more on making comparisons, see Chapter 13.

Once you have a basis for comparison, the first step in deciding the criteria for your evaluation is to look over your invention work and consider what you have learned so far about your subject. Try to answer these questions:

- What do you consider the most important aspect of your subject?

- What other qualities, either positive or negative, does this subject have?

- If you are evaluating a subject for its usefulness, what must it do?

- If you are evaluating a product or service, think about what you will use it for. If you are evaluating a child's car seat, for example, the most important criterion will probably be safety. What do you mean by the term *safe*, and how can you tell if a particular car seat is safe?

- If a product or service needs to be reliable, what do you mean by that term, and how can you determine reliability?

- What criteria are absolutely necessary for the subject to possess? What criteria are important, but perhaps not as necessary?

- What research might help with your evaluation? Will a search of the Web help? What would you gain from talking with others or conducting a survey?

> **Writing** Activity
>
> ## Constructing and Supporting Criteria
>
> Construct a list of possible criteria for your evaluation. For each of your criteria, explain, in no more than one sentence, why it is important in evaluating your subject. Also, in no more than one sentence, outline what kind of evidence you might use to support each criterion.

Annlee Lawrence's Criteria

STUDENT WRITING EXAMPLES

Brainstorming (pp. 177, 343, 617)

Freewriting (pp. 134, 256, 344, 393)

Criteria (p. 300)

Listing (p. 97)

Answers to Reporter's Questions (p. 256)

Organization (pp. 98, 182, 647)

Clustering (pp. 135, 298)

Interviewing (p. 216)

Research (pp. 136, 137, 178, 179, 217, 218, 258, 259, 302, 343, 346, 396)

Reflection (p. 12)

After Annlee Lawrence completed some brainstorming and freewriting about her subject, she made a list of the criteria for evaluating fast-food restaurants and did some additional freewriting to discover what they meant and what she thought about each one. Here is an excerpt:

- Why should anyone care about eating a burger?
- What does "obesity" mean? Who says it's important?
- Why is "fat" bad and are there different kinds of fat?
- How does cholesterol hurt people? And I read somewhere that there is both good and bad cholesterol—I wonder if any of each is in a burger?
- And everyone knows that we want to consume fewer calories, right?
- Does any of this affect taste?
- I keep hearing about high blood pressure and sodium—is that salt?
- What about the other stuff we usually eat with a burger? Fries? A Coke?

> I guess I know it's important to not be overweight and all, but I wonder if eating a burger now and then really matters. Aren't there some people who eat them all the time, though? I mean, with fries and all? How bad could that be? I need to learn more about fat and calories and things, so I can point to what is bad (and if anything is good) about America's burgers.
>
> Once I learn some stuff—now, where can I learn the fat content, etc. of burgers? Does McDonald's and Wendy's and Burger King post them somewhere? Online? It'd be kind of funny if I had to go and buy a burger at each place, just to find out how unhealthy it might be!
>
> And once I have some information, how can I present it so readers can understand and make a wise choice, based on my evaluation?

For help with locating sources of information and with field research, see Chapter 19; for help with taking notes and documenting your sources, see Chapter 20.

Exploring Your Ideas with Research

Although personal opinions are sometimes sufficient evidence for an evaluation, in more formal settings, you will need to support your claims with outside research. One advantage of conducting research is that the information you find will help you form your judgment about your subject. It's important not to make that judgment too soon; often you won't know what you really think until you have done a lot of invention work, conducted much of your research, and have even written a draft or two.

Research, of course, can give you solid evidence—verifiable information, such as figures, statistics, data, or expert testimony—to help support your final evaluation. The kind and amount of research you will need to do will vary according to the rhetorical situation: who your audience is and what you are trying to accomplish. Use the reporter's questions of *who, what, when, where, why,* and *how* to get started on your research. After you have determined the information you need, decide what kind of research you should conduct to gather that information, in the library and on the Internet. You may also need to do field research.

As you review your notes, look for information that will help you show to what degree your subject does, or does not, meet a given criterion. Look as well for any conclusions that others have drawn about the subject of your evaluation—and consider if and how your evaluation differs from theirs. While you can use others' opinions in support of your conclusion, hearing and reading what others have said will often provide new ideas and suggest additional avenues for research.

As you conduct your research, you may find that other writers have reached judgments that differ from yours. You will want to address—and counter—their opinions in your comments, in order to strengthen your evaluation.

Writing Activity

Conducting Research

Using the list of qualities of effective evaluative writing on pages 286–288, review your invention writing and your list of criteria, and note what you already know about your subject. Next, determine whether you need to do research to come up with additional criteria or evidence, learn more about similar subjects, or muster stronger counterarguments.

In no more than two pages, outline a research plan. In your plan, indicate the following:

- What you already know about your subject
- What questions you still have
- Who or what sources might answer your questions
- Who might provide other perspectives on your subject
- Where you might look for further information
- When you plan to conduct your research

Gather, read, and take notes on your subject from these outside sources. Use an electronic journal to record images, URLs, and other information that you find as you conduct your research.

Annlee Lawrence's Research Strategy

Annlee Lawrence needed to research the nutritional content of typical meals available from the three restaurants she was evaluating. She developed the following research plan:

- I'll check both online and at the stores themselves, to see if the information is provided.
- I need to try to compare apples to apples as much as I can—that is, I want to compare similar-size hamburgers, and similar-size fries and drinks (otherwise it would be an unfair evaluation and my readers would not benefit and probably wouldn't believe me).
- I should check in the library for information on why these things (calories, fat, sodium, cholesterol) are bad for people.
- I may also find in the library some useful information about the companies I'm focusing on (McDonald's, Wendy's, Burger King). I know there are others (Sonic, A&W), but I want to concentrate on the big three, because they're everywhere.

Writing Activity

Considering Your Research and Focusing Your Ideas

Examine the notes you have taken from your research. Then, using your criteria as a starting point, see how your information matches the criteria you have established.

Reviewing Your Invention and Research

After you have conducted your research, review your invention work and notes and think about the information you collected from outside sources and how that information matches the criteria you have for your evaluation. You may be ready to decide on a working thesis statement—a statement that summarizes the main point of your evaluation—at this point. Even though you might already have a general idea of the conclusion your evaluation is leading you to, your thesis should come *from* your complete evaluation. It is best to decide on your thesis when you have done a lot of invention work (listing, brainstorming, clustering, and other strategies) and research. You might even wait until after you construct your first draft.

Organizing Your Evaluation

Once you have some sense of the criteria you will use and how your subject matches those criteria, consider how you might organize your evaluation. Here are some questions to ask yourself when deciding on your organization:

- Who is the audience for your evaluation?
- Why might readers be interested in your evaluation, or how you can make them interested in it?
- What is your purpose for writing—that is, what will your readers learn about your subject by reading your evaluation? How will that knowledge help them as they write their own evaluations?

For more on design
and visuals, including
examples of different
kinds of graphics, see
Chapter 18.

🔊 **USING DIGITAL TECHNOLOGIES** | **Using Computer Software to Create Hierarchies**

If there's one thing computers are good at, it's establishing hierarchies (systems of ranking, prioritizing, and organizing things). When you're writing an essay that evaluates something, the computer screen can serve as a workshop space, where you can move around ideas and concepts.

You can use a variety of software programs—and sometimes different windows within the same software application—to design charts, outlines, tables, Venn diagrams, time lines, and other visual space holders for your information. Use color, line, shape, and space to code information, defining categories and interesting interrelations among your ideas and segments of information.

The answers to these questions can help you decide what you need to emphasize, which in turn will help you choose an organizational approach.

Here is a brief outline of three possible organizational approaches for writing an evaluation:

For more on the
inductive and
deductive methods,
see Chapter 9.

Options FOR Organization
Options for Organizing Evaluations

First Inductive Approach	Second Inductive Approach	Deductive Approach
Outline why you are making the evaluation.	Begin with a discussion of the subject or subjects that you are evaluating.	Begin with the conclusion that you have reached about the subject or subjects (your thesis statement).
Discuss/explain the criteria.	Explain its or their strengths and weaknesses.	Explain why and how you reached that conclusion using a compare-and-contrast format; compare and contrast each aspect of what you are evaluating in relation to the criteria.
Explain how well your subject or subjects match (or fail to match) the various criteria.	Outline how the positive and negative points match each of your criteria.	
Discuss which subjects are "best," according to the evaluative criteria you have established. Explain your thesis statement in your conclusion.	Explain how the subject or subjects you are evaluating fulfill those criteria (this, then, is your thesis statement).	

Constructing a Complete Draft

Once you have generated some initial thoughts and ideas, selected the criteria for judging your subject, and reviewed your notes from your reading and research, your next step is to write a first draft, which is often called a working draft. Your first draft is your opportunity to expand, explain, and develop your ideas.

Before beginning your draft, review the writing you have done so far. What are the relative advantages of evaluating several items or of concentrating on just one? Why? Review the criteria that you have developed and decide which you want to emphasize. If your instructor and/or peers have given you suggestions, consider how you will incorporate their advice into your evaluation. As you prepare to write, ask yourself the following questions:

- What is the most effective way to explain my criteria?
- In what ways does the subject of my evaluation match up with (or fail to match up with) the criteria I have selected?
- What is my final evaluation?
- How can I express my main point effectively as a thesis statement?

As you draft your evaluation, stop occasionally to read your work, imagining that you are reading it for the first time. Because your draft is an exploratory text, ask yourself the following questions:

- How have I compared my subject with similar items?
- How effectively have I added details demonstrating how well the subject matches my criteria?
- What visual information might I use to explain my evaluation?
- How clear is my final judgment?

For more on comparison, definition, and description, see Chapter 13.

INTEGRATING SOURCES

Including Others' Perspectives in Narratives (p. 99)

Quoting Sources (p. 139)

Paraphrasing Sources (p. 182)

Incorporating Numerical Data (p. 220)

Incorporating Partial Quotes (p. 262)

Designing Visuals to Show Your Data (p. 304)

Summarizing Information from Sources (p. 349)

Including Research Information (p. 398)

Synthesizing and Integrating Sources into Your Draft: Designing Visuals to Show Your Data

In many ways, simply doing an evaluation is a kind of synthesis—the act of taking pieces of information and putting them together to form a new way of looking at your subject. The specific details of the subject that you are evaluating, taken together, will enable you to make the determining judgments needed for your evaluation. These details from your research will then help your readers follow your line of thought and understand the reasoning behind your judgments.

When researching and writing an evaluation, you may find that some of your evaluation will be based on numerical data. One useful way to show those data is in the form of a graph or a table. We can see how Annlee Lawrence incorporates numerical data into her evaluative narrative both to explain to and to show her readers the total caloric intake of some popular fast-food meals:

> When I researched the nutritional content of these three meals, I found that all three have high calorie content (see fig. 1). The Whopper Combo from Burger King has been a favorite of Americans for generations. But is it as good for your body as it is to your taste buds? When I researched the nutritional information, I discovered that this meal has a grand total of 1350 calories. In contrast, Wendy's Classic Single Combo has 1180 calories, and McDonald's Quarter Pounder Combo has 1060.

Lawrence lists the meals in descending order based on number of calories. Some readers simply get overwhelmed with reading numbers, however. One way to make a clearer argument is to do what Lawrence did: incorporate numbers into your narrative, but also use graphs or tables to visually depict the data. Lawrence could total the caloric intake of each of the fast-food meals and show the results in a table, for example:

Table 1   Calories in a Fast Food Meal

Fast-Food Meal	Total calories
Burger King's Whopper Combo	1350
Wendy's Dave's Hot & juicy [TM] 1/4 Single Combo	1180
McDonald's Quarter Pounder Combo	1100

Consider how such a table makes it easy for readers to see what Lawrence found out about the calorie content of various fast-food combination meals.

Parts of a Complete Draft

Introduction: One of the qualities of a successful evaluation is that it grabs and holds readers' attention. Strategies that will help you hook your readers include the following:

- **Begin by explaining why you are making the evaluation—your rhetorical purpose—followed by a discussion of your criteria.** It is also often helpful to include an explanation of why you selected these criteria. This is usually the approach taken by articles in consumer magazines such as *Consumer Reports*. Mary Beth Griggs uses this approach in "This Is How *Jurassic World*'s Velociraptors Should Have Looked." She begins by showing a scene from the film depicting unfeathered dinosaurs. She then goes on to evaluate the representation of the velociraptors in the movie based on the scientific evidence she presents.

- **Indicate your conclusion at the beginning.** You will then explain in the body of your text why and how you reached that conclusion. Dennis Baron uses this type of introduction in his blog post. He ends his first paragraph with the sentence, "I would like to offer a modest alternative: don't make English official, ban it instead."

- **Set the scene for your evaluation.** Depending on your topic, you might open your evaluation with a description of your subject.

Body: If you are using the inductive approach, indicate what you want to evaluate and on what basis at the beginning, and then work through the process (and through the body of your evaluation) as you go. If you are using the deductive method, begin by stating your judgment, and then use the body of your paper to support it, often by comparing and contrasting your subject with other subjects of the same type.

Conclusion: Regardless of the organizational method you employ, make sure that your judgment of your subject—your evaluation—is clearly stated. Remember that in an evaluation, your ultimate conclusion is usually your thesis statement, or main point, but your conclusion can serve other purposes as well. A conclusion in evaluative writing often does the following:

- **Summarizes how each supporting piece of evidence helps support your main point.** In a lengthy, detailed evaluation, a summary of your findings can help readers recall the main points that you are making.

- **Reaches out to your audience.** An appeal to the audience is an especially effective way to end an evaluation, as often you want them not only to agree with your evaluation but also to do something with what they have learned.

Title: As you compose your evaluative writing, a title should emerge at some point—perhaps late in the process. The title should reflect your judgment of your subject, and it should catch your readers' attention and make them want to read your essay.

 USING DIGITAL TECHNOLOGIES   **Storing Image Files**

It is always a good idea to store the photographs you find in your research in a separate computer file, so you will have easy access to them when you start constructing your evaluation. Name your images and folders so that you can easily find the pictures you wish to use. For example: "Rodeo_rider. jpg," or "calfroper1.gif" will help you more easily find images you've saved than "pic1" or "image_3."

Be aware that image files come in different formats: .jpg, .gif, .bmp, and .tif are some common image file extensions. If a picture will not open on your computer, it may be because you don't have a program on your computer that is capable of handling that image's format.

VISUAL *Thinking* | Going Beyond Words to Achieve Your Goals

As a result of her research, Annlee Lawrence found a number of statistics that she wanted to use in her paper to help readers understand her evaluation.

For more on using visuals, see Chapter 18.

While writers can often present statistical information in sentences within their text, presenting that information in a table organizes the data for readers and makes it easier for them to understand. For example, the information on calories, sodium, and fat in the fifth paragraph of Lawrence's first draft (see page 309) could be presented like this:

Food item	calories	fat (grams)	milligrams of sodium
Whopper	650	37	910
Medium fries (salted)	410	18	570
Medium Coke	190		

She could also put her information in the form of a column or bar graph, or if Lawrence wanted to show how the total calories of these three food items make up a meal, she could use a pie chart.

- While Lawrence selected a pie chart to display this data, would a line or bar chart be as effective?

- What other kind of visual—such as a drawing or photograph— might help readers understand this information?

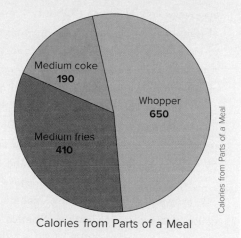

Calories from Parts of a Meal

Writing Activity

Constructing a Full Draft

After reviewing your notes, invention activities, and research and carefully considering all of the information that you generated and the comments you received, construct a complete first draft of your evaluation, using the organizational approach that you have decided on. Remember that your evaluation will evolve as you write, so your ideas will most likely change as you compose this first draft. Remember also that you will be learning as you write. While you may have some sense of whether your subject fits your criteria, expect to modify your position as you develop your evaluation essay.

Annlee Lawrence's First Draft

After deciding on an organizational approach and a tentative thesis, Annlee Lawrence was ready to begin her first, or working, draft. She did not worry about errors and instead concentrated on getting her main ideas on paper. Note that she started her paper by outlining what she was going to do, without revealing her conclusions. This inductive approach is one of the possible organizational methods described on page 303. As she wrote, Lawrence did not worry about grammar, punctuation, and mechanics; instead, she concentrated on getting her main ideas into her draft. (The numbers in circles refer to peer comments, which follow the draft on page 310.)

Who Has the Better Burger?
Annlee Lawrence

Dr. Julie Gerberding, former director of the USA's Centers for Disease Control and Prevention (CDC) argues that statistics show that 65% of US adults are overweight or obese ("Obesity"). And Janelle Stanish writes that "Millions of people in the United States are considered obese. As waistlines continue to increase, people are asking the question: Who is to blame? Is it because Americans have become lazy and are more irresponsible with their food choices? Are fast food chains the 'bad guys'?"

If the fast food chains are indeed the "bad guys," they are huge and serve lots of people: Did you know that McDonald's operates more than 36,000 restaurants in more than one hundred countries? McDonald's feeds more than 69 million people a day—more than the entire population of Spain!

Are fast food chains the "bad guys"? That is the question I also want to ask, as evidently obesity, if left unabated, will surpass smoking as the leading cause of preventable death in America. So why is it that we can't seem to stay away from our beloved Big Macs or Whoppers? Probably because our lives demand it at times. We don't have time to prepare a full-blown meal, so we have created fast food to fit with our fast-paced lives. So unfortunately, obesity can't be helped in today's society, but can be avoided through moderation of consumption.

Generally speaking, much fast food is unhealthy. But if you had to pick one that was the healthiest, which would it be? I felt that for this evaluation, the most important criteria for determining a "healthy" burger should be calories, total fat, and sodium. I chose some of the favorite meals to evaluate: the Whopper Combo from Burger King, Wendy's Dave's Hot & Juicy™ Single, and McDonald's Quarter Pounder Combo. ❶

The Whopper Combo from Burger King has been a favorite of Americans for generations. But is it as good to your body as it is to your taste buds? When I researched the nutritional information, I discovered that the sandwich itself has 650 calories, 37 grams of total fat, and 910 milligrams of sodium. A medium order of salted fries has 410 calories, 18 grams of fat, and 570 milligrams of sodium. Not to mention the medium Coke that contains 190 calories. All this adds up to be a grand total of 1350 calories, 55 grams of fat, and 1480 milligrams of sodium (BK USA Nutritionals). ❷

Because I used the Burger King Whopper, I picked a similar sandwich from Wendy's, Dave's Hot 'N Juicy™ 1/4 lb. Single. The burger has 530 calories, 31 grams of total fat, and 1220 grams of sodium. A medium "Value-Cut" fry has 410 calories, 20 grams of fat, and 440 milligrams of sodium; a medium coke has 240 calories. This all adds up to 1180 calories, 51 grams of total fat, and 1660 milligrams of sodium (Wendy's Nutrition Facts).

Last but not least, there is the McDonald's Quarter Pounder with cheese. Despite popular opinion, this burger is the best for you. It has 520 calories, 16 grams of fat, and 1110 milligrams of sodium, which is 50% of what people are supposed to have, each day, salt-wise. A medium fry has 240 calories, 19 grams of fat, and 190 milligrams of sodium. And a 16 ounce Coke has 340 calories. The total calories would be 1100, total fat 35, and total sodium of 1300, which is about 60% of the recommended daily sodium intake ("Get the Nutrition").

So if you do get caught up in a hurry and feel like grabbing a burger and you are counting calories, then get the McDonald's Quarter Pounder. The McDonald's Quarter Pounder has 130 fewer calories than the Burger King Whopper. Even their fries have 170 fewer calories than Wendy's. This doesn't mean that you should go and buy out McDonald's. Obviously, as the movie Super-Size Me proved, even the "healthy" fast food isn't good for you. But if eaten in moderation, fast food is one of the best things to happen to America.❸

Works Cited ❹

"BK USA Nutritionals." *Burger King*, 2015, www.bk.com/pdfs/ nutrition.pdf. Accessed 21 Apr. 2016.

McDonald's. Home page. 2016, www.mcdonalds.com/us/en/home.html. Accessed 21 Apr. 2016.

---. "McDonald's USA Nutrition Facts for Popular Menu Items." 2016, nutrition.mcdonalds.com/getnutrition/nutritionfacts.pdf. Accessed 21 Apr. 2016.

"Obesity Number One Health Problem in US Say CDC." *World Health*, 10 Nov. 2003, www.worldhealth.net/news/obesity_number_one_health_problem_in_ us_/. Accessed 21 Apr. 2016.

Stanish, Janelle R. "The Obesity Epidemic in America and the Responsibility of Big Food Manufacturers." *Student Pulse*, 2010. www.studentpulse.com. Accessed 21 Apr. 2016.

"Wendy's Nutrition Facts & Topics." *Wendy's*, 2016, www.wendys.com/food/Nutrition. jsp.mcdon. Accessed 21 Apr. 2016.

Student Comments on Annlee Lawrence's First Draft

❶ "These seem like good criteria, but why did you choose them? Do you need a stronger reason for your criteria here?"

❷ "These are a lot of statistics to digest at once (sorry!). I got lost. Can you give all this in a table or chart?"

❸ "Seems like the ending contradicts the rest of your essay. Why is fast food good for America? The ending seems wrong here."

❹ "You should check your formatting here. I think the dates might be wrong."

Revising

Once you have a full draft of your evaluation, you still have much to do. First, however, you should set the draft aside so that you can gain some critical distance. You can then read it with fresh eyes.

As you revise your early drafts, hold off on doing a great deal of heavy editing. When you revise, you will probably change the content and structure of your paper, so time spent working to fix problems with grammar, punctuation, or mechanics at this stage is often wasted.

When you reread the first draft of your evaluation, here are some questions to ask yourself:

- How effectively have I explained or indicated my criteria?

- What else might my audience want or need to know about my subject?

- How else might I interest my audience in my evaluation of this subject?

- What did I find out about my subject that I did not include in my evaluation?

- How clearly have I defined any terms my readers might not know?

- Could some aspects of my evaluation be more effectively presented as a graph or chart?

WRITER'S *Workshop* | Responding to Full Drafts

Working with one or two other classmates, read each evaluation and offer comments and questions that will help each of you see your papers' strengths and weaknesses. Consider the following questions as you do:

- What is your first impression of this draft? How effective is the title at drawing you in? Why? What are your overall suggestions for improvement? What part(s) of the text are especially strong?

- How clear and understandable is the point of the evaluation?

- How has the writer explained the subject of the evaluation? How might he or she develop the explanation further to make it more effective?

- How clearly and thoroughly has the writer explained and justified the criteria? What details need to be added or clarified?

- How effectively has the writer applied his or her criteria?

- How adequately are all assertions supported with evidence?

- If the writer makes comparisons, how clear are they? Where might additional comparisons be called for?

- How could the writer more clearly match the criteria to the subject? Are there any criteria that the writer discusses but never applies to the subject?

- What terms need to be defined?

- How effective is the organization of this evaluation? Why?

- How might visuals help the writer support his or her criteria more effectively?

- How clearly does the writer present and discuss any opposing points of view on this subject?

- How adequately is the writer's overall evaluation supported by the evidence he or she has presented?

Technology can help you revise and edit your writing more easily. Use your word processor's track-changes tool to try out revisions and editing changes. After you have had time to think about the possible changes, you can "accept" or "reject" them. Also, you can use your word processor's comment tool to write reminders to yourself when you get stuck with a revision or some editing task.

Because it is so difficult even for experienced writers to see their emerging writing with a fresh eye, it is almost always useful to ask classmates, friends, or family members to read drafts of your evaluative writing.

Responding to Readers' Comments

Once they have received feedback on their writing from peers, instructors, friends, and others, all writers have to decide what to do with that feedback. Since your writing is your responsibility, you must determine how to deal with reader responses to your work.

The first thing to do with any feedback is to consider carefully what your readers have to say about your text. For example, Annlee Lawrence's readers had the following reactions:

- One reader wondered why she chose the criteria she did. Lawrence needs to think about whether she needs to justify her criteria for her readers.

- Another reader felt overwhelmed by all of the statistical information in the paper and suggested a chart. Lawrence needs to think about what one or more charts might add to her paper, and what type of chart or graph she might use.

- A reader felt dissatisfied with her ending. How might Lawrence improve her conclusion?

- A reader pointed out problems with Lawrence's documentation, which affected the credibility of her evaluation.

You may decide to reject some comments, of course; other comments, though, may deserve your attention. You may find that comments from more than one reader contradict each other. In that case, use your judgment to decide which reader's comments are on the right track.

In the final version of her paper on pages 313–316, you can see how Annlee Lawrence responded to her readers' comments.

KNOWLEDGE OF CONVENTIONS

When effective writers edit their work, they attend to genre conventions, documentation, format, usage, grammar, and mechanics. By attending to these conventions in your writing, you make reading a more pleasant experience for readers.

Editing

After you revise, you have one more important step—editing and polishing. When you edit and polish, you make changes to your sentence structure and word choice to improve your style and to make your writing clearer and more concise. You also check your work to make sure it adheres to conventions of grammar, usage, punctuation, mechanics, and spelling. If you have used sources in your paper, you should make sure you are following the documentation style your instructor requires.

Because it is sometimes difficult to identify small problems in a familiar text, it often helps to distance yourself so that you can approach your draft with fresh eyes. Some people read from the last sentence to the first so that the content, and their familiarity with it, doesn't cause them to overlook an error. We strongly recommend that you ask classmates, friends, and tutors to read your work to help you find editing problems that you may not see.

See Chapter 20 for more on documenting sources using MLA or APA style.

To assist you with editing, we offer here a round-robin editing activity focused on careful word choice, which is a common concern in writing to evaluate.

WRITER'S *Workshop*	Round-Robin Editing with a Focus on Careful Word Choice

ROUND-ROBIN EDITING WITH A FOCUS ON

Fragments (p. 146)

Modifiers (p. 190)

Wordiness (p. 228)

Citing Sources (p. 270)

Careful Word Choice (p. 313)

Subordinate Clauses (p. 357)

Inclusive Language (p. 409)

Evaluative writing often requires careful word choice (diction). It is critical to select words that clearly represent what you intend to say. For example, notice how the revision to this sentence improves its clarity:

> We don't have time to prepare a full-blown meal, so we ~~have created~~ fast food to fit with our fast-paced lives.
>
> *rely on*
> ∧

People in general have not "created" fast food, but they have come to rely on the convenience that it provides.

Working with several peers, consult a good college dictionary and the portion of a handbook that covers word choice. If you are uncertain about a specific word choice, ask your instructor for help.

Genres, Documentation, and Format

If you are writing an academic paper in response to Scenarios 1 or 2, you will need to follow the conventions for the discipline in which you are writing and the requirements of your instructor. If you are working on Scenario 3, a review, you can be somewhat more informal than you would be in an academic paper.

If you have used material from outside sources, including visuals, you will need to give credit to those sources, using the documentation style required by the discipline you are working in and by your instructor.

For advice on writing in different genres, see the Appendix C. For guidelines for formatting and documenting papers in MLA or APA style, see Chapter 20.

A Writer Achieves Her Goal: Annlee Lawrence's Final Draft

Here is Annlee Lawrence's final draft. Note that she has addressed the questions and concerns that her classmates had.

ANNLEE LAWRENCE

Who Has the Healthier Burger?

EVALUATIVE ESSAY

Dr. Julie Gerberding, former director of the USA's Centers for Disease Control and Prevention (CDC) argues that statistics show that 65% of US adults are overweight or obese ("Obesity"). And Janelle Stanish writes that "Millions of people in the United States are considered obese. As waistlines continue to increase, people are asking the question: Who is to blame? Is it   1

Notice how Lawrence offers support for her criteria: information from the United States government

because Americans have become lazy and are more irresponsible with their food choices? Are fast food chains the 'bad guys'?"

If the fast food chains are indeed the "bad guys," they are huge and serve lots of people: Did you know that McDonald's operates more than 36,000 restaurants in more than one hundred countries? McDonald's feeds more than 69 million people a day—more than the entire population of Spain!   2

Are fast food chains the "bad guys"? That is the question I also want to ask, as evidently obesity, if left unabated, will surpass smoking as the leading cause of preventable death in America. So why is it that we can't seem to stay away from our beloved Big Macs or Whoppers? Probably because our lives demand it at times. We don't have time to prepare a full-blown meal, so we rely on fast food to fit with our fast-paced lives. So unfortunately, obesity can't be helped in today's society, but can be avoided through moderation of consumption.   3

Generally speaking, much fast food is unhealthy. But if you had to pick one that was the healthiest, which would it be? I felt that for this evaluation, the most important criteria for determining a "healthy" burger should be calories, total fat, and sodium. Since most everyone is concerned with calories, I wanted to focus on those, but know that sodium and fat are also important, so I collected information on those too.   4

I chose some of the favorite meals to evaluate: the Whopper Combo from Burger King, Wendy's Dave's Hot & Juicy™ Single, and McDonald's Quarter Pounder Combo.   5 6

When I researched the nutritional information for a Whopper meal, I discovered that this burger (with fries and a Coke) has a grand total of 1350 calories. Wendy's "Dave's Hot and Juicy" meal has 1180 calories, and the McDonald's Quarter Pounder with cheese combo has fewer calories, at 1100.   7

<div class="margin-notes">
One of Lawrence's classmates commented on her criteria:

These seem like good criteria, but why did you choose them? Do you need a stronger reason for your criteria here?

Lawrence has added information about why she chose calories as a criterion in response to this comment.

In the following section, Lawrence has incorporated information from external sources to support her thesis.

One peer reviewer had this comment

These are a lot of statistics . . . Can you maybe give all this in a table or chart?

Note how Lawrence put that data into three charts.
</div>

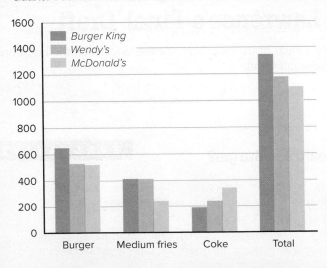

Fig. 1 Total calories in three fast-food meals

The "total fat" picture is similar with BK and Wendy's having the highest   8
fat content and McDonald's with the lowest—see Figure 2.

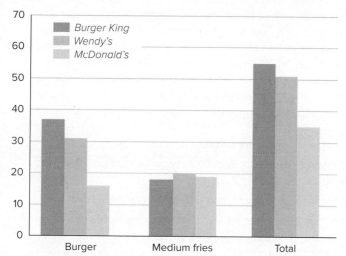

Fig. 2   Total fat in three fast-food meals

Last but not least is the sodium content (see fig. 3). Americans generally   9
take in way too much sodium: the government's Centers for Disease Control
recommends that the average person's daily sodium intake should be no more
than 2300 milligrams per day.

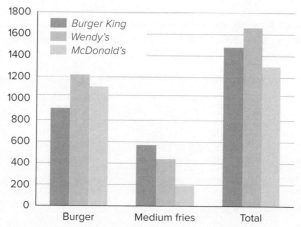

Fig. 3   Total sodium in three fast-food meals

Wendy's hamburger has more sodium than either of the other two burgers. 10
Note that Wendy's burger alone has about half the sodium that the average
person should have for an entire day.

So if you do get caught up in a hurry and feel like grabbing a burger and 11
you are counting calories, then get the McDonald's Quarter Pounder. The
McDonald's Quarter Pounder has 130 fewer calories than the Burger King 12
Whopper. Even their fries have 170 fewer calories than Wendy's. This doesn't
mean that you should go and buy out McDonald's. Obviously, as the movie
Super Size Me proved, even the "healthy" fast food isn't good for you. But if
eaten in moderation, fast food is one of the best things to happen to America.

Works Cited

"BK USA Nutritionals." *Burger King*, Apr. 2015, www.bk.com/pdfs/nutrition
.pdf, Accessed 21 Apr. 2016.

McDonald's. Home page. 2016, www.mcdonalds.com/us/ en/home.html

"McDonald's USA Nutrition Facts for Popular Menu Items." *McDonald's*,
2016,   nutrition.mcdonalds.com/getnutrition/nutritionfacts.pdf.
Accessed 21 Apr. 2016.

"Most Americans Should Consume Less Sodium." *Centers for Disease
Control*, 7 Apr. 2015, www.cdc.gov/salt/. Accessed 1 May 2016.

"Obesity Number One Health Problem in US Say CDC." *World Health.net*,
30 Jan. 2004, www.worldhealth.net/news/obesity_number_one_
health_ problem_in_us_1/. Accessed 21 Apr. 2016

Stanish, Janelle R. "The Obesity Epidemic in America and the
Responsibility of Big Food Manufacturers." 2010. www.studentpulse.
com/. Accessed 21 Apr. 2016.

Super Size Me, directed by Morgan Spurlock, Hart Sharp Video, 2004.

"Wendy's Nutrition Facts & Topics." 2016, www.wendys.com/food/
Nutrition.jsp.mcdon. Accessed 21 Apr. 2016.

This paper follows
MLA guidelines for
in-text citations and
works cited.

UNDERSTANDING A WRITER'S GOALS: QUESTIONS TO CONSIDER AND DISCUSS

Rhetorical Knowledge: The Writer's Situation and Rhetoric

1. **Audience:** Who do you see as Lawrence's audience?

2. **Purpose:** Lawrence seems to have another purpose for her evaluation, in addition to writing this paper for a class assignment: to help her classmates. How well does she fulfill that larger purpose?

3. **Voice and tone:** How does Lawrence use voice and tone to establish her *ethos?*

4. **Responsibility:** How effectively does Lawrence represent the facts about sodium and other nutritional data in her evaluation?

5. **Context, format, and genre:** Lawrence is writing as a college student who eats fast food. How does that affect her credibility in this evaluation? Can you tell what genre Lawrence's evaluation might be? Is it a report? While Lawrence makes effective use of graphs—usually a sign of a report— she does not use heads or subheads.

Critical Thinking: The Writer's Ideas and Your Personal Response

6. What is your initial response to Lawrence's essay?

7. Lawrence focuses on only three criteria for her evaluation. How sufficient are they, do you think, for her to construct an effective evaluation? Why?

Composing Processes and Knowledge of Conventions: The Writer's Strategies

8. How effective is the evidence that Lawrence provides? What other evidence might she have used?

9. How effectively does Lawrence use the quotation and information from the former director of the CDC?

Inquiry and Research: Ideas for Further Exploration

10. Interview several of your classmates, explaining Lawrence's conclusions. What is their reaction to her evaluation? Might it influence their dining decisions in the future?

Self-Assessment: Reflecting on Your Goals

Now that you have constructed a piece of evaluative writing, go back and reconsider your goals. To help reflect on the goals that you have achieved, respond in writing to the following questions:

 ## Rhetorical Knowledge

- *Audience:* What have you learned about addressing an audience in evaluative writing?
- *Purpose:* What have you learned about the purposes for constructing an evaluation?
- *Rhetorical situation:* How did the writing context affect your evaluative text? How did your choice of subject affect the research you conducted and the way you presented your evaluation?
- *Voice and tone:* How would you describe your voice in this essay? Your tone? How do they contribute to the effectiveness of your evaluation?
- *Context, medium, and genre:* How did your context determine the medium and genre you chose, and how did those decisions affect your writing?

 ## Critical Thinking, Reading, and Writing

- *Learning/inquiry:* What process did you go through to focus on a main idea, or thesis? How did you judge what was the most and least important criterion in your evaluation?
- *Responsibility:* How did you fulfill your responsibility to your readers?
- *Reading and research:* What did you learn about evaluative writing from the reading selections in this chapter? What research did you conduct? How sufficient was the research you did?
- *Skills:* As a result of writing this evaluation, how have you become a more critical thinker, reader, and writer? What skills do you hope to develop further in your next writing project?

Writing Processes

- *Invention:* What invention strategies were most useful to you?

- *Organizing your ideas and details:* What organization did you use? How successful was it?

- *Revising:* What are the strongest and the weakest parts of your essay? Why? If you could go back and make an additional revision, what would it be?

- *Working with peers:* How did your instructor or peer readers help you by making comments and suggestions about your writing? List some examples of useful comments that you received. How could you have made better use of the comments and suggestions you received?

- *Visuals:* Did you use photographs or other visuals to help explain your evaluation to readers? If so, what did you learn about incorporating these elements?

- *Writing habits:* What "writerly habits" have you developed, modified, or improved on as you constructed the writing assignment for this chapter? How will you change your future writing activities, based on what you have learned about yourself?

 Knowledge of Conventions

- *Editing:* What sentence problem did you find most frequently in your writing? How will you avoid that problem in future assignments?

- *Genre:* What conventions of the genre you were using, if any, gave you problems?

- *Documentation:* Did you use sources for your paper? If so, what documentation style did you use? What problems, if any, did you have with it?

If you are preparing a course portfolio, file your written reflections so that you can return to them when you next work on your portfolio. Refer to Chapter 1 (page 12) for a sample reflection by a student.

Text Credits

p. 288: "How Safe Are Worn Tires?", April 2014, *Consumer Reports*. **p. 289:** Baron, Dennis, "Don't Make English Official, Ban It Instead" The Web of Language, https://illinois.edu/blog/view/25/130039 Copyright © 2015 by Dennis Baron. Used with permission. **p. 293:** Macfarlane, Steve, "Jurassic World," *Slant Magazine*, June 10, 2015. Copyright © 2015 by Slant Magazine. Used with permission. **p. 295:** Griggs, Mary Beth, "This Is How Jurassic World's Velociraptors Should Have Looked" *Popular Science* online, July 17, 2015. Copyright © 2015 by Popular Science. Used with permission. **p. 313:** Courtesy of Annlee Lawrence.

Writing to Explain Causes and Effects

We are often curious about how and why things happen. We wonder what causes natural phenomena such as the northern lights (aurora borealis) that sometimes blaze across the night sky, we want to know what caused the extinction of certain species, and we have a vested interest in knowing the causes of diseases such as cancer, Alzheimer's, or schizophrenia.

Consider the events that take place in your life: You are surrounded by *changes* that occur, *trends* you can observe (and wonder why they happen), *behavior* that is unusual or surprising. All have *causes*, reasons why they happened or are hap-

pening. In fact, *why* is probably the best question you can ask as you explore any cause-and-effect relationship.

In some cases, discovering the cause is an end in itself. For instance, we may one day know precisely why the dinosaurs became extinct about 60 million years ago, but we may not be able to use that information to change life as it is currently lived on Earth. In other cases, though, we can use information gained from causal analysis to eliminate or avoid the causes of certain effects. For instance, in recent years, scientists have come to understand—and share with the public—the

strong cause-and-effect relationship between tobacco use and certain kinds of cancer. Although identifying and understanding relationships between causes and effects can be challenging, the act of writing will help you to become more aware of them. Because life includes many causes and effects, writing about them can help you to make sense of sequences of related events. As you work your way through your college or university classes, you will likely see a cause-and-effect relationship between a class or classes you are taking and your views about the job you eventually hope to have.

321

Setting Your Goals for *Causal Analysis*

Rhetorical Knowledge (pp. 324–328)

- **Audience:** Your success will partially depend on how well you have analyzed your audience. How can you make your audience interested in this cause-and-effect relationship?
- **Purpose:** Your main purpose is to convince readers that a cause-and-effect relationship exists. Your purpose may be to identify a cause and determine its effect(s). Or your purpose may be to determine a series of causes and effects—often called a causal chain.
- **Rhetorical situation:** Think about the factors that affect where you stand in relation to your subject.
- **Voice and tone:** Present yourself as a logical writer who provides reliable information.
- **Context, medium, and genre:** Decide on the most effective medium and genre to use to present your causal analysis. Visuals such as flowcharts are often an effective way of helping audiences understand causal relationships.

Critical Thinking, Reading, and Writing (pp. 328–342)

- **Learning/inquiry:** Think critically about whether an actual cause-and-effect relationship exists. It may be coincidental that one event happens right after another or that two phenomena often occur together.
- **Responsibility:** Recognize that causes and effects may be more complex than you first realize. Any given phenomenon or event is likely to have many causes and to produce many effects.
- **Reading and research:** As you conduct research about a causal relationship, make sure you understand the nature of the relationship well enough to be able to document the causality. Think about the ways technology can help you with your research.

Writing Processes (pp. 343-356)

- **Invention:** Begin by recording possible answers to the question you are considering, using an invention strategy such as brainstorming or listing.
- **Organizing your ideas and details:** Once you have recorded some ideas, think about how to organize your main points and what supporting evidence you need to provide.
- **Revising:** Read your work with a critical eye, to make certain that it displays the qualities of a good causal analysis.
- **Working with peers:** Peer review is a crucial part of the process of writing a causal analysis because it enables you to get a sense of how an audience will respond to your claim that a cause-and-effect relationship exists.

Knowledge of Conventions (pp. 356-363)

- **Editing:** When you edit a causal analysis, make sure that the subordinate clauses are attached to independent clauses and are therefore part of complete sentences.
- **Genres for cause-and-effect writing:** In your college classes, you will be required to follow the conventions for an academic essay. Other, nonacademic writing situations may call for a variety of genres.
- **Documentation:** You will probably need to rely on sources outside of your experience, and if you are writing an academic essay, you will be required to cite them using the appropriate documentation style. Consider how software can help you properly and accurately document your sources.

RHETORICAL KNOWLEDGE

When you write about causes and effects, you need to have a specific purpose in mind, some sense of your audience, and an idea of an effective way to substantiate the cause-and-effect relationships you are considering. How can you prove your claim that a cause-and-effect relationship exists?

As you read the material in this chapter, and as you discuss and write about it, consider the ways in which you can apply what you are learning to the writing you will do in other classes.

 ## Writing about Causes and Effects in Your College Classes

Many of the assignments for your college classes will ask you to determine the causes of an event, a trend, or a phenomenon. Here are some examples:

- Your theater history instructor may ask you to explain why and how a type of stage has evolved over time.
- Your biology instructor may ask you to explain what causes leaves to turn color and drop from trees in certain parts of the world in the fall.
- In a sociology course, you might investigate the possible effects of anti poverty programs on the crime rate in low-income neighborhoods.

The "Ways of Writing" feature on page 326 presents different genres that can be used when writing about causes and effects in your college classes.

 ## Writing about Causes and Effects for Life

Much of the writing constructed in professional settings is designed to solve problems. The first step in solving any problem is determining why the problem exists. Many professionals in the work world spend a good deal of their time determining causes and effects:

- A team of medical researchers writes a paper reporting on a study that reveals a cause-and-effect relationship between vitamin C deficiency and osteoporosis.
- A teacher wonders why some students have difficulty reading and studies them to find out the causes of their problems.

When writers focus on community issues, they often need to find and explain answers to *why* questions:

- A citizens' group submits a written report to the county health board arguing that more restaurant inspections lead to fewer incidences of *E. coli* food poisoning.

- A homeowner writes a letter to the editor of a county newspaper arguing that a nearby large "factory farm" is the source of the chemical residue recently discovered in local well water.

You will also encounter many occasions for thinking and writing about causes and effects in personal settings. It is critical to understand why things happen, and journals are an excellent place to explore such cause-and-effect relationships. For example, a young couple might keep a daily journal on the activities of their infant daughter. After a few weeks, when they reread their entries, they might notice a pattern suggesting that when they feed their daughter one kind of formula, she sleeps fewer hours at night.

The "Ways of Writing" feature on page 326 presents different genres that can be used when writing about causes and effects in life.

Scenarios for Writing | Assignment Options

Your instructor may ask you to complete one or both of the following assignments, in the form of scenarios, that call for writing about causes and effects. Each scenario gives you a sense of who your audience is and what you need to accomplish with your causal analysis.

Starting on page 343, you will find guidelines for responding to whatever scenarios you decide—or are asked—to complete. Additional scenarios for college and life may be found online.

Writing for College

SCENARIO 1 Academic Paper: Causes and Effects in One of Your Other College Courses

Consider the topics that you are studying this semester that involve causes and effects. Choose a topic that interests you, and then come up with a question about that topic that will lead you to investigate causes and/or effects. Here are some possibilities:

- **Geology:** What causes an earthquake?
- **Music:** How did hip-hop change popular music?
- **Art:** How did the invention of the camera affect the kinds of painting that artists did in the nineteenth century?
- **Physics:** What causes the lift that makes it possible for airplanes to fly?

Alternatively, you might consider some general cause-and-effect relationships that you have noticed. Here are a few examples:

- **College:** Why does the cost of attending college always seem to increase?
- **Community:** Why do some neighbors around the college resent having students rent homes nearby?
- **Classroom:** Why do some students take so long to finish college?

Ways of Writing to Explain Cause and Effect

Genres for Your College Classes	Sample Situation	Advantages of the Genre	Limitations of the Genre
Academic essay	Your health and wellness professor asks you to explain the possible causes of eating disorders in college-age female students.	In an academic essay you can examine an important issue in detail to determine cause.	Effective academic essays require substantial supporting evidence.
PowerPoint presentation	Your writing professor asks you to prepare a presentation on how professional athletes influence the actions of teenage males.	A PowerPoint presentation allows you to provide visuals that accompany your talk.	You'll need to be careful not to offer too many or too few details.
Brochure	To promote an expanded campus recycling program, your brochure needs to explain the cause(s) for the expanded program and its benefits.	A brochure is an effective medium for concisely presenting material in words and visuals.	A brochure allows only limited space for presenting an argument.
Formal laboratory report	Your botany professor asks you to construct a formal lab report showing the relationship of a warmer climate to the recent increase in the number of elm trees infested with bark beetles in your community.	A formal lab report is a common venue for showing such a cause-and-effect relationship.	Lab reports typically do not appeal to a wide audience.

Genres for Life	Sample Situation	Advantages of the Genre	Limitations of the Genre
Brochure	You decide to construct a brochure that explains why a certain stretch of highway is dangerous and causes more accidents.	A brochure gives readers a quick overview of your topic.	A brochure provides limited space to explain causes and effects.
Formal business plan	To get a loan for a new product line, you construct a business plan showing how these new products will increase profits.	Lending institutions often require a formal business plan before they decide whether to offer a loan.	Some intangibles—such as the work ethic of employees—cannot easily be documented in a business plan.
Poster	To help children understand that they need to wash their hands before eating, you construct a poster showing how germs can cause them to become sick.	A poster is a useful visual teaching tool for young readers.	Posters offer limited space for presenting material.
Web site	You want to create a Web site that explains how high school dropouts hurt the community because they often cannot find jobs that pay well.	A Web site can have a large school-age readership.	Constructing effective Web sites is time-consuming, and a Web site might not reach the entire target group.
Editorial	By writing an editorial, you hope to convince residents of your town that a slight increase in the sales tax will benefit the community.	An editorial lets you outline details about the cause-and-effect relationship between the small tax increase and the benefits for your community.	Because editorials tend to be short, it can be difficult to present enough evidence to support your position.

Writing Assignment: For this assignment, you can choose among several options. One possibility is to select an effect and then write about its causes. Another possibility is to select a cause and then write about its effects. Your goal is to convince an audience of instructors and students in the discipline that your causal analysis is credible. Photographs, charts, or drawings may help to visually show the cause-and-effect relationship you are outlining in this assignment.

SCENARIO 2   Laboratory Report

You are likely to be asked to construct laboratory reports during your college career, especially in your science classes. Although your instructor will give you specific guidelines for the report he or she asks you to construct, lab reports generally are just what the name implies: written observations.

Lab reports typically include these main headings:

- **Introduction**: a general guide to your experiment and the report that follows
- **Method:** a step-by-step outline of the process followed so that your experient could be replicated (sometimes a flowchart or other similar type of illustration helps readers understand the method)
- **Results:** your findings, often including presentations of data in tables and graphs
- **Analysis:** an explanation and outline of the mathematics involved
- **Discussion:** the relevance of your findings in relation to those of others, as well as any problems with your lab work
- **Conclusion:** a discussion of the extent to which the experiment met your initial goals

Lab reports can also include an abstract (a brief summary) and a review of the current literature (results of related studies and experiments). All sources (textbooks, papers, and so on) must be cited.

Writing Assignment: For one of your science classes, construct a formal laboratory report based on an experiment that you conducted. Your instructor will provide specific guidelines for you to follow.

Rhetorical Considerations in Cause-and-Effect Writing

Audience: While your instructor and classmates are your initial audience, you should also consider other audiences for your causal analysis. What evidence will convince your readers that you are making a valid claim about a cause-and-effect relationship?

Purpose: Your general purpose is to convince readers that a cause-and-effect relationship exists. How can you establish the causes of something (an effect), establish the effects of something (a cause), or show how a series of causes and effects are related?

Voice, tone, and point of view: Why are you interested in the cause-and-effect relationship that you have chosen to write about? What preconceptions about it do you have? What are your attitudes toward the topic and the audience? How will you convey those attitudes?

For more on choosing a medium and genre, see Chapter 17 and Appendix C.

Context, medium, and genre: Keeping the context of the assignment in mind, decide on a medium and a genre for your writing. How will your writing be used? If you are writing for an audience beyond the classroom, consider what will be the most effective way to present your information to this audience.

 # CRITICAL THINKING, READING, AND WRITING

Before you begin to write your causal analysis, read examples of writing about causes and effects to get a feel for this kind of writing. The qualities of writing about causes and/or effects include a focused presentation of the effect(s) or cause(s), a clearly stated claim that a cause-and-effect relationship exists, and sufficient evidence to support the claim. The writer also has the responsibility to research carefully, to avoid logical fallacies, and to consider other points of view.

 ## Learning the Qualities of Effective Writing about Causes and Effects

When you consider what causes what, or what the effects of something are, you need to convince others that the relationship you see in fact exists. Here are the qualities of writing that analyzes causes and/or effects successfully:

- Presentation of focused cause(s) or effect(s). At the beginning of your essay, introduce the event, activity, or phenomenon for which you wish to establish cause(s), or effect(s), or both. To focus the causes or effects, you should limit the time period that you are considering. This does not mean you cannot write about long periods of time (for a geology paper, you often have to do so). Rather, keep the time period in mind as you determine exactly what to focus on so you can reasonably cover your topic given the limits of your assignment.

- A clearly stated claim that a cause-and-effect relationship exists. After you have done enough research to be certain that a cause-and-effect relationship exists, you will be prepared to state the nature of that relationship. State the claim so that readers understand it, especially because they may know little or nothing about your topic. For example, "The terrorist attack on September 11, 2001, led to tighter security screening at airports in the United States" asserts a clear cause-and-effect relation-ship.

- Sufficient evidence to support your claim. To support your claim, present evidence that readers will consider persuasive. Such evidence may consist of the following:

  - The results of empirical studies or historical research found in scholarly and popular books, in journals, and on Web sites

  - Your own observations, experience, or reading

  - Testimony from interested or affected parties ("Interviews with other students indicate that . . .") or experts ("Professor X, a noted authority, asserts that . . .")

  - The use of examples that demonstrate that your suggested cause or causes actually do cause the effect

- Clear, logical thinking. People often jump to conclusions when they see two events happening at the same time and assume there is a cause-and-effect relationship (see the discussion of *post hoc, ergo propter hoc* in the box on page 347, and also the logical fallacy known as attributing false causes on pages 467–468). So consider these issues as you search for cause-and-effect relationships:

  - **Does the effect have a single cause, or multiple causes?** Things are rarely as simple as they first appear to be. More often than not, an effect will have multiple causes. Carefully analyze and research all the causes that may contribute to a particular effect.

  - **What are the contributing causes, and do they lead to a precipitating cause?** Often, a number of causes together contribute to what might be called a **precipitating cause,** the final cause that sets the effect in motion. Several contributing causes might set up a single precipitating cause. Although the football fan might blame the kicker who missed a last-second field goal for the team's loss of the important game, there surely were many other reasons that contributed to the loss (for example, dropped passes, poor execution of running plays, missed tackles).

  - **Is a particular cause remote or immediate?** It is sometimes useful to examine a chain of causes so that you understand what came first, what happened next, and so on. Writing down the sequence of causes and effects will help you see the events in the **causal chain** as they happened over time.

  - **Is a particular cause necessary or sufficient?** A **necessary cause** is one that must be present for the effect to occur. A **sufficient cause** is one that, if present, always triggers a particular effect. For example, for a teenager to be able to borrow the family car, his or her family must have a car—that cause is *necessary* to the effect of the teenager being able to borrow it. The teenager's forgetting to put gas into the family car before bringing it back, however, is a *sufficient* cause for the parents to refuse to lend it again; other causes would be sufficient as well (bringing the car home dirty or running into a utility pole and denting the fender are also possible causes for the parents' decision), so forgetfulness is not a necessary cause.

For more on writing effective arguments, including claims, evidence, types of appeals, and counterarguments, see Chapter 14.

- Anticipation of possible objections or alternative explanations. Although your causal analysis may be highly plausible, there are often other possible causes for the same effect or other possible effects of the cause that you are considering. Be prepared to acknowledge those other potential causes or effects and to show why your causes or effects are more likely.

Reading, Inquiry, and Research: Learning from Texts That Explain Cause-and-Effect Relationships

The readings that follow are examples of writing about causes and effects. As you read them, consider the following questions:

- To what extent has the writer focused on causes, on effects, or on both causes and effects?
- What parts of the selection seem the strongest? Why do you think so?
- How can you use the techniques of cause-and-effect writing exemplified here in your writing?

JUAN WILLIAMS

The Ruling That Changed America   CAUSE-AND-EFFECT ESSAY

Fifty years later, the *Brown* decision looks different. At a distance from the volcanic heat of May 17, 1954, the real impact of the legal, political, and cultural eruption that changed America is not exactly what it first appeared to be.

On that Monday in May, the high court's ruling outlawing school segregation in the United States generated urgent news flashes on the radio and frenzied black headlines in special editions of afternoon newspapers. One swift and unanimous decision by the top judges in the land was going to end segregation in public schools. Southern politicians reacted with such fury and fear that they immediately called the day "Black Monday."

South Carolina Gov. James Byrnes, who rose to political power with passionate advocacy of segregation, said the decision was "the end of civilization in the South as we have known it." Georgia Gov. Herman Talmadge struck an angry tone. He said Georgia had no intention of allowing "mixed race" schools as long as he was governor. And he touched on Confederate pride from the days when the South went to war with the federal government over slavery by telling supporters that the Supreme Court's ruling was not law in his state; he said it was "the first step toward national suicide." The *Brown* decision should be regarded, he said, as nothing but a "mere scrap of paper."

Meanwhile, newspapers for black readers reacted with exultation. "The Supreme Court decision is the greatest victory for the Negro people since the Emancipation Proclamation," said Harlem's *Amsterdam News.* A writer in the *Chicago Defender* explained, "neither the atomic bomb nor the hydrogen bomb will ever be as meaningful to our democracy." And Thurgood Marshall, the NAACP lawyer who directed the legal fight that led to *Brown*, predicted the end of segregation in all American public schools by the fall of 1955.

Juan Williams is the author of *Thurgood Marshall: American Revolutionary*, the nonfiction bestseller *Eyes on the Prize: America's Civil Rights Years, 1954–1965*, and *This Far by Faith: Stories from the African American Religious Experience*. He was born in Colon, Panama, but moved to Brooklyn, New York, in 1958. In an interview for the Web site Tolerance.org, Williams said, "Since I was born in 1954 my whole education is tied to the *Brown* case. I attended public schools in Brooklyn, New York, during the 1960s [and] those schools were very integrated. . . . I went to schools with Jewish children, Irish children, Italian children, and a stunning range of immigrant children from around the world."

Williams attended Haverford College and graduated with a degree in philosophy in 1976. For more than twenty years, Williams was an editorial writer, op-ed contributor, and White House reporter for *The Washington Post*. His work has appeared in *Newsweek, Fortune, Atlantic Monthly, Ebony, Gentlemen's Quarterly,* and *The New Republic.* Williams is currently a political analyst for Fox News and a panelist on Fox News *Sunday.*

This essay originally appeared in the April 2004 issue of the *American School Board Journal.*

1

2

3

4

Slow Progress, Backward Steps

Ten years later, however, very little school integration had taken place. True to   5
the defiant words of segregationist governors, the Southern states had hunkered

down in a massive resistance campaign against school integration. Some Southern counties closed their schools instead of allowing blacks and whites into the same classrooms. In other towns, segregationist academies opened, and most if not all of the white children left the public schools for the racially exclusive alternatives. And in most places, the governors, mayors, and school boards found it easy enough to just ask for more time before integrating schools.

That slow-as-molasses approach worked. In 1957, President Eisenhower 6
had to send troops from the 101st Airborne into Little Rock just to get nine black children safely into Central High School. Only in the late '60s, under the threat of losing federal funding, did large-scale school integration begin in Southern public schools. And in many places, in both the North and the South, black and white students did not go to school together until a federal court ordered schoolchildren to ride buses across town to bring the races together.

Today, 50 years later, a study by the Civil Rights Project at Harvard University 7
finds that the percentage of white students attending public schools with Hispanic or black students has steadily declined since 1988. In fact, the report concludes that school integration in the United States is "lower in 2000 than in 1970, before busing for racial balance began." In the South, home to the majority of America's black population, there is now less school integration than there was in 1970. The Harvard report concluded, "At the beginning of the 21st century, American schools are now 12 years into the process of continuous resegregation."

Today, America's schools are so heavily segregated that more than two- 8
thirds of black and Hispanic students are in schools where a majority of the students are not white. And today, most of the nation's white children attend a school that is almost 80 percent white. Hispanics are now the most segregated group of students in the nation because they live in highly concentrated clusters.

At the start of the new century, 50 years after *Brown* shook the nation, 9
segregated housing patterns and an increase in the number of black and brown immigrants have concentrated minorities in impoverished big cities and created a new reality of public schools segregated by race and class.

The Real Impact of Brown

So, if *Brown* didn't break apart school segregation, was it really the earthquake 10
that it first appeared to be?

Yes. Today, it is hard to even remember America before *Brown* because 11
the ruling completely changed the nation. It still stands as the laser beam that first signaled that the federal government no longer gave its support to racial segregation among Americans.

Before *Brown*, the federal government lent its power to enforcing the laws 12
of segregation under an 1896 Supreme Court ruling that permitted "separate but equal" treatment of blacks and whites. Blacks and whites who tried to integrate factories, unions, public buses and trains, parks, the military, restaurants,

department stores, and more found that the power of the federal government was with the segregationists.

Before *Brown*, the federal government had struggled even to pass a law banning lynching. 13

But after the Supreme Court ruled that segregation in public schools was a violation of the Constitution, the federal attitude toward enforcing second-class citizenship for blacks shifted on the scale of a change in the ocean's tide or a movement in the plates of the continents. Once the highest court in the land said equal treatment for all did not allow for segregation, then the lower courts, the Justice Department, and federal prosecutors, as well as the FBI, all switched sides. They didn't always act to promote integration, but they no longer used their power to stop it. 14

An irreversible shift had begun, and it was the direct result of the *Brown* decision. 15

The change in the attitude of federal officials created a wave of anticipation among black people, who became alert to the possibility of achieving the long-desired goal of racial equality. There is no way to offer a hard measure of a change in attitude. But the year after *Brown*, Rosa Parks refused to give up her seat to a white man on a racially segregated bus in Montgomery, Ala. That led to a yearlong bus boycott and the emergence of massive, nonviolent protests for equal rights. That same year, Martin Luther King Jr. emerged as the nation's prophet of civil rights for all Americans. 16

Even when a black 14-year-old, Emmit Till, was killed in Mississippi for supposedly whistling at a white woman, there was a new reaction to old racial brutality. One of Till's elderly relatives broke with small-town Southern tradition and dared to take the witness stand and testify against the white men he saw abduct the boy. Until *Brown*, the simple act of a black man standing up to speak against a white man in Mississippi was viewed as futile and likely to result in more white-on-black violence. 17

The sense among black people—and many whites as well—that a new era had opened created a new boldness. Most black parents in Little Rock did not want to risk harm to their children by allowing them to join in efforts to integrate Central High. But working with local NAACP officials, the parents of nine children decided it was a new day and time to make history. That same spirit of new horizons was at work in 1962 when James Meredith became the first black student to enroll at the University of Mississippi. And in another lurch away from the traditional support of segregation, the federal government sent troops as well as Justice Department officials to the university to protect Meredith's rights. 18

The next year, when Alabama Gov. George Wallace felt the political necessity of making a public stand against integration at the University of Alabama, he stood only briefly in the door to block black students and then stepped aside in the face of federal authority. That was another shift toward a world of high 19 hopes for racial equality; again, from the perspective of the 21st century, it looks like another aftershock of the *Brown* decision.

The same psychology of hope infected young people, black and white, nationwide in the early '60s. The Freedom Rides, lunch-counter sit-ins, and protest marches for voting rights all find their roots in *Brown*. So, too, did the racially integrated 1963 March on Washington at which Martin Luther King Jr. famously said he had a vision of a promised land where the sons of slaves and the sons of slave owners could finally join together in peace. The desire for change became a demand for change in the impatient voice of Malcolm X, the militant Black Muslim who called for immediate change by violent means if necessary.   20

In 1964, a decade after *Brown*, the Civil Rights Act was passed by a Congress beginning to respond to the changing politics brought about by the landmark decision. The next year, 1965, the wave of change had swelled to the point that Congress passed the Voting Rights Act.   21

Closer to the Mountaintop

This sea change in black and white attitudes toward race also had an impact on culture. Churches began to grapple with the Christian and Jewish principles of loving thy neighbor, even if thy neighbor had a different color skin. Major league baseball teams no longer feared a fan revolt if they allowed more than one black player on a team. Black writers, actors, athletes, and musicians—ranging from James Baldwin to the Supremes and Muhammad Ali—began to cross over into the mainstream of American culture.   22

The other side of the change in racial attitudes was white support for equal rights. College-educated young white people in the '60s often defined themselves by their willingness to embrace racial equality. Bob Dylan sang about the changing times as answers "blowing in the wind." Movies like "Guess Who's Coming to Dinner" found major audiences among all races. And previously all-white private colleges and universities began opening their doors to black students. The resulting arguments over affirmative action in college admissions led to the Supreme Court's 1978 decision in the *Bakke* case, which outlawed the use of quotas, and its recent ruling that the University of Michigan can take race into account as one factor in admitting students to its law school. The court has also had to deal with affirmative action in the business world, in both hiring and contracts—again as a result of questions of equality under the Constitution raised by *Brown*.   23

But the most important legacy of the *Brown* decision, by far, is the growth of an educated black middle class. The number of black people graduating from high school and college has soared since *Brown*, and the incomes of blacks have climbed steadily as a result. Home ownership and investment in the stock market among black Americans have rocketed since the 1980s. The political and economic clout of that black middle class continues to bring America   24 closer to the mountaintop vision of racial equality that Dr. King might have dreamed of 50 years ago.

The Supreme Court's May 17, 1954, ruling in *Brown* remains a landmark legal decision. But it is much more than that. It is the "Big Bang" of all American history in the 20th century.   25

UNDERSTANDING A WRITER'S GOALS: QUESTIONS TO CONSIDER AND DISCUSS

Rhetorical Knowledge: The Writer's Situation and Rhetoric

1. **Audience:** Williams is writing for an audience that, more likely than not, takes the decision in *Brown v. Board of Education* for granted. How does he show his audience the real importance of the decision?

2. **Purpose:** Williams wants readers to understand that even if U.S. public schools are still largely segregated, *Brown v. Board of Education* was perhaps the most important Supreme Court decision of the twentieth century. How successful is he in convincing you?

3. **Voice and tone:** Williams begins his article with measured language, much as you'd expect from a newspaper reporter. He then intersperses his reporting with several short, one-sentence paragraphs of commentary (for example, see paragraphs 13 and 15). How does this tone affect your response to what you read?

4. **Responsibility:** Williams needs to make sure his readers understand the social situation in the United States in 1954. How effectively does he do that?

5. **Context, format, and genre:** This essay is written as a retrospective, looking back over U.S. history in the fifty years since the Supreme Court decision. How sufficiently does Williams provide the historical background for you as readers today? How well does he establish the appropriate context? How does he use the conventions of an academic essay?

Critical Thinking: The Writer's Ideas and Your Personal Response

6. Before reading Williams's article, how aware were you of the impact of *Brown v. Board of Education?* Can you think of another Supreme Court ruling that has had as significant an impact?

7. At the end, Williams asserts that *Brown v. Board of Education* was instrumental in helping to establish the emerging black middle class. How do your experiences relate to Williams's observation?

Composing Processes and Knowledge of Conventions: The Writer's Strategies

8. Because for many people, fifty years after the fact, *Brown v. Board of Education* is simply an entry in history books, how does Williams make the decision real for his current readers?

9. Williams structures his argument to show that *Brown v. Board of Education* did not accomplish what it intended, but that it eventually did more. How effective is his argument? Why?

Inquiry and Research: Ideas for Further Exploration

10. Investigate other Supreme Court decisions. Which seem to have had a greater impact than expected at the time they were made?

NEAL GABLER

CAUSE-AND-EFFECT ESSAY

How Urban Myths Reveal Society's Fears

A well-known film critic and television personality, Neal Gabler has written articles for a number of publications, including *The New York Times*, *Esquire*, *New York Magazine*, *Vogue*, *Salon*, *Us*, and *Playboy*. His books include *An Empire of Their Own: How the Jews Invented Hollywood* (1988), *Winchell: Gossip, Power and the Culture of Celebrity* (1994), *Life the Movie: How Entertainment Conquered Reality* (1998), and *Walt Disney: The Triumph of American Imagination* (2006). The following essay was originally published in the *Los Angeles Times* in 1995. It offers insights into the origins of some popular urban myths.

The story goes like this: During dinner at 1 an opulent wedding reception, the groom rises from the head table and shushes the crowd. Everyone naturally assumes he is about to toast his bride and thank his guests. Instead, he solemnly announces that there has been a change of plan. He and his bride will be taking separate honeymoons and, when they return, the marriage will be annulled. The reason for this sudden turn of events, he says, is taped to the bottom of everyone's plate. The stunned guests quickly flip their dinnerware to discover a photo—of the bride *in flagrante*[1] with the best man.

At least that is the story that has been 2 recently making the rounds up and down the Eastern seaboard and as far west as Chicago. Did this really happen? A *Washington Post* reporter who tracked the story was told by one source that it happened at a New Hampshire hotel. But then another source swears it happened in Medford, Mass. Then again another suggests a banquet hall outside Schenectady, N.Y. Meanwhile, a sophisticated couple in Manhattan has heard it happened at the Pierre.

In short, the whole thing appears to be another urban myth, one of those 3 weird tales that periodically catch the public imagination. Alligators swarming the sewers after people have flushed the baby reptiles down the toilet. The babysitter who gets threatening phone calls that turn out to be coming from inside the house. The woman who turns out to have a nest of black-widow spiders in her beehive hairdo. The man who fails asleep and awakens to find his kidney has been removed. The rat that gets deep fried and served by a fast-food outlet. Or, in a variation, the mouse that has somehow drowned in a closed Coca-Cola bottle.

These tales are preposterous, but in a mass society like ours, where stories 4 are usually manufactured by Hollywood, they just may be the most genuine form of folklore we have. Like traditional folklore, they are narratives crafted by the collective consciousness. Like traditional folklore, they give expression to the national mind. And like traditional folklore, they blend the fantastic with

---

[1]Caught in the act of being unfaithful with the best man.

the routine, if only to demonstrate, in the words of University of Utah folklorist Jan Harold Brunvand, the nation's leading expert on urban legends, "that the prosaic contemporary scene is capable of producing shocking or amazing occurrences."

Shocking and amazing, yes. But in these stories, anything can happen not because the world is a magical place rich with wonder—as in folk tales of yore—but because our world is so utterly terrifying. Here, nothing is reliable and no laws of morality govern. The alligators in the sewers present an image of an urban hell inhabited by beasts—an image that might have come directly from Hades and the River Styx in Greek mythology. The babysitter and the man upstairs exploits fears that we are not even safe in our own homes these days. The spider in the hairdo says that even on our own persons, dangers lurk. The man who loses his kidney plays to our fears of the night and the real bogymen who prowl them. The mouse in the soda warns us of the perils of an impersonal mass-production society. 5

As for the wedding-reception tale, which one hacker on the Internet has dubbed "Wedding Revenge," it may address the greatest terror of all: that love and commitment are chimerical and even friendship is meaningless. These are timeless issues, but the sudden promulgation of the tale suggests its special relevance in the age of AIDS, when commitment means even more than it used to, and in the age of feminism, when some men are feeling increasingly threatened by women's freedom. Thus, the groom not only suffers betrayal and humiliation; his plight carries the hint of danger and emasculation, too. Surely, a legend for our time. 6

Of course, folklore and fairy tales have long subsisted on terror, and even the treacly cartoons of Walt Disney are actually, when you parse them, dark and complex expressions of fear—from Snow White racing through the treacherous forest to Pinocchio gobbled by the whale to Dumbo being separated from his mother. But these crystallize the fears of childhood, the fears one must overcome to make the difficult transition to adulthood. Thus, the haunted forest of the fairy tales is a trope for haunted adolescence; the witch or crone, a trope for the spent generation one must vanquish to claim one's place in the world; and the prince who comes to the rescue, a trope for the adult responsibilities that the heroine must now assume. 7

Though urban legends frequently originate with college students about to enter the real world, they are different from traditional fairy tales because their terrors are not really obstacles on the road to understanding, and they are different from folklore because they cannot even be interpreted as cautionary. In urban legends, obstacles aren't overcome, perhaps can't be overcome, and there is nothing we can do differently to avoid the consequences. The woman, not knowing any better, eats the fried rat. The babysitter is terrorized by the stranger hiding in the house. The black widow bites the woman with 8 the beehive hairdo. The alligators prowl the sewers. The marriage in Wedding Revenge breaks up.

It is not just our fears, then, that these stories exploit. Like so much else in modern life—tabloids, exploitalk programs, real-life crime best-sellers—urban legends testify to an overwhelming condition of fear and to a sense of our own impotence within it. That is why there is no accommodation in these stories, no lesson or wisdom imparted. What there is, is the stark impression that our world is anomic. We live in a haunted forest of skyscrapers or of suburban lawns and ranch houses, but there is no one to exorcise the evil and no prince to break the spell.

Given the pressures of modern life, it isn't surprising that we have created myths to express our malaise. But what is surprising is how many people seem committed to these myths. The *Post* reporter found people insisting they personally knew someone who had attended the doomed wedding reception. Others went further. They maintained they had actually attended the reception—though no such reception ever took place. Yet even those who didn't claim to have been personally involved seemed to feel duty bound to assert the tale's plausibility.

Why this insistence? Perhaps the short answer is that people want to believe in a cosmology of dysfunction because it is the best way of explaining the inexplicable in our lives. A world in which alligators roam sewers and wedding receptions end in shock is at once terrifying and soothing—terrifying because these things happen, soothing because we are absolved of any responsibility for them. It is just the way it is.

But there may be an additional reason why some people seem so willing to suspend their disbelief in the face of logic. This one has less to do with the content of these tales than with their creation. However they start, urban legends rapidly enter a national conversation in which they are embellished, heightened, reconfigured. Everyone can participate—from the people who spread the tale on talk radio to the people who discuss it on the Internet to the people who tell it to their neighbors. In effect, these legends are the product of a giant campfire around which we trade tales of terror.

If this makes each of us a co-creator of the tales, it also provides us with a certain pride of authorship. Like all authors, we don't want to see the spell of our creation broken—especially when we have formed a little community around it. It doesn't matter whether these tales are true or not. What matters is that they plausibly reflect our world, that they have been generated from the grass roots and that we can pass them along.

In a way, then, these tales of powerlessness ultimately assert a kind of authority. Urban legends permit us to become our own Stephen Kings, terrorizing ourselves to confirm one of the few powers we still possess: the power to tell stories about our world.

UNDERSTANDING A WRITER'S GOALS: QUESTIONS TO CONSIDER AND DISCUSS

Rhetorical Knowledge: The Writer's Situation and Rhetoric

1. **Audience:** When we selected Gabler's essay for this textbook, we thought it was about a topic that college students would be interested in. To what extent do you agree or disagree? Why?

2. **Purpose:** What do you see as Gabler's purpose in writing this essay?

3. **Voice and tone:** How would you describe Gabler's tone in this essay?

4. **Responsibility:** How does Gabler's use of Disney characters (paragraph 7) help or hurt his credibility?

5. **Context, format, and genre:** Because Gabler's essay was originally published in a newspaper, it is fairly brief, as most newspaper articles are. How does that conciseness affect how Gabler presents his information? What additional information would you like to have? Why? How does Gabler use the conventions of an essay?

Critical Thinking: The Writer's Ideas and Your Personal Response

6. Do you agree with Gabler that urban myths are the current version of "the most genuine form of folklore [traditional beliefs, myths, legends, and tales that are shared orally] we have" (paragraph 4)? Why or why not?

7. Gabler argues that urban myths require us to "suspend . . . disbelief in the face of logic" (paragraph 12). What instances can you think of in your life where you have suspended your disbelief? How willingly do you suspend disbelief? Why?

Composing Processes and Knowledge of Conventions: The Writer's Strategies

8. What kind of evidence in Gabler's essay do you find the most convincing? The least?

9. Gabler says that urban myths allow us each to become "a co-creator of the tales" (paragraph 13) and that they "permit us to become our own Stephen Kings, terrorizing ourselves . . ." (paragraph 14). How effective is this cause-and-effect argument?

Inquiry and Research: Ideas for Further Exploration

10. Interview several of your friends about myths they are familiar with. Outline them and make a brief report to your class.

11. Have you heard of any urban myths? List any that you know about, and be ready to explain them to the rest of your classmates.

12. Do an Internet search for "urban myths" and examine several that you find. Be ready to discuss them in front of your class.

GENRES *Up Close*   *Writing an Educational Poster*

Because people are busy juggling the demands of the professional, civic, and personal areas of their lives, they sometimes do not have time to read lengthy texts such as full academic essays. At other times, writers need to grab readers' attention when they are on the go—walking on sidewalks or down hallways, riding on buses or trains, or standing in a check-out line at a store or diner. To reach busy readers on the go, writers sometimes use educational posters, which provide information in a condensed form, with a mix of visual and verbal elements. Effective educational posters have the following features:

- **A focus on a single narrow topic.** A typical poster only has room for one very specific message.
- **A balance of elements.** Words, images, and white space (space without words or images) all appear in harmony, without clutter.
- **Relatively few words.** They include just enough to make a point.
- **Large type.** They can be read from a distance—at least ten feet away—when displayed on a wall.

The type size should be at least 24-point.

As you read the following poster, consider how these features are implemented.

APRILYUS

Anti-Smoking Poster

CAUSE-AND-EFFECT POSTER

Octavian, also known as Aprilyus, is an art student in Romania. His favorite art style is Impressionism, and his favorite artists are Grigorescu, Edgar Degas, and Igor Vieru. He enjoys digital arts and photography and believes that "a good artist is like an encyclopedia." We chose this poster by Aprilyus because it demonstrates the power of using both words and visual elements in texts.

SMOKING CAUSES LUNG CANCER

Courtesy of Aprilyus, deviantart.com

The poster focuses on a single, narrow topic—why you should not smoke.

The words, images, and white space in the poster are balanced.

The type size is large enough to be read at a distance.

UNDERSTANDING A WRITER'S GOALS: QUESTIONS TO CONSIDER AND DISCUSS

Rhetorical Knowledge: The Writer's Situation and Rhetoric

1. **Audience:** What effect will this poster have on smokers? What effect will it have on nonsmokers of various ages?

2. **Purpose:** What is the primary purpose for this poster? Is it to encourage smokers to quit? Is it to prevent people from starting smoking? How does it establish a cause-and-effect relationship?

3. **Voice and tone:** What is Aprilyus's attitude toward the topic?

4. **Responsibility:** What does Aprilyus consider his responsibilities to be? Why do you think that?

5. **Context, format, and genre:** If you were asked to convert this poster to a magazine ad, what changes would you make? Why?

Critical Thinking: The Writer's Ideas and Your Personal Response

6. How to you respond to this poster? Why?

7. What is the most striking feature of the poster? What makes you think that?

Composing Process and Knowledge of Conventions: The Writer's Strategies

8. How do the image and the words on the poster reflect Aprilyus's interest in Impressionism?

9. Why does Aprilyus use so few words on the poster?

Inquiry and Research: Ideas for Further Exploration

10. Find other works by Aprilyus. What common elements run through his work?

11. Conduct a Web search to learn more about the causes of lung cancer.

WRITING PROCESSES

As you work on your assignment, revisit the qualities of an effective cause-and-effect paper (see pages 328–330), and remember that the writing process is recursive—that is, writers move back and forth among all of the activities. After you engage in invention strategies and conduct some research, you may start writing, or you may decide to do some more research.

■ Invention: Getting Started

As you work, try to answer these questions:

- What do I already know about this event, phenomenon, or trend?
- Have I learned anything in any of my other classes that might inform my cause-and-effect paper?
- What do I know about its cause(s) or effect(s)?
- Where can I learn more about the causal relationships involved? What relevant personal experiences or observations can I contribute?
- What might my audience already know about the cause-and-effect relationship I am exploring?
- What might my audience's point of view be?
- What questions do I have? What do I want and need to find out?

As with any kind of writing, invention activities improve with peer feedback and suggestions. Consider sharing the invention work you have done so far with several classmates or friends in order to understand your rhetorical situation more clearly and to generate more useful information.

Writing Activity

Brainstorming

rainstorming is an invention technique that can help you focus your causal analysis and come up with possible causes and/or effects. Working with the questions above, spend a few minutes writing everything you can think of about the causal relationship you plan to discuss. Don't worry about putting this information into sentences or paragraphs; simply record it using any words that come to mind.

Hanna Lake's Research and Brainstorming

Earlier in her writing course, Hanna Lake wrote a paper about Irish and Norwegian customs in her family's history. Her interest in family history led her to wonder how people develop their definitions of family. She became particularly interested in how life experiences shaped the concepts of family for Black Hawk,

STUDENT WRITING EXAMPLES

Brainstorming (pp. 117, 343)

Freewriting (pp. 134, 256, 344, 393)

Criteria (p. 300)

Listing (p. 97)

Answers to Reporter's Questions (p. 256)

Organization (pp. 98, 182, 647)

Clustering (pp. 135, 298)

Interviewing (p. 216)

Research (pp. 136, 137, 178, 179, 217, 218, 258, 259, 302, 343, 346, 396, 396)

Reflection (p. 12)

the famous Sauk leader, and Harriet Jacobs, a nineteenth-century slave born in North Carolina, two figures she had learned about in her American history course.

Lake began by brainstorming the following lists. Notice that she is working to understand Black Hawk's and Harriet Jacobs' definitions of "family."

"Family"

Black Hawk:
Definition: ???
Evidence:

- British are their father (45); "furnished them with goods"
- French are their father (45); those who supply/provide for them
- Americans are their brother
- not all Indian tribes are automatically their brethren (47)
- their tribe is a united front (48)
- Spanish father has always been a good friend (51)
- "myself or nation" (54) uses "we" a lot

Role:

Not so much the nuclear family
The entire tribe, who holds a common interest
Anyone who offers help*

Jacobs:
Definition: ???
Evidence: ???
Role:
Nuclear family is her support system
Masters can be "like" family
Anyone who offers help*
Chapter 14 pg 525
The family is a haven in a heartless world. ~ Attributed to Christopher Lasch

My response:
Strange that both Jacobs and Black Hawk would see those who have power over them as "family."

Hanna Lake's Freewriting: A Letter to Her Grandfather

To organize her thinking for her project, Hanna Lake wrote a short letter to her grandfather because she knew that he was interested in family and family history. Note how she describes her project in this brief note.

> Hi, Grandpa. For my class, I am writing about what caused a Native American leader named Black Hawk and a slave named Harriet Jacobs to develop their concepts of family. I'm looking at what family means to them and what roles family plays in their lives.

As for Black Hawk, I think that family was a broad concept. Family ties were different from what I have experienced in my life. He was not as close to his wife and children, but he did consider his whole tribe and some Europeans as loosely affiliated family members. He has Spanish "fathers," and the U.S. President is known as the "Great Father." I know this sounds kind of weird, but I think using the "family metaphor" was the best way he could relate to other people. He also felt that the son of one of his old friends was like an adopted son. He called his tribe (the Fox tribe) "our" tribe and they live in "our" village. This shows that his tribe was a big support network. However, not all Indian tribes were like family. They sometimes warred against other tribes. The terms "father" and "brother" are used frequently in his autobiography and tend to designate people who provided support and supplies for Black Hawk and his tribe. Basically, for Black Hawk family was a broad concept, encompassing blood relations, his tribe, and his allies.

Harriet Jacobs had a dissimilar concept of family. She spent most of her time with her grandma and other close kin. She mostly views family as her blood relations although there are some masters whom she seems to consider like family. Again, this is kind of weird, but it may be that Jacobs could relate to family relationships.

Exploring Your Ideas with Research

Usually, when you are writing about cause-and-effect relationships, you will need to provide evidence to support your claims. Although you may be able to draw on your own experience to provide evidence, you will also need to offer verifiable information such as facts, statistics, expert testimony, experimental results, and examples. For instance, if you were writing about cause-and-effect relationships in the areas of health or safety, two good sources of information are the Centers for Disease Control and the U.S. Department of Transportation, both of which have Web sites filled with reliable information.

To find evidence from outside of your own experience, you will need to do research to answer questions such as the following:

- What facts or other verifiable information will provide solid evidence that a cause-and-effect relationship actually exists? Where can I find this information? What sources will be most reliable?

- What expert testimony can I provide to support my thesis about causes or effects, or both? What authorities might I interview?

- What statistical data support my contention that a cause-and-effect relationship exists?

- How can I best explain the data to my readers so that (1) they can easily understand them and (2) my evidence supports my conclusions?

The subject you focus on, and the kind of essay you are constructing, helps to determine the kind of research you conduct. For example, for Scenario 1, in which you focus on a topic in one of your courses, interviewing classmates, professors, and/or administrators is a useful way to learn about different perspectives.

As we have seen, Hanna Lake already had an interest in Black Hawk and Harriet Jacobs and their ideas about family when she began her cause-and-effect assignment. She wanted to explore this topic in more depth and detail. At her college library, she searched the library's online catalog for sources using the keywords "Black Hawk" and "Harriet Jacobs" and found some books that might be helpful. Sources she located included the following slave narrative:

Brent, Linda. *Incidents in the Life of a Slave Girl.* Edited by L. Maria Child. *The Classic Slave Narratives,* edited by Henry Louis Gates, Jr., New American Library, 2002. pp. 437–668.

Writing Activity

Conducting Research

What sources could help you answer the questions you have about your topic and formulate a working thesis? The following questions will help you focus your research:

- What do you already know about the subject from your invention work?
- What cause-and-effect connections can you make?
- For what cause-and-effect connections do you need to provide some evidence?
- Whom might you quote as an expert?
- Where can you find statistics that will support your claim?
- Where might you look for more information and evidence?

Reviewing Your Invention and Research

After you have conducted your research, review your invention work and the information you collected from outside sources. Once you have a general idea of the cause(s) and/or effect(s) your research is leading you to, try to develop what is called a *working thesis statement:* If you had to explain the cause-and-effect relationship now, based on what you have learned, what would it be? Through the process of writing itself, you will learn more about your topic and possible cause-and-effect relationships, so you will modify and develop the working thesis statement as you draft and revise your text.

Writing Activity

Considering Your Research and Focusing Your Ideas

Examine the notes you have made based on your research. Then, using the *who, what, where, when, why,* and *how* questions as a starting point, see what information you have. For example, if you were preparing a brochure, PowerPoint, or Prezi presentation for a campus group that is working to make your campus

(continued)

Writing Activity

Considering Your Research and Focusing Your Ideas *(continued)*

smoke free, here are the kinds of questions you might ask to get started on your brochure:

- **Who:** Who is affected by smoking on campus?
- **What:** What are the effects of smoking on campus?
- **Where:** Where do people smoke on campus?
- **When:** When is smoking on campus most detrimental to the health of others?
- **Why:** Why is it important to make ours a smoke-free campus?
- **How:** How can making our campus smoke-free lead to a healthier place to study and to work?

Strategies FOR Success | Self-Reflection

Self-reflection, also called *metacognition,* is thinking about thinking. Effective writers, readers, thinkers, and learners reflect on what they do because they know that reflection leads to better performance. Writers, in particular, benefit from reflecting on what they do when they compose, as well as the texts that they produce. Reflection is especially important when you are writing about cause-and-effect relationships because it is important to think beyond the obvious: causes can have many effects and effects can have multiple causes. To help you reflect more critically on causes and effects, consider the following kinds of questions: What are all of the possible causes of this phenomenon? What are the most likely causes? What are the most obvious causes? What are some possible causes that may have been overlooked?

Events that happen at the same time may or may not be related causally—be sure you are not asserting a relationship that does not in fact exist, or mistaking a cause for an effect, or vice versa. A thoughtful writer works diligently to avoid the logical fallacy of *post hoc, ergo propter hoc,* a Latin phrase meaning "after this, therefore because of this." If you argue that X caused Y simply because X preceded Y, you are guilty of this logical fallacy. What are some examples of *post hoc, ergo propter hoc* thinking that you have recently witnessed?

Often, in cases where two events happen at the same time and are probably causally related, it still may not be obvious which is the cause and which is the effect. For instance, educational experts have observed that students with low self-esteem often underperform in school. But do people who have low self-esteem perform poorly in school because they have low self-esteem, as has been assumed in the past? Or do they have low self-esteem because they perform poorly in school, as some psychologists now believe? A reflective writer needs to consider both of these possibilities.

Organizing Your Cause-and-Effect Paper

Once you have a working thesis and supporting evidence for your cause-and-effect paper, you need to consider how you might organize your text. The questions to ask yourself are all rhetorical:

- Who is the audience for your paper?
- Why might they be interested in your reasoning about causes and/or effects, or how can you make them interested in it?
- What is your purpose for writing—that is, why do your readers need to understand this cause-and-effect relationship? What will your readers learn about your subject by reading your paper?

Once you have determined your purpose, you can choose the organizational approach that is best suited to it. Here are three possible organizational approaches that you might choose for your paper.

Options FOR Organization
Organizing a Cause-and-Effect Essay

Identify an Effect and Then Determine Its Cause(s)	Identify a Cause and Then Determine Its Effect(s)	Determine a Series of Causes and Effects
Introduce the effect.	Introduce the cause.	Introduce one of the causes or one of the effects.
Explain the importance of the effect.	Explain the importance of the cause.	Explain the importance of the cause or the effect that you have identified.
List possible causes.	List possible effects.	List possible causes and effects.
Assert probable cause-and-effect relationship(s).	Assert probable cause-and-effect relationship(s).	Assert probable chain of causes and effects.
Note that there may be several causes.	Note that there may be several effects.	Provide evidence to support your claim about series of causes and effects.
Provide evidence to support your claim about cause-and-effect relationship(s).	Provide evidence to support your claim about cause-and-effect relationship(s).	Address skeptics' doubts.
Address skeptics' doubts—others say these causes do not cause the effect, so address those objections.	If others might see different effects from your cause, address their objections.	Conclude by summarizing the cause-and-effect relationships you discussed in your paper.
Conclude by summarizing the cause-and-effect relationships you discussed in your paper.	Conclude by summarizing the cause-and-effect relationships you discussed in your paper.	

Constructing a Complete Draft

Once you have chosen the most effective organizational approach for your audience and purpose, you are ready to construct the rest of your draft. As you work, keep the following in mind:

- Draw on your invention work and your research. If necessary, do more invention work and/or more research.

- As you try out tentative ideas about possible causes and/or possible effects, ask peers about what they consider necessary to support your ideas.

- Ask yourself and peers whether visuals might help make your case.

For more on constructing visuals, see Chapter 18.

Synthesizing and Integrating Sources into Your Draft: Summarizing Information from Sources

When considering cause-and-effect relationships, effective writers integrate a variety of sources into their texts to support their claims. Although writers can quote or paraphrase source material, they often find it best to summarize source information about cause-and-effect relationships because such explanations can be too long to integrate effectively as quotations or paraphrases. As noted on page 554 in Chapter 20, summaries need to encapsulate others' ideas accurately and concisely.

On pages 357–362 in this chapter, Hanna Lake quotes, paraphrases, and summarizes source material in her essay on the causes of Black Hawk's and Harriet Jacobs's ideas about family. When she summarizes source material, she clearly strives to be accurate and concise, as illustrated in the following passage (paragraph 7) from her essay:

> As with many American Indian nations of the time, European powers played a large role in the everyday lives of Black Hawk and the Sauk. The Spanish, French, English, and Americans all engage in diplomacy with Black Hawk throughout his autobiography. The Europeans supplied the Sauk with goods, weaponry, and even luxury items in exchange for trade and alliances (Black Hawk 43, 45). Though today we would see the Europeans' treatment of the Native Americans as controlling and oppressive, Black Hawk viewed this system of support as akin to the care taken by parents looking after their children; their support earns the European ambassadors the moniker of "father," and the President of the United States is known as their "Great Father," who oversaw his "red and white children" (Black Hawk 150). The general population of American whites were the Sauk's brothers—a familial relationship characterized by alternating periods of amity and conflict—and those in power who provided aid, presents, and allegiance were considered the Sauk's fathers. Some of Black Hawk's struggles were due to conflicts with his white brothers, but his "fathers" aid Black Hawk with allegiance and supplies during these times of struggle. For Black Hawk, these relationships were just as important as veritable blood bonds.

Notice how the summary includes source citations, enclosed in parentheses to set them off from Lake's words. The citations indicate to readers that this

INTEGRATING SOURCES

Including Others' Perspectives in Narratives (p. 99)

Quoting Sources (p. 139)

Paraphrasing Sources (p. 182)

Incorporating Numerical Data (p. 220)

Incorporating Partial Quotes (p. 262)

Designing Visuals to Show Your Data (p. 304)

Summarizing Information from Sources (p. 349)

Including Research Information (p. 398)

paragraph is a summary of someone else's words and ideas, rather than Lake's original ideas. (The paragraph also includes quotations, which are integrated into Lake's sentence and set off with quotation marks.)

In short, when you summarize and integrate others' ideas into your texts, you should aim to do the following:

- Concisely condense the source material.
- Accurately encapsulate the information in the source material.
- Cite the source of the information.
- Indicate how the summary supports your claim(s).

Parts of a Complete Draft

Introduction: To write an introduction that captures readers' attention, you might want to try one of the following strategies:

- **Give your audience a reason for being interested by vividly portraying how this topic makes a difference in their lives.**
- **Make a statement that suggests the unexpected.** Juan Williams uses this strategy in "The Ruling That Changed America" (page 331):

  Fifty years later, the *Brown* decision looks different. At a distance from the volcanic heat of May 17, 1954, the real impact of the legal, political, and cultural eruption that changed America is not exactly what it first appeared to be.

- **Examine a surprising causal relationship (that you can substantiate) to hold an audience's interest.**

Body: There are many strategies you can use to show cause and effect. In the body of your causal analysis, you may list and discuss possible causes and effects. You will likely also refute skeptics' claims. For example, in a causal analysis on the dangers of smoking, you might note that while many smokers may feel their habit endangers only themselves, research data indicates the harmful effects of second-hand smoke. You could then present the data as evidence.

 USING DIGITAL TECHNOLOGIES **Using Graphics and Video to Explain Cause-and-Effect Relationships**

Graphics, and even video, can help you explain complex cause-and-effect relationships. If your instructor allows, see if you can find a short video clip (one to three minutes long) that shows the causal relationship you are explaining. Many Web search engines include video searches. Or you might explore a large video site such as YouTube (youtube.com). If you have access to a digital video camera or own a video-capable cell phone or smartphone, you can create a short video clip. For example, if you are writing about the effects of proper grip, motion, and follow-through on curveball execution in baseball, you could ask a campus baseball player to demonstrate while you record a video of various techniques. Consider recording a voice-over that explains the movements involved.

Conclusion: In your conclusion, you need to reinforce the connections between the causes and effects that you have established. Do not assume your reader will make the same connections you have. Ask yourself the following questions:

- How effectively have you shown that the effect was a result of the cause?
- How well have you tied together all of the different ideas you have been working with?
- How clearly have you articulated your perspective so your audience has no doubt about what you have been trying to prove?
- Have you given your reader a sense of closure?

Title: As you construct your cause-and-effect paper, a title should emerge at some point—often late in the process. The title should reflect the cause-and-effect claim that you are considering.

VISUAL *Thinking*	Going Beyond Words to Achieve Your Goals

For this assignment Hanna Lake wrote a causal analysis in which she examined how life experiences influenced Black Hawk's and Harriet Jacobs' concepts of family. Fortunately, painted portraits of Black Hawk and photographs of Harriet Jacobs exist, and Lake easily found them on the Web. She did need to make choices, however, because multiple images of these two historical figures are available. For Black Hawk, she chose an illustration that appears in *History of the Indian Tribes of North America,* a three-volume set published between 1836 and 1844. For Harriet Jacobs, Lake chose a photo that appears on the cover of an edition of Jacobs' autobiography. Lake considered these publications to be reliable sources of historically accurate images. By adding these visuals to her causal analysis, Lake made Black Hawk and Jacobs seem more real for readers.

For more on oral presentations, including the use of PowerPoint, see Chapter 16.

- What other criteria could Lake use to select visuals for her analysis?
- What visuals would you recommend that Lake use in her analysis?

Writing Activity

Constructing a Full Draft

After reviewing your notes and research and invention activities, and carefully considering all of the information that you have generated, you are ready to construct a first complete draft, using the organizational approach that you have decided on. Remember that your thinking about the nature of the cause-and-effect relationship may evolve as you draft your paper, so your ideas will most likely change as you compose the first draft of your essay.

As you draft, keep in mind that you are proving that something occurred as a direct result of something else. Make sure you have support for your claims about cause-and-effect relationships.

(continued)

Writing Activity

Constructing a Full Draft *(continued)*

There is no one right way to start composing. However, if you have an organizational plan that you are comfortable with, you might begin by filling in parts of the sections that you feel best about or those where you feel you have the best information. You can always put everything together later.

An Excerpt from Hanna Lake's Early Draft

In this excerpt from an early draft, note how Hanna Lake incorporates evidence from her sources to prove her claim. As she wrote, Lake did not worry about grammar, punctuation, and mechanics; instead, she concentrated on getting her main ideas onto paper. (The numbers in circles refer to peer comments, which follow the draft on page 354.)

Brothers, Brethren, and Kin: The Role of Family in the Lives of Harriet Jacobs and Black Hawk ❶

Hanna Lake

Family serves a valuable function in a person's life; it fosters personal identity, provides support, and functions as a group of loyal confidants. Family has no strict definition and varies from individual to individual. The mechanisms that act on one's interpretation of family are life forces and life-shaping events. Harriet Jacobs, who wrote under the pseudonym Linda Brent, is a female slave in a slave-holding Southern state in the mid-nineteenth century.❷ During her enslavement she must endure undue advances from her master, grueling labor, and seven years confined in an attic while she is trying to escape. For Jacobs, the institution of slavery is the main force that produces her unique view on family. Black Hawk is a member of the Sauk tribe in the Western territory of the United States near present-day Illinois (Black Hawk 41). He is a war chief in his tribe; this position brings him frequently to battle and into talks with various political and military leaders. Black Hawk's views on family are formed mostly in his relations with others—tribes, countries, and cultures. He considers family to be a broad term that encompasses his nuclear family (though less so than the traditional sense), any group with common interests, or who looks to help Black Hawk and his tribe. Indeed, Black Hawk's broad sense of family, and his use of familial terms to define nonfamilial relationships, may make modern readers of his autobiography uncomfortable. Harriet Jacobs views family in a slightly more traditional sense: her close blood relations, with some benevolent individuals passing into the realm of *family*. Jacobs and Black Hawk grew up in diametrically different environments and, thus, even their translations of family—one of the most basic concepts—are deviating.

Jacobs' Nuclear Family ❸

For Jacobs, her reality is bleak and wrought with turmoil. Slavery places her existence in the hands of white slaveholders who consider her property to be bought, sold, and mistreated—sexually and otherwise. It is because of this unfortunate circumstance that her view of family is more conventional. She needs a strong support system to keep her resolve firm and, luckily, she is blessed with the relatively uncommon opportunity to have her actual family on the same plantation. Her grandmother, Martha, is an industrious free Black woman who keeps her own home near the house of the Flint family plantation whom Harriet considers to be a "great treasure" (Jacobs 445); she serves as Harriet's rock and confidante throughout the narrative. MORE ABOUT PRESENT FAMILY. Even her mother and father, who both die when Jacobs is still an adolescent, remain on Jacobs' mind all throughout her everyday life.

Black Hawk's Lack of Close Family

While Jacobs clings to the blood-related family she does have, Black Hawk does not seem to have the similar deeply rooted ties to his nuclear family and thus, his definition of *family* is less nuclear family-centric. Children, his wife, and other close relations are rarely mentioned, save for mainly the opening narration of previous generations of men in his family (Black Hawk 41–46). And even then there is little emotion or affection shown towards his great grandfather and his progeny. On another occasion, Black Hawk offers to trade his son for the son of a friend in his tribe (Black Hawk 61). When his own son is mentioned, no name is given and no sadness is expressed over losing his son (his own flesh and blood!) for a time. And when this adopted son is later killed, Black Hawk is determined to avenge his death with the help of braves in his tribe (Black Hawk 70). However, when Black Hawk loses his father in a battle with the Cherokees, he "blacken[s] his face, fast[s], and pray[s] to the Great Spirit for five years." As stated in the footnotes, tradition in the Sauk nation calls for a mourning period for close kin of up to a year; Black Hawk quintuples this period to grieve for his father (Black Hawk 49). Later, Black Hawk loses both his son and daughter in a short span of time. He describes this as "a hard stroke, because [he] loved [his] children" and resolves to live in seclusion with his family—this is one of the few instances when he refers to his wife, children, or nuclear family at all (Black Hawk 96). These prolonged times of mourning demonstrate that Black Hawk is deeply affected by the deaths of his father and children. Also, these episodes show that he considers his nuclear family to hold a dearer place in his life than he indicates; maybe it is just more difficult for him to translate those strong emotions of love into words than it is for Jacobs.❹

Student Comments on Hanna Lake's Early Draft

❶ "I'd like to see what Jacobs and Black Hawk look like."

❷ "When you talk about events in Jacobs' and Black Hawk's lives, use past-tense verbs. However, when you refer to the autobiographies, you can use present-tense verbs because the texts still exist."

❸ "You might consider eliminating the headings in the paper so that it flows more smoothly."

❹ "Your essay needs a conclusion to tie some of your points together."

Revising

Once you have a draft, put it aside for a day or so. This break will give you the chance to come back to your text as a new reader might. Read through and revise your work, looking especially for ideas that are not explained completely, terms that are not defined, and other problem areas. As you revise your early drafts, hold off on doing a great deal of heavy editing.

When you reread the first draft of your paper, here are some questions to ask yourself:

- How effectively have I explained my thesis so the reader knows what I intend to prove?
- What else might my audience want or need to know about my subject?
- How else might I interest my audience in my causal analysis?
- What did I find out about my subject that I did not include in my causal analysis?
- Have I clearly explained and defined any terms my readers might not know?
- Would any aspects of my causal analysis be more effective if presented visually?

WRITER'S *Workshop* | Responding to Full Drafts

Working with one or two classmates, read each paper and offer comments and questions that will help each of you see your paper's strengths and weaknesses. Consider the following questions as you do:

- What is your first impression of this draft? How effectively does the title draw you into the paper? Why? What part(s) of the text are especially effective for showing a cause-and-effect relationship?

- How well does the writer stay on track? If he or she loses focus, where does it happen?

- How logical is the paper? What strengths and weaknesses do you see in the writer's logic?

- How effective is the introduction? What suggestions can you make to improve the introduction?

- What do you think is the author's thesis or main point? How could it be expressed or supported more effectively?

- In the main part of the paper, are there parts that need more explanation? Where would you like more details or examples?

- How credible is the writer's case that a relationship exists? How credible are his or her sources?

- Might visuals such as charts, tables, graphs, or photographs help the writer to explain or support his or her claims about causes and/or effects more simply and clearly?

- How clearly and effectively does the writer present any opposing points of view on this subject? How effectively does he or she answer opposing viewpoints?

- What could be added or changed to make the conclusion more effective? To what extent does it make you want to learn more about this topic?

- What are the main weaknesses of this paper?—How might the writer improve the text?

Use your word processor's track-changes tool to try out revisions and editing changes. After you've had time to think about the possible changes, you can "accept" or "reject" them. Also, you can use your word processor's comment tool to write reminders to yourself when you get stuck with a revision or some editing task.

Responding to Readers' Comments

Once they have received feedback on their writing from peers, teachers, friends, and others, writers have to figure out what to do with that feedback. Because your writing is your responsibility, you must determine how to deal with reader responses to your work. The first thing to do with any feedback is to consider seriously what your reader has to say. Then it is up to you, as the author, to decide *how* to come to terms with these suggestions as you revise your causal analysis. You may decide to reject some comments, of course; other comments, though, may deserve your attention. You may find that comments from several readers contradict each other. In that case, use your own judgment to decide which reader's comments are on the right track. It is especially important to determine how well you have helped readers understand a cause-and-effect relationship.

In the final version of Lake's paper on pages 358–362, you can see how she responded to her reader's comments, as well as to her own review of her early draft.

KNOWLEDGE OF CONVENTIONS

In your college classes, writing about a cause-and-effect relationship is usually academic writing, so you will be required to follow the conventions for an academic essay. Other situations may call for a variety of genres, including memos, essays, blog postings, letters to the editor, and even formal position papers. Such documents often include tables, charts, graphs, or photos. Be aware of the conventions for any genre you use.

Editing

See Chapter 20 for more on documenting sources using MLA or APA style.

After you revise, you have one more important task—editing and polishing. At the editing stage, make changes to your sentence structures and word choices to improve your style and to make your writing clearer and more concise. Also check your work to make sure it adheres to conventions of grammar, usage, punctuation, mechanics, and spelling. Use the spell-check function of your word-processing program, but be sure to double-check your spelling personally (your computer cannot tell the difference between, say, *compliment* and *complement*). If you have used sources in your paper, make sure you are following the documentation style your instructor requires.

As with overall revision of your work, this final editing and polishing is most effective if you can put your text aside for a few days and come back to it with fresh eyes. We strongly recommend that you ask classmates, friends, and tutors to read your work to find editing problems that you may not see. To assist you with editing, we offer here a round-robin editing activity focused on making sure that subordinate clauses are attached to independent clauses.

WRITER'S *Workshop* | **Round-Robin Editing with a Focus on Subordinate Clauses**

ROUND-ROBIN EDITING WITH A FOCUS ON

Fragments (p. 146)

Modifiers (p. 190)

Wordiness (p. 228)

Citing Sources (p. 270)

Careful Word Choice (p. 313)

Subordinate Clauses (p. 357)

Inclusive Language (p. 409)

Writing about causes and effects benefits from the careful use of **subordinate clauses.** A subordinate clause has a subject and a verb, but it cannot stand on its own because it begins with a subordinating conjunction such as *although, because, while, if,* or *since*). When it appears on its own, it is a sentence fragment:

FRAGMENT   *Because my car did not start this morning.*

Because subordinate clauses cannot stand on their own, they need to be attached to an independent clause:

SENTENCE   *Because my car did not start this morning,* I was late for class.

or

SENTENCE   I was late for class *because my car did not start this morning.*

Working with several classmates, look for the subordinate clauses in your papers, and make sure they are attached to independent clauses. If you are uncertain about a specific convention for using subordinate clauses, consult a handbook or ask your instructor.

Genres, Documentation, and Format

If you are writing an academic paper in response to Scenario 1, follow the conventions appropriate for the discipline in which you are writing and the requirements of your instructor.

If you have used material from outside sources, including visuals, give credit to those sources, using the documentation style required by the discipline you are working in and by your instructor.

For advice on writing in different genres, see Appendix C. For guidelines for formatting and documenting papers in MLA or APA style, see Chapter 20.

A Writer Achieves Her Goal: Hanna Lake's Final Draft

Here is Hanna Lake's finished cause-and-effect paper, in which she argues that life experiences shaped Harriet Jacobs' and Black Hawk's definitions of family.

HANNA LAKE

Brothers, Brethren, and Kin: The Role of Family in the Lives of Harriet Jacobs and Black Hawk

Harriet Jacobs, who wrote a famous narrative under the pseudonym Linda Brent, was a slave in a slaveholding Southern state in the mid-nineteenth century (fig. 1). During her enslavement she endured undue advances from her master, grueling labor, and confinement in an attic for seven years while trying to escape. For Jacobs, the institution of slavery was the major force that shaped her concept of family. Black Hawk (fig. 2) was a member of the Sauk tribe in the Western territory of the United States (Black Hawk 41). He was a war chief in his tribe, a position that brought him frequently into battle and into talks with political and military leaders. For Black Hawk, "family" represented a proud tradition that could help keep his tribe harmonious and strong, and he used the context of family strategically to move the Sauk forward on the national and world stage. "Family" for Jacobs, which included blood relations and a small number of benevolent whites, served as a source of great emotional strength, protection, and strategic help to break out of slavery. Harriet Jacobs and Black Hawk grew up in diametrically different environments and entered adulthood at extreme ends of the power spectrum—Jacobs as a powerless slave and Black Hawk as the leader of an independent nation. For these two nineteenth-century Americans, the challenges they faced in their adult lives shaped their perceptions of "family" and the role it played in their struggles.

Harriet Jacobs' reality was bleak and wrought with turmoil. Slavery placed her destiny in the hands of white slaveholders who considered her to be property that can be bought, sold, and mistreated—sexually and otherwise. Because of this unfortunate circumstance, her view of family was fairly conventional. She needed a strong support system to keep her resolve firm, and luckily she was blessed with the relatively uncommon opportunity to have her blood relatives on the same plantation. Her grandmother, Martha, was an industrious free Black woman

1

2

Lake has changed some verb tenses in her essay. When referring to the events in the lives of Jacobs and Black Hawk, she uses past-tense verbs. However, when she refers to the autobiographies, she uses present-tense verbs because the autobiographies still exist.

Because a classmate asked what Jacobs and Black Hawk looked like, Lake added a photo of Jacobs and a portrait of Black Hawk.

With thanks to Louisa Burnham

Fig. 1 Harriet Jacobs

Library of Congress [LC-DIG-pga-07527]

Fig. 2 Black Hawk

who kept her own home near the house of the Flint family plantation, and Harriet considered her to be a "great treasure" (Jacobs 445); she serves as Harriet's rock and confidante throughout the narrative. Her grandmother also alleviated part of the greatest struggle Harriet had to deal with: the unwanted advances from Dr. Flint. Because of her grandmother's demeanor and constant presence, Dr. Flint, out of fear, did not pursue Harriet (Jacobs 472).

However, Jacobs' family was so close-knit that Dr. Flint used their closeness to his advantage. When Harriet ran away, he jailed her two young children and her uncle Phillip, hoping to distress her so much that she would come out of hiding to rescue the family that she held so dear (Jacobs 553, 563). Even her mother and father, who both died when Jacobs was still an adolescent, remained on Jacobs' mind throughout her everyday life. She thought about her parents with fond memories and lamented that her own children "cannot remember [her] with such entire satisfaction as [she] remembered [her] mother" (Jacobs 541). "Family" in *Incidents in the Life of a Slave Girl* means family in the most literal and traditional sense of the word: parents, grandparents, children, and all other blood relations who love each other, look out for one another's well-being, and minimize the effects of constant struggles. For Harriet Jacobs, family was her source of strength and happiness in a life made hopeless by slavery.

While Jacobs clung to the blood-related family she did have, Black Hawk did not seem to have similarly deeply rooted ties to his nuclear family and, thus, his definition of "family" was less centered on them. Indeed, Black Hawk's broad sense of family, and his use of familial terms to define nonfamilial relationships, may make modern readers of his autobiography uncomfortable. He rarely mentions his wife, children, and other close relations in his autobiography. In the opening narration he does describe previous generations of men in his family (Black Hawk 41–46), but even then Black Hawk shows little emotion or affection toward his great-grandfather and his progeny. On another occasion in the narrative, Black Hawk offers to trade his son for the son of a friend in his tribe (Black Hawk 61). When he mentions his own son, he doesn't even give his name and expresses no sadness over losing him. But when his adopted son is later killed,

3

4

Lake removed the headings in her essay to make it flow more smoothly.

Black Hawk is determined to avenge his death with the help of braves in his tribe (Black Hawk 70), signifying a strong attachment. When Black Hawk loses his father in a battle with the Cherokees, he "blacken[s] his face, fast[s], and pray[s] to the Great Spirit for five years." As stated in the footnotes, Sauk tradition called for a mourning period for close kin of up to a year; Black Hawk quintupled this period to grieve for his father (Black Hawk 49). Later, Black Hawk lost both his son and daughter in a short span of time. He describes this as "a hard stroke, because [he] loved [his] children" and resolves to live in seclusion with his family—this is one of the few instances when he refers to his wife, children, or nuclear family (Black Hawk 96). These prolonged times of mourning demonstrate that Black Hawk was deeply affected by the deaths of his father and children and that his nuclear family might have held a dearer place in his life than he indicates elsewhere in his writings; maybe it was more difficult for him to translate strong emotions of love into words than it was for Jacobs. But, unlike Jacobs, Black Hawk's greatest challenges extended far beyond the realm of his personal well-being, so the solace and support that were vital to his struggles also went beyond what members of a nuclear family can offer.

While Black Hawk included his close blood relations in his idea of "family," he also included members of the Sauk tribe. This group is most important to Black Hawk's fight for his goals. He consistently uses the word *our*, which signifies a unity between Black Hawk and the other Sauks: "our village" and "our people" (Black Hawk 77, 69). They were a people of common ancestry; people who had the same father in Muk-a-tà-quet; people who owed their success to Na-nà-ma-kee, another late war chief (Black Hawk 129). This reference to their shared forefathers is interesting because Na-nà-ma-kee was also Black Hawk's great-grandfather (Black Hawk 41). The fact that Black Hawk does not mention this link while addressing the men of his tribe shows that their common roots were more important than his notable heritage. Even though there were disagreements among the Sauk, they generally stood as a united front against enemies, much like a family unit. Black Hawk found a constant source of support from his tribe in the ongoing struggles against land-grabbing whites and rival tribes; while his tribe was a close-knit family system, there were conflicts with nearby tribes such as the Osage and the Sioux (Black Hawk 47, 140). The tribe had common enemies, and they worked together to avenge deaths of murdered members of the tribe (Black Hawk 123).

Like Black Hawk, Harriet Jacobs did find some support beyond her nuclear family, and she expresses appreciation and fondness for the additional support she finds in benevolent whites. Early in life, Jacobs was graced with a kind mistress who had also been her mother's mistress before her death. This generous woman provided Harriet with a life similar to "that of any free-born white child" and even taught her how to read and write (Jacobs 448). Again, even during her harrowing time under the eye of Dr. Flint, Jacobs found some

5

6

Lake added the names *Osage* and *Sioux* after a peer reviewer suggested that this would be useful information.

solace in the "large, loyal heart" of Miss Fanny, the woman who set her grandmother free and who visits Harriet to ensure she is being treated well (Jacobs 539). And during her escape Jacobs receives help from compassionate white friends—at a time when she most needs it. A dear friend of her grandmother promises to keep Harriet hidden, despite the illegality of harboring fugitive slaves. When Jacobs first meets her, the benefactress assures her that "[she] will be safe here" (Jacobs 552). These words of encouragement, along with a promise of security, establish a backup family for Harriet—a family with more privilege who can help her escape the perils of slavery. These white women, while mentioned only a few times in the narrative, were extremely powerful in Jacobs' life. They provided assistance and useful tools not often available to a slave. To Jacobs these women were extensions of her family, like a kindly aunt or another strong grandmother. While they were not as consistently valuable to Jacobs emotionally as her immediate family, they did assist her with her greatest struggles at opportune times.

As with many American Indian nations of the time, European powers played a large role in the everyday lives of Black Hawk and the Sauk. The Spanish, French, English, and Americans all engage in diplomacy with Black Hawk throughout his autobiography. The Europeans supplied the Sauk with goods, weaponry, and even luxury items in exchange for trade and alliances (Black Hawk 43, 45). Though today we would say the Europeans' treatment of the Native Americans was controlling and oppressive, Black Hawk viewed this system of support as akin to the care taken by parents looking after their children; their support earns the European ambassadors the moniker of "father," and the president of the United States is known as their "Great Father," who oversaw his "red and white children" (Black Hawk 150). The general population of American whites were the Sauk's brothers—a familial relationship characterized by alternating periods of amity and conflict—and those in power who provided aid, presents, and allegiance were considered the Sauk's fathers. Again, this definition, which implies a subservience of one group to another, makes us uncomfortable. However, it becomes understandable in the context of Black Hawk's use of the "family metaphor" to define broad relationships. Also, as Native American scholar Mark Wallace notes, Black Hawk's voice was "mediated" and "restrained by whites before it was even conceived" (481). Further, as literary scholar J. Gerald Kennedy observes, "The restrained voice we hear in the narrative is that of an old man filled with pride, remorse, and anger" (xxi). Some of Black Hawk's struggles were due to conflicts with his white brothers, but his "fathers" aid Black Hawk with allegiance and supplies during these times of struggle. For Black Hawk, these relationships were just as important as veritable blood bonds.

The diverging opinions of the two authors about the definition and role of family in their lives can be attributed to their social foundations and basic

7

8

Lake consulted some other scholarly sources to provide context for some of Black Hawk's observations.

life experiences. For Jacobs, family was a constant source of support, but at the same time, its presence was always a matter of uncertainty. She could never be confident that her family members would be in her life from one day to the next. Since slavery was such a terrible institution, it hardened the slaves emotionally and limited the circle of those people they could trust and depend on. But the family system she did have aided her in her struggles with a life of hard labor, sexual harassment, and eventual escape. Although Black Hawk was imprisoned later in his life and witnessed horrible atrocities committed by whites (Trask), during his formative years he was not subjected to captivity as a slave on a Southern plantation. As a result, he viewed family as a broader support system. For Black Hawk, family also encompassed members of his tribe and nations who offered assistance. His family structure assisted in his struggles with enemies, which included the United States government during portions of his life, and advanced the well-being of the greater Sauk community. However, we need to keep in mind historian Kerry A. Trask's observation that in his autobiography "Black Hawk thereby unwittingly enabled white people to feel good about themselves" (303), replacing their guilt with admiration for the Sauk leader.

When a classmate noted that the essay stopped, rather than concluded, Lake added this paragraph.

Black Hawk and Jacobs had contrasting concepts of family, which reflected some of the differences in their life experiences. However, focusing on the differences may cause readers to overlook some similarities in their lives. For example, both of them came from oppressed groups who were treated unjustly. Perhaps most importantly, though, both of them wrote autobiographies that include many keen insights about the roles that families can play. Both of them offer observations that encourage contemporary readers to think about what it means to be part of a family, no matter how the term *family* is defined. 9

Works Cited

Black Hawk. *Black Hawk: An Autobiography.* Edited by Donald Jackson, U of Illinois, 1955.

Brent, Linda. *Incidents in the Life of a Slave Girl.* Edited by L. Maria Child. *The Classic Slave Narratives,* edited by Henry Louis Gates, Jr., New American Library, 2002 , pp. 437-668.

Kennedy, J. Gerald. Introduction. *Life of Black Hawk, or Mà-ka-tai-me-she-kià-kiàk: Dictated by Himself.* By Black Hawk, edited by J. Gerald Kennedy, Penguin, 2008 , pp. vii-xxviii.

Trask, Kerry A. *Black Hawk: The Battle for the Heart of America.* Holt, 2006.

Wallace, Mark. "Black Hawk's *An Autobiography*: The Production and Use of an 'Indian' Voice." *American Indian Quarterly*, vol. 18, 1994, pp. 481-94.

UNDERSTANDING A WRITER'S GOALS: QUESTIONS TO CONSIDER AND DISCUSS

Rhetorical Knowledge: The Writer's Situation and Rhetoric

1. **Audience:** How does Lake acknowledge what her audience does and does not already know?

2. **Purpose:** Although Lake has considered the concept of family by studying her own family's history, in this paper she studies the concepts of family for two people whose experiences differ dramatically from hers. What do you think she has accomplished by studying these diverse perspectives?

3. **Voice and tone:** What is Lake's attitude toward her subject?

4. **Responsibility:** How does Lake responsibly represent the content of the two autobiographies?

5. **Context, format, and genre:** Lake is aware that both Jacobs and Black Hawk come from different cultures and different contexts from those of twenty-first century Americans. Because Lake relies on autobiographical material, it is only natural that Jacobs' and Black Hawk's perspectives will be revealed and might be at odds with our own view. How adequately does Lake explain her sources' contexts? How might she do so even more effectively?

Critical Thinking: The Writer's Ideas and Your Personal Response

6. How does your concept of family compare or contrast with the two concepts that Lake describes?

7. Which of the two concepts of family is easier for you to understand? Why?

Composing Processes and Knowledge of Conventions: The Writer's Strategies

8. To write her causal analysis, Lake drew on two autobiographies—primary sources—as well as secondary sources. What does she gain by incorporating secondary sources?

9. How does Lake draw connections between Black Hawk's and Jacobs' life experiences and their view of family?

Inquiry and Research: Ideas for Further Exploration

10. Interview several friends to find out how their life experiences have shaped their ideas about family. Write about the similarities and differences that the interviews reveal.

Self-Assessment: Reflecting on Your Goals

Now that you have constructed a piece of writing that explains causes and effects, review your learning goals, which you and your classmates may have considered at the beginning of this chapter (see pages 322–323). To help reflect on the learning goals that you have achieved, respond in writing to the following questions:

 ## Rhetorical Knowledge

- *Audience:* What have you learned about addressing an audience in this kind of writing?
- *Purpose:* What have you learned about the purposes for writing about causes and effects?
- *Rhetorical situation:* How did the writing context affect your writing about cause(s) and/or effect(s)? How did your choice of subject affect the research you conducted?
- *Voice and tone:* How would you describe your voice in this essay? Your tone? How do they contribute to the effectiveness of your writing?
- *Context, medium, and genre:* How did your context determine the medium and genre you chose, and how did those decisions affect your writing?

 ## Critical Thinking, Reading, and Writing

- *Learning/inquiry:* While working on your paper, what did you learn about the causal relationship you focused on that you could generalize about?
- *Responsibility:* How did you show that the effect or effects you wrote about were really the result of the cause or causes you identified?
- *Reading and research:* What did you learn from the reading selections in this chapter? What research did you conduct? What additional research might you have done?
- *Skills:* What skills have you learned while you were engaged in this project? How do you hope to develop them further in your next writing project?

Writing Processes

- *Invention:* What invention skills have you learned in writing about causes and effects? Which skills were most useful to you?

- *Organizing your ideas and details:* Describe the process you used to identify the causes and then the effects you wrote about. How did you decide to organize your paper, and how successful was your organization?

- *Revising:* What one revision did you make that you are most satisfied with? If you could go back and make an additional revision, what would it be?

- *Working with peers:* How have you developed your skills in working with peers? How did you make use of feedback you received from both your instructor and your peers? How could your peer readers help you more with your next assignment? How might you help them more, in the future, with the comments and suggestions you make on their texts?

- *Visuals:* Did you use visuals to explain your cause(s) or effect(s) to readers? If so, what did you learn about incorporating these elements? What did you learn about using technology when you searched for and used visual aids for your paper?

- *Writing habits:* What "writerly habits" have you developed, modified, or improved on as you constructed the writing assignment for this chapter? How will you change your future writing activities, based on what you have learned about yourself?

Knowledge of Conventions

- *Editing:* What sentence problem did you find most frequently in your writing? How will you avoid that problem in future assignments?

- *Genre:* What conventions of the genre you were using, if any, gave you problems?

- *Documentation:* Did you use sources for your paper? If so, what documentation style did you use? What problems, if any, did you have with it?

If you are constructing a course portfolio, file your written reflections so that you can return to them when you next work on your portfolio. Refer to Chapter 1 (page 12) for a sample reflection by a student.

Text Credits

p. 331: Juan Williams, "The Ruling that Changed America." Reprinted with permission from American School Board Journal, April 2004. Copyright 2004 National School Boards Association. All rights reserved. Used with permission. **p. 336:** Neal Gabler, "How Urban Myths Reveal Society's Fears." *Los Angeles Times*, November 12, 1995. Used with permission of the author. **p. 358:** Courtesy of Hanna Lake.

Writing to Solve Problems

You see, hear, and read about problems and possible solutions to those problems all the time. In developing countries, governments and nongovernmental organizations struggle with problems such as widespread poverty or disease. Closer to home, your community might experience a high dropout rate in your local high school or a shortage of affordable housing. When you write to propose solutions, you first identify an existing problem and then suggest one or more possible ways to solve it. For example, the Web site for Accion International has identified world pov-

erty as a problem and has proposed a possible solution. Accion started its lending program more than forty years ago, providing loans to what it calls "microentrepreneurs," so those business owners can grow their own small companies. In turn, the interest they pay provides funding for even more small-business loans.

When you are faced with a smaller-scale problem than world poverty, perhaps one in your own life or your friends' lives, you will often propose your own solution to it. When you suggest counseling to an unhappy friend, you are proposing a solution—a

known treatment—to an emotional problem: depression. When you recommend a heating and air conditioning repair company to a friend with a broken furnace, you are proposing a solution—the repair company—to a more practical problem: the faulty furnace.

When you propose any solution, however, others may already have suggested different solutions to the same problem. Therefore, you must support your own proposal with convincing evidence—not just opinions—and demonstrate that the proposal has a reasonable chance of success.

ESPAÑOL Sign up for email alerts **Join** Loans in the U.S.

ACCION

| **Donate** | What We Do | Our Impact | News | About Us | Get Involved |

About Us

Vision and Strategy

Contact Us

Financials

Annual Reports

Management

Board of Directors

President's Circle

Our Supporters

History

About Us

Accion is a global nonprofit dedicated to building a financially inclusive world with economic opportunity for all, by giving people the financial tools they need to improve their lives. We are building the next generation of top-tier microfinance institutions, and over more than 50 years have helped build 64 such institutions in 32 countries on four continents that today reach millions of clients. Our impact investing initiatives are pushing beyond microfinance to catalyze more than 20 innovative start-ups dedicated to improving the efficiency, reach and scope of financial services for the poor. And our Center for Financial Inclusion is helping to build a stronger industry with high standards and broad engagement. Currently, our work spans nearly two dozen countries, including the U.S., where we are the nation's largest nonprofit microfinance network.

Read our information sheet to learn more about Accion.

About the Organization

Learn about Accion's past and present by exploring our founding principles and future directions.

Our Mission, Vision and Strategy | Our History | News

Leadership

Meet the individuals who are leading an organization on the cutting edge of the microfinance industry.

Management Team | Board of Directors | President's Circle

Source: accion.org

The Web site for Accion, an organization committed to fighting world poverty through its support for small businesses, demonstrates many great examples of writing to solve problems.

Setting Your Goals for a *Proposal*

Rhetorical Knowledge (pp. 370-374)

- **Audience:** To persuade your audience to accept your solution, pay careful attention to your readers' views on and attitudes toward the problem. Who will be interested in your solution? What are their needs, values, and resources? What arguments are most likely to convince this audience?
- **Purpose:** One purpose of any proposal is to convince readers of the existence of a problem and the need for a solution. Another purpose is to convince readers that the solution(s) you propose is (are) the best one(s) possible.
- **Rhetorical situation:** Think about the factors that affect where you stand in relation to your subject. What is compelling you to write your proposal essay?
- **Voice and tone:** When you write to solve problems, you will need to be persuasive. As a result, make sure your tone engages your readers and does not in any way threaten or offend them.
- **Context, medium, and genre:** Decide on the most effective medium and genre to use to present your proposal to the audience you want to reach. Visuals such as charts, graphs, and photographs may help you make your case.

Critical Thinking, Reading, and Writing (pp. 375-392)

- **Learning/inquiry:** When you propose a solution, you first need to think critically to determine whether the problem exists and needs to be solved and whether your proposed solution is viable. Also think critically about the kind of evidence that will convince your readers. Further, evaluate a range of possible solutions to find one or more that are not only viable but effective.
- **Responsibility:** As you read solutions proposed by others, you have the responsibility to consider their solutions fairly as well as critically. You cannot ignore other good ideas simply because you do not agree with them.
- **Reading and research:** Readers will find your solution more acceptable if you have carefully and critically examined the problem and the issues surrounding your solution, supporting it with strong evidence, not unproven assumptions and assertions.

Writing Processes (pp. 393-408)

- **Invention:** Start by recording the ideas that you have about your problem, using an invention strategy such as brainstorming or listing. After recording your initial ideas and findings, you will also need to conduct research.
- **Organizing your ideas and details:** Once you have some ideas down, think about how you might organize your main points, what evidence you might need to provide to support them, and how you might deal with competing solutions to the problem.
- **Revising:** As you write, you may change your opinion about your problem and solution. Once you have a draft, read your work with a critical eye to make certain that it displays the qualities of an effective proposal.
- **Working with peers:** "Test" your solution on your classmates.

Knowledge of Conventions (pp. 408-416)

- **Editing:** One of the hallmarks of effective proposals to solve problems is the use of inclusive language—language that makes diverse readers feel like part of the team that is solving the problem.
- **Genres for writing to solve problems:** In your college classes, proposing a solution usually involves academic writing, so you will probably be required to follow the conventions for an academic essay. Nonacademic writing situations may call for a variety of genres such as a formal proposal to provide funding for a specific solution or an informal memo to suggest an internal policy change.
- **Documentation:** When writing to solve problems, you will probably need to rely on sources outside of your own experience. Document them using the appropriate style. Consider the ways that software can help you cite correctly.

 # RHETORICAL KNOWLEDGE

Readers of any proposal may ask themselves, "Why should I believe *you?*" All successful proposals have one important aspect in common: the establishment of a credible *ethos*. The nature of your subject and your audience will help you decide how best to maintain a balance between logical arguments and appeals to your readers' emotions.

 ## Writing to Solve Problems in Your College Classes

In many of your college classes, your instructor will present you with a problem and ask you to propose a solution. For your classes, you will be expected to examine any problem in depth, with academic rigor and an appropriate level of detail so that readers understand the problem. After all, if readers cannot understand the problem and see how it affects them, then why should they pay any attention to your proposed solution(s)? Here are some examples of problems you could write about in your college classes:

- In your political science class, you may be asked to propose a solution to the problems associated with the electoral college.
- In a course in environmental studies, you might be asked to propose ways to reduce U.S. dependence on fossil fuels.
- In your geology course, you might be asked to write a research proposal to study the problem of erosion in a nearby canyon.
- In your botany course, you might be assigned a problem/solution paper to examine the effects of climate change on the oak trees that surround your county courthouse and plaza.

The "Ways of Writing" feature on page 372 presents different genres that can be used when writing to solve problems in your college classes.

 ## Writing to Solve Problems for Life

Writing to solve problems is prevalent in all areas of your life. Many people feel that all they ever do in their professional lives is propose solutions to problems. Consider the following examples:

- An employee writes to her company's personnel director to propose a solution to the high turnover rate in her division.
- A new member of a company's product development division writes to his supervisor to suggest ways to reduce the time and costs required to develop and test new products.

People who are active in their communities often propose solutions as part of their civic life. Because problems continually emerge, every community constantly needs ideas to help solve its problems. You might, for example, write a letter to a local newspaper in which you propose a plan for raising funds for a nonprofit organization.

In your personal life, you will also encounter problems that need to be solved. Some will no doubt be large and potentially life altering. Suppose your mother, who lives alone, is suffering from Alzheimer's disease. You might send an e-mail to your siblings, proposing several possible solutions that you will discuss in a conference call. Or suppose your child is having a problem at school. You might send a letter to your child's teacher.

The "Ways of Writing" feature on page 372 presents different genres that can be used when writing to solve problems in life.

Scenarios for Writing | Assignment Options

Your instructor may ask you to complete one or both of the following assignments that call for a solution to a problem. Each of these assignments is in the form of a *scenario*. The list of rhetorical considerations on page 374 encourages you to think about your audience; purpose; voice, tone, and point of view; and context, medium, and genre.

Starting on page 393, you will find guidelines for completing whatever scenario you decide—or are asked—to complete. Additional scenarios for college and life may be found online.

Writing for College

SCENARIO 1   Solving a Social Problem from One of Your Courses

Think about a problem that you have learned about in another class you are taking this term. To complete this assignment, assume that the instructor has asked you to choose a problem and propose a solution for it, which you will present to your classmates. You must first decide which problem you wish to address and then look at various options for solving the problem. Here are some possible social problems to consider:

- **Education:** In some states, the dropout rate is relatively high.
- **Criminal justice:** In some cities, motorists run red lights more frequently than they do in other communities.
- **Business administration:** In many sectors of the U.S. economy, relatively few women have attained high-level management positions.
- **Health:** The incidence of diabetes is relatively high among some segments of the population in the United States.

Writing Assignment: Propose a solution to the problem that you have selected. Be sure to focus on solving one aspect of the problem, thus narrowing it down to a manageable size.

Ways of Writing to Solve Problems

Genres for Your College Classes	Sample Situation	Advantages of the Genre	Limitations of the Genre
Academic essay	In your sociology class, your professor asks you to examine some social problem (the effect of television violence or advertising on young people; eating disorders; and so on) and suggest possible solutions.	Your research on both the problem and potential solutions will be useful to young people who may engage in potentially unhealthy behaviors.	Some societal problems are too large to cover in one paper.
Proposal	The professor in your college success class asks you to write a paper detailing why some students leave school and to propose some ways to keep them enrolled.	A proposal is a good way to define a problem and then present research on potential solutions.	To get information from your fellow students, you will need to interview them—perhaps many of them—which is time-consuming.
Oral presentation	Create an oral presentation for your international relations class outlining a problem in another country and suggesting some solutions to that problem.	This oral presentation will force you to define the problem succinctly and then present possible solutions to it.	Illustrations will be crucial, and some problems are difficult to define orally and to show visually.
Letter to your campus newspaper	Your writing professor asks you to draft a letter to the editor of your campus newspaper about a problem on campus (litter, speeding cars, and so on).	Your school newspaper is a useful arena to publicize the problem and to ask fellow students to help with the solution.	A letter allows only limited space, and some problems and solutions are hard to describe briefly. It might not be published.
Recommendation report	Your business instructor asks you to outline an unusual business problem and to suggest a solution.	Finding a unique problem in the business world may help you and your readers understand how to solve unusual issues.	To make a good recommendation you will need to choose from multiple solutions, which may be difficult if the problem is unique.

Genres for Life	Sample Situation	Advantages of the Genre	Limitations of the Genre
Brochure	With several neighbors, you decide to construct a brochure in which you outline a local problem and suggest possible solutions.	A brochure provides a quick and easy way to share information about the problem, as well as your proposed solution.	A brochure provides limited space to present both the problem and the solution.
Memo	You have been asked to write a memo to the president of your firm, telling her about a serious problem and suggesting possible solutions.	A memo forces you to write concisely and specifically.	A memo is restrictive in terms of space (no one wants to read a ten-page memo).
Wiki	You want to construct a wiki that allows people in your area to share information on problems that affect them (graffiti, dangerous intersections, and so on) and to suggest and comment on possible solutions.	A wiki is an easy and uncomplicated way for people to share what they know about problems and potential solutions.	Someone will need to monitor the wiki for improper comments; readers need a reason to return to read and post on the wiki.
Web page	Every five years your extended family has a large-scale reunion, but there are always problems (travel time and cost, location for the reunion, and so on). Construct a Web page outlining these problems and and suggesting possible solutions.	A Web page gives everyone the same information at the same time; you can constantly update it, and you can provide links so you do not need to type all details into the page.	A static Web page does not allow for interaction (as a wiki does).
Performance improvement plan	A person you supervise at work has low sales for the quarter. You need to explain the problem and suggest solutions to it.	You can use your plan to outline both the problem and suggested solutions in sufficient detail so your employee has a real opportunity to improve his performance.	If your "plan for improvement" is incomplete, your employee might not do what he needs to do to solve the problem.

SCENARIO 2 Academic Writing: A Problem That Matters to You

For this scenario, decide on a problem for which you would like to propose a solution. You may choose a problem from any area of your life. Here are some suggestions:

- Your campus lacks adequate services for students with various kinds of disabilities.
- Your college needs daycare facilities for students with children.
- Your city's public library has too few computers, which means that patrons often must wait a long time for one to become available.
- The hourly pay rate for student workers on campus is relatively low.
- The number of arrests for driving under the influence rises dramatically in your city during holiday weekends.

Writing Assignment: Do you have a problem on your mind? What do you think should be done about it? Answering these two questions may lead you to a topic that you will want to write about. Your audience will be the community affected by the problem as well as the person or organization that has the power and resources to implement your solution.

Writing for Life

SCENARIO 3 Civic Writing: Proposal to Solve a Community Problem

Think about some problem in your community, such as litter that does not get picked up, a shortage of shelters or food banks for the homeless, gang violence, job losses, high housing prices, a lack of parks, or big-box stores moving in or closing down. As you consider a local problem, keep in mind that you will need to define that problem and prove that it exists to your readers. Unless they can understand the problem, your solution will not make any sense. Figure 12.1 gives an example of one possible local problem.

Writing Assignment: Write a formal proposal, which you plan to present to the city council, outlining and explaining the problem, as well as your suggested solution. For more on the format of a formal proposal, see pages 375–376. In your proposal, be sure to do the following:

- State the problem in enough detail that readers will understand it and its importance to your community.
- If your research turns up any background information (what the causes of the problem are, how long it has been a problem, what others have done to try to solve the problem, and so on), also outline that back-ground information.
- List possible solutions with their strengths and weaknesses (and costs, if applicable).

FIGURE 12.1 An increase in the number of mortgage foreclosures during an economic downturn can be problematic in communities with high unemployment.

- Explain why your suggested solution is the most effective one to solve the problem.
- Ask for action of some kind (for example, further study or funding for the solution).

Rhetorical Considerations in Proposal Writing

Audience: Although your instructor and classmates will be the primary audience, you should also consider other audiences for your proposal, depending on the scenario you have chosen. What will your audience know about this problem? Why should they be concerned about it? How can you make your solution(s) seem reasonable to them? What kinds of responses would you expect them to have to your proposal?

Purpose: Your purpose is to identify a particular problem and propose a viable solution. How will you convince your audience the problem needs attention?

Voice, tone, and point of view: You may choose to write about a problem that you have strong feelings about. How much has your view of the problem—or even your view that it *is* a problem—been determined by your value system? How will you deal with your preconceptions about the problem, and how might these preconceptions affect your tone? What attitudes, if any, do you have toward members of your audience, and how might that affect how you present your information?

For more on choosing a medium and genre, see Chapter 17 and Appendix C.

Context, medium, and genre: Keeping the context of the assignment in mind, decide on a medium and a genre for your writing. How will your writing be used? If you are writing for an audience beyond the classroom, consider what will be the most effective way to present your proposal to this audience.

CRITICAL THINKING, READING, AND WRITING

Before you begin to write your proposal, consider the qualities of a successful proposal. It also helps to read one or more proposals to get a feel for this kind of writing.

Effective writing that solves problems contains a clearly defined problem and a well-articulated solution that is targeted for a specific audience. In addition, this kind of writing will include convincing evidence for the proposed solution's effectiveness, as well as a well-documented review of alternative solutions. Finally, an effective proposal will include a call to action.

 ## Learning the Qualities of Effective Proposals

A proposed solution to a problem should include the following qualities:

- **A clearly defined problem.** An effective proposal first establishes the existence of a problem that is both understandable and manageable within the scope of the assignment.

For more information on cause and effect, see Chapter 11.

- **An awareness of the audience.** Your readers need to believe that the problem you are writing about actually exists and that your proposed solution will work. Therefore, use what your audience already knows and believes to shape your proposal. For instance, if your audience readily accepts the existence and importance of the problem, you can focus almost exclusively on the proposed solution. If, however, your readers may be unaware of the problem, or may not believe it *is* a problem, you will need to spend time making them aware of it and convincing them to be concerned about it.

- **A well-explained solution.** Your readers need both to understand your solution and to find it reasonable. One way to help any audience understand your proposal is to use language that the audience understands and to provide definitions of unfamiliar terms.

- **Convincing evidence for the effectiveness of the solution.** You will need to prove that your solution is viable and that it is the best answer to the problem by supporting your assertions with evidence such as expert testimony, case studies, experimental studies, and examples of similar solutions to similar problems. A solution needs to be feasible, affordable, and effective.

  You will also need to anticipate readers' objections to your proposed solutions so that you can address them. The cost of any solution almost always comes up as an objection, so you need to be prepared to deal with that concern ("While this solution is expensive in the near future, I will demonstrate how paying the extra money now will actually save us money in the long run").

- A well-documented review of alternative solutions. Although your proposed solution should stand on its own merits, for your proposal to convince the most skeptical readers, you must also acknowledge alternative ways to solve the problem and then carefully show why the alternatives will not work, or work as well, thus demonstrating that your solution is the best option.

- A call to action. There is little point to proposing a solution to a problem unless someone actually implements that solution. At the end of your proposal, you should urge those who can take action to solve the problem to do so.

Reading, Inquiry, and Research: Learning from Texts That Propose Solutions

As you read the selections, consider the following questions:

- How effective is the writer at convincing you that there is a problem that needs to be addressed?

- To what extent has the writer offered a workable solution?

- How convincing is the evidence? Why?

- How effectively does the writer anticipate opposing views and look at alternative solutions?

- How can you use the techniques of proposal writing exemplified here in your own writing?

REBECCA VALLAS & MELISSA BOTEACH

The Top 10 Solutions to Cut Poverty and Grow the Middle Class

The Census Bureau released its annual income, poverty, and health insurance report yesterday, revealing that four years into the economic recovery, there has been some progress in the poverty rate as it fell from 15 percent in 2012 to 14.5 percent in 2013, but there was no statistically significant improvement in the number of Americans living in poverty. Furthermore, low- and middle-income workers have seen little to no income growth over the past decade, as the gains from economic growth have gone largely to the wealthiest Americans.

With flat incomes and inequality stuck at historically high levels, one might assume that chronic economic insecurity and an off-kilter economy are the new normal and that nothing can be done to fix it. But there is nothing normal or inevitable about elevated poverty levels and stagnant incomes. They are the direct result of policy choices that put wealth and income into the hands of a few at the expense of growing a strong middle class.

The good news is that different policy choices can bring different outcomes. When the government invests in jobs and policies to increase workers' wages and families' economic security, children and families see improved outcomes in both the short and long term.

Here are 10 steps Congress can take to cut poverty, boost economic security, and expand the middle class.

This essay originally appeared on the Web page of the Center for American Progress (CAP). This organization describes itself as a group that provides "progressive ideas for a strong, just, and free America." From just that catch-phrase, what do you think would be the group's political philosophy?

Author Rebecca Vallas is an attorney who currently serves as the managing director for the Poverty to Prosperity Program at CAP. Vallas is the author of numerous articles on poverty, income security, disability, and criminal justice policy, and often testifies before Congress.

Author Melissa Boteach is the vice president of the Poverty to Prosperity Program at CAP. She oversees its poverty policy development and analysis, as well as its advocacy and outreach work. Boteach earned a master's degree in equality studies from University College Dublin. She has appeared on MSNBC, Fox News, and C-SPAN; has been a guest on several radio shows; and is frequently cited in English and Spanish print and online media.

1. Create jobs

The best pathway out of poverty is a well-paying job. To get back to prerecession employment levels, we must create 5.6 million new jobs. At the current pace, however, we will not get there until July 2018. To kick-start job growth, the federal government should invest in job-creation strategies such as rebuilding our infrastructure; developing renewable energy sources; renovating abandoned housing; and making other common-sense investments that create jobs, revitalize neighborhoods, and boost our national economy. We should also build on proven models of subsidized employment to help the long-term unemployed and other disadvantaged workers re-enter the labor force.

In addition, the extension of federal unemployment insurance 6 would have created 200,000 new jobs in 2014, according to the Congressional Budget Office. Indeed, every $1 in benefits that flows to jobless workers yields more than $1.50 in economic activity. Unfortunately, Congress failed to extend federal unemployment insurance at the end of 2013, leaving 1.3 million Americans and their families without this vital economic lifeline.

2. Raise the minimum wage

In the late 1960s, a full-time worker earning the minimum wage could lift a 7 family of three out of poverty. Had the minimum wage back then been indexed to inflation, it would be $10.86 per hour today, compared to the current federal minimum wage of $7.25 per hour. Raising the minimum wage to $10.10 per hour and indexing it to inflation—as President Barack Obama and several members of Congress have called for—would lift more than 4 million Americans out of poverty. Nearly one in five children would see their parent get a raise. Recent action taken by cities and states—such as Seattle, Washington; California; Connecticut; and New Jersey—shows that boosting the minimum wage reduces poverty and increases wages.

3. Increase the Earned Income Tax Credit for childless workers

One of our nation's most effective anti-poverty tools, the Earned Income Tax 8 Credit, or EITC, helped more than 6.5 million Americans—including 3.3 million children—avoid poverty in 2012. It's also an investment that pays long-term dividends. Children who receive the EITC are more likely to graduate high school and to have higher earnings in adulthood. Yet childless workers largely miss out on the benefit, as the maximum EITC for these workers is less than one-tenth that awarded to workers with two children.

President Obama and policymakers across the political spectrum have 9 called for boosting the EITC in order to right this wrong. Importantly, this policy change should be combined with a hike in the minimum wage; one is not a substitute for the other.

4. Support pay equity

With female full-time workers earning just 78 cents for every $1 earned by men, 10 action must be taken to ensure equal pay for equal work. Closing the gender wage gap would cut poverty in half for working women and their families and add nearly half a trillion dollars to the nation's gross domestic product. Passing the Paycheck Fairness Act to hold employers accountable for discriminatory salary practices would be a key first step.

5. Provide paid leave and paid sick days

The United States is the only developed country in the world without paid fam- 11
ily and medical leave and paid sick days, making it very difficult for millions
of American families to balance work and family without having to sacrifice
needed income. Paid leave is an important anti-poverty policy, as having a
child is one of the leading causes of economic hardship. Additionally, nearly
4 in 10 private-sector workers—and 7 in 10 low-wage workers—do not have a
single paid sick day, putting them in the impossible position of having to forgo
needed income, or even their job, in order to care for a sick child. The Family
and Medical Insurance Leave Act, or FAMILY Act, would provide paid leave
protection to workers who need to take time off due to their own illness, the
illness of a family member, or the birth of a child. And the Healthy Families
Act would enable workers to earn up to seven job-protected sick days per year.

6. Establish work schedules that work

Low-wage and hourly jobs increasingly come with unpredictable and con- 12
stantly shifting work schedules, which means workers struggle even more to
balance erratic work hours with caring for their families. Ever-changing work
schedules make accessing child care even more difficult than it already is and
leave workers uncertain about their monthly income. Furthermore, things
many of us take for granted—such as scheduling a doctor's appointment or a
parent-teacher conference at school—become herculean tasks.

The Schedules That Work Act would require two weeks' advance notice of 13
worker schedules, which would allow employees to request needed schedule
changes. It would also protect them from retaliation for making such requests—
and provide guaranteed pay for cancelled or shortened shifts. These are all
important first steps to make balancing work and family possible.

7. Invest in affordable, high-quality child care and early education

The lack of affordable, high-quality child care serves as a major barrier to reach- 14
ing the middle class. In fact, one year of child care for an infant costs more than
one year of tuition at most states' four-year public colleges. On average, poor
families who pay out of pocket for child care spend one-third of their incomes
just to be able to work. Furthermore, federal child care assistance reaches only
one in six eligible children.

Boosting investments in Head Start and the Child Care and Develop- 15
ment Block Grant, as well as passing the Strong Start for America's Children
Act—which would invest in preschool, high-quality child care for infants and
toddlers, and home-visiting services for pregnant women and mothers with
infants—will help more struggling families obtain the child care they need in
order to work and improve the future economic mobility of America's children.

8. Expand Medicaid

Since it was signed into law in 2010, the Affordable Care Act has expanded   16
access to high-quality, affordable health coverage for millions of Americans.
However, 23 states continue to refuse to expand their Medicaid programs to
cover adults up to 138 percent of the federal poverty level—making the lives of
many families on the brink much harder. Expanding Medicaid would mean
more than just access to health care—it would free up limited household
income for other basic needs such as paying rent and putting food on the
table. Having health coverage is also an important buffer against the economic
consequences of illness and injury; unpaid medical bills are the leading cause
of bankruptcy. Studies link Medicaid coverage not only to improved health,
improved access to health care services, and lower mortality rates, but also to
reduced financial strain.

9. Reform the criminal justice system and enact policies that support successful re-entry

The United States incarcerates more of its citizens than any other country in   17
the world. Today, more than 1.5 million Americans are behind bars in state and
federal prisons, a figure that has increased fivefold since 1980. The impact on
communities of color is particularly staggering: One in four African American
children who grew up during this era of mass incarceration have had a parent
incarcerated.

Mass incarceration is a key driver of poverty. When a parent is incarcer-   18
ated, his or her family must find a way to make ends meet without a necessary source of income Additionally, even a minor criminal record comes with
significant collateral consequences that can serve as lifelong barriers to climb-
ing out of poverty. For example, people with criminal records face substantial
barriers to employment, housing, education, public assistance, and building
good credit. More than 90 percent of employers now use background checks
in hiring, and even an arrest without a conviction can prevent an individual
from getting a job. The "one strike and you're out" policy used by public housing authorities makes it difficult if not impossible for individuals with even
decades-old criminal records to obtain housing, which can stand in the way
of family reunification. Furthermore, a lifetime ban—for individuals with felony
drug convictions—on receiving certain types of public assistance persists in
more than half of U.S. states, making subsistence even more difficult for individuals seeking to regain their footing, and their families.

In addition to common-sense sentencing reform to ensure that we no   19
longer fill our nation's prisons with nonviolent, low-level offenders, policymakers should explore alternatives to incarceration, such as diversion programs for individuals with mental health and substance abuse challenges.

We must also remove barriers to employment, housing, education, and public assistance. A decades-old criminal record should not consign an individual to a life of poverty.

10. Do no harm

The across-the-board spending cuts known as sequestration—which took effect in 2013—slashed funding for programs and services that provide vital support to low-income families. Sequestration cost the U.S. economy as many as 1.6 million jobs between mid-2013 and 2014. Some relief was provided this January, when Congress passed the Consolidated Appropriations Act of 2014, but many important tools to help low-income individuals and families pave a path to the middle class—such as adult and youth education and training programs, child welfare, and community development programs—were on a downward funding trend even before sequestration took effect.   20

As Congress considers a continuing resolution to fund the federal government past October 1 and avoid another government shutdown, it should reject further cuts to programs and services such as the Special Supplemental Nutrition Program for Women, Infants, and Children, or WIC, which provides vital nutrition assistance to pregnant women and mothers with new babies. Thereafter, Congress should make permanent the important improvements made to the EITC and the Child Tax Credit as part of the American Recovery and Reinvestment Act of 2009, which are set to expire in 2017. And it should avoid additional cuts to vital programs such as the Supplemental Nutrition Assistance Program, or SNAP, formerly known as food stamps, which suffered two rounds of deep cuts in 2013 and 2014.   21

Conclusion

It is possible for America to dramatically cut poverty. Between 1959 and 1973, a strong economy, investments in family economic security, and new civil rights protections helped cut the U.S. poverty rate in half. Investments in nutrition assistance have improved educational attainment, earnings, and income among the young girls who were some of the food stamp program's first recipients. Expansions of public health insurance have lowered infant mortality rates and reduced the incidence of low birth rates. In more recent history, states that raised the minimum wage have illustrated the important role that policy plays in combating wage stagnation.   22

There is nothing inevitable about poverty. We just need to build the political will to enact the policies that will increase economic security, expand opportunities, and grow the middle class.   23

UNDERSTANDING A WRITER'S GOALS: QUESTIONS TO CONSIDER AND DISCUSS

Rhetorical Knowledge: The Writer's Situation and Rhetoric

1. **Audience:** Who do you think is Vallas and Boteach's audience? This essay originally appeared on the Center for American Progress's Web page. Is this article the kind of essay readers of that Web page might expect? Why?

2. **Purpose:** Vallas and Boteach seem to have a clear and obvious purpose: to argue for their suggested "10 Solutions to Cut Poverty." Do you think there are any other agendas present in this essay? If so, what might they be?

3. **Voice and tone:** Throughout the essay, Vallas and Boteach present readers with facts and statistics. As a reader, do you think these make the essay's voice and tone kind of "dry," or do they make the essay more compelling?

4. **Responsibility**: In many ways, Vallas and Boteach's entire essay is about the social responsibility we all have to improve life for all Americans. What role do you think the federal government should have in helping to achieve that goal?

5. **Context, format, and genre:** This essay is a call to action. What is the most important idea that they suggest, and do you believe it is possible to implement that suggestion?

Critical Thinking: The Writer's Ideas and Your Personal Response

6. Vallas and Boteach believe that all ten of their ideas are important and necessary, and note that "one is not a substitute for the other" (paragraph 9). To what extent do you agree?

7. What are some other ways to address the economic issues that Vallas and Boteach discuss?

Composing Processes and Knowledge of Conventions: The Writer's Strategies

8. Vallas and Boteach use statistics throughout their essay. How helpful are the numerical data? What data do they present that you find more compelling than any other?

9. Vallas and Boteach begin their essay with an argument that "different policy choices can bring different outcomes." To what extent do you think their "Top 10 Solutions" will make significant changes?

Inquiry and Research: Ideas for Further Exploration

10. Vallas and Boteach wrote this essay in 2014, and note that the "poverty rate … fell from 15 percent in 2012 to 14.5 percent in 2013. . . ." What is today's poverty rate, and is it improving?

11. Select one of Vallas and Boteach's "solutions" and, using the Internet, learn whether that solution has been implemented.

12. Interview a friend or relative, asking about some of Vallas and Boteach's ideas. How useful does the person think these solutions are? Why?

SAGA BRIGGS

Intellectual Humility: What Happens When You Love to Learn—From Others

OPINION PIECE

Saga Briggs has a degree in Creative Writing from Oberlin College and has both taught and tutored writing at the elementary, secondary, and post-secondary levels. Briggs currently lives in Portland, Oregon, where she works as a writer, editor, and educational consultant.

1   Why do we enjoy learning? Is it because we actually like the process of learning, which often involves a struggle and occasionally requires failure, or is it because we like the end result—namely, the prospect of being right?

2   I ask this question because I think the answer sheds light on a major issue plaguing education today: intellectual humility (or lack thereof). We don't like being wrong, and we don't allow our students to be wrong. That's how we end up with learners more interested in appearing intelligent than in actually being intelligent.

3   But things are changing. Employers are starting to value skills like creativity, innovation, and resourcefulness—skills that forgive, even require, missteps and mistakes. Even more importantly, they're starting to value humility, especially the kind that motivates us to consider other perspectives and admit when we are wrong.

4   One of the most desirable skills at Google is intellectual humility, or the willingness to learn from others.

5   "Without humility, you are unable to learn," says Laszlo Bock, VP of hiring. "Successful bright people rarely experience failure, and so they don't learn how to learn from that failure." Instead, he says, they commit the "fundamental attribution error," which means attributing positive results to your own genius and negative results to someone else's shortcomings (e.g., intellectual arrogance).

6   "What we've seen is that the people who are the most successful here, who we want to hire, will have a fierce position. They'll argue like hell. They'll be zealots about their point of view. But then you say, 'here's a new fact,' and they'll go, 'Oh, well, that changes things; you're right.'"

7   But most of us don't think this way. When it comes to learning, we don't derive pleasure simply from "knowing" something, from building our treasure trove of facts. We derive pleasure from the idea of bestowing our knowledge upon someone else. And while the urge to share what we've learned is natural and good, it has become one-sided in the sense that we enjoy learning for ourselves more than we value the input of others.

8   So what is intellectual humility, exactly, and where did it come from?

Were Our Ancestors Intellectually Humble?

9   Socrates, the patron saint of intellectual humility, said it is only when we understand the depth of our own ignorance, only when we appreciate how little we know, that we are ready to develop the lifelong habits that will best support learning.

Richard Paul, author of *The Art of Socratic Questioning*, writes, "Socrates   10
philosophised by joining in a discussion with another person who thought
he knew what justice, courage, or the like was. Under Socrates' questioning,
it became clear that neither [of the two] knew, and they cooperated in a new
effort, Socrates making interrogatory suggestions that were accepted or rejected
by his friend. They failed to solve the problem, but, now conscious of their lack
of knowledge, agreed to continue the search whenever possible."

Aware of the inconsistencies of his own thoughts, and shrewdly suspect-   11
ing that similar inconsistencies were to be found in other men, Socrates was
always careful to "place himself upon the standpoint of ignorance and to invite
others to join him there, in order that, proving all things, he and they might
hold fast to that which is good."

Benjamin Franklin was another model of intellectual humility. In 1787, polit-   12
ical delegates gathered in Philadelphia with the task of reaching consensus on a
United States Constitution. During the last day of deliberations, Benjamin Franklin urging fellow delegates to accept the document. He began by confessing,
"There are several parts of this constitution which I do not at present approve."
But, he continued, "I am not sure I shall never approve them. For having lived
long, I have experienced many instances of being obliged by better information, or fuller consideration, to change opinions even on important subjects."
Towards the end of his remarks, Franklin made a final request of delegates who,
like him, "may still have objections" to the Constitution: he urged each one to
"doubt a little in his own infallibility and sign," and soon after, the Constitution
was approved.

Often referred to as the Miracle at Philadelphia, some scholars have   13
attributed the success of the Constitutional Convention not to the near-divine
insights of individual delegates, but to the tone of intellectual humility that
Franklin and others helped establish (Webb 2012).

Drawing on the habits of historical figures like these, Paul outlines the   14
modern definition of intellectual humility as follows: 1) having a consciousness
of the limits of one's knowledge, including a sensitivity to circumstances in
which one's native egocentrism is likely to function self-deceptively; and 2)
having a sensitivity to bias, prejudice, and the limitations of one's viewpoint.

"Intellectual humility does not imply spinelessness or submissiveness,"   15
says Paul. "It implies the lack of intellectual pretentiousness, boastfulness, or
conceit, combined with insight into the logical foundations, or lack of such
foundations, of one's beliefs."

Simply put, Socrates and Franklin were trying to tell us not to claim more   16
knowledge than we have. But where has this advice landed us today?

How Does Intellectual Humility Aid Learning?

Post-doctoral researchers Ian Church and Peter Samuelson have been study-   17
ing intellectual humility for nearly a decade. Church and Samuelson define

intellectual humility as "holding a belief with the firmness the belief merits." Some beliefs, like the belief that $2 + 2 = 4$, merit being held with the utmost firmness; to do otherwise, such as to have serious, lingering doubts as to whether or not $2 + 2 = 4$, is to be intellectually diffident or intellectually self-deprecating. Other beliefs, like the beliefs regarding the number of gumdrops in a jar, merit being held with very little firmness; to do otherwise is to be intellectually arrogant. Intellectual humility can be seen as the sort of middle ground between the two.

So what's the difference between intellectual humility and general humility?   18

As part of a larger body of work to explore the science of intellectual humil-   19
ity, Church and Samuelson investigated the differences between two types of humility. The two types are each characterized by a cluster of traits: general humility by social traits, and intellectual humility by a composite of traits that add up to a love of learning.

"We were happy to discover that intellectual humility seems to be a con-   20
cept that has its own place in the minds of the general population distinct from general humility," Samuelson told Justin Munce of *The Speaker* in an interview. "By the same token, there are many shared characteristics between an gener-ally humble person and an intellectually humble person in the folk conception (such as modesty) which we expected."

What surprised the researchers was that intellectual humility was distinctly   21
tied together with love of learning, curiosity, and a desire to seek the truth. These were not words used by participants to describe wise people; they were unique descriptors of people viewed as intellectually humble.

"Intellectual humility uniquely impacts how a person learns and acquires   22
new knowledge," Samuelson says. "While characteristics of general humility may help a person be willing to learn from others and open to new knowledge, the unique characteristics of intellectual humility—such as an understanding of the limits of one's knowledge, a search for the truth, a love of learning, among others—can motivate learning beyond what general humility can."

Samuelson adds that these qualities are "sorely needed in an era when in   23
every sector of our society people seem quite sure they are right and those who disagree with them are wrong, who seem to want to listen to people who will only confirm what they already know." More research is being carried out by Yale, Stanford, and Brown Universities.

In four recent studies, to be presented at APS in New York this May,   24
Kristi Lockhart, Mariel Goddu, and Frank Keil from Yale University examined developmental shifts in perceptions of boasting during childhood. They found that, unlike older age groups, young children endorsed telling everyone about positive accomplishments and were less likely to show a preference for humble peers over accomplished boasters.

"As children mature," the researchers report, "they come to see boasting as   25
distasteful. Dislike of boasting (and boasters) in childhood may foster a prefer-ence for intellectual humility as individuals grow."

The Stanford research group, which included Tenelle Porter, Karina   26
Schumann, Kali Trzesniewski, and Carol Dweck, conducted a series of studies
on the implications of intellectual humility for learning among adolescents and
adults. The researchers found that intellectual humility was associated with
more teacher-reported engagement, higher math grades, and greater growth
in math achievement among high school students.

"These results suggest that adolescents are capable of exhibiting and   27
benefitting from intellectual humility," the authors write.

The researchers also found that intellectually humble adults expressed   28
more openness to learning from those with the opposing socio-political view,
exposed themselves to more socio-political positions that conflicted with
theirs, and were more interested in studying all sides of important social issues,
"including emotionally charged issues such as immigration reform, affirmative
action, and capital punishment."

At Brown University, Mark Ho and Steven Sloman found that exposing   29
adults to the limitations of their knowledge (what they call the "Illusion of
Explanatory Depth") can help mitigate intellectually arrogant tendencies and
curb extreme political attitudes. For example, participants who were asked to
provide in-depth causal explanations for complex public policies subsequently
adopted more moderate political attitudes.

"Findings suggest that exposing people to the illusion of explanatory depth   30
by asking them to generate in-depth causal explanations may be one way to
encourage intellectual humility and, ultimately, civility," Ho and Sloman write.

Studies like these are just the beginning of a long line of research on the
benefits of intellectual humility for personal, educational, and professional growth.

Why We Must Teach Intellectual Humility

Jason Baehr, a philosophy professor at Loyola Marymount University and   31
co-founder of the Intellectual Virtues Academy, says the concept of intellectual
humility guides the way he teaches, as well as the way he raises his own children.

"As parents, we should create opportunities for kids to ask good, thoughtful, insightful questions," Baehr says. "We can model curiosity and give our   32
children opportunities to do the same. From a very young age, kids can understand qualities like curiosity, attentiveness and tenacity, and we have to help
them understand what they look like."

At the Academy, a list of "Master Examples" reminds his students that to   33
be intellectually humble is to be like Socrates.

But there are obstacles to adopting this practice in full.   34

One of them, says Ian James Kidd of Durham University, is the practi-   35
cal reality of modern education, which "creates sub-optimal conditions for
edifying education." Obvious examples, he says, include increasing course
sizes, bureaucratization of educational practice and policy, top-down impera-

tives, and the decline, especially in higher education, of one-on-one-teaching. "These developments erode the edifying, humanistic conception of education as an arena for the cultivation and exercise of the virtues that are, for Plato and for Confucius, the grounds of social and civic life."

Fortunately, some educators are managing to break free of these barriers.   36

Duncan Pritchard, Professor of Philosophy at the University of Edinburgh   37
and Director of the Eidyn Research Centre, currently leads two projects on the topic of intellectual humility: an Intellectual Humility MOOC and a research project aimed at developing an anti-individualistic version of virtue episte-mology and to explore the relationship between epistemic dependency and intellectual humility.

"The MOOC will bring together researchers from across the world from   38
such diverse fields as philosophy, psychology, education, and divinity to discuss, in an accessible manner, the issues raised by intellectual humility," Pritchard explained in an interview. "The hope is that this free online course will promote a broader public understanding of this notion."

One topic Pritchard has become especially interested in over the last few   39
years is how education has been informed by issues in cognitive science. It's here that he sees a lot of overlap with the topic of intellectual humility.

"Although we typically credit our cognitive skills with producing our cog-   40
nitive successes, in many cases such successes are not due to these skills at all, but rather due to situational factors. If that's right, then we are radically overestimating our cognitive abilities, and a large dose of intellectual humility is in order."

This is why he believes it's important to question how we should approach   41
the current model of education, with its focus on developing a subject's cog-nitive abilities. If we don't, we run the risk of squandering our students' full learning potential.

In his 2006 paper "Humility as a Virtue in Teaching," William Hare   42
acknowledges that many of us have denied humility as a virtue in teaching. Some of us may find the idea problematic in the context of establishing author-ity or building self-esteem. But these reservations have resulted in "narrow approaches to teaching, or have spawned simplistic solutions which confuse humility with outright skepticism," he says. Ultimately, Hare says, rejecting the notion of intellectual humility translates to rejecting reason, and to abandoning all respect for a student's education.

In the words of Samuelson, "Developing the virtue of intellectual humility   43
will not only help us learn, but also help us collaborate and learn from each other, and could move the needle toward more civil discourse in our society and ultimately finding the best solutions to our intractable problems."   44

What could be better than that?   45

UNDERSTANDING A WRITER'S GOALS: QUESTIONS TO CONSIDER AND DISCUSS

Rhetorical Knowledge: The Writer's Situation and Rhetoric

1. **Audience:** Do you think Briggs is writing for a general population, or does she have a more specific audience in mind? What makes you think so?

2. **Purpose:** Briggs sees a problem with the way many people approach learning, leading to a lack of intellectual humility. To address the problem, she explains the relationship between intellectual humility and love of learning. She also gives specific examples of how intellectual humility can be incorporated into a range of learning models. Do you think Briggs accomplishes her purpose? Why or why not?

3. **Voice and tone:** Briggs is writing about a serious problem: a lack of intellectual humility in today's classrooms, and so also in today's workplaces. Do you feel her tone is appropriate for her topic? Why or why not?

4. **Responsibility:** Briggs quotes more than a dozen sources in her text but does not provide a list of works cited. A works cited list would allow readers to locate and read those sources for more information. How does this lack of such a list affect Briggs's credibility?

5. **Context, format, and genre:** This essay originally appeared as an opinion piece on a Web site for educators interested in the latest trends and ideas applied to learning technologies. Can you identify what also makes this a piece of writing that looks for a solution to solve a problem? What makes you come to your conclusion?

Critical Thinking: The Writer's Ideas and Your Personal Response

6. As a student who is looking to enter the workforce in the future, or who is currently balancing school and work, how do you feel about the problem Briggs describes and

her proposed solutions? How would you judge your own level of intellectual humility? How do you think you can further develop it?

7. How would you define intellectual humility? What skills and attributes does someone need to possess to be considered intellectually humble? Do you agree that it's possible to develop these skills and attributes?

Composing Processes and Knowledge of Conventions: The Writer's Strategies

8. Since Briggs is presenting solutions that researchers like Ian Church and Peter Samuelson have identified during their years of working on the subject, readers need to get a sense of both Briggs' and her sources' *ethos* on this topic. How does Briggs establish both her own *ethos* and her other sources' as well?

9. Explain what strategy Briggs uses to establish that a problem exists within education. Then describe how she encourages her audience to agree that the problem exists.

Inquiry and Research: Ideas for Further Exploration

10. Check out the *Learning Technology Effectiveness* report published by the U.S. Department of Education's Office of Educational Technology (http://tech.ed.gov/learning-technology-effectiveness/). How does the government's estimation of how technology will necessarily aid education match up with what Briggs is saying?

11. Throughout her essay, Briggs presents some possible solutions for developing intellectual humility, including listening to others' viewpoints and remaining open to collaboration. Should Briggs have offered her readers more options? Are her suggestions enough to resolve the problem, in your opinion?

GENRES *Up Close* *Writing a Proposal*

Proposals often offer solutions to problems, but they also can suggest actions to take in situations where there is no real problem. For example, you can propose that you and your friends watch a particular sporting event or attend an upcoming concert. If you and your friends have similar tastes in sports or music, you may not have to support your proposal with reasons—for example, "This is being billed as the most competitive game of the season" or "I've heard it's the group's best concert yet."

Other kinds of proposals can outline future research projects, suggest ways to improve a company's already strong productivity, put forward ideas for enhancing an organization's marketing procedures, or seek funding for a research project. Such proposals are not designed to solve problems; instead, they suggest ways to seize opportunities.

Whether you are writing a proposal to solve a problem or to seize an opportunity, the genre features are similar. In particular, proposals do the following:

- Define a problem to be solved or an opportunity to be seized.
- Delineate a plan of action for solving the problem or seizing the opportunity.
- Make the case that the proposed solution is the most practical, feasible, and effective.
- Anticipate questions, objections, and alternative solutions/methods of seizing opportunities.
- Conclude with what the writer would like to happen next.

How does the following proposal memo fit these conventions?

AMY BASKIN AND HEATHER FAWCETT

MEMO   # Request for a Work Schedule Change

Amy Baskin is a freelance writer who has published in magazines such as *Canadian Parent, Canadian Living, Today's Parent, Canadian Family,* and *Education Today.* She has also taught children and adults for more than two decades.

Heather Fawcett is a writer and an advocate for children with special needs. Early in her career, she was a technical writer in the computer industry. Her textbook *Techniques for Technical Communicators* has been used on college and university campuses in Canada and the United States.

This proposal memo is excerpted from Baskin and Fawcett's book *More Than a Mom—Living a Full and Balanced Life When Your Child Has Special Needs.* www.morethanamom.net.

Do you or someone you know have flexible work hours? What benefits and problems can you see with such an arrangement?

Background

1   **K**aren works weekdays 9:00 to 5:30 as a technical writer for an aerospace plant. Karen's husband, Murray, doesn't start work until 9:30, but often must work late into the evening. They have two school-age children. Their younger, Helen, has cerebral palsy.

2   Karen would like to work flextime, so that she can be home with her daughters after school. That would allow her to schedule more therapy appointments for Helen, as well as help the girls with their homework. It would also save the family significant babysitting costs.

3   She will request a 6:00 a.m. to 2:30 p.m. workday.

Proposal Memo

To: John Doe
From: Karen MacDonald
Re: Request for Flextime
Date: May 17, 2006

4   As a team member of HI-Tech's Technical Writing Division for six years, I'd like to propose changing my work hours to 6:00 a.m. to 2:30 p.m., instead of 9:00 to 5:30.

5   I believe that, with this earlier schedule, I would be able to improve my written output by at least a third. As I'm sure you know, writing and editing requires a great deal of solitary concentration. Although I enjoy the camaraderie of our open-concept office, I am frequently disrupted by nearby phone calls and discussions. With the earlier schedule, I would have several hours to work without distraction before most of my coworkers arrive each day.

6   An earlier schedule would also allow me to schedule my daughter's medical appointments after work, meaning I'd be able to take significantly less time off, yet still see to her needs.

Overview of the memo—defines the problem/opportunity.

I feel that my work record as a reliable, selfdirected, and self-disciplined employee makes me an ideal candidate for flextime work.   7

Since I rarely interact directly with customers, customer service should not be compromised. Should an urgent matter arise after I'd left work for the day, I would still be accessible by cell phone.   8

My meetings with engineers can be easily rescheduled to take place before 2:30. I could still arrange to work a later schedule on days when my presence would be critical in the late afternoon—for example, if a client requested a 3:00 meeting.   9

To ensure success, I propose we meet weekly in the first month to review the arrangement. I would continue to report on my progress in weekly department meetings.   10

We can use the timelines currently in our product schedule to track my projects and measure productivity.   11

I would like to discuss this proposal with you further to address any potential concerns you might have. I understand that you are responsible for the success of this department and must determine whether this plan works for our team as a whole. I suggest a trial period of one month, after which the arrangement could be assessed and revised, if necessary. I understand that if the plan is not working, I might be required to return to my original schedule.   12

Delineates a plan of action to solve the problem/seize the opportunity.

Anticipates questions and objections.

Concludes with what the writer would like to happen next.

UNDERSTANDING A WRITER'S GOALS: QUESTIONS TO CONSIDER AND DISCUSS

Rhetorical Knowledge: The Writer's Situation and Rhetoric

1. **Audience:** The audience for Karen Mac-Donald's proposal memo is her supervisor. How has MacDonald shaped the memo to address the supervisor's needs?

2. **Purpose:** MacDonald's goal is stated in the "Re" line—she is requesting flextime. Besides announcing her goal with the phrase "Request for Flextime," what other phrases might be effective in the "Re" line?

3. **Voice and tone:** How does MacDonald's tone affect the persuasiveness of her proposal memo?

4. **Responsibility:** How does MacDonald demonstrate that she is a responsible parent and employee?

5. **Context, format, and genre:** If Mac-Donald had decided to make this request in a face-to-face meeting rather than in a memo, what would be different? If there is a follow-up meeting with her supervisor to discuss the proposal, what more might MacDonald say to strengthen her case? If MacDonald had written a letter rather than a memo to make her proposal, how would the letter differ from the memo?

Critical Thinking: The Writer's Ideas and Your Personal Response

6. If you were MacDonald's supervisor, how would you respond to her proposal? Why?

7. What is the most compelling section of MacDonald's proposal?

Composing Processes and Knowledge of Conventions: The Writer's Strategies

8. How does MacDonald address potential objections to her proposal? How effectively does she do that?

9. How does MacDonald establish her *ethos* in the proposal? How effectively does she do that?

Inquiry and Research: Ideas for Further Exploration

10. Conduct a Web search to see how some companies use flextime. Who seems to benefit from flextime?

WRITING PROCESSES

As you work on your assignment, remember the qualities of an effective proposal (see page 375). Also recall the recursive nature of the writing process—that is, after you engage in invention and conduct some research, you may start writing, or you may decide to do some more research. In fact, the more writing experience you get, the more you will realize that no piece of writing is ever finished until your final draft.

■ Invention: Getting Started

As with any writing that you do, the more invention activities that you can draw on, the more effective your paper will be. Try to answer these questions while you do your invention work:

- What do I already know about the problem?
- What possible solutions do I already have in mind to propose?
- Where might I learn more about this problem? What personal experience might I have that is relevant?
- What might my audience already know about this problem?
- What might their point of view be?
- What questions do I have about the problem or about possible solutions?

Writing Activity

Freewriting

eeping the questions above in mind, freewrite to jot down everything you know about the problem. Be sure to list any questions you still have as well. Your freewriting and listing should give you a good sense of what research you still need to conduct. Once you jot down what you know about the problem, you not only can focus on what else you need to understand about it (through more research), but you also can start thinking about possible solutions. Do not worry about putting what you know, what questions you have, and so on into complete sentences; the idea is to get down on paper or in a computer fi le everything you know about the problem and potential solutions. That invention work will give you a useful starting point.

For more on freewriting and other strategies for discovery and learning, see Chapter 4.

Susan DeMedeiros's Freewriting

Student writer Susan DeMedeiros decided to look at the problem of identity theft caused by illegal skimming devices—as well as solutions to this problem. She began with the following short piece of freewriting:

> Who would have ever thought I'd have my identity stolen on vacation? And that I wouldn't even realize it until my husband and I got home? I never expected to

be a victim of a crime—especially a crime that was also taking place in our safe and comfortable suburb of Santa Clara, California. Yet that's exactly what happened. My husband and I both had our cards skimmed at a hotel restaurant. We were just like the unfortunate supermarket customers at a Lucky grocery store who used a self-service checkout machine that had an illegal skimming device embedded in it. I think consumers need to know how to protect themselves from this kind of identity theft.

Exploring Your Ideas with Research

Once you have used invention techniques to decide on a problem and explore what you know about it, you need to conduct research to investigate the problem further and develop possible solutions to it.

Although your own experience may provide some evidence for the effectiveness of your proposed solution, personal experience usually needs to be supplemented by other forms of evidence: quotations from experts, examples, statistics, and estimates of the time and financial resources needed to implement the solution drawn from reliable sources. One way to organize your research is to use the qualities of effective proposals to guide your research activities. Here are some possibilities:

- **A clearly defined problem:** As you do research on your problem, look at how others have defined it and narrowed it to make it more manageable.

- **An awareness of the audience:** Your research should give you a sense of how other writers have defined and addressed their audiences. Also, you should note how other writers have treated people's perceptions of the problem that you are trying to solve. What do they assume that people know about the problem? What do they assume that people do not know about the problem? How much do they assume that people care about the problem?

- **A well-articulated solution:** For most kinds of problems in the world, you will not be the first person to propose solutions. Look at how other writers have articulated their solutions.

- **Convincing evidence for the solution's effectiveness:** You will need to find evidence that your proposed solution is viable. Look for expert testimony, the results of experimental research, and case studies.

- **A well-documented review of alternative solutions:** You cannot be certain that your proposed solution is the most effective one unless you have carefully reviewed a range of possible solutions. As you consider them, keep an open mind—you might find a solution that is more effective than the one that you first offered.

- **A call to action:** As you do your research, look at the language that other writers have used to inspire their readers to action.

For advice on conducting primary research, see Chapter 19.

USING DIGITAL TECHNOLOGIES | **Conducting Primary Research Online**

Your writing about problems and solutions can be improved if you investigate the kinds of solutions that would satisfy the larger community. To do so, you can use online resources to conduct primary research. To collect data or feedback from members of the community that will be affected by your solution, you can create a survey to collect their opinions, observations, and ideas, either by developing a simple e-mail distribution list and sending a small number of questions to targeted respondents or taking advantage of free spaces for collecting peoples' opinions and reactions on popular sites such as Facebook, Twitter, or Survey-Monkey.

Writing Activity

Conducting Research

Using the list of qualities for effective writing to solve problems, begin by listing what you already know about the problem and potential solutions. Then note what research you still need to conduct and possible sources to consult.

Susan DeMedeiros's Notes on Her Research

Reminder to self: Don't forget to include all the citations for the sources that I'm planning to use. Do this for everything or I'll be sorry later.

A clearly defined problem: I learned about the problem first-hand by being a victim. I can see from information in the news and by talking to people at my bank that it's a big problem. However, to get more hard data the U.S. Bureau of Justice Statistics looks like a good place to check.

An awareness of the audience: I think that I have a pretty good handle on the audience for this; it's pretty much everyone who uses credit cards and debit cards. However, I should look at how others have addressed audiences. I think I can get an idea of this by looking at the articles in local and national newspapers.

A well-articulated solution: I need to read a little more here and talk to more people. I also want to think about this a little more. I have sort of a sense of what might be a possible solution, but I need to think about how to write about it. I definitely want to see what the professional law enforcement agencies and bank security experts have to say.

Convincing evidence for the solution's effectiveness: Here I need to read what people with multiple perspectives are writing. If I do that, I'll have more options at a potential solution. That article that talks about a former skimmer should help here. I also need to figure out if sites like Mint.com provide greater security or put you more at risk.

A well-documented review of alternative solutions: If I don't look at a range of solutions, I might miss a really good solution. I need to keep an open mind. Also, I'm aware the best solution for me might not be the best solution for everyone.

A call to action: I'll rely a lot on others here. I'll see how others have called for action—and how folks have responded to those calls. I think that conversations with the bank and police department will include calls to action.

STUDENT WRITING EXAMPLES

Brainstorming (pp. 177, 343)

Freewriting (pp. 134, 256, 344, 393)

Criteria (p. 300)

Listing (p. 97)

Answers to Reporter's Questions (p. 256)

Organization (pp. 98, 182, 647)

Clustering (pp. 135, 298)

Interviewing (p. 216)

Research (pp. 136, 137, 178, 179, 217, 218, 258, 259, 302, 343, 346, 396, 396)

Reflection (p. 12)

For more on developing a thesis, see Chapter 13.

Reviewing Your Invention and Research

After finding sources and reading them critically, reconsider your thinking about your problem and your proposed solution in light of the qualities of an effective solution. Also begin thinking about a tentative thesis—your statement of your proposed solution. Keep an open mind, though. As you draft and revise your proposal, you may continue to refine your thesis. In some cases, you might even change it drastically. People who develop the best solutions usually leave open the possibility that a better solution could occur to them at any time.

Susan DeMedeiros Considers Her Research and Focuses Her Ideas

After reading through various sources and taking notes, DeMedeiros wrote the following in her research journal:

> My reading has given me a better handle on the problem and its possible solutions. I think I'm ready to state that the best solution is text alerts, though I understand that there are other options. Even though I'm recommending text alerts, I'll mention the other options.

Strategies FOR Success | Flexibility

Successful writers are flexible, especially when they are proposing a solution to a problem. Often when looking at a problem and then proposing a solution, writers may be tempted to fall back on their preconceived ideas. However, successful writers are flexible enough to put aside their own preconceived perspectives and to be honest about the scope and magnitude of the problem. Once they are willing to do so, they may become aware of solutions that never would have occurred to them otherwise.

Likewise, it's important to be flexible about a range of viable solutions and to evaluate carefully the effectiveness, affordability, and limitations of each. By being flexible in this way, you establish your credibility with your readers by demonstrating that you have thoroughly investigated a range of solutions and have made a carefully considered recommendation. By presenting each option fairly and by showing how *your* solution is the best, you also make your own position more credible and believable.

▮ Organizing Your Information

Once you know the problem you will be writing about and the solution you will be proposing, you need to consider how you might organize this material. Here are some questions to ask yourself:

- Who is your audience?
- Why might they be concerned about the problem you are discussing, and why might they be willing to accept your solution? Is it in your audience's best interest to find a solution for your problem?

- What is your purpose for writing—that is, why do your readers need this solution?
- What is the most important aspect of the problem you are proposing to solve?

One method for organizing a solution to a problem is the **whole-problem pattern.** If you are following this pattern, you first grab the readers' attention and introduce the problem and then use the paragraphs that follow to explain and illustrate it. If you think that readers are already familiar with the problem, this part of the paper could be fairly short, consisting of only a paragraph or two. If you think that readers are not familiar with the problem, however, then you might need to devote several pages to explaining and illustrating it. Then offer your proposed solution or set of solutions, respond to objections that you think readers might have, and conclude with a call to action.

A second organizational approach is to **segment the problem.** This approach is useful if the problem is relatively complex and has several components. First, you explain and illustrate the problem, but in a general way. Next, you focus on each part of the problem that needs special attention, offering a solution and responding to objections that you anticipate that are specific to each part. Finally, you offer suggestions for implementation and conclude with a call to action.

A third organizational approach, which involves a **sequence of steps,** is appropriate if the solution has multiple steps. After introducing the problem, you offer an overview of a series of steps that will solve the problem. You then explain each step in detail, provide evidence that it will work, and address any objections to it.

Here is a summary of these three organizational structures.

Options FOR Organization
Organizing a Proposal Essay

Whole-Problem Pattern	Segmenting the Problem	Sequence of Steps
Introduce the problem and its background.	Introduce the problem and its background.	Introduce the problem and its background.
Explain the problem.	Explain the problem.	Explain the problem.
Offer a solution or set of solutions.	Explain one part of the problem, offer a solution, and respond to objections.	Offer a multistep solution with an overview of the steps.
Respond to anticipated objections to the solution.	Explain another part, offer a solution, and respond to objections.	Offer a detailed explanation of the first step.
Offer suggestions for implementing the solution.	Deal similarly with remaining parts.	Offer a detailed explanation of the second step.
Conclude with a call to action.	Offer suggestions for implementing the solution.	Deal with any additional steps that might be necessary.
	Conclude with a call to action.	Conclude with a call to action.

Constructing a Complete Draft

Once you have chosen the organizational approach that works best given your audience and purpose, you are ready to construct your draft. Remember that your thinking about the problem and its solution(s) will evolve as you write, so as you work on the draft, keep the following in mind:

- Draw on your invention work and your research. As you draft, you may discover that you need to do more invention work and/or more research.
- As you try out tentative solutions to the problem, ask peers about the kinds of evidence you need to demonstrate that the solution is viable.
- Ask yourself and peers whether visuals might help make your case.

Synthesizing and Integrating Sources into Your Draft: Including Research Information

If you are working on a large research assignment, you will end up with a wealth of information, so using that information in your text can be a challenge: How can you condense it to help the reader understand it? This problem is especially acute when some of your research comes from texts that provide you with a large amount of information. One way to condense such research is to summarize what you learn and then to use those summaries in your text (for more on summarizing, see page 554).

When faced with a mountain of information, student writers often try to use it all—and so the information overwhelms the text. The student has turned over control of the text to the ideas from the sources she or he found, and the text is no longer the writer's. You can avoid giving up control of your text by using summaries of information from sources to support your claims.

After gathering extensive information provided by the U.S. Bureau of Justice Statistics, Susan DeMedeiros might have been tempted to take on the entire problem of identity theft, a huge subject. However, since she was herself a victim of a skimming machine, similar to what had happened in her local supermarket, she was able to concentrate on this one particular method of identity theft and avoid the temptation of trying to attack the entire problem. Doing so helped DeMedeiros select the most important ideas and present that information to her readers in an understandable manner.

To get a better handle on the information she had learned and what part of that information she wanted to present to her readers, DeMedeiros summarized what she felt would be important for her readers to know. She was able to use her summaries as she began to draft her paper. Here is an example of what DeMedeiros summarized:

> I didn't realize the extent of identity theft until I found myself to be a victim. What was even worse was my bank tried to notify me by leaving voicemail on my home phone, but that happened when I was on vacation. I've since learned

that I was a victim of a skimming machine that had been placed in a card reader at a hotel restaurant. I've since learned that there are at least five different steps to take to protect yourself from identity theft:

- Pay close attention to card readers (Service, n.d.).

- Monitor all accounts using a consolidated service such as Mint.com (Crouch, 2011).

- Educate yourself about identity theft and ways to prevent it (Federal, 2012).

- Shred bills, receipts, and bank statements (Shapiro, 2012).

- Set up message alerts that inform you of unauthorized account transactions (Ayala, 2012).

Note that DeMedeiros has defined the problem and her personal connection with it and then lists the potential solutions in a format—a summary—that makes them clear and understandable to the reader. DeMedeiros will end up recommending the final solution she lists.

To use summaries in your writing, do the following:

- Introduce the summarized information (never just put it into your text without some of your words as an introduction).

- Connect the summary back to your main point, so your readers can easily see how the summarized information supports your argument.

- Accurately report and document where the information came from.

See Chapter 20 for more on documenting sources using MLA or APA style.

Parts of a Complete Draft

Introduction: Regardless of your organizational approach, begin with a strong introduction to capture your readers' attention and introduce the problem that you are proposing to solve. To accomplish these two goals, you might do one or more of the following:

- **Provide a brief history of the problem.**

- **Quote an authority who knows the problem well.** Early on in her article, Briggs quotes Google's vice president of hiring on the correlation between humility and professional success.

- **Cite salient statistics that demonstrate the nature of the problem.** Vallas and Boteach begin their report by citing statistics showing that progress toward improving the lives of poor and middle-income families has stagnated.

- **Provide information about the problem that will surprise—and possibly concern—readers.** Susan DeMeideros begins her article (page 409) by stating that "In 2010, 8.6 million households had at least one person who was a victim of identity theft."

Body: When you propose a solution to a problem, you should determine the most effective organizational approach for the purpose you are trying to achieve and the audience you are addressing. The reading selections in this chapter, for example, use the organizational approaches outlined on page 397 to good effect. Whether you present a whole problem, segment the problem, or give a step-by-step solution, be sure to show why other solutions will not work or have already failed. Sometimes a problem has not been solved because previous solutions addressed only its symptoms, not its root cause. If this is the case, you need to show that your solution will take care of the root problem.

- **Present a whole problem and then give solutions.** Student writer DeMedeiros outlines a national problem—identity theft—and then shows how it is a local problem, provides historical background information, and then suggests what consumers must do to protect themselves.
- **Give a segmented view of the problem and solutions.** Vallas and Boteach briefly outline the problem of stagnating wages for what we call the middle class. Then they detail ten "solutions" that, even if enacted individually, mght improve parts of the problem.

Conclusion: In your conclusion, review your proposed solution, reach out to your audience, and, usually, call for readers to take action to implement the proposal. Your conclusion could include the following:

- An outline of the problem you are working to solve
- A summary of your main points, with an explanation of why your solution would work
- A call to action—what you would like your reader to *do* now that he or she knows about the problem and your suggested solution

Title: As you compose your proposal, a title should emerge at some point—often very late in the process. The title should, of course, reflect the problem that you are addressing and might or might not hint at the solution. If you hint at a controversial solution in the title, however, you risk alienating readers whom you might otherwise win over with the strength of your argument.

Writing Activity

Constructing a Complete Draft

After reviewing your notes, invention activities, and research, and carefully considering the possible solutions you have generated, write a complete first draft of your paper. Be sure to explain your problem in detail and to outline your solution and explain why it is the best way to solve the problem your paper focuses on.

Susan DeMedeiros's First Draft

In her first draft, note how Susan DeMedeiros presents the problem to her audience. As she wrote, DeMedeiros did not worry about grammar, usage, punctuation, and mechanics; instead, she concentrated on getting her main ideas into her draft. (The numbers in circles refer to peer comments, which follow the student draft on page 406.)

VISUAL *Thinking* | Going Beyond Words to Achieve Your Goals

While researching her proposal on preventing identity theft, Susan DeMedeiros found the report "Identity Theft Reported by Households, 2005–2010" on the Web site of the Bureau of Justice Statistics, a part of the U.S. Department of Justice. Along with other statistical data, she found the following figures and table shown below and on page 402.

You can see that these three visuals, for the most part, present the same information in three different formats: a table, a stacked bar chart, and a line graph.

Type of identity theft experienced by victimized households, and total financial loss attributed to each type of identity theft, 2010

| | | Financial Loss | |
Types of identity theft	Percent of identify theft victimizations*	Total loss (in thousands)	Percent of total loss
All types	100.0%	$13,257,487	100.0%
Existing credit card	54.0	$4,214,848	31.8
Other existing account	25.6	$2,306,165	17.4
Personal information	9.0	$3,901,016	29.4
Multiple types	11.4	$2,835,459	21.4

*Percent of identity theft victimizations by type of theft does not match the percentages by type shown in Figure 2 due to the inclusion of the multiple types category.

Percent of households that experienced identity theft, by type of theft, 2005, 2007, 2009, and 2010

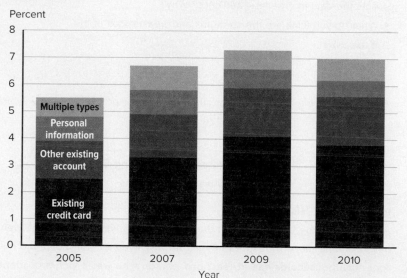

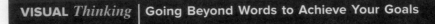

VISUAL *Thinking* │ **Going Beyond Words to Achieve Your Goals**

Household identity theft victimizations, 2005, 2007, 2009, and 2010

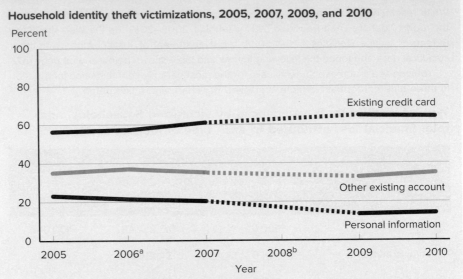

aDue to methodological changes in the 2006 NCVS, use caution when comparing 2006 criminal victimizaton estimates to other years. See Criminal Victimization, 2006, http://www.bjs.gov, for more information.

bAnnual estimates are not available for 2008 because six months of identity theft data were collected.

From "Identity Theft Reported by Households, 2005–2010," by L Langton, November 2011, Crime Data Brief, Bureau of Justice Statistics, U.S. Department of Justice. Retrieved from http://bjs.ojp.usdoj.gov/content/pub/pdf/itrh0510.pdf

- Which of these three visual representations do you think most effectively presents the data to a general audience? Why?

- What do you think are the strengths and weaknesses of the

  - bar chart

  - line graph

  - table

- Which do you think DeMedeiros should use in her proposal? (To see which one she did use, turn to page 411.)

Staying Ahead of Skimming Scams
Susan DeMedeiros

Identity Theft History ➊

According to the U.S. Bureau of Justice Statistics, various forms of identity theft have become more widespread over the past five years. In 2010, 8.6 million American households had at least one person who was a victim of identity theft. Five years earlier, in 2005, persons in 6.4 million households were victimized

(Langton, 2011). In 2012, "approximately 16.6 million persons or 7% of all U.S. residents age 16 or older, were victims of one or more incidents of identity theft" (Harrell & Langton, 2013). This increase is primarily due to the growing unauthorized use of credit and debit cards. Identity theft is defined by the Bureau of Justice as having three components: unauthorized use of credit and debit cards, fraudulently impersonating another for the purpose of opening new accounts, and a combination of the two components. It is a global problem. ❷

What Is Skimming?

Criminals use a tactic called "skimming" to steal personal information from consumers who swipe their cards at locations such as ATMs, grocery stores, and gas pumps. Skimming is when thieves attach data reading devices on digital card readers either internally or externally, or use handheld magnetic readers to collect the personal data stored in the magnetic stripe on the back of credit or debit cards. They then sell this data to higher-end criminals who use encoders to transfer consumers' data to counterfeit cards, which they, in turn, sell for up to $100. (Paganini, 2014). This creates a nightmare for the consumer. Not only does this create fraudulent charges on their credit cards, it swiftly wipes out cash from their bank accounts.

My Story

Visiting New York was a trip my husband and I had looked forward to for many months. I was excited about experiencing the energy of the Big Apple and shopping on 5th Avenue. My husband could not wait to listen to jazz music at the Village Vanguard. We stayed in a nice hotel on Long Island, and took the railroad into the city each day. When we returned home to California, there was a voice mail message from our bank to contact them regarding possible fraud on our account. I went online to view our bank account and discovered, to my horror, there were hundreds of dollars missing. I informed my bank that they were indeed fraudulent transactions. My husband's debit card was skimmed as well. Both cards were skimmed at the hotel restaurant where we had stayed, as we later discovered. The excitement from our vacation was replaced by anger and shock. Thieves ruined our vacation.

What Consumers Can Do

There are several possible solutions to this problem for consumers to consider:
- Pay close attention to card readers (Service, 2012).
- Monitor all accounts using a consolidated service such as Mint.com (Schultz).
- Educate yourself about identity theft and ways to prevent it (Federal, 2012).
- Shred bills, receipts and bank statements (Shapiro, 2012).
- Set up message alerts that inform you of unauthorized account transactions (Ayala, 2012).

Let's examine each one of these options . . .

The U.S. Secret Service suggests paying close attention to card readers.
Although it is important to know what a tampered device may look like, there have been card readers found with no external modifications such as the ones removed from Lucky grocery stores in California. Those units had internal cameras and electronics added to the circuitry that were discovered by the grocery employees during scheduled machine maintenance only after the units were opened. In such cases, the consumer would not see any difference in the external view of the card reader and would not know if it had been tampered with (Service, 2012).

Former skimmer suggests monitoring your accounts using Mint.com.
Convicted skimmer Dan DeFelippe now helps the government fight identity theft. Although he makes an important point of being vigilant about monitoring bank account activity, consolidating accounts at Mint.com has its drawbacks. At Mint.com, the user is required to provide all of their user names and passwords, so this solution may not be safe enough for the consumer even though the company claims they encrypt the data stored on their servers (Schultz). Providing private account log in data and passwords to an outside company makes sensitive data vulnerable to a breach. Furthermore, referring consumers to outside account consolidation services does not respond directly to consumer actions against card skimming at point of sale purchases.

The Federal Trade Commission promotes consumer education.
The Federal Trade Commission does indeed have an informative website www.ftc.gov, which offers the consumers a plethora of helpful information. However, if credit or debit cards have been compromised due to skimming of digital card readers, the FTC offers solutions only after the consumer has been notified of the breach by their respective financial institutions (Federal, 2012).

The Santa Clara Police Department suggests shredding sensitive documents.
The SCPD focuses on careful handling of paper items such as shredding bills, receipts, bank statements, and watching your mail (Shapiro, 2012).

The Best Solution? ❸

Message Alerts
Wells Fargo Bank suggests message alerts delivered to your email or mobile device. Wells Fargo Bank offers customers the best solution to protect their accounts. The Rapid Alerts program offers consumers free message alerts delivered by email or text. Alerts notify customers instantly of transactions to their accounts. This empowers consumers to take action should they see unauthorized activity (Ayala, 2012).

- Consumers can instantly detect fraudulent transactions and take immediate action.
- Rapid Alerts identify the merchant, date, amount, and location.
- Transactions originating from international locations are instantly identified
- Consumers are instantly alerted of online purchases, ATM withdrawals, and telephone transactions.

Are message alerts effective?

According to a Wells Fargo press release (2011), "Rapid Alerts allow consumers to better manage and track their consumer credit card spending while also providing them with near real-time detection of potentially fraudulent activity." However, it is important to remember that there are limitations with such an option:

Why would receiving a text message be the solution to focus on?

What is the point if the thieves already have my card data?

What do message alerts NOT do?

Message alerts do not prevent someone from opening new accounts in your name. Message alerts do not lock or close your account. It's up to you to take action. ❹

Solution	Benefit	Cost ❺
Look for fake card readers	You choose not to swipe your card if the reader looks suspicious. The benefit is that your card is not tampered with if you don't swipe it.	Many card skimming devices are internal and cannot be seen externally, so the cost is not using your card at pay-point locations.
Consolidate accounts on Mint.com	One stop shopping. Monitor all of your accounts on one site.	Loss of privacy and security of your user names and passwords carries risk of breaching all your accounts.
Sign up for credit reports	Can view activity to see if someone is opening up accounts in your name, or using your cards fraudulently.	From $12.00 to $40.00 per month. Reports are sent monthly or quarterly, not instantly.
Shred mail	Thieves cannot go through trash and retrieve your personal data to open accounts of their own if your mail is shredded.	Shredders and shredding services run from $25 to thousands of dollars depending on the level of quality. Shredding has no impact on card skimming.
Monitor accounts and bank statements	Keeps you up to date with the status of your accounts.	Fraud can occur at anytime day or night. The consumer won't know when it happens and can miss it unless they go into their bank sites constantly, which is impractical.
Text and E-mail alerts	Instant notification of unusual activity monitored by the bank. Activity can be quickly ceased and reimbursed.	No cost courtesy service offered by most banks and financial institutions. Set up takes minutes and can be done online.

The point is this . . . ❻

1. Text message alerts are the first line of defense. You will be alerted the moment unusual activity occurs.

2. Bank software programs keep track of your purchasing habits and can detect when activity does not fit your patterns.

3. Without message alerts, if your card is compromised, the potential for thieves to charge up your account or deplete your cash increases as time ticks on. ❼, ❽, ❾

Student Comments on Susan DeMedeiros' First Draft

❶ "You probably need an introduction that grabs our attention more than this does."

❷ "I think some kind of graphic might help explain all these numbers."

❸ "Why isn't the 'most effective solution' in with the other solutions?"

❹ "I really like the way you present information in this table but is it in the best place?"

❺ "Sometimes your benefit and your cost seem like they're saying the same thing."

❻ "These are important points. Is this the best way to introduce them?"

❼ "You need some sort of conclusion to tie things up more."

❽ "Of course, in your revised version, you'll need to include all of your citations."

❾ "Why are you using numbers here instead of bullet points like you use everywhere else?"

Revising

Once you have a draft, put it aside for a day or so. This break will give you the chance to come back to your text as a new reader might. Reread and revise your work, looking especially for ideas that are not explained completely, terms that are not defined, and other problem areas. As you work to revise your early drafts, postpone doing a great deal of heavy editing. When you revise, you will probably change the content and structure of your paper, so time spent working to fix problems with sentence style or grammar, punctuation, or mechanics at this stage is often wasted.

As you revise, here are some questions to ask yourself:

• How effectively have I explained and outlined the problem(s), so my readers can understand those issues?

• What else might my audience want or need to know about my subject?

• How might I explain my solution(s) in sufficient detail and with enough examples so my readers can see how my ideas are logical solutions to the problem?

- How clearly have I explained and defined any terms my readers might not know?
- What other visual aids might help explain the problem and/or my solution(s)?

Responding to Readers' Comments

Once you have received feedback from your classmates, your instructor, and others about how to improve your text, you have to determine what to *do* with their suggestions and ideas. The first thing to do with any feedback is to really listen to it and consider carefully what your readers have to say. For example, how might Susan DeMedeiros have responded to these reader suggestions?

- One reader was not drawn in by DeMedeiros's introduction. When a peer reviewer indicates that an introduction does not excite him or her, that comment means that *some* readers might just stop reading at that point.
- Another reader asked about the possibility of using a graphic to help explain data.
- A reader requested a conclusion that ties all of DeMedeiros's information together.

WRITER'S *Workshop* | Responding to Full Drafts

Working with one or two other classmates, read each paper and offer comments and questions that will help each of you see your papers' strengths and weaknesses. Consider the following questions as you do:

- What is your first impression of this draft? How effectively does the title draw you into the paper? What part(s) of the text are especially effective at explaining the problem or the writer's proposed solution?

- How successfully does the introduction grab readers' attention? What other attention grabbers might the writer try?

- How well has the writer explained the problem to someone who is unfamiliar with it? How might the writer explain it more effectively?

- How effective is the organizational approach?

- How carefully did the writer document sources in this draft?

- How well has the writer explained the proposed solution(s)?

- How well has the writer addressed objections that skeptics might raise?

- How has the writer suggested ways to implement the proposed solution(s)?

- Might visuals help the writer to present the problem or its solution(s) more effectively?

- How effectively does the conclusion call people to action?

- What do you see as the main weaknesses of this paper? How might the writer improve the text?

All of these questions or concerns were issues that DeMedeiros needed to address.

As with any feedback, it is important to listen to it carefully and consider what your reader has to say. Then it is up to you, as the author, to decide *how* to deal with these suggestions. You may decide to reject some of them and respond to others. You may find that comments from more than one reader contradict each other. In that case, you need to use your own judgment to decide which reader's comments are on the right track.

In the final version of her paper on pages 409–416, you can see how Susan DeMedeiros responded to her readers' comments, as well as to her own review of her first draft.

KNOWLEDGE OF CONVENTIONS

By paying attention to conventions when they edit their work, effective writers help to meet their readers' expectations. Experienced readers expect proposals to follow accepted conventions.

Editing

When you edit and polish your writing, you make changes to improve your style and to make your writing clearer and more concise. You also check your work to make sure it adheres to conventions of grammar, usage, punctuation, mechanics, and spelling. If you have used sources in your paper, make sure you are following the documentation style your instructor requires.

Because it can be difficult to identify small problems in a familiar text, it often helps to distance yourself from it so that you can approach the draft with fresh eyes. Some people like to put the text aside for a day or so; others try reading aloud; and some even read from the last sentence to the first so that the content, and their familiarity with it, doesn't cause them to overlook an error. We strongly recommend that you ask classmates, friends, and tutors to read your work to help find editing problems.

To assist you with editing, we offer here a round-robin editing activity on inclusive language.

WRITER'S *Workshop* | **Round-Robin Editing with a Focus on Inclusive Language**

When you propose solutions to problems, be especially careful to use inclusive language—language that does not exclude people based on gender, ethnicity, marital status, or disability. Using inclusive language makes readers feel that they are included in the group that is solving the problem.

Look for instances in your work where you may have inadvertently used language that excludes a group based on gender, ethnicity, marital status, or disability. If you are uncertain about whether a particular word or phrase is a problem, consult a grammar handbook or ask your instructor.

> **ROUND-ROBIN EDITING WITH A FOCUS ON**
>
> Fragments (p. 146)
> Modifiers (p. 190)
> Wordiness (p. 228)
> Citing Sources (p. 270)
> Careful Word Choice (p. 313)
> Subordinate Clauses (p. 357)
> Inclusive Language (p. 409)

Genres, Documentation, and Format

If you are writing an academic paper in response to Scenarios 1 or 2, you will need to follow the conventions appropriate for the discipline in which you are writing. For Scenario 3, you may need to follow the conventions of a formal proposal.

For advice on writing in different genres, see Appendix C. For guidelines for formatting and documenting papers in MLA or APA style, see Chapter 20.

A Writer Achieves Her Goal: Susan DeMedeiros' Final Draft

Below is the final draft of Susan DeMedeiros' proposal. As you read her essay, consider whether you think her solutions will work.

SUSAN DEMEDEIROS

Staying Ahead of Skimming Scams

PROPOSAL ESSAY

Abstract

On November 11, 2011, California-based Lucky grocery stores discovered   1
skimming devices embedded in their self-service check-out machines during routine maintenance. Readers in 24 stores in California were breached. Two of them were in my community, and one is at the store where I shop regularly. This incident is the inspiration for my topic for this project. I interviewed the Santa Clara store manager where the tampering occurred, the police, and the local Wells Fargo Bank for their perspective and advice. In

One of DeMedeiros's classmates made the following comment on her initial draft:

You probably need an introduction that grabs our attention more than this does.

DeMedeiros responded with a new opening paragraph that attempts to catch the reader's attention by presenting the situation that led to her interest in the topic.

addition to offering members of the public what I think is the best solution to protect their assets, I include statistical data on the prevalence of identity theft, information on card skimming, and a list of other possible solutions.

Staying Ahead of Skimming Scams

Santa Clara, California, is one of the safest places to live, but it is not immune to card skimming thieves. In November 2011, store employees discovered tampered card readers in check-out stands at the Lucky grocery store on Saratoga Avenue (S. Fein, personal communication, February 4, 2012). These card readers contained internal skimming devices that recorded credit and debit card data the moment they were swiped. Local shoppers were swindled out of thousands of dollars, but this turned out to be more than a local problem. Skimming devices were discovered in 24 Lucky stores throughout California (Delevett, 2011; Tumposky, 2011). In fact, these scams are a growing issue nationwide. Take Florida, for example, where recently 103 skimming devices were found in gas pumps across the state (Korn & Dendy, 2015). 2

Individuals need to learn how to protect themselves from this growing problem. These days, people use credit and debit cards regularly at pay-point locations such as grocery stores, gas pumps, ATMs, and movie theaters. To protect themselves, consumers should be vigilant and know what to do to avoid becoming victims of fraud. Several solutions are available, all of them outlined below, but the one that is most effective is setting up text and e-mail alerts that instantly notify consumers the moment an unauthorized transaction is attempted on their accounts. This solution is not only fast, easy, and inexpensive, it is critical. 3

Identity Theft History

According to the U.S. Bureau of Justice Statistics, various forms of identity theft have become more widespread over the past several years. In 2005, persons in 6.4 million American households had at least one person who was a victim of identity theft; by 2010, that number had risen to 8.6 million households (Langton, 2011). As of 2012, the most recent year for which such data are available, "approximately 16.6 million persons or 7% of all U.S. residents age 16 or older, were victims of one or more incidents of identity theft" (Harrell & Langton, 2013). This increase is primarily due to the growing unauthorized use of credit and debit cards. Identity theft is defined by the Bureau of Justice as having three components: unauthorized use of credit and debit cards, fraudulently impersonating another for the purpose of opening new accounts, and a combination of the two components. It is a global problem. We can see the growth of identity theft from 2005 to 2010 (no similar graphic data are available for 2012) in the chart from the U.S. Bureau of Justice Statistics shown in Figure 1 (Langton, 2011). 4

DeMedeiros received this comment from a classmate:

I think some kind of graphic might help explain all these numbers.

Her response was to add this graphic.

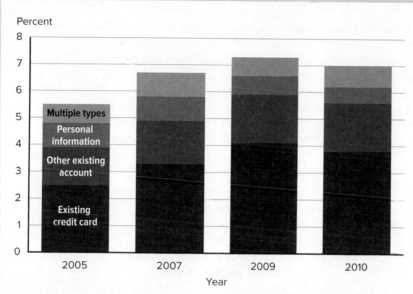

Percent

Fig. 1 Percent of households that experienced identity theft, by type of identity theft, 2005, 2007, 2009, and 2010. From "Identity Theft Reported by Households, 2005–2010," by L. Langton, November 2011, *Crime Data Brief*, Bureau of Justice Statistics, U.S. Department of Justice. Retrieved from http://bjs.ojp.usdoj.gov/content/pub/pdf/itrh0510.pdf

What Is Skimming?

Criminals use a tactic called "skimming" to steal personal information from consumers who swipe their cards at locations such as ATMs, grocery stores, and gas pumps. Skimming happens when thieves attach data-reading devices to digital card readers, either internally or externally, or use handheld magnetic readers to collect the personal data stored in the magnetic strip on the back of credit or debit cards. They then sell these data to higher-end criminals who use encoders to transfer consumers' data to counterfeit cards, which they, in turn, sell for up to $100. (Paganini, 2014). This results in a nightmare for the consumer. Not only does skimming create fraudulent charges on their credit cards, it swiftly wipes out cash from their bank accounts.

My Story

I have had my own experience with this type of identity theft. Visiting New York was a trip my husband and I had looked forward to for many months. I was excited about experiencing the energy of the Big Apple and shopping on 5th Avenue. My husband could not wait to listen to jazz music at the Village Vanguard. We stayed in a comfortable hotel on Long Island and took the

5

6

railroad into the city each day. When we returned home to California, there was a voicemail message from our bank asking us to contact them regarding possible fraud on our account. I went online to view our bank account and discovered, to my horror, that hundreds of dollars were missing. I informed my bank that the transactions were indeed fraudulent. My husband's debit card had been skimmed as well. We later discovered that both of our cards had been skimmed at the restaurant of the hotel where we had stayed. Thieves had caused the excitement from our vacation to be replaced by anger and shock.

What Consumers Can Do

Consumers can consider several possible solutions to this problem. Each of these options has advantages and disadvantages, as indicated by the following review and table:

The U.S. Secret Service suggests paying close attention to card readers.

Although it is important to know what a tampered device may look like, some card readers have no external modifications, such as the ones removed from Lucky grocery stores in California. Those units, which had internal cameras and electronics added to the circuitry, were discovered by the grocery employees during scheduled machine maintenance only after the units were opened. In such cases, the consumer would not see any difference in the external view of the card reader and would not know if it had been tampered with (U.S. Secret Service, 2012).

A former skimmer suggests monitoring your accounts using *Mint.com*.

Convicted skimmer Dan DeFelippe (Crouch, 2011) now helps the government fight identity theft. Although he makes an important point about being vigilant and monitoring all bank account activity, consolidating accounts at *Mint.com* (a Web site that manages money and monitors all of its users' financial accounts) has its drawbacks. At *Mint.com*, the user is required to provide the user names and passwords to all of their accounts, so this solution may not be safe enough for the consumer even though the company claims they encrypt the data stored on their servers (Duffy, 2013; Schultz, 2010). Providing private account log-in data and passwords to an outside company makes sensitive data vulnerable to a breach. Furthermore, outside account consolidation services do not protect consumers directly from card skimming during point-of-sale purchases.

The Federal Trade Commission promotes consumer education.

The Federal Trade Commission has an informative Web site (www.identitytheft. gov) that offers consumers a wide range of helpful information. However, if credit or debit cards have been compromised due to skimming of digital card readers,

7

8

9

10

the FTC offers assistance only after the consumer has been notified of the breach by the respective financial institutions (Federal Trade Commission, 2015).

The Santa Clara Police Department suggests shredding sensitive documents.

The SCPD advises consumers to shred all paper items such as bills, receipts, and bank statements, and to watch their mail carefully (C. Shapiro, personal communication, February 12, 2012). 11

Wells Fargo Bank suggests message alerts delivered to your e-mail or mobile device.

Wells Fargo Bank offers customers the most effective solution to protect their accounts. The Rapid Alerts program offers consumers free message alerts delivered by e-mail or text. Alerts notify customers instantly of unusual transactions to their accounts. This service empowers consumers to take action should they see unauthorized activity (M. Ayala, personal communication, February 4, 2012). 12

- Consumers can instantly detect fraudulent transactions and take immediate action.
- Rapid Alerts identify the merchant, date, amount, and location.
- Transactions originating from international locations are instantly identified.
- Consumers are instantly alerted of online purchases, ATM withdrawals, and telephone transactions.

I think receiving message alerts is the best solution. However, the following table presents the benefits and costs of each solution. 13

Solution	Benefit	Cost
Look for fake card readers	You can choose not to swipe your card if the reader looks suspicious. The benefit is that your card is not tampered with if you do not swipe it.	Many card-skimming devices are internal and cannot be seen externally, so the cost is the risk of not identifying a skimming device.
Consolidate accounts on *Mint.com*	This solution offers one-stop shopping. You can monitor all your accounts on one site.	This solution requires loss of privacy and the security of your user names and passwords; it carries the risk of breaching all your accounts.

(continued)

Here one of DeMedeiros' classmates asked the following question:

Why isn't the "most effective solution" in with the other solutions?

DeMedeiros responded by placing her "best solution" in with the others.

Here one of DeMedeiros' classmates wondered if the table were placed in the best spot:

I really like the way you present information in this table but is it in the best place?

DeMedeiros moved the table up to where its placement made more sense.

A classmate pointed out that the wording in DeMedeiros' chart was confusing because she seemed to be saying the same thing for both cost and benefit. DeMedeiros clarified her language so that the benefit and the cost were distinct from one another. She also made sure the benefit was positive and the cost was negative.

Solution	Benefit	Cost
Sign up for credit reports	You can view activity to see if someone is opening accounts in your name or using your cards fraudulently.	Credit reports cost from $12.00 to $40.00 per month. Reports are sent monthly or quarterly, not instantly.
Shred mail	Thieves cannot go through trash and retrieve your personal data to open accounts of their own if your mail is shredded.	Shredders and shredding services run from $25 to thousands of dollars, depending on quality. Shredding has no impact on card skimming.
Monitor accounts and bank statements	This solution keeps you up to date on the status of your accounts.	Fraud can occur at any time, day or night. Consumers will not know when it happens and can miss it unless they go into their bank sites constantly, which is impractical.
Text and e-mail alerts	This no-cost courtesy service allows instant notification of unusual activity monitored by the bank. Fraud can be quickly stopped and losses reimbursed. Setup takes minutes and can be done online.	This solution may not be offered by all banks and financial institutions. You have to take the time and initiative to set it up yourself.

Are Message Alerts Effective?

According to a Wells Fargo press release (2011), "Rapid Alerts allow consumers   14
to better manage and track their consumer credit card spending while also
providing them with near real-time detection of potentially fraudulent activity."
However, it is important to remember that there are limitations with such an
option. For instance, message alerts do not prevent someone from opening new
accounts in your name. They also do not lock or close your account. It is up to
you to take action.

Even with their limitations, message alerts can protect you in the following   15
ways:

- Text message alerts are the first line of defense. You will be alerted the
  moment unusual activity occurs.

One of DeMedeiros' classmates asked:

These are important points. Is this the best way to introduce them?

DeMedeiros changed her introduction to these points to make it more formal.

- Bank software programs keep track of your purchasing habits and can detect when activity does not fit your patterns.

- You will be alerted if your card is compromised, so the potential for thieves to charge items to your account or deplete your cash as time passes is greatly reduced.

Take Action

The sooner people take action, the better. Consumers should call or visit their financial institution today and sign up for message alerts to be sent to their cell phones or e-mail addresses. The public must be vigilant and protect their assets and credit by taking advantage of the tools that are available to help them stay ahead of the countless thieves who commit these crimes.

16

References

Crouch, M. (2011, January 6). Secrets of a former credit card thief. CreditCards.com. Retrieved from http://www.creditcards.com/credit-card-news/secrets-former-credit-card-thief-dan-defelippi-1282.php.

Delevett, P. (2011, December 6). Lucky urges some customers to close bank accounts in wake of hacking. *San Jose Mercury News*. Retrieved from http://www.mercurynews.com/business/ci_19480050.

Duffy, J. (2013, March 14). *Mint.com* review. *PC Mag*. Retrieved from http://www.pcmag.com/article2/0,2817,2344432,00.asp.

Federal Trade Commission. (2015). Identity theft. Retrieved from http://www.consumer.ftc.gov/features/feature-0014-identity-theft.

Harrell, E. & Langton, L. (2013, December). Victims of identity theft, 2012. Retrieved from U.S. Bureau of Justice Statistics: http://www.bjs.gov/content/pub/pdf/vit12.pdf.

Korn, L., & Dendy, M. (2015, May 19). 103 credit card skimmers found at Florida gas pumps: Officials inspect more than 7,500 gas stations across state. *WKMG Orlando*. Retrieved from http://www.clickorlando.com/news/103-credit-card-skimmers-found-at-florida-gas-pumps/33107150.

Langton, L. (2011, November). Identity theft reported by households, 2005–2010. Retrieved from U.S. Bureau of Justice Statistics: http://www.bjs.gov/content/pub/pdf/itrh0510.pdf.

Paganini, P. (2014, January 14). Introduction to the business of stolen card data. *Infosec Institute*. Retrieved from http://resources.infosecinstitute.com/introduction-business-stolen-card-data/.

Schultz, J. (2010, July 6). Should you trust Mint.com? *The New York Times*. Retrieved from http://bucks.blogs.nytimes.com/2010/07/06/should-you-trust-mint-com/.

Here a classmate questioned why DeMedeiros used a numbered list:

Why are you using numbers here instead of bullet points like you use everywhere *else*?

DeMedeiros recognized the inconsistency and addressed it.

One classmate pointed out that DeMedeiros didn't really have a conclusion in her initial draft. She responded with a concluding paragraph.

The paper follows APA guidelines for in-text citations and references. Since the draft originally submitted to classmates didn't contain any formal documentation, one classmate reminded DeMedeiros to add it:

Of course, in your revised version, you'll need to include all of your citations.

DeMedeiros included a formal list of references in her final draft.

Tumposky, E. (2011, December 9). Lucky's customers hit by card-skimming thieves. Retrieved from ABC News Web site: http://abcnews.go.com/US/luckys-supermarket-chain-hit-card-skimmer-thieves/story?id=15123679#.Ty3bb1wV3gU.

U.S. Secret Service. (n.d.). Beware of skimming fraud. Retrieved from http://www.secretservice.gov/Skimming-Fraud.pdf.

Wells Fargo. (2011, September 21). Wells Fargo enhances free rapid alerts service for mobile phone customers. Retrieved from https://www.wellsfargo.com/credit-cards/alerts/.

UNDERSTANDING A WRITER'S GOALS: QUESTIONS TO CONSIDER AND DISCUSS

Rhetorical Knowledge: The Writer's Situation and Rhetoric

1. **Audience:** Who is the intended audience for DeMedeiros' proposal? What makes you think that?

2. **Purpose:** What does DeMedeiros hope will happen when people read her proposal?

3. **Voice and tone:** How has DeMedeiros used language to help establish her *ethos* as someone who is knowledgeable about the problem of this particular form of identity theft?

4. **Responsibility:** Comment on DeMedeiros' use of sources to support her proposal. How responsibly has she used her sources? Why?

5. **Context, format, and genre:** DeMedeiros wrote this paper for a first-year writing course. If she were to convert this piece of writing to an article for her local newspaper, what revisions would she need to make? Effective problem/solution papers feature a well-defined problem and then present a viable solution. Does DeMedeiros do both in her paper? If so, how? If not, what could she do?

Critical Thinking: The Writer's Ideas and Your Personal Response

6. What is your initial response to DeMedeiros' proposal?

7. How is DeMedeiros' paper similar to other proposed solutions that you have read?

Composing Processes and Knowledge of Conventions: The Writer's Strategies

8. How effectively does DeMedeiros organize her proposal? What other organization would have worked?

9. Do you find the table that DeMedeiros uses to explain the different security options to be helpful? Can you think of any other visuals DeMedeiros might have used to help her argument? What might they be?

Inquiry and Research: Ideas for Further Exploration

10. Interview family members and neighbors about their feelings on how identity theft is affecting them and what measures they are taking to avoid it.

Self-Assessment: Reflecting on Your Goals

Having finished your proposal assignment, take some time to reflect on the thinking and writing you have done. It is often useful to go back and reconsider your learning goals (see pages 368–369). To better reflect on these learning goals, respond in writing to the following questions:

Rhetorical Knowledge

- *Purpose:* What have you learned about the purposes for writing a proposal?
- *Audience:* What have you learned about addressing an audience for a proposal?
- *Rhetorical situation:* How did the writing context affect your writing about the problem you chose and the solution you proposed? How did your choice of problem and solution affect the research you conducted and how you made your case to your readers?
- *Voice and tone:* What have you learned about the writer's voice in writing a proposal?

Critical Thinking, Reading, and Writing

- *Learning/inquiry:* As a result of writing a proposal, how have you become a more critical thinker, reader, and writer?
- *Responsibility:* What have you learned about a writer's responsibility to propose a good and workable solution?
- *Reading and research:* What research did you conduct for your proposal? Why? What additional research might you have done?
- *Skills:* What critical thinking, reading, and writing skills do you hope to develop further in your next writing project? How will you work on them?

Writing Processes

- *Invention:* What process did you go through to identify the problem and the solution you wrote about? How helpful was this process? What research skills have you developed while writing your proposal?

- *Organizing your ideas and details:* How successful was your organization? What drafting skills have you improved? How will you continue to improve them?

- *Revising:* What revising skills have you improved? If you could go back and make an additional revision, what would it be?

- *Working with peers:* How did you make use of the feedback you received? How have you developed your skills in working with peers? How could your peer readers help you more on your next assignment? How might you help them more?

- *Visuals:* Did you use visuals to help explain your problem and solution? If so, what did you learn about incorporating these elements?

- *Writing habits:* What "writerly habits" have you developed, modified, or improved on as you constructed the writing assignment for this chapter? How will you change your future writing activities, based on what you have learned about yourself?

 Knowledge of Conventions

- *Editing:* What sentence problem did you find most frequently in your writing? How will you avoid that problem in future assignments?

- *Genre:* What conventions of the genre you were using, if any, gave you problems?

- *Documentation:* Did you use sources for your paper? If so, what documentation style did you use? What problems, if any, did you have with it?

If you are constructing a course portfolio, file your written reflections so that you can return to them when you next work on your portfolio. Refer to Chapter 1 (page 12) for a sample reflection by a student.

Text Credits

p. 377: Vallas, Rebecca and Boteach, Melissa, "Top 10 Solutions to Cut Poverty and Grow the Middle Class" Center for American Progress, September 17, 2014. Copyright © 2014 Center for American Progess. www.americanprogress.org. **p. 383:** Briggs, Saga, "Intellectual Humility: What Happens When You Love to Learn—From Others" *InformEd*, April 18, 2015. Copyright © 2015 InformED, a blog by Open Colleges. https://opencolleges.edu.au/careers/ Used with permission. **p. 383:** Laszlo Bock, quoted in Bryant, Adam, "In Head-Hunting, Big Data May Not Be Such a Big Deal" *New York Times*, June 19, 2013. **p. 384:** Paul, Richard and Elder, Linda, *The Thinker's Guide to The Art of Socratic Questioning* (Tomales, CA: Foundation for Critical Thinking Press, 2006). **p. 384:** Benjamin Franklin, The Madison Debates, September 17, 1787. **p. 385:** Peter Samuelson, quoted in Munce, Justin, "Intellectual humility distinct from general humity, study finds" *The Speaker News*, January 6, 2015. **p. 385:** Lockhart, K.L., Goddu, M.K. & Keil, F.C. (in press) "Overoptimism about Future Knowledge: Early Arrogance?" *Positive Psychology* May 4, 2016. **p. 387:** Kidd, Ian James, "Educating for Intellectual Humility" in Jason Baehr (ed) Intellectual Virtues and Education: Essays in Applied Virtue Epistemology (New York: Routledge, 2015) pp 54–71. **p. 387:** Hare, W. (1992) "Humility as a Virtue in Teaching" *Journal of Philosophy of Education,* 26 (2): 277–236. **p. 390:** Amy Baskin and Heather Fawcett, "Request for a Work Schedule Change." *More Than a Mom—Living a Full and Balanced Life When Your Child Has Special Needs.* www.morethanamom.net. Used with permission of the authors. **p. 401:** From "Identity Theft Reported by Households, 2005–2010," by L Langton, November 2011, Crime Data Brief, Bureau of Justice Statistics, U.S. Department of Justice. Retrieved from http://bjs.ojp.usdoj.gov/content/pub/pdf/itrh0510.pdf. **p. 402:** From "Identity Theft Reported by Households, 2005–2010," by L Langton, November 2011, Crime Data Brief, Bureau of Justice Statistics, U.S. Department of Justice. Retrieved from http://bjs.ojp.usdoj.gov/content/pub/pdf/itrh0510.pdf. **p. 402:** Courtesy of Susan DeMedeiros. **p. 409:** Courtesy of Susan DeMedeiros.

CHAPTER 5

Using Strategies That Guide Readers

Whatever your purpose, you can use a range of rhetorical strategies to help readers understand your writing. Whether you use them within a sentence, a paragraph, or a complete piece of writing, these strategies help readers make connections. This chapter starts by focusing on the basic building blocks of any piece of writing— the thesis statement and the paragraph. Next, we look at how to link sentences and paragraphs together using cohesive devices. Then we explore strategies to narrate, describe, define, classify, compare, and contrast. Finally, we look at different ways you can outline and map your writing to ensure that the writing strategies you use are effective. All of these strategies can be used for the writing projects in Chapters 5–12.

© Banana Stock/Jupiter Images RF

■ Announcing a Thesis or Controlling Idea

A **thesis** announces the main point, major claim, or controlling idea in an essay. A clear thesis helps readers because it prepares them for what they will be reading.

Although a thesis statement can focus your attention as you write, it is usually helpful to write your thesis statement after you have done invention work and research. Invention activities can help you clarify your thinking about a topic. Research can help you learn more about it. Once you have done invention and research, a thesis statement can help you construct a well-focused draft. Of course, the exact wording of your thesis statement might change as you draft your paper.

The most effective thesis statements are limited and focused and offer some sense of the support that is forthcoming. If your thesis statement merely states a fact, it just informs the reader about that fact; it is not arguable. If you offer a personal feeling as a thesis ("I don't like coffee"), people could certainly argue with it, but your evidence would be purely subjective ("I don't care for the flavor") and therefore not persuasive. If your thesis statement is general and vague ("Movies are more expensive now than they were last year"), you probably won't be able to write much in support for it. Providing two figures—the average price of movies last year and the average price this year—proves your assertion.

Here are two examples of weak thesis statements that have been revised to make them stronger:

WEAK   I can't stand war movies.

REVISED   *Letters from Iwo Jima* is an effective war movie because it forces Americans to view, and even sympathize with, combatants traditionally seen as enemies.

REASON   There is no way to support your personal feeling—that you do not like war movies—with evidence. But you could provide evidence for the ways *Letters from Iwo Jima* helps viewers see enemy combatants in a new light.

WEAK   The National Football League is in trouble.

REVISED   The National Football League is in trouble because of highly publicized head injuries.

REASON   The weak version is too general and vague. The revised version gives a specific reason for the trouble.

It is important to *qualify* your thesis statement by using terms such as *probably* or *likely* to make it more acceptable to an audience.

EXAMPLE   Abraham Lincoln probably experienced more stress than any other U.S. president.

Writing Activity

Revising Weak Thesis Statements

Revise each of the following thesis statements, and explain how your revision has strengthened each statement.

New York City has a larger population than Chicago.
Pizza is better than pasta.
There are many weight-loss drugs available to consumers.
I don't like windy days.
Women's sports are growing in popularity.

Writing Paragraphs

A **paragraph** is a collection of connected sentences that focus on a single idea. With few exceptions, your writing projects will consist of paragraphs, each developing an idea related to your topic. In your writing, you need to think about both the effectiveness of individual paragraphs and the way they are organized and connected to support your purpose. Consider the following example, which might appear in a paper about Abraham Lincoln's career:

> <u>During his years as president, 1861–1865, Abraham Lincoln experienced great stress from a combination of causes.</u> **First,** the Civil War, which broke out weeks after his March 1861 inauguration, wore on him daily until its end in April 1865. **Second,** typhoid took the life of Willie, his beloved eleven-year-old son, in February 1862. **Third,** his wife, Mary Todd Lincoln, suffered from depression and other forms of mental illness, problems that became more acute during the years in the White House.

Although the specifics may vary, effective paragraphs generally have the following features:

- A focus on a single main idea. The more tightly you focus a paragraph on a main idea, the more you will help readers navigate the paragraph. Note that in the example paragraph every sentence is focused on the causes of Lincoln's stress. If you want to alert your readers to other information that will come later in your paper, use a *forecasting sentence.* In the example about Lincoln, the sentence that mentions Mary Lincoln's depression could forecast that the paper will have more to say about that topic.

- A topic sentence. A topic sentence guides readers by expressing a paragraph's main idea, the idea that the other sentences in the paragraph support or develop. In the example about Lincoln, the first sentence, which is underlined, serves as the topic sentence.

- Different levels of specificity. All paragraphs have at least two levels of specificity. In the paragraph about Lincoln, the topic sentence clearly introduces the idea of stress and its various causes, and the second, third, and fourth sentences are more specific.
- Connective words and phrases. Used within a paragraph, connective words and phrases, discussed in more detail on pages 425–427, can show precisely how the sentences in the paragraph support the topic sentence and relate to one another. In the example paragraph, the words *First, Second,* and *Third* (in bold type) tell readers that each of the sentences they begin offers a separate cause of Lincoln's stress.
- A logical connection to the next paragraph. When readers finish a paragraph, they expect that the next paragraph will be connected to it in some readily apparent way. After reading the paragraph that focuses on the sources of stress that Lincoln experienced, readers expect that the next paragraph will also be related to Lincoln's stress.

Placement of Topic Sentences

In the paragraph about Lincoln, the topic sentence is the first sentence, a placement that lets readers know right away what the paragraph will be about. Sometimes, however, a topic sentence is more effective at the end of a paragraph, where it can serve to develop suspense or summarize information. This strategy can be especially useful in persuasive writing because it allows the writer to present evidence before making an assertion. Here is an example:

> Less than a quarter of our agricultural land is used to feed people directly. The rest is devoted to grazing and growing food for animals. Ecosystems of forest, wetland and grassland have been decimated to fuel the demand for land. Using so much land heightens topsoil loss, the use of harsh fertilizers and pesticides, and the need for irrigation water from dammed rivers. <u>If people can shift away from meat, much of this land could be converted back to wilderness.</u>
>
> Joseph Pace, "Let's Go Veggie!"

Sometimes when the point is fairly clear to readers, a writer may decide to leave it unstated. In the following paragraph, the implied (unstated) topic sentence could be something like, "I am learning what it means to live as a woman in poverty":

> Sometime around four in the morning it dawns on me that it's not just that I'm a wimp. Poor women—perhaps especially single ones and even those who are just temporarily living among the poor for whatever reason—really do have more to fear than women who have houses with double locks and alarm systems and husbands or dogs. I must have known this theoretically or at least heard it stated, but now for the first time the lesson takes hold.
>
> Barbara Ehrenreich, *Nickel and Dimed: On (Not) Getting By in America*

Moving to a New Paragraph

Paragraph breaks signal that a writer is moving from one idea to another. Consider again the example paragraph on Lincoln in which every sentence is related to causes of stress. We could develop that paragraph further by adding sentences that maintain that focus. Look at what happens, though, when we add a sentence that does not fit the focus on causes of stress:

> . . . Third, his wife, Mary Todd Lincoln, suffered from depression and other forms of mental illness, problems that became more acute during the years in the White House. <u>To alleviate the stress, Lincoln often read the plays of Shakespeare.</u>

The last sentence in this paragraph does fit the general topic of Lincoln's experience with stress, but it does not fit the tight focus on causes in this paragraph. Instead, it introduces a related but new idea. The solution is to make the last sentence the topic sentence of the next paragraph:

> . . . Third, his wife, Mary Todd Lincoln, suffered from depression and other forms of mental illness, problems that became more acute during the years in the White House.
>
> <u>To alleviate the stress, Lincoln often read the plays of Shakespeare.</u> Among those that he read most frequently were *King Lear, Richard III, Henry VIII, Hamlet,* and *Macbeth.* About his favorite play, *Macbeth,* he wrote the following in a letter to the actor James H. Hackett on August 17, 1863: "I think nothing equals *Macbeth.* It is wonderful."

Notice that this new paragraph provides details about Lincoln and stress that are even more specific than the ones in the preceding paragraph.

Opening Paragraphs

The opening paragraphs of an essay announce the topic and the writer's approach to it. In an opening paragraph the writer needs to establish a relationship with readers and help them connect the topic to what they already know and care about. Some common strategies for opening paragraphs include the following:

- Tell an interesting anecdote.
- Raise a thought-provoking question.
- Provide salient background information.
- Offer a view that the writer and readers hold in common.
- Forecast the rest of the essay.

Writing Activity

Introductions

For each of the following excerpts from opening paragraphs, describe the strategy that the writer is using. Does it make you want to read more? Why or why not?

The official poverty rate in 2003 was 12.5 percent, up from 12.1 percent in 2002. In 2003, 35.9 million people were in poverty, up 1.3 million from 2002. For children under 18 years old, both the poverty rate and the number in poverty rose between 2002 and 2003, from 16.7 percent to 17.6 percent, and from 12.1 million to 12.9 million, respectively.

U.S. Census Bureau, "Poverty: 2003 Highlights"

American environmental policy faces a sobering reality: The United States has enacted and implemented some of the world's most effective wildlife conservation laws, yet U.S. wildlife populations are still in perilous decline. One in five animal and plant species in the United States—nearly 1,300 total species—is at risk of extinction. Among mammals, the populations of more than two-thirds of all imperiled species in the United States, from the wolverine to the polar bear, are falling.

Center for American Progress, "Confronting America's
Wildlife Extinction Crisis"

Tina Taylor was a model of what welfare reform was supposed to do. Taylor, 44, a single mother, had spent six years on public assistance. After 1996, when changes were made in welfare law to push people into work, she got a job that paid $400 a week and allowed her family to live independently. For the first time in a long time, she could afford to clothe and feed her two children, and even rent a duplex on the beach in Norfolk.

Griff Witte, "Poverty Up as Welfare Enrollment Declines; Nation's
Social Safety Net in Tatters as More People Lose Their Jobs"

Concluding Paragraphs

Readers remember best what they read last. Although it is not that memorable to simply restate what your essay is about in your conclusion, you can use it to do the following:

- Restate your thesis and remind readers of your key points.
- Emphasize the significance of your perspective on your topic.
- Bring your writing to closure by recalling the opening.

> ### Writing Activity

Conclusions

For each of the following concluding paragraphs, explain what the writer has done and decide how effective you think each conclusion is.

> Each day of my life there are times when I reflect back to working on the farm. And every day people notice that I am different from the rest of my peers. At school, teachers and organization leaders are impressed by my time management skills and the amount of responsibility I take on. At work, my boss continues to ask me where he can find some more hard working people. I simply tell him, "Try hiring some farm girls. I hear they turn out pretty good."
>
> Jessica Hemauer, "Farm Girl"

> Throughout, Lawrence's epic Migration Series shifts with agile grace between struggle and resilience, the particular and the universal. Ultimately, it conveys clear-eyed optimism. Arriving at the final panel, "And the migrants kept coming," you feel that life in the North is the better way, but as the waiting travelers face you en masse for the first time in the series, looking across the train tracks, you imagine the wrenching stories they surely had to tell.
>
> Mary Proenza, "One-Way Ticket: Jacob Lawrence's Migration Series"

Using Cohesive Devices

Within paragraphs, effective writers use a variety of cohesive devices to show readers how sentences are connected to one another. The major devices include connective words and phrases, word repetition, and pronoun reference. To help readers understand how paragraphs are related to one another, writers use transitional sentences as well as headings.

Using Connective Words and Phrases

You can guide readers with logically connected sentences and paragraphs, making these connections explicit through the use of **connective words and phrases.** These connections fall into three main categories: temporal, spatial, and logical.

TEMPORAL CONNECTIONS

Time: now, then, during, meanwhile, at this moment

> I worked all weekend. <u>Meanwhile</u>, my colleagues watched football all day Saturday and Sunday.

Frequency: often, occasionally, frequently, sometimes

> Sally likes unplanned trips. <u>Sometimes</u>, she'll even show up at the airport and then decide where to fly for the weekend.

Temporal order: first, second …; next; before (that); after (that); last; finally

Let's eat dinner. <u>After that</u>, let's see a movie.

SPATIAL CONNECTIONS

Location: nearby, outside, inside

I stood by the window. <u>Outside</u>, a moose ran down the street.

Spatial order: first, second …; last, next

Jane sat in the corner. <u>Next to her</u> sat Jill.

LOGICAL CONNECTIONS

Addition: further, furthermore, moreover, additionally, in addition, and, also

Martha Flynn is a powerful council member in our city. <u>In addition</u>, she may be headed for other powerful positions in the future.

Opposition/contrast: on the other hand, however, in contrast, on the contrary, but, conversely, nevertheless, yet, instead, rather

I don't eat meat for ethical reasons. <u>On the other hand</u>, I do wear leather shoes.

Comparison: likewise, similarly, analogously

George H. W. Bush led the United States to war in the 1990s. <u>Likewise</u>, George W. Bush led the United States to war in 2001.

Causation: because, as a result, as a consequence, therefore, thus, accordingly, consequently, so, then, on account of

He didn't pay his phone bill. <u>As a result</u>, the phone company discontinued his service.

Clarification: in other words, that is,

He rarely does his homework. <u>In other words</u>, he's not a very good student.

Qualification: under the (these) circumstances, under other circumstances, under these conditions, in this context

John McCain spent years as a prisoner of war in North Vietnam. <u>Under these circumstances</u>, it's remarkable that he is so well adjusted.

Conclusion: finally, in summary, to sum up, in conclusion, therefore

The new Toyota Camry has been rated one of the safest cars on the road. <u>Therefore</u>, we should consider buying one.

Illustration: for example, for instance, in particular, specifically

Luz wears colorful clothes. <u>For example</u>, yesterday she wore a bright red sweater to her math class.

Using Word Repetition

Repeating a word or phrase from one sentence to the next helps readers make a connection between those two sentences:

> The ultimate goal is to stop dating violence before it starts. Strategies that promote healthy **relationships** are vital. During the preteen and teen years, young people are learning skills they need to form positive **relationships** with others. This is an ideal time to promote healthy **relationships** and prevent patterns of dating violence that can last into adulthood.
>
> CDC Fact Sheet, "Understanding Teen Dating Violence"

Using Pronoun Reference

Pronouns substitute for nouns. When writers use pronouns to replace nouns, those pronouns point backward or forward to the nouns that they replace:

> During **his** years as president, 1861–1865, Abraham Lincoln experienced great stress from a combination of causes. First, the Civil War, which broke out weeks after **his** March 1861 inauguration, wore on **him** daily until its end in April 1865. Second, typhoid took the life of Willie, **his** beloved eleven-year-old son, in February 1862. Third, **his** wife, Mary Todd Lincoln, suffered from depression and other forms of mental illness, problems that became more acute during the years in the White House.

Writing Activity

Focusing on Cohesive Words

Working alone or with one or two classmates, identify the cohesive devices (and lack of cohesive devices) in the following paragraph. Also, edit the paragraph by adding cohesive devices that you think might strengthen connections between sentences.

(continued)

Writing Activity

Focusing on Cohesive Words *(continued)*

> The want to consume is nothing new. It has been around for millennia. People need to consume resources to survive. However, consumption has evolved as people have ingeniously found ways to help make their lives simpler and/or to use their resources more efficiently. Of course, with this has come the want to control such means. Hence, the consumption patterns have evolved over time based on the influence of those who can control it. As a result, there is tremendous waste within this system, to maintain such control and such disparities.
>
> Anup Shaw, "Creating the Consumer"

Using Transitional Sentences and Paragraphs

Writers use **transitions** to help readers move from one section of an essay to another. These sentences or paragraphs often summarize what has come before and forecast what will come next. Here are two examples:

> Those are the advantages of an interest-only home loan. However, there are several disadvantages as well.

> Although after that presentation I admired her intellect even more, her next decision caused me seriously to question her judgment.

Using Headings

In short pieces of writing, you may not need to use headings. For longer pieces of writing and in certain genres, though, headings and even subheadings can help readers more quickly understand the focus of the paragraphs that follow them. They tell readers that the paragraphs they precede are a related group and are all on the same topic.

Keep the following guidelines in mind when you write headings:

- Generally, use only one level of heading for a five-page paper.
- Be sure all content under a heading relates to that heading.
- Make your headings specific.

VAGUE	Properties of Glass
SPECIFIC	Chemical Properties of Glass

- At each level, make headings parallel in grammatical structure, font, and level of specificity.

NOT PARALLEL	The Chemistry of Glass, Physical Properties
PARALLEL	Chemical Properties of Glass, Physical Properties of Glass

- Design headings so that they stand out from the text.

DOESN'T STAND OUT	Common Uses of Glass
DOES STAND OUT	**Common Uses of Glass**

If you are writing an academic paper, you should follow the requirements of the documentation style you are using for the style of your headings.

For more on headings in MLA and APA style, see Chapter 20.

Writing Activity

Focusing on Headings and Subheadings

Working on your own or with several classmates, consider the headings in "Staying ahead of Skimming Scams" (pages 409–416 in Chapter 12). How do the headings help guide readers?

Writing Narratives

Both in everyday speech and in many kinds of writing, **narration** is a common strategy. When you narrate, you relate an event or a series of events or, in the case of a process, you give a series of steps. Most narratives are organized by time, or **chronologically,** from the beginning to the end of an event, a series of events, or a process. Obviously, narration is relevant to much of our discourse in all areas of our lives because our lives are filled with events and processes:

- At dinner, you tell your family or friends about an event at school or work that day.

- In a science course, you record what happened when you conducted a laboratory experiment.

- As a witness to a traffic accident, you tell the investigating police officers what happened.

In this section we consider two kinds of narratives: narratives that relate an event or a series of events and narratives that relate a process.

Narrating Single Events or a Series of Events

Often in everyday conversation, you narrate single events. Narrating a single event is also a common way of organizing part or all of a piece of writing. You might write an essay about an event that affected your life, an article on the opening of a store in your neighborhood, or a research report on the Montgomery bus boycott in 1955. You can also narrate a series of events such as an account of your life, of the growth of the McDonald's restaurant chain, or of the American civil rights movement in the 1950s and 1960s.

For more on narrating an event or a series of events, see Chapter 5.

When you narrate an event or a series of events, you will most often order your details chronologically—what happened first, what happened next, and so on. As an alternative, however, you might discuss the importance of the event or events first, and then proceed to the details so that your readers will understand why they, too, ought to be interested in what happened.

Chronological Structure: Because life's events occur chronologically, it is usually easiest to narrate them that way. It is also usually easier for readers to process narratives mentally when they unfold chronologically. Even a short narrative paragraph such as the following one can suggest a chronological ordering of events:

> Once my aunt found a freckle on her chin, at a spot that the almanac said predestined her for unhappiness. She dug it out with a hot needle and washed the wound with peroxide.
>
> Maxine Hong Kingston, "No Name Woman"

Point of View: The narrator of a story can have any of several points of view, so when you construct a narrative, select a point of view to write from.

In the *first-person* point of view, the narrator tells the story from the perspective of a participant or character in the story:

> When I went to kindergarten and had to speak English for the first time, I became silent.
>
> Maxine Hong Kingston, "Tongue Tied"

In a narrative told from a *third-person* point of view, the narrator is not a participant or character in the story. The narrator consistently uses third-person pronouns or proper nouns to talk about the actions of characters:

> On December 1, 1963, shortly after President Kennedy's assassination, Malcolm X addressed a public rally in New York City. He was speaking as a replacement for Elijah Muhammad as he had done many times before. After the speech, during a question and answer period, Malcolm X made the remark that led to his suspension as a Muslim minister. In answer to a question, "What do you think about President Kennedy's assassination?" Malcolm X answered that he saw the case as "The chickens coming home to roost." Soon after the remark, Malcolm X was suspended by Elijah Muhammad and directed to stop speaking for ninety days.
>
> John Henrik Clarke, from the Introduction to
> *Malcolm X: The Man and His Times*

Developing Tension: Narrative tension is the feeling readers have when they are concerned about what will happen to a character. The more readers care about a character, the more they want to know how the character will get through a conflict. Narratives with tension are more interesting to readers. To establish tension in narratives, writers show conflicts between characters who hold differing values or perspectives. For example, the following sentences develop tension:

> My mother's parents didn't want her to marry my father, so the young couple eloped on a blustery day in November.

> Tom and I were best friends, but then one day I saw him stuff a DVD into his shirt in a department store.

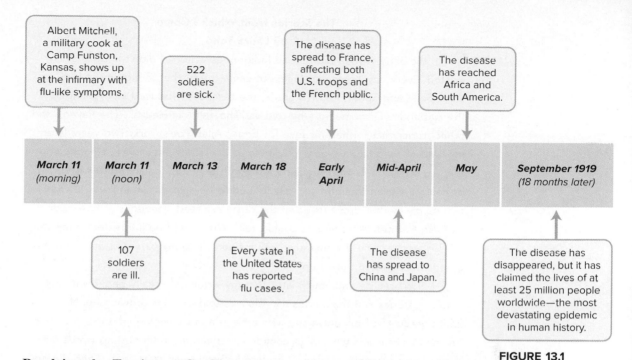

FIGURE 13.1
Time Line for the 1918 Flu Epidemic

Resolving the Tension or Conflict: Just as readers are intrigued by narrative tension, they are interested in seeing how tensions are resolved. Most readers look forward to a sense of closure by the end of the story.

Incorporating Visuals in Narratives: When you narrate a series of events, you have the opportunity to cover a significant period of time, as well as the complications involved in a more extended narration. If the chronology becomes complex, you might find it useful to guide readers with a summarizing visual such as a time line. Figure 13.1, for instance, is a brief time line for the flu epidemic of 1918.

Writing Activity

Analyzing Narrative Strategies

After reading the following narrative, respond in writing to the following questions:

1. What images do the references to Dick and Jane, the Edgar Allen Poe work, and Laura Ingalls Wilder evoke? How do you respond to those images and why?
2. At the conclusion, Tohe has achieved her childhood dream of becoming a writer, but it was a convoluted journey. Explain how she chronicles that journey.
3. The references to Presidents Kennedy and Johnson mean something to Tohe. What do they mean to you? Why? How interested are you in researching what impact Kennedy's assassination and Johnson's War on Poverty had on Americans in the 1960s? Why?
4. How do verb tenses function in the narrative?

For more on a type of writing that uses narration extensively, see Chapter 5,"Writing to Share Experiences."

The Stories from Which I Come
by Laura Tohe

In the early 1960s I didn't read Indigenous writers; I didn't know that any existed. Every day at reading time, out came the further monotony of Dick, Jane, Sally, and Spot. In fourth grade, the teacher introduced storytelling in the classroom. From memory he told us "The Tell-Tale Heart," "The Raven," and other stories that formed my love for Edgar Allen Poe's work. Two years later my teacher read Laura Ingalls Wilder to us every day after lunch. Hearing and reading stories in English regularly, I thought only non-Indians were writers or could be, even though I secretly longed to be a writer when I was 12 years old. As my mother drove us down the dusty rez road, I thought of how I could become a writer. What stories could I tell? Who would be interested in my stories? How does one become a writer? Instead I told my parents I wanted to be a pediatrician when I grew up.

I didn't realize until much later that my writing life really began with my mother's stories and the stories my relatives told as I was growing up. Not until I graduated from university with a degree in psychology did I stop writing "in secret." Fear and my lack of confidence stifled me from putting words on paper. I was growing up when President Kennedy was assassinated and during President Johnson's war on poverty, so I thought I could make a difference if I worked in the mental health field for my community. Though I didn't pursue a graduate degree in psychology, I think studying it as an undergraduate helped me understand something of human behavior. On our shopping trips "to town" Mom sometimes told my brothers and me stories that her great-grandmother told her. Most vivid is the one about a brother and sister who transformed into prairie dogs due to their parents' neglect and was the first story I wrote and published. My instructor and mentor told me I had a wealth of stories from my community and that I might write about that. I came to an epiphany—stories and storytellers had surrounded me all my life and I could write those stories.

Narrating Processes

When you narrate a process, you tell how something is done (informative/explanatory process narrative), or you tell others how to do something (instructional/directive process narrative).

Informative/Explanatory Process Narratives: Informative or explanatory process narratives tell readers how something is done so that they can understand a process, not so that they can replicate it. For example, you might write an informative process analysis to explain how a legislative bill becomes a law or how a seed germinates.

Instructional/Directive Process Narratives: In contrast to informative or explanatory process narratives, the purpose of instructional or directive process narratives is to help readers learn how to do something. For instance, you might explain how to make a great pizza or how to use the online library catalog at your school so that readers can replicate these processes.

USING DIGITAL TECHNOLOGIES | Constructing a Time Line

To construct a time line like the one in Figure 13.1, you can use a time line template in your word processor (you can download Microsoft programs from online resources by using the "help" feature to walk you through this process). It works best to construct your time line in a separate document and then copy and paste it into your project document. Alternatively, you can copy and paste the time line into a PowerPoint slide and then insert the slide into your document file. In addition to word-processing programs or PowerPoint, you may find more visually robust time lines in online time line programs like timetoast at https://www.timetoast.com/.

Writing Descriptions

When you describe, you sketch people, places, and things verbally. Usually, you will aim to establish an overall feeling about what you are describing, such as the feeling evoked in the following passage:

> A dark mist lay over the Black Hills, and the land was like iron. At the top of the ridge I caught sight of Devil's Tower upthrust against the gray sky as if in the birth time the core of the earth had broken through its crust and the motion of the world was begun. There are many things in nature that engender an awful quiet in the heart of man; Devil's Tower is one of them.
>
> N. Scott Momaday, *The Way to Rainy Mountain*

Because it is so common, **description** will be part of many of your writing projects. However, the approach you take to description will depend on what you are describing. Here we focus on three approaches that can be effective—naming people, things, or features; providing sensory details; and giving spatial dimensions.

Naming in Description

When you describe someone or something, you need to name that person or thing, as well as its features. For example, if you were to describe the room where you sleep, you might name objects such as the bed, dresser, chair, artwork, walls, ceiling, and floor. Consider the effect of naming in the following excerpt from Robert Sullivan's book *Rats:*

> A rat is a rodent, the most common mammal in the world. *Rattus norvegicus* is one of the approximately four hundred different kinds of rodents, and it is known by many names, each of which describes a trait or a perceived trait

or sometimes a habitat: the earth rat, the roving rat, the barn rat, the field rat, the migratory rat, the house rat, the sewer rat, the water rat, the wharf rat, the alley rat, the gray rat, the brown rat, and the common rat. The average brown rat is large and stocky; it grows to be approximately sixteen inches long from its nose to its tail—the size of a large adult human male's foot—and weighs about a pound, though brown rats have been measured by scientists and exterminators at twenty inches and up to two pounds. The brown rat is sometimes confused with the black rat, or *Rattus rattus,* which is smaller and once inhabited New York City and all of the cities of America but, since *Rattus norvegicus* pushed it out, is now relegated to a minor role.

A Sensory Approach to Description

A thorough sensory description includes details from all five senses—sight, hearing, taste, smell, and touch. In a vivid sensory description, the reader experiences vicariously what the writer has described. To generate such a description, you might use the questions in the following table. With minor modifications, you can use these questions to develop descriptions of a wide range of items.

Sense	Questions to Consider	Responses
Sight	What does it look like?	
	What do I see when I look at it?	
Hearing	What sounds does it make?	
	What sounds are associated with it?	
Taste	How does it taste?	
	What tastes are similar to it?	
	What tastes are associated with it?	
Smell	What does it smell like?	
	What smells are similar to it?	
	What smells are associated with it?	
Touch	What does it feel like to the touch?	
	What tactile associations do I have with it?	

Of course, for some subjects, you will rely on details from only one or two senses. The sense you will use most often when writing description is sight. Remember that other senses can also have an impact on readers, however. The sense of smell, for example, tends to evoke memory in humans more powerfully than any other sense.

In the following description, notice how the writer appeals to several senses:

> When I smell charcoal, I remember a meal at a folding table at the side of a river in Laos. A woman manned an oil drum cut in half, a hot blackened grill over its top, and coals spread in its belly. She grilled chicken legs, bones removed, until they were charred, their meat turned the color of dark honey. They were sent to the table with sticky rice, packed into little wicker baskets by her tough hands, along with ceramic crocks of red chili paste.
>
> Tamar Adler, *An Everlasting Meal*

A Spatial Approach to Description

When you describe something *spatially,* you describe it in terms of both its own physical dimensions and its relationship to the objects around it. An approach that is primarily spatial can include sensory details or a visual, which may even be the predominant part of the description. For example, Figure 13.2 is a photo of the World War II Memorial on Washington, D.C.'s National Mall. Below is a brief spatial description of the memorial.

> If you are walking east from the steps of the Lincoln Memorial, along the walkway bordering either side of the Reflecting Pool, you will cross paths with the World War II Veterans Memorial that abuts the pool at its southernmost edge. In fact, you cannot stroll along the historic pool's perimeter without intersecting the broad configuration of fountains, pillars, and pavilions, known somewhat popularly as the "Gem of the Mall." If you find it, as I did, wandering southeast from the

FIGURE 13.2
A Photo of the World War II Memorial in Washington, D.C.

© littleny/Shutterstock.com RF

Vietnam Veterans Memorial, you will pass through a tall, granite archway into a pavilion marked by the inscription "**ATLANTIC**," designating the Western theater of the war. Looking out and across, past the memorial's mechanized fountains and oval Rainbow Pool, you will see an identical pavilion, the Pacific theater. In two semi-circles that extend from either side of both pavilions stand fifty-six pillars, each named for a U.S. state or territory and adorned with a bronze wreath. Toward the top of each pavilion, where the arches meet, another larger wreath hangs from the beaks of four bronze American eagles.

Elizabeth Murphy, "The Gem of the Mall"

For more on two types of writing that use description extensively, see Chapter 5, "Writing to Share Experiences," and Chapter 8, "Writing to Analyze."

Writing Activity

Writing an Effective Description

Working on your own or with several classmates, choose a topic to describe. First, generate a list of questions that an interested reader might have about the topic. Second, answer each of the questions to generate descriptive details. Third, use those details to write a short descriptive paragraph, using the approaches described above.

Writing Definitions

Definitions help your readers understand the terms that you are using. Clear definitions are especially important if you are writing about a topic that you know more about than your readers do, about an issue over which there are differences of opinion—including over the meanings of terms—or about a topic for which precision is crucial. You will find occasions to use definitions in all four areas of life:

- In a letter to one of your U.S. senators, you define "the working poor" as you argue for legislation to assist low-income families.
- When you take a friend to a baseball game, you define "earned run average" when "ERA" appears after a pitcher's name on the big screen in left field.
- In an economics course, you define "gross domestic product" in a paper about economic growth in India and China.

Kinds of Definitions

You can use any of several kinds of definitions depending on how much information your readers need. Sometimes you can define a term simply by giving your readers a **synonym,** a more familiar word or phrase that could be used in place of the term you are defining. However, defining a word with a synonym has limitations. Consider some synonyms for the word *war: warfare, combat,* *conflict, fighting, confrontation, hostilities,* and *battle.* Depending on the context, these words cannot necessarily be used interchangeably.

More useful than a synonym in many cases is an essential definition. **Essential definitions** are sentence definitions that include three parts: (1) the name of what is being defined, (2) the general category for the item being defined, and (3) the form or function that distinguishes the item being defined from similar items in the same general category. Here are some examples:

Name	Category	Form or Function
A toaster	is a small kitchen appliance	that browns bread.
A mixer	is a small kitchen appliance	that combines ingredients.

If a synonym or an essential definition is insufficient, you can incorporate it in an extended definition. An **extended definition,** which can take up one or more paragraphs, may include both of these briefer types of definition, as well as additional information and examples. It is especially helpful when you need to define a concept that is abstract or complex. For instance, here is an extended definition of a *mugwump:*

This archetypal American word derives from the Algonquian dialect of a group of Native Americans in Massachusetts. In their language, it meant "war leader." The Puritan missionary John Eliot used it in his translation of the Bible into their language in 1661–63 to convey the English words *"officer"* and *"captain."*

Mugwump was brought into English in the early nineteenth century as a humorous term for a boss, bigwig, grand panjandrum, or other person in authority, often one of a minor and inconsequential sort. This example comes from a story in an 1867 issue of *Atlantic Monthly:* "I've got one of your gang in irons—the Great Mugwump himself, I reckon—strongly guarded by men armed to the teeth; so you just ride up here and surrender."

It hit the big time in 1884, during the presidential election that set Grover Cleveland against the Republican James G. Blaine. Some Republicans refused to support Blaine, changed sides, and the *New York Sun* labelled them *little mugwumps.* Almost overnight, the sense of the word changed to *turncoat.* Later, it came to mean a politician who either could not or would not make up his mind on some important issue, or who refused to take a stand when expected to do so. Hence the old joke that a mugwump is a person sitting on the fence, with his mug on one side and his wump on the other.

Michael Quinion, *World Wide Words*

Notice that the definition indicates what a mugwump is, explains the origin of the word and its history, and provides concrete examples.

Writing Activity

Identifying Features of a Definition

Consider the following definition of a Luddite:

For more on a type of writing that uses definitions extensively, see Chapter 9, "Writing to Convince."

> A Luddite is a person who fears or loathes technology, especially new forms of technology that threaten existing jobs. During the Industrial Revolution, textile workers in England who claimed to be following the example of a man named Ned Ludd destroyed factory equipment to protest changes in the workplace brought about by labor-saving technology. The term *Luddite* is derived from Ludd's surname. Today, the term *Luddite* is reserved for a person who regards technology as causing more harm than good in society, and who behaves accordingly.

Tech Target Network

1. What are the features of this definition?
2. How might you clarify the definition?

Writing Classifications

When you classify, you group—or divide—items into categories based on one or more of three principles—completeness, exclusiveness, or consistency:

- **Completeness** means that all items need to be included in a classification. If you were classifying automobiles, you would need to make certain that SUVs were included in your scheme.

- **Exclusiveness** means that none of your categories should overlap with any other category. If you were classifying movies, for example, the categories *movies about monsters* and *scary movies* don't work because some movies about monsters are scary (*The Thing*) and would fit in both categories.

- **Consistency** means that the same criteria need to be used to determine the contents of each category. If you are classifying animals and two of your categories are *mammals* and *birds,* your third category should not be *extinct animals* because that introduces different criteria into your system.

For more on a type of writing that uses classification extensively, see Chapter 8, "Writing to Analyze."

Many topics can be classified, which means that you will find classification a useful organizing strategy for many kinds of writing:

- Before purchasing a laptop computer for business travel, you might classify some possible laptops you are considering by weight—ultra-light (under three pounds), light (three to five pounds), moderate (six to eight pounds), and heavy (more than eight pounds).

FIGURE 13.3
The Five Food
Groups That Make
Up a Healthy Diet

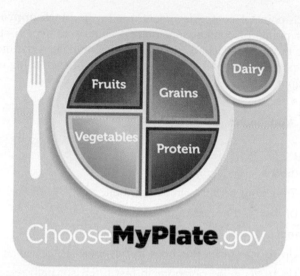

Source: www.choosemyplate.gov

- In deciding which candidates to support in an election, you might classify them according to their stated positions on issues that are important to you.

- As you write a menu for your next week's meals, you could use the categories in the diagram shown in Figure 13.3.

Writing about Comparisons and Contrasts

The related strategies of **comparison**—looking at how subjects are similar—and **contrast**—looking at how they are different—are common not just in writing but in thinking. People find that they are crucial tools in thinking about and differentiating many aspects of the world around them.

In all areas of life, you will use comparison and contrast:

- In an art history class, you might compare and contrast the features of two schools of art such as impressionism and surrealism.

- In an e-mail to a friend, you might compare and contrast two romantic comedies that you recently saw at movie theaters.

- You might compare and contrast the features of two network servers that your company is considering for purchase.

Approaches to Comparison and Contrast

The two major approaches to comparing and contrasting two items are point-by-point and block. In the **point-by-point approach,** you discuss the two items together for each point of comparison/contrast. In the **block approach,** you discuss all of your points of comparison/contrast about one item first and then all points about the other item second. Here are two abbreviated outlines for a paper comparing the sports of baseball and fast-pitch softball, each using one of the two organizational approaches.

Point-by-Point Approach

I.   Pitching
    A.   Method
        1.   Overhand or sidearm in baseball
        2.   Underhand in fast-pitch softball
    B.   Speed
        1.   Up to 100 miles per hour in baseball
        2.   Up to 70 miles per hour in fast-pitch softball

II.   Field dimensions
    A.   Mound
        1.   Elevated to about 12 inches in baseball
        2.   Level with the field in fast-pitch softball
    B.   Infield
        1.   Ninety feet between bases in baseball
        2.   Sixty feet between bases in fast-pitch softball
    C.   Outfield
        1.   Over 400 feet to the centerfield fence in baseball
        2.   Usually no more than 300 feet to the centerfield fence in fast-pitch softball

III.   Equipment
    A.   Balls
        1.   A baseball is approximately 2.75 inches in diameter
        2.   A fast-pitch softball is approximately 3.5 inches in diameter
    B.   Bats
        1.   Baseball bats are usually over 2.5 inches in diameter
        2.   Fast-pitch softball bats are usually under 2.3 inches in diameter

Block Approach

I. Baseball
    A. Pitching
        1. Overhand or sidearm
        2. Up to 100 miles per hour
    B. Field dimensions
        1. Pitcher's mound approximately 12 inches high
        2. Ninety feet between bases
        3. Over 400 feet to centerfield fence
    C. Equipment
        1. Baseball approximately 2.75 inches in diameter
        2. Bats usually over 2.5 inches in diameter

II. Fast-Pitch Softball
    A. Pitching
        1. Underhand
        2. Up to 70 miles per hour
    B. Field dimensions
        1. Pitcher's circle level with the field
        2. Sixty feet between bases
        3. Usually no more than 300 feet to centerfield fence
    C. Equipment
        1. Softball approximately 3.5 inches in diameter
        2. Bats usually under 2.3 inches in diameter

If you compare two items with many features, you should usually use the point-by-point approach. Regardless of the approach that you use, however, you can help guide your readers by doing the following:

- Focusing on the major similarities and differences
- Including the same points of comparison/contrast for both items
- Covering the points in the same order for both subjects
- Using transition words to move from point to point

Writing Activity

Comparing/Contrasting

Read "Just Go (to College)!" on pages 57–59 in Chapter 3, "Writing to Understand and Synthesize Texts." Construct an outline of the major points of comparison/contrast that Tracy Eckendorff offers when she compares arguments for earning a bachelor's degree. Does she use a point-by-point approach or a block approach?

Using Outlines and Maps to Organize Your Writing

Regardless of the organizing strategies that you use, outlines and visual maps can be helpful tools. Commonly used outlines and maps include scratch outlines, formal outlines, and tree diagrams.

Scratch Outlines

Scratch outlines work well early in the process of composing. As rough sketches of your thoughts, they can help you get ideas on paper without much concern for the final organization of the project. A scratch outline might be little more than a list of ideas in the order in which they might appear in the final project. Here is an example:

Solving the Problem of Childhood Obesit

- Open with a story about obesity to grab readers' attention.
- Provide some background/history.
- Describe the problem with statistics.
- Explain the causes of the problem: poor nutrition (five food groups), large serving sizes, lack of exercise.
- Describe the consequences of childhood obesity: diabetes, adult cardiovascular problems.
- For each cause, offer a possible solution: teaching parents how to read nutritional labels; educating children and parents about serving sizes; persuading schools to require physical education; and persuading parents to engage their children in more exercise.
- Conclude.

Formal Outlines

Formal outlines can be useful once you have done some invention work and research. In a formal outline, you arrange your ideas in a series of levels. The first level is marked with roman numerals (I, II, III), the second level with capital letters (A, B, C), the third level with numbers (1, 2, 3), and the fourth level with lowercase letters (a, b, c). Each level must have at least two entries. The entries in a formal outline can be in sentences (a sentence outline) or in words or phrases (a topic outline) as in the following example:

Solving the Problem of Childhood Obesity

I.   Opening story about obesity

II. Background/history of obesity

III. Description and explanation of the problem
  A. Statistical overview of the problem
  B. Causes of the problem
    1. Poor nutrition (five food groups)
    2. Large serving sizes
    3. Lack of exercise
  C. Consequences of problem
    1. Diabetes
    2. Cardiovascular problems in adulthood

IV. Possible solutions
  A. Instruction for parents on how to read nutritional labels
  B. Education for children and parents about serving sizes
  C. Recommendation that schools require physical education and that parents engage their children in more exercise

V. Conclusion

If you wanted a more detailed plan, with sentences that you could actually use in your paper, you could prepare a sentence outline like the following:

Solving the Problem of Childhood Obesity

I.   Many children, such as Heather H., begin the cycle of dieting and gaining weight as early as age 10.

II. Obesity has been increasing in the United States, especially among children and adolescents.

III. Here are some recent, and quite startling, statistics about childhood obesity.

IV. There are several reasons for this problem, including poor nutrition, ever increasing portion sizes, and children's reluctance to exercise.

(continued)

    A. The first reason is that today's children, who live in one of the wealthiest countries in the world, suffer from poor nutrition.

    B. Another reason is that we all seem to expect large serving sizes in every restaurant these days.

    C. Finally, many children don't exercise, preferring to stay indoors for video games and online chats with their friends.

V. The consequences of childhood obesity can be dire.

    A. Diabetes can be one major and severe consequence.

    B. Childhood obesity also leads to cardiovascular problems when children grow up.

VI. Fortunately, some doctors and other experts are turning their time and attention to this problem, and have come up with some unique ideas.

    A. Parents need to learn how to read food labels, so here are some instructions for doing so.

    B. Both children and parents need to understand what a reasonable "serving size" looks like.

    C. Several exercise programs are available that schools can provide to young students—exercise that will be fun and helpful to them.

VII. Childhood is too important a time to spend obsessing about weight, but children should be encouraged to eat a healthful diet and exercise regularly to avoid the dieting treadmill that Heather H. and others like her are on.

Tree Diagrams

FIGURE 13.4
Tree Diagram for a Paper on Childhood Obesity

Like outlines, **tree diagrams** show hierarchical relationships among ideas; Figure 13.4 gives an example.

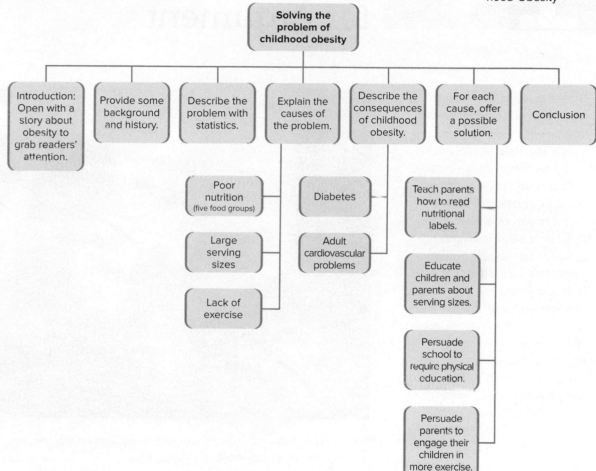

Text Credits

p. 422: Source: Pace, J. (1998), Let's Go Veggie! *Toronto Star.* May 27,1998. **p. 422:** Ehrenreich, Barbara, *Nickel and Dimed: On (Not) Getting by in America* Copyright © 2011 by Barbara Ehrenreich. Page 153. **p. 424:** Source: U.S. Census Bureau, "Poverty: 2003 Highlights". **p. 424:** Lee-Ashley, Matt and Gentile, Nicole, "Confronting America's Wildlife Extinction Crisis" Center for American Progress, October 19, 2015. Copyright © 2015 Center for American Progress. www.americanprogress.org. **p. 424:** Witte, Griff, "Poverty Up as Welfare Enrollment Declines; Nation's Social Safety Net in Tatters as More People Lose Their Jobs" *The Washington Post*, September 26, 2004. A3 **p. 425:** Courtesy of Jessica Hemauer. **p. 425:** Proenza, Mary, "One-Way Ticket: Jacob Lawrence's Migration Series" *The Brooklyn Rail*, June 3, 2015. Copyright © 2015 The Brooklyn Rail. Used with permission. **p. 427:** From "Understanding Teen Dating Violence" Fact Sheet, 2014. National Center for Injury Prevention and Control: Division of Violence Prevention, Centers for Disease Control and Prevention. http://www.cdc.gov/violenceprevention/pdf/teen-dating-violence-factsheet-a.pdf. **p. 428:** Anup Shaw, "Creating the Consumer" Global Issues, May 14, 2003 http://www.globalissues.org/article/236/creating-the-consumer. **p. 430:** Source: Kingston, M. H. (1976). *The Woman Warrior: Memoirs of a Girlhood Among Ghosts.* New York: Knopf. **p. 430:** Source: Kingston, M. H. (1976). *The Woman Warrior: Memoirs of a Girlhood Among Ghosts.* New York: Knopf. **p. 430:** Source: Clark, S. (1991). *Malcolm X: The Man and His Times.* Trenton: Africa World Press. **p. 432:** From Tohe, Laura, "The Stories From Which I Come" in *A Story Larger Than My Own: Women Writers Look Back on Their Lives and Careers,* edited by Janet Burroway. University of Chicago Press.Copyright © 2014 by Laura Tohe. Used with permission. **p. 433:** Momaday, N. S. (1976). *The Way to Rainy Mountain.* UNM Press. **p. 433:** Sullivan, R. (2012). *Rats: A Year With New York's Most Unwanted Inhabitants.* Granta Books. **p. 435:** Adler, Tamar, *An Everlasting Meal: Cooking with Economy and Grace* Scribner, 2011 p.143. **p. 435:** From Murphy, Elizabeth, "'As Having Life': Reflections on the Gem of the Mall" *The Straddler,* Summer 2013. Copyright © 2013 The Straddler. Used with permission. **p. 437:** Definition of "Mugwump" is used with permission of Michael Quinion, *World Wide Words.* www.worldwidewords.org. **p. 438:** Definition of " Luddite" from Tech Target Network is used with permission from Tech Target Network. **p. 439:** Source: http://www.choosemyplate.gov/index.html.

Using Strategies for Argument

Often in our culture, the word *argument* has a negative connotation, as if to *argue* really means to *fight* about something. But the term *argument* in many academic, professional, and civic settings and in most writing situations means to debate with someone about an issue or to attempt to persuade someone to accept your point of view. That does not mean your debating partners, listeners, or readers will end up agreeing with you (or you with them), but rather that, at the end of your argument, your audience will say, "I understand what you mean and can appreciate your position. I don't necessarily agree with everything you've said, but I can see where you're coming from." This kind of argument must have as its thesis an assertion that is debatable, not a certainty, and must generate responses somewhere on the following continuum:

Strongly Disgree ◄—————► **Strongly Agree**

Assertions that are capable of evoking such responses are appropriate **thesis statements** or **claims** for arguments. The fundamental aim of an argument is to move the audience along this continuum of responses toward agreement.

Effective arguers get to know their audiences well enough to understand where on this continuum their responses are likely to lie, and they choose argument strategies based on that knowledge. Of course, some members of the audience will be willing to move farther along the continuum than others.

If "winning" an argument means that the other side sees, understands, and appreciates your position, then your goal is to present your thesis and supporting evidence in a logical manner, so that your reader can at least understand—and perhaps agree with—your position.

© Juice Images/Cultura/Getty Images RF

Argument and Persuasion

When you present an argument, you want readers at a minimum to understand what you mean and to see your perspective. The concept of **argument,** then, is somewhat different from and broader than that of **persuasion.** When you have persuaded someone, you have convinced that person to believe something (this legislative bill is better than that one) or to do something (provide the funding needed for longer library hours).

In a sense, an argument is the means of persuasion: you cannot convince someone about anything without an effective argument. So although you certainly hope that you will be able to persuade the president of your school to increase the hours that the library is open, your overall goal is to construct and present a sound, effective argument. Put another way, after members of your audience read your argument, they may or may not agree with you in part or in full, but if your argument is effective, they will at least think, "I understand this writer's position, and he or she has made a strong case."

Each of the chapters in Part 3 of this book asks you to construct a certain kind of argument, with the goal of attempting to persuade your readers in a variety of ways. For example, Chapter 9 ("Writing to Convince") asks you to argue for a position on a controversial issue, while Chapter 10 ("Writing to Evaluate") asks for your judgment on the quality of a product, event, place, or other subject. In both cases, you may not necessarily cause your readers to change their minds—by switching sides on the issue or rushing out to see the film you recommended. Rather, they will understand your position and the reasons and evidence that support that position. Likewise, for Chapter 11 ("Writing to Explain Causes and Effects"), and Chapter 12 ("Writing to Solve Problems"), you are asked to argue a debatable claim, whether it be a cause-and-effect relationship or a solution to a problem. Readers may not completely agree with your claim, but if it is soundly argued, they should at least be willing to consider it.

Rhetorical Appeals

The philosopher Aristotle was one of the first to notice that effective speakers use three kinds of appeals to help make their arguments convincing. An **appeal** in this sense is a means of convincing your audience to agree with your argument, and perhaps of persuading them to do something. We introduced the three kinds of appeals—*logos, ethos,* and *pathos*—in Chapter 2 (pages 27–29) in the context of rhetorical analysis. Here we focus on using them to construct an effective written argument. You already use these various appeals when you want to persuade your friends to do something with you, for example, or to talk your parents or children into going somewhere.

Logical Appeals

Logical appeals, or, using the Greek word, *logos,* are appeals made through your use of solid reasoning and appropriate evidence, including statistical and other types of data, expert testimony, and illustrative examples.

No matter what kind of evidence you use to support your argument, that evidence must come from reliable sources. For more information on evaluating sources, see Chapter 19.

Consider what kind(s) of evidence will most effectively convince your audience. For example, if you are writing to evaluate something (perhaps a film, a restaurant, or an art museum), quoting known and accepted authorities on the subject is often persuasive. If you are writing to solve a problem, historical information also can be useful by demonstrating, for instance, how other communities have dealt with similar issues or problems.

Ethical Appeals

Ethical appeals, or appeals to *ethos,* focus on your character. When you establish your *ethos,* you communicate to readers that you are credible, intelligent, knowledgeable, fair, and perhaps even altruistic, concerned about the welfare of others. You can establish your ethos by doing the following:

- Present yourself as knowledgeable about your subject matter.
- Acknowledge points of view that differ from yours, and deal fairly with them. For example, you might write, "Other people might say that _____ is less costly than what I'm proposing, and they would be right—my plan does cost more. But the benefits far outweigh the cost, and here is why. . . ."
- Provide appropriate information, including facts and statistics. Some audiences will be receptive to statistical information; others will be more receptive to quotations from experts in the field. Still others might look for both types of evidence.

Emotional Appeals

Appeals to readers' emotions, or *pathos,* can help readers connect with and accept your argument. However, effective arguers use emotional appeals judiciously, avoiding appeals that astute readers might consider exploitive.

There are many ways to appeal to readers' emotions. Here are some possibilities:

- Identify who is or will be affected positively or negatively by a situation or course of action that you are arguing for and ask the audience to identify with them.
- Show how the situation or course of action has emotionally affected people elsewhere.
- Arouse indignation over a current situation by showing how it is inconsistent with a community's value or concerns.

You use all three appeals frequently in everyday life. To convince a friend to go to see a film with you, for example, you might mention that the film, although new and relatively unknown, received an award from the Sundance Film Festival, an appeal in which you draw on the *ethos* of the famous film festival; you might point out that the early showings cost only half as much as the nighttime shows (*logos*); or you might plead that you have no one else to go with and hate going to movies alone (*pathos*).

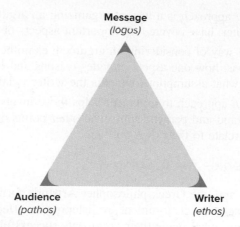

Message
(logos)

Audience
(pathos)

Writer
(ethos)

FIGURE 14.1 The Rhetorical Triangle

The Rhetorical Triangle: Considering the Appeals Together

Most effective arguments combine rhetorical appeals because audiences respond to a variety of appeals. The three kinds of appeal complement one another, as is suggested by the rhetorical triangle shown in Figure 14.1. Each aspect of an act of communication—the writer, the reader, the message—is connected to the other two aspects.

Writing Activity

Considering Your Audience

Construct two brief letters, each no longer than a page. For each letter, assume that you want twenty-four-hour, seven-day-a-week access to your college's library.

- For your first letter, your audience consists of your classmates. How would you argue for your position in a letter to them? What needs would you list, to show those you have in common?

- For your second letter, your audience is the president of your college or university. How would you argue for your position to him or her?

With several classmates, discuss the differences between your letters.

Three Approaches to Argument

In this chapter, we cover three ways to conceptualize argument: classical, Toulmin, and Rogerian. All three approaches are widely used as ways to think about and to design effective arguments. Understanding how they function will help you not only to understand the arguments you read or hear but also to construct your own written arguments.*

---

*Thanks to our good friend and colleague Doug Downs for reminding us of the differences among these three concepts.

- The *classical* approach is a way of organizing an argument to make sure you, as a writer, have covered all important aspects of your argument.
- The *Toulmin* way of considering an argument examines how the argument functions: how one aspect provides reasons and evidence for another and what assumptions underlie the writer's claims.
- The *Rogerian* approach to argument helps those involved in any argument understand and perhaps appreciate other points of view and how those might relate to their own positions.

Classical Strategies for Arguing

Aristotle © SuperStock/SuperStock

About 2,400 years ago, the Greek philosopher Aristotle formalized what we now call the **classical scheme** of argument by listening to effective public speakers and then figuring out what made their arguments successful. Amazingly, Aristotle's ideas remain relevant today. If you are using the classical scheme, this is the sequence you follow:

- Introduction
- Main claim
- Evidence supporting claim
- Discussion of other perspectives
- Conclusion

This approach is called the **deductive** way to reason because you state your claim and then help the reader understand (or deduce) how the evidence supports your claim. Here is a simplified example of how the deductive approach might work in asking for a raise:

- Introduction and main claim

  I'd like to talk with you about raising my salary. I've been with the company for two years now, and for several reasons I feel that I deserve a raise at this point in my career here.

- Evidence supporting claim

  First, I am very effective now at doing work in the office as well as working with customers outside the office.

  Second, I've taken classes to learn several new software programs, and I'm now fully proficient at using them.

  Third, I've shown that I can take on lots of responsibility because I've handled several important projects in the past two years.

  Fourth, my end-of-year rankings have consistently improved.

• Discussion of other perspectives (acknowledging, conceding, and/or refuting them)	Now, I know there was that one dissatisfied customer, but if you'll recall, I managed to satisfy her (at last!) by providing extra service.
• Conclusion	Therefore, I deserve a raise.

The advantage of the deductive method is that you state your position and make your case before your reader starts thinking about other perspectives. Because readers understand what your point is *early* in your text, they find it easier to follow your argument.

If you are using another method, commonly known as the **inductive** approach, you first present and explain all of your reasons and evidence, then draw your conclusion—your main claim. In other words, you provide the evidence first and then the conclusion at the end. The advantage is that your reader may come to the same conclusion before you explicitly state your position and will therefore be more inclined to agree with your view.

For more on deductive and inductive reasoning, see Chapter 9.

An inductive approach to asking for a raise could use the same evidence to support the claim, discussion of other perspectives, and conclusion, but begin without a main claim:

- • Introduction   I'd like to speak with you about my job performance here at our company now that I've been here for two years.

Parts of a Classical Argument

Thinking about the parts of an argument makes the task of arguing more manageable. When you put the parts together, the results can lead to an effective whole.

The classical argument as presented here has five parts occurring in a certain order. However, as you write your own arguments, you may find that not every part is essential in every case, and you may also find it useful to rearrange or combine the parts. The five parts are as follows:

1. **Introduction** (*exordium*): In the introduction, you gain the attention of the audience and begin to establish your credibility. To accomplish this task, you need to have analyzed your audience carefully. Your overall goal in the introduction is to prepare your audience to be receptive to your case.

    Here are some strategies that can work well in introductions for arguments:

    - • Show how the issue affects the audience.
    - • Show how the issue affects the community in general.
    - • Outline what a reader might do about the issue.
    - • Ask a question to grab the reader's attention.
    - • Explain what will happen if the reader does not get involved and take action.
    - • Begin with a compelling quotation.

USING DIGITAL TECHNOLOGIES   **Using Music in Arguments**

If you have ever listened closely to the words of popular songs, whether they are examples of rock, blues, jazz, musical theater, hip-hop, or rhythm and blues, you've probably noticed that many song lyrics follow the patterns of argument. Mining popular culture for examples that can help you build an argument can be quite effective.

If you are asked to write an essay that persuades, consider searching your music collection for interesting and powerful metaphors, statements, and stories you can use as quotations. Whether you collect CDs, download tunes, call up videos on YouTube, listen to podcasts, or even write and produce your own music, it is possible to consider your collection of music as a collection of arguments. Be careful, though, to provide context and reasons for choosing the particular quotations that seem to support your view.

Often, you can insert a sound file into a PowerPoint presentation, which can add an interesting dimension to a persuasive oral presentation. Additionally, you can produce an audio argument by using Audacity, a free audio editing program available online. Be cautious about posting any music online, however. All music—no matter how brief the excerpt—is protected by copyright and is not considered fair use unless it is in the public domain.

2. **Narration** (*narratio*): Here you briefly explain the issue and provide some background or context for the argument you will make, as well as explain why it is important. If your readers understand why the issue is important to *them,* they are more likely to be interested and involved in your argument. You can use a narrative to do the following:

   - State the crucial facts that are generally agreed on.
   - List the main issues or aspects that you will consider in your argument.
   - Introduce the main reasons that support your argument.

3. **Confirmation** (*confirmatio*): This is the main body of your argument. Here you offer evidence to support your thesis or claim. Evidence can consist of facts, statistics, expert opinion, and other information. For example, if you are arguing that students should get involved in the upcoming campus elections, statistics on an issue that affects them personally can help them understand the importance of the campaign.

4. **Refutation** (*refutatio*): If you can argue about a statement, that means ideas or values are in dispute—that is, an issue is undecided and there is another side to your argument. Dealing with that other side, or **counterargument,** is a crucial step: If you fail to deal with the opposition's counterarguments, your readers may think that you are unaware of them or that you are trying to conceal their existence.

   To refute counterarguments, you first need to discover what they are through research or audience analysis. For example, as you share ideas and drafts with your classmates, ask them what arguments the other side might make to address this issue or problem.

   As you consider opposing viewpoints, you need to decide how to handle them. Refutation is only one of several options. Some counterarguments may not be significant enough to merit further consideration;

it may be enough simply to acknowledge them. If you are trying to convince students to vote in a campus election, you might simply acknowledge the objection that one vote does not make a difference: "I understand what you mean, because I used to think that way. And it's true that one vote rarely makes 'the difference' in any election." Or you might decide to refute the objection, noting that "what one person can do is to talk to other people, and convince them that they need to vote, and talk to them about the issues, and then all of a sudden that one person has gotten a lot of other people involved."

Other ways to deal with objections to your argument include the following:

- Agree that *part* of the opposing view is valid, and then demonstrate how the rest of the argument is unsound.

- Accept that the opposing view is valid, but note that what the opposition suggests costs too much / is impractical / will not work because _____ has been tried and been unsuccessful in other places or has some other problem.

- Discredit any authorities they cite in their favor ("Since Jones wrote that, three studies have been published showing that his conclusions were incorrect. . .").

5. **Conclusion** (*peroration*): Here you conclude your argument and, possibly, call for action. In the conclusion, you can do one or more of the following:

- Summarize your case.
- Stir readers' emotions.
- Suggest an action or actions that the audience might take.
- Refer back to the start of your essay, tying everything together.
- List your main points, touching on your evidence for each.

Example: The Classical Scheme in Action

ELIZABETH BRAKE

Philosophers on the Supreme Court's Gay Marriage Ruling

An associate professor of philosophy at Arizona State University, Elizabeth Brake is the author of *Minimizing Marriage*, which won an honorable mention for the American Psychological Association's Book Prize in 2014. She writes about feminist ethics and political philosophy.

Introduction: Here Brake sets the stage, so to speak, as she introduces her argument for marriage equality.

The Supreme Court's decision deserves celebration. *If* there is to be a state-recognized and state-regulated institution of marriage, then equal treatment demands that it be extended to gays, lesbians, and bisexuals. In a context of marriage inequality, this decision is an important statement of legal equality. However, should there be a government-backed institution of marriage in the first place?

Narration: Brake supports her argument by pointing to the philosophical basis for marriage equality.

A number of philosophers have argued that the state should get out of the marriage business, leaving the celebration of weddings to churches and Vegas chapels, and allowing relationship partners to use the tools available in private contract to create enforceable property agreements. Some have argued that for the state to support—much less promote, as the U.S. does—an essentially religious or ethical institution is simply illiberal, just as supporting state-run baptisms or bar mitzvahs would be. Others have argued that the institution bears traces of its patriarchal heritage (in which women were legally subordinate within marriage) and that some provisions of marriage law, in some jurisdictions, facilitate domestic violence. Still others argue that marriage law wrongly imposes a single template for 'the good life' when in fact people seek intimacy in many forms. The state's preference for one form of relationship fails to treat citizens in different relationship forms—and with differing ideals of love relationships—evenhandedly.

Confirmation: Brake exemplifies the important functions served by caring relationships and thereby recognized marriages.

In my view, the state should recognize marriage relationships, because such recognition serves important functions. Most importantly, it protects and supports certain relationships in which people care for one another. Such caring relationships are widespread constituents of people's views of the good life, and they allow citizens to further their life plans in many ways. But not everyone wants, or finds, or idealizes dyadic, sexual, romantic, monogamous love relationships. People seek and find care and intimacy in many forms.

Two single female friends might cohabit, raising children together, or elderly friends might cohabit, providing mutual care. Some adults freely choose to enter polyamorous relationships, in which more than two parties share their sexual and emotional lives. Close, committed friends who share their lives, or small polyamorous groups, can provide the care that some marriages do.

Just as equal treatment demands that same-sex marriage be recognized, it requires that these other committed relationships be eligible for the support and protection which legal marriage provides. That is, if one of the main rationales for marriage law is the protection of devoted love and family life, love and family should be recognized in all their variety. This is not to say that friendships and polyamory should be styled as marriage: many would not want to be viewed as married, and it is important to keep alternate forms of civil recognition for those who oppose marriage on principle. However, such relationships deserve equivalent protection to marriages on grounds of equal treatment. In my view, recognizing and legally protecting the array of relationships in which people live would go a long way towards answering the arguments against legal marriage listed above.

Three caveats should be mentioned. First, while we are celebrating good marriages, we should recall that marriages can go bad—lethally bad—and that it is important to protect exit options. Second, the distribution of health benefits through marriage continues to be an injustice. Third, gays, lesbians, bisexuals, and polyamorists have important interests not covered by marriage law—such as protection against discrimination in employment. Marriage equality is an important step forward, but it is only one step towards full equality.

4

5

Objections and Refutations: Brake offers a possible objection to her argument and then refutes it giving specific examples.

Conclusion: Brake states the importance of marriage equality, but offers three caveats. Despite these caveats, marriage equality is, as she puts it, one step towards a greater equality for all.

Writing Activity

Identifying a Classical Argument

With several of your classmates, find an essay in a newsmagazine (such as *Time* or *The Week*) that is written in the form of a classical argument. Identify each part of the argument:

- Introduction
- Narration
- Confirmation
- Refutation
- Conclusion

Toulmin Approach to Argument

© Sijmen Hendriks

Stephen Toulmin

Another important approach to argument was developed by philosopher Stephen Toulmin in his 1958 book *The Uses of Argument*. As with Aristotle's classical scheme, you already use the main aspects of Toulmin's approach: Every day you make assertions ("All students need to be involved in the upcoming election") and then use "*because* statements" to provide support for those assertions ("because if they are not, they won't have their needs and positions represented to those in power"). Toulmin called your assertion a **claim** and the *because* statement **data.** For example, if you are trying to persuade your classmates to become involved in campus politics, you might claim that their involvement is vital to their own interests. But unless your classmates believe that getting involved will affect them (in amount of tuition they pay, for example), they will not be able to understand why they ought to take the time and make the effort to become involved. So you, as the person making the argument, must consider whether your audience will know why it is important for them to participate, and if you determine that they may not, it is up to you to provide those specific reasons.

What Toulmin adds to this fairly intuitive way of constructing any text is the notion of a **warrant:** *why* the data support the claim. Sometimes you need to say why explicitly; other times you can assume that your reader understands this connection.

In **Toulmin's model of argumentation,** then, three components are considered essential to any argument:

- **Claim:** the conclusion or point that you will argue and hope to convince readers to agree with. For example, your claim might be "A major objective of this country's space program should be to land a crew of astronauts on Mars."

- **Data:** the reasons you give to support your claim. Your data may take the form of *because* statements. You might support your claim about Mars by saying "because knowing about Mars will help us understand our own planet and the life it supports because Mars may have had water—and life—at one time."

- **Warrant:** the connection between the claim and the data, explaining why the data support the claim. Often this connection is obvious and can go unstated. For example, the data and claim above are connected by the idea that it is important that we understand our planet.

Three other components of an argument are considered optional: the backing, the rebuttal, and the qualifier:

- **Backing:** If you are not sure that your readers will see the connection between data and claim, you need to state the warrant and support it as well. The support for the warrant is the backing. If you felt you could not assume the warrant about understanding our planet, you might need to state it explicitly: "Understanding our own planet and the life it supports is crucial to our survival as a species, and knowing about Mars will help us gain that understanding."

• **Rebuttal:** When you rebut the opposition's position, you prove that your position is more effective—for example, that it is acceptable to more people. You might acknowledge the potential objection that space missions with astronauts are costly but argue that the potential benefits outweigh the costs: "While space flight with astronauts is expensive, in terms of our total economy those costs are small, and the possible knowledge that we would gain by putting a human being instead of a machine in charge of data collection is priceless."

• **Qualifier:** In response to opposing positions and points, you may need to in some way limit or modify, or qualify, your claim. You can do this by indicating precisely the conditions under which your claim does and does not apply. Qualifiers often include words such as *sometimes, possibly, may,* and *perhaps.*

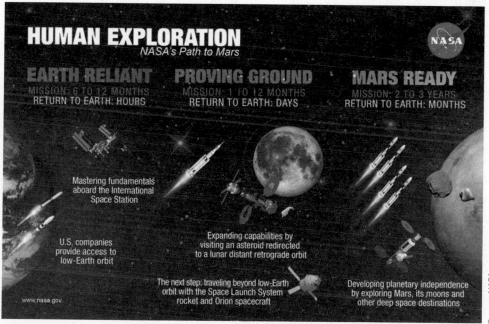

HUMAN EXPLORATION
NASA's Path to Mars

NASA

EARTH RELIANT
MISSION: 6 TO 12 MONTHS
RETURN TO EARTH: HOURS

PROVING GROUND
MISSION: 1 TO 12 MONTHS
RETURN TO EARTH: DAYS

MARS READY
MISSION: 2 TO 3 YEARS
RETURN TO EARTH: MONTHS

Mastering fundamentals aboard the International Space Station

U.S. companies provide access to low-Earth orbit

Expanding capabilities by visiting an asteroid redirected to a lunar distant retrograde orbit

The next step: traveling beyond low-Earth orbit with the Space Launch System rocket and Orion spacecraft

Developing planetary independence by exploring Mars, its moons and other deep space destinations

www.nasa.gov

Source: NASA

This image from NASA provides potential data for the argument presented above.

Example: The Toulmin Model in Action

Why Study Overseas

These excerpts from the Web page of the U.S. Department of State focus on issues related to studying overseas: why you should consider studying abroad and some of the possible issues you might face (and how to overcome them).

Claim: Studying abroad will be an enriching experience—and an experience you cannot get any other way.

Data: Overseas study is good because it helps you connect with new people.

Warrant: Connections with new people and new cultures are a good thing.

Backing: Through interacting with new cultures, you'll grow in understanding.

Data: Studying overseas is good because you'll learn new skills.

Warrant: Learning any new skill is beneficial.

Backing: You'll learn to effectively interact with people, and so will build new friendships.

Claim that will be rebutted: Studying abroad has some problems.

Why Participate?

When you experience a different culture, you gain a deeper understanding of yourself and those around you—deepening your knowledge about the world in a way that books, school assignments, and a professional career can never reveal.   1

Make Lasting Connections

Create lasting connections on your exchange experience when you connect with members of your host family or the friends you will meet at your host institution. The world is full of new people to meet, so be sure to reach out and make an effort to smile, talk to people, and make time to cultivate friendships you may have the rest of your life. By doing this, you become aware of the inner concerns, hopes, and dreams of a family, a neighborhood or city, a nation, and global community. And with this realization comes the corresponding knowledge of what it means to belong to your own particular country and culture.   2

Learn New Skills

As an exchange participant you will develop leadership skills, self-confidence, and a greater understanding of the complexities of the world around you. Getting to know the local citizens, experiencing their culture, and living as they do: these are things tourists miss, and this is where you really discover the way of life in another country with all its subtleties.   3

Embark on your educational or cultural exchange program and gain knowledge about another country and its language and culture. Experience building new friendships, taking responsibility for yourself, respecting differences, and tolerating the beliefs of others.   4

Culture Shock

Once abroad you may face an adjustment period referred to as "culture shock." Moving to a new country can be a very stressful experience. Everything is unfamiliar: from weather, landscape, and language to food, fashion, values, and customs.   5

The degree of "shock" depends on such factors as length of study abroad,   6
flexibility, tolerance for ambiguity, degree of difference between home and host
culture, prior experience abroad, and his or her expectations. Culture shock is a
normal part of study abroad, and it shows that your daughter or son is experiencing the differences between American culture and that of the host country.

Symptoms of culture shock can include: 7

- homesickness;
- depression;
- feeling lost and out of place;
- frustration;
- irritability;
- and fatigue.

The following information may be helpful to understand the three phases   8
that occur in culture shock:

Three Phases of Culture Shock

Phase I: The Honeymoon

During this initial period participants often feel excited to embark on   9
their new journey. You are open to trying new things and exploring your host
country.

Phase II: The Rejection

- You may miss your usual ways of dealing with school, work, relation-   10
  ships, and everyday life.
- You may find yourself studying for hours, longer than your classmates
  and colleagues because of language differences. If you are trying to
  speak and listen to a new language every day and trying to understand how things are done, it may feel like an overwhelming effort.
- You may feel homesick and idealize your life back home, while being
  highly critical of life in your new community. Feeling frustrated,
  angry, anxious, or even depressed is not uncommon.
- You may experience minor health problems and/or disruptions in
  sleeping and eating patterns.
- Your motivation may diminish, and you may feel like withdrawing
  from your new friends. This is a natural reaction to living in a new
  culture.
- You may contemplate going home early before completing your
  program, degree or research.
- You may be angry at not finding what you had expected.
- Helping your spouse and children adjust to life in their new culture
  may pose an additional challenge.

Qualifier: Some of the problems some students experience may not apply to you or your children; there are solutions that will help with culture shock.

Data: These are the phases most students go through **because** they are part of the process

Backing: we know this because other students experience this sequence

Backing: You'll end up enjoying and learning from the experience, as others have.

Phase III: The Recovery

- It is important to understand that as time passes you will be better able to enjoy your new surroundings.   11
- Your feelings and attitudes about living in a new country may improve, but you may never get to the high level experienced during the first phase.
- You may become more relaxed, regain your self-confidence, and enjoy life in your new country. Major obstacles that occurred in the earlier phases, such as misunderstandings and mistakes, will be easily understood and resolved.

Ways to Diminish Feelings of Culture Shock

Data: There are ways to help, so use them **because** they will make your experience better and you'll get over culture shock more quickly.

- "Plunge" into your host culture and wrestle with the differences.   12
- Keep an open mind; it is natural to have preconceived ideas and beliefs that come into question while abroad.
- Athletic activities like team sports or taking walks may be helpful.
- Get to know others at your host school or organization.
- Do not isolate yourself.
- Find a local person with whom you can discuss your frustrations and encounters.
- Learn as much as you can about your host culture.
- Maintain a support structure with others, particularly those going through the same experience. However, do not retreat into an American "clique" to avoid the discomfort of culture shock.
- Keep a journal. Record your impressions of new experiences and the transformations that are occurring within you.

> ## **Writing** Activity
>
> ## Using a Toulmin Argument
>
> Consider an issue you think is important to your classmates. Construct a brief Toulmin argument in which you identify your claim and the warrants your classmates need to believe in order to accept your argument. This issue could be something of local interest, such as online courses, or a matter of national significance, such as health care.

Rogerian Strategies for Arguing

Rogerian argument, which is based on the work of psychologist and mediator Carl Rogers, allows for the fact that at times we will take perspectives on issues that conflict with the views of people with whom we have important relationships. Suppose you and a close friend disagree about how to solve the problem of alcohol-related traffic fatalities. Although you could use classical argumentative strategies to win this argument, in the long term, your relationship might be better served by a conversation in which you try to see the other point of view.

Carl Rogers

Differences of opinion occur in all four areas of life—the academic, the professional, the civic, and the personal. And in all four areas, we have relationships that we want to maintain. We might therefore do better to resolve our differences without trying to "win." Although the strategies of classical argument may work well in settings where the participants are clearly opponents trying to convince a third party (two lawyers making their case to a jury, for instance), they do not work so well when the participants need to maintain a collegial, friendly, or even loving relationship. And although such strategies may work well when your topic is relatively uncontroversial or your audience is disposed to agree with your claim, they may be more likely to alienate than to persuade your audience when your topic is controversial and your audience is hostile to your claim. You might think of Rogerian argument as a "kinder, gentler" way to argue—and one that might often serve you well.

The ultimate goal of Rogerian argument is to negotiate differences and cooperate to reach a resolution that benefits or is in some way acceptable to both parties. Thus, in Rogerian argument, it is useful to begin by thinking about commonalities—that is, by thinking about and understanding opposing views and asking yourself, "Even though we may have some differences, what do we have in common?" or "Even though we may not think alike, how can we work together effectively to solve this problem?" Rogerian argument asks you to "feed back" opposing arguments. This approach requires you to understand the other person's position and to think enough about that position to articulate it. Stating the other person's position does not mean that you agree with it, of course, but that you understand it and that you recognize the other side of the argument.

Rogerian arguments have several components:

- **Introduction:** The introduction includes a description of the issue you hope to come to a consensus on. As you state a goal, keep your tone positive and invite others to participate in solving the problem or reaching agreement.

- **Summary of opposing views:** Be as accurate and as neutral as you can in stating the views of those who may disagree with you. Show that you have the skills, character, and fairness to see and appreciate the merits of opposing views.

- **Statement of understanding:** After you have stated the opposing views, demonstrate that you understand why others might hold such views. If possible, indicate the conditions under which you too could share those views.

- **Statement of writer's position:** The previous three parts have prepared your readers to listen to your views, and here is the place to state them. Invite your audience to consider your views in the same way that you have considered theirs.

- **Statement of contexts:** Building on the statement of your position, be specific about the kinds of conditions under which you hope others will find merit in your position.

- **Statement of benefit:** Explain how your position or solution will benefit those who might oppose you. End on a positive and hopeful note.

Example: Rogerian Strategies in Action

DANIEL H. COHEN

For Argument's Sake

Daniel H. Cohen is a professor of philosophy at Colby College, where he teaches courses in argumentation, logic, and medieval philosophy. The transcript of his TED talk appears below. (You can watch his TED talk at www.ted.com/talks/daniel_h_cohen_for_argument_s_sake). In his talk, Cohen argues that the usual ways we argue often focus on "argument as war," and that we could benefit from a new model, a new approach to argumentation, one in which the arguers learn from the argument.

1　My name is Dan Cohen, and I am academic, as he said. And what that means is that I argue. It's an important part of my life, and I like to argue. And I'm not just an academic, I'm a philosopher, so I like to think that I'm actually pretty good at arguing. But I also like to think a lot about arguing.

2　And thinking about arguing, I've come across some puzzles, and one of the puzzles is that as I've been thinking about arguing over the years, and it's been decades now, I've gotten better at arguing, but the more that I argue and the better I get at arguing, the more that I lose. And that's a puzzle. And the other puzzle is that I'm actually okay with that. Why is it that I'm okay with losing and why is it that I think that good arguers are actually better at losing?

3　Well, there's some other puzzles. One is, why do we argue? Who benefits from arguments? And when I think about arguments now, I'm talking about, let's call them academic arguments or cognitive arguments, where something cognitive is at stake. Is this proposition true? Is this theory a good theory? Is this a viable interpretation of the data or the text? And so on. I'm not interested really in arguments about whose turn it is to do the dishes or who has to take out the garbage. Yeah, we have those arguments too. I tend to win those arguments, because I know the tricks. But those aren't the important arguments I'm interested in academic arguments today, and here are the things that puzzle me.

4　First, what do good arguers win when they win an argument? What do I win if I convince you that utilitarianism isn't really the right framework for thinking about ethical theories? So what do we win when we win an argument? Even before that, what does it matter to me whether you have this idea that Kant's theory works or Mill's the right ethicist to follow? It's no skin off my back whether you think functionalism is a viable theory of mind. So why do

Discusses the focus of his talk: arguing.

Introduction: The better he gets at arguing, the more arguments Cohen loses. Why is it okay to lose, and what does "winning" an argument really mean?

Cohen continues to wonder about losing and wonders who benefits from a losing argument. He says he wants to focus on academic arguments and has some questions.

Cohen states more questions: What does someone win if they "win" an argument? Is it just convincing the other person to believe something that persons doesn't want to believe? What are the effects of doing that?

we even try to argue? Why do we try to convince other people to believe things that they don't want to believe? And is that even a nice thing to do? Is that a nice way to treat another human being, try and make them think something they don't want to think?

Cohen outlines three methods of argumentation, which he hopes we all can all agree on. The first model: argument as war.

Well, my answer is going to make reference to three models for arguments. 5 The first model, let's call this the dialectical model, is that we think of arguments as war, and you know what that's like. There's a lot of screaming and shouting and winning and losing, and that's not really a very helpful model for arguing but it's a pretty common and entrenched model for arguing.

His second model: a mathematical approach.

But there's a second model for arguing: arguments as proofs. Think of a 6 mathematician's argument. Here's my argument. Does it work? Is it any good? Are the premises warranted? Are the inferences valid? Does the conclusion follow from the premises? No opposition, no adversariality, not necessarily any arguing in the adversarial sense.

Cohen suggests a third model of argumentation: argument as performance (an attorney trying to convince a jury, for example).

But there's a third model to keep in mind that I think is going to be very 7 helpful, and that is arguments as performances, arguments as being in front of an audience. We can think of a politician trying to present a position, trying to convince the audience of something. But there's another twist on this model that I really think is important, namely that when we argue before an audience, sometimes the audience has a more participatory role in the argument, that is, arguments are also audiences in front of juries who make a judgment and decide the case. Let's call this the rhetorical model, where you have to tailor your argument to the audience at hand. You know, presenting a sound, well-argued, tight argument in English before a francophone audience just isn't going to work. So we have these models—argument as war, argument as proof, and argument as performance.

Argument as war is the dominant model, even down to the wording we often use when we talk about argumentation

Of those three, the argument as war is the dominant one. It dominates 8 how we talk about arguments, it dominates how we think about arguments, and because of that, it shapes how we argue, our actual conduct in arguments.

But, Cohen argues, the "argument as war" approach actually doesn't work well as a way to effectively argue, and he explains why.

Now, when we talk about arguments, yeah, we talk in a very militaristic 9 language. We want strong arguments, arguments that have a lot of punch, arguments that are right on target. We want to have our defenses up and our strategies all in order. We want killer arguments. That's the kind of argument we want. It is the dominant way of thinking about arguments. When I'm talking about arguments, that's probably what you thought of, the adversarial model. But the war metaphor, the war paradigm or model for thinking about arguments, has, I think, deforming effects on how we argue.

The "argument as war" approach has only negative benefits.

First it elevates tactics over substance. You can take a class in logic, argu- 10 mentation. You learn all about the subterfuges that people use to try and win arguments, the false steps. It magnifies the us-versus-them aspect of it. It makes it adversarial. It's polarizing. And the only foreseeable outcomes are triumph, glorious triumph, or abject, ignominious defeat. I think those are deforming effects, and worst of all, it seems to prevent things like negotiation or deliberation or compromise or collaboration. Think about that one. Have you ever entered an argument thinking, "Let's see if we can hash something out rather than fight it out. What can we work out together?" And I think the argument-as-war metaphor inhibits those other kinds of resolutions to argumentation. And finally, this is really the worst thing, arguments don't seem to get us anywhere. They're dead ends. They are roundabouts or traffic jams or gridlock in conversation. We don't get anywhere.

Oh, and one more thing, and as an educator, this is the one that really bothers me. If argument is war, then there's an implicit equation of learning with losing. And let me explain what I mean. Suppose you and I have an argument. You believe a proposition, P, and I don't. And I say, "Well why do you believe P?" And you give me your reasons. And I object and say, "Well, what about . . . ?" And you answer my objection. And I have a question: "Well, what do you mean? How does it apply over here?" And you answer my question. Now, suppose at the end of the day, I've objected, I've questioned, I've raised all sorts of counter-considerations, and in every case you've responded to my satisfaction. And so at the end of the day, I say, "You know what? I guess you're right. P." So I have a new belief. And it's not just any belief, but it's a well-articulated, examined, it's a battle-tested belief.

Great cognitive gain. Okay. Who won that argument? Well, the war metaphor seems to force us into saying you won, even though I'm the only one who made any cognitive gain. What did you gain cognitively from convincing me? Sure, you got some pleasure out of it, maybe your ego stroked, maybe you get some professional status in the field. This guy's a good arguer. But cognitively, now—just from a cognitive point of view—who was the winner? The war metaphor forces us into thinking that you're the winner and I lost, even though I gained. And there's something wrong with that picture. And that's the picture I really want to change if we can.

So how can we find ways to make arguments yield something positive? What we need is new exit strategies for arguments. But we're not going to have new exit strategies for arguments until we have new entry approaches to arguments. We need to think of new kinds of arguments. In order to do that, well, I don't know how to do that. That's the bad news. The argument-as-war metaphor is just, it's a monster. It's just taken up habitation in our mind, and there's no magic bullet that's going to kill it. There's no magic wand that's going to make it disappear. I don't have an answer. But I have some suggestions, and here's my suggestion.

If we want to think of new kinds of arguments, what we need to do is think of new kinds of arguers. So try this. Think of all the roles that people play in arguments. There's the proponent and the opponent in an adversarial, dialectical argument. There's the audience in rhetorical arguments. There's the

11

12

13

14

Benefit: now the "loser" has a "well-articulated, examined . . . belief"

In the "argument as war" approach, what does the "winner" gain? Some self-satisfaction, perhaps, but the "loser" actually makes the cognitive gain!

Cohen asks how we can change the way we argue, and he suggests we need new exit strategies.

But, Cohen argues, we need to see ourselves as the arguer and the audience: that would be the real benefit to learning a new way to argue.

reasoner in arguments as proofs. All these different roles. Now, can you imagine an argument in which you are the arguer, but you're also in the audience watching yourself argue? Can you imagine yourself watching yourself argue, losing the argument, and yet still, at the end of the argument, say, "Wow, that was a good argument." Can you do that? I think you can. And I think, if you can imagine that kind of argument where the loser says to the winner and the audience and the jury can say, "Yeah, that was a good argument," then you have imagined a good argument. And more than that, I think you've imagined a good arguer, an arguer that's worthy of the kind of arguer you should try to be.

Now, I lose a lot of arguments. It takes practice to become a good arguer   15
in the sense of being able to benefit from losing, but fortunately, I've had many, many colleagues who have been willing to step up and provide that practice for me.

Thank you.

Writing Activity

Constructing a Rogerian Argument

With several of your classmates, construct a Rogerian argument, focusing on some campus or national issue or problem.

Some Common Flaws in Arguments

Any argument, no matter how effective, can be marred by **logical fallacies,** or flaws in reasoning. Although sometimes introduced deliberately into an argument with the aim of misleading readers, such flaws are often inadvertent, and avoiding them requires the kinds of critical thinking discussed in Chapter 2. The following list includes the most common and easily avoided fallacies.

- **Appealing to irrational fears:** All humans have fears, and it is often easy to exploit those fears. Someone making the argument that cattle ranchers should test each cow every month, even though there have been only a few isolated cases of mad cow disease in the United States, would be exploiting an irrational fear.

- **Appealing to pity:** Although appeals to pity and other emotions can be justified at times, this kind of appeal can mask an otherwise weak case. If a student who is failing a course because she has missed many classes and performed poorly on exams appeals to her instructor by pleading, "If I fail this course, I won't graduate on time," she is obviously masking a weak case.

- **Appealing to prejudice:** Also known as *ad populum,* this fallacy occurs when the writer appeals to a preexisting prejudice. A common example is the practice of putting an image of the American flag on a bumper sticker that advocates a particular product or stance, with an appeal to patriotism thus substituting for an argument for the product or stance. For example, Figure 14.2 is an advertisement for the American Civil Liberties Union (ACLU) that uses the American flag to indicate that their cause is patriotic. How does this image influence your initial reaction to the ad?

- **Appealing to tradition:** The most common form of this appeal is the statement "We've always done it this way in the past."

- **Arguing from a lack of knowledge or evidence:** We can illustrate both forms of this flaw with the following example: You have looked for a needle in a haystack, and your search has been unsuccessful. From this lack of evidence, one person might argue that there must be a needle in that haystack if you would only search more carefully. From the same lack of evidence, a second person might argue that there is no needle in the haystack. In reality, of course, neither conclusion can be supported.

- **Attacking the opponent's character:** Often called an *ad hominem* attack, this fallacy is sometimes used in an attempt to direct attention away from the logic of a case—usually a strong case—by evoking a negative emotional response to the person making the case. In an effort to make an opponent seem like a hypocrite, a person might say, "My opponent argues that vegetarianism is a moral choice, but I notice that he wears leather shoes—so it is acceptable to *wear* part of an animal, but not to eat part of one? That is hypocritical!" The opposite fallacy (*pro hominem*), which is also common, involves directing attention away from a case—usually a weak case—by evoking a positive emotional response to the person making it. A legislator might appeal to the public to support an unworthy bill by praising the record of the colleague who introduced it: "Because Representative Smithers has advocated good ideas in the past, we should vote for her plan to drill for oil in Central Park."

- **Attributing false causes:** Usually called *post hoc, ergo propter hoc*

FIGURE 14.2 An Advertisement for the ACLU, Using the Familiar Stars and Stripes as Part of Its Appeal

("after this, therefore because of this"), this fallacy occurs when someone assumes that event A caused event B because event A occurred before event B. A common example is superstitious thinking: "I've been having so much bad luck recently because I broke a mirror/walked under a ladder/crossed the path of a black cat." This fallacy is common in civic life. In political campaigns, for example, an incumbent will often claim that his or her policies have caused the economy to improve, whereas a challenger will charge that the incumbent's policies have caused crime rates to increase. All sorts of events occur before other events in the world, but that does not mean that they cause those other events.

- **Bandwagon appeal:** Here the arguer is essentially saying, "Many people are doing it, especially people whom you admire, so it must be a good thing to do. You should do it too." Television beer commercials frequently use this appeal when they show a group of young, attractive people having a great time at a party: if those people are having such a good time drinking that brand of beer, anyone who drinks it will also have a good time.

- **Begging the question (circular reasoning):** This fallacy treats a questionable assertion as if it has already been answered or fully explained, as in the following example: "My friend would never cheat because he's an honest person." To assert that someone is honest is not to provide evidence that he did not or would not cheat; this assertion merely restates the idea that the person would not cheat but has nothing to do with whether he actually did cheat.

- **Complex question:** In this ploy, an arguer asks a question that actually has two parts and demands a one-part response. For instance, the question "When did you stop beating your dog?" has embedded in it the assumption that you used to beat your dog. The person to whom it is addressed would be right to reply, "Hold on. Let's first establish whether I have ever beaten my dog in the first place."

- **Either-or reasoning:** Also known as "false dichotomy," this fallacy occurs when writers give readers two opposing choices (either A or B) when other possibilities also exist. For instance, a person might state, "You can major in business administration, or you can plan on getting a crummy job."

- **Faulty analogy:** In this fallacy, the writer makes a comparison that is in some way misleading or incomplete—or that does not even relate to the topic being discussed. A columnist who writes, "Leading a country is like running a business. In both cases, the bottom line is the most important consideration" is using a faulty analogy because governments and businesses are different in significant ways.

- **Guilt by association:** This fallacy occurs when a writer seeks to discredit an opponent by associating the opponent with some unpopular person, group, or idea, as when politicians attempt to brand their opponents with labels such as "free-spending liberal" or "hard-right conservative." Such labels imply that *all* liberals are "free spending" or that all conservatives are "hard-right"—and both labels have negative connotations.

- **Overgeneralization:** This fallacy occurs when someone reaches a conclusion based on insufficient evidence, especially atypical examples. For instance, your friend engages in overgeneralization when, after an automobile accident in which she was not wearing a seat belt but sustained only minor injuries, she says, "See? Seat belts aren't necessary."

- **Oversimplification:** People sometimes search for simple answers to complex problems. For instance, some might say that the solution to gang violence in high schools would be simply to require students to wear uniforms in school. Of course, the problem of gang violence is complex, and its solution will not be that easy.

- **Red herring (or non sequitur):** This fallacy occurs when the writer introduces an irrelevant point to divert attention from the issue being considered. The fallacy gets its name from the practice of dragging a red herring—a fish—along the ground to distract hunting dogs from the scent that they are following. A student who says to his teacher, "I know that I was late for class today, but I've been on time every other day" is using a red herring to throw the teacher off the scent of the real issue: The student is late.

- **Slippery slope:** This fallacy claims that once something starts, it must continue, just like a person sliding down a slippery slope. An example is the student who says, "We've got to fight that proposed fee for using the computer center. If that fee is enacted, pretty soon they'll be charging fees for using the restrooms on campus."

- **Stacking the deck:** Here the writer presents evidence for only one side of the case. A student who says, "I should get an A because I handed in all my homework," while neglecting to mention that she got a C on the midterm and final exams, is stacking the deck.

- **Straw person:** This fallacy occurs when an arguer distorts the opponent's argument and then attacks that distorted argument. For instance, a few decades ago, when equal rights for women was a hotly contested issue, some people made statements such as "Equal rights for women means that women will have the right to use men's restrooms. What is this country coming to?" Unisex restrooms were not part of what women's rights advocates were arguing for.

- **Universal statements:** Such statements often include words such as *always, never, all, everyone, everybody, none,* or *no one.* Of course, some statements that include those words are true—for instance, "All humans are mammals." However, when writers use those words to describe human behavior or beliefs, those statements are usually problematic. For example, the statement "Men never share their feelings, but women always do" could be easily contradicted with just one or two cases.

Writing Activity

Searching for Logical Fallacies

To help you learn to identify logical fallacies, find several instances of them in your local or campus newspaper. (Hint: Often, letters to the editor provide rich material!). Bring copies to class, share them, and explain the logical fallacies to your classmates.

Text Credits

p. 454: Brake, Elizabeth, Philosophers on the Supreme Court's Gay Marriage Ruling" *Daily Nous*, June 29, 2015. Copyright © 2015 by Elizabeth Brake. Used with permission. **p. 458:** "Adjusting to a New Culture," Bureau of Educational and Cultural Affairs Exchange Programs, U.S. Department of State. Exchanges.state.gov/us/adjusting-new-culture. **p. 463:** Cohen, Daniel H. "For Argument's Sake" TEDxColby College, Filmed February 2013. Copyright © Daniel H. Cohen. Reprinted by permission.

Using Strategies for Collaboration

Although writing can be a solitary activity, it is often a collaborative endeavor. For instance, researchers in the sciences, education, and engineering often coauthor research proposals and reports. In business, teams often write project proposals and reports. In local, state, or national legislatures, many people collaborate to write bills to present to their colleagues. When groups of neighbors or parents are concerned about some local problem, they will often collaborate on a letter to the editor of their local newspaper or to the school board. In your writing classroom, you will probably have the opportunity to get feedback from your classmates, and in other courses, you are likely to encounter assignments that require you to work as part of a team.

© Banana Stock/Jupiter Images RF

Working with Peers on Your Single-Authored Projects

As you craft your own writing projects, working with peers can yield many benefits. Early in the process of crafting a project, peers can help you generate ideas by challenging you to consider other perspectives. Later in the process, peers can point out ways to revise your writing so that readers will find it more understandable, informative, or persuasive. Peers can also help edit your prose.

In the chapters in Parts 2 and 3 of this book, "Writer's Workshop" activities help you solicit feedback from peers. It is your responsibility to encourage peers to offer candid assessments of your work. Peers should not be nasty, of course, but they *should* give you a clear sense of how well your writing is fulfilling its purpose.

Strategies for Working with Peers on Your Projects

Feedback from peers can help you at any point in a project. Although it is important to seek and use the perspectives that peers can offer, it is equally important to remember that *you* are ultimately responsible for the project. Given this principle, the following guidelines can be useful:

- Peers can indicate what is working well—and not so well. When peers ask for more information, you should consider adding that information to your next draft.
- Peers' questions are usually more helpful than their suggestions.

Using Digital Technologies for Peer Review

If it is difficult to find time to meet face-to-face with peers outside of class, digital technologies for peer review can help. Even if it is easy to meet face-to-face, though, writers still can use digital tools. Here are some common tools that you can use:

- The track-changes feature of your word-processing software makes it easy to see the changes that different reviewers are suggesting in a document. You can then accept or reject any or all suggested changes.
- The comment feature of most word-processing software makes it easy to offer a suggestion or pose a question to the writer.
- Many instructors use a course-management system such as Blackboard or Canvas to offer courses either completely or partially online.
- Wikis offer writers the opportunity for peer review. Changes to documents in wikis are automatically tracked. Changes can easily be made by anyone with access to the document.
- More and more instructors are using technological tools such as Google Docs to facilitate peer collaboration.

Working with Peers on Multiple-Authored Projects

Working with your classmates on multiple-authored projects can have many benefits. One long-term benefit is that it will prepare you for coauthoring documents with your colleagues in the workplace. Another benefit is that working with a group can infuse a project with a rich array of perspectives.

Group work also presents challenges, however. Some members of the writing team may be inclined to contribute too much to the project while others sometimes seem to contribute too little. Some coauthors may insist on doing things their way without listening to potentially effective ideas from others.

Strategies for Working with Peers Effectively

Working with peers can be challenging because they may question your thinking in new and sometimes uncomfortable ways. In college, this kind of interaction is especially likely because your classmates may have personalities and/or cultural backgrounds that differ substantially from yours. Although encountering a variety of backgrounds and perspectives can move you out of your comfort zone, it can also be a catalyst for learning.

Collaboration can take place in several ways. You might find yourself working on an entire project with the same team. Or you might find yourself using one classmate or a small group of your classmates as peer reviewers for drafts of one another's works. The "Writer's Workshop" sections in Parts 2 and 3 suggest strategies for peer review of single-authored works.

To make the most of your work with peers, try the following strategies:

- **Listen empathically to your group members' comments and questions.** Empathetic listeners strive to understand why someone is making a particular comment or raising a particular question.

- **Assign roles to members of the group.** One member of the group can be the *recorder*, whose duty is to keep track of who says what. Another member of the group can be the *question-asker*, posing questions to encourage everyone to think more critically or deeply. Yet another group member can be the *facilitator*, whose role is to keep the discussion focused and moving forward. It is important that every group member have some *specific responsibility* to perform.

- **Provide positive and constructive feedback.** Every piece of feedback can be stated more or less negatively or more or less positively. Further, every negative or less-positive statement can be recast into a more positive form:

USING DIGITAL TECHNOLOGIES | Using a Wiki to Collaborate

Working in groups can be a challenge, especially when you are in an online class or your group members are trying to schedule out-of-class work time together. You might want to consider using a free online groupware site, or even a wiki. A wiki is an interactive Web site that allows members to create, add, delete, and change content. Each group member can edit existing content and develop separate materials on linked pages. Wikis and groupware document sites eliminate the confusion of keeping track of multiple e-mails in your inbox. Some popular sites to try out free of charge include *Google Groups* (groups.google.com), *Google Docs* (docs.google.com), *Wikidot* (www.wikidot.com/), and *Wikispaces* (www.wikispaces.com).

Less Positive

There's an error in this sentence.

This paragraph is underdeveloped.

You don't have a conclusion.

More Positive

You could edit the sentence this way:

You could develop this paragraph by adding this:

What are you planning to say in the conclusion?

- **Pay attention to interpersonal dynamics.** Before the group begins discussing the assigned topic, ask each member of the group to respond to the following kinds of questions:
- What can the group do to function most effectively?
- What seems to impede our group from functioning effectively?
- What encourages you to contribute effectively to the group?

- **Do round-robin sharing.** To ensure that every member of the group contributes equally, go around the table clockwise, with each person contributing one after the other. Do this as many times as necessary to solicit everyone's contributions.

- **If possible, keep the group relatively small—three or four members.** Larger groups become hard to manage, and it becomes difficult to coordinate calendars or to reach consensus.

- **Consider your class and your peer group to be intertwined communities.** Make a commitment to improve the work of each community and each member of the community. If every member makes such a commitment, everyone will benefit.

- **Celebrate your accomplishment.** When the project is completed, treat yourselves, perhaps by enjoying coffee or lunch together.

- **Never take peer comments personally.** Comments and suggestions are directed at your paper, not at you. So if a classmate says, "this part of your paper is confusing," the comment is about the paper—not about you.

One way to ensure the success of any group endeavor is to plan. The tasks that follow will help you to plan various aspects of your work with your group.

DEFINE SUCCESS FOR THE GROUP

What will count as success, and how can the group achieve it? You might use the following chart, for example, to define success and to identify the means for achieving it.

Defining Group Success	
Sign of Success	**Method(s) for Achieving**
Everyone shows up for our meetings at the agreed-on time.	Add meetings to daily planners and/or smartphones.
Everyone participates equally.	Use a round-robin approach for sharing ideas during discussions.

DEVELOP A PLAN FOR DEALING WITH GROUP PROBLEMS

Potential problems include a group member who dominates a discussion, doesn't carry a fair share of the load, or misses a deadline. If a problem does surface, deal with it immediately. Dealing with small problems immediately can keep them from becoming bigger problems. If a problem arises, do *not* focus on who is to blame; instead, focus on finding a solution.

SET SHORT-TERM AND LONG-TERM GOALS

Before the group begins a particular work session, decide what you want to accomplish in the session—your short-term goal. As you work, stay focused on that goal until you achieve it. If the group will work together over multiple sessions, decide on a long-term goal to achieve by the last session. Then establish short-term goals for each session along the way.

Project Goals	
Long-Term Goals	**Short-Term Goals**
Complete the project by November 16.	Complete library research by October 3.
	Complete interviews by October 10.

DEVELOP A PLAN FOR COMPLETING THE PROJECT

Identify the subtasks that need to be completed along the way, as well as a time line for completing each subtask. Write down who is responsible for each task, and make certain that each member of the group has a list of everyone's responsibilities. As each deadline for a subtask approaches, ask the responsible member or members to report on progress.

MAKE A CALENDAR OF GROUP MEETINGS

Group meetings can be held face-to-face, by telephone, or in online chat rooms. For each meeting, establish an agenda and identify what each person needs to do before the meeting. Also, decide who will serve as the discussion leader for each meeting, and assign a different discussion leader for each meeting.

Calendar for Meetings

Meeting Date	Agenda Item(s)	Individuals' Preparation	Discussion Leader
October 11	Examine interviews	Hanna: Bring three copies of transcripts of interviews with rental-property owners.	Hanna
		Molly: Bring three copies of transcripts of interviews with renters.	
		Meghan: Bring three copies of transcript of interview with city attorney.	

Using Digital Technologies to Facilitate Multiple-Authored Projects

Whether or not collaborative meetings are held in person, digital tools can support the process. Here are some tried-and-true suggestions for using digital tools:

• Agree on a sequence for working on each digital file to avoid duplication of effort.

• For revising, use the track-changes and comment features of your word-processing software. That way other members of the group can see the changes that you are making.

• When you send a file to another member of the group for revising or editing, copy the other members of the group so that they can be certain who is working on the document and can see the progress on the project.

• When you name files, include the current date in the file name, such as "rental_paper_10–18–16." Don't delete older versions of files because you may need them to recover a deleted paragraph or to recover a file that has become corrupted. You might also include the initials of the team member who worked on the most recent version— e.g., "rental_paper_DHR_10-19-16."

Making Effective Oral Presentations

Along with invention, arrangement, memory, and style, *delivery*—the way you present a message—is one of the five canons of rhetoric. In most of this book, we have dealt with written or visual forms of delivery. In this chapter, however, we will consider oral presentations, a form of delivery that is becoming increasingly important in all areas of life.

- In your academic life, you will be asked to make presentations in some of your classes.
- In your professional life, you will often be asked to present your ideas to your colleagues and to clients.
- In your civic life, you may speak before the local school board, or to the city council, or in front of any number of civic or political organizations.
- In your personal life, you may be called on to give a speech at an occasion such as a wedding, a funeral, or a school reunion, or you may speak at a less formal gathering of your family or friends.

© Image Source/Getty Images RF

As with written communication, oral presentations are *rhetorical acts*. To prepare an effective oral presentation, you need to ask yourself the same questions that you would ask for any writing situation:

- What do I want to accomplish? In other words, what is the purpose of this presentation?
- Who is my audience? What do they already know about my topic?
- What is the context surrounding this presentation?

- How much do I already know about my topic, and what else do I need to learn about it?

Once you have decided what you want to accomplish with a particular audience on a specific occasion, you will have a better understanding of how you need to prepare: what kind of research you need to conduct, what types of information you need to collect, and what kinds of visuals you should prepare.

Developing Your Presentation

You can use several approaches to develop an oral presentation. For more formal presentations on complex topics, you might decide to write the full text of your presentation. In some situations, you might choose to read your full text, especially if you have to use specific words at specific moments during your presentation. In other situations, you might write the full text and then prepare an outline of it. You might then speak from that outline, which is written on a sheet of paper, appears on a set of PowerPoint slides, or both.

 ## Establishing a Clear Structure

As with any piece of discourse that you construct, an oral presentation needs to have a clear organization that helps you to achieve your purpose. For most oral presentations, you will need to do the following:

- Construct an effective, thought-provoking, and attention-grabbing *introduction*. Remember that during your presentation, your listeners may be tempted to let their attention wander. Therefore, part of your job is to draw them in, to tell them something that will interest them, and to indicate quickly how your topic affects them.

- Let your audience know the *main point(s)* that you plan to make. Often called **forecasting,** this technique is especially important in oral presentations. If you have five main points that you want to cover, name them. Each time you move to the next point, make note of that, too ("The third point I want to make is . . . "). It often helps to provide the audience with a written outline of your points.

For more on supporting claims with evidence, see Chapters 9 and 14.

For more on using transitions, see Chapter 13.

- Include sufficient evidence to *support* each of your claims. You will be much more credible as a speaker if you support your claims with facts, examples, statistics, and testimony from experts.

- *Point back* to your main point so that it will be easy for your listeners to understand exactly how each point that you make or piece of information that you provide relates to your thesis.

- Use *visual aids* to outline the structure of your talk, if the situation calls for them. Your PowerPoint or Prezi slides should outline the points you want to make, which you will then elaborate on. The message of each visual needs to be readily apparent.

- Use your *conclusion* to summarize and emphasize your main point, and to outline briefly how everything in your presentation supports it.

VISUAL *Thinking* | **PowerPoint or Prezi Presentations**

Consider the most *ineffective* ways to use or a PowerPoint or Prezi presentation:

- The speaker uses very small type, so any text would be difficult for the audience to read.
- The speaker spends part of the designated speaking time setting up or becoming familiar with the projection equipment.
- The speaker simply reads the visuals to the audience.
- The speaker uses every PowerPoint or Prezi special effect on every slide.
- The speaker faces *away from* the audience while reading the text on the screen.
- The speaker walks to the screen and uses a finger to point to words on the screen.

Now contrast that presentation with an effective one:

- Each visual aid uses appropriate type sizes, colors, and graphics to illustrate the speaker's main points.
- Before the presentation, the speaker learns how to use the equipment and sets it up.
- The speaker talks directly to the audience, using the text on each visual only as a starting point, which he or she then elaborates and explains.
- The speaker uses PowerPoint or Prezi special effects sparingly.
- The speaker talks directly to the audience, making eye contact and looking for signs that the audience is "getting" what the presentation is about.
- If necessary, the speaker uses an inexpensive laser pointer to point to specific words on the screen.

Suppose you were assigned to write an academic paper focusing on whether students litter on your campus, and you needed to prepare an oral presentation as part of that assignment. The slide in Figure 16.1 on page 480 is one possible way for you to start a PowerPoint or Prezi presentation on that topic.

The photograph can help you get your audience's attention and focus them on your topic. Each subsequent slide can contain the same heading but provide the points you want to discuss in your presentation. Your second slide (Figure 16.2) might offer examples that suggest that students really are *not* slobs.

You will elaborate on these **talking points** as you make your presentation, discussing each one in detail and providing more information to support each point as you make it. For example, for the first point you could add the following information:

For more on visuals for presentations, see Chapter 18.

- Student organizations collect all recycled products in classrooms and office buildings.
- Student groups make money through this recycling effort.

(continued)

(continued)

Are students really slobs?

© Kent Matthews/The Image Bank/Getty Images

FIGURE 16.1   An Opening Slide for a Presentation

Are students really slobs?

Not necessarily. At our college, students

- help with the campus recycling program.
- are responsible for cleaning their dorm rooms.
- are subject to weekly inspections.
- are fined if their bathrooms are not clean.
- serve on a task force to keep our campus beautiful.

FIGURE 16.2   A Second Slide

- Students work together in the dorms to collect recycled products.
- Several student leaders serve on the Campus Recycling Board (CRB).

As you speak, then, you will flesh out each point with specific examples that are not on the slide but that provide information and details for your audience.

Considering Your Audience

Your *audience* is your primary concern as you plan, develop, and deliver your presentation. Every decision you make depends on your awareness of that audience, from considering what they already know about your subject, to what they need to know to believe what you tell them, to how you should present yourself to that audience. So consider: How do you want to come across to your audience? As informed and logical? As thoughtful? Probably. Or as someone shouting at them? Or droning at them? Probably not.

USING DIGITAL TECHNOLOGIES ── **Enhancing Oral Presentations with Visuals and Audio**

Using graphic, audio, and video files to enhance your oral presentations is not just a good idea—in this day and age, it's often expected. Audiences are not usually critical of video that is less than perfect as long as it illustrates an important point. Before incorporating media into your oral presentation, however, use the following checklist to make sure your presentation goes smoothly:

- Examine the room, lecture hall, or space where you will be presenting. Note the size and shape of the room, the seating arrangements, and the available equipment.

- If you are using video or sound media, make sure you have allowed enough time for the video or audio clip to play.

- Keep it brief. Do not give the audience time to get uncomfortable or restless while the video or sound is playing.

- *Always* plan a fallback handout, visual chart, or anecdote in the event that the technologies available in the room suddenly fail.

- Choose music, video clips, and images that are relevant to your presentation and that strengthen your claims and positions.

- Practice your presentation, including the time it takes to start and stop each video or sound element.

- Once you feel that you have developed and practiced your presentation sufficiently, ask a friend, coworker, or classmate to be your test audience. Be open to this person's feedback. Video and sound elements should illustrate, add meaning to, and clarify main points, not distract or confuse your audience. If your test audience tells you that it's not clear why you have incorporated media, ask for comments and suggestions.

- Give the audience time to react. If they *do* enjoy the media you've incorporated, give them a moment to laugh or applaud before you continue with your presentation.

One way to move your audience in the direction you would like them to go is through what magician and author Steve Cohen calls "command [of] the room." He recommends that you do the following:

- Look listeners in the eye. This might seem hard to do, especially if you are speaking before a large crowd, but you can always find someone to look at and speak to directly. Find these folks in several parts of your audience, and soon it will look like you are speaking personally to *everyone* in that audience.

- Hold that eye contact longer than you might expect to.

- Speak in a conversational tone and manner.

- Remember the 45-degree rule: If you are concerned that you might wobble as you speak, make sure to put one foot in front of the other, at about a 45-degree angle. It's impossible to wobble when you stand that way.

Finally, always make certain that your listeners can hear you, projecting your voice to the farthest member of your audience. To make certain that the audience can hear you, begin your presentation by asking, "Can folks in the back of the room hear me if I speak at this volume?" It's also a good idea to ask people to raise their hands and cup their ears if they can't hear you.

Writing Activity

Analyzing and Evaluating a Speech

Author Dale Dauten suggests listening to the "top 100 speeches" and other speeches available at www.americanrhetoric.com/. Visit that Web site and listen to a famous speech. In no more than two pages, write a brief analysis by responding to the following questions:

- What do you think made this speech famous?
- How effective do you think it was? Why?
- How effective do you think its original audience found it? Why?
- How was it organized?
- What were the main points of the speech?

Eliminating the Fear of Speaking in Public

The fear of speaking in public is often at or close to the top of lists of common fears. However, a bit of nervousness before a presentation can be a positive thing. If you are not nervous, you can be overconfident and not do a very effective job. Here are some techniques that can help you overcome stage fright:

- Be overprepared. Know what you want to say. Know your subject. If you plan to use visual aids, be prepared for the unexpected—for example, a broken projector.

- Practice *out loud* several times before your presentation. The more you practice, the better your presentation will be, period. *Thinking* what you want to say and actually *saying it aloud* are really two different things. When you just think about a presentation, your mind tends to fill in the words you leave out. But when you force yourself to practice out loud, you will end up with a much more polished presentation.

- Time your presentation so you know that it fits whatever time parameters you have been given. You want to avoid having your host hold up a sign that says "TWO MINUTES LEFT" when you still have eight minutes of material to deliver in your presentation.

- Another way to eliminate the fear of speaking, or at least to avoid showing that fear, is to use a clipboard to hold your notes. A piece of paper held in your hand might shake, but a clipboard will not.

- *Visualize* making a successful presentation before you make it. *See yourself* in front of your audience. *Listen* to them applaud. *See* audience members nod in agreement. *See yourself speaking with them* afterward. Picture what you want to happen, and it will.

- As you speak, do not let minor distractions bother you. If you hear noise from an adjoining room or from the street outside, ignore it. Do not assume that the person in the back row who appears to be laughing is laughing at you. Any number of things will distract you. You need to ignore them and concentrate on what you want to say.

Other Tips for Making Effective Oral Presentations

- Show enthusiasm.
- Use hand gestures purposefully.
- Become aware of any tics (such as saying "um," playing with your hair, or rubbing your nose) and eliminate them. One strategy is to video record your speech and then watch it with a friend or classmate. Another strategy is to watch for these distracting behaviors while practicing in front of a mirror.
- Before a presentation and immediately following it, invite members of the audience to ask questions at the end of the presentation.
- Do not rely solely on visuals, especially a PowerPoint or Prezi presentation. Because digital technology can fail, be prepared to give a presentation even if the computer or the projector fails to function properly.
- After practicing your presentation with a script or notes, also practice giving it with a bulleted list of your main points. Put that list on a 3″ × 5″ card.
- Always say "thank you" at the end of your presentation. You will find it to be surprisingly effective (and thoughtful).

Online Presentations

It's not uncommon for people to make online presentations. Whether you're taking an online class or being asked to make a presentation to a group of people who can't gather in the same place at the same time, you can now use digital technologies to record and deliver a presentation. (You might use the recording function in PowerPoint or choose a screen recording program such as Quicktime Player or Camtasia.) When you develop an online presentation, follow the same general guidelines you would use when making a face-to-face presentation. However, make sure to pay close attention to the following points.

- Make sure your audio track matches the text on each slide.
- Use visuals that enhance the point you are trying to make.
- Script your presentation before you record it. Then practice reading it several times before recording it. You are much more likely to give a professional-sounding presentation if it's scripted and you have practiced it.
- Keep your digital presentation under eight minutes. People tend to stop paying attention to online presentations that last longer than eight minutes.

Writing Activity

Making an Oral Presentation

Using one of the projects that you wrote for Part 2 or 3 of this textbook, prepare and deliver an oral presentation. Revise and adapt your project to suit your new medium and purpose by establishing a clear structure, using effective visual aids, and considering your audience according to the strategies described in this chapter.

If you have a video camera and can record your presentation so you can play it back and critique yourself, so much the better. But in any case, when you practice, think of your work as *rehearsal:* Go through your presentation from start to finish, without stopping. If you mispronounce a word or drop your notes or the projector does not work, just continue as if you were actually giving your speech.

Choosing a Medium, Genre, and Technology for Your Communication

© Bridgeman Images

As long as humans have recorded their experiences, they have used technologies that act as tools to record their ideas.

The image that opens this chapter is a portion of a prehistoric cave painting from caves in Lascaux, France. The paintings are approximately 17,000 years old. Although we know little about the person or people who made this image, we can surmise that painting was a useful technology for communicating with the intended audience. We do know that this medium (painting on a cave wall) allowed ancient humans to record images that might be decorative, might be symbolic, might tell a story, or might have performed a combination of these functions. Although cave painting is a type of communication—or **genre**—that has been lost, its medium is certainly durable, having survived for thousands of years.

Communication technologies are as varied as paint on a cave wall or a canvas, a piece of chalk, a ballpoint pen, or a word-processing program. Whatever a writer's purpose, the availability of a particular tool often helps to

determine what **medium**—method of delivery—that writer uses to communicate.

When writers use a specific communication technology, they need to understand the impact that the technology will have on that communication. You do not always have a choice of which technology or medium you can use. But when you do, you need to understand the potential and limitations of each, and you need to make your choice in a rhetorically sound way. This

chapter will provide an overview of communication technologies, suggestions on evaluating publishing options, and guidelines for choosing the most effective genre and medium for your work. This chapter will also discuss design considerations and computer-mediated technologies.

Communication Technologies

Consider Figure 17.1. This rock next to the Rio Grande river in New Mexico appears to show some ancient petroglyphs. Is the more recent writing on the rock a revision or new text? Is this "rock writing" an example of using a technology?

Communication technology is not necessarily an electronic device. Because writing is itself a technology, every tool that we use to compose is a kind of communication technology. Some communication technologies, such as word-processing software, encourage revision while others, such as pen and paper, make revision more difficult. On the other hand, a handwritten letter, while difficult to revise, may make a more personal connection with your reader than a word-processed document. And pens and notepaper are easier to carry than laptop computers and do not require an electrical outlet, a battery, or an Internet connection to function.

For an overview of digital technologies for computer-mediated communication, see pages 490–496.

Writing is inextricably linked to the technology that produces it. Understanding your own process and what communication technologies will work most effectively and efficiently for you in a given writing situation is important to your success as a writer. One of the goals of any writing course—such as the one you're now taking—is to help you determine which technologies to use for the writing situations that you encounter, and to help you learn how to use them effectively.

© Greg Glau

FIGURE 17.1 Rock with petroglyphs and other writing

Publishing Your Work

When you write letters or even when you write for an academic purpose, you are usually writing to one person or to a small number of people. As a result, your communication is generally private. When you *publish* your written work, however, you make it public. You can publish your writing in a variety of ways, from printing a newsletter and distributing copies to a limited group of people to constructing a page on the Web that is accessible to anyone. Although publishing your work can be exciting, it also involves both responsibilities and risks.

As recently as the 1970s, the only way to publish a piece of writing was in some kind of print medium. Publishing meant typesetting a manuscript and reproducing it on a printing press, a process that was both time-consuming and expensive. With the advent of the Internet, specifically the hypertext environment of the Web, today's students have technology and publishing options and opportunities that were unheard of in the past. Now anyone who constructs a Web page on a server connected to the Internet publishes a document that is available to the entire world. If you are like our students, for example, you probably spend some time on Facebook and Twitter. While these are not academic "publishing" by any means, they are a way for you—a student—to publish and share information with students everywhere.

If you publish to a broad audience, and especially if you publish online, you need to remember that those who view your work will be forming an opinion of you and your ideas that is based solely on what they see and read. Comments made in haste, without thought and reflection, can sometimes come back to haunt their authors. Members of your audience will also respond in some way to the design of your document or Web page—to the colors, the typeface, the size of type, the arrangement of items on the page or screen, and so on. If you make assertions, they will expect you to provide proof. As with any other form of written communication, they will also expect you to follow the conventions of spelling, grammar, punctuation, and mechanics. If you do not, you will weaken your credibility. Whether you publish in print or in an electronic medium, you will enhance your credibility if you choose an appropriate genre.

Selecting a Genre and a Medium

At the beginning of any writing task that has an audience beyond their immediate circle, writers need to decide which established form, or genre, to write in and the best medium in which to publish their work.

In choosing a genre and medium, you need to consider carefully the audience, the context, and the purpose for your writing. For example, if you are writing a set of instructions for the operation of a propane camp stove, you can expect that the people who will read those instructions will usually be outdoors and often in isolated locations. The instructions will be more useful and effective if they are published in print and in a size that is easy to pack and carry. On the other hand, if you are providing information about the academic support resources available on your campus and most of the students on the campus have high-speed Internet access, the best way to reach this audience may be to publish the information on a Web site.

The chapters in Parts 2 and 3 include further details about genres.

Deciding on a Genre for Your Work

The genre you use for your writing is usually determined by your rhetorical purpose: Who is your audience, and what are you trying to accomplish with that audience? Sometimes, of course, whoever asks you to write will dictate the genre:

- Your employer asks you to construct a formal proposal.
- Your art teacher asks you to construct and present an oral report that uses visuals in the form of handouts or a PowerPoint or Prezi presentation (for more on presentation software, see page 495).
- Your Aunt Hanna asks you to send her a letter about your recent move to a new city, and she especially requests that you print photographs in the letter.
- Your college president requests e-mail responses to a proposed new student fee.

Much of the time, though, you will select the appropriate genre based on your audience and rhetorical purpose:

- If you want to suggest to the president of your college that your campus cafeteria needs a healthier selection of food, a formal letter or proposal is probably the best approach (Chapter 9 focuses on persuasive writing).
- If you want to provide information to your community about an upcoming campus art exhibit, a brochure or poster might be the best genre (Chapter 7 focuses on informative writing).

For more on some common genres, see Appendix C.

- If you want to analyze an upcoming proposal to raise school taxes, a wiki, blog, or Facebook page might be useful genres with which to present your analysis—and any one would allow others to chime in as well (Chapter 8 focuses on analytical writing; for more on blogs and wikis see pages 491–492).

Once you have decided on the genre, you will have to decide which medium will be the most effective in presenting the information (or your argument, evaluation, request, and so on). And your writing might take several forms. For example, if you are writing to share an experience (see Chapter 5), you might outline your shared experience in one of these forms:

- In print form, as an essay for your writing class or a newsletter to your extended family
- On the Web, including several pictures, to share with family and friends
- As a pdf file on the Web that readers can download and print
- In an audio or video clip that you can e-mail to readers and/or make available as a Web link

Deciding Whether to Use Print, Electronic, or Oral Media

Few academic papers are handwritten these days. Usually, you need to turn in an assignment printed in type on paper or in some kind of electronic medium. Often you have no choice; your instructor will specify a medium and format. However, in other situations your instructor might not specify the medium and format and instead will expect you to make the proper rhetorical choice.

Because the same information can usually be provided in both print and electronic forms, the medium you choose often depends on how that information is going to be used. Consider how each one also helps you accomplish different tasks better than the other.

Features of Paper and Electronic Documents

Criteria	Medium: Print on paper	Medium: Electronic
Portability	Easily portable	Can be sent almost instantly over the Internet; needs devices for portability such as a laptop, e-reader, or smartphone
Control of design	Relatively easy to control	Less easy to control—issues can be screen size and resolution
Ability to search	More difficult to search—needs a good index	Easy to search—can use linked keywords
Revision	Once printed, difficult to revise—have to go back to the electronic version	Easy to revise

Paper documents work best when you are providing information in a narrative or sequential organization. Much academic writing, which is often argumentative, works well in print form because argument, which involves stating and supporting a thesis, is best presented as a linear sequence of points. On the other hand, if you are providing information that does not need to be read sequentially or chronologically, then hypertextual electronic formats, in which readers can use links to move easily from one section to another, offer an advantage over paper documents.

Writing Activity

Selecting a Medium

With several of your classmates, consider the following writing tasks. For each one, decide what genre and medium might be appropriate to get your message across to the audience indicated.

- A group consisting of you and your neighbors wants to collect comments and information on a problem with what appears to be an illegal dump near a school and present them to the town council.

- To increase public awareness of the different organizations on campus, your group has been asked to send information to various civic clubs such as the Rotary, Kiwanis, and Elks. With the material will be a request for donations to your school organizations.

■ ## Considering Design

In addition to choosing a genre and medium for your work, you will need to decide on a design for it. We know that many people absorb information more readily when it is presented in a diagram or a chart. And we know that how a document looks will affect our response to it. Chapter 18 covers the principles of effective design and provides guidelines for incorporating visual material in your writing. No matter what design functions you use, your goal in using them should be to make your message more effective. Learning how to use the technologies that allow you to produce graphs and charts will help you in college as well as in your career.

 ■ ## Considering Digital Technologies

Your choice of a medium for your work may depend not only on the writing situation and the genre you have chosen but also on the availability of computers and the Internet to you and your audience, and on your—and their—comfort level with using them.

When you think about the way you use computers during your writing process, you probably think about using word-processing software to compose, revise, and edit your various drafts. Although these uses are important, they are not the only way that computers can help you during your writing process. You might use a computer to find information on the Internet or to access library databases. In addition, you can use word-processing software at other times besides composing, such as when you are taking notes or brainstorming, listing, and doing other invention work. You can even use other technologies, such as e-mail, blogs, wikis, or instant messages, for exploring topics and sharing ideas and drafts with peers.

The following technologies give you additional tools and options for writing and publishing your work.

E-mail

Many of us use e-mail frequently. Familiar though it may be, e-mail is a powerful technology. To make the best use of it, you need to be aware of some basic rhetorical issues.

- **Tone:** E-mail messages range from very informal to formal, depending on your audience. If you are writing to a close friend, a family member, or even a classmate, you may feel comfortable using nonstandard words such as *gonna* or *dunno* or acronyms such as *BTW* (by the way) or *ASAP* (as soon as possible). However, using nonstandard language in your e-mail correspondence with supervisors, instructors, or people you don't know may harm your credibility with your audience.

- **Audience:** Although you may send an e-mail to a specific person, *that* person might forward your e-mail or include it in another e-mail to someone you don't even know, so be aware of and cautious about what you say. If you have a sensitive message to convey or want to address serious issues, pick up the telephone.

- **Ethos:** Your e-mail address will be seen by everyone to whom you send e-mail. If you send e-mail from work or school, your address is often assigned to you—and usually consists of a form of your name. However, when you set up a personal e-mail account, you can choose your own address, which will therefore say something about you. Like a vanity license plate on a car, addresses that are overly cute are inappropriate in a professional environment. Consider using different personal addresses for different purposes. When you are looking for a job, use a personal e-mail address instead of your work e-mail because your current employer may have access to your e-mail account.

For more on e-mail as a genre, see Appendix C.

Threaded Discussions

A **threaded discussion** is simply e-mail that, instead of being sent to individual addresses, is posted on the virtual equivalent of a bulletin board. Participants add their comments in the appropriate place—either as an extension of a previous message or as a new topic or "thread." The advantage is that everyone can see what the other participants are saying.

Threaded discussions can help instructors and students perform a variety of writing tasks. If the class is being offered entirely online, threaded discussions are a substitute for in-class discussions. If the class meets face-to-face, threaded discussions are one way to work collaboratively on a class assignment or participate in a discussion outside of class.

Synchronous Chat

At its most basic level, **synchronous chat** is simply a way to communicate with someone else in real time using text. Synchronous chat brings individuals together in a space to communicate. Programs like Second Life allow you to "teleport" to a virtual world and interact through the use of avatars. These days most people who use synchronous chat are likely to be using some kind of instant messaging (IM).

Although instant messaging and other forms of synchronous chat are a great way to communicate with distant friends or relatives, you can also use the same technology for a variety of group or team activities, including classroom and workplace tasks. Synchronous chat provides an incredibly powerful environment for brainstorming. Because most chat software has a logging function, you can keep a written record of your conversation or brainstorming session and use it later in your writing. The convenience of having a record of what has been said can also be used by employers to terminate employees who misuse company equipment. When using IM in the workplace, always be professional and appropriate with your keystrokes.

For a definition of brainstorming, see Chapter 4, page 64.

Blogs

Blogs are a type of online journal. Like pen-and-paper journals, blogs often feature personal, reflective writing, but blogs are posted on the Web and are therefore public documents. Because blogs are consciously written as public documents, they are often about subjects that might interest large numbers of people, such as politics or sports or the entertainment industry. However, they tend to retain their personal flavor because there is seldom, if ever, any accountability for what gets written in a blog. Some blogs are the work of a single author; others are interactive. They allow, and even encourage, multiple writers to take part in the conversation.

Wikis

A **wiki** is "a page or collection of Web pages designed to enable anyone who accesses it to contribute or modify content" (http://en.wikipedia.org/wiki/Wiki). A wiki allows readers not only to read what is posted (as in a blog) but also to add or modify the content. In a real sense, then, a wiki is a living document that changes according to the thoughts about and written responses to information and ideas already posted. Although the most famous wiki is probably the online encyclopedia *Wikipedia,* there are many other uses for a wiki:

- Businesses use wikis to share information and to let employees add and correct information.
- Families, especially extended families, can use a wiki to post information on family members, family reunions, and important occasions.
- College students can use a wiki to share information, to work on collaborative writing assignments, and for other purposes related to their course work.
- Teachers use wikis to share curricular material, lesson plans, and assignment prompts and to encourage students to have online discussions about key topics in the discipline.

Word-Processing Software

Word processors such as Microsoft Word, OpenOffice, and Pages have always performed four basic functions: inserting text, deleting text, copying and moving text, and formatting text. One important advantage that word processors offer is that they are a very forgiving technology. Changes are easy to make. This ability to revise texts easily opens up all kinds of possibilities for writers. Major revisions become easier because moving chunks of text from one place to another takes only a few simple clicks. Editing your text becomes easier because you can make minor changes with just a few keystrokes, instead of having to retype or handwrite the entire paper. In addition, other functions allow a writer or writers to edit a text and peer reviewers to make comments on it. You will most likely do a lot of writing in your college classes, so *For more on effective* becoming familiar with the functions of your word-processing program will *document design and* serve you well.

the use of visuals, see   While all documents need to be well written, readers now expect word-
Chapter 18. processed documents to look professional as well. Formatting options include, but

are not limited to, type fonts and sizes, tables, boxes, and visual effects such as numbered and bulleted lists. If a writer needs to include graphics, they can be inserted directly into the word-processed document. Options for designing a document continue to increase as technology improves.

USING DIGITAL TECHNOLOGIES | **Learning New Software Programs**

Use the "barter system" to discover how you and your classmates can help one another become more proficient with various software applications. Make a list of all the computer programs (software applications) you have used, and compare the list with those made by your friends. Are there programs you would like to learn to use?

Are there programs you can show someone else how to use more effectively? Take advantage of any free time you have in the computer classroom or computer lab to help someone else—or ask for someone's help—in using unfamiliar programs that will aid your peers in their classes or on the job.

Writing Activity

Using Editing Features

Using whatever word-processing software you have available, investigate some of its editing features. Is there a track-changes feature? If so, try it. Is there a comment feature?

Working in teams of two, each student should write a paragraph or two on what you think is the most interesting or challenging feature of your word-processing program. Save your writing as an electronic file, and then share it with your teammate. Edit your teammate's file, using the track-changes and comment features.

Peer-Review Applications

As increasing numbers of writers use computer software to collaborate, the software keeps improving. The programs that writers use for this purpose fall into two distinct categories: collaborative tools built into standard word-processing programs, as discussed on page 492, and Web-based editing programs.

One type of Web-based editing program is a wiki—software that allows open editing of Web documents. A wiki is useful when writing teams work over distance and do not necessarily share the same computer operating systems or Web-browsing software. This flexibility makes wikis useful for student projects. You may also find Google Docs helpful; the "see revision history" feature allows collaborators to return to previous drafts and see what changes have been made to the file. More and more writing teachers are using Google Docs (or a similar program), so it will benefit you to learn how to use such technology.

One Web-based program that allows peers to comment on your work is available to you as part of Connect Composition, which is available with this text. This software permits you and the other members of your assigned peer group to make comments about one another's writing and to view and respond to those comments.

Graphics Software

Today, it is possible to enhance your documents using a variety of visual information: tables, charts, graphs, photos, drawings, and other visual images. Although you can design some tables using a word-processing program and graphs and charts using a spreadsheet, other images need to be digitized (that is, put into a form that can be read by a computer). The easiest way to render many visuals in a digital format is to use a graphics program such as PaintShop-Pro or Illustrator. If you are taking photographs yourself, you can use a digital camera. If you have a printed image, however, you can easily digitize it by using a scanner.

Once the image is digitized, you can manipulate it by using graphic editing software such as PhotoShop. Image-editing software allows you to change the size or resolution of the digital image, crop out unneeded elements, or change the contrast. However, image-editing software also makes it possible to change images inappropriately. Just because it is easy to change a photo does not mean that you *should* change it. The ease with which we can alter images raises serious ethical questions.

 USING DIGITAL TECHNOLOGIES | **Protecting Your Computer**

Letting someone use your computer can result in downloads and icons you don't want or need popping up on your screen or freezing your computer when you least expect it. Especially when your school computer is used for "recreational" purposes, files and programs can clog up your machine, causing resource issues that can mean an expensive trip to the tech support service. It's better to limit the number of people who use your computer and to resist the urge to use someone else's computer. Most colleges provide computer labs on campus, and the staff at the computer lab can usually help you with any problems that arise. In order to avoid corruption and loss of your data, be sure to back up all of your documents often. Besides saving documents to an external device, you can e-mail copies of documents to yourself.

We have all seen examples of famous photographs that have been altered to include a person who was not in the original image or to change a person's appearance in some way. Some doctored photos might be considered funny, or may make some point, as in the photo shown in Figure 17.2. One of the more famous "doctored" photographs shows Russian dictator Joseph Stalin walking with a group of men . . . and in the bottom photograph, the man on Stalin's left has disappeared. These and other altered photographs are detailed in David King's book, *The Commissar Vanishes: The Falsification of Photographs & Art in Stalin's Russia.*

Desktop Publishing Software

Desktop publishing software such as Quark and InDesign allows writers to produce documents on their personal computers that are ready to be professionally printed. Although people who are comfortable with computers and have some

© Fine Art Images/Superstock

© RIA-NOVOSTI/AFP/Getty Images

FIGURE 17.2 This Figure of Joseph Stalin was modified so that one person "disappeared" from the original print—perhaps to make a political point?

training in layout and design can readily do some simple desktop publishing tasks, most people need training or practice in its use. Most desktop publishing programs are designed to construct short documents, and people often use them to prepare flyers, brochures, and newsletters. Such software gives you control over your document, including more precision in placing and manipulating images and more control over *leading* (the spacing between the lines) and *kerning* (the spacing between letters).

VISUAL *Thinking* | **Using Image-Editing Software Ethically**

If you are thinking of altering a photo, the first question you need to ask yourself has both ethical and legal implications: do I have the right to change someone else's image without that person's permission? Unless you already own the image or have the owner's permission to use it and alter it, making changes may very well violate the creator's copyright. Because you will need the owner's permission to use the image, make sure you also get permission to change the image if you would like to do so. You may think that cropping out what you consider to be unnecessary parts of a photo might not be an issue, but the copyright owner might see the situation differently. Second, you need to be sure that by making changes you are not misrepresenting your subject or misleading your readers.

Presentation Software

At some point in their careers, almost all professionals make oral presentations. Sometimes professionals need to make a presentation to an audience of peers or higher-level employees. At other times they may need to do a sales presentation or present a report on a project in a more informal setting. Most professional presenters include some kind of visual component to help keep their audience's attention focused on the presentation. In the past, presenters often used large charts or posters, slides, or overhead transparencies. Now, most professionals use presentation software such as PowerPoint or Prezi. Presentation software allows you to format slides for a presentation easily and professionally. If you do not have access to PowerPoint, you can use Impress, a compatible, open-source (free) program that is part of the OpenOffice desktop software suite. Google Docs, another free Web-based presentation program, allows you to import PowerPoint files and easily share and collaborate on presentations online.

For more on oral presentations and presentation software, see Chapter 16.

When using presentation software, you need to remember that your slides should complement your presentation, not be its focus. When you give a presentation, you want your listeners to focus primarily on what you say. If you use a graphic, the graphic should add to, not detract from, the content of the slide. Think of your bullet points as "talking points" or even as hyperlinks. What you actually say is the equivalent of clicking on a link in a Web page for more information. Take care not to use your slides as speaking notes for your presentation, and use only a limited amount of text on each slide.

Technologies for Constructing Web Pages

Web pages are computer files that can be viewed using software called a **browser.** Examples of browsers are Chrome, Safari, and Firefox. Web pages are coded using hypertext markup language (html). The html coding places information in the document that allows the browser to display the page properly. There are many ways to construct a Web page:

- Use the "save as a Web page" option in your word-processing software. This option has the advantage of being easy and is appropriate for very simple, straightforward Web pages.

- "Hand code" the hypertext markup language (html) (this means writing the actual mark-up tags in a text editor like Notepad or TextEdit). This option gives you more control over the design of your site, but it is time-consuming.

- Use an html editor like Dreamweaver. Because html has become increasingly complex, most professionals now use html editors.

- Use a Web-based page construction tool like Google Sites. Web-based tools usually have both visual (word processor–like) and html editor modes. They have the added advantage of instantly providing you with an opportunity to view your page exactly as it will appear online before you publish it.

For more on writing Web pages, see Appendix C.

Although you need to be sensitive to the look and feel of your Web pages, ultimately what will matter most is their content. The most important question will be, "How effectively am I getting my message across to the audience that I am targeting?"

Communicating with Design and Visuals

The two documents on this page combine written and visual elements. The poster at the top of the page was crafted with specialized graphics software, commonly available in university or college computing labs. The flyer below uses one of several widely available word-processing software programs.

Whether you are designing an elaborate poster or a simpler one, you can use the same standard design principles that are the focus of this chapter.

When you apply the principles of design, you need to consider your writing situation and make rhetorical choices. Here are some questions to consider:

- What are you trying to accomplish with your text, and how might design and images help you achieve your goals?
- What kind(s) of design elements and images might appeal to your audience?
- How will the available technology affect the design and image choices you make?

© National Organization for Women

For a discussion of reading visuals critically, see Chapter 2.

BEAUTIFUL**WOMEN**

1999 Love Your Body Campaign
www.nowfoundation.org

Recollections of a Pioneer

The birth and development of aviation as seen by Igor Sikorsky

Presentation by Sergei Sikorsky
Tuesday, March 29, 6 p.m.
Cooley Ballroom C, Student Union, ASU's Polytechnic campus

Sergei Sikorsky retired as vice president for special projects with Sikorsky Aircraft in 1992, after a 50-year career in the industry, but remains an active consultant. His career also included service in the U.S. Coast Guard — participating in early helicopter search and rescue missions near the end of World War II — and 14 years with United Technologies, where his language skills in French, German, Italian, and Russian led to assignments in Europe and Asia, aiding production of Sikorsky models in Japan and Germany, and the marketing of civil and military helicopters — from Iceland to pre-revolutionary Iran.

Come discover the **evolution of aviation** through the eyes of one of its pioneers. **Igor Sikorsky** was a brilliant engineer and visionary who developed some of the world's most sophisticated airplanes and helicopters. His son will discuss the birth and development of aviation as seen through his father, in addition to examining recent developments in aviation technology.

cls.asu.edu

Source: ASU Events

ASU COLLEGE of LETTERS & SCIENCES
ARIZONA STATE UNIVERSITY

Principles of Document Design

Whatever their rhetorical choices might be, writers can use the design principles of proximity, contrast, alignment, and repetition to craft more effective texts.

Proximity

Whenever you vary the amount of space between and around text elements so that related items are close to one another and unrelated items are separated from one another, you are employing the principle of **proximity.** For instance, consider the following three versions of a shopping list:

Version A	Version B	Version C
wireless network router	wireless network router	wireless network router
watercolors	wireless mouse	wireless mouse
English dictionary	blank CDs	blank CDs
blank CDs	English dictionary	
pastels	thesaurus	English dictionary
thesaurus	book of quotations	thesaurus
wireless mouse	oil paints	book of quotations
oil paints	watercolors	oil paints
book of quotations	pastels	watercolors
		pastels

Which list would make it easier for you to find these nine items in the shortest amount of time? Most people would probably find the third list easiest to use because the information is organized into three categories. We might label those categories "Computer Equipment," "Reference Books," and "Art Supplies." The spaces between the three categories help separate one group from another.

For some documents, such as brochures and newsletters, writers can also use borders and color to group common items and separate them from dissimilar items. (Colored type may not be appropriate for many academic papers.)

As illustrated by the poster advertising the "Love Your Body" campaign, at the beginning of this chapter, a dark background and bright colors can make your poster stand out.

Contrast

Contrast is the design feature that sets some aspects of a page apart from others. You can use contrast by employing design features such as bold or italic type, underlining, indentation, and color to indicate the hierarchy of importance among

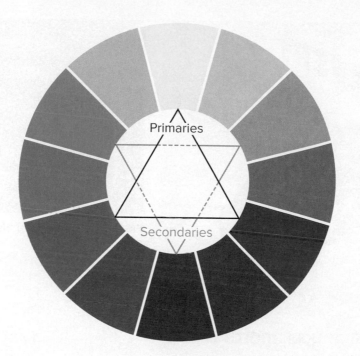

FIGURE 18.1
The Color Wheel

text elements and to produce certain effects. For instance, you can use contrast to make headings at different levels of importance visually distinct.

Color can also add visual interest and contrast to your texts. If you use more than one color in a document, however, consult the color wheel shown in Figure 18.1 to determine which colors work best together.

As the color wheel indicates, the **primary colors** are red, yellow, and blue. The **secondary colors,** located at points halfway between the three primary colors on the wheel, are formed by combining primary colors: Red and yellow combine to make orange; blue and yellow combine to make green; and red and blue combine to make violet. Other colors are formed by combining primary colors with secondary colors.

Complementary colors are directly across from each other on the wheel—for instance, yellow and violet, red and green, and blue and orange. Placing complementary colors next to each other has the effect of *jarring* the reader. Placing adjacent colors together, on the other hand, has a *pleasing* effect. Pairing colors separated by two or three positions on the color wheel can have a *vivid* or *bold* effect.

Colors are sometimes considered to be warm and cool. *Warm* colors—red, orange, and yellow—are energetic and bold. *Cool* colors—green, blue, and violet—sometimes have a soothing, calming effect. Consider the poster shown in

FIGURE 18.3 A Poster Using Cool Colors

Source: National Archives

© Kim Peasley

FIGURE 18.2 A Poster Using Warm Colors

Figure 18.2 above. Two warm colors, yellow and red, appear together in this poster. Because red and yellow are also both primary colors, the red text on the yellow background is especially eye-catching.

Now consider the poster shown in Figure 18.3. The background for this poster is in shades of blue and the turtle is mostly green, both cool colors that have a calming effect.

Alignment

Alignment is the design feature that provides consistency in the placement of text and graphical elements on a page. Writers also use alignment to indicate relationships among text elements. As readers of English, we are accustomed to text that is aligned on the left side of the page. Other alignments are possible, however, and you can vary alignments to achieve different effects.

Unless your text is very brief, your best choice for most academic writing is usually to align your text at the left margin to make it easier for your readers to process. For other contexts—for example, a professional report—you might align your text at both margins, or *justify* it, for a professional look; most books and periodicals make extensive use of this type of alignment. If your text is short and you want to achieve an eye-catching effect on a poster or a brochure, you might consider using right or center alignment.

Repetition (or Consistency)

When you use **repetition** or **consistency,** you apply the same design features to text elements with similar rhetorical functions, doing so consistently throughout the text. Note how the consistent use of bullets in front of the items in our shopping list sets them off even more for readers.

Shopping List

Computer Store	Bookstore	Art Supply Store
• Wireless network router	• English dictionary	• Oil paints
• Wireless mouse	• Thesaurus	• Watercolors
• Blank CDs	• Book of quotations	• Pastels

There are many ways to adhere to the principle of repetition or consistency in a document: following a documentation style accurately; designing to make text easier to read; using typefaces and fonts consistently; using a carefully developed heading structure; and using bullets, numbers, letters, graphics, and white space consistently.

USING A SINGLE DOCUMENTATION FORMAT

Chapter 20 provides guidelines for citing sources and formatting academic papers. Following a single, consistent format throughout your paper makes it easier for readers to determine the type of source you are citing, find it in your works-cited or references list, and consult it themselves if they choose to do so.

DESIGNING TO MAKE DOCUMENTS EASIER TO READ

The principles of proximity, contrast, alignment, and repetition aren't the only means that document designers use to help make texts more readable. The appropriate typeface (serif for print, sans serif for electronic), and the use of headings, bullets, and white space (any space that does not have text or graphics) all act to shape a document that is easier to read. While good design principles help readers read more quickly, they also enable readers to find information in longer documents more easily.

USING TYPEFACES AND TYPE SIZES CONSISTENTLY

A **typeface** is a design for the letters of the alphabet, numbers, and other symbols. A **type font** consists of all the available styles and sizes of a typeface. For most academic documents, you should use no more than two typefaces. Typefaces belong to one of two general categories: serif and sans serif. A **serif** typeface has small strokes or extenders at the top and the bottom of the letter, and letters may vary in thickness. **Sans serif** (without serif) type has no small strokes or extenders, and the letters may have a uniform thickness. Usually, serif type is considered easier to read, especially in longer texts. For that reason, most newspapers, magazines, and books, including this one, use serif type for body text and sans serif type in headings and other kinds of displayed type, for contrast. Here are some examples of serif and sans serif type:

Serif Typefaces	Sample Sentence
Times New Roman	Carefully select the typeface that you use in your texts because the type can affect how easily readers can process your text.
Cambria	Carefully select the typeface that you use in your texts because the type can affect how easily readers can process your text.

Sans Serif Typefaces	Sample Sentence
Arial	Carefully select the typeface that you use in your texts because the type can affect how easily readers can process your text.
Calibri	Carefully select the typeface that you use in your texts because the type can affect how easily readers can process your text.

All of the samples above are in 12-point type, which is a standard size for academic papers (1 point is equivalent to 1/72 of an inch). Notice that different typefaces take up different amounts of space. In some writing situations, space costs money; if so, you should consider a smaller face such as Times New Roman or Calibri over a larger one such as Cambria or Arial. In other situations, such as a slide presentation, you may need a larger face.

Most computer programs offer a wide range of typefaces to choose from, including unusual and ornate varieties. You should use these typefaces sparingly, however, because they can be difficult to read, especially for longer texts.

USING HEADINGS CONSISTENTLY

Headings signal the content of your paper and help readers understand its organization. When headings are worded and styled consistently, readers know which sections are at a higher or lower level of generality than others. You can use different sizes of type; different typefaces; and underlining, bold, and italic type to signal different levels of generality. Treat headings at the same level the same way—the same font size and style, the same location on the page, and the same capitalization.

You should also use parallel structure for all headings at a given level, as in the following example:

Parts of the City

    Shopping in the Business District

    Discovering the Residential Areas

    Enjoying the Waterfront

    Relaxing in the Parks

 USING DIGITAL TECHNOLOGIES | **Integrating Visual and Graphical Elements**

Projects written for digital media should integrate visual and graphical elements in ways that make logical and rhetorical sense. Here are some suggestions:

- Choose appropriate color schemes. See the discussion of contrast on pages 498–500.

- Use *labels* and *captions* that clarify visual information.

- Use elements that *explain* and *establish context* for images, video, and sound that you use. Use media that *support* your main ideas and arguments, rather than simply accompanying them.

- Be prepared to prove ownership and/or rights to the media you have incorporated.

USING BULLETS, NUMBERS, ROMAN NUMERALS, AND LETTERS CONSISTENTLY

You can use bullets, numbers, Roman numerals, or letters—or some combination of these elements—for a variety of purposes. Most frequently, they are used to indicate items in a list or an outline. Any of these markers can be effective for a short list of items, as shown on page 504.

If you are presenting steps in a process or items in a certain order, numbers are usually a more effective choice, and a combination of Roman numerals, letters, and numbers is standard in outlines. Bullets can be used to set off the items in a list effectively, although they can be problematic in longer lists because readers may have to count down the list of items if they need to discuss a particular point in the list. Of course, you should use bullets, numbers, Roman numerals, and/or letters consistently throughout a text.

For more on how to construct an outline, see Chapter 13.

USING WHITE SPACE CONSISTENTLY

White space is any part of a document that is not covered by type or graphics. The margins at the edges of a document are white space, as are the spaces between lines and above and below titles, headings, and other elements. Use white space consistently and intentionally throughout a document to help readers process information. You should always leave the same amount of space above headings at the same level. (If you are using MLA or APA style, you will need to follow the guidelines provided by the style you are following for margins and spacing—see Chapter 20.)

Bullets	Numbers (with Bullets)	Roman Numerals (with Letters)	Letters (with Numbers)
Car Models	Car Models	Car Models	Car Models
• Ford	1. Ford	I. Ford	A. Ford
• Taurus	• Taurus	A. Taurus	1. Taurus
• Focus	• Focus	B. Focus	2. Focus
• Mustang	• Mustang	C. Mustang	3. Mustang
• Chevrolet	2. Chevrolet	II. Chevrolet	B. Chevrolet
• Impala	• Impala	A. Impala	1. Impala
• Malibu	• Malibu	B. Malibu	2. Malibu
• Corvette	• Corvette	C. Corvette	3. Corvette

USING GRAPHICS EFFECTIVELY

Graphics can appear in academic papers as well as a number of other types of documents. The different kinds of graphics are discussed on pages 506–517. Generally, you should use the same kind of graphic to illustrate similar points or concepts. To achieve consistency, you need to consider the following:

- What you want to accomplish with each graphic
- What the overall look of each image is
- How the graphics are marked with labels and captions
- How you should introduce the graphics within your text

Select the kind of graphic that best accomplishes your purpose. To most effectively indicate the composition of a pizza, for example, you might choose a pie chart like the one in Figure 18.4, which shows the ingredients used to make a sausage and mushroom pizza weighing 1.6 kg. The sum of the numbers in the segments equals 1.6 kg, the weight of the pizza. The size of each slice shows us

FIGURE 18.4
A Pie Chart Showing the Composition of Pizza
Source: Math League[1]

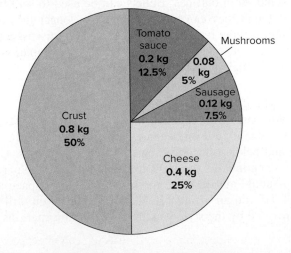

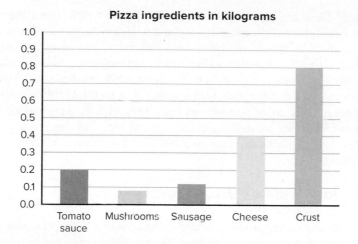

FIGURE 18.5
A Bar Graph Presenting the Same Data as the Pie Chart

the fraction of the pizza made up from that ingredient. Figure 18.5 shows the same data but displayed as a bar graph—as you can tell, the bar graph does not explain or present the information as effectively as the pie chart does.

To present graphics effectively, follow these guidelines:

- **Give the graphics in your document a consistent look.** For example, use one-color or multicolor drawings rather than mixing one-color and multicolor drawings. If you use multiple colors, use the same ones in each graphic (for more on the use of color, see pages 498–500).

- **Introduce and explain each graphic.** Think about the meaning you intend to convey to readers with the graphic. If you do not do so, then it is possible that your readers will not understand why you have included the image. For the bar graph in Figure 18.5, for example, you should introduce it before it appears in your text ("This next graph shows how mushrooms make up the least amount, in weight, of the ingredients in a typical pizza") and follow the image with an explanation of how the bar graph connects to your topic.

- **Place graphics in a document strategically.** Place each visual as close as possible to the text discussion that refers to it. If you are following APA style, however, you have the option of placing visuals at the end of your paper.

 ## Designing New Media

Most of the principles of good design for print texts still hold for new media with minor exceptions. For example, serif fonts appear to be more readable in print, while sans serif fonts are more readable online. Whether you are crafting Web pages, PowerPoint presentations (meant to be presented as static presentations or as videos), or any other forms of new digital media, you should keep basic principles of effective design in mind.

There is a school of thought, championed by Web usability expert Jakob Neilsen, recommending that Web pages should err on the side of simplicity and avoid "bells and whistles." There are valid arguments for this point of view. However, remember that design is a rhetorical decision. How you design anything, whether it is a static Web page or a video, should be driven by your understanding of how to get your message across to your intended audience most effectively. Strike a balance: you want your work to be engaging and eye-catching while not being overpowering.

The best way to achieve this visual balance is to think rhetorically. Is your target audience likely to respond more positively to a background of bright or muted colors? Will they most likely prefer to read long passages of text, or might they respond better to salient points in a bulleted list accompanied by a carefully scripted audio track?

Common Kinds of Visual Texts

When you consider adding a visual image or images to a document, you should do so to help accomplish your overall purpose. Do not add a visual just to have a picture or chart or table in your text; rather, use it as a way to support your thesis and achieve your goal for that piece of writing. Visuals such as tables, bar and line graphs, charts, photographs, drawings, diagrams, maps, and cartoons can be effective tools.

Tables

Tables organize information in columns and rows for readers, helping them make comparisons between or among pieces of information or sets of numerical data. Consider, for instance, Table 18.1, which compares health care in seven countries based on quality, efficiency, access, length and health of people's lives, and expenditures per capita. The same data given in a paragraph would be difficult to compare. By reviewing the table, however, readers can easily make comparisons up and down rows, across columns, and across rows and columns. The table makes it easy to see that although the United States spends significantly more per person for health care, it clearly gets much less for its money.

USING TABLES EFFECTIVELY IN YOUR TEXTS

Word-processing programs will usually allow you to format information into tables automatically—consult the Help screen for the program you are using. Spreadsheet programs also allow you to construct tables.

To decide whether a table will be appropriate for your purpose and audience, answer the following questions:

- Do I have data or information that could appear in tabular form?
- How would a table help me organize this data or information for readers?
- How can I organize the data or information in the table so that readers can find the information they need and make the comparisons I want them to see?

Bar and Line Graphs

Bar and line graphs provide another way to present numerical information to your readers. Both types of graphs plot data along a horizontal line (the *x*-axis) and a vertical

Table 18.1   The United States Ranks Last among Seven Countries on Health Sysytem Performance Based on Measures of Quality, Efficiency, Access, Equity, and Healthy Lives

	AUS	CAN	GER	NETH	NZ	UK	US
OVERALL RANKING (2010)	3	6	4	1	5	2	7
Quality Care	4	7	5	2	1	3	6
Effective Care	2	7	6	3	5	1	4
Safe Care	6	5	3	1	4	2	7
Coordinated Care	4	5	7	2	1	3	6
Patient-Centered Care	2	5	3	6	1	7	4
Access	6.5	5	3	1	4	2	6.5
Cost-Related problem	6	3.5	3.5	2	5	1	7
Timeliness of Care	6	7	2	1	3	4	5
Efficiency	2	6	5	3	4	1	7
Equity	4	5	3	1	6	2	7
Long, Healthy, Productive Lives	1	2	3	4	5	6	7
Health Expenditures/Capita, 2007	$3,357	$3,895	$3,588	$3,837*	$2,454	$2,992	$7,290

Note:*Estimate, Expenditure shown in $US PPP (Purchasing power parity)
Source: Calculated by The Commonwealth Fund based on 2007 International Health Policy Survey; 2008 International Health Policy Survey of Sicker Adults, 2009 International Health Policy Survey of Primary Care Physicians; Commonwealth Fund Commission on a High Performance Health System National Scorecard; and Organization for Economic Cooperation and Development, OECD Health Data, 2009 (Paris: OECD, Nov. 2009). www.commonwealthfund.org/News/News-Releases/2010/Jun/US-Ranks-Last-Among-Seven-Countries.aspx

line (the *y*-axis). Like a table, a **bar graph** allows readers to make comparisons. For example, the graph in Figure 18.6 on page 508 allows readers to compare actual or projected energy use in three different parts of the world over a period of fifty years.

Writing Activity

Analyzing Bar and Line Graphs

Analyze the bar and line graphs on page 508 by responding to the following questions:

- What are the components of the graphs?
- How has the writer used color in the bar graph?
- How has the writer organized the data in the graphs?
- What would happen if the writer reversed the x-axis and the *y*-axis in either of the graphs?
- What stories do these graphs tell?

FIGURE 18.6
Bar Graph
Showing Energy
Consumption in
the World from
1970 to 2020

Source: U.S. Government
Energy Information
Administration

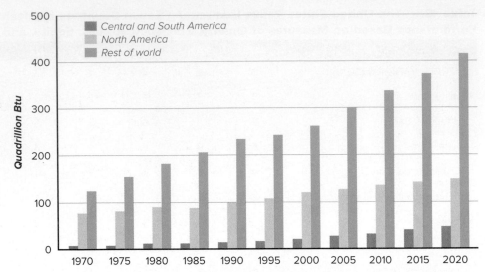

FIGURE 18.7
A Line Graph
Illustrating the
Relationship
between Mileage
and Value

Source: Math League

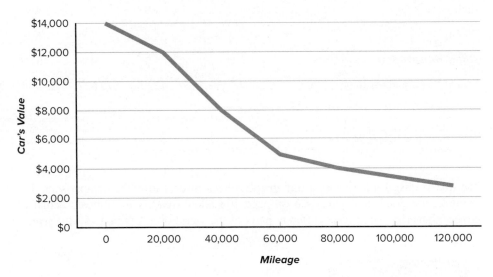

A **line graph** shows readers a change or changes over a period of time. Figure 18.7 is a line graph illustrating the relationship between a car's mileage and its value.

USING GRAPHS EFFECTIVELY IN YOUR TEXTS

You can use bar or line graphs that have been constructed by others in your project as long as you give proper credit to the source. You can also use a spreadsheet program, like Excel, or PowerPoint to construct graphs from data you have discovered or generated on your own. Consider using an online graphing site, such as "Create a Graph" (http://nces.ed.gov/nceskids/Graphing/), hosted by the National Center for Educational Statistics. If you do not have access to a computer, however, you can construct the graph yourself, using graph paper. If you use data from a source to construct your graph, you need to give credit to that source.

To use bar and line graphs effectively in your texts, consider the following questions:

See Chapter 20 for help with citing sources for your data.

- Do I have sets of numerical data that I would like readers to compare?
- Do I have data that indicate a change over a period of time?
- What could a bar or line graph add to my text?
- If I am using a bar graph, how should I organize it?
- How should I explain the graph in my text?
- Do I have access to the technology (a color printer, for example) that will enable me to construct the graph and present it effectively?

Charts

A **chart** is a visual text that allows you to show the relationships among different items or among the parts of a whole. Consider Figure 18.8, which shows the measure of greenhouse gases (GHGs) related to the manufacture of a variety of everyday products. Notice how the chart allows readers to make consistent comparisons among products and their effects on the environment.

Two kinds of charts that are very common in academic writing, as well as in writing for other areas, are pie charts and flowcharts. A **pie chart** shows readers the components that make up the whole of something. Pie charts, like the one shown in Figure 18.4 (page 504), are ideal for showing the percentages of each part of an item.

A **flowchart** shows how a process works. Many readers find it easier to understand processes when they see flowcharts. Figure 18.9 on page 510 illustrates the complex process of launching a water rocket. Notice that the chart is also a kind of *decision tree,* with yes or no responses that direct readers' progress through the chart.

Product Carbon Footprints (GHGs released during manufacture)

275 kg Computer and Monitor	**5 kg** Hamburger	**490 g** 1kg Wheat Flour
22 kg iPod touch	**9 kg** 1kg Tomatoes (Greenhouse)	**240 g** 1kg Potatoes
3 kg T-shirt	**4 kg** 1kg Cheese	**27 g** 1 Egg

FIGURE 18.8   Chart Showing Greenhouse Gas Emissions by Product

FIGURE 18.9
Flowchart That Is
Also a Decision
Tree

Source: Gary Ensmenger

H_2O Rocket Launcher Flowchart
(when alternative propellants are available)

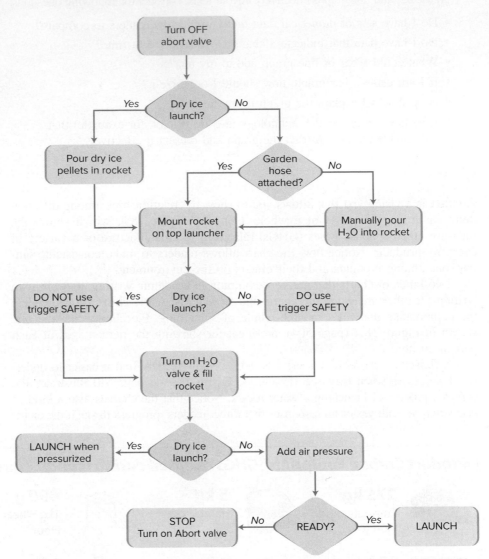

USING CHARTS EFFECTIVELY IN YOUR TEXTS

As with graphs, you can use charts that have been produced by others in your paper as long as you give proper credit to the source. You can construct your own charts the old-fashioned way—drawing them by hand—or you can use a drawing program. Spreadsheet programs and PowerPoint also enable you to produce charts and import them into your paper.

To use charts effectively in your texts, consider the following questions:

- Is there a process, a key relationship, or the components of something within my text that I could illustrate with a chart?

- How will the chart help my audience better understand a particular point in my paper?

- How can I organize the chart so that readers can see patterns in the information?

- Do I have access to the technology (a color printer, for example) that will enable me to construct the chart and present it effectively?

Photographs

Photographs are common in our lives. We see them daily in magazines and newspapers, as well as on Web sites, billboards, and posters. Because photographs are filled with details, a single photograph can replace hundreds or even thousands of words. Imagine how difficult it would be to describe your best friend's physical appearance to a stranger using words alone. On the other hand, a photograph could not give your reader a detailed view of your friend's personality.

Consider two well-known photographs of Abraham Lincoln. The first Figure 18.10) portrays Lincoln with his son Tad. The second (Figure 18.11) portrays Lincoln with Allan Pinkerton, who headed the Union spying operations, and Major General John A. McClernand. A writer could use either photograph to illustrate what Lincoln's life was like during the Civil War years, which corresponded with his years in the White House. The photograph that shows Lincoln with his son gives readers a sense of his personal life. It does not tell the whole story, however, including his love for Tad and his other two children—Willie and Robert—and his heartbreak when his favorite child, Willie, died from typhoid fever in 1862, at age eleven. These are details that a writer would include in the text. Similarly, the photograph of Lincoln with Pinkerton and McClernand does not give a complete picture of his working relationship with them; for that, words are needed.

Source: Library of Congress [LC-DIG-cwpb-04326]

FIGURE 18.10 Abraham Lincoln with His Son Tad

© Royalty-Free/Corbis

FIGURE 18.11 Lincoln with Allan Pinkerton (left) and Major General John A. McClernand

Writing Activity

Considering Photos

With your classmates, prepare a list of six well-known places, people, or objects. Bring one photograph of each place, person, or object to class. Compare and contrast your photos with those that other students have brought by responding to the following questions:

- What does each photograph reveal about its subject? What does each photograph leave out?
- What does each photograph reveal about the person who took it?
- How could you use each photograph in a piece of writing?
- What purposes could each photograph have in a given type of writing?

USING PHOTOGRAPHS EFFECTIVELY IN YOUR WRITING PROJECTS

With the advent of inexpensive digital photography, it is easy to store, retrieve, manipulate, and send photographs. Although it is easy to integrate digital photographs into your documents, note that low-resolution photos are grainy when printed on paper. *Resolution* refers to the number of pixels (or dots) in the image. High-resolution photos have more pixels per inch than low-resolution photos. The following table gives the recommended resolutions (300 dots per inch) for several photograph sizes:

Size of Photo	Recommended Resolution for Printed Photograph
2″ × 2″	600 × 600 pixels
2″ × 3″	600 × 900 pixels
4″ × 6″	1200 × 1800 pixels
5″ × 7″	1500 × 2100 pixels

In your written texts, you may use photographs that have been produced by others if you give proper credit to the source of the photograph. If you are publishing the photograph on a Web site or in some other print or electronic medium, you will need to obtain permission to use it from the copyright holder unless it is in the public domain. If a photograph is in the **public domain,** no one owns the copyright for the image, and you may use it without obtaining permission. You may find photos available for public use in Creative Commons (http://creative commons.org/).

To decide when and how to use photographs in your writing, consider the following questions:

- What kind of photograph will most effectively support my purpose?
- What impact will a photograph have on my text?

- How will my audience respond to each of the photographs that I am considering?
- Where might I place the photograph in my text? Why?
- Do I need permission to use a particular photograph?
- How might I ethically manipulate the photograph to use in my text? For example, can I crop, or cut out, part of the photograph that includes extraneous material?
- If the photograph is an electronic document, is the resolution high enough for use in a print document?
- Will the technology that is available to me accurately reproduce the photograph?

Drawings

Like photographs, **drawings** enable readers to visualize a subject. Drawings are common in technical and scientific writing because writers in those fields frequently need to give readers detailed descriptions of objects, many of which are so small or so far away that it is difficult to see and photograph them. Consider the drawing of a cell nucleus in Figure 18.12. Notice how this drawing includes **labels**—words that name its parts. What is missing from this drawing, however, is an explanation of the functions of the nucleus and its many parts. Only words can provide that information. In other words, the visual and verbal elements in a text should serve to complement and supplement each other.

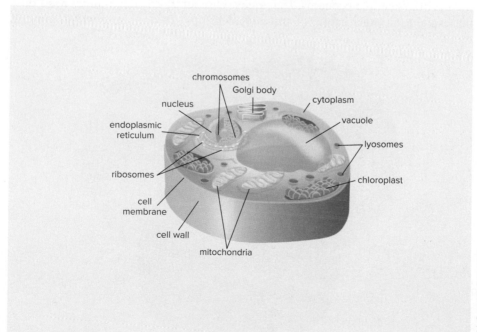

FIGURE 18.12
Drawing of a Cell Nucleus

Considering Drawings

Find an example of a drawing in one of your textbooks, in a newspaper or magazine, or on a Web site. Discuss how successfully the text and drawing you have found work together to achieve the writer's purpose.

USING DRAWINGS EFFECTIVELY IN YOUR TEXTS

You can produce a drawing by hand. If you have access to a scanner, you can then scan your finished drawing, generating a computer file. Or you can use a drawing program that allows you to generate a digital file directly on your computer. If you pick up a drawing from a source for use in your paper, you will need to give proper credit to that source. If you are publishing the drawing, you will need to obtain permission to use it.

To use drawings effectively in your texts, consider the following questions:

- What in my text could I illustrate with a drawing?
- How could a drawing meet the needs of my audience?
- Can I use an existing drawing, or do I need to construct one?
- Do I need permission to use an existing drawing?
- Do I have access to software that I can use to construct the drawing?

Diagrams

Diagrams are drawings that illustrate and explain the arrangement of and relationships among parts of a system. Venn diagrams, for example, consist of circles representing relationships among sets. Consider the Venn diagram in Figure 18.13, which illustrates how sustainable development depends on relationships among the environment, the economy, and equity. Of course, this diagram by itself does not explain the exact nature of these relationships. To do that, a writer needs to

FIGURE 18.13
Venn Diagram
Illustrating
Sustainable
Development

Source: Manchester Development Education Project

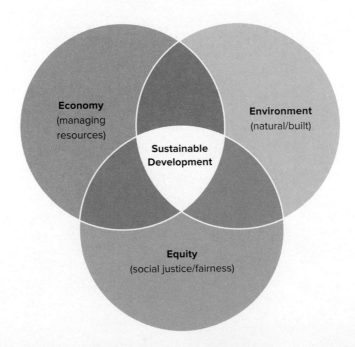

define each of the terms in the diagram—*environment, economy, equity*—and then explain how they interact to form sustainable development.

USING DIAGRAMS EFFECTIVELY IN YOUR WRITING

As with drawings, you can either construct a diagram by hand and scan it or use a drawing program. If you use a diagram from a source, you will need to give proper credit to that source. If you are publishing the diagram, you will need to obtain permission to use it.

To use diagrams effectively in your writing, consider the following questions:

- What in my text could I illustrate with a diagram?
- What effect will the diagram have on my readers?
- Can I use an existing diagram, or do I need to construct one?
- Do I need permission to use an existing diagram?
- Do I have access to software that I can use to construct the diagram?

Maps

Cartographers use **maps** to record and show where countries, cities, streets, buildings, colleges, lakes, rivers, and mountains are located in the world or in a particular part of it. Of course, consumers of maps use them to find these places. We use printed or downloaded maps to drive from one location to another. On the evening news, we see maps showing where events take place and what kind of weather is occurring in neighboring states and countries. We even use maps to help us visualize fictional places such as the territories described in the *Lord of the Rings* trilogy (Figure 18.14).

FIGURE 18.14
Map from the
Lord of the Rings
Trilogy

FIGURE 18.15
Neanderthal
Range Map

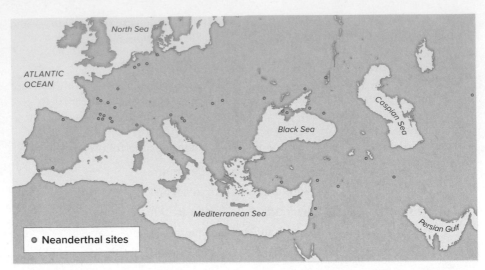

Maps are used in many different academic disciplines, including sociology, political science, history, and geology. Anthropologists use maps to illustrate where species have lived, as in Figure 18.15, which shows the range of the Neanderthals—an extinct species of humans—in Europe.

Writing Activity

Analyzing Maps

Choose one of the two maps in Figures 18.14 and 18.15 or a map in one of your textbooks and respond to the following questions:

- What is the purpose of this map?
- What additional information would make the map more useful?
- What would a writer need to explain to readers so that readers could use the map effectively?
- How does the map adhere to the principles of proximity and contrast (see pages 498–500)?
- How might the captions for the maps be revised to be more informative?

USING MAPS EFFECTIVELY IN YOUR TEXTS

In most cases, you will need to use maps from other sources, giving credit and obtaining permission to use them if necessary. To use maps effectively in your texts, consider the following questions:

- What information could a map offer to my audience?
- If there is an existing map that will serve my purpose, do I need permission to use it?
- If I have to draw my own map, what tools do I need?

- What data do I need to construct the map?
- What information do I need to include in the caption for the map?
- What technology do I need to present the map effectively?

Cartoons

To find evidence of how much people enjoy cartoons, you need only walk the halls of any office building on your campus. You will notice that people display cartoons on their office doors, cubicle walls, and bulletin boards. **Cartoons** make humorous—and sometimes poignant—observations about people and events. Consider the cartoon in Figure 18.16. One feature of most cartoons is that their visual and verbal elements complement each other. The visual part of the cartoon gives the topic a human or humanlike face, and the verbal part offers a specific comment.

USING CARTOONS EFFECTIVELY IN YOUR TEXTS

In most cases, when you use cartoons in your text, they probably will have been produced by other people. Make sure that you are able to give the source information for any cartoon that you include. If you are publishing your project online or in another medium, you will need to obtain permission to use the cartoon from the copyright holder. If you draw your own cartoon, you will need to do so by hand and then scan it to produce a computer file that you can incorporate into your text.

To use cartoons effectively in your texts, consider the following questions:

- How will a cartoon support my purpose?
- Given that readers usually associate cartoons with humor or satire, how might humor or satire affect my readers?
- Do I need permission to use a published cartoon, or is it in the public domain?

"First, I want to give you an overview of what I will tell you over and over again during the entire presentation."

FIGURE 18.16
Cartoon

Text Credits:
Drew Dernavich The New Yorker Collection/ The Cartoon Bank.

Using Visuals Rhetorically

See Chapter 1 for a discussion of audience, purpose, and the rhetorical situation.

As you consider using visuals, think about using them rhetorically to achieve a specific purpose with a specific audience.

Considering Your Audience

Readers are more likely to expect visuals in some genres than in others. Lab reports, for example, commonly include tables and graphs. This principle applies to any visuals that you plan to use in your writing. As you consider using a particular visual, ask yourself the following questions:

- Does my audience need this visual, or is it showing something that my readers already know very well? What information might a visual add?
- How will this audience respond to this visual?
- What other visual might they respond to more favorably?
- Will this audience understand the subtleties of this visual?
- How do I need to explain this visual for this particular audience?

Considering Your Purpose

As we saw in Parts 2 and 3 of this book, you will have a general purpose for any writing project—to record and share experiences, to explore, to inform, to analyze, to convince or persuade, to evaluate, to explain causes and effects, or to solve problems. To the extent possible, every part of your paper should contribute to that purpose. Any phrase, clause, sentence, paragraph, or section of your paper that does not support your purpose needs to be revised or deleted. The same principle applies to any visual that you are considering. Diagrams, for example, most often have an informative purpose. A cartoon, in contrast, is almost always

FIGURE 18.17
A Photograph from the Web Page for Feed the Children, a Charitable Organization

Courtesy of Feed the Children

humorous but often makes a statement. Photographs are often used to make the rhetorical appeal of *pathos*, as they can evoke an emotional response in the reader. Figure 18.17, for example, is a photograph from the Web page for Feed the Children, a charitable organization.

Before using any visual, ask yourself these questions:

- How will this visual support my purpose?
- How might this visual detract from my purpose?
- Why is this visual necessary?
- What other visual or visuals might support my purpose more effectively?

Using Visuals Responsibly

Just as you need to consider the purpose for using any visual, you also need to consider how using visuals responsibly will enhance your credibility as a writer.

Permissions

Whenever you plan to use a visual, you need to make certain that you have permission to use it. If you have constructed a table, graph, or chart from data that you have gathered, then permission is not needed. If you use a visual prepared by someone else, or use data from a source to produce a visual, you should always give credit to your source, even if the visual or data are from a government source or are in the public domain (that is, outside of copyright and available to anyone who wants to use them). For most academic papers, it is usually not necessary to request permission to use a visual. However, if your writing will be made available to an audience beyond your classroom, including online, you will need to ask for permission to use any visual from a source that you include. Some visuals that you find on the Web are in the public domain, but if you are in doubt about a particular visual, contact the Web manager of the site where you found it to ask what permissions are required.

The subjects of photographs have certain rights as well. If you take a photograph of a friend, you need to ask your friend for permission to use it if your project will have an audience beyond the two of you. If your friend does not want the photo used in a course paper or on a Web site, you are ethically and legally obligated to honor those wishes. To be certain that there is no misunderstanding, ask your friend to sign an agreement granting you permission to use the photo for clearly specified purposes. If you later want to use the photo for other purposes, ask your friend to sign another agreement. But you should never put undue pressure on someone to sign such an agreement.

Distortions

Just as you should not distort quoted or paraphrased material (see Chapter 20), you should also be careful not to distort the content and the physical properties of any visuals you include in your paper. Sometimes the data in charts and graphs is misrepresented—consider, for example, Figure 18.18, which shows the pass rates for students in English 101. Clearly, the pass rate improved by year 3 and remained fairly stable afterward. *If* this chart maker wants to show a dramatic improvement in the pass rate, then it makes sense to use a scale that runs from 75% to 95%. On the other hand, a full scale (from 0 to 100%) makes the improvement in pass rates much less obvious and dramatic, as shown in Figure 18.19.

There may be times, however, when some forms of distortion can be helpful and ethical. For instance, consider the two maps shown in Figure 18.20. The first one shows the forty-eight contiguous states as they typically appear on a map. Such maps show the relative sizes—measured in square miles—of the states. The second map is designed to show the distribution of wire-service news stories about certain cities and states. Notice that New York and Washington, D.C., get lots of attention in wire-service news stories. This deliberately distorted image helps to make a serious point about the news.

Writing Activity

Analyzing Visual Distortions

Do a Web search to find a distorted map that presents information in a way that you think is interesting and useful. Write a brief explanation of why the distorted map is useful to share with friends who might also find the map interesting.

FIGURE 18.18
Chart That Distorts Information

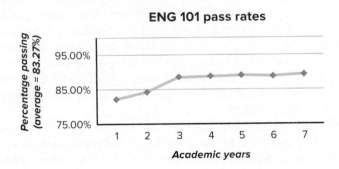

FIGURE 18.19
Chart That Presents the Same Information Honestly

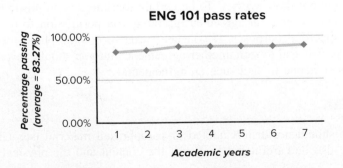

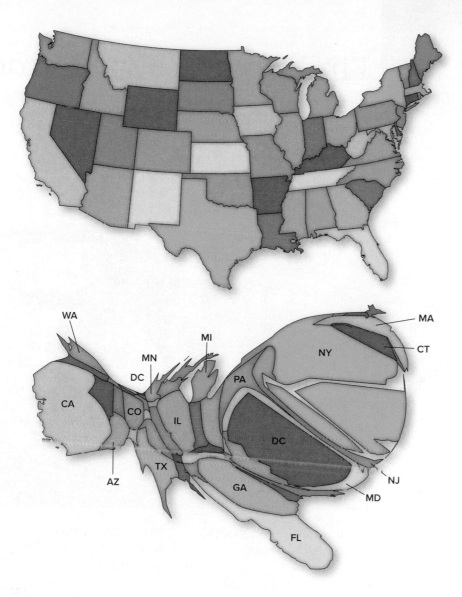

FIGURE 18.20
Regular Map of
the United States
and Distorted Map
That Illustrates
a Point about
the News

Text Credits

Finding and Evaluating Information

In the past, **research** meant searching through actual library stacks. Because of the almost instant access to a wealth of sources that technology makes possible, finding information today may appear to be much easier than it was in the past, but the reality is that it is simply different. Although you can still find books and print journals on library shelves, and they are still useful resources, today researchers often start a project with a search of the library's online catalog or database or a search of the World Wide Web. In fact, many of us these days refer to searching as "Googling" a word or phrase. "Just Google it" is a common way to request that someone look something up. But a simple search on the Internet will result in a lot more information than you need, and some (often much) of what you find is simply inaccurate.

Before the advent of electronic sources, researchers usually assumed that they could rely on the accuracy of the printed texts found in college or university libraries. Although

© Anderson Ross/Getty Images RF

those sources still exist, anyone can now publish anything on the Web or more easily self-publish content as a book. So much information is available on the Internet that it is vital to focus your search as carefully as possible so that you turn up only the most relevant sources. It is also more critical than ever for you to evaluate the quality of what you do find.

Also, many researchers go out into the field to conduct other kinds of research. Depending on the project and the discipline, you might gather information through observation or experimentation. If you are working with human subjects, you might use interviews and surveys.

Conducting Effective Library and Web-Based Research: An Example

You already have plenty of experience in conducting research. Have you ever used a classmate's opinion of an author or a band to influence a friend to read that author's book or to see that band? If so, you were using the results of a type of field research called **interviewing** as evidence.

For more on field research, see pages 541–546.

The research that you do for any writing task is a rhetorical act. That is, you conduct research for a specific purpose, with a particular audience in mind, in a specific writing situation. Consider how you might approach the following assignment for a psychology class:

> Respond to this question: Why do adolescent males (and sometimes females) change their behavior when they join a gang? Based on your research, write a 3- to 4-page paper that provides compelling reasons for this behavior, providing specific evidence to support your position.

This assignment is fairly straightforward: Your purpose is to fulfill this assignment, and your audience is your psychology professor. The assignment even provides you with a **research question.** Your answer to this question will form the thesis of your research paper. But where will you find the evidence that will help you decide on your answer to this question—your thesis—and support that thesis? How will you locate it? How will you be able to tell if the evidence is credible and reliable?

Often it will be your responsibility to formulate a research question. When you find yourself in that situation, keep these principles in mind:

- Keep the question focused. For example, "What caused the Civil War?" is a huge question. However, "Why did Confederate forces fire on Fort Sumter on April 12, 1861?" is much more manageable.

- Make sure you will be able to get good information on your question. You may be interested in the role Venezuelan oil plays in the U.S. economy, especially from the Venezuelan perspective. However, if you discover that most of the information for this topic is in Spanish and you can't read that language, you will probably not be able to go forward with this question.

- Consider whether you can find an adequate number of resources to answer your question. For example, are the people you hope to interview available and willing to speak with you? Can you really arrange to do field research at some far-off location?

Library Research

Usually the first place to look when conducting research to answer a question is the reference section of your college library. There you will find sources such as general and specialized encyclopedias and dictionaries. For example, you might start your research for the psychology paper about gangs and adolescents by defin-ing "adolescent," perhaps by looking it up in a medical dictionary:

> A young person who has undergone puberty but who has not reached full matu-rity; a teenager.
>
> —American Heritage Medical Dictionary®

Based on this definition, you determine that your research will focus on males and females between the ages of thirteen and nineteen. You decide to conduct a search in your online college library catalog. (Librarians are also available online in many libraries.) Almost every library has a reference librarian, and he or she is a truly useful resource. It is always helpful to discuss your research question with the reference librarian. He or she will probably be able to point you to some reference sources that might be useful.

All college libraries have a book **catalog** of some kind. In addition to the book catalog, your library probably subscribes to various electronic **databases** such as *Academic Search Complete*. Databases are indexes of articles that are available in periodicals; many also provide complete texts of the articles them-selves. To look for articles in popular or trade magazines, for instance, you would search one database, while you would use another database to find articles in academic journals, and still another database for articles in newspapers.

 USING DIGITAL TECHNOLOGIES   **Using Academic Databases**

The following are popular academic data-bases that can help you with research in dif-ferent disciplines. Keep in mind that the names of academic databases do change; your ref-erence librarian can help you find a database that will be useful for your particular project.

- *Academic Search Complete*
- *ERIC*

- *General Science Index*
- *Google Scholar*
- *Humanities Index*
- *JSTOR*
- *LexisNexis Academic*
- *Social Science Index*

SEARCHING A LIBRARY CATALOG

For any electronic search, you need to come up with an appropriate word or phrase, or **keyword,** that will be found in the kind of source you are seeking. To find useful keywords for a search of your library's catalog, it is often a good idea to start by consulting the *Library of Congress Subject Headings (LCSH),* a book that lists subject headings in use in most library systems. It will tell you how subject areas are categorized in the library and will therefore help you come up with search terms that will turn up books on your subject.

Note that the search term "gang behavior" is just one of a range of possibil-ities. It is often useful to use a number of search terms. You can also pull up more information on each entry and examine other relevant references that might be useful to your research.

Here is a research hint: Whenever you find a book on your research subject in your college library, spend a few minutes examining the *other* texts that surround the one you just located. Books about the same topic are shelved together, so once you find one book on the topic you are researching, many others will be nearby.

SEARCHING AN ONLINE DATABASE

Now that you have several books that you might want to examine for information on gang behavior, you should also search one or more of the databases your college's library subscribes to. A search of a typical database—in this case, *Academic Search Complete*—using the keywords "male" and "gang" might turn up abstracts (summaries) of articles like this one:

<u>"GANG WORLD".</u> By: Papachristos, Andrew V. Foreign Policy, Mar/Apr2005 Issue 147, p48–55, 8p, 3c, 1bw; Abstract: The article discusses the rise of street **gangs** around the world. The image of a young, minority, "innercity," **male gang** member is transmitted, exploited, and glamorized across the world. The increasing mobility of information via cyberspace, films, and music makes it easy for **gangs, gang** members, and others to get information, adapt personalities, and distort **gang** behaviors. Two images of street **gangs** dominate the popular consciousness—**gangs** as posses of drug-dealing thugs and, more recently, **gangs** as terrorist organizations. Although the media like to link **gangs** and drugs, only a small portion of all **gangs** actually deal in them. Similarly, the name Jose Padilla is inevitably followed by two epithets—al Qaeda terror suspect and street **gang** member. The link between the two is extremely misleading. One of the most urgent challenges for policymakers is distinguishing between the average street **gang** and groups that operate as criminal networks. Globalization and street **gangs** exist in a paradox: **Gangs** are a global phenomenon not because the groups themselves have become transnational organizations, but because of the recent hypermobility of **gang** members and their culture. Individual **gangs** flaunt their Internet savvy by posting complex Web sites, including some with password protection. As the global economy creates a growing number of disenfranchised groups, some will inevitably meet their needs in a **gang.** INSETS: Want to Know More?; When **Gangs** Go Bad.; (*AN 16195307*)
📄 **HTML Full Text** 📄 **PDF Full Text** (**1.7 MB**)

Note that the abstract indicates that this article deals with "gang culture," so this one seems especially promising (and because the full text of the article is available online, you can print the essay with a click of your mouse). Note also that *Academic Search Complete,* the search database we used for this search, may not be available in all libraries. We use it here to illustrate a possible search database; your college or university will provide a similar search database.

Another online database that many colleges offer their students is *JStor,* which indexes a wide range of academic journals (about 2000). Figure 19.1 shows the first part of a search using the keyword "adolescent gangs."

Several of the articles listed by *JStor* appear to be potentially useful. Because they are available as full-text articles, you can click on the title and immediately check them

FIGURE 19.1
Search of the
JStor database
using the search
term "adolescent
gangs"

Source: jstor.org

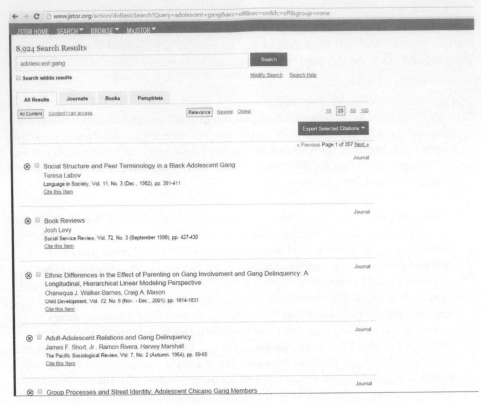

for relevance. Generally, you should also look for recent articles because their information will be more up to date. Note that in the *JStor* screenshot in Figure 19.1 users can sort their search information so the newest articles rise to the top of the screen.

Research on the Web

You continue your search on the Web, which is the largest part of the global network of computers known as the Internet. The Web is hyperlinked, which means that one useful site will often provide links to many more.

If you have conducted Web searches, you probably quickly learned that different **search engines,** software programs that find sites on the Web, locate different information—that the results provided by Google (www.google.com), Yahoo! (www.yahoo.com), and Bing (www.bing.com) often vary. You may also have used a "meta-search" engine such as Dogpile (www.dogpile.com), which searches *other* search engines, so the results you retrieve are from a range of searches. Usually, it is helpful to use several different search engines.

A search of the Web using Google and the keywords *gang behavior*, for example, yields 57 *million* hits. This result provides an unmanageable number of choices. The most effective way to limit the number of hits that a search engine returns is to narrow what the search engine is looking for. You can narrow your search easily on Google by enclosing multiple keywords within quotation marks so that the search engine looks for them when they appear together as a phrase. Simply by enclosing the search term "gang behavior" in quotation marks, you can limit the result to 33,700 hits, for example. This helps, but 33,700 options are still far too many. As a next step, you might qualify the search even more. If you are looking for information about female gangs, for example, you might try searching with the keywords "gang behavior" and "female." Doing so gives you a list of 21,200 hits. Although that number is better, it's still not really good enough. You can then modify the search even further by trying this combination of keywords: "gang behavior" and "adolescent female." This time the response, shown in Figure 19.2, is only 171 hits, a more manageable number. By closely defining your search terms and using them in combination, you can narrow your search and come up with the best possible online sources.

One other option you might consider if you are working on an academic paper is Google Scholar, which searches only scholarly Web sites. Searching Google Scholar using the keywords "gang behavior" and "adolescent female" gives you the result shown in Figure 19.3. You can also search for images on the Web. Using an image search on Google, for example, you may find a photo of gang activity that you can use to illustrate your paper.

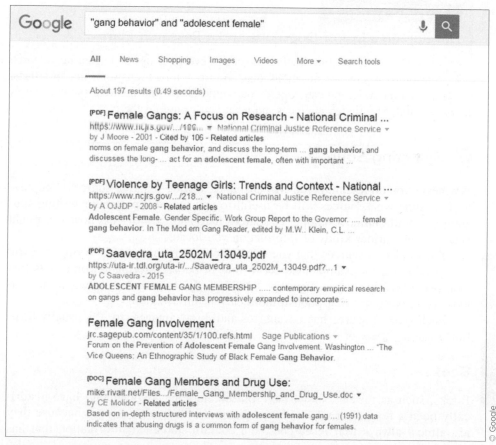

FIGURE 19.2
Result of a search using the Google search engine and the keywords "gang behavior" and "adolescent female"

FIGURE 19.3
Result of a search using the Google Scholar search engine and the keywords "gang behavior" and "adolescent female"

Google   "gang behavior" and "adolescent female"

Scholar   About 46 results (0.03 sec)

Articles
Case law
My library

Female gang involvement
GD Curry - Journal of Research in Crime and Delinquency, 1998 - jrc.sagepub.com
... can be a form of liberation. A research agenda is proposed that offers examples of
how a common set of theoretical issues might guide studies of both male and female
gang behavior. Female participation in gang-related crime ...
Cited by 98   Related articles   All 4 versions   Cite   Save

Any time
Since 2015
Since 2014
Since 2011
Custom range..

[BOOK] Female gangs: A focus on research   [PDF] from asu.edu
JW Moore, J Hagedorn - 2001 - west.asu.edu
... delin- quency and criminal activity of female gang members, examines how ethnicity and gender
norms may influence female **gang behavior**, and discusses ... however, that joining a
gang—regardless of the gang's structure—is a significant act for an **adolescent female**, often ...
Cited by 106   Related articles   All 34 versions   Cite   Save   More

Sort by relevance
Sort by date

Female juvenile delinquency and the problem of sexual authority in America, 1945-1965
R Devlin - Yale JL & Human., 1997 - HeinOnline
... 1997] Devlin 159 enhancing the perception, first articulated by Hoover, of the potential for
adolescent female criminality ... by the extent and significance of female gang delinquency, attempted
to perform some controlled scientific investigations into female **gang behavior** in working ...
Cited by 35   Related articles   All 3 versions   Cite   Save

☑ include patents
☑ include citations

[BOOK] Violence by teenage girls: Trends and context   [PDF] from demoiselle2femme.org
MA Zahn - 2008 - demoiselle2femme.org
Page 1. US Department of Justice Office of Justice Programs Office of Juvenile Justice
and Delinquency Prevention MAY 2008 ' Study Group Understanding and Responding
to Girls' Delinquency _I. Hol)cr1' l-*l0]'t= -.$, t.lr'ninisr ...
Cited by 51   Related articles   All 3 versions   Cite   Save   More

✉ Create alert

Collective violence: comparisons between youths and chimpanzees   [PDF] from researchgate.net
RW Wrangham, ML Wilson - Annals of the New York Academy ..., 2004 - Wiley Online Library
... society. We stress that our proposal is not intended to represent a complete account
of **gang behavior**. It ... composition. Males are least likely to act aggressively if the
stranger is an **adolescent female** with a sexual swelling. Males ...
Cited by 51   Related articles   All 13 versions   Cite   Save

© Google

Writing Activity

Developing a List of Questions and a Research Plan

For one of your current writing projects, develop a list of intriguing research questions. These are questions that require complex answers, not just facts. After each question, indicate where you would go to find answers (your library's online catalog? a search engine?) and what you would do there.

Selecting Sources

Whenever you do research, you will encounter a wide range of sources. You have to determine what sources will be useful to you for your particular writing situation. We will outline a number of sources here and then discuss how you might *evaluate* the various kinds of information you locate.

The kind(s) of sources that you select depend on what you are trying to learn. You would not, for example, expect to find in books information on events that took place less than a year ago. For that kind of information, you would need to look for publications that publish more current information.

Each type of source has advantages and disadvantages, so it is usually helpful to use a variety of sources.

Books

Books, such as the one shown here on female gang involvement, have historically been a researcher's first choice for much academic research because they are almost always well researched and contain statistical information that has

Book from Oxford University Press

been validated. However, even books have to be subjected to more intensive questioning these days because it is now relatively easy and inexpensive for just about anyone to publish a book. Books in an academic library, however, have been carefully evaluated by librarians and are usually reputable. One disadvantage of the research you will find in a printed book is that it often takes several years to write, review, and publish a book—so the information often is not as current as that contained in other sources.

Academic Journals

Academic essays appear in **journals** such as *The American Journal of Psychiatry*. Journals are most often sponsored by universities. Essays in most academic journals are written by scholars in the field and are "peer reviewed," which means that other scholars have read the article, commented on it, and made a judgment about its validity and usefulness. Journal articles are usually well researched. Also, academic essays usually come with a "works cited" or "references" page, which lists all of the sources the writer used. Often, these lists point to useful sources about the topic you are working on.

For example, your library search focusing on adolescent males and females and gangs might turn up this essay, published in *The American Journal of Psychiatry:* "What Happens to 'Bad' Girls? A Review of the Adult Outcomes of Antisocial Adolescent Girls" by Kathleen A. Pajer, M.D., M.P.H. In addition to the essay, you find a "works cited" section with eighty-three entries, references to other journal articles and books that Dr. Pajer used in her text. These will lead you to more information about teenage gangs.

Newspapers

Newspapers, especially those with a national focus such as *The New York Times,* are considered reliable sources. Often, local papers will get their information from national sources.

LexisNexis is a database that indexes newspapers, other periodicals, and a wide range of other kinds of documents. A *LexisNexis* search for newspaper articles on a topic will provide you with recent information. You need to remember, however, that while newspapers are very current sources, because they are following stories in progress, sometimes the information they provide may change as more complete information on a story becomes available. Many Web sources will now indicate when an article was updated with new information.

Popular Magazines

Magazines, especially newsmagazines such as *Time* and *Newsweek,* have a broad perspective on national and international issues and often provide useful background and historical information, as well as their own editorial commentary. Many make the contents of the print magazine available online. Often the magazine will offer additional content online, as well as forums for readers to respond to articles and to one another.

The New York Times newspaper

© The McGraw-Hill Companies, Inc./ John Fournoy, photographer

Newsweek magazine

Source: Newsweek

FIGURE 19.4
Search of the
Newsweek.com
Web site using
the keyword
"gangs"

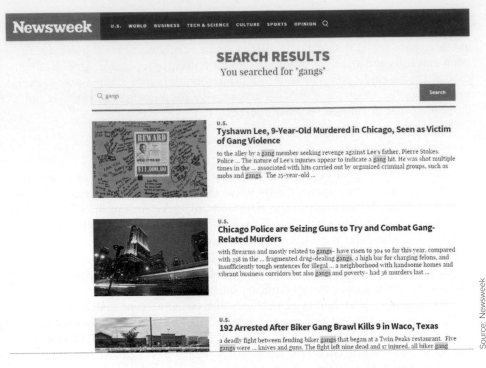

Source: Newsweek

Automotive News
magazine

Source: Automotive News

Foreign Affairs
magazine
Reprinted by permission of
FOREIGN AFFAIRS, July/
August 2012. Copyright
2012 by the Council on
Foreign Relations, Inc.
www.ForeignAffairs.com

Source: Council on Foreign Relations, Inc.

A search at Newsweek.com for example, turns up possible sources for your paper on gangs, as shown in Figure 19.4.

Trade or Commercial Magazines

Trade or commercial/professional magazines, such as *Automotive News,* have a specific audience, which consists of the members of a group with a common interest or profession. If the magazine is published for a professional organization, a portion of the members' dues usually pays for the magazine. Other magazines are for-profit publications that serve the industry as a whole. These publications often are written specifically for their target audience. They also can provide lots of information from an insider's perspective, so you may need to be very familiar with the field.

Public Affairs Magazines

Magazines that focus on public affairs, such as *Foreign Affairs,* generally publish articles on national issues, so they are useful sources for papers about these issues. Their essays are usually thoughtfully researched and documented.

Specialty Magazines

Magazines about travel, different regions of the country, cooking, and other specialized topics are often useful if you are searching for the kinds of information they provide. Examples include *Arizona Highways*. Others, such as *BusinessWeek*, cater to a specific field and often have useful statistics and other types of information related to that field.

The Internet

Arizona Highways magazine

Courtesy Arizona Highways

The Internet, especially the Web, offers a huge range of information, all available very quickly. As you will see on pages 534–541, it sometimes takes a bit of work to figure out exactly who controls a Web site and the information it presents, so information you obtain from the Web must be used with caution.

It is extremely difficult to generalize about the Internet because it remains a dynamic, ever-evolving source of information and, often, misinformation. Any attempt to categorize Internet sources is, at best, a rough estimate, but we can point to at least five different kinds of online resources.

- **Web sites that serve as what used to be called the "home page" of an organization.** Most of these are now much more complex and sophisticated than they were in the early years of the Web, but they may very well be the first place you choose to look for information about any organization or group. Although the quality of the information you find on these Web sites may be good, you need to remember that because they are maintained by the organization itself, they tend to give a very positive view of the organization.

- **Web sites that provide information to the general public.** Many of these Web sites are maintained by government agencies. Their subject matter and complexity vary depending on whether they are constructed and maintained by local municipalities, state agencies, or the federal government. In most instances, the information found on these sites is very reliable. Figure 19.5, for example, is the home page for the site maintained by the Internal Revenue Service.

- **Online periodicals and newspapers.** As noted earlier, almost every print publication now has an online version. Some local newspapers have a free news section that is available to all and a section that is available only for paid subscribers. Subscribers to *The New York Times* print edition receive the digital edition of the *Times* free. The *Times* also offers digital-only subscription plans (www.nytimes.com). Many magazines allow online viewers to read most of their articles, while others publish snippets online and allow full access only to subscribers.

  Some academic journals, such as *Kairos* (http://english.ttu.edu/Kairos/), are published only online. Like most academic journals, they are peer-reviewed, and the information in them is as reliable as that found in print academic journals.

- **Blogs.** A blog is usually maintained by one person who shares his or her thoughts on a given topic or set of topics and may post links to other sites on the Web as well as comments from other writers. While some

FIGURE 19.5
Home page for
the Internal
Revenue Service

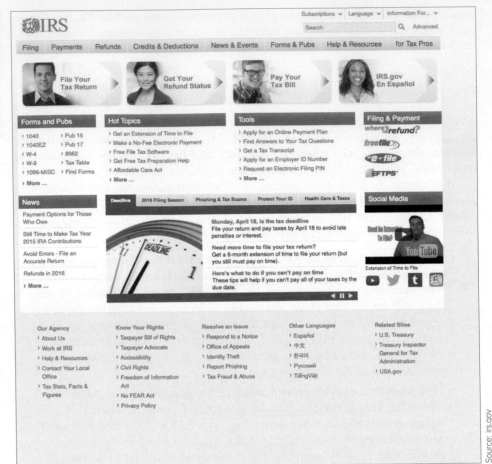

Source: irs.gov

blogs are maintained by experts in a particular field, others are written by people who want to communicate their own point of view on anything from politics to what kind of software is better. Be cautious about using them as sources. Figure 19.6 is an example of a blog on cooking. While you need to be cautious using blogs as sources, they often provide interesting information about the person who writes the blog. An example is shown in Figure 19.6, where Giovanina Bucci discusses a recent cooking class on her blog.

*For more information
on evaluating sources
see pages 534–541.*

- **Wikipedia.** Wikipedia is a collaborative online encyclopedia. The articles on Wikipedia are written by volunteers, and it is possible for anyone to edit already existing articles. Although there are some safeguards to protect certain pages, some information found on Wikipedia may be suspect. You may think of it as a good starting place, in much the same way that a traditional encyclopedia is a place to start for background, but you should not rely on it for all of your information on a topic. It is wise to look for additional sources of information beyond Wikipedia. You should also be cautious about citing it as a source in your academic papers. Figure 19.7 shows the Wikipedia entry for "higher education."

Tuesday, July 27, 2010

Home Grown Tomatoes: Turnin' Up the Heat

Cookin', Teachin', and Laughin'

Home Grown Tomatoes is a weekly Vegan/Vegetarian column written by Giovanina Bucci

Can you believe it? I survived. I *actually* survived the cooking class and it went great! The class was full, which meant I fed 12 hungry bellies two appetizers, a first course, an entree, and dessert. Ruth, Angela, Rachel, Kathy, Karen, Bob, Deb, Kristen, Tammy, Quinton, Marsha, and Molly all joined me for a really wonderful evening of cooking, teaching, laughing, and for what I would consider, a really splendid night! Two things that I learned: talk more about the food, ingredients, and directions as I'm throwing things together and get a new pair of sneakers. Oh, and one other thing. Gazpacho doesn't have to taste like you're drinking cold salsa.

The group was really positive and fun, which I think helped ease the pressure of the situation immensely. The owner of the Seasoned Kitchen, Tony, was also there helping to keep things running smoothly - and he also did the dishes, which was awesome! I forgot to bust out my camera in the beginning, so these pictures are a little late in the game, but nonetheless, some eye candy for you.

FIGURE 19.6
Page from *Home Grown Tomatoes* blog

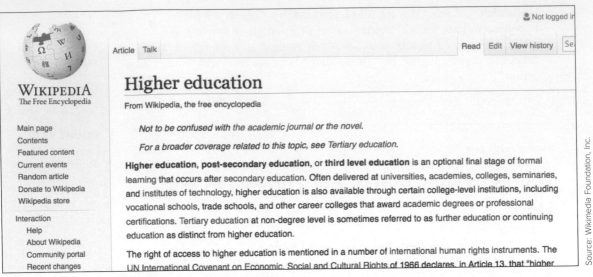

FIGURE 19.7 Wikipedia entry for "Higher Education"

Writing Activity

Planning Your Research

For a college class in which you have been asked to conduct research on a particular topic, select a potential topic, and then list the sources you might look at and what you might expect to find in them. Also plan when and where you will conduct your research.

Evaluating Your Sources: Asking the Reporter's Questions

Finding sources is only the beginning of your task in conducting research; you also need to evaluate the information you locate. How do you determine that a source is credible and accurate? Usually, asking the questions reporters ask when they are working on a story will help you.

Who Is the Author?

Who is the author of the research? What can you learn about that author? If the work is an essay or an entire book, you may be able to find biographical information about the author or authors. For example, let's say you are conducting research on gangs and find this book in your college library: *Teen Gangs: A Global View*, edited by Maureen P. Duffy and Scott Edward Gillig, and published by Greenwood Press, now ABC-CLIO/Greenwood. Here is what you are able to find out about the two editors from examining the book:

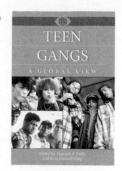

MAUREEN P. DUFFY is associate professor and chair of the counseling department at Barry University, Miami Shores, Florida.

SCOTT EDWARD GILLIG is professor and coordinator of the mental health counseling specialization at Barry University.

Both editors are university professors, which means the book most likely contains thoroughly researched and well-documented articles by respected authors. If you examine ABC-CLIO/Greenwood's catalog or Web site, you will see that it specializes in nonfiction books primarily for schools and that it also publishes library reference titles. Your investigation indicates that the editors are both professors and the book is not self-published. Although you cannot tell much about the reputation of ABC-CLIO/Greenwood from its Web site alone, all of the information you have found suggests that the articles in this text were probably written by people who are credible authorities in their field.

Scholarly book on the subject of gangs

What Is the Text About? What Is the Quality of the Information?

To determine the answer to this question, you will need to ask the following additional questions:

- What is the focus of the printed or online text you are considering?
- How thoughtful and research based is it?
- Does the text take a balanced, thoughtful approach?

You'll also want to make sure the text is relevant to your topic.

For instance, in your research on why adolescent males or females change their behavior when they join gangs, suppose you visit the Web site from the American Academy of Child and Adolescent Psychiatry that presents facts about children and gangs (shown in Figure 19.8 on page 536). How would you answer the three questions above about the information provided on this Web site?

If you do check out this Web site, at the bottom you will read:

The American Academy of Child and Adolescent Psychiatry (AACAP) represents over 8,700 child and adolescent psychiatrists who are physicians with at least five years of additional training beyond medical school in general (adult) and child and adolescent psychiatry.

This statement adds to the credibility of the Web site.

Although this Web site and its information appear to be credible, you (as the writer of a paper on how behaviors change when youths join gangs) have to ask, how relevant is this information to my paper? In this instance, although the facts presented on the Web site seem credible and useful, they do not discuss the focus of your own paper—changing behavior after joining a gang. Therefore, although the information might be helpful and interesting, it does not seem to fit your own paper.

FIGURE 19.8
Facts for Families about children and gangs

Source: American Academy of Child & Adolescent Psychiatry

Although the information shown in Figure 19.8 comes from a professional association (and thus is credible), even at sites or blogs maintained by individuals, you can sometimes learn valuable information and find useful links. For example, Streetgangs.com offers, through its "resources" section, an extensive list of gang intervention and prevention programs in the Los Angeles area. Of course you would need to assess the reliability of all such sources.

When Was the Text Published or the Web Site Last Updated?

Generally, the more current the information a source provides, the more useful it is to you. In academic research, new data are generally a response to *older* data. In fact, one of the benefits of reading books and articles by university scholars is that they almost always refer to earlier research as they outline how their new research relates to it.

At www.streetgangs.com/contacts/copyrights, there is no notice of when the Web page was last updated, but there are many links to 2015 articles about gangs and gang members, so (as this book is being written), this Web page is current.

Why Was This Information Published?

What can you determine about why the information was published? What is the text's purpose? Who appears to be the target audience? If you can determine to whom the text appeals, you might gain a sense of its purpose.

You cannot know for sure why an essay was published, or a book printed, or a Web site constructed, but you can make some good guesses:

- **Essays in academic journals** are often published to share new knowledge. This is especially true of articles in scientific journals, which publish the results of scientific research, but even in journals that focus on the humanities or on professional fields, professors publish what they have learned from their reading and thinking.

  Because articles in academic journals are peer-reviewed, other scholars in the field will get the chance to comment on, make suggestions about, and offer criticisms of any essay before it is published. So generally you can expect the information in journal articles to be credible. Journals are also major venues that scholars and practitioners use to communicate and share information within professional and scientific fields.

- **Academic books** provide professors with a way to distribute large amounts of information and insight to their peers, and while some make money for their author and publisher, many do not, so the profit motive is not a strong factor in publishing an academic text. Academic texts are also peer-reviewed, so other scholars in the field will have examined the information, data, and conclusions in a text prior to publication. During the publishing process, those peer reviewers will have the opportunity to contribute their ideas, criticisms, and suggestions. Academic texts are generally published by university presses.

- **Articles in newsmagazines and newspapers** present items in the local, national, or worldwide news. Most often, editors work diligently to present the news in an unbiased manner, but most newspapers and even some magazines have editorial pages or sections.

  As with anyone else, newspaper and magazine editors and writers have their own particular viewpoints and ways of looking at what they report on—in other words, there is always *some* bias in anything that is said or written. At any particular time and place, you might be able to label newspapers and magazines according to their general tendencies. But these ways of seeing and writing about the news vary over time, as editors and writers come and go.

  How can you, as a reader, get some sense of the biases of the news-magazines and newspapers you read for your research? One way is to compare how the same information is presented in different magazines or newspapers. Read two or more editorials on the same topic. Look for facts related to a story that appear in one publication but not in the other: What might the omission or inclusion of an important fact tell you about each newpaper's or magazine's biases? Consider how the same story is presented in two different publications. How big is the headline? How much space is devoted to the article? Is it on the front page or on an interior page?

- **Web sites** provide all kinds of information. However, not all Web sites give completely accurate and reliable information. You have to evaluate a Web site just as you would any other source. For information on evaluating Web sites, see "Using Digital Technologies" (page 541).

Writing Activity

Analyzing Newspapers

Most newspapers have a particular political slant, which is often clear in their editorials but is also evident in the way various news stories are presented. If you examine the newspapers from several large cities, such differences will be readily apparent. Select a major story that is currently in the news, and compare how three newspapers cover it. What kind of photographs accompany the story? What do their editorials say about it? How much "newsprint" or online space is devoted to the story? Where do the stories appear?

Compare what you have learned with the information that several of your classmates have gathered about coverage of the same story or a similar story.

Writing Activity

Examining a Web Site to Determine Its Audience

Select one of the following Web sites and, in no more than two pages, outline who you think is the intended audience for the site, what you think its purpose is, and why you make that assertion. Indicate who maintains the site (if you can tell) and when it was last updated.

ojp.gov/programs/yvp_gangs.htm
www.csun.edu/~hcchs006/gang.html
www.bigonion.com/tours/gangs-of-ny/

Where Was the Item Published?

It is becoming increasingly difficult to differentiate between library research and online research because so many traditional library resources are now located online. In addition, many libraries provide portals to online databases and other online sites. As a result, whether information resides in a physical building or is stored on a server, you will need your critical thinking skills more than ever to determine its value.

As with any research activity, your decision about where to search for information depends on what you are trying to learn. If the answer to your research question requires demographic data, you might find that all the reliable and most current census information is on different Web sites maintained by various agencies of the U.S. government. Web-based research is rarely sufficient for a project of any depth, however. For example, you probably can learn more about local census trends and data from your local newspaper (which may also be available on the Web).

Articles and other source materials published on the Web can appear professional and unbiased, but it is often difficult to find information that allows you to fully evaluate the credibility of a Web page. To do so, you need to determine what person, company, or organization constructed the site and stands behind it. If you learn that you are examining a personal Web site instead of one sponsored by a government agency or a university, you need to take that fact into account. Although organizations will often have their own agenda, they usually can devote more resources to the construction and maintenance of a Web site than an individual can. Web suffixes generally indicate the source of a Web site:

- **.edu** indicates an educational institution. Information you find at such a location has generally been approved by the school. However, many colleges and universities also provide Web space for students and faculty members, and those individuals may post information that has *not* necessarily been approved by the school.

- **.com** indicates a for-profit company. The suffix *.com* is a shortened form of *commercial* and usually designates a business-oriented site.

- **.org** indicates an organization. The *.org* Web suffix is generally used for nonprofit organizations.

- **.gov** indicates some level of government (state, national, or local).

- **.net** indicates Web sites generally used by Internet service providers (ISPs) and companies that provide Web hosting, like www.concentric.net. Some commercial businesses also use the *.net* extension, but usually not as their main Web site. Some Internet service providers allow their customers to use their "net" extension for sharing things like photographs, such as www.photo.net.

- **.biz** is most often used for small-business Web sites.

- **.info** is, like *.com,* an unrestricted domain: anyone can use it. According to Network Associates, the company that assigns and allocates Web addresses, *.info* is the most popular extension beyond *.com, .net,* and *.org.*

There are also additional domains available—for some of the newer ones, see Figure 19.9, which shows a section of the Networks Solutions Web page.

For more information on Web suffixes and addresses, see www.networksolutions. com/. Network Solutions offers a "WhoIs" search function for nearly all sites on the Web except personal ones. Conducting a "WhoIs" search will give you information

FIGURE 19.9
Examples of new domains available

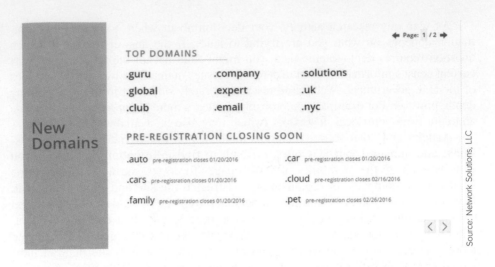

about the sponsor of any particular Web page. This search not only tells you who "owns" the domain name, but also provides e-mail contact information. If the Web page you're looking for is not listed, then it is probably a personal page.[1]

How Accurate Is the Information in This Source?

Anyone who stands in a supermarket check-out line and sees tabloid headlines about aliens and Elvis sightings understands that not all news stories that appear in print are necessarily accurate. How do you know what information to believe and what information to view with skepticism?

- One of the best ways of determining the accuracy of the information in any publication is to find out who published it. As we have noted, books published by university presses and articles published in academic journals are peer reviewed. You can usually expect that large newspapers, such as *The New York Times*, will print the most accurate information available at the time each issue is published. Over time, some information published in reliable periodicals or newspapers may change or need to be corrected. The publication is then likely to publish the updated information.

- Another way of determining accuracy is to investigate the author's track record. Of course, it's important to make sure that the author's area of expertise is in the subject you are researching. A famous actor who writes a diet book may or may not be a credible source of information on proper nutrition.

---

[1]Thanks to William Sherman, University of Northern Colorado, for this information.

To determine the accuracy of information on a Web site, you might consider the Web sites it provides links to. Often, following some of the links will give you information about the site's credibility. For example, as this is being written, all of the articles on the Web site Streetgangs.com showed 2015 dates.

Links that connect to reputable newspapers or television stations would indicate that whoever is maintaining the Web site is providing readers with connections to legitimate news articles, thus adding to the credibility of the Web site. However, sometimes links just lead to stories that have bylines but give little indication of what organization the writer works for. What impact do links such as these have on the way you view the information available on this site?

 USING DIGITAL TECHNOLOGIES **Evaluating Web Sites**

Ask yourself the following questions when evaluating the credibility of a Web site.

- Who is the author or sponsor of the site? What can you find out about the author or sponsor? Why might this person or organization sponsor the site? What benefit might the sponsor receive from the Web site?

- What does the site's address tell you about it? What does the suffix that appears at the end of the address tell you about it: *.edu* for educational, for example, or *.com* for commercial? Is there a tilde (~) in the address, which indicates a personal site?

- What is the purpose of the site? Is the purpose to provide information? To sell a product or service? To persuade readers to accept a particular point of view?

- How professional is the tone, and how well designed is the site? How carefully has it been edited and proofread? How many grammatical and spelling errors are there?

- Consider the quality of the author's arguments. Does the content contain logical fallacies? How fairly does the author deal with opposing views?

- Can you find a date when the site was published or most recently updated?

- What kinds of links does the site provide? How legitimate or credible are the sites the links lead to?

Field Research

As we have seen, much of the time you will gather information for your research projects from books, periodicals, the Web, and other preexisting sources. At other times, you may need to gather firsthand information. Sometimes you can get the information you need by simply observing people, wildlife, or natural phenomena. At other times, the best method of gathering information from human subjects may be to ask questions of individual people or groups of people, either directly or in writing. However you do it, the act of gathering information on your own is called **field research** because you need to go out "into the field." The most common kinds of field research you might find yourself doing are observation, personal interviews, and surveys.

Working with Human Participants

Much field research has to do with human behavior. Any time you are doing research that involves human participants, you are expected to behave ethically and to do or say nothing that might in any way harm your participants. To ensure that researchers follow ethical practices, all academic institutions (and many private organizations) have Institutional Review Boards (IRBs). All research projects that use human participants must be approved by your organization's IRB or its designated representative. All IRBs have their own rules. Check with your instructor about your school's human participants policy.

Informed Consent

Whether you are required to submit a formal proposal to your school's IRB or simply need to work closely with your instructor, if you are going to be working with human participants, you need to get their permission by having all of the participants in your field research sign an Informed Consent Form. Most institutions have templates for these forms readily available.

Observations

Watching and recording what you see might be the most effective way to help you answer your research question. If viewing people, animals, or other phenomena over a short time will provide you with useful information, you may choose observation as your research method.

OBSERVING HUMANS

If you are writing an informative or analytical paper, you may need to observe human behavior as part of your research. To make your observations, you might station yourself at a particular place in a shopping mall, at an athletic event, or at a busy intersection and record, in detail, certain behaviors. For example, you might record how many vehicles passing through an intersection near your college actually come to a complete stop at the stop sign. You would need to keep track of the total number of vehicles passing by as well as the specific number of vehicles that demonstrate the particular behavior you are watching for. It is, of course, possible to make even more detailed observations, such as what car models drivers who run stop signs are driving. To make detailed observations such as these, it helps to prepare by setting up categories. Once you are in the field observing and recording, you probably won't have time to develop new ones.

OBSERVING OTHER PHENOMENA

For writing projects that lend themselves to observation, see Chapters 6, 7, and 8.

You can also observe other natural and human-influenced phenomena. Some researchers observe animal behavior; others watch tornadoes and other weather patterns. The specific nature of what you are observing will determine the tools you will need and the methods you will use.

Writing Activity

Conducting an Observation

People often comment on how students are tied to technology. How valid is this assertion? One way to test this assumption might be to sit for an hour in your student union or some other place where students from your campus gather. Watch the behavior of the students. Are they talking with one another in person, or are they using technology to communicate, listen to music, or watch videos? Take notes of what you see. You might want to establish some categories. Are students talking on cell phones? Are they texting? Are they using laptops? Are they listening to iPods? Write a short report on your findings.

Interviews

Because most of us are comfortable talking with other people, we often think that interviewing someone will be easy. However, interviews are rarely an easy way to do meaningful research. Effective interviews that yield useful information happen only when the interviewer prepares ahead of time. As you prepare, it's important to remember that some of the interviews you may see on television or hear on the radio are not necessarily good examples of interviewing.

You can employ several strategies to prepare and conduct a successful interview:

- Call ahead to make an appointment instead of just showing up in your interviewee's office. You might obtain more information than you might otherwise have been able to get.

- Do your homework ahead of time so that you have good questions ready to ask, have anticipated the nature of the responses, and have good follow-up questions at hand. Being able to anticipate the nature of the interview will enable you to steer it in the direction in which you need it to go.

- Be prepared to take notes. Before you interview someone for an assignment, practice (using your interview questions) with a classmate or a friend.

- Consider bringing along some kind of recording device. If you plan to record the interview, make sure you have your subject's permission before the interview begins. Some people are willing to talk but do not wish to be recorded.

- Be polite and friendly during the interview. It is usually a good idea to follow up an interview with a thank-you note.

Although your specific interview questions will depend on your topic and the person you are interviewing, you will usually want to prepare two kinds of questions: open-ended and directed. **Open-ended questions** let the person being interviewed develop his or her answers at length. **Directed questions** seek more specific kinds of information. As part of her research for a paper on violence in the movies, for example, Magda was interested in learning about how people react when they are watching violent movies. To find out, she decided to interview the local manager of a theater chain that sometimes shows violent, R-rated movies. To prepare for the interview, Magda developed the following list of questions:

1. What would you consider a violent movie?
2. What specific content in a movie makes it violent?
3. Are all movies that contain scenes with (the content from the previous questions) necessarily violent? If not, why not? What's the determining factor?
4. Do you show many movies like that? If so, how many per month?
5. Why do you think people watch violent movies?
6. What age groups seem to watch violent movies?
7. Do audiences at violent movies behave differently from audiences at other types of movies, such as comedies?
8. Are audiences at violent movies more or less likely to buy more at the concession stand?
9. Do audiences at violent movies leave behind more or less trash in the theater?
10. Are audiences at violent movies more or less likely to leave through an unauthorized exit?
11. Are audiences at violent movies generally noisier or quieter?

Some of the questions in Magda's list, such as 1–3, were open-ended. Others, such as questions 7–11, were more directed, perhaps indicating the direction of her thinking as she developed her thesis.

Avoid what can be called "forced-choice questions," questions that presuppose only a few specific choices and force your subject to answer one of them. Asking "Do you think the football team is bad or just plain awful this year?" assumes the team really is bad and that your subject will agree. A better question would be "What's your opinion of the football team this year?"

Also stay away from leading questions that have built-in *assumptions* the person you are interviewing might not agree with. A question like "Don't you think that conducting surveys provides a richness that other research methods can't match?" assumes (1) that the interviewee will interpret "richness" in the same way you do, and (2) that both of your definitions of "can't match" will also agree. It would be more effective to ask the question in a more neutral way: "Are there any advantages, in your view, to surveys over other kinds of field research? If so, what might they be?"

Writing Activity

Conducting an Interview

Assume that you are a reporter for your school's newspaper. Your editor has assigned you to interview the president of your campus on a topic of your choice. Develop a list of ten questions, some open-ended, some directed, that you want to ask the president.

Surveys

Although interviews are useful sources of information and have the advantage of enabling a direct exchange between the subject and the interviewer, the number of people that one person can interview is limited. Some research projects require you to collect information from a larger number of people than you could possibly interview. To get information from a large number of people quickly and efficiently, you can use a **survey.** Although on the surface a survey may look like just a set of questions, an effective survey is carefully designed, and its questions are very specifically framed. A good survey will either target a particular group of people or solicit information about the participants to provide you with a context for their answers.

CONSTRUCTING A SURVEY

Several strategies will enable you to put together an effective survey:

- Keep the survey a reasonable length. Ask only those questions that are necessary. Many people think that all surveys need to start with questions that ask for certain basic demographic information, but you need gather only information that is important for your research.

- Make sure the questions you ask call for an appropriate response. If a reasonable answer to the question is "yes," or "no," make sure there are only two possible responses. If a wider range of responses is appropriate, a scale such as "strongly agree, agree, no opinion, disagree, strongly disagree" may be more useful.

- Consider whether you want to ask only *closed-ended* or *directed* questions that call for specific answers, such as "List your age," or if you also want to ask *open-ended* questions, such as "Describe your experience at the Math Testing Center." Closed-ended questions are easier to tabulate, but open-ended questions will provide you with more examples and narrative detail.

- If you ask open-ended questions that call for written responses, give your respondents enough room on the form to answer fully.

- The question itself should not influence the response. Asking a question like "Do you think there are not enough parking spaces on campus?" leads the respondent to say "yes." A more effective way to get the same information would be to ask, "What is your opinion of the campus parking situation?"

- Have a strategy for tabulating the open-ended responses. Are you going to try to categorize them? Are you planning to use them as anecdotal examples?

- Consider using an electronic survey, such as those provided by SurveyMonkey.com. These companies often allow you to conduct free surveys but limit the number of responses you can receive to 100 or so. An electronic survey lets you reach a wider audience: You can simply e-mail the survey link. Also, you may find that those you want to complete your survey are more likely to fill out an electronic form than a paper one—and the electronic survey will help you collect and collate your data. Do not hesitate to ask teachers if they will allow you to survey students in your class. Conducting a survey in one of your classes about a subject you are writing about in another class is a great way to help "see" the connections between the classes you are taking.

ADMINISTERING YOUR SURVEY

Test your survey before you administer it. That way, if a question or two proves to be faulty, you can make changes. Have several people respond to your survey, asking them to indicate any confusing questions. Also consider whom you would like to respond to your survey, targeting your audience as specifically as possible. A general rule of thumb is that the more people you can ask to take your survey— the larger the data set—the more useful the results will be. It is also important to make sure that you are surveying the right population. If you are looking for information on what kind of coffee drinks are most popular on your campus, for example, you should survey only coffee drinkers.

Writing Activity

Developing a Survey

Often people who are thinking of opening a small business conduct a survey of their potential clientele to test their business plan's chances for success. Think of a possible product or service that seems to be lacking in your community. Then identify the customers your business will serve. Develop a set of survey questions that will give you a good sense of whether others share your perceived need for this business.

Text Credits

p. 524: Source: Definition of "adolescent" adapted and reproduced from *The American Heritage® Medical Dictionary*. Copyright © 2007 Houghton Mifflin. **p. 525:** Abstract: "Gang World" by: Papachristos, Andrew V. *Foreign Policy*, Mar/Apr2005 Issue 147, p48–55, from Academic Search Complete. Copyright © 2005 by Foreign Policy. **p. 535:** Source: Blurb about authors Duffy and Gillig from the Greenwood Press online catalog Greenwood Publishing Group, Inc., Westport, CT. **p. 535:** From The Child Adolescent Psychiatrist, Facts for Families Pages, American Academy of Child & Adolescent Psychiatry. https://www.aacap.org/AACAP/Families_and_Youth/Facts_for_Families/Facts_for_Families_Pages/The_Child_And_Adolescent_Psychiatrist_00.aspx.

20

Synthesizing and Documenting Sources

Effective academic writing does not just emerge out of a writer's mind. Academic writers are expected to know what others have said about their topic, using the work of other writers to help establish a foundation for an argument, substantiate an argument, or set up a point that they will then challenge or support. This process of building your own arguments using support and arguments from other writers is called **synthesis**. As they synthesize ideas, academic writers need to use sources, acknowledging the thinking that already exists on an issue and giving credit to those who developed it. When developing an argument in an academic essay, for instance, you will be expected to review the relevant work of previous researchers and summarize their results.

You will then be able to build your own arguments, working from

© Hero Images/Getty Images, RF

theirs. And you will need to give these researchers credit. To help you synthesize other people's writing and document your sources, this chapter covers plagiarism, quotations, paraphrasing, and

summaries, as well as the MLA and APA documentation styles.

For more on synthesis, see Chapters 2 and 3.

An Overview of Documentation

When you document sources appropriately, you accomplish several important purposes:

- Documentation indicates what you as the writer did not produce—in effect, it indicates where you have used summary and paraphrase: "This isn't my idea and here is where it came from." Or it indicates a quotation: "These aren't my words, and here is the name of the person who wrote or said them."

- Documentation that follows a system such as the one recommended by the Modern Language Association (MLA) or the American Psychological Association (APA) provides readers with a list of sources—called the list of Works Cited in MLA style or References in APA style—so they can consult the works listed. Proper documentation, within the text and in the list of sources, makes it easy for the reader to locate and read a particular source the writer has cited or even a specific quotation in that source.

- Proper documentation of appropriate sources lends *ethos* (credibility) to you as a writer and enhances your argument.

Different academic disciplines have different style guides that offer a range of conventions for writers to follow, including conventions for documentation. Here we will present the conventions for documentation given in the style guides of the MLA and the APA. MLA style is used for papers in humanities disciplines, including English; APA style is used for papers in social science disciplines. The current editions of both manuals are as follows:

Modern Language Association, *MLA Handbook*. 8th ed., MLA, 2016.

American Psychological Association. (2010). *Publication manual of the American Psychological Association* (6th ed.). Washington, DC: Author.

Other disciplines recommend a variety of styles. Here are some of those other options:

- *Scientific Style and Format: The CSE Manual for Authors, Editors and Publishers* (7th ed.). If your academic work is in the sciences, you may be required to use the style suggested by the Council of Scientific Editors (CSE), formerly the Council of Biology Editors (CBE).

- *Information for Authors.* This volume, published by the Institute of Electrical and Electronics Engineers (IEEE), is used by engineers.

- *The Chicago Manual of Style* (16th ed.). *CMS* is another widely used style. In fact, if you are expected to do on-the-job writing that requires documentation, more likely than not you will use *CMS*.

When you use information from sources to support your thesis, you must be careful to give appropriate credit to the author of each source. Failing to do so is plagiarism. You can choose from among several options for presenting information that you have taken from other writers' work: quotations, paraphrases, or summaries.

Plagiarism

We've all heard lots of discussion about plagiarism. It's important, however, to have a firm grasp of exactly what constitutes plagiarism, which can mean different things to different people. The best definition of **plagiarism** is from the Council of Writing Program Administrators in their "Defining and Avoiding Plagiarism: The WPA Statement on Best Practices": "In an instructional setting, plagiarism occurs when a writer deliberately uses someone else's language, ideas, or other original (not common-knowledge) material without acknowledging its source" (www.wpacouncil.org/positions/WPAplagiarism.pdf). As the statement implies, the key concept in plagiarism is the *intent to deceive*: the act of knowingly submitting someone else's work as your own is the basic ingredient of what constitutes plagiarism. There are two somewhat related problems that students, especially those who are new to using research in their writing, often have problems with: inadequate or incorrect citations, and "patchwriting."

Inadequate or Incorrect Citations

One of the most common problems students have when they are integrating material from sources into their writing is inadequate or incorrect citations. Citation systems such as MLA can be confusing to new researchers, and instructors often see students make mistakes when they are citing sources. If you are integrating material from sources, whether you are using a direct quotation, a paraphrase, or a summary, you must cite it appropriately. You'll also need to have the appropriate citation in your list of works cited or references at the end of your paper. Refer to the guidelines on pages 556–578 for MLA or pages 579–598 for APA, and ask your instructor or a tutor in the writing center if you are unsure about how to cite a specific source.

Patchwriting

Rhetoric and composition scholar Rebecca Moore Howard uses the term *patchwriting* to describe what happens when students unintentionally put passages from sources into their own writing without proper attribution. This problem commonly occurs when students use paraphrases or summaries inappropriately or simply aren't quite sure how to incorporate the ideas of others into their work. To avoid patchwriting, make sure your paraphrases and summaries are in your own words and are properly cited when you incorporate the ideas of others into your work.

Anti-plagiarism Software

Search technologies that enable all of us to find information more quickly and thoroughly on the Internet than ever before can also be used by instructors to check whether the writing students are turning in is original or taken from another writer's work. Anyone who finds a suspicious passage in a piece of writing can easily enter the passage into a search engine such as Google, making sure the whole passage is enclosed in quotation marks, to see if it appears elsewhere on the Internet. Using similar search technologies, some companies have marketed what has come to be called anti-plagiarism software such as Turnitin or Safe-Assign, which is part of Blackboard. Instructors who use this kind of software commonly let their students know that they are going to submit the students' papers. In fact, many instructors encourage their students to submit drafts of assignments so that the software can point out potentially problematic passages and inadequate citation. Using anti-plagiarism software in this way gives students the opportunity to have their drafts checked for both patchwriting and inadequate citation, so they can revise their papers before submitting the final draft.

Quotations

When the most effective way to make a point is to use another author's exact words, you are using a **quotation.** Use a direct quotation in the following situations:

- When the exact wording is particularly striking
- When the author is considered to be especially authoritative
- When you take issue with the author's statement

If you are using MLA style and your quotation is shorter than five lines, you should enclose it in quotation marks and incorporate it into your text. Because the quotation is incorporated into the sentence, a comma is used after the introductory phrase. At first it might feel a bit awkward or clumsy when you integrate quoted material into your writing; however, you will get better with practice. Using verbs such as *notes, comments, observes,* and *explains* will help you introduce quotations smoothly and meaningfully.

For information on how to cite quotations, paraphrases, and summaries within text, see pages 556–578 for MLA style and pages 579–598 for APA style.

Commenting on the early days of Barack Obama's presidency, David Corn notes, "Politics is not a meritocracy, and Obama realized no president was guaranteed credit or lucky bounces" (15).

When the quotation is longer than four lines and you are using MLA style, start the quotation on a new line and indent all lines of the quotation one-half inch. The quotation should be double-spaced and does not need to be enclosed in quotation marks. If the quotation is introduced with an independent clause, that clause is followed by a colon.

A political observer explains an analogy from the early days of Barack Obama's presidency:

> Politics is not a meritocracy, and Obama realized no president was guaranteed credit or lucky bounces. But at times he couldn't help feeling, as he told one associate, a kinship with the protagonist in Ernest Hemingway's *The Old Man and the Sea.* He had, against tremendous odds, caught a big fish, but on the long voyage back to shore, his prized catch had been picked to pieces by sharks. (Corn 15)

If you are using APA style, quotations of fewer than forty words should be enclosed in quotation marks and incorporated into the text, as follows:

> Commenting on the early days of Barack Obama's presidency, David Corn (2012) notes, "Politics is not a meritocracy, and Obama realized no president was guaranteed credit or lucky bounces" (p. 15).

Block quotations are used in APA style when the quotation is at least forty words long. They are indented only five spaces and double spaced, and are not enclosed in quotation marks.

> A political observer explains an analogy from the early days of Barack Obama's presidency:
>
>> Politics is not a meritocracy, and Obama realized no president was guaranteed credit or lucky bounces. But at times he couldn't help feeling, as he told one associate, a kinship with the protagonist in Ernest Hemingway's *The Old Man and the Sea*. He had, against tremendous odds, caught a big fish, but on the long voyage back to shore, his prized catch had been picked to pieces by sharks. (Corn, 2012, p. 15)

Ellipses

If you decide that a quotation is too long and want to condense it, you can do so by placing an ellipsis (three periods with a space between each) in place of the omitted words. If the ellipsis occurs at the end of the sentence, you will need to place the sentence's period before the first ellipsis with a space between the period and the first ellipsis point. Make sure when you use an ellipsis that you do not change the meaning of the original quotation. For example, compare the original quotation from Marshall McLuhan and the condensed version to see how an ellipsis should be used properly.

ORIGINAL QUOTATION

> As the alphabet neutralized the divergencies of primitive cultures by translation of their complexities into simple visual terms, so representative money reduced the moral values in the nineteenth century.

CONDENSED VERSION

> In *Understanding Media*, Marshall McLuhan compares the visual technology inherent in the alphabet with money, saying, "As the alphabet neutralized the divergencies of primitive cultures . . . so representative money reduced moral values in the nineteenth century" (141).

Brackets

If you find that a quotation is not clear and you need to add information so that your readers will understand it better, you can do so by using square brackets [ ]:

> In their book *Freakonomics*, Steven D. Leavitt and Stephen J. Dubner confirm that often commonly held stereotypes seem to apply to reality:
>> For instance, men [on online dating sites] who say they want a longterm relationship do much better than men looking for an occasional lover. But women [on the same sites] looking for an occasional lover do great. (82)

Paraphrases

Use a **paraphrase** to put someone else's ideas into your own words. Because you are using someone else's ideas, you need to include an appropriate citation. However, in a paraphrase you need to use your own words and sentence structure. If you choose to borrow unique phrases from the original, those phrases should be placed in quotation marks. Here, for example, is a block quotation in MLA style:

> In his book *The World Is Flat*, *The New York Times* columnist Thomas L. Friedman notes that when Netscape went public in 1995, it had significant ramifications for the emerging global economy:
>> Looking back, what enabled Netscape to take off was the existence, from the earlier phase, of millions of PC's, many already equipped with modems. Those are the shoulders Netscape stood on. What Netscape did was bring a new killer app—the browser—to this installed base of PC's making the computer and its connectivity inherently more useful for millions of people. (57)

If you don't want to use a direct quotation, you can paraphrase Friedman's information by changing it into your own words. However, in paraphrasing, you need to be careful that you do not commit **plagiarism** by using language, sentence structures, or both that are too close to the original. The following paraphrase uses language that too closely mimics the original.

Faulty Paraphrase

> In *The World Is Flat*, Thomas L. Friedman looks back to 1995 and notes that what enabled Netscape to take off when it went public was that it could stand on the shoulders of the millions of already existing PC's, many already equipped with modems. Its new killer app—the browser—helped millions of people make connecting more useful (57).

In contrast, the following paraphrase is entirely in the writer's own words and sentence structures:

Acceptable Paraphrase

> In *The World Is Flat*, Thomas L. Friedman looks back to 1995 and notes that Netscape could make a significant impact on the emerging global economy when it went public because of its browser. When Netscape brought this new software application—the browser—to the users of modem-enhanced PC's, it made those connected computers much more useful (57).

Suppose you were writing about Asperger's syndrome and found a definition at the National Institute of Neurological Disorder and Stroke Web page. Here is part of that definition:

> Two core features of autism are: a) social and communication deficits and b) fixated interests and repetitive behaviors. The social communication deficits in highly functioning persons with Asperger's syndrome include lack of the normal back and forth conversation; lack of typical eye contact, body language, and facial expression; and trouble maintaining relationships. Fixated interests and repetitive behaviors include repetitive use of objects or phrases, stereotyped movements, and excessive attachment to routines, objects, or interests. Persons with ASD may also respond to sensory aspects of their environment with unusual indifference or excessive interest.

Faulty Paraphrase

A faulty paraphrase of the first sentence would mimic the sentence structure in the original text and would look similar:

> According to the National Institute of Neurological Disorder and Stroke, the main core features of autism are: a) poor communication skills and b) fixating on the same things repeatedly.

The following acceptable version conveys the idea but with a different sentence structure.

Acceptable Paraphrase

> According to the National Institute of Neurological Disorder and Stroke, two main features of autism are awkward communication skills and fixated, repetitive interests.

USING DIGITAL TECHNOLOGIES   **Managing Research Notes**

You can use a Word document while you are conducting research to help record notes and to document your research sources. Use an outline of your project to help organize information. While you may be tempted to copy and paste information from your sources, it is best to paraphrase or summarize from them and note why the information is relevant to your project's topic as well as the exact source the information came from. You can record source documentation for your list of works cited (MLA) or references (APA) in a Word file as you proceed.

Summaries

When you include a **summary** of your source's ideas, you condense the material presented by another author into a briefer form. Although similar to paraphrasing, summaries reduce information into a substantially smaller number of words. You might summarize a paragraph or even a page of material in only a sentence or two. To summarize a chapter, you might need several paragraphs. A summary of a larger work might be several pages in length. Once again, however, the summary must be entirely in your own words and sentence structures to avoid plagiarizing the original. Here are faulty and acceptable summaries of the National Institute of Neurological Disorder and Stroke passage.

Faulty Summary

There are two core features of autism that include (a) social and communication deficits and (b) fixated interests and repetitive behaviors.

Acceptable Summary

Autistic behavior usually includes communication issues as well as behavior that is both fixated and repetitive.

For more on writing a summary, see Chapter 2, pages 23–25.

Note that if you use phrases from the original in your summary, you should enclose them in quotation marks.

Syntheses

As noted on pages 25–26 in Chapter 2, **synthesis** is the act of blending information from multiple sources and melding it with the writer's own ideas. A synthesis could involve quoting, paraphrasing, and/or summarizing source material. To avoid plagiarism when synthesizing source material, you need to clarify which ideas are taken from which sources and which ideas are your own. For example, in the opening paragraph of his essay on gangs and adolescent behaviors (page 595), writer Aaron Zook reviews some of the literature on the topic:

> Since the early 1920s, researchers have closely studied the relationship between street gangs and violent crime from a variety of perspectives: criminological, socio-logical, and psychological (Thabit, 2005). Whatever the underlying causes for gang membership, the results seem clear; members of street gangs admit to a far greater rate of serious crime, and to far more severe acts of violence (Penly Hall, Thornberry, & Lizotte, 2006) than non-gang members of the same age, race, and socioeconomic background. According to the Web site Safeyouth.org (n.d.), gang violence is certainly cause for concern:
>
> > Gang members are responsible for much of the serious violence in the United States. . . . Teens that are gang members are much more likely than other teens to commit serious and violent crimes. For example, a survey in Denver found that while only 14% of teens were gang members, they were responsible for committing 89% of the serious violent crimes.
>
> Many researchers have therefore come to the conclusion that gangs necessarily cause violence and deviant behavior.

For more on synthesis, see Chapter 3.

Notice how Zook uses parenthetical citations to identify the sources for information that he has taken from multiple sources. Notice too in the last sentence that Zook uses his own words to draw a conclusion from the material that he summarized and quoted earlier in the paragraph. However, if his sentence had read, "Many researchers have therefore come to the conclusion that gang members are responsible for much of the serious violence in the United States," he would have been plagiarizing because the sentence includes exact words and phrases from the original block quotation.

Faulty Synthesis

Many researchers have therefore come to the conclusion that gang members are responsible for much of the serious violence in the United States.

Acceptable Synthesis

Many researchers have therefore come to the conclusion that gangs necessarily cause violence and deviant behavior.

or

Many researchers have therefore come to the conclusion that "gang members are responsible for much of the serious violence in the United States."

MLA Documentation Style

There are two components to MLA style: parenthetical in-text citations and a works-cited list that appears at the end of the paper. Every source cited within the body of the paper appears in the works-cited list.

MLA Style: In-Text Citation

In MLA style, parenthetical in-text citations are used in conjunction with the list of works cited to give readers the information they would need to locate the sources that you have quoted, paraphrased, or summarized. The intent in MLA style is to give only as much information in the text as the reader needs to find the detailed bibliographical information in the list of works cited—generally, the author and the page number of the material cited. The following are examples of how to cite different types of sources within your text using MLA style, starting with the most basic citation: a work with one author.

A WORK WITH ONE AUTHOR

Suppose that you quote from page 173 of *Midnight Rising* by Tony Horwitz, published in 2011. In MLA style, your in-text citation would be "(Horwitz 173)." MLA in-text citations do not include punctuation, and the page number is given simply as a number.

The parenthetical citation is placed directly after the cited material. Here is an example using a block quotation in MLA style:

> The scene at Harpers Ferry, Virginia, in 1859 is described as one of confusion:
>> When the word of trouble in Harpers Ferry first spread on the morning of October 17, the response of white Virginians nearby was swift and instinctive. Their neighbors were under attack, blacks were rumored to be rising up, and that was all any able-bodied man needed to know before grabbing a gun and rushing to the scene. (Horwitz 173)

In this example, the author's name is not mentioned in the text that precedes the quotation. When the author's name is mentioned in the sentence preceding a quote, however, the parenthetical citation includes only the page number, as in the following example:

> Tony Horwitz describes the first reaction to rumors by those living near Harpers Ferry, Virginia, as both "swift and instinctive" (173).

If a parenthetical citation follows a quotation that ends a sentence, place the period after the parenthetical citation. However, if the quotation appears as a block (see above), place the period before the citation.

A WORK WITH MORE THAN ONE AUTHOR

Use all the authors' last names. If there are three or more authors, use the first author's last name with *et al.* following it.

> Glassick et al. state that "teaching, too, must in the end be judged not merely by process but by results, however eloquent a teacher's performance" (29).

> Ultimately, it is the results of teaching, not the method or the quality of the performance, that we must evaluate (Glassick et al. 29).

TWO OR MORE WORKS BY THE SAME AUTHOR

If you are citing ideas from two or more works by the same author, use the title of the work, shortened, to distinguish which source you are citing.

> It is important to establish good relations with the people you work with by engaging in non-work related conversation. Both men and women do so, but the subjects of their conversations differ (Tannen, *Talking* 64).

AN UNKNOWN AUTHOR

Use a shortened version of the title.

> Employees of Google believe their corporate culture to be antithetical to that of Microsoft ("Google" 15).

A GOVERNMENT AGENCY OR A CORPORATE AUTHOR

Use the name of the organization.

> Policy makers and citizens are warned that "Arizona is not positioned well to attract and keep the knowledge workers it needs" (Morrison Institute 6).

AN ANTHOLOGIZED WORK

Cite the author of the anthologized piece, not the editor of the collection. However, give the page numbers used in the collection.

> John Perry Barlow asks the important question: "The enigma is this: If our property can be infinitely reproduced and instantaneously distributed all over the planet without cost, without our knowledge, without its even leaving our possession, how can we protect it?" (319).

A SECONDARY SOURCE

Whenever possible, cite the original source. However, if you do need to use a quotation from a secondary source, use *qtd. in.*

Jonathan Shaw muses, "I don't think mankind is ready, spiritually or mentally, for the transformations it's undergoing in the technological era: tattooing is a mute plea for a return to human values" (qtd. in Dery 284).

AN ONLINE SOURCE

Unless your source has some kind of numbering system or is a pdf file, you will not usually be able to provide page numbers for your quotation or paraphrase. Give the author or, if the author's name is not available, the title of the online work you are citing.

According to Christopher Beam, there are a number of methods that Internet service providers can use to block Web sites if a government orders them to do so.

MLA Style: Constructing a List of Works Cited

Because the list of works cited at the end of your paper is intended to work together with your in-text citations, it includes only the sources you cite within your text, not the works that you read but did not cite. The list should be double-spaced, and its entries are listed alphabetically by the last name of the first author. The first line of each entry is even with the left margin; any subsequent lines are indented one-half inch.

All entries in the list are formatted according to the same rules. In the following pages, you will find, for each common type of entry, a sample entry for a work in MLA style and, on pages 582–592, for many of the same works in APA style. First, though, to see some important differences between the two styles, consider these pairs of entries:

MLA   Horwitz, Tony. *Midnight Rising*. Henry Holt, 2012.

APA   Horwitz, T. (2012). *Midnight rising*. New York: Henry Holt and Company.

MLA   Stine, Linda J. "Teaching Basic Writing in a Web-Enhanced Environment." *Journal of Basic Writing*, vol. 29, no. 1, 2010, pp. 33–55.

APA   Stine, L. J. (2010). Teaching basic writing in a web-enhanced environment. *Journal of Basic Writing* 29(1), 33–55.

Notice in particular the following:

- In both styles, entries consist of three essential pieces of information: author, source, and publication information for the source. Note the difference in the placement of information: In APA style, the year of publication follows the author's name rather than coming later in the entry as it does in MLA style.

- In MLA style, authors' first and middle names are given in full if that is how they are given in the source; in APA style, only initials are given.

- In MLA style, all major words in titles are capitalized; in APA style, only the first word, words following a colon, and proper nouns are capitalized in the titles of books and articles. All major words are capitalized in the titles of periodicals, however.

- In both styles, titles of books and periodicals are given in italics. In MLA style, titles of articles are enclosed in quotation marks; in APA style, they are not.

The section that follows includes model entries for different types of print and nonprint sources in MLA style. Figure 20.1 provides you with a flowchart that will help you find the model entry that is closest to the source that you need to cite.

PRINT DOCUMENTS

Books

The basic items in an entry for a book are the author's name or authors' names, the title, and the publication information, consisting of the publisher and date of publication. See Figure 20.2 on pages 562–563 for guidelines on where to find the elements of a works-cited entry for a book in MLA style.

1. Book with one author: The most basic form includes the author's name, the title of the book, in italics, and the publication information.

publication information

author   title publisher date

Maddow, Rachel. *Drift*. Crown, 2012.

2. Two books by the same author: In MLA style, the author's name appears only in the first entry. For all subsequent entries, three hyphens are used instead of the name. The entries are listed in alphabetical order according to title.

Kissinger, Henry. *On China*. Penguin, 2011.

- - -. *White House Years*. Simon, 1979.

3. Book with multiple authors: In a book with two authors, provide the first author's name (last name, first), followed by a comma and the word "and." Then add the second author (first and last name), followed by a period. If a book has three or more authors, give the name of the first author followed by *et al.* (For an example of the use of *et al.*, see no. 8.)

Plame, Valerie, and Sarah Lovett. *Burned: A Vanessa Pierson Novel*.
    Penguin, 2014.

Grafton, Anthony, et al. *The Classical Tradition*. Harvard UP, 2010.

4. Book by a corporate entity or organization:

Adobe Systems Inc. *Adobe Acrobat 5.0: Getting Started*. Adobe, 2001.

FIGURE 20.1

MLA Style: A Flowchart for Determining the Model Works Cited Entry You Need

Is My Source a Complete Print Book or Part of a Print Book?

No	Yes, go to the next question below.	Go to this entry.
	Is it a book with only one author?	1
	Are you citing more than one book by this author?	2
	Is it a book with multiple authors?	3
	Is the book by an organization of some kind?	4
	Is the author unknown or unnamed?	5
	Does the book also have a translator?	11
	Is it a later publication or edition of the book?	6, 7
	Is it a multivolume work or part of a multivolume work?	13
	Is it part of a series?	14
	Does the book have an editor or a translator?	8, 11
	Is the book an edited collection or anthology?	8
	Is it a work in a collection or an anthology?	9
	Is it an introduction, a preface, a foreword, or an afterword?	12
	Is it an entry in a dictionary or reference work?	22
	Is it a published interview?	10

Is My Source from a Print Periodical Such as a Journal, a Magazine, or a Newspaper?

No	Yes, go to the next question below.	Go to this entry.
	Is it from a scholarly journal?	
	Is it a journal with volume and issue numbers?	15
	Is it a journal with only issue numbers?	16
	Is it from a magazine?	17
	Is it a review?	20
	Is it from a newspaper?	18
	Is it an editorial?	19
	Is it a letter to the editor?	21

Is My Source a Print Source but Not from a Journal, a Magazine, or a Newspaper?

No	Yes, go to the next question below.	Go to this entry.
	Is it an entry in a dictionary or reference work?	22
	Is it a government document?	23
	Is it a pamphlet?	24
	Is it the proceedings from a conference?	25
	Is it an unpublished doctoral dissertation?	26
	Is it a published or an unpublished letter?	27
	Is it a map or chart?	28
	Is it a cartoon?	29
	Is it an advertisement?	30

Is My Source a Nonprint Source from an Online Subscription Database or the World Wide Web?

No	Yes, go to the next question below.	Go to this entry.
	Is it a professional or personal Web site?	31
	Is it an article?	
	Is it a scholarly article retrieved from a database?	32
	Is it an article from an online journal?	34
	Is it an article from an online magazine?	35
	Is it an article from an online newspaper?	36
	Is it an online book?	33
	Is it a blog entry?	37
	Is it an entry on a wiki?	38
	Is it a posting to an electronic forum?	39
	Is it an e-mail message?	40

Is My Source a Nonprint Source That Is Not Published Online?

No	Yes, go to the next question below.	Go to this entry.
	Is it a television or radio program?	41
	Is it an audio recording?	42
	Is it a film, DVD, or Blu-ray?	43
	Is it a nonperiodical publication on CD-ROM?	44
	Is it a personal, e-mail, or telephone interview?	45
	Is it an oral presentation?	46
	Is it a performance?	47
	Is it a work of art?	48

Consult with Your Instructor about How to Cite Your Source.

5. Book by an unknown author:

> *The Chicago Manual of Style: The Essential Guide for Writers, Editors, and Publishers.* 16th ed., Chicago UP, 2010.

6. Republished book: Including the original date of publication is optional in MLA style. If you do include this date, place it immediately following the title.

> Darwin, Charles. *On the Origin of Species.* 1859. Sterling, 2008.

7. Book in a later edition:

> Roen, Duane H., et al. *The McGraw-Hill Guide to Writing: Writing for College, Writing for Life.* 4th ed., McGraw-Hill, 2017.

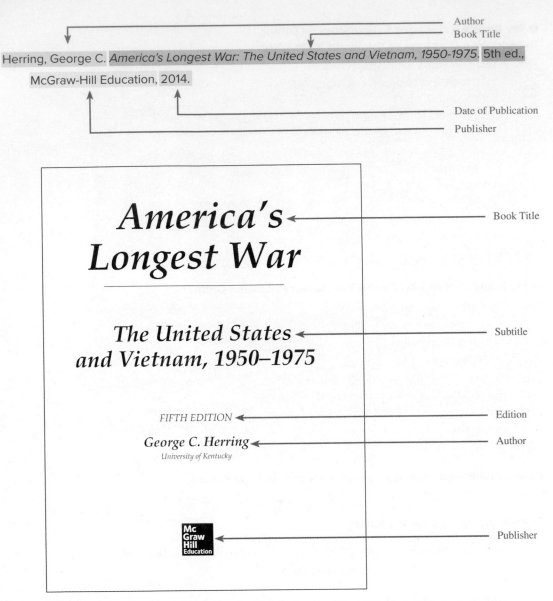

FIGURE 20.2   The Parts of a Works-Cited Entry for a Book in MLA Style

8. Edited collection:

Behm, Nicholas N., et al., editors. *The WPA Outcomes Statement—A Decade Later.* Parlor Press, 2013.

Harrington, Susanmarie, et al., editors. *The Outcomes Book: Debate and Consensus after the WPA Outcomes Statement.* Utah State UP, 2005.

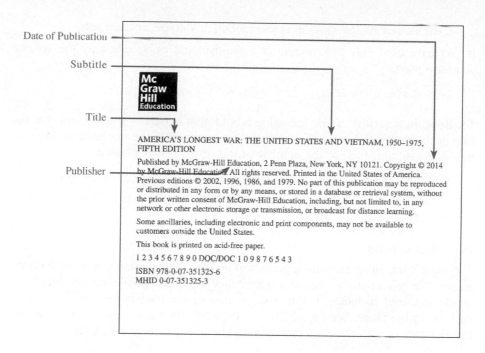

FIGURE 20.2
The Parts of a
Works-Cited Entry
for a Book in
MLA Style
(*Continued*)

9. Work in a collection or an anthology: Include the full range of pages for the work you are citing, not just the pages you used or quoted from.

> Callaway, Micheal. "The WPA Learning Outcomes: What Role Should
> Technology Play?" *The WPA Outcomes Statement—A Decade Later,*
> edited by Nicholas N. Behm et al. Parlor Press, 2013, pp. 271-84.

10. Published interview:

> Banderas, Antonio. "America's Hottest Husband." Interview by Meg Grant. *AARP
> The Magazine,* Nov. 2011, p. 64.

11. Translation:

> Larsson, Stieg. *The Girl Who Kicked the Hornet's Nest.* Translated by
> Reg Keeland, Alfred A. Knopf, 2010.

12. Introduction, preface, foreword, or afterword:

> Campbell, T. Colin. Foreword. *Prevent and Reverse Heart Disease,* by Caldwell
> B. Esselstyn, Jr., Avery, 2008, pp. viii-ix.

13. Multivolume work: If you have used more than one volume of a multivolume work, note the total number of volumes in the work (Refer to the actual volume and page numbers used in your in-text citation.)

> Caro, Robert A. *The Years of Lyndon Johnson.* Vintage, 2003. 4 vols.

If you have used only one volume of a multivolume work, cite only the volume you have used.

> Elias, Norbert. *The History of Manners.* Vol. 1, Pantheon, 1982.

14. Book in a series: If you are using a book that is part of a series, include the title of the series with no italics or quotation marks after the publication information and medium. Include the number of the series if it is present.

> Shortand, Michael, editor. *Science and Nature: Essays in the History of the Environmental Sciences.* British Society for the History of Science, 1993. BSHS Monograph Ser. 8.

Periodical Articles

The basic items in an entry for a periodical article are the author's name or authors' names, the title of the article, and information about the publication in which the article appeared, including its title, volume number and issue number (if applicable), date, and page range. See Figure 20.3 on page 565 for guidelines on where to find the elements of a works-cited entry for a periodical article in MLA style.

15. Article in a scholarly journal with volume and issue numbers:

author   title of article

> Peters, Bradley. "Lessons about Writing to Learn from a University-High School Partnership." *WPA: Journal of the Council of Writing Program Administrators,* vol. 34, no 2, 2011, pp. 59–88.

volume and issue no. and date   page range   title of periodical

16. Article in a scholarly journal that has only issue numbers: Include only the issue number following the title of the journal.

> Lousley, Cheryl. "Knowledge, Power, and Place." *Canadian Literature,* no. 195, 2007, pp. 11-30.

17. Magazine article: Magazines may or may not include volume and issue numbers. In any case, in MLA style, volume numbers are not given. Instead, dates are provided. If magazines are published weekly or biweekly, the day is included along with the month, which is abbreviated. If the entire article does not appear on consecutive pages, give the first page number and a plus sign (+).

> Foust, Dean, et al. "AFLAC: Its Ducks Are Not in a Row." *BusinessWeek,* 2 Feb. 2004, pp. 52-53.

> Wilson, Chauncey E. "Usability and User Experience Design: The Next Decade." *Intercom,* 1 Jan. 2005, pp. 6-9.

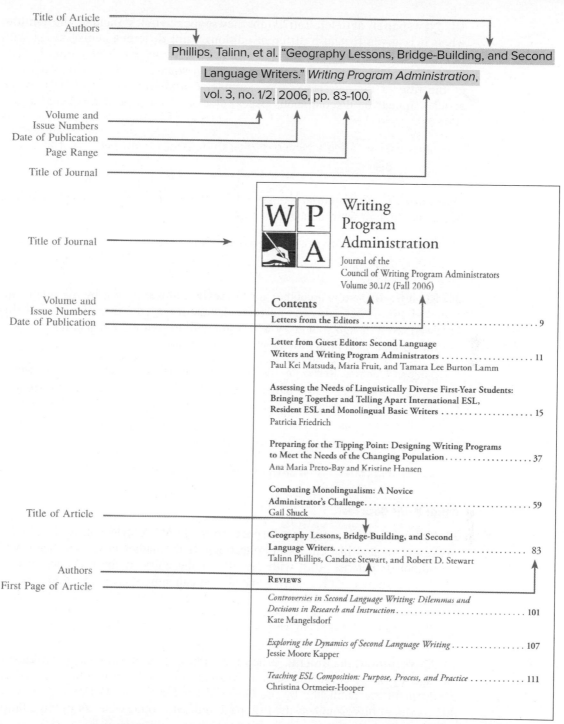

FIGURE 20.3 The Parts of a Works-Cited Entry for a Journal Article in MLA Style

18. Newspaper article: Entries for newspaper articles include the edition, when it is given (because different editions print different items), along with the date of publication and the section and page numbers. You should include the city of origin of a local newspaper within square brackets if it is not part of the title of the newspaper (for example, *Capital Times* [Madison]). When articles appear on discontinuous pages, give the first page number and a plus sign (+).

> Fatsis, Stefan. "A More Modern Masters." *The Wall Street Journal,* 9 Apr. 2002, p. B1+.

19. Editorial: If an editorial is unsigned, use the form below. For signed editorials, begin the citation with the author's name.

> "U.S. and Mexico Share a Lot More than a Border." Editorial. *Arizona Republic* [Phoenix], 22 Nov. 2015, p. 5F.

20. Review: If there is no author for the review, alphabetize it by the title of the review. If the review also has no title, alphabetize by the title of what is being reviewed, even though your entry will begin with *Review of.* When citing a review, use the format appropriate for its place of publication.

> Jablonski, Jeffrey. Review of *The New Careers: Individual Action and Economic Change,* by Michael B. Arthur et al. *Technical Communication Quarterly,* vol. 12, 2003, pp. 230-34.

21. Letter to the editor:

> Lewis, Jeff. Letter. *Arizona Republic* [Phoenix], 22 Nov. 2015, p. 6F.

Other Print Sources

22. Entry in a dictionary or reference work: In MLA style, entries in reference works are treated like entries in collections. If the author is known, begin with the author. Otherwise, start with the title of the entry. If the reference work is commonly known and regularly updated, you can simply give the edition and the date of publication.

> "Express Mail." *Merriam-Webster's Collegiate Dictionary.* 11th ed., 2003.

23. Government document: When the author of the document is not known, the agency is given as the author. Most publications from the U.S. federal government are published by the Government Publishing Office (GPO). Give that as the publisher unless the title page indicates otherwise, as in the citation below.

United States, Department of Health and Human Services, National Institutes
of Health. *Toxicology and Carcinogenesis Studies of Resorcinal (CAS No.
108-46-3) in F344/N Rats and B6C3F₁ Mice (Gavage Studies)*. National
Institutes of Health, 1992.

24. Pamphlet or brochure: Pamphlets and brochures are short documents and
are usually held together by staples rather than a more formal binding. They are
treated as books.

A Guide to Visiting the Lands of Many Nations & to the Lewis & Clark
Bicentennial. National Council of the Lewis & Clark Bicentennial, 2004.

25. Published conference proceedings: The entire collection is treated as a
book. Individual articles are treated as though they were in a collection by different authors.

Buchanan, Elizabeth, and Nancy Morris. "Designing a Web-Based Program in
Clinical Bioethics: Strategies and Procedures." *Proceedings of the 15th
Annual Conference on Distance Teaching & Learning*, U of Wisconsin,
1999, pp. 65-70.

26. Unpublished doctoral dissertation:

Edminster, Judith R. "The Diffusion of New Media Scholarship: Power, Innovation, and Resistance in Academe." Dissertation. U of South Florida, 2002.

27. Letter: If the letter you are citing has been published, treat it as you would
a work in an anthology, but also include the date.

Hemingway, Ernest. "To Maxwell Perkins." 7 February 1936. *Ernest Hemingway:
Selected Letters, 1917-1961*, edited by Carlos Baker. Scribner, 1981, pp. 437–38.

If the letter you are citing is a personal letter, start with the writer's name followed
by "Letter to the author" and the date.

Morris, Patricia M. Letter to the author. 28 Dec. 2015.

28. Map or chart:

San Francisco Bay. California State Automobile Association, 2004.

29. Cartoon:

Benson, Steve. Cartoon. *Arizona Republic*, 28 Dec. 2006, p. 17.

30. Advertisement: Identify the product or company being advertised. Give the
appropriate publication information and include the word "Advertisement."

The Great Courses. Advertisement. *Time*. 30 Nov. 2015, p. 79.

ONLINE SOURCES

Because online sources change constantly, citing them is more complicated than citing print sources. In addition to the author's name (if known) and the title of the document and overall Web site, provide publication information (if known, such as the sponsoring organization. URLs should be included at the end of citations. See Figure 20.4 for guidelines on where to find the elements of a works-cited entry for an article accessed from an online database.

31. Basic professional or personal Web site:

American Medical Association. 1995-2016. www.ama-assn.org/ama.

Publication Information about the Print Version of the Article → Hayes, Matt. "College Football Inside Dish." *Sporting News,* 29 Sept. 2003, p. 31.

Online Subscription Service → *Academic Search Premier,* connection.ebscohost.com/c/articles/20079892/ big-time-college-football-indisde-dish.

Full URL of article

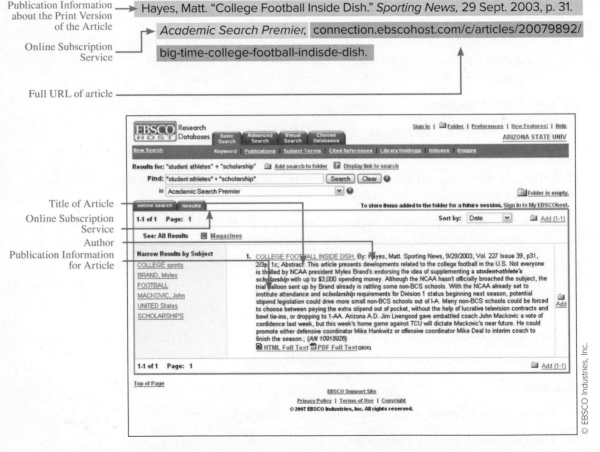

Title of Article
Online Subscription Service
Author
Publication Information for Article

FIGURE 20.4 The Parts of a Works-Cited Entry for a Periodical Article Accessed from an Online Subscription Database

USING DIGITAL TECHNOLOGIES | Using Microsoft Word to Develop Citations

Within newer versions of Microsoft Word, you can build citations with the bibliographic information you've gathered about your sources. Select "Insert" and then the "Document Elements" tab at the top, and then select the citation style you want to use—either MLA or APA. Choose "Insert Citation" (for Word 2010) or the tool icon and "Citation Source Manager." Make sure you choose the correct source type: book, article in a journal, Web site, or whatever is appropriate. From here you can enter the bibliographic information for your source by following the prompts. Each time you use a new source in the body of your project, add a new entry to the citations list, and Word will automatically track your sources. It is a good idea to review your project carefully before you submit it to ensure that every source that appears in the project has both an in-text citation and an entry in the works-cited (MLA) or reference (APA) page and that the format for each citation is correct.

32. Scholarly article retrieved from a database:

author   title of article   title of journal

Johansen, Donald. "Microwave Propulsion Ionizer." *International Journal*

database

of Aerospace Innovations, vol. 3, no. 2, 2011, pp. 85-92. *EBSCOHost*,

vol./issue
no., date,

connection.ebscohost.com/c/articles/63543106/microwave-propulsion-ionizer. page range

Full URL of article

33. Online book:

author   title of online book   title of the Web site

Howells, William Dean. *Familiar Spanish Travels*. 1913. *Project Gutenberg*.

1 Nov. 2012, www.gutenberg.org/ebooks/7430.

For books that you download to a digital device, include the version (Kindle, iPad, etc.) after the title of the book:

Slawenski, Kenneth. *J.D. Salinger: A Life*. Kindle ed., Random House, 2011.

34. Article from an online journal:
When the online article is a digitized version of a print document, include the page numbers that you would find in print. However, if the document appears only in electronic form, page numbers may not exist. Always include the URL or DOI for the full article at the end of the citation.

Salvo, Michael J. "Deafened to Their Demands: An Ethnographic Study of
Accommodation." *Kairos*, vol. 7, no. 1, 2002, english.ttu.edu/kairos/7.1/
binder2.html?coverweb/salvo/map.htm.

35. Article from an online magazine:

Plait, Phil. "The Milky Way, in 46 *Billion* Pixels." *Slate*, 22 Nov. 2015, www.slate.com/
blogs/bad_astronomy/2015/11/22/milky_way_huge_interactive_photo_of_
the_galaxy.html.

36. Article from an online newspaper:

Zernike, Kate. "Massachusetts's Rejection of Common Core Test Signals Shift in
U.S." *The New York Times*, 21 Nov. 2015, www.nytimes.com/2015/11/22/us/
rejecting-test-massachusetts-shifts-its-model.html?_r=0.

37. Blog entry: Use the MLA format for general Web sites. Include the name of the author (bloggers often use pseudonyms); the name of the entry, enclosed in quotation marks; the name of the blog; the date and time of the entry (if available); and the full URL of the blog entry.

jrice. "Misplaced Identities." *Yellow Dog*, 10 Jan. 2015, 8:53 a.m., ydog.net/.

38. Wiki entry: Include the title of the entry, in quotation marks; the title of the wiki (italicized), the date and time the page was last updated (if available), and the full URL for the entry.

"Rhetoric." *Wikipedia*, 6 Apr. 2016, 11:35, en.wikipedia.org/wiki/Rhetoric.

39. Posting to an electronic forum such as a mailing list (listserv): This basic format is used for all online forums including Web-based postings.

Ztang. "How a Career in Technical Communication Ruined Me as a Letter
Writer." *Reddit: Rhetcomp*, 15 Apr. 2016, i.imgur.com/Qr2ueBi.jpg?1.

40. E-mail message:

Bernhardt, Stephen B. "Re: Congrats!" Received by Greg Glau, 18 Apr. 2016.

OTHER NONPRINT SOURCES

41. Television and radio programs: The basic elements for entries that cite radio and television programs include the title of the episode, the title of the program, or series, the name of the network, and the broadcast date.

"Dogs and More Dogs." *Nova*, narrated by John Lithgow, PBS, 3 Feb. 2004.

"Scientists Succeed in Cloning Human Embryo." *All Things Considered*, NPR,
12 Feb. 2004.

42. Audio recording: A citation emphasizing a particular song would follow the format below.

> Underwood, Carrie. "Blown Away." *Blown Away*, 19 Recordings Limited, 2012. *iTunes*, itunes.apple.com/us/album/blown-away/id510168255.

43. Film, DVD, or Blu-ray: In MLA style, the citation usually starts with the title and the director. The distributor and year of release are necessary. Other items, such as performers, are optional.

> *The Lord of the Rings: The Two Towers*. Directed by Peter Jackson, performances by Elijah Wood and Ian McKellan, New Line Home Entertainment, 2003.

44. Nonperiodical publication on a CD-ROM:

> *The OWL Construction and Maintenance Guide*. Edited by James A. Inman and Clinton Gardner. IWCA, 2002.

45. Personal, e-mail, or telephone interview: Indicate whether the interview was conducted in person, by e-mail, or by telephone following the name of the person you interviewed.

> Schwalm, David. Personal interview. 21 Feb. 2004.

46. Oral presentation:

> Russell, David R. "Teacher's Perception of Genre across the Curriculum: Making Classroom/Culture Connections Visible." Conference on College Composition and Communication Convention, 26 Mar. 1999, Atlanta Hilton.

47. Performance: If you are citing a play, an opera, a concert, or a ballet performance, start with the author, followed by the title, and include any other pertinent information (such as the director), the performance date and the location of the performance, and the city (if it is not named in the location).

> Jones, Jerry. *The Norse Family*. Directed by Walter Onger, 28 Dec. 2007, Mesa Performing Arts Center.

48. Work of art:

> di Chirico, Giorgio. *The Philosopher's Conquest*. 1914. Art Institute of Chicago.

MLA Style: Sample Student Paper

Follow these guidelines if you are required to use MLA style:

- Note that a separate title page is not required. Instead, on the first page, put your name, your professor's name, the course number, and the date in the upper-left-hand corner, one inch from the top of the page, and follow with the title of your paper. The title should be centered, with major words capitalized (not articles and prepositions), and it should not be underlined or in a special typeface.

- Double-space the entire paper, including the information mentioned above, block quotations, and your list of works cited.

- Leave one-inch margins on all sides.

- Put page numbers in the upper-right-hand corner, one-half inch from the top. Just before each page number, put your last name.

- Indent the first line of paragraphs one-half inch from the left-hand margin.

- Begin your list of works cited on a new, consecutively numbered page. Include the title *Works Cited* one inch from the top. Center the title; do not use a special typeface for it.

The student paper that follows, "Money for Nothing" by Jessie Katz, is an example of a research project that uses MLA style.

1"

1"

1/2"

Katz   1

Jessie Katz

Professor Wilson

English 105

April 16, 2012

Money for Nothing

For followers of college sports, February is a particularly exciting time of year. With the recent culmination of the football season in the bowl games and the anticipation of upcoming March Madness, all eyes seem glued to ESPN and the sports section of the newspaper as the drama of the season's games, rivalries, and players unfolds. In this charged atmosphere, the public turns its attention toward student-athletes and has ample occasion to contemplate the extraordinary lives that these young people lead. Indeed, some student-athletes apparently have it all: Aside from their national recognition and virtual stardom on and off of their campuses, these athletes also often receive special on-campus housing, the use of state-of-the-art training facilities, and, perhaps most notably, substantial scholarships from their schools.

1"

According to the National Collegiate Athletic Association (NCAA), colleges and universities award $1 billion in athletic scholarships annually to over 126,000 student-athletes (*NCAA*). NCAA defines athletic aid as "a grant, scholarship, tuition waiver, or other assistance from a college or university that is awarded on the basis of a student's athletic ability"; and a student-athlete is a member of the student body who receives athletic aid from his or her school sometime during his or her freshman year. Regardless of financial need or academic promise, athletic scholarships may cover tuition, fees, room and board, and books. Although nearly all Division I and Division II schools grant athletic scholarships, awarding this type of aid does little to benefit the academic prestige, community, or economic condition of colleges or universities. Giving scholarships based solely on athletic merit may in fact undermine the purpose of institutions of higher education, so colleges and universities need to reexamine the extraordinary amounts of money they currently spend on athletic aid to their students.

Like any social institution, colleges and universities exist to promote a certain set of goals. Even though mission statements differ from school to school, these organizations usually share three major objectives: academic scholarship through instruction

1"

Student's name.

Professor's name.

Course title.

Date.

Title centered; major words capitalized.

Shortened version of title of source enclosed in parentheses.

Thesis statement.

Katz   2

and research, service to the university's community, and economic development of the university and its surroundings. For instance, Arizona State University, one of the nation's premier research institutions and a member of the Pac-12, defines its current mission through the vision it calls "The New American University." The Board of Regents for Arizona's Public Universities' *(Board of Regents)* Web site explains this vision as follows:

> Arizona State University has developed a new model for the American research university, creating an institution that is committed to excellence, access and impact. ASU pursues research that contributes to the public good; and ASU assumes major responsibility for the economic, social and cultural vitality of the communities that surround it.

Universities, including ASU, promote their goals through their facilities, through their academic and community programs, and especially through their people, the large majority of whom are students. Students represent both a college's main source of income and its main product; and when a school awards a scholarship, it makes an investment in an individual who it feels will make a special contribution to its goals. However, granting athletes aid does not directly contribute to the three primary goals that most colleges and universities share.

Although they are part of institutions that society entrusts with the passage and creation of knowledge through scholarship and research, athletic departments often appear to disregard the academic success of student-athletes. Certainly not all student-athletes fit the "dumb jock" stereotype, but an alarming amount of data shows that these individuals fall behind their peers in the classroom. Academic underachievement in student-athletes starts at the recruitment level. To become a member of the NCAA and gain the privilege of practicing and playing sports and obtaining a sports scholarship at a Division I or Division II college, incoming freshmen must graduate from high school, complete at least fourteen core courses (including English, math, and physical and social sciences), have a minimum grade point average of 2.0, and achieve a minimum score of 820 on the SAT (*NCAA*). While these requirements appear reasonable, NCAA receives too many applicants and has a staff that is too small to carefully examine each potential student's high school record. In the most extreme cases of academic under-preparedness, student-athletes enter institutes of "higher" education

Quotation longer than four lines indented 1/2 inch and double-spaced. Sentence that introduces it ends with colon. Page number not included because this is a Web source.

Katz   3

without basic literacy and math skills. Since NCAA evaluates high school courses rather than college courses, after student-athletes are accepted into college, the regulation of student-athlete academic education becomes less centralized, falling to the universities' athletic departments, which may be motivated to keep student-athletes in the game and not on the academic chopping block. Instances abound in which advisors recommend lenient professors and classes with titles like Leisure and the Quality of Life, Sports Officiating, and Popular Music (Board of Regents). Surely, if and when academic education becomes subordinate to athletics, colleges and universities are counterproductive in funding their student-athletes' "scholarship."

Organization as author.

One of the most disturbing facts concerning athletics in colleges and universities is that a substantial number of athletes are leaving these schools without a degree. In an effort to remedy the academic deficiencies prevalent in college sports, NCAA instituted the Academic Progress Rate (APR) program in 2004 (Bartter 1). Using a complex formula to assign each team an APR, NCAA supports teams with an APR of 925, the minimum value that predicts that the team will graduate at least half of its athletes, and higher. According to a recent study by the University of Central Florida, of the fifty-six Division I football teams selected to play in the 2006 Bowl games, twenty-three teams (including the previous national champion, University of Southern California) received an APR below 925, and twenty-seven teams had a graduation rate under 50%. For all Division I student-athletes, the U.S. Department of Education reports a 62% graduation rate, although the graduation rates for "the elite sports" (men's basketball and football) are considerably lower, with a basketball graduation rate of 44% and a football graduation rate of 54% (Wolverton). Admittedly, the total student-athlete graduation rate exceeds the graduation rate (60%) of non-athletes, but the success of many of these student-athletes may be bolstered by the financial support they receive. Consequently, a vast sum of the money that colleges give to their athletic students does not support the achievement of a degree, the most important tangible reward that a college or university can give a student. Indeed, unlike academic or music scholarships, which directly contribute to a college degree, athletic scholarships fund a pursuit unrelated, and at times even counterproductive, to what ASU's mission statement calls "fundamental fields of inquiry." Thus,

Source cited in parentheses, with page number.

Katz cites studies to support her thesis about athletic aid.

Katz   4

granting athletic scholarships does not necessarily lead to academic returns for the university or the student-athlete.

Despite the academic arguments against granting athletic scholarships, some institutions defend their awarding of financial aid based solely upon athletic performance with the argument that athletics contribute to the community service facet of a college's or university's stated mission. Certainly, a strong athletic program may benefit the community in a variety of healthy ways; a winning team engenders school spirit in its students and faculty, entices the citizens who live near the college to take an active interest in at least one aspect of the school, and earns state and national recognition and exposure, which may attract students and lead to increased enrollment. However, college athletics can be seen as having as many detrimental as positive effects on its community. In some instances, the same school spirit that fills the students with a sense of pride and place leads to very disreputable, unsportsmanlike conduct in the student body. In 2003, University of West Virginia students set over 100 fires and rioted in the streets after their football team defeated Virginia Tech (French 89). More recently, rioters set over forty fires and one person was shot after the University of Kentucky men's basketball team won the NCAA Championship in April 2012 (Kindelan). The athletes themselves also sometimes engage in activities that harm the communities; underage drinking and drug use occur in the athlete population as they do the general college population, and more serious events (such as allegations of rape against members of the University of Colorado football team in 2001 and the 2005 Baylor University incident in which one basketball player murdered his teammate) become highly publicized scandals. These events weaken considerably the positive impacts college athletics may have on schools' communities and undermine other community services, such as volunteer work, that students without any sort of scholarship perform. While athletics may benefit the community in many ways, they also have too many harmful effects on the community for colleges to justify the current levels of spending that many of them devote to athletic scholarships.

Perhaps the most common justification for granting student-athletes athletic scholarships is that college athletics is a major source of revenue for institutes of higher learning: through scholarships, athletes are allowed a portion of the money that they bring to their schools. This justification operates on the assumption that athletics do indeed attract capital to colleges and universities; yet an increasing amount of evidence

Katz responds to counterargument about possible benefits of student athletics.

shows that athletics departments actually cause a substantial deficit to the institutions that house them. The financial information from college athletics departments can be very misleading: in 1994, NCAA reported that Division I-A athletics programs earned an average of about $13,632,000 and spent about $12,972,000, yielding an apparent profit of $660,000 (French 80). These numbers, though, did not account for the fact that some universities subsidized their athletic departments. If the direct transfers to athletics programs from their universities that year were subtracted from the average earnings, the result would reveal that these programs actually had a $174,000 deficit. In fact, some athletics departments had so little money that they could not even afford to fund their athletes' scholarships; instead, there is evidence of some universities dipping into the scholarship funds reserved for students with demonstrated financial need or academic merit (French 82).

Another misconception about athletic funding is that winning teams attract more monetary gifts from donors and alumni. A study by Cornell University management and economics professor Robert Frank, discussed in a 2004 *Sports Illustrated* article, demonstrates that "the presumed indirect benefits of sports, such as the spike in alumni giving and an enlarged applicant pool, are by all indications minimal." In fact, Frank discovered that most big-time athletic programs have to be subsidized by the university. Therefore, even if a profit from student athletics is earned, universities usually cannot and do not use the money to advance their missions. Southern Methodist University President Gerald Turner confirms these conclusions: "I've been a university president now for about 20 years and I have never found any relationship between alumni giving to academic programs and the success of the athletic program" (qtd. in Fish). When colleges and universities award athletic scholarships, it may be less of a sound financial investment than boosters hope.

Without a doubt, athletics have an important entertainment role in a university setting. Yet, behind the Rose Bowl and March Madness, athletics programs are not as beneficial to their scholarly institutions as they may seem. It's time for colleges and universities to concentrate on their central missions—to promote academic scholarship, service to the university's community, and economic development of the university and its surroundings—instead of justifying the exorbitant expenditures of funds on programs that are more popular than they are useful to the school, the student, and the community at large.

Source cited in parentheses, with page number.

Information from authoritative source introduced by signal phrase within text.

Katz responds to two additional counterarguments; she responds to second counterargument by citing study and quoting expert.

Secondary source introduced in text, with *qtd. in* used in parenthetical citation.

Katz   6

Works Cited

Bartter, Jessica. "Institute Study by Lapchick Looks at APR Rates and Graduation Rates for 2005–06 Bowl-Bound Teams." Devos Sport Business Management Program, College of Business Administration, U of Central Florida, 5 Dec. 2005, business.ucf.edu/devos/newsroom/spotlights-lapchick-study/.

Board of Regents: Arizona's Public Universities. *ASU Strategic Plan and Updates*. 2016, www.azregents.edu/impact-arizona/asu-strategic-plan-and-updates.

Fish, Mike. "Separate Worlds: Studies Show Big-Time Athletics Don't Impact Academic Donations." *Sports Illustrated*, 14 Sept. 2004, pp. 59–62.

French, Peter A. *Ethics and College Sports: Ethics, Sports, and the University*. Rowman, 2004.

Kindelan, Katie. "Kentucky Students Riot after NCAA Championship Win." *ABCNews.com*, 3 April 2012, abcnews.go.com/blogs/headlines/2012/04/kentucky-students-riot-after-ncaa-championship-win/.

National Collegiate Athletic Association. 2016, www.ncaa.org.

Wolverton, Brad. "Under New Formula, Graduation Rates Rise." *Chronicle of Higher Education*, 6 Jan. 2006, chronicle.com/article/Under-New-Formula-Graduation/28460.

New page, title centered; double-space between title and first line of works-cited list.

Entries double-spaced, in alphabetical order.

First line of each entry at left margin; all other lines indented 1/2 inch.

Note that URLs are included for Web sources.

APA Documentation Style

APA Style: In-Text Citation

In APA style, parenthetical in-text citations are used in conjunction with the list of references at the end of a paper to give readers the information they would need to locate the sources that you have quoted, paraphrased, or summarized. In-text citations include year of publication along with the author and page number. Suppose, for example, that you are quoting from page 282 of Deborah Tannen's *You Just Don't Understand: Woman and Men in Conversation,* published in 1990. In APA style, a parenthetical in-text citation would be "(Tannen, 1990, p. 282)." If you give the author's name within your sentence, however, the date appears in parentheses following the name. APA parenthetical citations have commas between the elements and "p." before the page number. Page numbers are needed only when you are citing a quotation or specific information.

The following are examples of how to cite different types of sources within your text using APA style.

A WORK WITH ONE AUTHOR

Tony Horwitz (2012) describes the first reaction to rumors of an attack by those living near Harpers Ferry, Virginia, as both "swift and instinctive" (p. 173).

A WORK WITH MORE THAN ONE AUTHOR

For a source with up to five authors, use all the authors' last names in the first citation. If you give their names in parentheses, put an ampersand (&) between the last two names. After the first citation, use the first author's name followed by *et al.* for a work by three or more authors.

Grafton, Most, and Settis (2010) write that "Chaucer's admiration of classical poetry, and the lessons he learned from it about irony, tragedy, history, fate, and love, made him a major conduit, and fashioner, of the classical tradition in England" (p. 193).

Ever since the middle of the 20th century, nations have considered democracy as the only legitimate form of national government (Grafton, Most, & Settis, 2010, p. 256).

For a source with six or more authors, use *et al.* with every citation, including the first.

AN UNKNOWN AUTHOR

Use a shortened version of the title.

Employees of Google believe their corporate culture to be antithetical to that of Microsoft ("Google," 2006).

A GOVERNMENT AGENCY OR A CORPORATE AUTHOR

Give the complete name of most organizations every time you use them. After the first use, however, you can use an abbreviation for organizations with unwieldy names and well-known or easily understood abbreviations.

The Federal Emergency Management Agency (FEMA, 2007) offers officials many suggestions in a new brochure. You can obtain a copy of FEMA's brochure at our main office.

A SECONDARY SOURCE

If you need to use a quotation from a secondary source, use *as cited in* to let your readers know that you are doing so.

Aristotle noted that tiny animals can be found "in books, some of them similar to those found in clothes, others like tailless scorpions, very small indeed" (as cited in Greenblatt, 2011, p. 83).

AN ONLINE SOURCE

Cite in the same way that you would cite a print source. For a source with paragraph numbers, use *para.* or ¶. If you cannot find a date for the source, use the abbreviation *n.d.* (for "no date").

According to Christopher Beam (2006), there are a number of methods that Internet service providers can use to block Web sites if a government orders them to.

A BLOCK QUOTATION

In APA style, block quotations are used for quotations of more than forty words and are indented one-half inch or five spaces, as in the following example:

A political observer explains an analogy from the early days of Barack Obama's presidency:

Politics is not a meritocracy, and Obama realized no president was guaranteed credit or lucky bounces. But at times he couldn't help feeling, as he told one associate, a kinship with the protagonist in Ernest Hemingway's *The Old Man and the Sea*. He had, against tremendous odds, caught a big fish, but on the long voyage back to shore, his prized catch had been picked to pieces by sharks. (Corn, 2012, p. 15)

If the author's last name and year of publication are not included in the sentence that introduces the quotation, they should be provided in parentheses following the quotation along with the page number, as shown here.

APA Style: Constructing a References List

The section that follows includes model entries for different types of print and nonprint sources in APA style. Figure 20.5 provides you with a flowchart that will help you find the model entry that is closest to the source that you need to cite.

For a comparison of the MLA and APA styles for citing books and periodical articles, see pages 558–559.

FIGURE 20.5
APA Style: A Flow-chart for Deter-mining the Model References Entry You Need

Is My Source a Complete Print Book or Part of a Print Book?

No	Yes, go to the next question below.	Go to this entry.
	Is it a book with only one author?	1
	Are you citing more than one book by this author?	2
	Is it a book with multiple authors?	3
	Is the book by an organization of some kind?	4
	Is the author unknown or unnamed?	5
	Does the book also have a translator?	10
	Is it a later publication or edition of the book?	6, 7
	Is it a multivolume work?	12
	Does the book have an editor or a translator?	8,10
	Is the book an edited collection or anthology?	8, 9
	Is it a work in a collection or an anthology?	9
	Is it an introduction, a preface, a foreword, or an afterword?	11
	Is it a published interview?	13
	Is it an entry in a dictionary or reference work?	22

Is My Source from a Print Periodical Such as a Journal, a Magazine, or a Newspaper?

No	Yes, go to the next question below.	Go to this entry.
	Is it from a scholarly journal?	
	Do the journal's page numbers continue from one issue to the next?	14
	Does each issue start with page 1?	15
	Is it from a magazine?	16
	Is it a review?	19
	Is it from a newspaper?	17
	Is it an editorial?	18
	Is it a letter to the editor?	20
	Is it an article in a newsletter?	21

Is My Source a Print Source but Not from a Journal, a Magazine, or a Newspaper?

No	Yes, go to the next question below.	Go to this entry.
	Is it an entry in a dictionary or reference work?	22
	Is it a government document?	23
	Is it an unpublished doctoral dissertation?	24
	Is it an academic report?	25

Is My Source a Nonprint Source from the Internet?

No	Yes, go to the next question below.	Go to this entry.
	Is it a professional or personal Web site?	26
	Is it an article?	
	Is it a scholarly article?	27, 28
	Is it from an online magazine?	30
	Is it from an online newspaper?	31
	Is it an online book?	29
	Is it a posting to an electronic forum?	32
	Is it an e-mail message?	33
	Is it a blog entry?	34
	Is it an entry in a wiki?	35
	Is it a podcast?	36

Is My Source a Nonprint Source That Is Not Published Online?

No	Yes, go to the next question below.	Go to this entry.
	Is it a television or radio program?	37
	Is it an audio recording?	38
	Is it a film, DVD, or Blu-ray?	39
	Is it an oral presentation?	40

Consult with Your Instructor about How to Cite Your Source.

PRINT DOCUMENTS

Books

The basic elements in an entry for a book are the author's name or authors' names, the date of publication, the title, and the publication information, consisting of the place of publication and the publisher. See Figure 20.6 on pages 583–584 for guidelines on where to find the elements of an entry in a list of references for an edited collection in APA style.

Book Title and Subtitle
Date of Publication
Editors

Duffy, M. P., & Gillig, S. E. (Eds.). (2004). *Teen gangs: A global view.*
Westport, CT: Greenwood.

City of Publication
Publisher

Book Title

TEEN GANGS

Subtitle

A GLOBAL VIEW

Editors

Edited by
Maureen P. Duffy and
Scott Edward Gillig

A World View of Social Issues
Andrew L. Cherry, Series Adviser

Publisher

Greenwood Press
Westport, Connecticut • London

City of Publication

FIGURE 20.6   The Parts of a Reference Entry for an Edited Collection

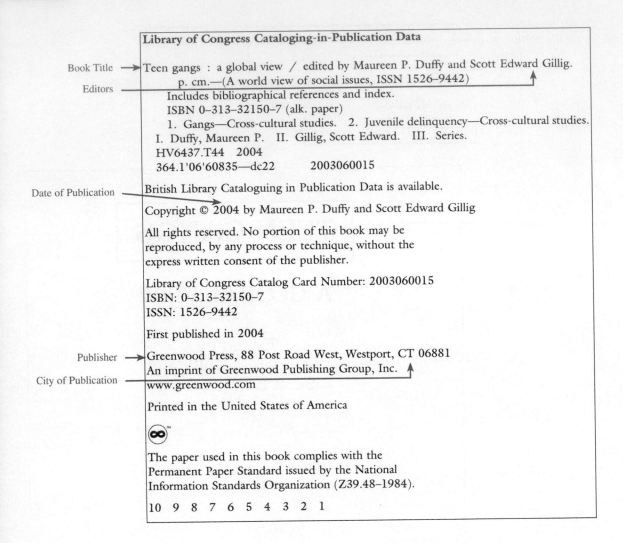

Book Title →
Editors
Date of Publication
Publisher →
City of Publication

Library of Congress Cataloging-in-Publication Data

Teen gangs : a global view / edited by Maureen P. Duffy and Scott Edward Gillig.
    p. cm.—(A world view of social issues, ISSN 1526–9442)
    Includes bibliographical references and index.
    ISBN 0–313–32150–7 (alk. paper)
    1. Gangs—Cross-cultural studies. 2. Juvenile delinquency—Cross-cultural studies.
    I. Duffy, Maureen P.   II. Gillig, Scott Edward.   III. Series.
    HV6437.T44   2004
    364.1'06'60835—dc22   2003060015

British Library Cataloguing in Publication Data is available.

Copyright © 2004 by Maureen P. Duffy and Scott Edward Gillig

All rights reserved. No portion of this book may be
reproduced, by any process or technique, without the
express written consent of the publisher.

Library of Congress Catalog Card Number: 2003060015
ISBN: 0–313–32150–7
ISSN: 1526–9442

First published in 2004

Greenwood Press, 88 Post Road West, Westport, CT 06881
An imprint of Greenwood Publishing Group, Inc.
www.greenwood.com

Printed in the United States of America

The paper used in this book complies with the
Permanent Paper Standard issued by the National
Information Standards Organization (Z39.48–1984).

10 9 8 7 6 5 4 3 2 1

1. Book with one author: In APA style, the date of publication follows the author's name. The author's first and middle name are given as initials, and the title of the book is italicized. Only the first word of the title is capitalized, as well as any proper nouns and the first word following a colon.

              date of
  author publication title   city   state publisher
Greenblatt, S. (2011). *The swerve.* New York, NY: Norton.

2. Two entries by the same author: The entries are listed in chronological order, with the earliest publication first. If more than one work was published in the same year, the works are ordered alphabetically based on the first letter of the title. Each work is given a lowercase letter after the date: for example, "(2004a)" for the first entry published in 2004 and "(2004b)" for the second entry. These letters would appear with the dates in the in-text citations.

> Greenblatt, S. (2004). *Will in the world: How Shakespeare became Shakespeare.* New York, NY: Norton.
>
> Greenblatt, S. (2011). *The swerve.* New York, NY: Norton.

3. Book with multiple authors: All authors' names are inverted. Use an ampersand to separate the last two entries. Give the names of all authors up to seven; if there are eight or more authors, follow the sixth name with an ellipsis, then the last author's name.

> Bellah, R. N., Madsen, R., Sullivan, W. M., Swidler, A., & Tipton, S. M. (2007). *Habits of the heart: Individualism and commitment in American life* (3rd ed.). Berkeley, CA: University of California Press.

4. Book by a corporate entity or organization: When the publisher is the same as the author, use the word *Author* where the publisher's name is usually given.

> Adobe Systems Inc. (2001). *Adobe Acrobat 5.0: Getting started.* San Jose, CA: Author.

5. Book by an unknown author:

> *The Chicago manual of style: The essential guide for writers, editors, and publishers* (16th ed.). (2010). Chicago, IL: University of Chicago Press.

6. Republished book: The original date of publication must be included.

> Dickens, C. (1969). *Hard times.* (D. Craig, Ed.). Baltimore, MD: Penguin Books. (Original work published 1854)

7. Book in a later edition:

> Corbett, E. P. J. (1990). *Classical rhetoric for the modern student* (3rd ed.). New York, NY: Oxford University Press.

8. Edited collection:

> Inman, J. A., & Sewell, D. N. (Eds.). (2000). *Taking flight with owls: Examining electronic writing center work.* Mahwah, NJ: Erlbaum.

See also Figure 20.6 on pages 583–584.

9. Work in a collection or an anthology: In APA style, the page numbers come after the title and before the publication information.

> Callaway, M. (2013). The WPA learning outcomes: What role should technology play? In Behm et al. (Eds.) *The WPA Outcomes Statement—A Decade Later* (pp. 271-284). Anderson, SC: Parlor Press.

10. Translation:

> Larsson, S. (2010). *The girl who kicked the hornet's nest* (R. Keeland, Trans.). New York, NY: Knopf. (Original work published 2007)

11. Introduction, preface, foreword, or afterword:

> Campbell, T. C. (2008). Foreword. In C.B. Esselstyn, *Prevent and reverse heart disease* (pp. viii-ix). New York, NY: Avery.

12. A multivolume work published over more than one year:

> Campbell, J. (1959-1968). *The masks of god* (Vols. 1-4). New York, NY: Viking.

13. Published interview:

> Blair, K., & Takayoshi, P. (1999). Making the map: An interview with Gail Hawisher [Interview with G. Hawisher]. In K. Blair & P. Takayoshi (Eds.), *Feminist cyberspaces: Mapping gendered academic spaces* (pp. 177-191). Stamford, CT: Ablex.

You should cite an interview published in a periodical as you would a periodical article (see nos. 14, 15, and 16). APA categorizes personal interviews as personal communications: because such an interview cannot be recovered, there is no need to include an entry for it in a reference list, but the interview should be cited in the body of the text (see nos. 33 and 40).

Periodical Articles

The basic items in an entry for a periodical article are the author's name or authors' names, the date of publication in parentheses, the title of the article, and information about the publication in which the article appeared, including its title, volume and issue number (if applicable), and the page range for the article. See Figure 20.7 for guidelines.

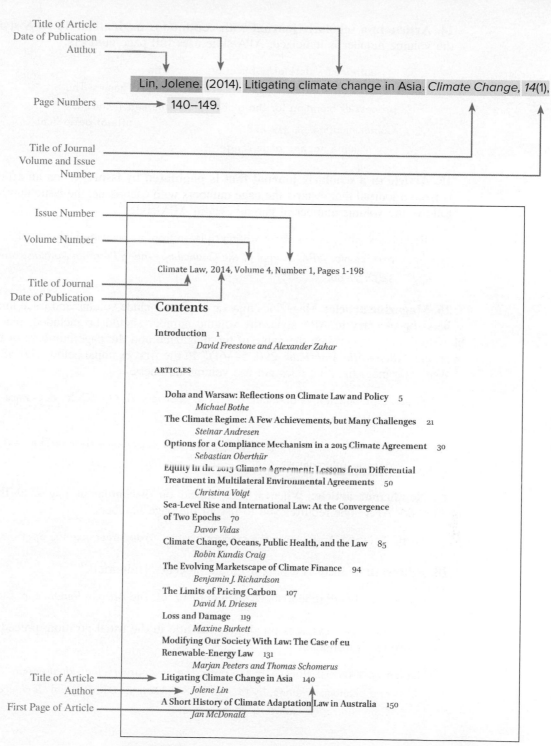

Title of Article
Date of Publication
Author

Lin, Jolene. (2014). Litigating climate change in Asia. *Climate Change, 14*(1),

Page Numbers — 140–149.

Title of Journal
Volume and Issue
Number

Issue Number

Volume Number

Climate Law, 2014, Volume 4, Number 1, Pages 1-198

Title of Journal
Date of Publication

Contents

Introduction 1
    David Freestone and Alexander Zahar

ARTICLES

    Doha and Warsaw: Reflections on Climate Law and Policy 5
    Michael Bothe
    The Climate Regime: A Few Achievements, but Many Challenges 21
    Steinar Andresen
    Options for a Compliance Mechanism in a 2015 Climate Agreement 30
    Sebastian Oberthür
    Equity in the 2015 Climate Agreement: Lessons from Differential
    Treatment in Multilateral Environmental Agreements 50
    Christina Voigt
    Sea-Level Rise and International Law: At the Convergence
    of Two Epochs 70
    Davor Vidas
    Climate Change, Oceans, Public Health, and the Law 85
    Robin Kundis Craig
    The Evolving Marketscape of Climate Finance 94
    Benjamin J. Richardson
    The Limits of Pricing Carbon 107
    David M. Driesen
    Loss and Damage 119
    Maxine Burkett
    Modifying Our Society With Law: The Case of eu
    Renewable-Energy Law 131
    Marjan Peeters and Thomas Schomerus
    Litigating Climate Change in Asia 140
    Jolene Lin
    A Short History of Climate Adaptation Law in Australia 150
    Jan McDonald

Title of Article
Author
First Page of Article

FIGURE 20.7 The Parts of a Reference Entry for a Journal Article

14. Article in a scholarly journal with continuous pagination: In APA style, the volume number is italicized. APA style uses full page numbers.

authors   date of publication   title

Thayer, A., & Kolko, B. E. (2004). Localization of digital games: The

process of blending for the global games market. *Technical*

Communication, 51, 477–488.   title of periodical

volume no. and page range

15. Article in a scholarly journal that is paginated by issue: When an article is from a journal that restarts the page numbers with each issue, the issue number follows the volume number in parentheses in APA style.

Peters, B. (2011). Lessons about writing to learn from a university-high school

partnership. *WPA: Journal of the Council of Writing Program Administrators,*

34(2), 59–88.

16. Magazine article: Magazines may or may not include volume and issue numbers. In an entry in APA style, the volume number should be included, placed within commas between the name of the magazine and the page numbers of the article: "(*Scientific American, 290,* 54–61)." In the first example below, *Business-Week* is a magazine that does not use volume numbers.

Foust, D., Eidem, M., & Bremner, B. (2004, February 2). AFLAC: Its ducks are

not in a row. *BusinessWeek,* 52–53.

Wilson, C. E. (2005, January). Usability and user experience design: The next

decade. *Intercom, 52,* 6–9.

17. Newspaper article: When articles appear on discontinuous pages, as they often do, APA style requires you to list all the page numbers.

Fatsis, S. (2002, April 9). A more modern masters. *Wall Street Journal,* pp. B1, B4.

18. Editorial: If there is a title, it should precede "[Editorial]."

Moral scoreboard [Editorial]. (2004, February 18). *The Arizona Republic,* p. B10.

19. Review: If the review is titled, give the title in the usual position, preceding the bracketed information.

Jablonski, J. (2003). [Review of the book *The new careers: Individual action*

and economic change, by M. Arthur, K. Inkson, & J. K. Pringle]. *Technical*

Communication Quarterly, 12, 230–234.

20. Letter to the editor:

> Rosati, C. (2004, February 18). Let's throw the book at Valley street racers [Letter to the editor]. *The Arizona Republic*, p. B10.

21. Newsletter article, no author: Unsigned articles should be alphabetized in the list of references by the first word of the title. If there is a volume number, place it between the name of the publication and the page numbers, separated by commas. The following example from the newsletter of the Heard Museum of Native Cultures and Art has no volume number.

> Shared images: The jewelry of Yazzie Johnson and Gail Bird. (2007, January/February). *Earthsong*, 8.

Other Print Sources

22. Entry in a dictionary or reference work: APA style uses page numbers even when the entries are alphabetical.

> Express Mail. (1993). In *Merriam-Webster's new collegiate dictionary* (p. 411). Springfield, MA: Merriam-Webster.

> Pfeiffer, R. H. (1974). Sumerian poetry. In *Princeton encyclopedia of poetry and poetics* (pp. 820–821). Princeton, NJ: Princeton University Press.

23. Government document: Like MLA style, APA style lists the agency as the author of the report when the author is not known. If you list a subdepartment or agency, make certain that you also list the higher department if the subdepartment is not well known. If the publisher is not the Government Printing Office (GPO), list the highest known agency or department as the author. If the document has a specific publication number, list it after the title.

> National Institutes of Health. (1992). *Toxicology and carcinogenesis studies of Resorcinol (CAS No. 108-46-3) in F344/N rats and B6C3F$_1$ mice (Gavage Studies)* (NIH Publication No. 92-2858). Research Triangle Park, NC: Author.

24. Unpublished doctoral dissertation:

> Edminster, J. R. (2002). *The diffusion of new media scholarship: Power, innovation, and resistance in academe* (Unpublished doctoral dissertation). University of South Florida.

25. Academic report:

> Melnick, R., Welch, N., & Hart, B. (2005). *How Arizona compares: Real numbers and hot topics*. Tempe: Arizona State University, Morrison Institute for Public Policy.

ONLINE SOURCES

APA style requires including the Digital Object Identifier (DOI) for online sources, if one is available. Regulated by the International DOI Foundation (IDF), the DOI is a unique number that is registered with a specific agency that follows the standards of the IDF. It works similarly to the system that registers domain names on the Internet and helps people locate a specific reference, such as a journal article or an online book.

If there is no DOI, then include the home page URL using the format "Retrieved from http://www.xxxxx/" (with no period at the end).

26. Basic professional or personal Web site:

American Medical Association. (2004). Home page. Retrieved from http://www
.ama-assn.org/

27. Article from an online journal with a Digital Object Identifier (DOI): Include the issue number as well as the volume number; provide the DOI at the end of the entry.

authors   date of publication   title of article

Maylath, B., Grabill, J., & Gurak, L. (2010). Intellectual fit and programmatic power:
Organizational profiles of four professional/technical/scientific communication programs. *Technical Communication Quarterly, 19*(3), 262–280.
doi:10.1080/10572252.2010.481535
DOI

title of journal
volume and issue nos.
page range

28. Article from an online journal without a DOI: In APA style, the volume number is italicized.

> Salvo, M. J. (2002). Deafened to their demands: An ethnographic study of accommodation. *Kairos 7*(1). Retrieved from http://english.ttu.edu/kairos/7.1/binder2.html?coverweb/salvo/ctx.html

Note: If you retrieved the article from an online database, include the URL of the home page for the database only if the article would be difficult to find otherwise (for example, "Retrieved from PsycARTICLES database: http://psycnet.apa.org)."

29. Online book:

> Wolfe, T. (1998). *A man in full* [Kindle edition]. New York, NY: Farrar, Straus, and Giroux. Kindle file.

APA suggests that you include in the reference list the author, date, title (with e-reader book type in square brackets if applicable); that you italicize the title but not the bracketed material, and source (DOI or URL, if available):

> Leonard, E. (2012). *Raylan.* [iBooks edition]. Retrieved from iBooks.

If you acquired the book through an online library (Google Books, ebrary, NetLibrary) and not on an e-reader device, omit the bracketed information from the reference.

30. Article from an online magazine:

> Cooper, M., & Tumulty, K. (2004, February 16). Bring on the cash! *Time.* Retrieved from http://www.time.com

31. Article from an online newspaper:

> Novovitch, B. (2004, February 17). It's home stupid home, but the "clods" can read. *New York Times.* Retrieved from http://www.nytimes.com

32. Posting to an electronic forum such as a mailing list (listserv): In APA style, list only electronic references that have been archived and are retrievable.

> Peckham, I. (2004, February 17). Update on AP and dual enrollment [Electronic mailing list message]. Retrieved from http://lists.asu.edu/cgi-bin/wa?A2=ind0309&L=wpal&D=1&O=D&F=&S=&P=52156

33. E-mail message: In APA style, e-mail is cited only in the text as "personal communication," followed by the date of the e-mail.

34. Blog entry: Provide the name of the author (bloggers often use pseudonyms), date, title of entry, the words "Message posted to," name of blog, and the URL.

Rice, J. (2007, March 30). Network academics [Web log post]. Retrieved from
http://ydog.net/?page_id5345

35. Wiki entry:

Rhetoric. (n.d.). Retrieved March 30, 2007, from http://en.wikipedia.org/wiki/
Rhetoric

36. Podcast:

Sharot, T. (Writer). (2012). *The optimism bias* [Video podcast]. Retrieved from
http://www.ted.com

OTHER NONPRINT SOURCES

37. Television and radio programs: In APA style the names of the writers,
directors, and producers are given as appropriate. Indicate whether the source is
a television or radio broadcast in square brackets.

Buckner, N., & Whittlesey, R. (Writers, Directors, Producers). (2004, February 3).
Dogs and more dogs. *Nova* [Television broadcast]. Boston, MA, and
Washington, DC: Public Broadcasting Service.

Turpin, C. (Executive Producer). (2004, February 12). Scientists succeed
in cloning human embryo. *All things considered* [Radio broadcast].
Washington, DC: National Public Radio.

38. Audio recording:

Thompkins, C., & Kear, J. (2012). Blown away [Recorded by C. Underwood]. On
Blown away [CD]. Nashville, TN: Sony Nashville/Arista.

39. Film, DVD, or Blu-ray:

Jackson, P. (Director). (2002). *The lord of the rings: The two towers* [DVD].
United States: New Line Home Entertainment.

40. Oral presentation: Because live lectures are not recoverable data, in APA
style, they are cited parenthetically in the text but are not included in the list of
references. However, when professional presentations are made from texts that
can be recovered, they are cited.

Russell, D. R. (1999, March). *Teacher's perception of genre across the curriculum:
Making classroom/culture connections visible.* Paper presented at the
Conference on College Composition and Communication Convention,
Atlanta, GA.

APA Style: Sample Student Paper

The student paper that follows, "How Do Gangs Affect Adolescent Behavior?" by Aaron Zook, is an example of a paper that uses APA style.

If you write a paper using APA style, follow these guidelines:

- Include a separate title page. Center the title one-third of the way down the page, using capital and lowercase letters; do not use a special typeface for it. Give your name, the course name and number, and the date, all also centered and double-spaced, on separate lines below the title. In the upper-right-hand corner, give the page number. In the upper-left-hand corner, type "Running head:" followed by a shortened version of the title in all capital letters. The words "Running head" should appear on the title page only; the shortened version of the title goes on all subsequent pages.

- On the second page of your paper, provide an abstract of the paper if your instructor requires one. An abstract is a brief (approximately 100–120 words) summary of your paper's contents. If you include an abstract, the paper itself begins on the third page. Repeat the title on the first page of your paper, centering it one inch from the top. Double-space to the first line of your text.

- Double-space the entire paper, including any block quotations and the items in your list of references.

- Leave one-inch margins on all sides.

- Place page numbers in the upper-right-hand corner after the running head, five spaces after the shortened version of the title.

- Indent paragraphs and block quotations one-half inch from the left margin.

- Note that some papers use headings to label sections of the text. If you use headings, center them and double-space above and below them.

- Put your list of references on a new page, with the title "References" centered at the top.

Running head
is a shortened ver-
sion of the
title (preceded by
"Running head:"
on the first
page only).

Running head: HOW DO GANGS AFFECT BEHAVIOR?   1

Title is centered,
one-third of the
way down the
page.

Name, title of
course, name of
professor, and
date are centered
and double-spaced
on separate lines
below the title.

How Do Gangs Affect Adolescent Behavior?

Aaron Zook

Psychology 101

Professor Jones

March 23, 2016

↕ ½"
1"

How Do Gangs Affect Adolescent Behavior?

Since the early 1920s, researchers have closely studied the relationship between street gangs and violent crime from a variety of perspectives: criminological, socio-logical, and psychological (Thabit, 2005). Whatever the underlying causes for gang membership, the results seem clear; members of street gangs admit to a far greater rate of serious crime, and to far more severe acts of violence (Penly Hall, Thornberry, & Lizotte, 2006) than non-gang members of the same age, race, and socioeconomic background. According to the Web site Safeyouth.org (n.d.), gang violence is certainly cause for concern:

> Gang members are responsible for much of the serious violence in the United States.... Teens that are gang members are much more likely than other teens to commit serious and violent crimes. For example, a survey in Denver found that while only 14% of teens were gang members, they were responsible for committing 89% of the serious violent crimes.

Many researchers have therefore come to the conclusion that gangs necessarily cause violence and deviant behavior. As a matter of policy, then, it seems clear that the solution to a number of social ills is to break up, disrupt, or prevent the formation of gangs. Other programs seek to prevent young people from joining gangs through interventions of various types and levels of effectiveness. Most of these efforts take it as a given that gangs seriously distort behavior, even among individuals who already belong to "high-risk" demographic groups. Adolescents living in poverty or other disadvantaged circumstances; those attending violent and/or failing schools; members of criminalized peer groups; and children from violent and/or extremely dysfunctional households or demonstrating a predisposition toward antisocial behavior all seem to be at greater risk for future gang membership, but a number of studies have shown that their own behaviors are considerably more violent while they belong to a gang than they were before or after membership (Gordon et al., 2004). After years of study, researchers still do not clearly understand how and why gangs exert such a powerful influence on behavior. A crucial answer might be found in the typical composition of a gang. Overwhelmingly, gangs are made up of adolescents and young adults. The me-dian age of violent gang members has been estimated to be eighteen; members tend to join in their late teens, and contrary to popular fallacies and urban legends, youths

1"

Title repeated on first page of paper, centered.

Double-space from title to first line of paper.

Information from sources cited with parenthetical references.

Quotation longer than forty words indented 1/2 inch or 5 spaces and double-spaced. Introductory sentence ends with a colon. Because no date is given in source, abbreviation *n.d.* is included.

Et al. used for first citation of work with six authors.

Zook presents synthesis of his findings.

HOW DO GANGS AFFECT BEHAVIOR?   3

Opening paragraph
sets up the issue.

generally leave a gang with few or no consequences within a year of joining (Thomas,
2005). Clearly, then, the gang problem can and should be understood in large part as
a youth problem; researchers might come to a deeper understanding of the nature
and impact of gangs by shifting some emphasis in their research from violence to
adolescent adjustment behaviors.

First point:
difficulty of
defining gangs.

The research community has by no means reached a consensus as to the precise
definition of street gangs, however. The telltale sign that a group is a gang—one that
most researchers, police organizations, the popular media, and gang members themselves agree on—is a tendency to commit violent acts (Katz & Jackson-Jacobs, 2004),
but violence is not an adequate condition in itself. Why, for example, are Crips and
Bloods considered gangs, but not Skinheads? Likewise, organized crime is now rarely
considered "gang behavior," though early studies included these types of organizations.
Yet all of these form distinct social groups and are involved in criminal behaviors
(Thomas, 2005). One common distinction researchers draw is based on the motivation
behind the group's violent activities. Does the group sell drugs or stolen merchandise?
Do they operate according to an ideology or shared set of racial or cultural prejudices?
Or are they primarily concerned with "turf," status, or violence for its own sake?
Contemporary studies tend to maintain that only the latter group of motives typify
"gangs" and have been particularly concerned with the seemingly random nature of the
various criminal behaviors that many such gangs exhibit. The criminal acts seem to have
largely symbolic value that is consistent with the way many street gangs are associated
with the use of emblems, dress, and a shared name easily identified by all of their
members (Katz & Jackson-Jacobs, 2004).

Experts in gang behavior have advanced numerous explanations for the most
troubling examples of violent gang behavior: random drive-by shootings, seemingly
unmotivated killings and aggravated assaults, carjackings, and so on. Ritual initiations,
turf wars, cycles of retribution between competing gangs, and intragang status are
obvious motivators. Yet another explanation has involved the culpability of the media
and the police in promoting gang imagery: The very definition of gangs as violent
entities increases members' levels of violence. In other words, certain youths seek
the rewards they think gang membership will afford them—status; protection; group

HOW DO GANGS AFFECT BEHAVIOR? 4

identity; and entertainment, drugs, and sex (U.S. Department of Education, n.d.)—and are willing to engage in violent acts because "that's what a gang is." The image is reinforced by the news and popular media and by the folklore of the gang itself. It has also been argued that both gang members' own accounts of their activities and police statistics may be misleading. Because of the status violence confers on a perpetrator, a subject could conceivably exaggerate his or her criminal behavior in surveys and interviews as a means of bragging. Further, crime statistics reflect arrest and incarceration rates which, considering the general conspicuousness of gang members and police efforts to target these groups, could conceivably skew higher for gang offenders than for criminals who do not belong to gangs. A number of studies, less sensational in their findings and therefore less visible in the mainstream media, have found that most gang members spend the majority of their time simply "hanging out," albeit often within the context of drug or alcohol use (Katz & Jackson-Jacobs, 2004). In a sense, then, lacking any overarching objective such as profit or ideology, some gangs may see continued violence as a means of justifying their own existence and retaining members who would otherwise grow restless and leave.

If retention is indeed the motivation for violent gang behavior, then it seems unlikely that some special feature of gangs in their day-to-day operation enables violent extremes of behavior; rather, it is the symbolic value of the gang "family" that makes them sufficiently attractive to justify violence, the risk of death or imprisonment, and the common perception (however false) that one can never leave the gang. It seems likely that certain characteristics typical of adolescents—the desire to create a self-identity, establish a sense of belonging, and both derive status from and earn status within groups (Ausubel, 2002)—make them vulnerable to the allure of such symbolism. It also seems likely that, in addition to environmental and psychological factors such as peer pressure and/or facilitation (Gifford-Smith, Dodge, Dishion, & McCord, 2005), cultural factors also aggravate the problem of gang violence. That is to say, while many studies have rightly focused on how crumbling inner cities, poverty, and lack or loss of opportunity and hope affect a teen's predisposition toward gang affiliation, it might be worthwhile to examine how society itself provides gangs with false or mythical status that might add to their attraction.

Second point: various explanations of gang behavior, leading to most satisfactory one.

Concludes with assertion that his arguments have led to: cultural factors contribute to gang violence.

HOW DO GANGS AFFECT BEHAVIOR? 5

References

Ausubel, D. P. (2002). *Theory and problems of adolescent development* (2nd ed.). Lincoln, NE: iUniverse.

Gifford-Smith, M., Dodge, K. A., Dishion, T. J., & McCord, J. (2005). Peer influence in children and adolescents: Crossing the bridge from developmental to intervention science. *Journal of Abnormal Child Psychology, 33*(3), 255–265.

Gordon, R. A., Lahey, B. B., Kawai, E., Loeber, R., Stouthamer-Loeber, M., & Farrington, D. P. (2004). Antisocial behavior and youth gang membership. *Criminology, 42*(1), 55–88. Abstract retrieved from Selection and Socialization database: http://onlinelibrary.wiley.com

Katz, J., & Jackson-Jacobs, C. (2004). The criminologists' gang. In C. Sumner (Ed.), *The Blackwell companion to criminology*. Malden, MA: Blackwell Publishers.

National Youth Violence Prevention Center. (n.d.). *Youth gangs*. Retrieved from http://www.safeyouth.org/scripts/teens/gangs.asp

Penly Hall, G., Thornberry, T. P., & Lizotte, A. J. (2006). The gang facilitation effect and neighborhood risk: Do gangs have a stronger influence on delinquency in disadvantaged areas? In J. F. Short, Jr., & L. Hughes (Eds.), *Studying youth gangs*. Lanham, MD: Altamira Press.

Thabit, W. (2005). How did East New York become a ghetto? Retrieved from http://muse.jhu.edu/books/9780814783412

Thomas, C. (2005). Serious delinquency and gang membership. *Psychiatric Times 22*(4). Retrieved from http://www.psychiatrictimes.com

U.S. Department of Education. (n.d.). *Youth gangs: Going beyond the myths to address a critical problem*. Retrieved from http://www.ed.gov/admins/lead/safety/training/gangs/problem_pg3.html

New page, title centered; double-space between title and first line of reference list.

Entries double-spaced, in alphabetical order.

First line of each entry at left margin; all other lines indented 1/2 inch or 5 spaces.

Text Credits

Constructing a writing portfolio gives you the opportunity to select, display, and reflect on the work you have done in this course. Although there are many ways to construct a portfolio, this chapter offers you some common suggestions and guidelines that others have found useful. An important purpose for constructing the portfolio is to provide you with support for the claims that you will make about your writing in the course. In short, a portfolio helps you support this statement: "Here is what I have learned this semester, and here is the evidence that I have learned these writing strategies and conventions."

Your instructor will provide guidelines on how much evidence to include in the portfolio to support your claims about what you have learned. For some claims, a single example of your work will be sufficient evidence. In other cases, you may need to provide several examples. For instance, to demonstrate that you know how to adapt a message for a particular audience, you might need to show how you have done so for two or three different audiences.

What Is a Portfolio and Why Should I Construct One?

In the past, graphic artists and photographers were the only professionals who tended to keep portfolios of their work. These artists used portfolios to show potential clients their previous work and to give them a sense of what to expect in the future. More recently, many other professionals, such as technical or professional writers, have found that keeping a portfolio is helpful when they look for work.

Although no one will deny that the quality of the final product is important, from an educational perspective, how you arrived at that final product may be just as important as, or even more important than, the result you achieved. By looking at your process (the path you took to get to your endpoint) in a portfolio, your instructor can better assess your strengths and weaknesses as a writer.

When instructors or other readers look at a single piece of your writing, they may come away with a narrow view of your writing capabilities. They may see only a particular kind of writing, with its strengths and weaknesses. However, when readers look at a portfolio of your work, they gain a fuller picture of the writing you have accomplished.

Because the portfolio represents what you have learned throughout the course, the ideal time to read this appendix and to begin constructing your portfolio is during the first week of classes. Starting early will give you many opportunities to select and reflect on your work while that work is still fresh in your mind. Students who construct the most effective portfolios usually work on them a little each week.

Selecting Materials for Your Portfolio

As you decide what to include in your portfolio, ask yourself these questions:

- What have I learned about writing in each of the four areas of life—academic, professional, civic, and personal?
- What have I learned about writing for various purposes?
- What rhetorical skills and knowledge have I developed?
- What critical reading skills have I developed?
- What critical thinking skills have I developed?
- What have I learned about composing processes—invention, drafting, revising, and editing?
- What have I learned about working effectively with peers?
- What knowledge of conventions have I developed?
- What have I learned about strategies that will help me succeed as a writer?
- What have I learned about using digital technologies?

As you respond to each of the questions listed above, consider a follow-up question: *What evidence will demonstrate that I have developed this set of skills or knowledge?* Think about all the work that you have done in the course. Among the print or electronic evidence—tangible evidence—available to you are the following:

- Invention work (listing, brainstorming, clustering, and freewriting)
- Research notes (from your library and online research, field research, and interviews)
- Reading notes (comments you made on the reading you did for the class)
- Drafts of papers
- Peers' written comments on your work
- Online discussions about your work
- Polished versions of your papers
- Reflections on your papers (that you write when you submit your papers)

Among the evidence that may not appear on paper or electronically are the following:

- Discussions with peers about your writing
- Discussions with your instructor about your writing

You will, of course, need to transcribe evidence that exists only in your memory so that you can make it available to those who read your portfolio.

Reflecting on What You Have Written

As noted earlier, it is useful to reflect on your work regularly throughout the semester while that work is fresh in your mind. A week or a month later, you may not remember why you followed up on a peer's comments or how you might approach the topic differently if you were to write about it again. Remember that *reflective writing* asks you to do just what its name suggests: to think back on, to consider, to reflect on the work you did for the course. Consider answering the questions at the end of each chapter in Parts 2 and 3 of this book as a way to start that reflective process.

There are several ways to keep track of your reflective writing. You may choose to keep a handwritten or electronic journal, or you may want to keep your own course blog where you regularly reflect on your course writing.

For more on journals, see pages 22–23.

As you reflect on the work that you use as evidence in your portfolio, you might consider another question: *Why does this piece of evidence effectively demonstrate that I have developed a certain set of skills or knowledge?* Your response to that question should also appear in your portfolio because it illustrates that you are confident about what you have learned during the course.

As you reflect on your polished essays, you might wish to include a paragraph for each that begins, "If I had the opportunity to revise this paper further, I would. . . ." This kind of statement acknowledges the situation that exists in most courses: there is rarely enough time to revise as thoughtfully as you could even if the course were two semesters long.

Organizing Your Portfolio

There are many ways to organize your portfolio, and your instructor will let you know how he or she would like your portfolio to be arranged and organized. Some colleges and universities have specific portfolio requirements; if yours does, you will receive guidance on what you need to do.

Sometimes, your instructor will ask you to organize your portfolio in a *chronological* manner, starting with the first piece of writing you did for the class and ending with your final piece of writing. Other organizational schemes you may find especially useful include the following:

- **By learning goals:** This is an efficient and effective way to organize your portfolio. For example, the Writing Program Administrators Outcomes Statement (see page xl–xlii), which is prominent in this book, includes four categories of learning goals: (1) rhetorical knowledge; (2) critical thinking, reading, and writing; (3) processes; and (4) knowledge of conventions. If you use this scheme, you may wish to follow the order given here, or you may wish to reorganize the categories to reflect what you consider to be most important. Once you have decided on the order of the learning goals, those goals can become headings in your portfolio. Under each heading, then, you could respond to the three questions noted earlier:

  - What have I learned? How have I grown as a writer?

For an example from a writing portfolio organized by learning goals, see pages 604–606.

- What evidence demonstrates that I have learned this—that I have grown?
- Why is this evidence the most convincing evidence that I can choose?
- How can I use my knowledge and skills in other parts of my life?
- How did I use what I learned in my writing class in my other college writing assignments?

- **By purpose:** If you use this organizational scheme, you could list the chapter titles from Parts 2 and 3 of this book as your headings—for example, "Writing to Explore," "Writing to Convince," "Writing to Solve Problems," and so on. This pattern may allow you to focus on each purpose more fully, but it also may cause you to repeat statements about learning goals. That is, for each purpose, you might have to say, "Here's how I learned to adapt my message to an audience." If you do use this organizational pattern, you still can use the same questions:

  - What have I learned? How have I grown as a writer?
  - What evidence demonstrates that I have learned this—that I have grown?
  - Why is this evidence the most convincing evidence that I can choose?
  - How can I use my knowledge and skills in other parts of my life?
  - How did I use what I learned in my writing class in my other college writing assignments?

 ## Portfolio Formats

You may decide to submit—or your instructor may request that you submit— your portfolio in one of the following formats:

- **As a print document** in a three-ring binder.
- **As an electronic file,** either on a flash drive or CD. If you use this format, consider constructing a hypertext document so that readers can click on links to see other parts of your portfolio.
- **As a Web site.** This format enables you to provide links to other parts of your portfolio, as well as links to other Web sites or pages that you have found useful during the semester.

In the example shown in Figure A.1, note how student Eileen Holland has organized her electronic portfolio. As background for her work in her first-year writing course, she provided examples of her writing from elementary and secondary school. Because she was an avid reader who believed that reading helped her as a writer, she provided information about several of her favorite writers. Then she included materials to demonstrate that she learned skills and knowledge from the four areas of the Writing Program Administrators Outcomes Statement. Finally, she looked to the future by projecting what she hoped to learn in upcoming semesters.

**Electronic Portfolio
Introduction and Table of Contents**
by Eileen Holland

My Writing in Elementary School	Welcome to my writing portfolio for first-year composition. As my contents indicate, I've been interested in writing since elementary school because my teachers gave me fun writing projects and lots of encouragement. In high school, I was fortunate enough to work with teachers who offered me lots of constructive feedback; some of my friends did the same. I've also been inspired by writers such as Garrison Keillor, Jared Diamond, and Sarah Vowell.

My Writing in High School

My Favorite Writers

Garrison Keillor

Jared Diamond

Sarah Vowell

Categories of Learning

Rhetorical Knowledge

Critical Thinking, Reading, and Writing

Processes

Knowledge of Conventions

Using Digital Technologies

Transfer: My Future Goals for Learning to Write

Welcome to my writing portfolio for first-year composition. As my contents indicate, I've been interested in writing since elementary school because my teachers gave me fun writing projects and lots of encouragement. In high school, I was fortunate enough to work with teachers who offered me lots of constructive feedback; some of my friends did the same. I've also been inspired by writers such as Garrison Keillor, Jared Diamond, and Sarah Vowell.

In this portfolio I demonstrate how I have developed skills and knowledge in this course. In particular, I demonstrate how I have learned in four areas: (1) Rhetorical Knowledge; (2) Critical Thinking, Reading, and Writing; (3) Processes; and (4) Knowledge of Conventions. I also talk about how I use digital technologies. In addition to describing what I have learned, I also offer evidence from my work this semester to prove that I have learned the kinds of knowledge and skills that we have studied.

When I finished high school, I thought that I knew all that I needed to know about writing. In this course, though, I have come to appreciate that learning to write is a never-ending journey. My teacher, who has been writing for more than five decades and teaching writing for almost three decades, told us that she's still learning to write. In class we talked about all sorts of people who keep learning to perform well in their fields until they retire— teachers, professional athletes, entertainers, engineers, painters, architects. People keep on learning.

A Portion of a Sample Portfolio

The portfolio excerpt shown here comes from Chelsea Rundle, who constructed it in a second-semester writing course. Note how she used the Writing Program Administrators Outcomes Statement to organize her portfolio. Also note how she used evidence from her work to demonstrate what she had learned.

PORTFOLIO

Chelsea Rundle

I cannot believe the semester is coming to a close already. Even though it has seemed quite short, I have learned a lot over the course of this semester. In English 102, I learned that a good paper topic is one that I am passionate about and is feasible. Picking topics that were particular to my major—applied biology—helped me explore different issues/trends in the field of biology and medical science through writing my English papers.

In my first paper, I explored the concept of personalized medicine by researching what others thought about it and then stepping back and forming my opinion on the topic. For the second paper, writing to convince, I addressed a topic I am very passionate about—CT scans causing radiation cancer. I was able to look at how these two topics affect one another because CT scans are an integral process in personalized medicine.

The topic for my evaluation was the biology program at ASU Tempe versus the biology program at another ASU campus. I picked this topic because I am planning on attending one campus for one more year, but I do not know what campus to attend after that. Even though in my evaluation I came to the conclusion that the other campus's biology program would be better for me—I am still not sure. You made the comment on one of my drafts that I should try taking a biology course at ASU Tempe. I may take your advice and try taking a course over there before making a final decision regarding which university to attend. Also, I am not certain what future career I want to enter into. It may be best for me to figure that out before picking which campus I want to attend.

For my proposing a solution paper, I chose a topic that I am passionate about but is not particular to my major. Instead, I chose a topic personal to me and those living in my neighborhood—a new parking regulation passed by the Home Owner's Association (HOA) that does not allow any vehicles to be parked on the street. I chose this topic because my sister will be getting her driver's license soon and I just bought a new truck, so my family will have too many vehicles to fit in our garage and driveway. You suggested that I go to the city council with my final paper, and I just might. The parking regulation has been a problem for a number of families in my neighborhood. If I get enough people to side with me and show the HOA why the regulation is a problem and what some possible solutions to the problem are, I have faith we can get the HOA to change their minds. We'll see.

While writing these four papers and revising them, I have expanded my writing knowledge and have learned how to strengthen my writing skills. I will demonstrate what I have learned in this portfolio. In the portfolio for writing goals and objectives, I used only examples from English 102 because it is the only class I took this semester in which I learned about writing.

RHETORICAL KNOWLEDGE

• Focus on a Purpose

In writing the first argument, I stayed focused on a purpose: persuading the audience to see the dangers of CT scans. To do this, I used a claim, support for my claim, and the refutation of counterarguments. In refuting counterarguments I addressed multiple viewpoints on the issue while showing the reader why my claim is correct. The following is a refutation of a counter-argument I used to strengthen the paper:

> Some argue that radiation cancer is not caused by CT scans, but can be caused by other factors. This is absolutely true, for radiation, or the release of energy, can be given off by a number of sources including household electrical appliances, heaters, the sun, and x-ray machines. For example, I recall my parents telling me that they were always warned as children not to stand too close to the microwave, or they would get cancer. This is hardly the case, for the type of radiation given off by electrical appliances and heaters isn't harmful enough to cause cancer. However, radiation cancer is caused by high exposure to the sun and x-ray machines. Therefore, as exposure to CT scans—a form of x-ray technology—increases, so does the risk of radiation cancer.

• Respond to the Needs of Different Audiences

When writing a paper particular to my major, I had to think about the needs of my audience. It is important to explain a topic and give background information at the beginning of the paper to avoid confusion. It is hard for readers to form an opinion from reading your paper if they don't understand the topic you are writing about. It is also important not to offend your audience, so the writer must determine how to use the three appeals—logos (logic), ethos (ethics), and pathos (emotions)—appropriately. Balancing logos, ethos, and pathos is a major challenge in writing an effective paper. Peer reviews helped me determine where more background information was needed.

To provide background information to the reader in a draft of my argument on the topic of CT scans, I wrote:

> The word *tomography* originates from the Greek word *tomos*, meaning "slice," and *graphia*, or "describing." CT scans, a form of tomography, have been used for years as the predominant method for medical imaging. The scans produce a three-dimensional image of an object's internal structure based on several x-ray images. Original uses of CT scans are to diagnose different cancers, guide biopsies and similar procedures, and to plan surgery or radiation treatment ("Computed").

Also regarding how to respond to the needs of audiences—I learned that it is crucial to maintain a negotiable stance while writing an argument. Arguments are rarely two-sided, so it is important to be open to all sides. If you form an opinion without getting all the facts and hearing other viewpoints, you can't honestly say your claim is correct. It is difficult to persuade your audience to see things from your perspective if you don't know all the perspectives yourself. . . .

Text Credit

p. 604: Courtesy of Chelsea Rundle.

In many of your college classes, you will be asked to take essay examinations—to sit and write (sometimes on a computer, more often by hand), for a specified period of time, about the material you have learned. Writing essay exams differs in several ways from writing academic papers that you might work on for several weeks. When you write an essay exam, you will find that the following is true:

- You usually have to rely on your memory.
- You don't have much time to figure out what you would like to say.
- You can't get feedback from your instructor and classmates.
- You usually do not have much time for revision.

It is no wonder, then, that some students worry about in-class essay examinations. Our purpose here is to help you overcome any possible concerns about essay examinations by giving you some specific strategies to use before and during such tests.

Keep in mind that situations that are similar to essay exams may come along throughout your life. In your career or in a civic organization, for example, you may be asked to write quickly and without the luxury of invention work or peer feedback:

- As a small-business owner, you might have to draft and complete a cost estimate and quotation in a customer's home.
- As a member of a city council or town board, you may need to comment on a political issue at a town meeting or in response to a question from the media.
- If you write advertising copy or are a journalist, you will frequently have tight deadlines to contend with.

Think of college essay examinations as a way of preparing for life after college, when you often will have to write from memory in a short period of time.

To write an effective response to a question on an essay examination, you will need to do the following:

- Know and understand the information that the examination will cover.
- Be able to relate that information to other topics and ideas you have read about and discussed in class.
- Analyze and understand the question(s) that you are asked to address.
- Construct a thoughtful answer to the question(s), and get your ideas onto paper in the available time.

- Deal with any pre-exam stress issues that you might have. Much of what causes stress for any kind of examination occurs when students are not prepared for the exam, so just being ready can make a big difference in your anxiety level.

- Deal with the examination *scene*—whether you are writing by hand or on a computer, what distractions there might be (other students, noise), and so on.

Getting Ready: Information Gathering, Storage, and Retrieval

When you read and take notes for your college classes, remember that one day you probably will be tested on this information.

Chapter 2 provides useful strategies for reading effectively, and Chapter 4 offers strategies for writing about course material, so we suggest that you revisit those chapters with an eye to using them to help prepare you for essay examinations. Instructors don't expect students to remember everything covered in their classes, but they do expect them to recall and understand the main concepts and to relate those concepts to other ideas. As you read and listen in class, make note of the major concepts, and be sure you can explain them.

For more on annotating, see Chapter 2, pages 17–18.

One reading strategy, for instance, requires you to annotate what you read, not only listing the main points but also jotting down any comments and questions you have about the text. This "talking back" to the text helps you remember what you've read and develop your own ideas and positions on the issues you read about—positions you may be asked to argue in an in-class essay examination.

Considering Questions

As you read and listen to class lectures and participate in class discussions, consider the kinds of questions an instructor might ask you to write about. What are the big issues or ideas that have been covered in class or that you have encountered in your reading? As you think of possible questions, record them in your journal. Then set aside some time to write responses to those questions.

For example, in a humanities class where you are considering various periods in the world of art, it is quite possible that, for an in-class essay examination, your instructor will ask you to situate a group of specific artists in the historical context in which they lived and worked. In a political science class, you may be asked to write about how the specific political issues of the day influenced a particular political party or movement. In your history class, you may be asked to explain how the historical events that took place over a period of time led to the start of a war. It is important to recognize that you probably can make a good guess at what questions an instructor will ask on an essay examination, so it is worthwhile for you to consider what those questions might be—before the exam—and how you might answer them.

Analyzing Questions

In addition to thinking about and predicting what questions you might be asked, it is important to understand what the questions are asking you to do.

Because instructors know that students have limited time to respond to an essay examination, they generally will ask questions that have a narrow focus. For example, in a history class, a question for a major writing assignment might be worded like this:

Discuss the events that led up to the second Iraq war.

For an in-class examination, where students have only a brief time to respond, however, a question might be worded like this:

In no more than two pages, explain what was defined as Iraq's "no fly zone."

The following question is a writing prompt designed to elicit a brief response and is similar to prompts used on placement examinations—those tests that determine which writing class is appropriate for a student. How might you answer it?

Ernest Hemingway once commented, "As you get older, it is harder to have heroes, but it is sort of necessary." To what extent do you agree or disagree with his observation? Why? Support your opinion with specific examples.

What is this essay question asking you to *do*? If you have not studied Hemingway, this question might worry you, but consider this: The question is not about Hemingway; rather, it asks for your response to what he said about having heroes. Do you think that, to construct an effective essay, you might want to define what a hero is to you? That you might want to provide some examples of your own heroes? That when you answer the real question—whether you agree with Hemingway's comment—you will need to provide some specific examples to show what you mean?

When you see the test question(s) for your essay examination, ask yourself what the question(s) asks you to *do*:

- Does it ask you to analyze something—to explain how the parts make up the whole? Consider how you might answer this question:

  Analyze the use of the magic of flying in relation to the other illusions in the Harry Potter films.

  For more on analysis, see Chapter 8.

- Does the question ask you to *evaluate* an idea or text or work of art? Consider how you might answer this question:

  Of the short stories you read in English class this semester, explain which makes the most effective use of imagery.

  For more on evaluation, see Chapter 10.

- Does the exam question ask you to *show connections* between historical trends, or causal chains—to demonstrate that one event led to or caused other events? Here, of course, your answer will need to show clearly the connections that you see. How might you answer this question?

  How did the Gulf of Tonkin incident influence the start of the Vietnam War?

  For more on cause and effect, see Chapter 11.

- Does the test ask you to compare one or more ideas or texts with others? Or does it ask you to *contrast* concepts or ideas or texts? If you are asked to

For more on comparison and contrast, see Chapter 13.

compare things, then you will look for similarities between them; if you are asked to contrast, then you will look for (and provide examples of) differences. How might you answer the following question, from a political science class?

Briefly compare Canada's and Australia's reactions to the second Iraq war.

- Does the question ask you to *define* something? When you define something, you most often explain what you think it is, and then also set it against what it is *not*. Usually, questions that deal with definitions ask for more than just a dictionary definition.

For more on definition, see Chapter 13.

- Does the question ask that you *discuss* an idea, a concept, or a text? In examination terms, "discuss" means to present the most important features of an idea or a concept and then analyze them. You will need to provide examples or other kinds of evidence to support your analysis. "Discuss" in an examination question also leaves your options fairly open—that is, you can discuss briefly or discuss in detail. In an essay *exam*, you can only discuss *briefly*, so consider only the main points you want to make and how you can support those specific points.

- Does the question ask you to *illustrate* something—that is, to provide specific examples to explain the characteristics of the idea or concept?

- Does the examination ask you to *explain* an idea or concept? Think about how you might answer this question:

Explain the significance of rills on the lunar surface.

- Does the exam ask you to *critique* something (a work of art, a short story, a poem, an idea), outlining and explaining its strengths and weaknesses? Consider how you might answer this question:

Critique William Faulkner's use of time in "A Rose for Emily."

For more on rhetorical analysis, see pages 26–29.

- Does the exam question ask that you *review* or *summarize* a particular philosophy or train of thought?

- Does the exam ask you to *analyze* a topic (a text, a local agency, a business plan), to explain how the various aspects of that topic function and work together? Does it ask you to construct a *rhetorical analysis*?

If you are faced with a multiple-part question that seems difficult to answer, draw some lines between each section—in effect, break down the question into its component parts. For example, here is a multipart question:

Noting the recent changes in campus safety problems, argue that your campus needs more or less police protection, but without causing a siege or locked-in mentality for the student body.

Go through and mark each part of the question:

1. Noting the recent changes in campus safety problems
2. argue that your campus needs more or less police protection
3. but without causing a siege
4. or locked-in mentality for the student body

Part 1 asks that you outline what changes in campus safety issues have recently taken place.

Part 2 asks that you take a position on the amount of police protection your campus needs. (If you argue for more protection, what does that increase mean: more police on campus? More police on foot patrol? Bicycle police? Should they be more heavily armed? Should police dogs be deployed on campus?)

Part 3 asks that you define what a "siege mentality" would be for the students. Part 4 asks much the same: for a definition and explanation of what a "locked-in mentality" is.

Breaking down a complex question in this manner allows you to see and thus consider each part of the question, an analysis that helps ensure that you will answer all of its parts.

Constructing Thoughtful Answers

Once you understand exactly what the question is asking you, it is helpful to jot down your main ideas. Then think about what organizational method you might use.

Also think about whether it is a *short-* or *long-answer* essay exam. If you have an hour for the essay exam, for example, and there are ten questions, that gives you an average of six minutes to answer each question, a fairly good tipoff that you are working with a short-answer examination. For your answers to be effective, you will need to get right to the point and then state any supporting evidence as concisely as possible.

On the other hand, if you have ninety minutes to respond to one question on an exam, then you have time to brainstorm the ideas you might want to present, to construct a brief cluster diagram of how the parts of your answer relate to each other, and to do other invention work. And as you are writing the exam, you will have time to explain each aspect of your answer in greater detail than on a short-answer exam.

Often, the test question itself will give you a strong clue about what kind of organization might be effective. For example, consider this sample question from a history class:

An understanding of the past is necessary for understanding the current situation.

Explain what you think the above statement means. Discuss the similarities between the 1964 presidential election, in which Lyndon Johnson soundly defeated Barry Goldwater, and the 2008 presidential election, in which Barack Obama soundly defeated John McCain. How does an understanding of past events help us to understand what happens in the present?

This is a three-part question, which means that a three-part answer might be the most efficient and effective strategy. If you break down the question into its parts, you have the following:

- *Explain* what the statement means. The first part of your answer should do just what the question asks, in your own words and from your own perspective: What do you think the statement means?

- *Discuss* the similarities, as the question asks you to do. What historical trends and events brought about Lyndon Johnson's election? What similar trends and events contributed to Barack Obama's election?
- *Discuss* how past events (in this case, the 1964 presidential election) help us understand a similar event that took place forty-four years later. Do these two events mean a similar election might happen again in 2052?

One type of organization that works well for essay examinations is what is commonly called the "classical scheme." This method of organizing ideas dates back at least to Aristotle, who noticed that effective speakers most often do the following:

1. State their position and what is important (what is "at stake" in the argument).
   a. State their first piece of evidence, always connecting it back to the main point
   b. State their second piece of evidence, connecting it back to the main point
   c. State the third piece of evidence …
   d. And so on
2. Briefly outline any objections to the main point; then explain why those objections are incorrect, or at least show how their position can accommodate the objection.
3. Summarize their position, restating their main points.

For more on the classical scheme, see Chapter 14.

If you follow the classical scheme, you will do the following:
- Construct a solid thesis statement, clearly indicating the main point that you want to make in your answer.
- Provide an effective and logical organizational pattern to follow.
- State your main point right at the start, forcing yourself to use supporting details that always relate back to that main idea. (If an idea or piece of supporting evidence does *not* help you accomplish what the test question asks you to do, then why is it there?)
- Acknowledge the other side of an issue or situation or idea, which tells your instructor that you are aware that there are other perspectives or approaches.
- Tie everything together at the end (which is what a conclusion should do).

Dealing with the Examination Scene

You probably have your favorite place to write, where it is quiet (or there is music playing), and where everything you need is at hand (computer, paper, pencil, pen, erasers, coffee). But you *rarely* will have such an ideal setting for an in-class examination—unless you construct it.

Because you usually know when an exam will take place, it's a good idea to prepare your test-taking environment as best you can, so the writing situation the examination presents is as normal and comfortable as possible. If you usually use a pencil to write, then make sure you have several sharpened pencils with you—or better yet, a good-quality mechanical pencil. If you are allowed to use notes as you write the exam, make sure your notes are clearly written and legible. Here are some other ways to prepare to construct an effective essay examination:

- Know the material that you will be tested on by using effective studying techniques (for example, recording and then listening to your notes; rewriting your in-class notes on your computer to help impress them in your memory and also to make them available in readable form; working with others in study groups).

- Consider what questions you might be asked by constructing your own test questions. This activity forces you to look at the material from a different viewpoint (teacher rather than student), by asking, "What would I like my students to know and understand about this material? What might be the best way for them to demonstrate that knowledge?"

- *Before* taking the exam, think about how you will spend the time you are allotted. Surprisingly, few students really think about how they will spend the hour or ninety minutes or whatever time they will be given for the exam. If you have a plan going into the exam, then you will use your time more wisely. So think about how to use the time you will be allowed effectively, and then consider how much time you might spend on each of these tasks:
  - Understanding the question
  - Getting some ideas onto paper
  - Organizing those ideas
  - Actually writing the exam
  - Revising your response, once you have it on paper
  - Editing your work
  - Proofreading your work

See Chapter 4, "Writing to Discover and to Learn," for more on study strategies.

Note whether some questions are worth more points than others; if so, then it makes sense to spend *more time* on the questions that are worth more. If you encounter a question that you cannot immediately answer, skip it and go on to other questions. That strategy gives you some time to think about it as you work on other answers.

Terry Dolan Writes an Essay Examination

College student Terry Dolan received this prompt for a sixty-minute essay examination:

PROMPT

In his 2005 book *The World Is Flat*, Thomas Friedman talks of "ten forces that flattened the world." Name three of Friedman's ten forces, and explain how they helped to flatten the world.

TERRY DOLAN'S RESPONSE

In his book *The World Is Flat*, Thomas Friedman talks of ten forces that flattened the world. I will discuss how three of these forces—the fall of the Berlin Wall, Netscape going public, and open-sourcing—helped to flatten the twenty-first-century world.

On November 9, 1989, the Berlin Wall fell. While this was a major victory for the forces of democracy in East Berlin and East Germany, it also stood as a symbol for the eventual fall of communism in all of Europe. By opening up Eastern Europe, and eventually the old Soviet Union, to free market capitalism, the end of the Berlin Wall was Friedman's first "flattener." Friedman also talks about the IBM PC computer and how its introduction helped to facilitate the flattening process begun by the fall of the Berlin Wall. The computer with a modem helped to connect people in the old communist bloc with new computer and economic networks.

Friedman's second flattening force happened when the browser Netscape went public. Netscape was a major force because it really opened up the World Wide Web and the Internet for the general population. Before Netscape, the only way people had access to the Internet was in text-only environments. Although that type of access may have been interesting, it mainly attracted scientists and educators. Netscape let people use graphics, and eventually sound and video, online as well. One of the important advantages Netscape offered is that it could be used on any type of computer—PCs, Macs, or Unix boxes.

One important off-shoot of Netscape that helped flatten the world was the fact that when people began to send pictures, audio, and video files over the Internet, they needed more bandwidth. To accommodate this need, companies started laying more fiber optic cable. As a result, phone prices started dropping as well, enabling people to communicate more and faster.

Another flattener, according to Friedman, is the open-source movement. Unlike most software, you can download open-source software for free. Friedman explains that it works on the same model as scientific peer review. People participate in developing the software for the good of the group and the notoriety it gives them. The main open-source software that Friedman discusses is the Apache Web server. Friedman talks about how many of the main Internet Web sites run on Apache servers. Because there is no cost involved in buying the software, just about anyone who knows how can run a Web server.

An even more important example of open-source software is probably the Linux operating system. Linux is a kind of Unix, a powerful computer operating system. The advantage to Linux is that it's cheap (you can download it for free) and flexible (lots of computer people are constantly working to make it even better). The disadvantage to Linux is that most software is written to run on PCs. But more and more open-source software is being written to run on Linux boxes. You can now get Open Office and similar open-source programs that will let you do just about anything you could do with Microsoft software. All the open-source programs are free. You can also get Firefox, a web browser that runs on Linux. In other parts of the world, lots of computers run on Linux and use open-source software.

Finally, what I think is the most interesting point about all of Friedman's flatteners is that they're all about technology, mainly computer technology, and how that helps all of us connect to one another faster and better. Technology is what's making the world flat.

Appendix C
Standard Document Forms

Selecting and using a particular "form" for your text involves making rhetorical choices. Before selecting any kind of format for your text, then, you first need to ask (and answer) the following questions:

- What do you want your writing to accomplish? Do you want to inform your reader, persuade your reader to do something, or evaluate a product, service, or creative work for your reader?
- What form will best serve your purpose?
- Who is your audience?

You already make these kinds of decisions about form all the time when you communicate with your friends, family members, and professors. For some communications (a letter to your great-aunt), a handwritten, personal letter will suffice; for others (asking a professor for a letter of recommendation to get into law school), a more formal business letter is a better choice.

In addition, you also select the size and kind of font to use as well as photographs and drawings, charts and graphs, and other visual aids; you decide whether to use headings in your document, whether bulleted or numbered lists are appropriate and useful, where a colored background or type is useful, and so on. These are all rhetorical choices that you as a writer make, whatever document you are constructing.

This appendix presents guidelines for designing ten different types of print or online documents, along with examples of each type.

Features of an Effective Business Letter

The audience for any piece of business writing will have specific expectations. The most obvious expectation is that you should address your colleagues more formally than you address your college classmates. As with any text, business letters (and memos—see p. 624) have real audiences and purposes, and the form that you use needs to fit your readers' concept of business correspondence:

- Use margins of at least one inch on all four sides of the letter.
- Use a standard 12-point font such as Times New Roman.
- Single-space addresses and paragraphs.
- If you use a block or modified block format (see Figure C.1), double-space between sections of the letter—return address of sender, date, name and address of person to whom the letter is being sent, salutation, paragraphs, and closing. If you use an indented format, you do not need to double-space between paragraphs.

- Use a colon after the salutation.
- Use formal, but not stilted, language.
- After the closing (usually "Sincerely"), use a comma.
- After the closing, include four blank lines for your signature; then type your name, and give your professional title, if applicable. If you are using your company's letterhead, then of course you do not need to duplicate the address, telephone numbers, and so on that are already printed on the letterhead.
- After your name and professional title, include a "cc:" (copy) line, an "Enc:" (enclosure) line, or both if necessary.

Hanna Olsen 1111 Lutefisk Lane Olso, WI 55555	Return address of sender Double-space between sections
October 1, 2016	Date
Kirsti Anderson, Director Office of the Registrar 413 Lefse Hall Oslo College Oslo, WI 55555	Name and address of person to whom letter is being sent
Dear Ms. Anderson:	Salutation

I am writing to request that you adjust my tuition payment for this semester. Because of health problems, I have been forced to withdraw from two of my courses. I am requesting a partial tuition refund for those six credit hours.

Double-space between paragraphs

Three weeks after the semester began, I was diagnosed with mononucleosis, which has limited the number of hours that I can attend class and study. Fortunately, I am doing well in my other two courses, and I am confident that I will be able to carry a full course load next semester.

To document my illness, I have attached a note from the Campus Medical Center. If you need further evidence, I will be happy to provide it.

I look forward to hearing from you soon.

Sincerely,	Closing
	4 blank lines
Hanna Olsen	Signature
Hanna Olsen	Name
Enc: Note from Campus Medical Center	Enclosure line

FIGURE C.1
Business Letter,
Block Format

- Because error-free letters give readers a positive impression, proofread your letter carefully and ask a friend or colleague to proofread it if possible. A second set of eyes is an effective insurance policy.
- Be sure to keep thc electronic version of the letter. Back it up—just as you would for any important document.

Features of an Effective Letter of Application

Your purpose in writing a letter of application is just what you would expect it to be: you want your letter to get something for you—most often a job interview (and sometimes even the job itself).

- Use the features of the business-letter format described on pages 616–618.
- Use the exact job title from the job announcement to indicate the position for which you are applying. Businesses sometimes advertise for more than one position at a time, so it is crucial to get the job title right.
- Briefly summarize your qualifications for the job. Don't simply repeat what is on your résumé, which will be attached to your letter.
- If the job announcement includes "required qualifications" and "desired qualifications," you must discuss all of the required ones, and you should discuss as many of the desired ones as possible.
- Indicate how you can meet the needs of the hiring organization. Show that you are eager but not desperate.
- Subtly show that you have done your homework in learning as much as possible about the organization, the unit within the organization that you would be working for, and the job itself.
- Never misrepresent your skills, knowledge, or background. Honesty is the best approach.

Figure C.2 on page 619 is an example of a letter of application.

Features of an Effective Résumé

At first glance, writing a résumé might seem easy: just list your work history and when you did it. But constructing an effective résumé involves a great deal of time and effort. To begin with, you need to consider carefully the audience to which you are addressing your résumé: Who will see your résumé? What information will they need, and what format should it be in? Should it be a paper résumé, or should it be in an electronic form? If you are adapting your résumé for a specific position, what does the job advertisement call for? You want to ensure that everything the advertisement asks for is included.

- You may—or may not—choose to include a concise career objective at the beginning of your résumé. Although such job objectives were common until recently, some experts now advise résumé writers not to include an objective because the objective is to acquire the job for which you are applying.

FIGURE C.2
Letter of
Application

Kirsti Brones
1234 Raaen Way
Modum, MN 55555

Return address of sender

Double-space between sections

July 5, 2016

Date

Anna Drolsum
Personnel Director
Super Computer Company, Inc.
2222 E. Cyberspace Dr.
Minneapolis, MN 55444

Name and address of person to
whom letter is being sent

Dear Ms. Drolsum:

Salutation

I am writing to apply for the sales representative position recently advertised
in the *Minneapolis Star-Tribune*. The skills that I have developed in my
degree program support my strong interest in the position.

Double-space between paragraphs

In my recent internship with Excellent Computer Company, I had sales
responsibilities similar to those described in your advertisement and on your
Web site. Thus, I gained experience in maintaining sales accounts and in
making cold calls to prospective corporate customers. Prior to my internship,
I learned how to handle customer concerns by working for several years at
the Customer Service desk of a Bull's-Eye Department Store.

I am especially interested in working for Super Computer Company because
you have such a strong reputation for offering quality products and being
responsive to customers' needs.

I am eager to speak with you about the sales representative position. If you
have any questions about my enclosed résumé, please call me at
400-555-4371. Thank you for considering my application.

Sincerely,

Kirsti Brones

Closing

Signature

Kirsti Brones

Name

Enclosure

Enclosure line

- Include current contact information—name, mailing address, e-mail address,
  phone numbers.

- Use descriptive headings to label the sections of your résumé, such as "Education,"
  "Work Experience," "Skills," "Activities," "Awards," and "References." Include

activities if they demonstrate additional skills, such as leadership. Include awards that reveal qualities or achievements that are an asset to the job you are seeking.

- Do not include personal information such as age, race, ethnicity, marital status, sexual orientation, or health status because employers are not allowed to consider such information.

- If requested to do so, list your references. Before you list someone as a reference, make certain that he or she knows your work and feels comfortable recommending you for a job. As an alternative, you can add the line "References available upon request." If you post your résumé on a Web site, do not list your references.

- If you limit your résumé to a single page, hiring personnel can read it quickly. However, it is more important to include the information that will help you get a job—even if it takes several pages—so consider your audience and what they expect from you. In business, for example, one-page résumés are common; in colleges and universities, résumés are usually much longer and more detailed.

- Use good quality paper.

- A résumé must not have any errors, so be sure to proofread carefully. Ask friends to help with this task if possible. Do not rely solely on the spell-check function of your word-processing program.

- If you post your résumé on a Web site, keep in mind that readers will see it one screen at a time rather than one page at a time.

- Although it is easy to embellish an online résumé with ornate graphics, a simple online résumé is actually more effective.

- Because employers sometimes conduct Web searches for résumés, adding some key terms such as the word "résumé" itself to your online résumé will make it more likely that a search engine will detect your résumé.

Different Kinds of Résumés

The two most common kinds of résumés are the **chronological résumé** and the **functional résumé.** In a chronological résumé, you list all of the jobs you have held in the past in reverse chronological order with the most recent listed first. Your work history should appear just below your personal information. Figure C.3 on page 621 is an example of a chronological résumé. In a functional résumé, you make sure to highlight skills you possess or tasks you have accomplished in previous jobs. Another option is to combine the two formats by listing jobs chronologically and highlighting the tasks that you performed while employed in each job. Figure C.4 on page 622 is an example of a résumé that is both chronological and functional.

 ## Electronic Résumés

As you enter today's employment market, you are likely to encounter employers who ask you to submit electronic résumés. Sometimes the electronic résumé can be nothing more than a digital copy (a Word document or a PDF) of your paper résumé. However, you might be asked to fill out a Web form that will serve as a résumé. When you are submitting an

Kirsti Brones

1234 Raaen Way
Modum, MN 55555
400-555-6981
kbrones@email.com

Work Experience

Marketing Intern, Excellent Computer Company, Anoka, MN, Spring 2016
Customer Service Representative, Bull's-Eye Department Store, Edina, MN, 2012–2015

Education

Bachelor of Science, Marketing, College of Business, University of Minnesota, 2016

Activities

President, Undergraduate Student Marketing Club, University of Minnesota, 2015–2016
Volunteer, Habitat for Humanity, 2014
Volunteer, Boys and Girls Club of America, Edina, MN, 2012–2014

References

Available upon request

Name, centered and bold font
Contact information, centered

Heading, flush left and in bold

Double-space before and after headings

FIGURE C.3 A Chronological Résumé

electronic résumé of any kind, in all likelihood the first reader of your résumé will not be a human but a machine. When they read résumés, machines are programmed to search for predetermined keywords or phrases. That means that every résumé that contains the right keyword or phrase will go on to the next phase of screening—maybe by a human. Reading job ads closely will give you a good idea of what keywords or phrases might be important for the specific job you're applying for. While you already know the importance of proofreading a paper résumé, proofreading becomes even more important with electronic résumés. A human reader might forgive one small typo in a paper résumé. A machine can't forgive a typo because unless the words are all spelled correctly, they won't match the words the program is looking for. Keywords are highlighted in Figure C.4.

Features of an Effective E-mail Message

Especially in business environments, e-mail is everywhere. It has become the primary means of communication in many—if not most—businesses. To construct an effective e-mail, like any other kind of text, you need to consider the rhetorical situation, who your audience is, and what you want the e-mail to accomplish.

Name, centered
and bold font

Contact
information,
centered

Heading, flush
left and in bold

Double-space
before and
after headings

Kirsti Brones

1234 Raaen Way
Modum, MN 55555
400-555-6981

Work Experience

Marketing Intern, Excellent Computer Company, Anoka, MN, Spring 2016

➤ Facilated focus groups
➤ Wrote questions for focus groups
➤ Wrote brochure copy
➤ Assisted with marketing research

Customer service Representative, Bull's-Eye Department Store,
    Edina, MN, 2012–2015

➤ Helped solve problems for customers
➤ Responsible for inventory of returns

Education

Bachelor of Science, Marketing, College of Business,
    University of Minnesota, 2016

Activities

President, Undergraduate Student Marketing Club, University of Minnesota,
    2015–2016
Volunteer, Habitat for Humanity, 2014

➤ Coordinated volunteers
➤ Trained new volunteers in reading blueprints

Volunteer, Boys and Girls Club of America, Edina, MN, 2012–2014

References

Available upon request

FIGURE C.4   A Mixed Chronological and Functional Résumé

In addition, because it is so easy to forward an e-mail (readers do not even need to cut and paste any of the text), it is important to understand that what you say to one person in an e-mail might be shared widely with people whom you did not intend to receive it.

- Use relatively short block paragraphs to make it easier for your readers to read the message. Single-space, and include a blank line between paragraphs.

- Be very careful when using "reply to all" when you respond to an e-mail message, especially on listservs or online discussion forums.

- Before sending a "BCC" (blind copy) to people other than the primary recipients of your message, think carefully about the ethical implications of secretly sharing this message.

Date: Thu, 26 May 2016 16:58:31 -0400
From: O_DOOL@XYandZ.com
To: needshybrid@cox.net
Subject: Your new vehicle

I am happy to tell you that your new Toyota Prius has arrived. We will have it prepared for you to pick up after 5:00 pm tomorrow evening.

I think you'll find the colors you chose to your liking.

Please respond to this e-mail to tell us when you'll pick up your new Prius. Could you also please make sure to bring a copy of your proof of insurance card? Our finance officer forgot to make a copy when she was doing your paperwork. We do need a copy for the files.

Thanks for your business,

Oscar Doolittle
Sales Manager
X, Y, & Z Toyota/Scion
Yuma, AZ 85365
(928) 555-4567

FIGURE C.5
E-mail Message

- Use a font that is easy to read on a screen, such as 10-point or 12-point Times New Roman or Arial.

- If you use an electronic signature for your e-mail, make certain that it includes relevant contact information. For business messages, use a signature that is suitable for business. Don't use a font that is too flashy, and if you do include a photograph or drawing, make sure it is not so large that downloading your message takes a long time.

- In business e-mail, it is best to not use emoticons such as smiley faces.

- If you intend to attach a file to the message, develop a system that helps you remember to attach the file. Also make certain that the file is free of viruses.

Figure C.5 is an example of an e-mail.

Features of an Effective Memo

As with business letters, business memos have their own specific requirements as to format—and memos, too, always have a rhetorical purpose. Ask yourself the following questions when writing a memo:

- What do I want this memo to accomplish?

- Who is my audience? What will my readers already know about my topic? What additional information do I need to provide to accomplish my goals?

- What is the situation or context in which I'm writing this memo? How does that context affect what I write and how I write it?

FIGURE C.6
Memo

Date: March 29, 2016

   To: Information Technology Staff

From: Norman Jones, Assistant Director, Division of Information Technology

   RE: Latest Windows Migration

This July, all computers in the Division of Research and Development will be migrated to the new Windows operating system. The migration will be conducted over the course of the week of July 16.

Because we need to have the new Windows operating system installed and fully operational by the end of July, **all members of the information technology staff need to be on the job between July 16 and July 31.** For that reason, I cannot approve any requests for vacation time during that period.

I hope that this early notice affords you ample time to plan your summer vacations accordingly. I regret any inconvenience that this migration to a new operating system might cause.

Thank you for your good work.

cc: Linda Searcy, Director, Division of Information Technology

---

- If your office or organization has a memo template, use that format. If it does not, follow the generic format: Include separate lines for a "To" entry, a "From" entry, the date, and a "Regarding" or "RE" designation.
- For printed memos, use margins of at least one inch on all four sides.
- In the "RE" line, use a clear, concise subject heading.
- For printed memos that have legal significance, include your initials or legal signature, in ink.
- For memos that need to be shared with other people besides the primary recipient(s), add a "cc" (copy) line after the body of the memo.
- Use bold type sparingly for emphasis and to highlight any information that requires immediate attention.

In today's workplace, memos are usually attached to e-mail messages and are rarely distributed in print form. Figure C.6 is an example of a memo.

 ## Threaded Discussion Groups and Listserv Postings

A number of publicly available Web sites such as Yahoo!, MSN, and Google offer online discussion groups (sometimes called **threaded discussions**). Organized by topic or interest area, these groups allow members to view and participate in written

discussions over the Web. After a member posts a message about a particular topic, others may then post their responses. As the discussion proceeds, a Web page is automatically built around the discussion. Threaded discussions allow members to see all the postings in context on one Web page. This makes participating in and viewing the discussion easy.

A **Listserv** is another kind of online forum. Although the word *Listserv* technically should be capitalized because it is a registered trademark of a company called L-Soft International, Inc., the word is increasingly used as a common noun—in the way that "kleenex" is often used to mean "facial tissue," rather than as a brand name, Kleenex. A listserv distributes e-mail to the addresses of all people who have subscribed to that listserv. That is, when a subscriber sends a message to a listserv, the listserv automatically distributes it to all other subscribers. Listservs allow participants to transmit information to large numbers of people who share an interest or are involved in an organization, and they are an effective way to discuss important issues, share ideas, and make announcements. Figure C.7 is an example of a listserv posting.

From: Duane Roen <Duane.Roen@asu.edu>

Subject: **Final Version of CWPA Conference Schedule: Thanks**

Date: May 25, 2012 9:26:10 AM MST

To: Writing Program Administration <WPA-L@ASU.EDU>

Reply-To: Writing Program Administration <WPA-L@asu.edu>

Dear Colleagues,

Dave Blakesley let us make some last-minute changes in the CWPA conference schedule before he begins printing the program. Thanks, Dave.

Here is the final (and we mean final) version of the CWPA conference schedule: wpacouncil.org/node/3813#attachments

I thank all the people who proposed such interesting presentations.

I also thank those who helped with the program. It's been a wonderfully collaborative effort!

Best,

Duane

Duane Roen

President, Council of Writing Program Administrators

FIGURE C.7
Listserv Posting

Features of an Effective Threaded Discussion or Listserv Posting

- If you are posting a message as part of an ongoing discussion in a threaded discussion group or on a listserv, become familiar with previous postings on the topic so that you don't repeat what has already been written. Repetition may annoy other subscribers.

- Stay on the topic at hand unless it is appropriate to move to a new topic.

- If you disagree with someone's opinion on a topic, express your views clearly and politely. Do not engage in personal attacks (called flaming).

- Because server space costs money and online readers do not enjoy scrolling through prior messages, do not include in your posting the message to which you are responding. If you want to respond to a specific section of a previous posting, copy and paste the specific text instead, making sure to distinguish the text so that it is not confused with your own.

- Do not post personal messages ("thanks for that information, Joe") to the group or listserv, when that message is intended for just one person.

- Above all, be sure that you want to reply to the group or listserv as a whole rather than to an individual. Sometimes, people post a reply to a group or list that was intended for an individual. As you might imagine, such messages can be embarrassing.

- Keep your messages as brief as possible. Just as with an e-mail message, readers usually do not want to read a discussion posting that is longer than one screen of text.

Features of an Effective Brochure

As with a résumé, a brochure needs to accomplish something: to sell a product or service (or to get a reader interested in a product or service), perhaps, or to provide information (a voter's guide, for example).

- Include an informative and attention-getting headline.

- Include a visual element such as a photo or drawing if it grabs readers' attention and adds to the content of the brochure.

- If the brochure advertises an event, make certain that you include all relevant information—date, time, place, cost (if any), and a phone number interested parties can call or Web site address they can visit for further information.

- Your layout will depend on the number of folds that your brochure has. If you are using standard 8-1/2″ × 11″ paper, you may decide to have no fold, a bi-fold, or a tri-fold. A no-fold sheet fits well into a notebook. A tri-fold can fit into a shirt pocket.

FIGURE C.8
A Brochure About
How to Stop
Bullies Online

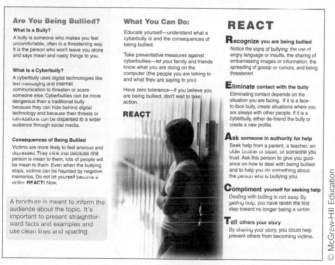

- Consider the principles of proximity, contrast, alignment, and repetition. (See Chapter 18 for more on these design concepts.)
- If you use photos or graphics that are not your own, make certain that you have permission to display them publicly.

Figure C.8 is an example of a brochure.

Features of an Effective Poster

While posters often seem to be only large sheets of paper with a small amount of text and lots of illustrations and a colored background, they also have a rhetorical purpose: to convey a message to an audience. If you are preparing a poster, you need to answer

©Elizabeth Murphy

FIGURE C.9
A Poster Advertising
an Event

questions such as these: What do you want your poster to do? Provide information? Show people how to get somewhere? Explain something?

- Include a headline that is informative and will grab viewers' attention.

- Include a visual element such as a photograph or drawing if it grabs viewers' attention and adds to the content of the poster.

- Because you will often need to reproduce a large quantity of posters, depending on the needs of your project, the quality, color, and size of the paper you use will affect your printing costs. At a certain point, you need to consider how much you are willing to spend in terms of your overall budget.

- Because using colored ink can also affect cost, keep your budget in mind when you determine whether your poster should be in color.

- Determine what size poster and what size font will be necessary for readers. Both will depend on the location of the poster and how close to the poster readers will be. Will they be whizzing by on their bikes, or will they be walking within a few feet of it?

- Consider the principles of proximity, contrast, alignment, and repetition described in Chapter 18.

- If you use photos or stock graphics, make certain that you have permission to display them publicly.

- If the poster advertises an event, make certain that you include all relevant information—date, time, place, cost (if any), and a phone number or Web site address where further information is available (if applicable).

Figure C.9 is an example of an effective poster.

Features of an Effective Newsletter

Newsletters most often have a specific audience (usually employees or members of a club or organization of some kind). Those who produce newsletters for a group also have specific purposes. At our university, for example, we get newsletters from a number of places (often in electronic form), including the following:

- The university itself, including a "wellness newsletter," which tells of various workshops employees can attend to lose weight, stop smoking, and so on, as well as information on how to become better managers, learn new computer software, and other useful advice.

- The faculty senate, which lets us know about political issues on campus.
- Our department, letting us know about upcoming speakers, recent publications by our colleagues, and other news of interest.

For an effective newsletter, consider the following:

- Determine who your readers will be in order to select information that will be interesting and useful to those readers.
- Determine a purpose for the newsletter, and keep that purpose in mind as you decide what to include and what to exclude.
- Use headlines that clearly indicate the content of the stories that follow them.
- Consider the principles of proximity, contrast, alignment, and repetition. (See Chapter 18 for more on these design principles.)
- If you use photos or graphics that are not your own, make certain that you have permission to include them in your publication.

Figure C.10 is an example of an online newsletter, which demonstrates all of these criteria.

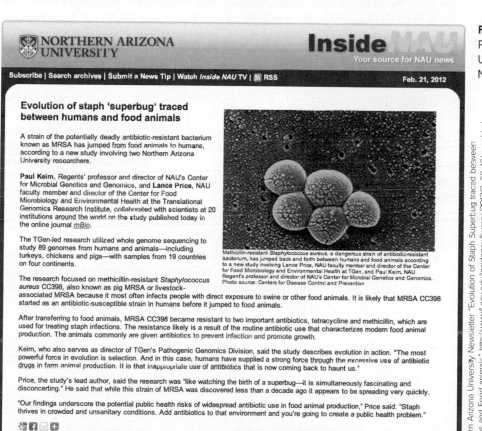

FIGURE C.10
Part of a University Newsletter

Northern Arizona University Newsletter "Evolution of Staph Superbug traced between Humans and Food animals." http://www4.nau.edu/insidenau/bumps/2012/2_20_12/mrsa.html. Reprinted by permission of Northern Arizona University.

Features of an Effective Web Site

Do you have your own Web site (a collection of Web pages)? Would you like to? These days, more and more of us do have Web sites. For example, as a student you might develop a portfolio in which you display your work as a Web site. (See Appendix A.) As a member of an organization, you might develop a Web site that describes the activities of the organization. Or, like many people do these days, you might develop a Web site in which you tell your family's history.

As with any text, one primary consideration is audience—and for a Web site, that can mean just about anyone. Consider the following questions as you create your Web site:

- What do you want your Web site to do? To tell about you and who you are? About the work you do?
- What do you want to include on your Web site? Photos? Drawings?

When designing a Web site, you should keep several points in mind. First of all, you need to consider both the purpose of the site and its intended audience. You will design a personal Web site, intended to be viewed by your friends and family, very differently from a Web site that is intended to portray you as a professional. On your personal Web site you might display photographs of your family, your friends, your pets, or some of your favorite places. You might provide links to restaurants you enjoy or the Web sites of your favorite sports teams. On the other hand, on a professional Web site you might include your résumé as well as links to a professional organization to which you belong. Both sites, however, should provide those who visit them with a clear sense of how to navigate the site. You might have a navigation bar along the top or on the side, with buttons that link to different pages on the site, including the home page.

One other factor to keep in mind when designing a Web site is that although we call the parts of a Web site *Web pages*, we are really talking about screens. While paper pages are a uniform size, Web pages can vary in size depending on the size and resolution of the monitor on which they appear.

- Break text into smaller chunks, and write as concisely as possible. Give readers "breathers." Bulleted lists work especially well on the Web.
- Graphics can enhance the informational value and aesthetic appeal of Web pages, but they can also cause pages to download more slowly. Use graphics if they highlight, elaborate on, or can substitute for words on the screen.
- Try to design each page of your site so that readers can view the entire page with only a minimal amount of scrolling.
- To make pages usable to a wide audience, make them accessible to people with visual impairments. To determine whether your site is accessible, you can consult accessible.org (www.bobby-approved.com/). There are links on the site to further information on how to design your site so that it is more accessible.
- Each page on your Web site should have a design that is consistent with the other pages on your site. Although you have more flexibility on a personal Web

FIGURE C.11
The Web Site for
an Independent
Publisher

site than with a professional site, you still want to give each page the same overall look and feel. A lack of consistency may make your viewers suspect that they have left your site for another.

- Organization and navigation work hand-in-hand on the Web. Organize material on the site so that the organizational principle is apparent to readers. Web designers frequently organize sites either sequentially or hierarchically. You might choose to organize the site sequentially, an organization similar to that of a numbered list. Or you might choose to organize hierarchically, where you begin with the most important or most general topic and then have your viewers "drill down" further into the site for the specific details.

- If you include links to external sites, periodically check to see if any links are "dead"—links to sites that are no longer active.

- Regularly examine the page to make certain that the information is current. Including a "last date updated" line helps to assure your viewers that you are keeping the site current.

Figure C.11 is an example of an effective home page for a publisher's Web site.

Index